THE CLASSICS
OF WESTERN
SPIRITUALITY

THE CLASSICS OF WESTERN SPIRITUALITY
A Library of the Great Spiritual Masters

President and Publisher
Kevin A. Lynch, C.S.P.

EDITORIAL BOARD

Meister Eckhart
TEACHER AND PREACHER

EDITED BY
BERNARD MCGINN

WITH THE COLLABORATION OF
FRANK TOBIN AND ELVIRA BORGSTADT

PREFACE BY
KENNETH NORTHCOTT

PAULIST PRESS
NEW YORK • MAHWAH • TORONTO

Copyright © 1986 by
Bernard McGinn

Library of Congress Cataloging-in-Publication Data

Eckhart, Meister, d. 1327.
    Meister Eckhart, teacher and preacher.

    (The Classics of Western spirituality)
    Includes bibliographies and index.
    Contents: Eckhart the teacher / translated by
Bernard McGinn. Commentary on Exodus. Selections
from the Commentary on the Book of wisdom, from the
Sermons and lectures on Ecclesiasticus, and from the
Commentary on John—Eckhart the preacher. Latin
sermons / translated by Bernard McGinn. German
sermons / translated by Frank Tobin—The "Sister
Catherine" treatise / translated by Elvira Borgstädt.
    1. Spiritual life—Middle Ages, 600–1500.

I. McGinn, Bernard, 1937–   .   II. Tobin, Frank J.
III. Borgstädt. Elvira.   IV. Title.   V. Series.
BV5080.E3213   1986   252'.02   86-22487
ISBN 0-8091-0377-X
ISBN 0-8091-2827-6 (pbk.)

Published by Paulist Press
997 Macarthur Boulevard
Mahwah, New Jersey 07430

Printed and bound in the United States of America

CONTENTS

CONTENTS

PART TWO: ECKHART THE PREACHER

Editor of this Volume

BERNARD McGINN is Professor of Historical Theology and of the History of Christianity at the Divinity School of the University of Chicago and is a member of the university's Committee on Medieval Studies. Born in Yonkers, New York, in 1937, McGinn received a licentiate in sacred theology from the Pontifical Gregorian University in 1963 and a Ph.D. in history of ideas from Brandeis University in 1970. His books include *The Golden Chain*, *Visions of the End*, and *The Calabrian Abbot*. In this series he has been the editor of *Apocalyptic Spirituality*, and, along with Edmund Colledge, of *Meister Eckhart: The Essential Sermons, Commentaries, Treatises, and Defense*. Most recently, he collaborated with John Meyendorff in editing *Christian Spirituality: Origins to the Twelfth Century*.

Collaborators of this Volume

FRANK TOBIN is Professor of German at the University of Nevada, Reno, and serves on the editorial board of the *German Quarterly*. Born in Omaha, Nebraska, in 1935, Tobin received a licentiate in philosophy from the Berchmanskolleg in Munich in 1960, an M.A. in German from Marquette University in 1964, and a Ph.D. in German from Stanford in 1967. His publications include books and articles on medieval German literature, especially on Meister Eckhart. His volume *Meister Eckhart: Thought and Language* appreared in 1986 from the University of Pennsylvania Press.

ELVIRA BORGSTÄDT is a native of Heilbronn, West Germany. Trained in the diverse fields of chemistry, creative writing, medieval mysticism, and commercial real estate, she now resides with her family in the mythical community of University Village in Chicago's First Ward.

Author of the Preface

KENNETH NORTHCOTT is Professor of Older High German Literature and of Comparative Literature at the University of Chicago. His major interests are the literature of the High Middle Ages in Germany, especially the *Minnesang*, Latin poetry, and Parzifal, and of the Late Middle High and Early New High German periods. He has published extensively in all these areas. More recently he has become interested in sociology and was responsible for the English translation of Arnold Hauser's *The Sociology of Art*.

DEDICATED TO THE MEMORY OF
BERNARD LONERGAN, S.J.
ANOTHER GREAT TEACHER AND MAN OF GOD

FOREWORD

This is the second volume devoted to Meister Eckhart to appear in the Classics of Western Spirituality Series, and were Eckhart less significant a figure in the history of spirituality there might be need to defend the reasons for including another volume on this difficult and to some dangerous thinker. Difficult Eckhart certainly remains. The present volume, for all its apparatus, no more solves the problems and puzzles connected with his thought than any earlier translation or interpretation has. Meister Eckhart's writings invite us to share in a mystery. This volume has no other intention beyond that of helping to spread the invitation.

Despite the dangers that many have found implied or expressed in Eckhart's thought, both in the fourteenth century and afterward, his appeal has been widespread in many ages. In his own era many devout religious, as well as large groups of laypersons, were nourished by his vernacular preaching. Learned theologians and mystics like John Tauler, Henry Suso, and later Nicholas of Cusa pondered the depths of his Latin works. Since his rediscovery in the early nineteenth century, he has inspired and influenced thousands, both famous philosophers and theologians and humble, holy seekers known only to God. Perhaps no Western mystic has appealed so strongly or offered so fruitful a conversation to the great mystical traditions of Asia.

It remains to express gratitude to those who have made this volume possible: first of all to Frank Tobin, whose labors in behalf of this book extend far beyond the excellent translations of the Middle High German sermons he has provided; second, to Elvira Borgstädt, for her fine translation of the "Sister Catherine" treatise, and to my friend and colleague Kenneth Northcott for his Preface. Finally, I would like to thank Ellen Babinsky for help regarding the preparation and editing of the manuscript.

PREFACE

It is a particular pleasure for me to write this Preface to the second volume of the works of Meister Eckhart, though my concerns with the work of the Meister are of a somewhat different, though I hope complementary, nature from those of Bernard McGinn and Frank Tobin. My approach to Eckhart is by way of the literature of the earlier Middle High German period—the classical "High Middle Ages"—and my interest in his works stemmed originally from the phenomenon of Eckhart as a writer and a master of the written Middle High German word. The very fact that he was one of those rare phenomena who appear from time to time—a man who could write masterful prose in two languages—bears testimony to the linguistic skill that lies behind so much of his thinking.

Professor McGinn has rightly pointed out that the "influence" of Eckhart on the Middle High German and, subsequently, the New High German languages has in the past been exaggerated, but nevertheless it is his German writings that make us aware of the power of the Middle High German language to express theological and philosophical notions without recourse to Latin borrowings. Furthermore, it is Eckhart's rare, if not unique, concern with wordplay, as Professor McGinn has pointed out, that makes the literary as well as the theological scholar aware of the potential richness and polyvalence of the vocabulary of the late Middle High German period. In this regard Tobin's article on the meaning of *eigenschaft* gives us a fascinating and essential insight into the ambiguities of a word that may on the face of it seem simple enough to comprehend. We see that the apparent abstraction is grounded very firmly in a series of concrete meanings.

There is, however, a further matter of interest for the literary scholar and the student of language, and that is Eckhart's adaptation of the secular language of the *Minnesang*, the poetry of courty love, to his theological purposes. Here we are faced with an interesting turn of the wheel of literary history. It was around the year 1160 that Middle High German written literature became "secularized," that is to say it ceased to be the purview of monks and clerics and passed into the hands of the *ministeriales* and the nobility. From this secularization arose the great epics of the late twelfth and early thirteenth centuries and the poetry of courtly love, which I have already mentioned. This latter poetry developed a terminology that was peculiar to its own needs and that in its own way "secularized" an earlier poetic language that had expressed the love of man for God and the love of God for man. In the hands of the *Minnesänger* this language became solely the expression of the love of man for woman and, in some cases, of woman for man. The vocabulary is limited and highly charged so that it develops almost into a poetic jargon. It was Eckhart, the Dominican, who a century after the period when the *Minnesang* flourished most spectacularly took this vocabulary and used it once more for the expression of the relationship of God to man, at once a dangerous and a bold strike that in the hands of a less consummate literary artist—and I use this term advisedly—could have led to a confusion of thought and meaning. Eckhart never leaves us in doubt that this secular love vocabulary has now been restored to a theological purpose, but has, at the same time, lost none of the meanings that had accrued to it during its secular use.

It will of course not be possible to do more than hint at this rather technical poetic event in a translation into English, but I think it important for the English-speaking reader to understand from this one example (and many more that could be adduced) that the writer whose works have been so lovingly and painstakingly translated by McGinn and Tobin is not just "another theological thinker" but a literary force of the highest magnitude. He is ready to speak to, and startle, his audience into thought by this adaptation of terminology to his main purposes and it is in this linguistic and literary command that much of the effect of his teachings may be sought. Perhaps the fascination with his thought and expression will persuade the reader to try to reach back and read Eckhart in the original Middle High German—the effort will be well repaid.

In any case this new volume adds a wealth not only of theology but of literature to the stock-in-trade of the English-speaking reader. I am delighted that it is being published.

KEY TO ABBREVIATIONS

I. The abbreviations used for the books of the Bible follow the practice of the Jerusalem Bible. The translations of scriptural texts, however, have been made directly from Eckhart's Latin and German, which is usually close to the Vulgate text. In addition, the Vulgate numbering of the Psalms has been followed.

II. Frequently cited works will be abbreviated as follows:

A. Eckhart's Works. Unless otherwise noted, all Eckhart's works are cited and have been translated from the edition of the Deutsche Forschungsgemeinschaft under the general editorship of J. Quint for the German works and J. Koch for the Latin works. This edition, *Meister Eckhart: Die deutschen und lateinischen Werke* (Stuttgart and Berlin: W. Kohlhammer, 1936–) is hereafter abbreviated as DW and LW, followed by the volume number. The letters n. and nn. will refer to the numbered section(s) of the Latin edition. The editor of this volume and the editors of the Classics of Western Spirituality Series wish to take this opportunity to express their sincere gratitude to the directors of the Deutsche Forschungsgemeinschaft for their permission to make use of the critical text as the basis for this translation.

Individual works appear as follows:

LW. *Book of the Parables of Genesis (Par. Gen.)*
Commentary on Exodus (Comm. Ex.)
Commentary on Genesis (Comm. Gen.)
Commentary on John (Comm. Jn.)
Commentary on Wisdom (Comm. Wis.)
Parisian Questions (Par. Quest.)
Sermons and Lectures on Ecclesiasticus (Comm Ecc.)
Sermons, Latin (Sermon with Roman numerals)

KEY TO ABBREVIATIONS

DW. Book *"Benedictus"* 1 and 2 *(Bened.)*
Counsels on Discernment (Couns.)
On Detachment (Detach.)
Sermons, German (Sermon with Arabic numerals)

Essential Eckhart. This is the short reference for the companion volume to this one, *Meister Eckhart: The Essential Sermons, Commentaries, Treatises, and Defense* (translation and Introduction by Edmund Colledge, O.S.A., and Bernard McGinn; Preface by Huston Smith; New York: Paulist Press, 1981; Classics of Western Spirituality Series).

Théry. Stands for the edition of the Cologne Trial documents by G. Théry, "Édition critique des pièces relatives au procès d'Eckhart contenues dans le manuscrit 33b de la Bibliothèque de Soest," *Archives d'histoire doctrinale et littéraire du moyen âge* 1 (1926): 129–268.

B. Other Authors

1. Aristotle:
   Categories (Cat.)
   Metaphysics (Met.)
   On the Soul (Soul)
   Physics (Phy.)
   Posterior Analytics (Post. Anal.)
   Topics (Top.)

2. Augustine
   Confessions (Conf.)
   Literal Commentary on Genesis (Lit. Comm. Gen.)
   Christian Doctrine (Christ. Doct.)
   Trinity (Trin.)

3. Moses Maimonides
   Guide for the Perplexed (Guide)

4. Thomas Aquinas
   Commentary on the Sentences (In Sent.)

KEY TO ABBREVIATIONS

Summa against the Gentiles (SCG)
Summa of Theology (STh). The subdivisions are indicated as follows: Ia.
12. 3 = First Part, question 12, article 3.

The abbreviation **MHG** = Middle High German

INTRODUCTION

In 1981 Edmund Colledge, O.S.A., and I collaborated on the first volume devoted to Meister Eckhart in The Classics of Western Spirituality series. This volume, *Meister Eckhart: The Essential Sermons, Commentaries, Treatises, and Defense* (hereafter referred to under the short title of the *Essential Eckhart*), was designed to present the main lines of the German Dominican's teaching on the basis of a judicious selection of both the Latin and the Middle High German writings. All too often then, as now, some interpreters try to pit the vibrant and creative vernacular preacher against the supposedly dry and uninteresting scholastic writer and so continue to misunderstand Eckhart and his special place in the history of Christian spirituality.

From the beginning, the *Essential Eckhart* was designed to be complemented by one or more volumes that would make further riches of Eckhart's teaching and preaching available to the English-speaking public. The current extraordinary interest in Meister Eckhart has resulted in a number of new translations of Eckhart's vernacular sermons into English,[1] as well as an excellent version of the *Parisian Questions* and the "Prologues" to the *Three-Part Work*, Eckhart's vast unfinished project for a systematic theology;[2] but no other attempts to illustrate the full range of his contribution by coordinated presentations of both sides of his literary efforts have been made. Hence the present volume, intended to continue and enrich the work begun with the *Essential Eckhart*. Due to constraints of time and space, the *Essential Eckhart* was able to offer translations of only nine of the vernacular sermons, though the nine were judged to be among the most important for understanding the fundamental lines of Eckhart's mysticism. The present volume is designed to do more justice to Eckhart the preacher by including thirty sermons, twenty-four translated from the MHG vernacular and six from the Latin. Once again, the structure of the volume tries to show that the profound and daring teaching found in the Meister's scholastic writings, especially in the scriptural commentaries that form the bulk of these, is the source

1

INTRODUCTION

and often the necessary gloss for what he preached. Eckhart the teacher and Eckhart the preacher should never be separated.

The Introduction to the *Essential Eckhart* contained an account of Eckhart's life and subsequent influence written by Edmund Colledge, as well as an attempt to sketch the main lines of Eckhart's thought, written by me.[3] There is no need to repeat here what was said there. The past five years, of course, have seen the publication of a number of notable studies, especially of Eckhart's thought.[4] While these serve to enrich our understanding of the ever-elusive Meister, I have not seen in them reasons for altering the basic position I attempted to set out in the 1981 Introduction and in two articles published at that time.[5] Nevertheless, the Introduction to this companion volume can help to flesh out some of the points made in the *Essential Eckhart*, not only by commenting on the texts contained here in a general way, but also by taking up one of the most crucial issues in interpreting Eckhart's thought—the problem of speaking about God.

1. The Selections in This Volume

As explained above, the two-part structure of this volume grew out of the intention to show how both aspects of Eckhart's life as a Dominican, his formal teaching in the schools and his activity as a preacher, were intimately related. The selections presented in Parts I and II have no simple one-to-one correlation; but an attentive reading, helped by the notes, which try to cross-reference themes to other texts both in this volume and in the *Essential Eckhart*, will demonstrate how illuminating it is to read Eckhart in this way. Since Eckhart's influence was so vital to the MHG mystical texts of the later Middle Ages, I have also decided to add by way of an Appendix the most striking and controversial of all the texts once ascribed to the German Dominican, but now known to be by a follower, the famous "Sister Catherine" treatise.

PART I. ECKHART THE TEACHER

Although the importance of the *Parisian Questions* and the "Prologues" to the *Three-Part Work* cannot be denied, the overwhelming preponderance

INTRODUCTION

of what remains of Eckhart's scholastic writings consists of the scriptural commentaries he wrote for the training and use of preachers. These survive in what is doubtless a fragmentary but still impressive form, filling three large volumes of the critical edition (LW I–III). We cannot be sure when any of them was written. Most likely, they were begun during Eckhart's second period as teaching Master in Paris (1311–1313), when he planned the *Three-Part Work*, and they were continued when he found the opportunity during the years 1314–1326 when he taught and preached in Strassburg and Cologne.

The lengthiest of these is the great *Commentary on John*, Eckhart's only surviving interpretation of a New Testament book. Here, as in all his commentaries, Eckhart does not provide a continuous exposition in the manner of his predecessor Thomas Aquinas, but elects to choose key verses to illustrate the essential speculative and moral truths found in the text. Still, this work comes closest of all his efforts to a finished and exhaustive treatment. It also contains some of the most profound and important sections in all his writings, notably the part devoted to the Johannine Prologue (Jn. 1:1–14), translated in the *Essential Eckhart*.[6] Many other sections of this commentary are rich sources for Eckhart's thought,[7] and one other key passage is translated in this volume.

The Old Testament commentaries comprise two devoted to Genesis, one each to Exodus and Wisdom, and a mixture of exegesis and preaching called the *Sermons and Lectures on Ecclesiasticus* (or Sirach). Selections from the two Genesis commentaries (the first is devoted more to the literal meaning, the second to the "parabolical," or hidden meaning) were given in the *Essential Eckhart*.[8]

For this volume I have decided to translate the whole of Eckhart's *Commentary on Exodus*, because of its intrinsic value and also to provide a better sense of one of Eckhart's exegetical works taken in its entirety. Both the Exodus and the Wisdom commentaries stand out among the Dominican's Old Testament expositions, but the *Commentary on Exodus* is special for a number of reasons. First, it contains Eckhart's commentary on Exodus 3:14 ("I am who am . . . He who is sent me"), the text that for centuries was the key scriptural reference for Jewish and Christian understandings of the nature of God as that of pure being or existence (*esse*).[9] Meister Eckhart's understanding of the term *existence* and how it may and may not be said to apply to God is a highly complex one, as already suggested in the Introduction to the *Essential Eckhart*.[10] No other text in all his writings comes closer to a general summary of his position than this part of the *Commentary on Exodus*. A

3

number of other sections of the exposition also have an important bearing on the Meister's understanding of *esse*.[11]

An even more important reason for selecting the *Commentary on Exodus* for complete translation is the lengthy treatment it gives to the issue of proper speech about God in its interpretations of Exodus 15:3 ("Almighty is his name") and 20:7 ("You shall not take the name of your God in vain").[12] It is clear from Eckhart's own remarks that he meant these two sections to be taken together as a single extended treatise on this key theological issue, *De nominibus Dei*, "On the Names of God." The second part of this Introduction will study this treatise in detail, comparing it with the treatments of Maimonides and Thomas Aquinas, as well as with the homiletic presentation found in one of the vernacular sermons translated here.

I have argued elsewhere in more detail that while both predication and analogy are important for understanding the shifting contexts of the ways in which Eckhart speaks about God, it is a deeply Neoplatonic form of dialectic thought that is most essential to his metaphysical position.[13] Recent publications of other Eckhart scholars have supported and enriched this hermeneutical line.[14] Therefore, the explicitly dialectical texts in Eckhart's writings provide an indispensable clue for the correct interpretation of the different ways he talks about God and creation in various contexts. One of the most important of these dialectical texts occurs in the *Commentary on Exodus* in his remarks on how God can be said to be both similar and dissimilar to creatures.[15] Although some of the later portions of the commentary are less interesting, it should be evident from what has been said why the *Commentary on Exodus* deserves its place in the part of this volume devoted to Eckhart the teacher.

Reasons of space made it impossible to include the whole of the *Commentary on Wisdom*, the other gem among Meister Eckhart's expositions on the Old Testament. The Wisdom literature in general exercised a powerful influence on the German Dominican, as can be seen from the frequency with which he cites all the Wisdom books. To complement the Exodus text, I have chosen four key passages from the *Commentary on Wisdom*, one from the *Sermons and Lectures on Ecclesiasticus*, and one from the *Commentary on John* for translation in Part I. Each of these illustrates one or more of the most essential themes of Eckhart's speculative thought. Taken together they constitute a kind of *summa* of his theology.

The first text, Eckhart's remarks on Wisdom 1:14 ("He created all things that they might be"), deals with the Meister's understanding of creation and thus can be compared with the texts from the two Genesis commentaries found in the *Essential Eckhart*. What it adds to these is a more detailed treatment of the final cause of creation than that found anywhere else in the Dominican's writings. The second selection concerns Wisdom 7:11 ("All good things came to me together with her," that is, Wisdom, "moral integrity not to be counted through her hands"). It highlights the unity and equality of all goodness and love in God and in those to whom God comes, and in its second half deals with the nature of moral goodness, or the *honestum*.

The third text is Eckhart's famous exposition of Wisdom 7:27 ("And since it is one, it can do all things"), the greatest of the dialectical texts referred to before. Vladimir Lossky first drew attention to this difficult but crucial passage;[16] since his time it has been studied and commented on by many scholars. In claiming a priority for God conceived of as the One (that is, the "not-to-be-distinguished") in that the One shows how God is the more distinct insofar as he is indistinct (we might say, "the more transcendent to things insofar as he is immanent in them"), Eckhart does not mean to deny his insistence elsewhere on the privileged place of existence (*esse*) as a proper name for God. What he wants to make clear is that the true meaning of divine existence insofar as we can grasp it is rooted in an incomprehensible dialectical mystery of Absolute Unity.[17]

The fourth selection is the comment on Wisdom 18:14 concerning the silence in which the Almighty Word comes into the world. In this text Eckhart deals with a number of essential themes: the birth of the Word in the soul, the indistinction of God, the notion of the image as a formal emanation or "inner boiling" (*bullitio*) in God, and the necessity for union without a medium. The passage explaining Ecclesiasticus 24:29 ("They that eat me, shall yet hunger") is perhaps the most powerful text that Eckhart ever wrote on the way in which all things both "eat" God insofar as their being depends utterly on him and yet will always "hunger for him" because they can never exhaust his immeasurable existence. This text also contains Eckhart's most detailed treatment of analogy, and thus forms an important complement to the dialectical texts translated here. Finally, the sixth text, taken from the *Commentary on John*, is among the major passages for the Meister's theology of the Trinity. It deals with the way the Father, as the source of the divine emanations, is also the satisfaction of all things.

PART II.   ECKHART THE PREACHER

About 1270, Robert Kilwardby, another Dominican theologian who like Eckhart served as a provincial, wrote to the Dominican novices under his charge:

5

INTRODUCTION

There are indeed people in other states of life who preach, but they do not do so in the same way. For the friars of the Order of Preachers do it by virtue of the very institution of their Order, by virtue of their job which gives them their name.[18]

The young Eckhart, who entered the order a few years after these words were written, was doubtless steeped in this understanding of the Dominican mission, and it was this that he sought to express in his own preaching activity. Eckhart preached extensively in both Latin and the vernacular. In the critical edition of the Latin works fifty-six sermons, some in several parts, were edited by Ernst Benz, Bruno Decker, and Josef Koch (LW IV). Although we cannot tie these sermons down to specific places and audiences, we can imagine that most of them were delivered to clerical audiences usually consisting of Eckhart's fellow Dominicans. Many of them are mere sermon notes; others are either fairly arid or add little to what can be found in more detail in the other Latin works. Nevertheless, some of these sermons are among the most impressive of all Eckhart's efforts as a preacher. Six of this group are translated here.

Sermon IV.1–2 is based on one of Meister Eckhart's favorite scriptural texts, Romans 11:36: "All things are from him, through him, and in him." It deals with God as one and three, but especially with the Holy Spirit. Sermon VI consists of four fragments dealing with *caritas*, or divine love, of which only the first two are translated here. Sermon XXV.1–2 is a key passage for Eckhart's doctrine of grace, about which there has been considerable controversy and not a little confusion. Sermon XXIX is justly regarded as the greatest of Eckhart's Latin sermons (and is one of the few to have been translated into English before). As an extended consideration of the mystery of God as the One who is to be identified with pure Intellect, it bears comparison with such other key texts as question 1 of the *Parisian Questions* ("Are Existence and Understanding the Same in God?") and the dialectical text on *unum* from the *Commentary on Wisdom*.

Sermon XLV is one of the longest of Eckhart's sermons, and at first glance somewhat atypical. Though it does not lack some speculative insights, it is primarily moral in tone. This carefully structured homiletical piece, with its beautiful "collation" on four ways in which Christians must learn how to follow Christ by bearing their own cross, is a reminder that Eckhart's preaching, however speculative and difficult, was never divorced from moral application. The three brief sections that constitute Sermon XLIX dealing with Matthew 22:20 ("Whose are this image and inscription?") form an important source for Eckhart's teaching on the nature of the *imago*,

6

and bear interesting comparison with the many vernacular sermons (e.g., Sermons 16b, 69, and 70) that also consider this central notion.

Eckhart's vernacular sermons are more numerous and with justice more widely known than his Latin offerings. The richness of their manuscript witnesses show that it was primarily through his vernacular preaching that his influence spread. Although previous claims about Eckhart's role as *the* originator of MHG philosophical and theological vocabulary have been exaggerated,[19] the power of Eckhart's daring formulations and the subtlety of his use of language make him one of the great—if difficult—masters of German prose style.[20]

Franz Pfeiffer's landmark edition of Eckhart in 1857 contained over a hundred sermons. Subsequent investigators uncovered scores of others they claimed were products of the Meister's preaching. The indefatigable efforts of Josef Quint (1898–1976), the editor of the critical edition contained in DW I–III, reduced the number of authentic sermons to eighty-six. Quint did not live to complete DW IV, which is to contain possibly authentic sermons, as well as sayings, legends, and other materials; hence some uncertainty still exists about a number of pieces that are very much in the style of Eckhart, if not certainly by him.[21] In both the *Essential Eckhart* and the present volume only sermons from Quint's critical edition of eighty-six have been included.

Meister Eckhart's vernacular sermons rarely follow one particular line of thought through to the end. Rather, they might be better described as sets of variations on a few central themes.[22] In a noted passage from Sermon 53, Eckhart summarized the basic content of his German preaching under four headings:

> When I preach, I am accustomed to speak about detachment, and that man should be free of himself and of all things; second, that a man should be formed again into that simple good which is God; third, that he should reflect on the great nobility with which God has endowed his soul, so that in this way he may come again to wonder at God; fourth, about the purity of the divine nature, for the brightness of the divine nature is beyond words. God is a word, a word unspoken.[23]

While these four themes are an admirable summary of the main lines of Eckhart's vernacular preaching, it is important to point out that each is so rich in implications, so varied in formulations, that an adequate exegesis of any of them would demand an extensive analysis of scores of sermons.

Eckhart's Latin commentaries demonstrate how central the work of exegesis was to all his thought. The same is true of his sermons, both in Latin and in the vernacular. However abstruse and subtle his thought, it always finds its professed root in the text of the scriptures. Every sermon of Eckhart's begins from a scriptural text and cannot be understood apart from it. In the rapidly shifting development of most of his sermons, the scriptural text is frequently the most important clue to the inner development of his thought. Eckhart's use of scripture was unusual, even for his time. The Meister assumes a freedom in relation to the text that scandalizes modern exegetes even more than his speculative principles did the inquisitors who condemned him. In the Latin works, his freedom was restricted to readings discovered through the letter of the Vulgate or its liturgical equivalents, or at times to those he found in Maimonides's interpretations of the Hebrew text; in the MHG sermons he was free to make his own versions to suit the point intended, and many of these sermons are based on extended wordplay that is better read than summarized. Eckhart's attitude toward the "word" of scripture, then, is a paradigm for his treatment of all words—they are useful but partial and imperfect revelations of the Word that can never be fully grasped.

The twenty-four MHG sermons chosen for this volume are designed to present a fuller range of Eckhart's contribution as a popular preacher than what was available in the *Essential Eckhart*. It is not so much the limited number of themes as the ingenious way in which Eckhart adopts his rhetoric to present them that guarantees these generally brief pieces an honored place among the great texts of Christian mysticism. The choice of these particular sermons is the result of collaboration between myself and Frank Tobin of the University of Nevada at Reno, one of the foremost experts on Eckhart and his thought. Tobin's help in bringing the *Essential Eckhart* volume to completion was invaluable, and I am more than grateful that he consented to prepare the translations and notes for the MHG sermons found in this volume.

It would scarcely be productive to try to give full introductions to each of these twenty-four sermons, not least because there can be no substitute for reading the sermons themselves. The largest number of the pieces presented here, like those found in the *Essential Eckhart*, are taken from the first volume of Quint's edition and represent sermons whose ascription to Meister Eckhart, in one way or another, is most assured. These eleven sermons ring the changes on many of the four central themes outlined in Sermon 53. Sermon 1, for instance, deals with the way in which the soul as the temple of God must be free of all things in order to receive Jesus, and thus illustrates the first theme, that of detachment (*abegescheidenheit*). Sermon 3, on the other hand, emphasizes the way which the soul, as endowed with knowledge, can "break through" to the pure and ineffable divine nature, and thus is more illustrative of the fourth theme.

Sermon 4 deals with the birth of the Word in the soul, the most pervasive theme in Eckhart's vernacular preaching.[24] Sermon 7 is one of the many that talks about the nature of our union with God, or, in the words of Sermon 53, how we are "formed anew into the simple goodness that is God." It insists that although love unites us with God in work and intellect unites us with God's pure being, the divine ground lies even deeper. Sermon 9, one of Eckhart's most noted pieces, is a profound exercise in apophatic or negative speech about God and will be described in more detail in the second part of this introduction.

Sermons 10, 14, and 16b all deal in various ways with the third of the themes mentioned in Eckhart's summary statement, that is, with the "nobility of the soul." They speak of how the powers of the soul and especially the soul's ground are related to God both as one and three, and how the birth of the Word in the soul brings true unity that allows the "just person" to be spoken of as divine. Sermon 12 is a particularly rich and daring offering that resumes many of Eckhart's more provocative statements about the soul's divine nature, including the assertion condemned at Avignon that there is "something" in the soul of such a nature that "if a person were completely like this, he would be completely uncreated and uncreateable."[25] A similar assertion is found in Sermon 24, included here. Also from the first volume of Quint's edition is Sermon 21, a profound presentation of God as one and of the relation of intellect and will to the divine unity. This sermon is also unusual in being the only place in the vernacular writings that refers to God as "the negation of negation," a key theme of the Latin works.[26]

The remaining thirteen sermons are taken from those found in the second and third volumes of Quint's edition, comprising pieces that cannot be proven authentic on the grounds of citation in the proceedings of Eckhart's trial at Cologne or on the basis of parallels with the Latin works, but whose style and content argue that they truly belong to the Dominican preacher. Sermon 29 speaks of the birth of the Word in the soul and the "uncreated something" found there. It also reminds us of the famous Sermon 52 in referring to a "breaking through" into the hidden Godhead where God and the soul live "without a why."[27] Sermon 30 is a dialectical text about the soul's unity with God that ends with a fitting moral application. Sermon 39 deals with the theme of the "just person" and the work of the Trinity in the soul, and Sermon 40 is a careful statement of Eckhart's understanding of union with God. Sermon 46 is a brief but significant piece that investigates the role of the Incarnation in the return of the soul to God. Sermon 59 is a deeply pastoral text in which many of the themes of the Meister's preaching are combined.

Sermons 69 and 70 deal with the text "A little while" (or "a little bit," as Eckhart takes it) "and you will not see me" (Jn. 16:16). They deal with the issue of union without a medium, of the nature of the image, and of the properties of the intellect. Sermon 71 is one of the most noted expressions of Eckhart's apophatic theology—a meditation on the various meanings of nothingness suggested by the text "Paul rose from the ground and with eyes open saw nothing" (Ac. 9:8). Sermon 76 returns to the pervasive themes of the birth of the Word in the soul and the relation of our sonship to that of Christ. Sermon 80 concerns the divine plenitude filling all things, and Sermon 84 deals with how the soul must rise above itself to be united with God. Finally, the noted Sermon 86, one of Eckhart's most difficult texts, reverses the traditional interpretations of the Mary and Martha story from Luke 10 to show that Martha is a type of the person who has "learned life," combining both action and contemplation, and is thus superior to Mary, the pure contemplative.[28]

APPENDIX. THE "SISTER CATHERINE" TREATISE

The broad lines of the influence of Meister Eckhart on late medieval spiritual literature were surveyed by Edmund Colledge in the Introduction to the *Essential Eckhart*.[29] The marks of Eckhart's teaching are found not only in other major mystics, such as John Tauler and Henry Suso, but also in a rich body of sermons and treatises, many of which circulated under the Meister's name. Franz Pfeiffer's ground-breaking edition of 1857 included no less than eighteen treatises, but Josef Quint reduced this to three.[30]

Among the treatises mistakenly edited by Pfeiffer under Eckhart's name, perhaps the most interesting is the text known as "Schwester Katrei," or "Sister Catherine," from the title it bears in some manuscripts, "Daz ist Swester Katrei Meister Eckehartes Tohter von Strâzburc."[31] The title, as well as the general theme of a mysterious woman who comes to the Dominican cloister to give instruction to Friar Eckhart, is obviously related to one of the popular Eckhart Legends, called "Meister Eckhart's Daughter."[32]

The text has enjoyed considerable attention, not only because of its discovery in a number of different manuscripts (at least seventeen) and in several variants, but also because it has been frequently seen as a heretical work belonging to the so-called Brethren of the Free Spirit. In Norman Cohn's exaggerated account of the Free Spirit ("An Elite of Amoral Supermen," as his chapter title has it), the "Schwester Katrei" treatise is one of the three basic pieces of evidence used to support this view.[33] Even in Gordon Leff's more carefully argued treatment in his *Heresy in the Later Middle Ages* we are told: "Nowhere is this transition to open heresy to be seen more clearly than in the partly heretical treatise known as *Schwester Katrei.*"[34] Leff admits that the text does not counsel the amoral activity associated with the Free Spirit, and that it contains much of the basic teaching associated with Eckhart; but he insists that the sister's claim to identity with God is "outright pantheism," and he concludes that "in leaping the gulf between God and man it opened up the way to all the excesses which were made to follow from the claim to divinity."[35]

The traditional picture of the Free Spirit movement has been challenged by Robert E. Lerner in his important book *The Heresy of the Free Spirit in the Later Middle Ages* (Berkeley: University of California Press, 1972). Here Lerner subjects "Sister Catherine" to a careful analysis that demonstrates that the work contains no antinomianism, and even steers clear of the passivity or "Quietism" that marks such other Free Spirit texts as Marguerite Porete's *Mirror of Simple Souls*, but he admits that the sister's claim of permanent unqualified union with God goes beyond the boundaries of traditional orthodox mysticism.[36]

This is not the place to discuss all the issues involved in the debate over the Free Spirit movement and its connections with Beguine mysticism. It is clear, however, that it was not only the Avignon papacy but also the mystics themselves who were worried about false mystical teaching. The evidence of Tauler and Suso in Germany, Jan van Ruusbroec in the Lowlands, Walter Hilton in England—and even of the "Sister Catherine" treatise itself—shows how much a part of fourteenth-century mysticism this issue was. Since the "Sister Catherine" text is so deeply marked by Eckhart's thought, and since the treatise has been so important to the discussion of orthodoxy and heterodoxy in fourteenth-century mysticism, I asked Elvira Borgstädt, a student of medieval literature, to prepare an English translation of the piece for inclusion in this volume.

The version chosen for the translation is not that found in Pfeiffer, but the new, critically edited text prepared by Franz-Josef Schweitzer on the basis of one of the key manuscripts (Karlsruhe, Landesbibliothek, St. Peter ms. pap. 19, f. 2r–39v).[37] Though this manuscript dates to 1472, it represents a fairly pure version of the original that appears to have been written in the Alemannic dialect, quite possibly in Strassburg, in the first half of the fourteenth century. (Eckhart was in Strassburg from about 1314 to 1323.) The form of the treatise is a dramatic dialogue, recounting a series of meetings between a friar confessor (probably, but not certainly, a Dominican) and a woman who is obviously a Beguine. In the initial meetings (see Sections I–IV) the woman begs the confessor to show her the fastest road to eternal happiness. His advice concerning poverty of life and the practice of the virtues, however, does not seem to be sufficient for what she desires. Following the guidance of the Holy Spirit, she becomes increasingly dissatisfied with the confessor's counsels and at the end of these interviews "goes off into exile" to seek a more perfect way. On her return the confessor does not recognize her. After hearing her confession, he joyfully announces to his brothers: "I have listened to [the confession of] a person and I'm not sure if she is a human being or an angel. . . . She knows and loves more than all the people I have ever known."[38] But still the "daughter" is not confirmed in permanent union with God, although her moments of enjoyment of God lead her to make the daring statement, "Father, rejoice with me, I have become God," a claim that is more reminiscent of some of the sayings of the Sufi mystics than those typical of most Christian mystics.[39] Finally, she is enraptured in a three-day trance in which she appears to be dead. When she awakes, she has achieved the state of permanent union that has caused so much difficulty for the interpreters of "Sister Catherine."

Now it is quite true that the main tradition of Christian mysticism, represented in the Latin West by such figures as Augustine and Bernard of Clairvaux, had insisted that any union with God that could be achieved in this life was always a temporary and partial one. But the thought of Eckhart, and even that of such later orthodox mystics as Teresa of Avila, the first female Doctor of the Church, suggests other possibilities. Meister Eckhart's notion of union as perfect awareness of the soul's virtual identity with the divine ground and the ability to live "without a why" on the basis of this awareness seems to imply at least the possibility of what we could call a permanent mystical state, or what the "Sister Catherine" text speaks of as "being established in God."[40] Eckhart, of course, very seldom ties this to the kind of ecstatic experience involving the suspension of the senses found in this text, and here "Sister Catherine" doubtless reflects the Beguine piety of the late Middle Ages in which ecstasy played such a large role. But it must be noted that the three-day ecstasy is not the goal, but only the penultimate stage. The path to union dramatized here is not unlike that described by the mature Teresa in *The Interior Castle*, where rapture and the suspension of the faculties are found in the sixth dwelling place, or "mansion," but the highest, seventh dwelling place of the spiritual marriage is a permanent state of union beyond rapture in which Mary and Martha, that is, the contemplative and active lives, are perfectly joined.[41] This is not to say that "Sister Catherine's"

INTRODUCTION

view of union is the same as Teresa's, or that it is necessarily orthodox in all particulars; but it does suggest that just because it does not conform to the views of *some* Christian mystics, it does not need to be immediately dismissed as heretical.

The longer part of the text consists of the extended sixth section dealing with conversations between the daughter and the confessor in which the traditional roles of male adviser and female disciple are reversed. It is now the "established" daughter who takes the lead and gives instruction, though not in any crude or domineering way. The confessor is still a learned priest, and a fair portion of the instruction in these lengthy discourses is put in his mouth. The difference, to put it in Cardinal Newman's terms, is that he has only "notional" knowledge of the heavenly mysteries of which he speaks; the daughter, who has the "real" knowledge of one who has actually experienced them, must now be seen as the higher authority. This is surely one of the most daring aspects of this provocative text, but should it really be called heretical? The author felt that giving spiritual authority to a woman was not unusual in Christian history. The example of Mary Magdalene, that great lover of Christ and popular medieval saint,[42] is analyzed in detail throughout the latter part of the work and serves to provide both a model and a warrant for the daughter's role reversal.

The picture drawn of the daughter after her establishment is on the whole an orthodox one. She is far from being an antinomian or even a laxist. In a passage misused by Norman Cohn, the confessor (perhaps by way of testing the authenticity of her spiritual claims) tells her: "You should eat when you are hungry and drink when you are thirsty. You should wear a soft gown and sleep in a soft bed. . . . If you want to enjoy all creatures you should rightfully do so, because any creature you choose to enjoy is brought back to its origin." This might imply merely giving up severe asceticism and making use of the things of the world, or it might be a lurking invitation to something worse. In any case, the daughter replies: "I know that you speak the truth. However, you must know that I will never desire anything else but to be a poor person until my death."[43]

The daughter's attitude toward the church and the traditional means of salvation is considerably more orthodox than another text that has been used as evidence of the Free Spirit, Marguerite Porete's *Mirror of Simple Souls*. It is the confessor, rather than she, who criticizes the friars for not living up to the example set by St. Dominic and St. Francis, complaints that were quite common in the fourteenth century.[44] At the moment of her establishment in union she is quick to insist, "I have attained by grace what Christ is by nature,"[45] a point also stressed by Eckhart.[46] Like Eckhart's followers

Suso and Tauler, a strong Christocentric and not merely "Logocentric" emphasis is found in the treatise.[47] There is also some attention given to the role of Christ in the Eucharist, a characteristic theme of Beguine piety.[48] Finally, we have already remarked on how the anonymous author, like other early disciples of Eckhart, took pains to condemn as "true heretics" those who have false notions of union and who "engage in sinful behavior . . . because they do not take sin for sin."[49]

This is not to say that all aspects of the teaching of the "Schwester Katrei" are beyond question. First of all, as the notes to the translation will make clear, the treatise is rich with many of the daring ideas and formulations of Meister Eckhart. The virtual existence of all things in God, the identity of the highest powers of the soul with the Godhead, the dynamic process of "flowing out" and return, the notion of union without a medium, and many others, are all evident. Most of the questions and problems that confront the interpretation of Eckhart's mysticism of the "God beyond God" can also be raised against the "Sister Catherine."

Even more interesting, however, are the problematic aspects of the teaching of the treatise that appear to be peculiar to it, rather than drawn directly from Meister Eckhart. The Dominican Master, as we know,[50] had little interest in visionary experiences of any kind. "Sister Catherine" seems to take this a step further in a developed polemic against any kind of bodily vision of God.[51] The deeply Neoplatonic basis of the work's mysticism also seems to be the source for two of the more questionable aspects of the text's teaching, both of which go beyond anything that Eckhart ever set forth in explicit fashion. The first is the daughter's detailed response to the confessor's request to explain the nature of hell, which she says is "nothing but a state of being" already present in sinners' attachment to the things of this world.[52] This discussion leads into a daring denial of bodily ascension or resurrection, a point in which "Sister Catherine" comes very close, if in a general way, to the position adopted in one of the great classics of Christian Neoplatonism, the *Periphyseon* of John the Scot.[53] It is difficult to know, both in the case of Meister Eckhart and in that of his anonymous disciple, whether we can speak of direct knowledge of the *Periphyseon* or not.

The many questions raised by the fascinating "Sister Catherine" treatise cannot be solved here, but await the ongoing collaborative work of students of language and literature, as well as those interested in the history of mysticism. Enough has been said, I hope, to indicate why this text deserves inclusion in this volume. My special thanks are due to Elvira Borgstädt for her excellent translation of this difficult piece, as well as her help in thinking about many of its problems.

INTRODUCTION

2. Meister Eckhart on Speaking about God[54]

The problem of speaking about God has never been more cogently put than by Augustine in a text from his *Christian Doctrine* that Eckhart loved to cite:

> Have we spoken or announced anything worthy of God? Rather I feel that I have done nothing but wish to speak: if I have spoken, I have not said what I wish to say. Whence do I know this, except because God is ineffable? If what I said were ineffable, it would not be said. And for this reason God should not be said to be ineffable, for when this is said something is said. And a contradiction in terms is created, since if that is ineffable which cannot be spoken, then that is not ineffable which can be called ineffable. This contradiction is to be passed over in silence rather than resolved verbally. For God, although nothing worthy may be spoken of him, has accepted the tribute of human voice and wished us to take joy in praising him with our words.[55]

The African doctor's recognition of the need for continuing praise of God despite his ineffability has been seconded by all Christian theologians, but his advice that "the contradiction is to be passed over in silence" was followed neither by him nor by his successors. While few Christian thinkers have claimed to be able to resolve this paradox, most have felt the need to discuss it. The incomprehensibility of the God of philosophical theology and the hiddenness of the God who reveals himself in Christ—two aspects of the same mystery, as Karl Rahner has argued[56]—have been with Christianity from the beginning. Nor is the problem of discourse on what by definition lies beyond speech absent from the other world religions, especially Christianity's neighbors, Judaism and Islam.

Meister Eckhart wrestled with this problem throughout his life, and he also has the distinction of being the first major theologian to deal with Augustine's paradox within the framework of two languages rather than one, that is, both in the technical Latin of the schools and in the vernacular of preaching and piety. It would be too lengthy to survey the whole range of Eckhart's reflections on the proper ways of speaking about God here, but the presence of the *Commentary on Exodus* and its treatise "On the Names of God" in this volume allows for an analysis of this central text and a comparison of such a formal theological treatment with Eckhart's homiletical practice as reflected in Sermon 9.

15

INTRODUCTION

First, a word about the tradition of treatments of the divine names or names of God (*de nominibus Dei*). Since the days of the Greeks, Western philosophers have been accustomed to ponder what kinds of attributes can be predicated of the supreme nature and how they can be used. Harry A. Wolfson, in a series of papers reprinted in his *Studies in the History of Philosophy and Religion*, has provided a wealth of material on pagan, Jewish, Christian, and Islamic speculation on the divine attributes.[57] In his piece "St. Thomas on Divine Attributes," Wolfson sketches the background to the five ways known to medieval scholastics like Aquinas and Eckhart in which terms may be applied to God.[58] These "ways" (*viae*) provide a helpful entry into the analysis of Eckhart's treatise. They are: (1) the way of univocation or equivocation, that is, that the terms we use of things can be applied to God either in exactly the same sense or in a completely different sense (positions rejected by Eckhart and by Thomas Aquinas); (2) the way of negation (*via negationis*), that is, the terms we use of things must be denied of God; (3) the way of causality (*via causalitatis*), which says that the terms we use of things apply to God insofar as he is the cause of all; (4) the way of eminence (*via eminentiae*), namely, that the terms we use of things apply in some higher way to God; and finally, (5) the way of analogy (closely allied to the way of eminence), which states that terms used of both creatures and God are partly the same and partly different.

It is important to note that the concern of medieval theologians like Thomas Aquinas and Meister Eckhart with speaking about God was not merely a philosophical exercise, a treatment of abstract "attributes" of God, but was actually a treatment of the "names of God," that is, the titles and descriptions that the God of revelation had used to describe himself in the Bible. As "hearers of the Word," believers were placed in a "linguistic situation" in which they were addressed by God and invited to respond to him in fitting fashion.[59] Two things follow from this. First, Christian believers begin with a fact, not a possibility, that is, with certain names that God has used of himself, not merely with names that *might* be used; and second, because these revealed names are both more diverse and sometimes more scandalously anthropomorphic and material than those allowed by the philosophers, Christian theology demands a more complicated hermeneutic of divine titles than the ancient thinkers had evolved. The desire to organize the divine names into fitting categories and to work out the dynamics of how they function was implicit in Christian belief from the beginning and became explicit in the age of the great Fathers of the fourth century. Around the year 500 the mysterious writer known today as the Pseudo-Dionysius in

16

his treatise *Divine Names* provided a treatment that was to be classic in both the East and the West.[60]

Concern with the names or titles of God was not unique to Christianity. Both Jewish and Muslim religious thinkers were also addressed by God in their revealed books and therefore also felt called upon to analyze the divine names and to study the proper rules for using them. Some of the Muslim thinkers, especially Avicenna and Averroes, were well known to Meister Eckhart and the scholastic authors in general; but the greatest non-Christian resource for scholastic authors on this issue was to be found in the *Guide for the Perplexed* of the Jewish philosopher and religious thinker Moses Maimonides (1135–1204), or Rabbi Moses as Eckhart always called him. Maimonides's *Guide* was translated into Latin about 1240 and was an important resource for many scholastic authors, especially Thomas Aquinas in his *Summa of Theology*.[61] No Christian author of the Middle Ages, however, knew Maimonides better or reflected greater sympathy for his views than did Meister Eckhart. To the best of my recollection, Eckhart never criticizes Maimonides the way he does Avicenna or others. In his theory of exegesis,[62] in many aspects of his interpretation of particular scriptural passages, but above all in his treatment of how to speak correctly about God, Eckhart is deeply influenced by the great Jewish thinker. In fact, the Meister's "Treatise on the Names of God" might be best described as a three-way conversation among Rabbi Moses, Friar Thomas, and Eckhart.

The first part of Eckhart's treatment is in his commentary on Exodus 15:3, "Almighty is his name." After examining how God is all-powerful although it is said that there are some things that he cannot do,[63] the Meister then launches into the treatise that he says will consist of four sections:

> The first is what some philosophers and Jewish authors think of this question and of the attributes which name God. . . . Second, there is a brief summary of what Catholic writers think of these predications or names. Third, why do Boethius and the theologians generally teach that only two kinds of categories, substance and relation, can be used of divinity? Fourth, we will speak about the name more proper and especially particular to God, that is, the "Tetragrammaton," below under Chapter 20 on the verse "You shall not take the name of your God in vain" (Ex. 20:7).[64]

Eckhart's consideration of the philosophers and Jewish authors (nn. 35–53) begins with an emphasis on the way of eminence (*via eminentiae*). Authorities are cited to show that God is not so much indescribable as above description, not so much unnameable as "omninameable," because he precontains all inferior perfections in himself in a more excellent way (n. 35). Avicenna's doctrine of God as existence is noted and it too seems to be understood in an eminent way (n. 36). But when Eckhart shifts to a lengthy summary of the position of Maimonides, it is the way of negation (*via negationis*) rather than that of eminence that predominates.[65] Like the Pseudo-Dionysius, Rabbi Moses held that negative propositions about the Creator are true, but that affirmative propositions are "partly equivocal." Eckhart summarizes his teaching on the five modes of positive attribution or denomination, showing that only the fifth, denomination from the effect (the *via causalitatis*), can be said to apply to God. In other words, we can only talk about what God has done, not what he is, and since this fifth mode posits nothing in God himself, it is described as "unsuitable, improper and not in keeping with the truth" (n. 44). The Meister concludes with the startling apophatic statement: "Hence all things that are positively said of God, even though they are perfections in us, are no longer so in God and are not more perfect than their opposites" (n. 44), though he seems to hold out an exception for the term existence (*esse*), at least insofar as it is conceived of as God's perfect self-sufficient being and not our own powerless one.

The second half of this first part of the treatise "On the Names of God" (nn. 45–53) is a deeper penetration of the reasons why Maimonides and other non-Christian thinkers held that positive propositions could not be properly predicated of God. Once again, Eckhart shows a deep knowledge of and profound respect for Maimonides as he paraphrases and summarizes the Guide's argument concerning the impossibility of any dispositions (*dispositiones*) being added to God.[66] To the Rabbi's seven proofs Eckhart adds an eighth—dispositions are added to things to make up for defects, something that cannot be true of God as *ipsummet esse* (n. 51).

In the second section of the treatise (nn. 54–61) Eckhart moves on "to take a summary glance at what our Christian teachers hand down on this" (n. 54). There are four essential principles for understanding their teaching. First, "there is one way of speaking and thinking about beings or things and their existence and another way about the categories of things and how we make use of them" (n. 54). Substance alone is being; all other things are being only analogously. Second, "expressions or propositions primarily and necessarily are in accord with the concepts of things and not with the things themselves" (n. 55). Third, "act proceeds from essence according to the ideas and properties of the attributes" (n. 56), so that while Paternity is identical with God's essence, we say that the Father and not the essence begets. The fourth principle is that all our knowledge arises from the senses, a good Aristotelian and Thomistic axiom (n. 57).

At this point Eckhart's thought appears to take an abrupt turn as he suddenly begins an analysis of how perfections exist in God "as necessarily and simply one and one thing" (n. 57). The point is to underline the priority of negation in speaking of God. If all our knowledge arises from the sense world in which perfections are multiple, can we really know how all perfections are absolutely one in God? "Anyone who would see God himself through himself . . . would see a single perfection. . . . If the onlooker were to give a name to that which he sees and through which and in which he sees, it would necessarily be the One" (n. 57)—but can we really ever see God this way in this life?[67]

On this basis Eckhart proceeds to address "that knotty and famous question whether there is a distinction of attributes in God or only in our intellect's way of grasping" in nn. 58–61. Here again his answer relies heavily on Maimonides. All distinction of divine attributes is totally on the side of the receiving intellect that "draws knowledge of such things from and through creatures" (n. 58). Thomas Aquinas, arguing on the basis of the priority of the way of eminence, thought differently, holding that the distinction of divine attributes had a real foundation in the overflowing richness of the divine nature.[68] Eckhart, even though he admits that "distinct attributes of this kind are not vain and false because they relate to something that is true and real in God" (n. 61), so stresses God's absolute unity that he affirms that "no distinction can exist *or be understood* in God himself" (n. 60). This not only distances him from Thomas Aquinas, but it also seems to have been the reason why this phrase, plus the two Maimonides citations preceding it, were singled out for condemnation in the papal bull of 1329.[69] It should be pointed out, however, that this extract was put among the second class of condemned articles, that is, those "suspect of heresy, though with many explanations and additions they might take on or possess a Catholic meaning."

The third section of Eckhart's treatise (nn. 62–78) continues his treatment of the Catholic writers by investigating why Augustine, Boethius, and others affirm that two of Aristotle's ten categories, substance and relation, and not just substance alone, can be legitimately applied to God. The answer comes through an appeal to two principles. First, "Relation, even though it is an accident, still does not signify in the manner of an accident, because it does not do so as inhering in a subject or substance" (n. 63). The *esse* of a relation is *adesse* ("being toward") rather than *inesse* ("being in"), the charac-

INTRODUCTION

teristic mode of an accident. Consequently, and second, "relation perdures in the Godhead according to the mode of signifying and predicating which constitutes its own genus as a category" (n. 64). Meister Eckhart goes on to expound further reasons for the appropriateness of the use of relation language for the Trinity. Although his teaching here is in substantial agreement with that of Thomas Aquinas, Eckhart's emphasis on the priority of Absolute Unity in God leads to some real differences, as when he cites without disapproval the formula of Gilbert of Poitiers, rejected by Thomas, that the relations as it were remain "standing on the outside" of the divine substance (n. 65).[70]

Eckhart then adds a fifth principle to the four already invoked as rules for speaking about God, namely, that "the ten categories . . . are distinguished from each other first and necessarily and immediately by themselves according to their ideas and ways of predicating," but that this is not true of the species (i.e., particular examples) of these categories (n. 67). The application of this axiom shows that all qualities ascribed to God (e.g., goodness, justice, etc.) are reducible to substance and therefore to the same mode of predication—that is, that "in the Godhead the Father knows by means of the same thing by which he is and by which he is God, namely, his substance" (n. 68). But since the concepts of substance and relation are not the same in the case of God, "God is not simply and by the same idea God the Father and God as substance, but he is God as substance by one idea and Father by another" (n. 70).

Now this distinction of the concepts of substance and relation in the case of God may seem to contradict Eckhart's earlier statement that "no distinction can exist or be understood in God himself." The Meister does not provide us with an answer to this seeming contradiction, but two responses seem possible. First, we might say that relation does not posit a distinction *in* God, because that would conceive of relation as implying "existence in" (*inesse*) rather than "existence in relation to" (*adesse*). But even if we were to dismiss this and claim that the difference in the notions of substance and relation still imply some kind of duality, a response might be framed on the basis of Eckhart's distinction between the triune God and the hidden divine ground, or Godhead. That is, the conceptual distinction between substance and relation is legitimate in thinking about God as three-who-are-one, but is not in any way applicable to the hidden Godhead.[71] Certainly, the conceptual distinction accepted here in no way suggests any distinction in being. Since the concept of relation in itself does not connote either *esse* or *inesse*, but is defined solely by what it is related to (*adesse*, e.g., a father as father is a father only insofar as he has a son), relation creates no distinction of essence and existence—the existence of the Father is not other than the existence that is identical with the divine essence.

A sixth and final principle is then invoked by Eckhart, the scholastic commonplace originating in Aristotle "that the truth of an affirmative proposition always subsists in the identity of terms, but the truth of a negative one subsists in the difference or distinction of terms" (n. 73). Since the "truth of an affirmation consists in the existence of what is" (n. 73), "the affirmation that consists in the existence and identity of the terms properly belongs to God" (n. 74). God alone is full and pure existence; creatures are both "being and nonbeing." No negation, nothing negative, belongs to God, except the "negation of negation," which is how the One is predicated in the *via negationis*. Thus, the negation of negation signifies the purest and fullest affirmation, the famous "I am who am" of Exodus 3:14 (n. 74).[72] Existence can deny itself nothing and to nothing, and for this reason it is almighty—"His name is almighty," as the base text says.

Eckhart's Neoplatonic dialectic of the "negation of negation" stands on its head the Maimonidean insistence that only negative propositions can be legitimately used of God. This is confirmed by his response to an objection drawn from the Pseudo-Dionysius that "negations about God are true, but affirmations are unsuitable" (n. 78).[73] Following Thomas Aquinas in *STh* Ia. 13. 3, Eckhart holds that this is true of the mode of signifying, but not of the perfections signified. Eckhart here, like his mentor Thomas, is a clear proponent of the *via eminentiae* rather than the *via negationis*, but the way in which he arrives at his position is different from that of Thomas.

The picture gets even more complex when we turn to the fourth part of Meister Eckhart's treatise "On the Divine Names," the section found under the commentary on Exodus 20:7 in nn. 143–184.[74] This part, based largely on Maimonides, is an extended consideration first of the Hebrew names for God (nn. 143–60), then of Christian understandings of the name "Who is" (*Qui est*) in nn. 161–69, and finally of the basic hermeneutics of applying all positive and negative names to God (nn. 170–84). Here, at least at first glance, Meister Eckhart seems to take back what we have just seen, so that the *via negationis* appears to triumph once more over the *via eminentiae*. Before we can deal with this problem, a brief summary of the argument is in order.

Eckhart begins by investigating the name Adonai and those similar to it, following Maimonides's *Guide* 1.61–64. Then he turns his attention to the "Tetragrammaton," or name of four letters (YHVH, our "Yahweh"), which he interprets as a circumlocution for the "ineffable name of God" that signifies the divine substance itself (nn. 146–48).[75] The importance of the Tetragrammaton had been known to Latin authors since the time of Jerome, but under the influence of Maimonides both Thomas Aquinas and Meister Eckhart gave it special prominence.[76] In *STh* Ia. 13. 9 and 11 Thomas had modified his earlier views by giving the Tetragrammaton a position of parity with the traditional term *Qui est*. If the latter is favored from the viewpoint of origin (God is pure *esse*), the four-letter name is preferred to any other as signifying "the incommunicable and, if we could say such a thing, individual substance of God" (Ia. 13. 11c). Eckhart, as we shall see, does not invoke this distinction and tends to link the two names more closely than does Thomas.

The names of twelve letters and of forty-two letters that Eckhart next discusses (nn. 149–54) are taken over from Maimonides. The first refers to the blessing of Aaron and his sons in Numbers 6:24–26 where the sacred Tetragrammaton is used three times (3 × 4 = 12), and the second refers to the forty-two letters in the words of Genesis 1:1–2a. A treatment of the names of two letters and that of Shaddai or *sufficientia* follows (nn. 155–60). Eckhart closes his remarks on the Hebrew names by noting with Maimonides that except for the mysterious Tetragrammaton all these names are derived from God's activities or effects and tell us nothing about the divine nature.

Eckhart then turns to a summary of Christian teaching, based on Thomas Aquinas and John Damascene, of the meaning of *Qui est* as the privileged name of God (nn. 161–69).[77] Of the four reasons he gives for the preeminence of this name the most interesting is the second, because it shows that the Dominican thought that *Qui est* was probably the inner meaning of the Tetragrammaton insofar as it signified what was most proper to God. Both Avicenna and Aquinas are cited to support this claim (n. 164). The fourth reason given for the priority of *Qui est* is typically Eckhartian— "That which is above every name excludes no name, but universally includes all names and in an equally indistinct way" (n. 166). This note brings us back to the beginning of the treatise where the role of existence as the indistinct *nomen omninominabile* was emphasized (cf. n. 36).

In the final part of the fourth section of the treatise Meister Eckhart broadens the perspective to embrace both positive and negative divine names in nn. 170–84. Rabbi Moses is once again the guide, as the analysis of the positive names begins with a lengthy paraphrase of the four errors the Jewish thinker finds committed by those who ascribe affirmative predicates of God (nn. 171–73, following *Guide* 1.60). Eckhart then proceeds to assign three reasons of his own to corroborate his Jewish source (nn. 174–77). The first of these (n. 175) expresses one of the essential themes of Eckhart's metaphysics, the virtual existence of all things in God.[78] All the perfections that exist formally in creatures are found virtually in God—God is not a circle or mutable, but the idea of a circle and the idea of mutability exist in him forever. Therefore, the idea (*ratio*) of anything at all is pure perfection in the divine Intellect (n. 176), but not as it exists in external reality. Third, "Existence receives nothing, since it is last, and it is not received in anything, since it is first. . . . Therefore, nothing is positively received by God nor apprehended truly in him, but it is empty and incorrect" (n. 177). This final reason does not exclude affirming existence of God, but only denies positing any of the *determinations* of existence of him.

Eckhart concludes with a study of why the saints and doctors say that only negations can be properly predicated of God, and of how negations can be said to differ from affirmations if neither really places anything in the divine nature (nn. 178–83). Once again, the authority of Maimonides (*Guide* 1.59, 58) forms a starting point, but the Meister adds to it an appeal to Christian authors and to his own arguments.

Negations differ from affirmations in respect to God by showing that nothing of what our senses apprehend in things is to be found in him (nn. 179–80). The advantages of negations are two. First (nn. 181–82), since all negations are founded on affirmation (i.e., every negation presupposes some act of affirmation), every negation (e.g., God is not material) leads to some positive conclusion (e.g., God has none of the attributes that are connected with matter). The second advantage (n. 183, based on *Guide* 1.59), is that those who use negative names at the very least come to know more about God than those whose ignorance prevents them from removing imperfections from their conception of him. A progressive removal of terms (e.g., corporality, temporality, creatureliness) thus leads to a gradual "locating" of God within a logical space framed by negations that is similar to one argued by Thomas Aquinas in an early work, his *Commentary on The Trinity of Boethius*, where he says: "The more negations we know of them [immaterial substances], the less vaguely we understand them, for subsequent negations limit and determine a previous negation as differences do a remote genus."[79] Eckhart then ends his "Treatise on the Names of God" with a summary of non-Christian authorities who all agree that "the one thing I know about God is that I do not know him" (n. 184).

Eckhart's extensive analysis of the problem of speaking about God merits comparison with the most noted scholastic treatment, question 13 of the First Part of Thomas Aquinas's *Summa of Theology*. A full comparison cannot be attempted here, but article 2, where Thomas addresses the question "whether any name can be used of God in a substantial way," provides an important starting point for the investigation of Eckhart's relation to the Angelic Doctor. Thomas outlines three positions on the issue of whether affirmative names like "good," "wise," and "living" can be substantially applied to God. The first opinion is that of Maimonides, who argues that positive names are really negative, that is, to say that God is living means that he is not an inanimate being. The second position holds that such terms really signify the way of causality, that is, to say that God is good means that he is the cause of goodness. Aquinas considers these positions unfitting for three reasons,[80] and hence he decides on the priority of the way of eminence, that is, that perfective names like "good" are preeminently applied to God, but they do not represent him in the way he truly is due to the imperfection inherent in our way of signifying. "These words signify the divine substance, but imperfectly just as creatures represent God imperfectly."[81]

At first glance, Thomas's position seems to be rather different from that of Eckhart, at least in those parts of his treatise where the German Dominican cites Maimonides so extensively and seems to agree with the Jewish philosopher's view that Thomas rejected. However, the situation becomes more complex in the case of all three thinkers once we penetrate beneath the surface. Did Maimonides reject all forms of analogy or eminent predication? Was he correctly understood by Thomas and Meister Eckhart? How seriously does Thomas Aquinas take the role of negation in our language about God? Where does Eckhart stand in relation to the two, and what is his own contribution? These are large questions, not to be exhausted here; but a few general remarks can be made to help guide some particular comparisons.

While it is true that Maimonides considered that all nonactional predicates referring to God must be taken as negations, Harry A. Wolfson has drawn attention to a passage in *Guide* 1.53 that concludes: "Some [attributes] may also be taken as expressive of the perfection of God by way of comparison with what we consider perfections in us," and thus has argued that the affirmative form of these propositions is not without meaning, though, of course, the fact that all such perfections are identical in God and separate in creation emphasizes their totally different modes of signification.[82] This possible opening to a doctrine of analogy implying the *via eminentiae* has been followed up by other scholars, notably David Burrell, who has tried to show that the distance between Maimonides and Aquinas may be not so great as imagined in the past.[83] Certainly, such an approach also finds confirmation from the strong tendency in a number of studies of Thomas over the past years that have emphasized the strength of the negative, apophatic, and, one might even say, "agnostic" element in his doctrine of God.[84] This is not to say that Maimonides, Aquinas, and Eckhart hold the same positions, but it does qualify any simple-minded contrasts. On the problem of speaking about God, the positions of all three might be best described as subtle combinations of the *via negationis* and the *via eminentiae*. Maimonides and Eckhart lay greater stress on the former, Thomas on the latter. Thomas's teaching is rooted in his highly nuanced analogy of being; Maimonides's background and the issues he dealt with seem to have precluded all but hints of a doctrine of analogy in his thought. Eckhart does make use of analogy, but the heart of how he speaks about God is expressed through his Neoplatonic dialectic of indistinction and the negation of negation.

Some particular comparisons between Eckhart and Aquinas will help to show the differences. First, it would be a mistake to see Meister Eckhart as merely siding with Maimonides against Aquinas, as some have done.[85] Eckhart never explicitly excludes the *via eminentiae*, and several times, both early and late in the treatise (e.g., nn. 35, 78, 178) he argues for its priority in explicit or implicit fashion.[86] But second, we must recognize that Eckhart's view of eminent predication is not the same as that of Aquinas for at least two reasons. In the text under consideration, Eckhart seems to suggest that *only* the term existence (*esse*) correctly signifies God's substance in an eminent way. Nowhere in the course of his treatment does he suggest that *esse indistinctum* is not a proper term for God, and more than once he affirms it (e.g., nn. 36, 44, 51, 161–69). *Esse indistinctum* can be understood as the same as *unum* or Absolute Unity, the negation of negation that is the purest form of affirmation, a position argued for here (nn. 57, 74), and elsewhere in the works translated in this volume.[87] But in restricting eminent terms to *esse-unum* and thus tending to exclude *bonum* and the like, Eckhart parts company with Thomas Aquinas.

The position taken in this text, of course, has to be compared with those found in other places in his writings to get the full picture. In the Prologue to the *Work of Propositions* the Meister put all four classic transcendental terms (*esse, unum, verum, bonum*) on the same level as preeminently applicable to God and only improperly predicated of creatures.[88] Earlier, in the *Commentary on Exodus*, he cited Augustine on God as good without any qualifying remark,[89] a statement that can be paralleled elsewhere in his works.[90] Passages from the *Commentary on John* translated below support the position of the *Commentary on Exodus* by ascribing *esse* to the divine ground and *unum* and *verum* to the Persons of the Father and the Son.[91] In most of his writings *esse* and *unum* are the terms properly predicated of the hidden Godhead; but on the basis of such texts as Sermons XXIX and 9, as well as the *Parisian Questions*, we cannot exclude *intellectus* as preeminently belonging to the divine ground. Even though for Eckhart, as for any good Neoplatonist, *bonum* always signifies what is "self-diffusive" (*diffusivum sui*) and thereby implies if not duality, at least duality's root (a reason for statements denying that God is good, as in an important passage from the *Commentary on John* translated here,[92] and also the text from Sermon 9 to be discussed below), there is a passage in Sermon XLIX.3 that identifies *bonitas* with the inner life of the Godhead involved in the emanation of Persons.[93] Thus, on the question of the most proper eminent predications for the divine being, there seem to be two tendencies in Eckhart's thought. It is not clear that he ever successfully reconciled them.

A second difference between Eckhart and Aquinas in the matter of eminent predication is evident in texts like nn. 44 and 175, where the Meister deals with the relation between perfections in God and those realized in us. For Thomas Aquinas, as is well known, this relation is expressed through the doctrine of analogy, specifically through an analogy that is both intrinsic and proportional.[94] In the Angelic Doctor the *via eminentiae* is founded on the *via analogiae*. While Eckhart does speak about analogy in a number of places, and while he even garbs his teaching in Thomistic language,[95] his understanding of analogy is that of an extrinsic relation based on dialectical opposition (what can be affirmed of God must be denied of creatures, and vice versa) rather than on intrinsic attribution and proportionality. "Analogates have nothing of the form according to which they are analogically ordered rooted in positive fashion in themselves," as Eckhart says in the noted text from the *Sermons and Lectures on Ecclesiasticus*.[96]

Eckhart's formal doctrine of analogy serves to set off the Absolute Unity of the divine perfections from the multiple perfections we know in the world around us. It divides virtual and formal existence (e.g., nn. 57, 175) in such a way that Eckhart can assert that "all things that are positively said of God, even though they are perfections in us, are no longer so in God and are not more perfect than their opposites" (n. 44)—a position that contradicts Aquinas's first objection to Maimonides in Ia. 13. 2.[97]

Still, even in the realm of analogy we must beware of overly simplified contrasts between Aquinas and Eckhart. If the formal content of their respective understandings of analogy are rather different, a number of recent Thomist scholars, such as David Burrell, have emphasized that for Aquinas analogy is far more a skill in using language to investigate what lies beyond conceptual grasp than it is a clearly defined doctrine rigidly adhered to in all situations.[98] Although the term *dialectic*, at least as understood in its Neoplatonic form,[99] is, I believe, a more appropriate word to characterize the dynamics of Eckhart's way of speaking about God, if we take analogy in the sense of attentiveness to the subtle play of language as it is used to both dis-

close and hide the divine mystery, then Eckhart must be thought of as a
master of the art of analogy, especially in his vernacular sermons.

All the sermons translated here demonstrate this, but it may be useful
to single out one of the most noted, Sermon 9 on the text from Ecclesiasticus
50:6–7, for a more detailed illustration, especially since this apophatic piece
contains a famous formulation of Eckhart's negative theology that was condemned by Pope John XXII.

This sermon, preached for the feast of St. Dominic, is a survey of various attributes of God showing affinities both with the *Parisian Questions* and
Latin Sermon XXIX in its stress on God as *intellectus,* or understanding, as
well with the "Treatise on the Names of God" in its highly apophatic character. It commences with a paraphrase of three of the definitions of God
from the twelfth-century compilation known as the *Book of the Twenty-Four
Philosophers.* Eckhart concentrates on the definition that asserts "God is something that is of necessity above being." An investigation of the implications
of this leads him to a statement of the dialectical relation of God and creatures similar to the more involved analyses found in the Latin works—by
the very fact that God is *in* all creatures, he is also *above* them all. [100]

Each thing can act or work within its own mode of being, but God
works above being in "nonbeing" (MHG *unwesen*) since he creates being
where none had previously existed. It is obvious that Eckhart is speaking
here about created or formally inhering being (*esse hoc et hoc*), and that this is
why he goes on to condemn those "unsophisticated teachers" who say that
"God is pure being." Eckhart's dialectical view of analogy leads him to say
that God "is as high above being as the highest angel is above a gnat," but
in typical fashion he immediately asserts the antithesis by saying "I have not
denied being to God; rather I have elevated it in him."[101] He goes on to approve Augustine's paradoxical formulations that God is "wise without wisdom, good without goodness, powerful without power."[102]

Eckhart next discusses the applicability of the ten categories to God,
claiming that "none of these modes touches God, but neither does he lack
any of them."[103] His argument here, though not always clear, is based on
the priority of the *via eminentiae,* that is, the categories as we know them are
not in God, but their higher, unknown reality is. In accordance with the
teaching put forth in the *Commentary on Exodus,* he singles out substance and
relation as properly applicable to God. This leads him to the passage whose
last two sentences were singled out for condemnation as heretical:

> In God the images of all things are alike, but they are the images of unlike
> things. The highest angel and the soul and a gnat have like images in

27

God.[104] God is neither being nor goodness. Goodness adheres to being and is not more extensive. If there were no being, neither would there be goodness. Yet being is purer than goodness. God is neither good nor better nor best of all. Whoever would say that God is good would be treating him as unjustly as though he were calling the sun black.[105]

Eckhart is aware of the daring nature of his statement, which seems to go against both tradition and scripture. In answer to the objection from Mark 10:18 ("No one is good but God alone") he says that God "shares most of all" because he gives himself in and to all things. But this seems to hint that goodness is not a name for God as he is in himself, but only a name for God as the source or cause of all things, that is, it is an expression of the *via causalitatis*. This reading is supported by the discussion that follows, in which Eckhart turns to other names of God and tries to locate them at different levels in the divine reality. Being (*wesen*) is God's antechamber (*vorbürge*), whereas intellect (*vernünfticheit*) is the temple in which he shines out as holy, "for he alone is there in his stillness."[106]

Since God and the soul have the same ground, the exposition easily moves next to talk about the spark of intellect within the soul. With the power of intellect "the soul works in nonbeing and so follows God who works in nonbeing."[107] To love God is to receive him under the "coat of goodness"; intellect draws aside this coat and "perceives him bare, as he is stripped of goodness and of being and of all names."[108] It is because God is intellect and because we know this that we can reach beatitude. The being of angels, and of all things, like an image in a mirror,[109] depends totally on that from which it comes, the divine Intellect.

Finally, Eckhart returns to his text ("As the morning star through the mist . . ." Si. 50:6–7) to reflect on the word *as* (*quasi*) as a "biwort," or both adverb and allegory, as we might put it. Since the most proper names that man can use of God (if not of the Godhead) are *wort* and *warheit*, we must learn to be like adverbs, ever near the Word, just as the morning star always stands near the sun.[110] The Meister identifies three different kinds of words: the word "brought forth," or uttered, that is, created being itself; the word that is "thought out and not brought forth," which is that by means of which we understand anything; and the Word that is "not brought forth and not thought out, that never comes forth. . . . It is continually being conceived in the Father who speaks it, and it remains within."[111] Intellect has all its power in inward unifying activity. "God's happiness depends on his understanding's working internally, where the Word remains within. There the soul should be an ad-verb and work one work with God in order to receive

28

its happiness in the same inwardly hovering knowledge where God is happy."[112]

The passage from this sermon denying the attribute goodness to God was cited in the second "rotulus" or list of errors handed to Eckhart at Cologne. He admitted that the statement was his and defended it by saying that "since God is above every name by which we are able to denominate him, he is more excellent than white in comparison with black."[113] Pressed harder at the Avignon trial, he retreated. The "votum theologicum" of the Avignon Commission reports:

> Even the Meister himself holds this article, as it sounds, erroneous; but on this issue he defends the point that God is above every name and superior to all discourse and higher than everything we understand. All utterance falls short of his proper nature (*proprietas*), and every name we use of God differs from this proper nature more than white from black, because these belong to a single univocal genus [i.e., color].[114]

The commission rejected Eckhart's defense for a set of interesting reasons. First, they objected on grounds that mirror the Dominican's own arguments in the "Prologue" to the *Work of Propositions* and elsewhere on the priority of the *via eminentiae*, saying, "Names ought not to be denied to God which belong more properly to him than to the creature, as that God is being, substance, God is good, just as we deny white is black." Second, the commission rejected Eckhart's claim that terms that are univocal in genus are inapplicable to both God and creatures by an appeal to something like Thomas Aquinas's first response to Maimonides's position on the superiority of the *via negationis*, that is, we must have some way of discriminating between relatively adequate and totally inadequate names. In the case of God, names that signify "one simple indistinct thing," such as *goodness* and *wisdom*, are therefore better than mutually opposed terms like *black* and *white*. It is clear from this exchange that the talk about black and white had rather confused the issue, and it is also evident that the full range of Eckhart's view of speaking about God, with its subtle combination of the *via negationis* and at least some elements of the *via eminentiae*, was capable of a stronger and more detailed defense than he provided, at least as far as our records show. The logic of theological condemnation, however, is antithetical to nuance and qualification, as Eckhart learned to his dismay.

Eckhart's appeal to the correctness of his intention in using such expressions was consistent with a major premise of his defense,[115] but it is puzzling that he did not appeal to that side of his teaching on speaking about God

INTRODUCTION

which allowed terms like *goodness* to be predicated of God, and perhaps even of the hidden Godhead. Equally inexplicable is why the bull of condemnation classed this passage from Sermon 9 among the two appended heretical articles that Eckhart denied saying, when all through both trials he admitted it as his own. Despite these puzzles, Sermon 9 is a good test case to show how Eckhart's subtle exposition of speaking about God set forth in such detail in the *Commentary on Exodus* helps us to gain a better understanding of some of his most difficult and daring vernacular texts. In this as in so much else Eckhart the teacher and Eckhart the preacher are one.

NOTES

1. Reiner Schürmann, *Meister Eckhart. Mystic and Philosopher* (Bloomington: Indiana University Press, 1978); Matthew Fox, *Breakthrough: Meister Eckhart's Creation Spirituality in New Translation* (Garden City, N.Y.: Doubleday, 1980); and especially M. O'C. Walshe, *Meister Eckhart: German Sermons and Treatises* (London and Dulverton: Watkins, 1979 and 1981), 2 volumes containing all the MHG sermons, but not the treatises.
2. Armand Maurer, *Master Eckhart: Parisian Questions and Prologues* (Toronto: Pontifical Institute of Mediaeval Studies, 1974), also includes a portion of the *Comm. Ex.* on Ex. 3:14.
3. See *Essential Eckhart*, pp. 5–23 and 24–61 respectively.
4. Among recent important studies: Alain de Libera, *Le problème de l'être chez Maître Eckhart: logique et métaphysique de l'analogie* (Geneva: Cahiers de la revue de théologie et de philosophie 4, 1980); Alain de Libera, "A propos de quelques théories logiques de Maître Eckhart: existe-t-il une tradition médiévale de la logique néo-platonicienne?," *Revue de théologie et de philosophie* 113 (1981): 1–24; Emilie zum Brunn and Alain de Libera, *Maître Eckhart: Métaphysique du verbe et théologie négative* (Paris: Beauchesne, 1984); Dietmar Mieth, "Meister Eckhart: Authentische Erfahrung als Einheit von Denken, Sein und Leben," *Das "einig Ein": Studien zu Theorie und Sprache der deutschen Mystik*, ed. Alois M. Haas and Heinrich Stirnimann (Freiburg, Switzerland: Universitätsverlag, 1980), pp. 11–61; Donald F. Duclow, " 'My Suffering is God': Meister Eckhart's *Book of Divine Consolation*," *Theological Studies* 44 (1983): 570–86; Alois M. Haas, *Geistliches Mittelalter* (Freiburg, Switzerland: Universitätsverlag, 1984), and most recently the same author's excellent summary article "Seinsspekulation und Geschöpflichkeit in der Mystik Meister Eckharts," *Sein und Nichts in der Abendländischen Mystik*, ed. Walter Strolz (Freiburg, Germany: Herder, 1984), pp. 33–58.
5. Bernard McGinn, "The God beyond God: Theology and Mysticism in the Thought of Meister Eckhart," *Journal of Religion* 61 (1981): 1–19; and "Meister

INTRODUCTION

Eckhart on God as Absolute Unity," in *Neoplatonism and Christian Thought*, ed. Dominic O'Meara (Albany: SUNY Press, 1982), pp. 128–39. More recently, see my general piece, "Meister Eckhart: An Introduction," in *An Introduction to the Medieval Mystics of Europe*, ed. Paul Szarmach (Albany: SUNY Press, 1984), pp. 237–57.

6. See *Comm. Jn.* nn. 1–131 (*Essential Eckhart*, pp. 122–73). This forms about one-sixth of the entire commentary.

7. Especially, *Comm. Jn.* nn. 199–222 (LW III, pp. 168–86) on how God can be said to dwell and not to dwell; nn. 357–69 (LW III, pp. 302–14), a brief treatise on the Trinity; and nn. 511–18 (LW III, pp. 442–48) on the transcendental terms in relation to God.

8. *Comm. Gen.* nn. 1–28 (*Essential Eckhart*, pp. 82–91) dealing with the general doctrine of creation; *Par. Gen.* nn. 1–40 (ibid., pp. 92–107) on the principles of exegesis and the hidden meanings of Gn. 1:1; and *Par. Gen.* nn. 135–65 (ibid., pp. 108–21) on Eckhart's anthropology.

9. For papers displaying an ecumenical approach to this tradition (unfortunately without a piece on Eckhart), see *Dieu et l'être: Exégèse d'Exode 3, 14 et de Coran 20, 11–24* (Paris: Études augustiniennes, 1978).

10. See *Essential Eckhart*, pp. 32–39.

11. E.g., *Comm. Ex.* nn. 104–05, 158–64 (see below, pp. 79–80, 94–96).

12. *Comm. Ex.* nn. 34–78 and 143–84 (pp. 53–70, 90–102), constituting almost a third of the whole commentary.

13. See especially McGinn, "Meister Eckhart on God as Absolute Unity" (note 5).

14. A. de Libera's article "A propos de quelques théories logiques de Maître Eckhart" (note 4) has valuable remarks on the meaning and background of Eckhart's teaching on predication; A. Haas's "Seinsspekulation und Geschöpflichkeit in der Mystik Meister Eckharts," pp. 33–34, 40–42, stresses the role of dialectic.

15. *Comm. Ex.* nn. 110–19 (pp. 81–83).

16. Vladimir Lossky, *Théologie négative et connaissance de Dieu chez Maître Eckhart* (Paris: Vrin, 1960), pp. 261–65.

17. For more on this see McGinn, "Meister Eckhart on God as Absolute Unity."

18. Quoted from *Early Dominicans: Selected Writings*, ed. and intro. by Simon Tugwell, O.P., Classics of Western Spirituality (New York: Paulist Press, 1982), p. 150.

19. See A. Haas, "Meister Eckhart und die Sprache, Sprachgeschichtliche und sprachtheologische Aspekte seiner Werke," *Geistliches Mittelalter*, pp. 194–200.

20. Eckhart's German style has been the subject of an extensive literature. For recent studies, see the papers of A. Haas in *Geistliches Mittelalter;* and Frank Tobin, "Meister Eckhart's German Sermons: Semantics and Grammar as Style," *Semasia: Beiträge zur Germanisch-Romanischen Sprachforschung* 3 (1976): 75–85, and "Meister Eckhart: Scholasticism, Mysticism and Poetic Style," *Amsterdamer Beiträge zur älteren Germanistik* 16 (1981): 111–33.

21. Walshe's two volumes (see note 1) contain ninety-seven sermons in all.

INTRODUCTION

22. On Eckhart's preaching, see the papers collected in *Meister Eckhart der Prediger: Festschrift zum Eckhart-Gedenkjahr*, ed. Udo Nix, O.P., and Raphael Öchslin, O.P. (Freiburg, Germany: Herder, 1960); and, more recently, A. Haas, "Meister Eckharts geistliches Predigtprogramm," *Geistliches Mittelalter*, pp. 317–37.
23. *Essential Eckhart*, p. 203.
24. See *Essential Eckhart*, pp. 51–55.
25. See below, p. 269. For this article in the Bull of condemnation ("In agro dominico"), see *Essential Eckhart*, p. 80, and the discussion in the Introduction (p. 42).
26. On the negation of negation, see *Essential Eckhart*, p. 34, and the Glossary at the end of this volume.
27. Sermon 52 is translated in *Essential Eckhart*, pp. 199–205.
28. On this sermon, see especially Dietmar Mieth, *Die Einheit von vita activa und vita contemplativa in den deutschen Predigten und Traktaten Meister Eckharts und bei Johannes Tauler* (Regensburg: Pustet, 1969).
29. *Essential Eckhart*, pp. 15–23.
30. The treatises appear in DW V. They were translated by Edmund Colledge in *Essential Eckhart*, pp. 209–94.
31. Franz Pfeiffer, *Deutsche Mystiker des Vierzehnten Jahrhunderts, Vol. 2: Meister Eckhart* (Leipzig: Göschen, 1857), pp. 448–75. This text was translated by C. de B. Evans, *Meister Eckhart by Franz Pfeiffer* (London: Watkins, 1924), pp. 312–34.
32. See Pfeiffer, *Deutsche Mystiker*, p. 625. There is an English translation of the Legend in Raymond B. Blakney, *Meister Eckhart* (New York: Harper and Row, 1941), pp. 252–53.
33. Norman Cohn, *The Pursuit of the Millennium*, rev. ed. (New York: Oxford University Press, 1970), pp. 149, 175, 178–79.
34. Gordon Leff, *Heresy in the Later Middle Ages* (New York: Barnes and Noble, 1967), Vol. 1, p. 401.
35. Ibid., pp. 401–04, for his discussion.
36. R. E. Lerner, *The Heresy of the Free Spirit in the Later Middle Ages*, pp. 215–21.
37. Franz-Josef Schweitzer, *Der Freiheitsbegriff der deutschen Mystik: Seine Beziehung zur Ketzerei der "Brüder und Schwestern vom Freien Geist," mit besonderer Rücksicht auf den pseudoeckhartischen Traktat "Schwester Katrei" (Edition)* (Frankfurt: Lang, 1981), pp. 322–70 for the edition.
38. See pp. 356–57.
39. See p. 358. Sufi mystics, such as the ninth-century al-Hallaj, shocked many by statements such as "I am the Absolute Truth." See Annemarie Schimmel, *Mystical Dimensions of Islam* (Chapel Hill: University of North Carolina Press, 1975), p. 72.
40. See, e.g., pp. 357, 360, 361–62, 368.
41. Teresa of Avila, *The Interior Castle*, Classics of Western Spirituality (New York: Paulist Press, 1979), especially 6.4–5, 10–11; and 7.1–2,4.

42. For an introduction to the Magdalene's role in Christianity, see Marjorie M. Malvern, *Venus in Sackcloth: The Magdalene's Origins and Metamorphoses* (Carbondale: Southern Illinois University Press, 1975).
43. See p. 366.
44. See pp. 365–66.
45. See p. 359; cf also p. 368.
46. *Essential Eckhart*, pp. 52–54.
47. For some passages, at times involving an *imitatio Christi* theme, see, e.g., pp. 353, 359, 367, 368, 371, 378–79, 381.
48. On the role of the Eucharist, see pp. 377, 382.
49. See p. 368.
50. *Essential Eckhart*, p. 61.
51. For the attack on visions, see pp. 375, 380, 381–82.
52. See pp. 363–64.
53. See pp. 363, 364–65. The discussion of the absorption of all materiality into spirit is found especially in *Periphyseon* 5.8. The parallels are discussed by Schweitzer, ibid., pp. 77–82.
54. This section is a revised version of a paper originally delivered at the International Conference of Medieval Studies held at Kalamazoo in May 1981, in a section on Medieval German Mysticism organized by Frank Gentry of the University of Wisconsin. My thanks are due to Frank Tobin for some useful suggestions.
55. Augustine, *Christ. Doct.* 1.6. I have used the translation of D. W. Robertson, Jr., *St. Augustine: On Christian Doctrine*, Library of Liberal Arts (Indianapolis: Bobbs-Merrill, 1958), pp. 10–11.
56. Karl Rahner, "The Hiddenness of God," *Theological Investigations*, Vol. 16 (New York: Seabury, 1979), pp. 228–31.
57. Eleven papers reprinted in Harry A. Wolfson, *Studies in the History of Philosophy and Religion*, 2 vols., ed. Isadore Twersky and George H. Williams (Cambridge, Mass.: Harvard University Press, 1973, 1977).
58. Ibid., vol. 2, pp. 497–524.
59. The phrase "linguistic situation" is taken from Gerhard Ebeling, "The Hermeneutical Locus of the Doctrine of God in Peter Lombard and Thomas Aquinas," *Distinctive Protestant and Catholic Themes Reconsidered* (New York: Harper and Row, 1967), pp. 70–111.
60. For a translation of *Divine Names*, see *Pseudo-Dionysius: The Complete Works*, trans. Colm Luibheid; Forward, Notes, collaboration in translation and Bibliography by Paul Rorem; Preface by René Roques; Introductions by Jaroslav Pelikan, Jean Leclercq and Karlfried Froehlich, Classics of Western Spirituality (New York: Paulist Press, forthcoming).
61. For an English version of the *Guide* I have made use of *The Guide for the Perplexed by Moses Maimonides*, trans. from the original Arabic text by M. Friedländer (New York: Dover, 1955; reprint of the second edition of 1904). For an analysis

of Maimonides's doctrine of the divine attributes, see the several papers in Wolfson's *Studies in the History of Philosophy and Religion*. On the Latin versions of Maimonides and their influence, the best studies are those of Wolfgang Kluxen, "Literargeschichtliches zum lateinischen Moses Maimonides," *Recherches de théologie ancienne et médiévale* 21 (1954): 23–50; and "Die Geschichte des Maimonides im lateinischen Abendland als Beispiel einer christlich-jüdischen Begegnung," *Miscellanea Mediaevalia 4: Judentum im Mittelalter*, ed. Paul Wilpert (Berlin: De Gruyter, 1966), pp. 146–66.

62. On Eckhart's principles of exegesis, see *Essential Eckhart*, pp. 27–29.

63. *Comm. Ex.* nn. 27–33 (pp. 50–53).

64. *Comm. Ex.* n. 34 (p. 53). In this passage Eckhart notes that Thomas Aquinas cited this same verse as the main authority for his treatment in *STh* Ia. 13. Eckhart also mentions treating the names of God in his comments on other passages of scripture, but none of these seems to have survived.

65. *Comm. Ex.* nn. 37–44 depend on *Guide* 1.52–58. (I follow the modern numeration of chapters; Eckhart's are usually lower by one in following the medieval Latin version.)

66. *Comm. Ex.* nn. 46–50, depending on *Guide* 1.55 and 51.

67. On God as One, see my article "Meister Eckhart on God as Absolute Unity" (note 5).

68. E.g., *In I Sent.* d. 2, q. 1, a. 3; and *STh* Ia. 13. 4.

69. This extract forms article 23 of the Bull "In agro dominico" (*Essential Eckhart*, p. 79).

70. For Thomas's position here, see *STh* Ia. 28. 2, and *On God's Power* 8. 2. On Eckhart's view and the possible influence of Maimonides, see J. Koch, "Meister Eckhart und die jüdische Religionsphilosophie des Mittelalters," *Jahresbericht der Schleschischen Gesellschaft. Philosophisch-psychologische Sektion* 101 (1928): 146–47.

71. On this distinction see my article "The God beyond God" (note 5).

72. For texts on the negation of negation, see, e.g., Sermon 21, *Comm. Ex.* n. 74, *Comm. Ecc.* n. 60, *Comm. Wis.* n. 148, and *Comm. Jn.* n. 556 (pp. 281, 68, 181, 167–68, 185).

73. This famous text is from the *Celestial Hierarchy* 2.

74. In the earlier portions of the treatise Eckhart twice affirmed that the fourth section would deal with the Tetragrammaton, though this is explicitly discussed only in nn. 146–48 (pp. 90–91). It is clear, however, that he has the whole commentary on Ex. 20:7 in mind as the conclusion to his treatise.

75. See the previous mention of the Tetragrammaton in *Comm. Ex.* n. 19 (p. 47).

76. For a survey article (which, however, does not discuss Joachim of Fiore and Eckhart, two of the most important witnesses), see Armand Maurer, "The Sacred Tetragrammaton in Medieval Thought," *Actas del V Congreso Internacional de Filosofía Medieval* (Madrid: Editora Nacional, 1979), Vol. 2, pp. 975–83.

77. To be compared with *Comm. Ex.* nn. 14–25 (pp. 45–49).

78. For some other appearances of this theme, see *Comm. Ex.* nn. 120–122; *Comm.*

Wis. n. 32 (pp. 83–84, 152); *Par. Gen.* n. 45 (LW I, p. 512); and *Par. Quest.* 1 (LW V, p. 45).

79. Thomas Aquinas, *Commentary on the Trinity of Boethius* q. 6, a. 3, a position that is superceded in *STh* Ia. 13. 2.

80. The reasons given in the corpus of 13. 2 are: (1) neither view gives us a reason why some names (e.g., goodness) should be more properly used of God than others (e.g., body); (2) as a result of these views everything said of God would be true only in a derived sense (*per posterius*); and (3) these views do not match the intention of those who speak about God.

81. *STh* Ia. 13. 2c. This was also the root of the position taken by Eckhart in *Comm. Ex.* n. 78 (p. 70) in his response to the objection drawn from the Pseudo-Dionysius.

82. See H. A. Wolfson, "Maimonides on Negative Attributes," *Studies in the History and Philosophy of Religion*, Vol. 2, pp. 226–29.

83. David B. Burrell, "Aquinas and Maimonides: A Conversation about Proper Speech," *Immanuel* 16 (1983): 70–85. Less cogent is Harold Joseph Johnson, "*Via negationis* and *Via analogiae*: Theological Agnosticism in Maimonides and Aquinas," *Actas del V Congreso Internacional de Filosofia Medieval*, vol. 2, pp. 843–55.

84. One of the first works to stress the apophatic element in Thomas's thought was that of Josef Pieper, *The Silence of St. Thomas* (New York: Pantheon, 1957; German original 1953). Since then, the issue has been approached from a number of perspectives. See, e.g., David B. Burrell, "Aquinas on Naming God," *Theological Studies* 24 (1963): 183–212; and more recently his *Aquinas: God and Action* (Notre Dame, Ind.: Notre Dame University Press, 1979); and Victor Preller, *Divine Science and the Science of God: A Reformulation of Thomas Aquinas* (Princeton, N.J.: Princeton University Press, 1967).

85. As Josef Koch seems to have done in his article "Meister Eckhart und die jüdische Religionsphilosophie des Mittelalters," pp. 142–45. For another survey of the influence of Maimonides on Eckhart, see H. Liebeschütz, "Meister Eckhart und Moses Maimonides," *Archiv für Kulturgeschichte* 54 (1972): 64–96.

86. For another assertion of the priority of the *via eminentiae*, cf. *Comm. Jn.* n. 86 (*Essential Eckhart*, p. 154).

87. See *Comm. Wis.* n. 148 (p. 167).

88. "Prologue" to the *Work of Propositions* nn. 4–8, 15 (LW I, pp. 167–70, 175–76).

89. *Comm. Ex.* n. 17 (p. 46), citing Augustine, *Trin.* 8. 3.

90. See, e.g., *Comm. Jn.* n. 114, Sermon 22, and *Bened.* 1 (*Essential Eckhart*, pp. 166, 195, 209–10).

91. E.g., *Comm. Jn.* nn. 562, 564 (pp. 187, 188).

92. Cf. *Comm. Jn.* n. 562 (p. 187).

93. Sermon XLIX. 3, n. 511 (p. 237).

94. The literature on Aquinas's notion of analogy is immense, and the differences among the interpreters great. For a solid textual study, see George Klubertanz,

INTRODUCTION

St. Thomas on Analogy (Chicago: Loyola University Press, 1960); and for a more theoretical approach, David B. Burrell, *Analogy and Philosophical Language* (New Haven: Yale University Press, 1975).

95. For Eckhart on analogy, see V. Lossky, *Théologie négative et connaissance de Dieu chez Maître Eckhart, passim*; Josef Koch, "Zur Analogielehre Meister Eckharts," *Mélanges offerts à Etienne Gilson* (Paris: Vrin, 1959), pp. 327–50; Maurice de Gandillac, "La 'dialectique' du Maître Eckhart," *La mystique rhénane* (Paris: Presses universitaires, 1963. Colloque Strassbourg 1961), pp. 83–86; Fernand Brunner, "L'analogie chez Maître Eckhart," *Freiburger Zeitschrift für Philosophie und Theologie* 16 (1969): 333–49; and Alain de Libera, *Le problème de l'être chez Maître Eckhart* (see note 4).

96. *Comm. Ecc.* n. 53 (p. 178).

97. Eckhart's position here is similar to that found in John the Scot, *Periphyseon* 1. See *Iohannis Scotti Eriugenae Periphyseon* (*De Divisione Naturae*): *Liber Primus*, ed. I. P. Sheldon-Williams (Dublin: The Dublin Institute for Advanced Studies, 1968), pp. 74–76.

98. See D. Burrell, *Analogy and Philosophical Language* and *Aquinas*.

99. See my paper, "Meister Eckhart on God as Absolute Unity," especially pp. 136–39.

100. Sermon 9 (p. 256). On the role of dialectic in this sermon, see V. Lossky, *Théologie négative et connaissance de Dieu*, pp. 202–07.

101. Compare with *Par. Quest.* 1, nn. 8–10 (LW V, pp. 45–46); and Sermon XI, n. 118 (LW IV, p. 112).

102. Distantly based on Augustine, *Trin.* 5. 1. 2.

103. See below p. 257.

104. A related passage on angel, soul, and fly occurs in Sermon 52 (*Essential Eckhart*, p. 200). Cf. *Comm. Wis.* n. 99 (p. 157).

105. See p. 257. The final two sentences form the second appended article of "In agro dominico" (*Essential Eckhart*, p. 80). The only difference is that the Latin text has "as if I were to call white black." Cf. Sermon 83 (*Essential Eckhart*, pp. 206–07).

106. Compare this passage on the priority of *intelligere* with Sermon XXIX nn. 301–04 (pp. 225–26), and *Par. Quest.* 1, nn. 4–5, 7 (LW V, pp. 40, 42, 43).

107. See p. 258 below.

108. At this point (p. 258) Eckhart refers to the debate he had in the schools with another Master on the priority of intellect over will, probably a reference to the dispute with the Franciscan Gonsalvo of Spain; cf. *Par. Quest.* 3 (LW V, pp. 59–71).

109. A favorite analogy, cf., e.g., *Comm. Jn.* nn. 23–24 (*Essential Eckhart*, p. 129).

110. See p. 259.

111. See p. 259.

112. See p. 260.

113. See Théry, p. 263.

INTRODUCTION

114. The text is found in Franz Pelster, "Ein Gutachten aus dem Eckehart-Prozess in Avignon," *Aus der Geisteswelt des Mittelalters: Festgabe Martin Grabmann* (Münster, 1935. Beiträge der Geschichte der Philosophie des Mittelalters. Supplement III), p. 1112.
115. See B. McGinn, "Meister Eckhart's Condemnation Reconsidered," *The Thomist* 44 (1980); 400–03.

Part One

Eckhart the Teacher

translated by
Bernard McGinn

I. COMMENTARY ON EXODUS

It should be noted that only a few passages in Exodus are interpreted here, both because they are handled in the *Glosses*[2] (and generally by the commentators), and also because the opportunity to discuss them is rather rare. For these reasons the same approach, that is, interpreting a few texts, will be followed throughout the whole Old Testament, except for the Psalter which is in daily use. . . .

Chapter 1. "These are the names of the children of Israel . . ." (v. 1). And below, "because the midwives feared God, he built them houses." (v. 21)

1. Through "houses" understand riches or worldly prosperity, as Augustine says in the second chapter of his book, *The Words of Exodus,*[3] and as it is here in the *Gloss.*[4] Second, note that these words are interpreted in different ways by various saints. Hence you should know that two things are to be considered in the action of these midwives: first, the devotion by which they saved the infants and "feared God"; and second, that they lied to Pharoah and feared for their lives.

2. By means of the first deed they merited both eternal reward and spiritual homes, as is written of St. Augustine that "he received . . . a home not made with hands . . . in heaven";[5] and it is expressed figuratively in Luke 16: "When I have been removed from my stewardship, they may receive me into their houses" (Lk. 16:4). That seems to be the opinion of Jerome,[6] and Augustine does not depart from it.[7] Still, in the *Gloss* Gregory says that in their case the eternal reward was changed into a temporal one due to the sin of lying, because "he built them houses," that is, worldly possessions.[8] However, this does not seem the case, because only mortal sin takes away eternal reward,[9] and even according to Gregory himself a "well-intentioned lie" is counted among the light and venial sins.[10]

3. By means of the second deed, that is, that they lied and feared for their lives, according to all the saints in general it is certain that they sinned both because they lied and also because in fearing for themselves they sought their own good, and so they received no merit at all, neither eternal nor temporal. Hence, if temporal possessions are to be understood through the houses that God built for them, one should rather say that they received not only an eternal reward, but at the same time also a temporal one from the first deed, that of devotion. Moses spoke of the temporal reward, both because what is spiritual is hidden to people and what is temporal appears to them outwardly, and also because the people to whom Moses was speaking had a taste for and sought what was carnal.

4. From what has been said notice the praise given devotion and the good work in general by which celestial and terrestrial goods are merited at the same time. Just as in every holy work there are two things—the interior motive and the exterior act[11]—so too in the prize or reward there are two, so that even in this case the text from Ecclesiasticus 33 is true: "Two against two" (Si. 33:15). Thomas explains and upholds Gregory's words, however, in IIaIIae, q. 101, a. 4, ad 3.[12] But one could say briefly from the beginning that the midwives did not lie, and so the whole question would vanish, for it could be true that many Jewish women knew midwifery.[13]

Chapter 2. "After this there went a man . . ." (v. 1). And below, "Who has appointed you judge over us?" (v. 14).

5. First note that no one can or ought to be a judge except one who is superior, more excellent and more perfect than others,[14] for he says "over us," and also first says "prince" and then adds to it "and judge." God and nature universally order and judge inferior things through superior ones; those who do otherwise, act against God and nature and hence sin seriously.

6. Note in the second place that he says "over us," not "over me," although he alone speaks who did the wrong (v. 13). From this it is clear that a judge is only able to judge those under him, and "ought not put his sickle into another's harvest," and also that "a verdict given by one who is not its judge has no validity."[15] So we see that neither sight nor taste judge about color and taste, but the "common sense" that is superior to both, as it says in the second book of the *Soul.*[16] Further, no individual sense has power to judge its own action, as it says there,[17] but this judgment belongs to the superior, that is, the "common sense." 7. From which comes the third point to be noted: that the judge ought to be shared and common to the parts, because the "common sense" that is not partial or individual judges the senses.

Fourth, note that the judge ought to judge with serenity, for he says "over us." Superiors always judge and rule inferiors with serenity and mildness.[18] "You, a master of power, judge with serenity" (Ws. 12:18); "He disposed all things mildly" (Ws. 8:1).

Chapter 3. "Moses fed the sheep" (v. 1).

8. First note that a prelate or pastor ought to feed the sheep, and not the sheep the pastor. "I do not seek what is yours, but you; for the children should not heap up treasure for the parents, but the parents for the children" (2 Co. 12:14). This is why in nature the nurturing and supporting power is prior to and joined to the generative power.[19] 9. Second, note that the pastor ought to feed the sheep, that is, in the first place to be intent on the good and the profit of the sheep and not his own advantage or honor, namely, to be a benefactor and not a master. Augustine says in the *Investigations with Orosius*, "He who desires to be a master and not a benefactor should know that he is no bishop."[20] He says, "He fed the sheep." The Psalm says: "He brought him from following the pregnant ewes to feed Jacob his servant" (Ps. 77:70–71); and 2 Corinthians 12: "I will most gladly spend and be spent myself for your souls" (2 Co. 12:15). Ezechiel 34 and John 10 write of these and like matters at length, and Bernard in the third book of *On Consideration* says: "On what grounds do you think yourself superior to those from whom you beg a favor? Hear the Lord, 'Those who have power over them are called benefactors' (Lk. 22:25). . . . You are lying if you intend to be in charge of benefactors rather than to be a benefactor. Only a small and mean spirit seeks its own gain rather than the advantage of its subjects."[21]

"Moses hid his face, etc." (v. 6).

10. Rabbi Moses in [the *Guide*] 1.5 introduces this text and says that it teaches us that divine matters are to be treated with great reverence and fear without presumption.[22] Hence there follows, "He dared not look at God." Another version puts it: "He was afraid to look at God." Rabbi Moses says that the wise Jewish teachers say that the vision by means of which he later saw God (Nb. 12:8) "was his reward because he hid his face in order not to look at God."[23]

At the beginning of the chapter he cites Aristotle on this saying, "When Aristotle, the prince of philosophers, began to investigate very deep matters, he said . . . 'He who would read my words should not accuse me of trusting in the strength of my intellect to speak of things I do not know, but should judge that I am doing this from desire and love of acquiring knowledge and attaining true wisdom according to man's capability.' "[24] Hence Rabbi Moses concludes that "a man should not presume to speak of God until he disciplines his soul in actions, purges his behavior to make it pure, extinguishes his passions, and does not prematurely try to comprehend God's secret. Rather, he should be ashamed and fear to draw near."[25] This is why it says, "And Moses hid his face." 11. In the second place, he cites in connection with this passage Ecclesiastes 4: "Guard your foot when you go into the house of God" (Qo. 4:17); and third, the example of the man who tries to behold something whose great brightness surpasses the powers of his sight. Fourth, he cites the text from Proverbs 25: "You have found honey; eat what is sufficient for you"; and below, ". . . a searcher of majesty shall be overwhelmed by glory" (Pr. 25:16, 27). He also uses the Psalm passage: "O Lord, my heart is not exalted" (Ps. 130:1), and Ecclesiasticus 3: "Do not seek things above you" (Si. 3:22). He notes that the wise men said: "It would be better for a person who does not respect the Creator's glory not to have come into the world." He also gives the example in Chapter 32 of the infant who should not immediately at the beginning eat bread and meat and wine,[26] in accordance with the text, "When I was with you, I fed you with milk" (1 Co. 3:2).

12. We can cite the passage from Avicenna, *Metaphysics* 9.7: "We neither experience nor examine nor are drawn to the more hidden and divine things unless we have first put the yoke of pleasure, wrath, and their sisters from our necks."[27] In the last chapter of Book I of the *Consolation* Boethius says:

> If you wish
> To see the truth
> By clear light, . . .
> Banish joys,
> Banish fear,
> Cast out hope,
> Be free of pain.
> Where these reign,
> The mind is clouded
> And bound with chains.[28]

As far as the literal sense goes, when the eye or the tongue of a sick person is covered by a coating, it functions badly;[29] hence visible objects seen through media of different transparency appear curved even though they are straight.[30] 13. It can also be said that Moses as he drew near or approached God "hid his face." Anyone who wishes to see the deep hidden things of God in the light of grace (i.e., in the spirit), must hold captive his own countenance, that is, natural intellect or reason. That is why these things are called supernatural. "Bringing every intellect into captivity in service to Christ" (2 Co. 10:5). "Darkness was above the face of the abyss" (Gn. 1:2)—"darkness" meaning the hidden things of God; "above the face of the abyss" meaning above all created reason. "He breathed into his face the breath of life" (Gn. 2:7), because grace enflames and elevates nature, and in a general way every superior does to its inferior, just as heat does by the power of the substantial form of fire, and even more by the power of the heavenly body and its animating principle,[31] and the sea by the moon's power, and the inferior spheres by the power of the *primum mobile*.[32] This is what Moses clearly says below in Chapter 33: "If I have found grace in your sight, show me your face that I may know you" (Ex. 33:13). A third literal meaning: Someone who wants to look at the sun or some lofty visible thing "hides his face" with a veil. "When Moses is read, a veil covers their hearts, but when they are converted to God, the veil will be taken away" (2 Co. 3:15–16). This is why he said earlier, "Not that we are sufficient of ourselves, but our sufficiency is from God" (2 Co. 3:15).

"I am who am" (v. 14a).

14. Four things are to be remarked upon here. The first is that these three words "I," "am," and "who" belong to God in the most proper sense.[33] The term "I" is the pronoun of the first person. A distinguishing pronoun signifies the pure substance[34]—pure, I say, without any accident, without anything foreign, the substance without quality, without this or that form, without this or that.[35] These things belong to God alone, who is above accident, species, and genus. I say they are his alone, so that he says in the Psalm: "I alone am" (Ps. 140:10). Further, the term "who" is a non-finite word—infinite and boundless existence belongs to God alone. 15. Also, the term "am" is a substantive word, a word in the sense of "the Word was God" (Jn. 1:1), and substantive in the sense of "upholding all things by the Word of his power" (Hb. 1:3).[36]

Second, note that the term "am" is here the predicate of the proposition when God says "I am," and it is in the second position.[37] As often as it occurs, it signifies that pure naked existence is in the subject, from the subject, and is the subject itself, that is, the essence of the subject. It also signifies that essence and existence are the same, which belongs to God alone whose "what-it-is" is his "that-it-is," as Avicenna says,[38] and who has no "what-it-is" beyond the "that-it-is" alone which signifies existence.

16. Third, note that the repetition (namely, that it says "I am who am") indicates the purity of affirmation excluding all negation from God. It also indicates a reflexive turning back of his existence into itself and upon itself and its dwelling and remaining fixed in itself. It further indicates a "boiling" or giving birth to itself—glowing in itself, and melting and boiling in and into itself, light that totally forces its whole being in light and into light and that is everywhere totally turned back and reflected upon itself,[39] according to that saying of the sage, "The monad gives birth to" (or gave birth to) "the monad, and reflected love or ardent desire back upon itself."[40] Therefore, John 1 says, "In him was life" (Jn. 1:4). "Life" expresses a type of "pushing out" by which something swells up in itself and first breaks out totally in itself, each part into each part, before it pours itself forth and "boils over" on the outside.[41] This is why the emanation of the persons in the Godhead is the prior ground of creation.[42] Thus in John 1 it says, "In the beginning was the Word," and then, "all things were made through him" (Jn. 1:1, 3).

17. Once more, "I am who am" is stated for the reason that Augustine gives in the *Trinity* 8.3: "God is not a good soul, or good angel or good heaven, but a good Good." And below: "When you hear about a particular good, . . . if you could leave aside these particularities and gaze upon what is Good through itself, you would behold God." And further, "It is nothing else than the Good itself, and for this reason also the Highest Good."[43] Therefore, the "good Good" signifies the unmixed and highest Good that is fixed in itself, depends on nothing, and returns upon itself in perfect fashion.[44] Thus the term "I am who am" indicates that existence is unmixed and full, as was said above.

18. Fourth, note that the term "who" may at times by an extended meaning inquire after a name, as Priscian says in his shorter part, citing the poet's verse: "Who, father, is that man who thus accompanies him on his way?"[45] It may even inquire about some other accidental circumstance, as in John 1: "Who are you?" (Jn. 1:19), and the like. Still, in the proper sense "who" and the term "what" ask about the "what-it-is" or essence of a thing, that which the name signifies and the concept or definition indicates.[46] Therefore, because in every created thing existence and essence differ, the former coming from something else and the latter not coming from something else,[47] the question whether something exists, which asks about the "that-it-is" or existence of a thing, is different from the question about what it is, which asks about the "what-it-is" or essence of the thing. That is why it is foolish to answer someone who asks what a man or an angel is by saying

"He is," or that a man or an angel exists. But in God where "that-it-is" is the "what-it-is" itself, a fitting answer to someone asking who or what is God is "God is," for God's existence is his "what-it-is." He says, "I am who am." On this point we have what Augustine says in the *Trinity* 8.2: "When you hear he is the Truth, do not ask what is truth." And below, "Remain, if you can, in that very first instant in which you were touched by something like a flash at the mention of 'Truth.' "[48] In *On Consideration* 5 Bernard says: "If you say that God is good, or great, or blessed, or wise, or anything, it is all summed up in the words 'he is,' because in his case existence is all these things. . . . In comparison with an existence that is so singular and so great would you not judge that whatever is not it is non-existence rather than existence?"[49] This is why he says "I am who am."

19. Again, fifth, note that Rabbi Moses in treating this passage "I am who am" seems to think that it is the name "Tetragrammaton" or one like it "which is sacred and separated, written, and not pronounced, and alone signifies the naked and pure substance of the creator."[50] I have more on this below concerning the text "You shall not take God's name in vain" (Ex. 20:7).[51] Rabbi Moses means that the term "I am" in the first instance signifies the thing's essence and is the subject or what is denominated. In the second instance, the repeated "I am" signifies existence and is the predicate or denominator and denomination.[52] Now it is generally true that what is denominated or the subject of a proposition is incomplete. The subject, as its name shows, is incomplete, just as matter is, and this is why Boethius says that "a simple form cannot be a subject."[53] The denominator and denomination always act as the form and perfection of the subject (as when someone is said to be just, good, wise, or the like) in cases where the essence is not self-sufficient, but is needy and wanting, requiring something else to perfect it.

20. Now to need something else and not to be self-sufficient is totally foreign to God's essence. "The First is rich through itself."[54] Therefore, when he says "I am who am," he teaches that the subject "I am" itself is the predicate "I am" that comes second, and that the denominator is what is denominated, the essence is the existence, the "what-it-is" is the "that-it-is," the essence is self-sufficient and its own sufficiency. That is to say he "does not need any creature's essence or anything outside himself to establish him or perfect him, but his essence is self-sufficient" to all things and in all things.[55] Such sufficiency is proper to God alone. In everything that is beneath God, the essence is not self-sufficient to and in all things. For example, an artist's nature is not sufficient for his work unless the will to work, and the power and knowledge and the like (things which are not the artist's nature itself) accompany it. Therefore, substance and power, existence and op-

eration are different in everything that is beneath God. Such divine sufficiency is signified when from God's Person we hear "I am who am"— "I" used discretely, I say. On this point we have what Rabbi Moses says in [*Guide*] 1.63: "The two-letter name taken from the name 'Tetragrammaton' pertains to the stability of the essence, and 'Shaddai' is derived from 'Dai' which means 'sufficiency.' "

21. Mark therefore that if any essence at all (e.g., that of man) had its existence as what it is, it would be a necessary existence. "Nothing abandons itself," or can abandon itself, as Augustine says in the *Immortality of the Soul*;[56] and nothing flees itself, as he says in the *Book of Eighty-Three Questions.*[57] It would then be always eternal, eternal always; it could not *not* exist and it would be necessary for it to exist. But God is his existence; he is "who is" as it says here: "I am who am; He who is, sent me." Hence he is necessary existence. This is why Avicenna in his *Metaphysics* generally calls God "necessary existence."[58] Existence itself needs nothing because it lacks nothing, but all things need it because there is nothing outside it. That which is nothing needs existence, just as the sick man needs health and is wanting. Health does not need the sick man; perfect health is to be lacking in what is sick, to have no infirmity. To lack nothing is the height of perfection, the most full and pure existence; and if existence is full, then it is also life and wisdom and every other perfection.[59] Just as he exists for himself and for all things, so too he is sufficient for himself and for them all; he is his own and everything's sufficiency. "Our sufficiency is from God" (2 Co. 3:5). God does not need existence, since he is existence itself. He does not need wisdom or power, or anything at all added or foreign, but on the contrary every perfection is in need of him who is existence itself, both because each of them in and of itself is essentially a mode of existence itself, depending upon it and inhering in it, and also because it would be nothing without existence, neither wisdom nor anything else, but pure nothing.[60] "Without him nothing was made" (Jn. 1:3), as if to say, even "what was made," what possesses and receives existence, such as wisdom and anything of this sort, would indeed be nothing without existence.

"He who is, sent me" (v. 14b).

22. Note that as Peter Lombard in the *Gloss* and the first book of the *Sentences* adduces, Jerome in the Letter to Marcellus says: "That of which we say 'it was' no longer is; that of which we say 'it will be' is not yet; but God only 'is' and knows no past or future existence. He alone truly exists to

whose essence ours is compared as non-existence."[61] In the fifth book of *On Consideration* Bernard says: "What is God? That without which nothing is. He is no more able to exist without himself than anything is able to be without him. He exists for himself and for all things, and through this in a certain sense he alone exists who is his own existence and that of all things."[62] "If it be not he, who is it then?" (Jb. 9:24), and "You who alone are," and "He alone is" (Jb. 14:4, 23:13). "They could not understand him that is" (Ws. 13:1); "Our God is one God" (Dt. 6:4), that is, he alone is. This is what it says here: "He who is, sent me."

23. On the text "The way of the wicked shall perish" (Ps. 1:6), Augustine says: " 'The way of the wicked shall perish' is the same as if to say 'The Lord has not known the way of the wicked,' but it expresses more clearly that to perish is not to be known by the Lord and to remain firm is to be known, so that existence belongs to God's knowledge and non-existence to what he does not know because the Lord says, 'I am who am,' and 'He who is, sent me.' "[63] Also in the text "You will destroy all that speak a lie" (Ps. 5:7) he says: "A lie belongs to what does not exist, not that which does. If I say what is, what is true is said; if I say what is not, it is a lie. Therefore he says, 'You will destroy all that speak a lie,' because they depart from what is and sink down to what is not."[64] In *True Religion* he says, "Falsity is to take something as existing which does not; . . . truth is that which shows what is."[65] 24. What John Damascene has in the *Orthodox Faith* 1.12 hints at what has been said: "The foremost of the names that are applied to God is existence—that he is," which is according to the text "He who is, sent me." "He contains the whole of existence in himself like an infinite ocean of substance."[66] I have said much more about this in the *Book of Questions* in treating of the divine names.[67]

25. In the last place this also is to be noted, namely, that it says, "He who is, sent me." No one ought to appropriate judgment, teaching, and preaching for himself unless he is sent by a superior who holds the place of the God "who is." "No man takes an honor to himself, but he takes it who is called by God, as Aaron was" (Hb. 5:4); "All who take the sword will perish by the sword" (Mt. 26:52). By receiving and appropriating what was not given to them by a superior they sin, and in the midst of the sin they perish in the act itself. "Receive the holy sword" (2 M. 15:16); "Come, I will send you" (Gn. 37:13), and in this chapter above "I will send you to Pharaoh" (Ex. 3:10). "Behold, I will send you" (Is. 6:8); and "The Lord has sent me and his spirit" (Is. 48:16). "I did not send prophets, and they ran" (Jr. 23:21); "How shall they preach, unless they be sent?" (Rm. 10:15).

"This is my name forever" (v. 15).

26. These words can be distinguished and ordered in three ways. First, "This name, 'he is' (add 'will be,' or 'belongs to') me forever." Second: " 'He is,' this name is mine forever," which has the same sense as the first distinction and order. Third: "He is forever," that is, being that is eternal and in security, "this is my name." "But you, O Lord, endure forever" (Ps. 101:13).

Chapter 15. "Then Moses sang this canticle . . ." (v. 1). And below, "Almighty is his name" (v. 3).

27. Note that the text says two things, namely, that God is almighty, and then that "his name" is "almighty."[68] As far as the first point goes there are two things to remark. First, that to be almighty belongs to God properly and he alone can do everything. He says, "Almighty is his name," and on this first point we must see how God can do everything. Second, how scripture, the theologians, and the saints say that there are some things that God cannot do.

28. The proof of the first remark is this. Every agent has natural power over those things (and through itself only over those things) which are contained under the form which is the principle of the agent's action.[69] But existence is the principle of every divine action. Therefore, God has power over everything that is or can be.[70] The major of the proposition is shown by reference to examples drawn from every agent of art and nature. Fire makes warm by its heat, and for this reason acts upon everything that can be heated and through itself on nothing that is not subject to heat and fire's form. Hence the fire that in its sphere is right next to the moon's sphere does not act upon it and does not touch it, although it is touched by it. Further, sight and sight alone is able to see all luminous and colored objects. All the soul's powers except that of sight are totally ignorant of color; and sight itself knows nothing in the visible object (think of the taste, odor, or the like of what it sees) save that it is colored and luminous. And again, in the world of art it is clear that from the form of the building that is in the mind the artist (e.g., an architect) produces every building in exterior reality and nothing else but buildings.[71] This is why Augustine says that the idea of man is created as the form of every man and of nothing that is not a man.[72] Again, as the better authorities say,[73] the power of begetting in the Father is in the essence rather than in Paternity, and this is why the Father begets God the Son but does not beget himself the Father. He gives the Son divine existence and the existence, wisdom, and power of the Father, but not the fact that

he is the Father. Rather he gives him the fact that he is Son by reason of a relation of opposition to the Father. Therefore, the major of the assigned syllogism is proven; but the minor, namely, that existence is the principle of every divine action, that is, the formal principle, is evident both because he himself is totally existence and also because in him there is nothing over and above existence.

29. The conclusion then is the one we want, namely, that God has power over everything that is or can be—simply and absolutely everything. This is what John 1 says: "All things were made through him, and without him was made nothing" (Jn. 1:3). How could anything be made or be something without existence? Or how can what has been made not have previously been a nothing that lacked existence? God is existence and he alone gives existence immediately to everything. Hence Gregory says that everything would fall back into nothing if the Creator's omnipotence did not hold it fast.[74] Augustine gives the example of light which is found in a medium when the sun is present.[75] That is what this text has, "Almighty is his name." "No word is impossible with God" (Lk. 1:37), for no word is formed or can be formed from what is not a being insofar as it is such. The reason is that being is the first thing known by the intellect, as Avicenna says.[76] How is what does not exist knowable, especially since according to the Philosopher knowledge is only of things that are true, and being and truth are interchangeable?[77] Further, the true, the knowable, and what is in any way understandable are all based on existence and included in it, just as two is based on one and qualified existence on simple existence.

Thus three things are clear: how "his name," that is, God's, "is almighty"; and how "all things were made through him, and without him was made nothing" (Jn. 1:3); and third how "no word is impossible with God" (Lk. 1:37). How could anything be impossible for existence within its compass? Existence itself is God, and "God was the Word" (Jn. 1:1). How can a word exist without the Word? How can what is "with God" and in the Word and produced by the Word as Principle not be a word? "In the beginning was the Word, and the Word was with God, and the Word was God. . . . All things were made through him" (Jn. 1:1, 3). So much for the first point, that God has power over everything.

30. Second, we have to see what and what sort of things God does not have power over, or rather is said not to have power over by common folk. From what has been said it is clear that God has power over everything, or all those things which exist and stand among beings and the number of all the things that are. God also has power over everything which is subject to potency, that is, which power can make. "Almighty" expresses two things:

"all" and "might,"[78] mighty over all or in all. Therefore, he has power over whatever is in the number of all the things that are and also over all that power can make, but he does not have power over whatever is not in the number of all things that are and what does not have the potency to be but rather not to be. "Everything," the universal affirmative, and "nothing," the universal negative, are opposed.[79] But God has power over everything, as proven above. Therefore, he does not have power over nothing, both because nothing is not in the number of all the things that are, but is the opposite and exclusion of all, and also because power over nothing is no power, but its total negation. "All things were made through him" in relation to that which can be, "and without him was made nothing" in relation to that which cannot be. This is the great importance of the text: "You love all things that are" in relation to the first point, "and you hate nothing," that is, the nothing itself, "of all the things you have made" (Ws. 11:25) in relation to the second. "Without him was made nothing" (Jn. 1:3). Nothing and everything are totally mutually opposed, and therefore to have power over nothing is to have no power at all.

31. Besides, both action and motion take their name and nature from their goal,[80] and whatever one does in nothing is nothing and becomes nothing. "Without him was made nothing" (Jn. 1:3). It is one thing to make something from nothing, another to make it in nothing. When I say that something is made from nothing, the term "nothing" is the starting point and existence is the goal. It is the opposite when something is said to be made *in* nothing. Furthermore and third, nothing cannot be the goal of any action whatsoever, for how could what does not exist be a goal?

32. Therefore, it is clear that according to the name "almighty" God has power over everything and can do whatever has the potential to be done. Conversely, when we say that something is not subject to God's power, this is said either because it does not exist, is not a being, or is not numbered among all things that are, being a kind of nothing, or because it is said that God cannot do it because to do something of this sort is not a power and does not belong to potency but to impotency. Thus, to be able to fail or to be able to be overcome comes from the impotency by which something cannot resist what destroys or overcomes it.

As far as the first kind of case is concerned, we say that God does not do anything that implies a contradiction.[81] If contradictories are set up as existing at the same time, it follows that neither of them will exist, for if the one does, the other will not, and vice versa. Therefore if both are, neither is. Second, we always say that God cannot do evil because evil as such is not a being and does not fall within the number of all the things that are. 33.

Further, God is said not to do what implies a contradiction and evil insofar as it is evil because power of this kind is not power or is power over nothing in that these are nothing or nonbeing. They are privations of all being and have no efficient cause since they are not effects, but they have a "deficient cause" since they are defects.[82] But God, in that he is existence, cannot fail in existence, cannot lose himself. "He cannot deny himself" (2 Tm. 2:13).

What the Philosopher says in the fourth book of the *Topics*—"God and the zealous person do wicked things"[83]—does not stand in the way of what has been said, as Thomas explains in three ways in Ia, q. 25, a. 2, ad 4.[84] One can say that the Philosopher says this to refute two errors. Socrates used to say that the wise man could not sin and the Stoics that the virtuous man could not.[85] Against these two the Philosopher says that a "god," that is, a virtuous person, and a zealous person, that is, a wise man, can do wicked things. Or it can be said that God and the zealous person can do whatever there is of act and being in a wicked deed, or that the Philosopher's saying is not true in itself but is true of the thing he is talking about.[86] This third explanation agrees with the second that Thomas gives. I have commented on this in treating the passage "Since it is one, it can do all things" (Ws. 7:27).[87] So much for the first topic, that God is called "almighty."

34. The second topic is to see why it says "Almighty is his name." Although I have remarked on the names of God in different places—first upon Genesis 13, second on the passage in Zachary, "Orient is his name" (Zc. 6:12), and on the text in Philippians "He gave him a name that is above every name" (Ph. 2:9)—[88] nevertheless, because Thomas in Ia, q. 13 bases his treatment of the names of God, whether God can be named, on this verse "Almighty is his name," I would like to note four things now. The first is what some philosophers and Jewish authors think of this question and of the attributes which name God, such as when God is called substance, or good, caring, generous, and the like. (You will find more on this here in the comment on the verse "You shall not take God's name in vain" in Chapter 20.)[89] Second, there is a brief summary of what Catholic writers think of these predications or names. Third, why do Boethius and the theologians generally teach that only two kinds of categories, substance and relation, can be used of divinity? Fourth, we will speak about the name more proper and especially particular to God, that is, the "Tetragrammaton," below under Chapter 20 on the verse "You shall not take the name of your God in vain" (Ex. 20:7).[90]

35. In relation to the first point, take as a beginning what the *Book of Causes* says: "The First Cause is above all description" (proposition 6), and "The First Cause is above every name" (proposition 22).[91] In the *Book of the*

Twenty-Four Philosophers it says: "God is that which by reason of excellence words alone do not signify and minds by reason of his unlikeness do not understand."[92] Remember that the *Book of Causes* does not say that God is indescribable, but that he is "above description," in accord with the Psalm verse, "You have magnified your holy name above all" (Ps. 137:2), and Philippians 2, "He has given him a name that is above every name" (Ph. 2:9). The superior is not deprived of the inferior's perfections, but precontains them all in a more excellent way.[93] Therefore the "Name that is above every name" is not unnameable, but "omninameable,"[94] so that Augustine in Sermon 13 on John speaking of the Psalm passage, "For with you is the fountain of life" (Ps. 35:10), says: "Everything can be said of God, but nothing can be worthily said. No gap is greater than this: to seek a fitting name and not to find it; to look for a way of speaking and to find all of them." Augustine's words.[95]

36. Second, take the word of Avicenna in the last chapter of *Metaphysics* 8 where he says: "The first property of God is that he is," that is, existence. "In the case of the other properties, in some it is 'existence with a relation,' in some it is 'existence with a negation.' " The reason is, as he says, "neither of these two groups of properties makes any kind of multiplicity or variation in God's essence." For example, when God is said to be "substance, existence in a subject is denied to him. When he is said to be one, all division is understood to be denied of him." When it is said that God "is the First, what is understood in him is the relation of his existence to the whole" or to all things. And the same with similar attributes.[96] This is clear in the many propositions and names that the philosophers have attributed to God, such as the one: "God is the Principle without principle, the process without change, the end without end"; or "God is the always moving immovable"; or "God is that from which whatever is is"; and many others like these.[97]

37. Third, take the opinion of Rabbi Moses who in *Guide* 1.57 says: "Know that a negative proposition concerning the Creator is true; there is nothing doubtful in it nor does it detract from the Creator's truth in any way. But an affirmative proposition about him is partly equivocal."[98] Earlier, in Chapter 51 he says: "Every attribution or denomination comes about by one of five ways." 38. First, when a definition is predicated of the thing defined, as "Man is a rational animal." Second, when a part of the definition is predicated, as "Man is an animal." Third, when "something is attributed to something which is outside its essence" and a disposition added to it, as an accident is. Fourth, when something is attributed to something with respect to something else, as when one is said to be a father or companion, or generally when something is compared with something else in any way. "The

fifth way of denomination or attribution is that by which something is denominated from its completed work, as when it is said, 'Peter is the one who built this gate or this tower.' "[99] Now it is manifest that a denomination or attribution in the first, second, or third ways does not belong to God because there is no definition of God (so much for the first and second ways), nor is there accident in him (so much for the third). But the fourth way by which something is denominated by comparison to something else seems to belong to God because this way implies no multiplicity or change in what is denominated by the comparison.

39. Still, Rabbi Moses says that this mode of attribution or denomination by comparison does not belong to God. His reason, given after Chapter 55,[100] is that every comparison is a form of likeness. Nothing is nor can be said to be like God, first, because he "has nothing in common with anything," but also in that "essence is predicated of God and other things in a purely equivocal way."[101] He proves the same thing in a second way thus. Every comparison is a likeness of things that agree in species or at least in genus; but God, since he is outside genus, agrees with nothing in species and genus. He explains the major premise through examples; the minor is self-evident. Therefore, the conclusion is that there is truly no likeness or comparison between God and creatures. His third proof of the same is that in itself comparison is an accident even though God does not enter into comparison with other things, but comparison relates to the things with which he is compared. Therefore, as he says, one could not avoid attributing an accident to God, since of its nature comparison is an accident.[102]

40. Perhaps a more subtle reason can be given why there is no comparison between God and a creature, and it is this. Every comparison implies that there are at least two things and that they are distinct, for nothing is compared to itself or is like itself.[103] Every created being taken or conceived apart as distinct in itself from God is not a being, but is nothing. What is separate and distinct from God is separate and distinct from existence, because whatever exists is from God himself, through him and in him. "Without him was made nothing" (Jn. 1:3); and "In him we live, and move and have our being" (Ac. 17:28). Through this we can well grasp what Jerome says: "Our existence is not compared with God's";[104] and we can explain many similar things that Bernard puts in Book 5 of *On Consideration* when he speaks of God and his existence, as well as many like texts in scripture and the words of the saints.

41. Among the ways given only the fifth way by which a thing is denominated from its completed work seems to belong to God. In being denominated according to this way no multiplicity or change is expressed in

him, nor does it describe anything added to the substance of the agent. This sort of thing is "removed from the substance denominated." 42. Maimonides shows by two examples that "one simple substance in which there is no multiplicity can be the agent of different works."[105] The first is in fire which is one in substance, having no "will or choice" added to its substance, and is still the agent of different works: melting, curdling, softening, blackening, bleaching, and burning. It is true to say that fire, a single agent in itself, "is a bleacher, a blackener, a burner, etc." If someone were ignorant of fire's nature, he might believe that there were diverse powers in it or dispositions added onto fire's substance "one of which blackened, another bleached," a third burned, a fourth melted, and so forth. "He who knows fire's nature believes that it does all the above through one active quality, namely heat. If this be the case in a natural agent without will, how much more in one who operates through will, and how much more in the Creator who is above all denomination? Of course, in us wisdom is different from power and power is different from will."[106] Therefore, we are wise through one property, have power through another, and will through a third. It is not so in the Creator, but in him wisdom is power itself and is will itself, so that he does not have wisdom through one property, power through another, will through a third, but is wise, powerful, and willing through the same thing, namely his substance. Hence the Rabbi says that those wise in the Law said: "God is powerful in his substance, alive in his substance, willing in his substance."[107]

43. The second example he gives is in man who by a single rational power "in which there is no multiplicity" does many different things. Through it he builds, cuts, covers, rules fellow citizens, knows arithmetic, and by the one rational power brings many things of this sort into existence. "If this be so, how will we remove from the power of the high and lofty Creator the different things he does that proceed from one simple substance in which there is no multiplicity nor anything added on? Therefore, all the denominations attributed to the Creator in books will name his works, not his substance, or else are put down to signify the perfection of those dispositions which in us are perfections added to the substance."[108]

44. This is what Rabbi Moses transmits about the names or attributes that are affirmatively predicated of God. He says that all positive statements about God are improper expressions, since they posit nothing in him. To posit nothing in something and still to speak positively about it is unsuitable, improper, and not in keeping with the truth. Hence all things that are positively said of God, even though they are perfections in us, are no longer so in God and are not more perfect than their opposites. For example, mercy,

devotion, and the like, are perfections in us, while anger, hatred, and the like, are imperfections. Just as saying that God is angry or hates, since these things are nothing, posits nothing at all in God save that he performs certain external actions which proceed from anger or hatred in us, so too the same is true of their opposites. Thus mercy and devotion posit nothing and are nothing in God, but God himself is called merciful only for the reason that he performs external works like those which mercy causes in us, according to the Psalm text, "As a father has mercy on his children, so the Lord has mercy on them that fear him" (Ps. 102:13). Therefore, although mercy, devotion, and the like, are perfections in us, they are not in God.[109]

For example, consider that in the fox craftiness joined to shrewdness is a perfection, just as savagery in a dog is not an evil because of the natural fidelity he has for all his master's possessions and hence the savagery shown to everything that is not his master's. Again, the avarice by which the ant gathers in summer what he lives on in winter, although he is not consciously providing for the winter, is a perfection in it.[110] These three things are not perfections in us, but imperfections. Thus how much more would our perfections—the remedies and aids of the imperfection by which our substance has no power of itself or from itself and cannot itself perform an act that is perfect and perfective of itself—be altogether useless if they were in and posited in God where his very substance of itself has power over everything and is sufficient to itself and other things? This is so both because he is existence, and existence and it alone suffices for itself and all things, and also because he is the First of all things, and "the First is rich in itself."[111] How can things that do not exist be in God? Or how can things that posit nothing be posited or positively predicated where they posit nothing? Third, how can perfections be where they do not perfect and are of no advantage, but rather corrupt and make multiple? Fourth, how can things be perfections rather than imperfections that do nothing and are not productive of anything?

45. After seeing what Rabbi Moses and the Jewish sages thought about the names that are positively attributed to God, the second main point to note is the root and reason the Greek and Arab philosophers and the Jewish sages give why nothing may be positively or affirmatively said to be in God or fittingly predicated of him. 46. The root and reason is twofold. One is that which Rabbi Moses writes in *Guide* 1.54 when he says that the root of this saying and opinion is because there are four things that have no connection with God.[112] The first is corporality and every property that implies corporality, for spirit and body, in being what they are, are totally opposed to each other. Now "God is spirit" (Jn. 4:24). The second is that in God there is no mutability, no potentiality that is not in act. Third is that there is no

privation or lack in him; fourth, that there is no similarity of God to creatures. "To whom have you likened God?" (Is. 40:18). "There is none among the gods like you, O Lord" (Ps. 85:8). Because all affirmative names of this sort imply and connote one of the above four it follows that they are unsuitable and discordant with the divine nature and with truth itself.

47. Again, in the second place, the root of what has been said is that which he puts down in *Guide* 1.50, that the universal rule is that in God there neither is nor can be any addition of dispositions whatever. But all affirmative names predicate or imply some addition which they posit about God; otherwise they would not be positive expressions. Therefore, nothing affirmative is properly and aptly said about God, but only unsuitably said. He demonstrates the major premise there, and on the basis of his words we can construct seven proofs.[113]

48. The first goes this way. Every disposition is a thing added on to the substance to which it is joined, but this is repugnant to the purity and unmixed character of the divine nature. "The light shines in the darkness and the darkness grasped it not" (Jn. 1:5); "God is light, and in him there is no darkness" (1 Jn. 1:5). Second, every disposition is outside the substance of that to which it is attributed, but this is repugnant to the fullness of the divine nature, which, since it is existence (Ex. 3:14), and hence the fullness of all existence, can have nothing outside it.

49. The third is this: Every disposition is an accident or flows from the genus of accident or betrays the nature of accident, but this is repugnant to the divine simplicity and its formality. As Boethius says, an accident can be joined to something that exists, but to the act of existence itself, or that by which a thing is,[114] nothing can be joined. Therefore, according to him, "The simple form cannot be a subject."[115] The fourth: If some disposition is in God and is other than God, there are already many eternal beings, but this is repugnant to the infinity of the divine nature, which has the property of uniqueness. This is because eternity is a persisting "now" that cannot be divided, because it is according to its name "outside boundaries"[116] and limits, and because it is impossible for there to be two infinite things. For that is infinite outside of which there is nothing. If many infinite things are posited, none of them will be infinite, because there will be something outside of each one of them.[117]

50. The fifth proof goes this way. Where there is disposition there is some multiplicity, but this is repugnant to the unity of the divine nature. "That is truly one, in which there is no number," as Boethius says;[118] and Rabbi Moses says that God is one "in every way and according to every respect," so that "no multiplicity either inside or outside the understanding"

can be found in him.[119] Sixth. If any disposition is posited in God, since God is existence and outside existence there is nothing, it will be a medium between existence and nothing, between being and nonbeing. But this is repugnant to the divine priority by which God is the first and last. "I am the first and the last" (Is. 44:6). The First can never have a medium. The seventh proof is from the same point. One of two things cannot be a medium between the two, for it would then be its own medium and the same thing would be medium and extreme. But every disposition by its nature is a medium between what it disposes and that to which it disposes it.[120]

51. Or give the clear and brief eighth proof that it is impossible for any disposition or addition or any number whatsoever to be found in God. The reason is that everything of that sort, such as disposition, addition, and number, exists for the sake of a defect in the sort of thing in which it is found. Hence only those things that are defective and are not able to be self-sustaining are multiplied and numbered. The case is different concerning other things such as the heavenly bodies and immaterial things. Thus, man's essence is not sufficient to understand or to know in itself, and for this reason the intellectual power and habit of knowledge are added to it. This is why the teachers say that a habit is properly not posited in those powers which are naturally sufficient to be moved to act.[121] God, as the First and Supreme, is self-sufficient to and in all things; therefore, no disposition, addition to his substance, or number can enter into him. The major and minor premises were proved above in the examples of fire and man's rational power. For this reason dispositions and numbers of this sort in created things are not perfections, but are the remedies and reinforcements of the imperfection and defect of some act of existence. This does not pertain to God, both because he is existence, because he is Existence Itself (Ex. 3), and because that is the First. "The First is rich in itself."[122]

52. On this eighth proof there are three things to note. The first is that because of this the teachers say that the light of glory is something added to the created intellect that disposes it to the vision of God's essence because created nature of itself is not sufficient for this.[123] The second is that in prime matter there is nothing added to the matter, because through its very essence it strives for and receives form without any power added to it. The third is that because the existence of things resembles the nature of God, "the First and Last," every substantial form, since it is existence and gives existence, is united to matter and perfects it immediately through itself. Therefore, the form is the intrinsic cause of the thing. It is different with an agent and goal which do not give themselves in substantial fashion, and whose substance matter does not look to or strive for either through its nature, matter, or

existence. For this reason an agent and goal are extrinsic causes of material things.[124] It is otherwise in the case of becoming in things. This stands apart from existence and apart from the generation which is the very existence of the thing.[125] Media, accidents, and added dispositions occur there—[the things] which alteration, as a kind of path to generation and existence, looks to.

Fourth. From these remarks the truth and the necessary reason why in every composite being there must be a single substantial form that gives existence is evident.[126] It is also clear how the dispositions that precede form in matter are not useless, but are necessary for becoming and alteration, imperfect as they are. After the form's introduction they no longer precede it but follow it in existence according to nature's order. And so the heat that precedes fire's form in a piece of wood is imperfect prior to fire's form. It is not fire's heat, but is the heat of what is lighted and is tending toward the existence and form of fire.

53. Therefore, the root and ground of what went before is evident and also how all affirmations or positive names in no way belong to God and how there is no disposition at all in him, either substantial or accidental, even those that are perfections in us, such as power, wisdom, life, and the like. Hence some wise man said that God is "powerful in his substance, alive in his substance,"[127] intelligent in his substance, and the like. For this reason the saints commonly said that God's greatness is his existence and his knowledge is his existence, and the same of the other attributes.[128] The reason is that he is powerful, lives, is wise, and the like by his very substance. Others said that God "exists, but not by essence, lives, but not by life, is powerful, but not by power, is wise, but not by wisdom."[129] In the *Trinity* 5.1 Augustine says: "Let us understand God, insofar as we can, as good without quality, great without quantity, . . . ruling but not from a position, embracing all things without external form, total everywhere without a place, eternal without time."[130] So much for the first part on what some philosophers and the Jewish sages have written about the names attributed to God positively or affirmatively.

54. In the second part it remains to take a summary glance at what our Christian teachers hand down on this. There are four points to clarify this. The first is that there is one way of speaking and thinking about beings or things and their existence and another way about the categories of things and how we make use of them. By not paying attention to this some people have fallen into many difficulties. The ten categories are not ten beings or ten things, nor are they the ten first beings and ten first things, but they are the first ten categories of things or beings.[131] They are in no way the first ten

beings, but one thing alone is being, namely, substance. Other things are not really beings, but are what belongs to a being (as *Metaphysics* Book 7 says);[132] they are beings only analogically by relation to the one absolute being which is substance.[133] Thus urine is called healthy not by reason of health inhering in it in a formal fashion, but only by analogy and with respect to the exterior health that is properly found in an animal. The same is true of the way wine is related to the circular sign that signifies that there is wine in the tavern or in the jug.[134] And so all nine of these [remaining] categories are not beings directly, but indirectly, that is, by way of a being.[135] The reason is that only substantial form gives existence; accidents universally do not give existence, but qualitative and quantitative existence, and things like these. Rather, an accident finds an existence that is already prior in nature in the subject and it does not give existence, but receives it in and through the subject. Hence the whole composite thing is one being, although there may be ten thousand accidents or accidental categories in it. Just as the whole composite thing is one qualified thing by means of quality alone, and one quantified thing by quantity alone, and so forth, so too it is a being by substance alone, that is, by substantial form. Everything of this sort is a being or thing in external fashion by an analogical relation to the one thing which is a being and a thing, that is, substance.

The categories are genera in a univocal not in an analogical sense; otherwise there would not be ten primary genera. The First as such does not hang on another, nor does it depend upon or have an analogical relation to something else.[136] So I say then that relation, although it is said to have the least being of the accidents, is nonetheless just as much a primary genus of category as substance itself. The very name "the First" shows it.[137] The difference between what is equivocal, univocal, and analogous is that the equivocal is distinguished by means of things that are different, the univocal by means of differences in the same thing,[138] while the analogous has neither the one nor the other, but is only distinguished through modes of existence of something that is one and the same in number and that already is found to exist in nature through the form that is substance.

55. The second preliminary remark is that expressions or propositions primarily and necessarily are in accord with the concepts of things and not with the things themselves, because words are the signs and "marks of the feelings that are in the soul."[139] For this reason they denote, indicate, and signify the concept, and are therefore judged true or false, as suitable or unsuitable discourses and propositions not on the basis of things or beings in the absolute sense, but on the basis of the concepts of things and beings— which they signify primarily and necessarily. Thus the power of sight does

not regard the visible object itself, the thing seen, except by accident. For this reason the substance of what is seen has no effect on the act of seeing itself in the way the proper visible object itself does, nor does it have any effect in relation to the manner of seeing, as does the common visible object, that is, quantity, movement, and the like.[140] A large thing is more easily seen than a small one, and something at rest than something moved.

56. The third preliminary notion is that act proceeds from essence according to the ideas and properties of the attributes. For example, Paternity in the Godhead is that thing which is the essence, and the essence in the Son is really that which is Filiation.[141] Nevertheless, we truly and properly say that the Father begets, not the essence, and that the Son is begotten, not the essence. Likewise in God existence and knowledge are the same; nevertheless, we say and grant that God knows evil, but we do not hold that he is evil. This is what the *Book of Causes* says in proposition 18 that "all things are beings because of First Being, and are living things . . . because of the First Life, and are intellectual things . . . through the First Intellect."[142] Augustine says in *To Orosius:* "Although the soul and reason are one, the soul does one thing, reason another. We live by the soul; we know by reason."[143] Bernard in *On Consideration* 5 says: "God loves as charity, knows as truth, . . . works as power, reveals as light."[144]

57. The fourth point is that all our knowledge arises from the senses so that a person who lacks a sense power from birth would be deprived of knowledge of that sensible object.[145] We name things from knowing them and according to the manner in which we know them. All perfections and those of all the genera, since they are in God as the First Cause of all things, are in him as necessarily and simply one and one thing, because "God is one" (Ga. 3:20). Everything that is in the One and in which the One is, is itself one. For "the One is that in which there is no number."[146] Thus there is one essence in the divine Persons because there is no number of essences in that essence. The Person of the Father is one because there is no number of persons in that person. Thus in God every perfection is one because in him there is no number of perfections. This is the reason why anyone who would see God himself through himself, that is, through his essence and not from other things nor through some other medium, would see a single perfection and would see all perfections in it and through it rather than it through them. This perfection would not be a particular perfection,[147] but a single one that is above all. If the onlooker were to give a name to that which he sees and through which and in which he sees, it would necessarily be the One, according to the text in the last chapter of Zacharias, "In that day there will be one Lord, and his name will be One" (Zc. 14:9). The One is not the name

for wisdom, or power, and the other individual attributes, but it is the One that is all, above all, and in which all are according to Philippians 2: "I have given him a name which is above every name" (Ph. 2:9). He says "name" in the singular because it is the One "which is above every name," because the perfections of all names that are divided in creatures are one thing and one perfection in it.

58. From this the true answer of that knotty and famous question whether there is a distinction of attributes in God or only in our intellect's way of grasping is clear and evident. It is certain that the distinction of divine attributes, for example, power, wisdom, goodness, and the like, is totally on the side of the intellect that receives and draws knowledge of such things from and through creatures.[148] Creatures, by the fact that they are from the One but below the One, necessarily fall into number, plurality, distinction, guilt, and fault, a condition by which they are numbered among all the things that are. That which commits an offense in the One and against the One incurs the guilt of distinction and falls into the all. This is one explanation of what is said in James 2: "He who offends in one point has been made guilty in all" (Jm. 2:10). The distinction which the term "all" implies is indeed guilt, fault, and defect in existence and unity. Everything that exists is either above all and above number, or is numbered among all things. But above all and outside number there is only the One. No difference at all is or can be in the One, but "All difference is below the One," as it says in the *Fountain of Life*, Book 5.[149] "That is truly one in which there is no number," as Boethius says.[150] And Rabbi Moses, as mentioned above, says that God is one "in all ways and according to every respect," so that any "multiplicity either in intellect or in reality," is not found in him.[151] Anyone who beholds [the number] two or who beholds distinction does not behold God, for God is one, outside and beyond number, and is not counted with anything.[152]

59. First, because he is outside number. Thus, what is not quantity does not make anything quantified nor greater than any quantified thing, nor does what is not quality cause something to be numbered with a qualified thing or a quality. Something quantified and something qualified are not two quantified things or two qualified things, nor two nonqualified or nonquantified things. 60. Second, because the unity which makes God one is not the unity which creates number or the principle that constitutes number. Hence, as often as you repeat that unity, it would never make a number or make something to be numbered. Third, because existence is not counted along with being, nor is form generally with the thing that is formed. Existence and every form is from God as the First Existence and the First

63

Form. Therefore, no distinction can exist or be understood in God himself. 61. And fourth: All distinction is repugnant to the infinite. But God is infinite. However, distinct attributions of this kind are not vain and false because they relate to something that is true and real in God.[153] Still, in God there is one thing, and, according to Bernard, "We may say, one in the highest degree."[154] This thing is most truly power, wisdom, goodness, and the like. It is evident that these kinds of names are not synonymous because they signify different ideas or conceptions of our intellect.[155]

62. From what went before, where we said that God is and does all things by his substance, it is clear that in him there is only one category, namely the substance by which he exists, is powerful, wise, good, and the like. In creatures these things belong to the nine categories of accident. But then comes the question how Augustine,[156] Boethius,[157] and the saints and teachers in harmony say that there are two categories, substance and relation, in the Godhead. 63. The response is from what was noted above. We said that we speak in one way about beings and things, in another way about categories, and also that the truth of a predication corresponds first and in itself not so much to things as to the conceptions of things and the ways of signifying. Relation, even though it is an accident, still does not signify in the manner of an accident, because it does not do so as inhering in a subject or substance. You can see an example in the case of whiteness and the white thing. Although whiteness exists in a subject and is an accident or something inhering in a subject, the term does not signify whiteness as something inhering. Just as the word "white" signifies the quality alone[158] (as does "whiteness"), it co-signifies or connotes the subject also, and for this reason signifies itself as an accident and something inhering.[159] This is why Avicenna is said to have thought that the term "white" principally signified the subject and secondarily the accident.[160]

64. You should know that "there are two things found in relation, namely, the way in which it refers to something else, which is what the idea of relation as a category consists of," and the further consideration "of the very existence of relation . . . by which it is rooted in something that belongs to a being, . . . such as quality, quantity, and the like."[161] By reason of its genus and the fact that it is a relation, relation posits nothing at all in the subject and does not say that anything exists or inheres,[162] but it posits that the thing that exists comes from another and is directed to another, that it originates there and dies there, and that it is "simultaneous in time, nature, and intellect"[163] with, in, and through that thing. Because relation as such is nothing positive in a subject, and because it signifies only what was said and in that way (this is true of relation alone among the nine categories), and

because as such it is not the principle of any of the subject's operations (for God is wise, good, almighty, and the like, by reason of his substance, but by his substance is not related to any other thing whatsoever),[164] hence relation perdures in the Godhead according to the mode of signifying and predicating which constitutes its own genus as a category. It is different with all the other eight kinds of accident, as is evident to one who considers them. Therefore, this is the reason why every kind of accident except for relation is absorbed into the substance in God.

65. There is another and neighboring reason and it is formulated thus: Every accident of a subject and in a subject has one existence with the subject, and this is the subject's own existence. This is true even if there were a thousand accidents. Their existence is inhering existence, that is, existence in a subject, and their existence is in the existence of the subject, for they do not have an existence apart from that of their subject.[165] Now in God Existence Itself is the same as the essence or substance,[166] and therefore in him all the accidental categories are absorbed into the substance according to the genus and manner of predication which they receive from the subject and from their connection with the subject. Relation alone does not receive its genus as a category from a subject nor through ordering to a subject, but rather to its opposite.[167] For this reason relation is the only kind of category that is not absorbed into substance in the Godhead, but it remains as it were standing on the outside. Hence the older theologians used to say that the relations "assist" and "stand by."[168] This is what *Metaphysics* 5 says: "Insofar as knowledge is a relation, it is of the thing known, not of the knower."[169]

66. Against this it seems that the category of action does not signify that something "is in the agent, but rather that it is from the agent,"[170] and by this same reason it would not be absorbed into the substance since it would not signify some inhering existence, but an existence from something. But this doubt is solved because even though action does not signify that something is in the agent, what it does signify is a something and is according to something found in the subject, that is, according to its principle.[171] This is not so with relation, but rather its origin and principle is not in the subject but in its opposite. There is an example of this in the act of virtue which insofar as its substance is concerned has its principle from its agent and receives the mark of goodness there where it also receives the existence which is controvertible with the good. Nevertheless, this act insofar as it is virtuous arises and has its principle totally from its end.[172] So much for the fourth of six preliminary remarks.

67. Fifth, note that the ten categories, as the first categories, are distinguished from each other first and necessarily and immediately by them-

selves according to their ideas and ways of predicating. This is not the case with the species of these genera. Hence, "Quality is not substance" is immediately distinct, but "Knowledge is not substance" is distinct mediately and not immediately.[173] The reason that knowledge is not substance is due to the fact that it is a quality, which quality, I repeat, is not a substance, but self-distinguished by being "contrary to substance." Then I can assume that every accidental form of category by its very idea is absorbed into substance except for the idea proper to relation (as has been said) because it does not receive this idea from a subject. Therefore, "What is said of the Godhead by way of relation has a different idea than the idea of substance," as well as a manner of predicating that is distinguished in opposition to substance.[174]

68. Thus it is clear, first, that "knowledge, goodness, and the like, which are in the other genera of accidents" are not distinguished by opposition to substance because the genera by reason of which they were distinguished from substance are absorbed into substance so that it serves in place of the genera for all of them. Hence it is clear, secondly, that knowledge in the Godhead is substance whereas in us it is a quality. And it is evident, thirdly, that just as the same thing in us makes us wise and that very thing and not another makes us like to and in possession of this quality, so in the Godhead the Father knows by means of the same thing by which he is and by which he is God, namely, his substance. The same is true of the Son and Holy Spirit. 69. Therefore, knowledge and substance in God belong to a single mental category, which is the idea of substance in both cases, just as in us knowledge and quality are of one mental category. This mental category is proper to the genus (quality), but not to the species (knowledge), except insofar as knowledge itself is a type of quality. But species does not provide the ground for predication, because species are not distinguished according to different ways of predicating, but according to the differences which the species of one common genus constitute under the same way of predicating.[175]

70. It is different with Paternity and similar relations in the Godhead, for the idea of substance and that of relation are not the same in the way that the ideas of knowledge and quality are in us. The relation in God keeps the genus of relation and is different from the idea of substance, just as in us the ideas of quality and of substance are different. Therefore, God is not simply and by the same idea God the Father and God as substance, but he is God as substance by one idea and Father by another. I say that different ideas are distinguished according to different genera, not only in the way species is distinguished from genus (e.g., knowledge from quality) where the difference is only imperfect.[176] 71. Further (and ingeniously) note that the idea

of relation is a genus, but since it is not existence or inhering existence, as said above, it creates no distinction of existence and essence, because insofar as it is a relation it does not regard existence, essence, or substance, but rather what is totally opposite to itself.[177] For this reason the existence of the Father and that of the essence are one in the Godhead, and the same is true of the relations that distinguish the persons of the Son and Holy Spirit. These relations are not directed to existence; they distinguish neither substance nor existence, but the mutually opposed persons.

72. I summarize briefly by saying that relation according to the idea of its genus is not absorbed into substance, both because God's substance does not imply the idea of a relation, and because it does not stand for a relation, as happens on the contrary with the remaining eight kinds of accident (e.g., quality in the Godhead is absorbed into the substance). Again, by its own special sufficiency God's substance is quality, acquires the idea and property of quality, and functions for him as a quality. By his very substance God is qualified, for example, knowing, good, and the like; but he is not related by his substance. For these two reasons relation alone among the accidents remains in its own genus in the Godhead. Now the idea of genus in itself is distinguished from the idea of the genus of substance, so that some things are predicated substantially and in the singular in God, while other things are predicated relatively and in the plural.[178] For there is one essence, one goodness and things of this sort in God, but many persons and real relations. Hence Boethius says that "the essence preserves the Unity, the relation supplies the Trinity."[179] Let us take the following example. As one who knows and is white Martin indeed possesses qualities, and if the quality were to be absorbed into his substance, or if his substance were sufficient to make him a knower and white and possessing qualities in a general way, then without doubt knowledge, whiteness, and quality in the general sense would be Martin's very substance. Also knowledge, whiteness, and the like, would be species of substance and would not belong to the category of quality or be species of it. The case is different with relation, which certainly would not be absorbed into Martin's substance nor into the mode of predication of substance. And so Martin would know and be white through substance, and knowledge and whiteness would be substance in him, but he would not be related or referred to anything through substance, but rather through relation according to the idea and property of the genus relation. So much on the fifth of the six remarks.

73. The sixth and last thing to be noted is that the truth of an affirmative proposition always subsists in the identity of the terms,[180] but the truth of a negative one subsists in the difference or distinction of terms. Hence the

Philosopher in *Metaphysics* 4 says that "truth is when what is said to be actually is, and what is not said to be is not."[181] And Augustine in *Soliloquies* 2, "Truth is that which is."[182] For example, everything that is gold is true gold, but what is not true gold is certainly not gold, because it is something other than gold, such as a mixture of gold and bronze. But even this, that is, the mixture of gold and bronze, does not exist as *this* unless it is true gold-bronze, and the same is true of other things. Truth and being are interchangeable. Truth then is the existence of what is and consequently the non-existence of what is not. Everything said beyond this comes from evil because it is from nonbeing and from what does not exist and is evil because it is false, idle, and in vain, useless, and superfluous, in accord with the text of Matthew 5: "Let your speech be 'Yes, yes'; 'No, no'; and whatever is beyond these comes from the evil one" (Mt. 5:37). The truth of affirmation consists in the existence of what is.

74. That this is proper to God and God alone was seen above on the text from this third chapter of Exodus, "I am who am." He says "I" by way of distinction; he is alone in the most superlative sense—"I am alone" (Ps. 140:10). He says, "I am who am," both because he is the fullness of existence and full existence, and also because he is nothing else but pure existence. The conclusion is that the affirmation that consists in the existence and identity of the terms properly belongs to God. What is more the same than existence and existence; "I am who am?" For this reason no proposition is more true than that by which the same is predicated of the same. Everything that is less than God, since it is less than existence, is [both] being and nonbeing, and some kind of existence is denied to it since it is below and less than existence. And so negation is a part of it. But to existence itself no existence is denied, just as to the genus animal no particular animal, such as a lion, is denied. Therefore, no negation, nothing negative, belongs to God, except for the negation of negation which is what the One signifies when expressed negatively.[183] "God is one" (Dt. 6:4; Ga. 3:20). The negation of negation is the purest and fullest affirmation—"I am who am." It returns upon itself "with a full return";[184] it rests upon itself, and through itself it is Existence Itself. So no negation belongs to God—"He cannot deny himself" (2 Tm. 2:13).[185] Existence cannot deny that it is Existence Itself: "Nothing abandons itself."[186] Nor can it deny itself to anything, according to the maxim "The First is rich in itself."[187] Further, it cannot deny anything, according to the text "He works all in all" (1 Co. 12:6). He says "in all" because he denies it to none; he says "all" because he denies none. Just as nothing is denied to Existence Itself, so too existence denies itself in nothing ("It cannot deny itself") and denies nothing. It accepts and gives freely.

75. On this point note that because it is freely done this act of giving or gift and generally any activity and work that are free are properly divine. What is not freely done, but is done for a reward, not given or donated but sold, is simony. "Every good gift and every perfect present is from above" (Jm. 1:17). "A good gift" is what is genuine, what is purely given and not sold. The same is true of a present, and therefore it is expressly said, "Freely you have received, freely give" (Mt. 10:8), and "He cast out all those who were buying and selling in the temple" (Mt. 21:12). He denies no one, according to the text "Everyone who asks, receives" (Mt. 7:8). He denies nothing, according to the text "Ask whatever you will and it shall be done to you" (Jn. 15:7). In *Confessions* 10 Augustine says that "he speaks to all" all things and about everything, but "not all hear";[188] and those who hear do not hear everything and about everything. God as existence gives existence to all things and all perfection, truth, and goodness, for these belong to existence. But evil, sin, lying, and everything that belongs to nonbeing and to nothing and reeks of nothing he denies. "You ask and you do not receive, because you ask amiss" (Jm. 4:3), because, as was said, he denies nothing. He also denies those who make such requests because they belong to nothing. Augustine on John says: "Sin is nothing, and men become nothing when they sin."[189] "God does not hear sinners" (Jn. 9:31). (Although Augustine says that this last word is that of the blind man who had not yet been fully illuminated.)[190]

76. From what has been said it is evident why God is commonly and frequently said to advise, command, and work good for us and in us, but to prohibit evil completely and not to perform it. Evil things do not come about through him—"Without him was made nothing" (Jn. 1:3); "You should know that I have done no wicked thing" (Jb. 10:7). Man, not God, does what is nothing, what is wicked. We see this as a universal rule in nature. For example, fire by nature inclines toward, encourages, advises, commands, and gives upward motion, and naturally withdraws from, discourages, detests, and prohibits downward motion. God as existence, goodness, truth encourages, inclines toward, commands, orders, and gives everything that is, that is good and that is true; but he prohibits and withdraws from everything that is evil, that is untrue and that belongs to nothing. 77. It is clear then that affirmation, since it belongs to existence, is proper to God and divine things insofar as they are divine. Negation is not proper, but foreign to him. The reason is briefly what was given above—affirmation possesses and includes existence. The term "is" is the copula of every affirmative statement, even if only by reduction.[191] Negative statements, and they alone, include nonexistence.

78. What Dionysius says in the Chapter 2 of the *Celestial Hierarchies*, that "Negations about God are true, but affirmations are unsuitable,"[192] does not contradict this, for it is true about the mode of signifying in such sentences.[193] Our intellect grasps the perfections which belong to existence from creatures where perfections of this kind are imperfect, divided, and scattered. It signifies them according to that mode. In these propositions there are two things to keep in mind, namely the perfections signified, such as goodness, truth, life, understanding, and the like—and these are suitable and true—and the mode of signifying in such cases—and these are unsuitable, as Dionysius says. There is another reason for saying that affirmative propositions are unsuitable and false, because, as Augustine says concerning Joshua 24:23 ("Put away strange gods") in his *Questions on the Heptateuch*: "Anyone who thinks of God in a way that is not true to him carries a false and alien God in his thought. Who is the man who thinks of God in the way in which he is?"[194] And so it stands that statements of this sort about God are unsuitable, false, and untrue. This is why it is said "Every man is a liar" (Ps. 115:11); "We see now . . . in an obscure manner . . . in part" (1 Co. 13:12), as the Apostle says. This is enough on the positive names that are commonly attributed to God in scripture.

The fourth point is a special look at the name that is the Tetragrammaton, but this will be treated below on Exodus 20:7: "You shall not take the name of your God in vain."[195]

"The Lord has reigned forever and ever." (v. 18).

79. The first thing to remark is that some manuscripts have "has reigned" in the past, others "will reign" in the future, and this seems to fit the text's intention better. But both are a single truth. First, in the Godhead past and future are the same; it is otherwise in our apprehension which "has no place in such excellent light."[196] Both are also true because God is "prior to eternity," as it says in the *Book of Causes*,[197] and so he "has reigned" prior to it. "He will reign" always afterwards, as Daniel 2 says: "His kingdom will last forever" (Dn. 2:44).

80. This said, we need to know that the question frequently directed to this passage is how or in what way there could be something beyond eternity, since eternity by its very name means "outside limits" whatever and without end. In the twentieth chapter of the *Proslogion* Anselm gives four arguments or responses to this question.

First, God is beyond anything eternal by causality,[198] because even if there were nothing eternal God would not be any less. But if God did not exist, such things would not and could not be. Second, the things we call eternal can be thought of as nonexistent or apart from the fact they are eternal; but God cannot be thought of as not existing or apart from the act of existence. Third, God is simply infinite and consequently eternal; the other things we call eternal are composed of "the finite and the infinite," as the *Book of Causes* says in its commentary on the fourth proposition. Fourth, God is "beyond" the eternal by reason of his presentiality. His entire eternity is present to God simultaneously, so that his past is as present to him as his present, and the same is true of his future.[199] The whole duration—past, present, future—is present to God himself; it is not excluded from him, but rather included and contained. This is not the case in the other things that are said to be eternal, according to Anselm, because they no longer have present the part of their duration that is past. The same is true of the future.

81. Although these explanations at first glance are pleasing, they do not accord with the text's intention. In this passage Moses wished to say that the Lord "has reigned" without end previously and "will reign" without end or term afterwards. This is why he speaks of eternity insofar as it is a kind of duration. These explanations show that God is more excellent in nature than the other things that are called eternal. What he says in the fourth explanation about the presentiality of the past and future as different in God and in other eternal things is not quite subtle enough. As Boethius says in the fifth book of the *Consolation of Philosophy*, the difference is based upon motion, even if the world and motion be thought of as eternal.[200]

82. The fifth interpretation of this text "forever and ever" concerns eternity insofar as it is a duration in creatures and one that they participate in with God as its eminent author and cause.[201] Augustine proves this in his chapter on the Father and the Son in the *Book of Eighty-Three Questions*,[202] where he discusses the example of chastity in itself and chastity in those who are chaste from, through, and in it. Augustine also says there that God is the author of eternity, who makes created things eternal. The second proposition in the *Book of Causes* says that existence in its primary stage is "higher than and prior to eternity." It is universally true that a cause is prior to what comes from it and its end prior to what is dependent on it. Ecclesiastes 1 says ". . . to the place whence the rivers come, they return" (Qo. 1:7), in relation to the end. And in Book 3 of the *Consolation of Philosophy* Boethius says:

Everything repeats its proper course,
And rejoices in returning to its origin.[203]

83. The passage is explained briefly and clearly in a sixth way by saying that "eternal" is here taken for any finite duration which is the period used to describe the life span of something. Thomas has this explanation as well as the fifth.[204] This is why another translation has, "The Lord will reign for future ages and beyond."[205] Augustine also uses this interpretation on the basis of the Greek text in commenting on Josue 4, and in commenting on Genesis 31 he cites a line of Horace: "He who does not know how to be content with little will be a slave forever."[206] In the *Gloss* at this point Origen says, "When it says 'forever,' it means a length of time, but with some end. . . . And when it says 'forever and ever,' it still indicates an end, though one unknown to us."[207] Rabbi Moses says that when it has "forever," or "forever and ever," an end is indicated; but when it says "forever and ever and ever," it is to be understood as without an end.[208]

84. Still, we can assign a seventh explanation as follows. "Words are the signs of acts undergone in the soul."[209] Hence, the modes of signification and consequently of predication are formed according to the manner of understanding, as we said above in the case of the passage "Almighty is his name."[210] "Eternal" signifies eternity in the concrete, that is, the form alone, as in "white signifies quality and nothing further."[211] Even though it does not signify the subject, it nonetheless connotes and suggests it. The subject is related to the form as something passive to something active,[212] as effect to cause. It is clear that something white owes the fact that it is white to whiteness, and so whiteness is prior to what is white as its cause and author, and is beyond or after what is white as the end and term of the whitening by which the thing is white.

85. Again, there is an eighth argument as follows. Eternity and every duration in general concerns the very existence of things, for everything is said to last as long as its existence remains. Thus, the modes of duration are distinguished according to the different forms of existence: Eternity [refers to] the divine existence; "aeon" to the existence of unchangeable created things; and time to the existence of changeable things.[213] It then follows that duration, in itself, primarily and formally concerns the very act of existence. The existence of created things is not their essence, but is something posterior to it in the order of understanding.[214] Therefore, the duration of God, whose existence is his very substance, is something prior to eternity. But if it is prior, it is also posterior, because the First or Principle and the End always coincide and agree with each other.[215] This is what is said here: "The Lord has reigned forever and ever." The Primal Eternity by its mode of signification is related to the "eternal" as "source" is to "essence."[216] But

"source" is proper to God, and "essence" is proper to the creature, as is clear from the treatise "On the Source."[217]

86. Finally, the passage "The Lord has reigned forever and ever" plainly and briefly intends to say that his kingdom will always and infinitely stand beyond any measure of counting or conceiving. Thomas has a wonderful saying that accords with this in his [*Summa of Theology*] Ia, q. 14, a. 20, about the infinity of the thoughts and affections of hearts that are known by God with the knowledge of vision. This is obscure to many, and I cannot remember anyone before Thomas who said it.[218] Not even Thomas himself in other places says this about the knowledge of vision, but only about the knowledge of simple understanding.[219] I have spoken about this plainly and fully in the *Work of Questions*.[220] Let us say then that the Lord has known "forever" by the knowledge of vision as far as knowing can reach into eternity, and that he has known "beyond that" by the knowledge of simple understanding. And what goes for God's knowledge is equally true about his kingdom and rule. "We will walk in the name of the Lord our God forever and beyond that" (Mi. 4:5).

Chapter 16. "They set out from Elim, etc." (v. 1).

87. This is where the sixteenth chapter is generally marked, but some begin it a little later at the words "the fifteenth day." These interpreters also have what follows in verse 2 ("They murmured") without the conjunction "and."[221] "Neither had he more who had gathered more, nor did he find less who had provided less" (v. 18).

88. This passage can be explained in three ways. The first is this. Rabbi Moses in his [*Guide*] 3.13 cites this passage and says that it can be verified literally, because a poor person, who seems to have less, is as well supplied as the rich person who has more if we look at what is necessary and not merely a matter of greed. Boethius in Book 2 of the *Consolation of Philosophy* says, "Nature is content with a few little things; if you want to pile them up to a superfluous overflow, it would be either unpleasant or harmful."[222] The Psalm says, "I have not seen the just forsaken, nor his seed seeking bread" (Ps. 36:25). In Book 10 of the *Confessions* Augustine says that food should be taken like medicine;[223] and Cicero's *Tusculan Disputations*, Book 5, says: "Nature is satisfied with a little attention"; and shortly after, "Nature needs things few and small."[224] This is especially true since it is a command of the law in Deuteronomy 15 that "There shall be no poor nor beggar among you" (Dt. 15:4). Thus those who have less will be helped by those

who are rich, "since we are all members of one another" (Ep. 4:25). Members naturally help each other. According to Aristotle, nature has enough of what is necessary and does not abound in what is unnecessary.[225] "Give what is left over as alms" (Lk. 11:41). I have spoken of this earlier on the text "If God shall be with me . . ." (Gn. 28:20).[226]

89. The second explanation is this. The matter involved in things that can be generated is no more satisfied by the most noble of forms, such as that of humanity, than by that of the least, such as an ant, which it has already received (although it always strives for some form, even the least). Further, the eye does not see less for the foot's sake and more for its own, but equally for both, because it is first and foremost for the whole body and whole person. This is what is said by way of a parable, "He who gathered more, did not have more, nor he who gathered less have less." Solomon describes matter in the same way in the parable of the adulterous woman in Proverbs 5.[227]

90. The third explanation goes this way: Manna, as any heavenly and divine gift, has this characteristic—if and insofar as it is divine, it is equally attractive, sweet, and soothing for the hunger of the just and perfect person, be it great or little. It is not more for the one or less for the other, for what is more for one and less for another is no longer divine. In the case where one person takes less and another more, there is nothing just, divine, good, nor done in love.

The first reason is that such a person does not love God alone in the things he loves, nor love them in God. "God is one" (Ga. 3:20); he is the One. But in the One there is no more or less, because every "difference is below the One," as was said above.[228] Second, because such a person does not love the good as such, but particular goods. For him the good in itself is not the formal object of his will willed for its own sake. Therefore the good itself does not form and inform him, but something outside and apart from the good. What is outside and apart from the good is certainly evil, and consequently it forms and makes the lover evil, or rather deforms him, deprives him of the good and hence of God.

91. Third, in God there is no giving more or less, rather, the things that in themselves possess more or less become and receive in him and through him, as in the One, one existence. That is why it expressly says here, "He who gathered more, did not possess more, nor he who gathered less have less." Something that in itself has the appearance of more or less becomes and is one in God, both because what is divided in the inferior is always one in the superior, and because everything that is in the One and

one with it is certainly one. With his whole being God is present whole and entire as much in the least thing as in the greatest. Thus the just person who loves God in all things would seek in vain for something more or greater when he has some little thing in which the God whom he loves alone to the exclusion of everything else is totally present. There is no "greater" or "less" in God nor in the One; they are below and outside God and the One. And thus someone who sees, seeks, and loves what is more or less is not as such divine. This is the meaning of the axiom in the *Book of the Twenty-Four Philosophers:* "God is the infinite intellectual sphere with as many circumferences as centers and whose center is everywhere and circumference nowhere. He is entire in his least part."[229]

92. There is an example of this in the sacrament of the Lord's Body which is entire in the smallest part of the consecrated host, and also in every substantial form, in that it is found entire through essence and its "whatness" in the least part of the subject. Every part of fire is fire, and the whole soul is found in the smallest part of the body it gives life to.[230] From what has been said the meaning of the passage in Luke 15 is clear: "There is joy in heaven over one, more than over ninety-nine" (Lk. 15:7); and Matthew 10: "He who loves more . . . is not worthy of me" (Mt. 10:37); and Matthew 25: "What you have done for one of these, the least of my brethren, you have done for me" (Mt. 25:40); and many like passages. For this reason Truth itself teaches us to pray that "your will be done" for us "on earth as it is in heaven" (Mt. 6:10), that is, in the lowest and least as well as in the greatest and highest.

Chapter 18. "And when Jethro the priest had heard . . ." (v. 1). And below, "Hear my words and counsels" (v. 19).

93. There are four points from Augustine to be noted here,[231] and they are found in the *Gloss* but scattered and spread out.[232] First, "An example of humility is suggested here, for Moses with whom God spoke did not disdain to take advice from a foreigner."[233] Second, "Scripture warns us that true advice can be given through anyone and should not be rejected."[234] Third, those who hold the high position of judge should beware of pride and greed and follow after truth.[235] Fourth, "A spirit that cares little about human actions is open to God, and will be more filled by him the more freely it reaches out to high eternal things."[236] Note in the fifth place that when one single person wants to have honor on the grounds of his high state he often becomes harmful and hurtful to others unless he entrusts something to them.

Chapter 20. "The Lord has spoken" (v. 1).

94. The *Gloss* and Thomas in IaIIae, q. 100, have enough on the sufficiency, order, and distinction of the ten commandments.[237] For the present five points can be made.

First, why is there no mention of the commandment of love among the commandments? John 15 says of it, "This is my commandment, that you love one another" (Jn. 15:12), and Matthew 22 says, "This is the first and greatest commandment" (Mt. 22:38). 95. On this point note first that no art gives rules about the end, but about the means by which the end is acquired.[238] The doctor attends to health as perfectly as he can without [limiting himself] to means or measure, but he gives his potions and pills with both means and measure.[239] The art of medicine provides rules for calculating and measuring such things. "The goal of the commandment is love" (1 Tm. 1:5).

96. Again, the end in every case lies outside what it is the end of—movement is not the end of movement, the line is not the end of the line, time is not the end of time, and so forth. This is why love, which is the "goal of the commandment," as 1 Timothy 1 says, ought not to be numbered among the commandments.

In Ia IIae, q. 100, a. 3, Thomas gives another reason, saying that love of God and neighbor, that is, the act of charity, "is contained in the ten commandments as a principle is contained in its conclusions." We believe conclusions because of principles, and not vice versa. An end in the realm of actions acts like a principle in the realm of knowing.[240] "Love," therefore, since it is "the goal of the commandment," ought not to have a commandment given about it or to be itself numbered among the commandments, but is to be included in all the other commandments like a principle in a conclusion.

You should know that things can pertain to a commandment of the law in two ways: Some pertain to the substance of the commandment; others not to the substance, but as preambles without which the commandment does not apply.[241] Because all the commandments of the divine law are ordered to the goal that the human mind be united to God (which is the property of charity), it is evident that no command of the divine law applies without charity, and that without it they are of no value (cf. 1 Co. 13:3). This is why faith and hope do not belong to the substance of the law and are not numbered among the ten commandments, but are necessary preambles to the law's commands. Unless a person believes that God exists and hopes to receive something from him by obeying the law's commands, one would not be inclined or prepared to receive and undergo the yoke and burden of the commandments. On Matthew 5, Chrysostom says, "Justice is a nuisance for those living in the flesh; the burden of the work is not undertaken without hope of reward."[242] This is what is written in Hebrews 11: "Someone who comes to God must believe that he exists" (as far as the first point), "and that he rewards those who seek him" (as far as the second) (Hb. 11:6). This is why faith is especially proposed as a preamble "by way of proclamation," and hope "by way of promise,"[243] as is clear from Chapters 6 and 19 where it says, "Say and announce to the children of Israel" (Ex. 6:6, 19:3)—and this relates to faith—and "If you will hear my voice, you shall be my peculiar possession above all people" (Ex. 19:5)—and this concerns hope. As far as substance goes, the ten commandments are set forth in this twentieth chapter as precepts to be obeyed.

97. The third point to be noted is that Rabbi Moses in [*Guide*] 2.34 treats of the legislation described in Chapter 20 and says that according to the text itself and the opinion of the learned, the people heard a voice speaking, but only Moses heard the words themselves. This was also probably the case with Paul's conversion and fall in Acts 9, where it says, "Those who accompanied him stood amazed, hearing a voice, but seeing no one" (Ac. 9:7). We often see someone standing far off, who because of the distance or weakness of hearing hears a voice or sound in a confused and indistinct way, and who is unable to catch the words and meaning distinctly. Rabbi Moses says that the text "I am the Lord your God and you shall have no other god" (Ex. 20:2–3) signifies "two principle beliefs: that he is the creator and that he is one." Made ready with Moses (cf. Ex. 19:11, 15), the whole people of Israel heard from God's mouth, because these commands can be grasped demonstratively by the human intellect and do not need the mediation of prophecy or prophet. "The wise men have used this explanation for David's saying, 'God has spoken once and for all, but I have heard these two things,' because power belongs to God. O Lord, you will render unto every man according to his works (Ps. 61:12–13)."[244]

98. There is a fourth reason why it seems very fitting that the commandment of love is not placed among the ten commandments spoken of here. This is because the old law is one of fear, the new law that of love or charity. Augustine says, "In brief, the difference between the old and the new law is that between fear and love."[245] John 13 says, "I give you a new commandment, that you love one another" (Jn. 13:34); and John 15, "This is my commandment, that you love one another" (Jn. 15:12). The Son, the

Word Incarnate, says "mine." "You have not received a spirit of bondage in fear, but you have received a spirit of adoption as sons" (Rm. 8:15), that is, one of love. "Son" comes from "philos," that is, love.[246]

99. The proof and sign of what has been said is that in the whole Mosaic law I do not remember any place where the love of God is put forward under the imperative or prescriptive mode, so that it says "You must love." Deuteronomy 6 says "You shall love" (Dt. 6:5), which pertains more to exhortations or promises. This is why Chapter 20 says, ". . . mercy unto them that love me" (Ex. 20:6), and why God's Son, the "beloved Son," says in Matthew 5: "It was said, 'You shall love'; but I say to you 'Love!' " that is, the imperative (Mt. 5:43–44).

It is also worth remarking that the words "you shall love" in Deuteronomy 6 are not only not put in the imperative as a command, but are set out as a promise or a reward, the fruit and "goal of the commandment" (cf. 1 Tm. 1:5). The reason is that anyone who loves his neighbor as he loves himself (Mt. 22:39), or like himself (Mk. 12:31), that is, just as much as himself (the word "like" means "just as much as"),[247] possesses everything that his neighbor has, whether by way of merit or reward, just as if he himself had done the meritorious work and gained the prize. I have expanded on this in a rich way in relation to Matthew 22, "You shall love your neighbor as yourself" (Mt. 22:39);[248] and to 1 Corinthians 3, "All things are yours" (1 Co. 3:22).[249]

"You shall have no strange gods" (v. 3).

100. Two important things are said. First, "You shall have no strange gods" in the plural. To declare and to have many gods implies a contradiction, an opposition between noun and attribute. "If there are many gods, there is no god."[250] Second, it says "strange gods," because if God exists, he is not strange. If he is strange, he is not God.

101. For the present I prove the first point as follows. Every multitude or plurality descends from the One and participates in it.[251] From this first point it follows that what descends or falls is not God, and every multitude is of this nature.[252] The second thing that follows is that everything that participates in any way is not God, and every plurality is of this nature. The third thing is that everything that descends or falls has something above it and prior to it, and hence is not God; every plurality is of this nature. Fourth, what participates in existence is not full existence, nor truly simple, and hence is not God. But every plurality is of this nature, because it participates in the One and consequently in existence.

102. The fifth conclusion. Existence Itself is the cause of everything that is a being, just as whiteness itself is the cause of everything white. But God is Existence Itself in its most powerful, most general, and most simple sense. Any God whatsoever, if he exists, will be the cause of all other beings. Therefore, the other things put up as gods either do not exist, or are not beings, or have the other God as their cause, that is, the God who is Existence. The sixth point is this—if there were many gods, each of them would be Simple Existence Itself and there would be nothing to distinguish them. Therefore, they would be indistinct and thus one or the One.[253] Seventh. If anyone were both man and this man by means of the same thing, it would necessarily follow that there could only be one man. But God, if he exists, is, is God, and is this God by means of the same thing, because he is absolutely simple.

103. Eighth. Anything said or held to be God and not to be Existence Itself, but something else, will either be a being without existence, or else will have existence from another. But the first is impossible; and if you hold the second, the thing that receives existence from another can no longer be God. I have said much about this in commenting on the text "God is one" (Dt. 6:4).[254] This is what 1 Corinthians 8 says, "If indeed there are many gods and many lords," according to the gentiles' errors, "nevertheless for you there is one God" (1 Co. 8:5–6). I have said more on this in commenting on Deuteronomy 32, "See that I am alone and that there is none other beside me" (Dt. 32:39). All this concerns the first point—that it says "you shall not have strange gods" in the plural.

104. The second issue to study is why it says "strange gods." You must recognize that God is foreign to no being, and this for six reasons.

The first is because he is existence and every act of existence comes immediately from him. Existence is foreign to no being—that to which existence is foreign is nothing.[255] The second reason is that "God is infinite."[256] The infinite is foreign to no being, but only to nothing, since outside it there is nothing, or, more properly speaking, outside it is only nothing. Acts 17 says, "He is not far from any one of us; in him we live, and move and have our being" (Ac. 17:27–28). Augustine in the *Morals of the Manichaeans* near the beginning says: "Existence has no contrary save non-existence."[257] The third reason is this. Indistinction belongs properly to God, distinction to creatures, as touched on above.[258] Nothing that is indistinct from something is foreign to it.

105. The fourth reason. Nothing is less foreign than that which is inmost in things, totally penetrating them. But this is existence, which is God, the fullness of existence.[259] The fifth reason is that nothing is less foreign

79

than that which sinks down into the essences of things. But this is existence and it alone. Essence as such looks to nothing else but existence, as its name shows. Sixth. Nothing is less foreign than that which "is the first of all to come to things and the last to leave."[260] This is that which God is insofar as he is the First Cause flowing into [all things] with himself in the first instance.[261] Romans 8: "He has given us everything with himself" (Rm. 8:32); Romans 5: "The love of God has been poured out in our hearts through the Holy Spirit . . . living in them" (Rm. 5:5, 8:11)—the Holy Spirit is the first gift. Also Wisdom 7: "All good things came to me together with her" (Ws. 7:11). 106. Every created thing, on the contrary, in that it is distinct and different from existence, is foreign. ("Foreign" comes from "other.")[262] Therefore, it is clear that every essence is foreign to or other than every other essence, as something distinct in relation to what it is distinguished from.[263] But existence is indistinct from being and essence.[264]

107. This is evident in every composite thing in this world, where under one indistinct act of existence the essences of the various categories remain distinct. In a piece of wood that is one in its act of existence the essences of the form, the matter, the quantity, quality, and the like remain distinct. Speaking to God, Augustine says, "You were with me, but I was not with you."[265] God is with us as indistinct; we are not with him as distinct, because created and limited. Since God is unlimited he is subject to no definition, as Avicenna says.[266] Definition pertains to limits. And so, if God is foreign, he does not exist. This is what Genesis 35 says, "Cast away strange gods" (Gn. 35:2); and Joshua 24, "Put away strange gods" (Jos. 24:23). Just as everything that is similar attracts its like, on the contrary, what is foreign, since it is dissimilar, rejects it. By rejecting what is foreign we will become similar— "We will be similar to him, for we shall see him as he is" (1 Jn. 3:2).

108. Nothing is so easy and so worthwhile as renouncing what is foreign and rejecting what is from without, whose nature is external, foreign, adverse. The Psalm says, "Foreigners have risen up against me" (Ps. 53:5), and so the Psalmist prays, "Save your servant from foreigners" (Ps. 18:4). Treating the text "Put away strange gods" from Joshua, Augustine says: "Anyone who thinks of God in a way that he is not, has a false and foreign god in his thoughts."[267] Because none of the faithful in this life is able to conceive of God as he is ("Every man is a liar": Ps. 115:11), we always have to say "Put away strange gods." This is what the *Gloss* has.[268]

109. The reason for the addition "before me" in "You shall have no strange gods before me" is that many people do not appear to have "strange gods" from the outside, who nonetheless before God who "sees the heart" (1 K. 16:7), truly worship many gods. "This people honors me with their

lips, but their heart is far from me" (Mt. 15:8, following Is. 29:13). Everything which anyone makes his end is a god for him, because God alone is "the first and last, the beginning and end" (Rv. 22:13), "although there are many gods and many lords" (1 Co. 8:5).

"Nor any likeness which is in heaven above, or on the earth beneath" (v. 4).

110. Two things are to be noted here: first, that it is forbidden to make a likeness of God; second, that it says "in heaven above, or on the earth beneath."

111. In relation to the first point, scripture frequently condemns those who set up likenesses, as Isaiah 44 reproaches some and says, "To whom have you likened God, or what image will you make for him?" (actually Is. 40:18); and the Psalm says, "There is none like you among the gods, O Lord" (Ps. 85:8). This is the reason why no image or likeness at all was put in the tabernacle over the propitiatory, which was like a chair, though the likeness of the cherubim was below it (Ex. 25:17–22). How could a visible likeness stand for the Infinite, the Immense, the Invisible, or the figure of an image for the Uncreatable? Hence some older authorities held that God could not be seen in himself even by the blessed, but only by means of certain theophanies.[269] And even today the more learned theologians say that God cannot be represented by any likeness of a lower order, so that by its mediation the divine essence could be seen in it and through it.[270] However, in Genesis 1 God says: "Let us make man to our image and likeness" (Gn. 1:26); and 1 John 3 has: "We will be like him, and we will see him as he is" (1 Jn. 3:2).

112. You should know that nothing is as dissimilar as the Creator and any creature. In the second place, nothing is as similar as the Creator and any creature. And in the third place, nothing is as equally dissimilar and similar to anything else as God and the creature are dissimilar and similar in the same degree.[271]

113. The first proposition is evident from this: What is as dissimilar as the indistinct and the distinct? These are more distinguished and more dissimilar than any two distinct things that are similar, just as man and non-man are more distinguished than any two men, or something colored and something not colored than any two colored things insofar as they are colored. But God is indistinct from every being, just as Existence Itself is indistinct from any being, as said above.[272] But everything created, by the very fact that it is created, is distinct. 114. A further, second proof. What is as dissimilar as the infinite and the finite? And a third: What is as dissimilar as that which has no genus in common with another thing? But God, insofar

81

as he is outside every genus, has no common genus with anything.[273] From these three arguments the first proposition, that nothing is as dissimilar as God and the creature, is evident.

115. Nothing is as similar as God and the creature. What is as similar to something else as that which possesses and receives its total existence from the order and relation it has to something else, a thing whose total act of existence is drawn from this other and has this as an exemplar?[274] But this is the way that the creature is related to God, as Boethius says in Book 3 of the *Consolation of Philosophy*, when he says of God: "As Form of the Good lacking all malice, you draw forth all things from the supernal exemplar. . . . bearing the world in your mind and forming it like the Image."[275] Second, what is as similar to something as that which is assimilated to another thing in and according to its inmost reality, that is, existence, truth, goodness, and the like? Other things are similar in relation to extrinsic reality, like heat, color, taste, shape, and the like. 116. Further and third, what is as similar to something else as that which "lives, and moves and has its being" in it (Ac. 17:28), whose existence is to be in it and in nothing else? In the first book of the *Soliloquies* Augustine says, "God, from whom to be turned away is to fall, to whom to be turned back is to rise, in whom to remain is to stand firm. God, from whom to depart is to die, in whom to return is to revive, in whom to dwell is to live."[276] From these three arguments the second proposition, that nothing is as similar to anything else as God and the creature, is evident.

117. The third proposition is that nothing is both as dissimilar and similar to anything else as God and the creature. What is as dissimilar and similar to something else as that whose "dissimilitude" is its very "similitude," whose indistinction is its very distinction? God is distinguished from everything created, distinct, and finite by his indistinction and his infinity, as is evident from Ia, q. 7, a. 1, ad 3.[277] Therefore, because he is distinguished by indistinction, is assimilated by dissimilitude, the more dissimilar he is the more similar he becomes. Thus, the more that one tries to speak about the ineffable, the less that one says about it as ineffable, as Augustine says in *Christian Doctrine*.[278] Again, someone who denies time actually posits it, as Averroes says, because to deny time happens in time.[279]

118. Therefore, no likeness to God can be established, because the more one posits it the less one posits it and the more dissimilar it becomes. Hence Augustine's *Free Choice* Book 2 says, "No visible likeness of an invisible thing can be completely fitting."[280] 119. Second, to be similar to God is also to be more dissimilar—and in more ways—as the saints and theolo-

gians commonly say. The more ways that something is like God, the more it is unlike him.

120. Third. Things themselves and their forms are not in God, but the ideas of things and of forms.[281] God is the Word, that is, the Logos, which is the Idea. John 1: "The Word was God" (Jn. 1:1). But nothing is as equally similar and dissimilar as the idea of something and the thing itself, for an idea is not truly and affirmatively predicated of a thing (e.g., "rational animal" of man) unless it is similar to it, or rather the same, as claimed above.[282] But on the other hand what is as dissimilar as the eternal uncreatable and the temporal created? This is the way it is with a thing and its idea. The idea of a corruptible circle is eternal;[283] and further, the idea of a circle is not a circle nor circular itself. Therefore, the idea of likeness is not like, but unlike, and it would not be like anything unless the idea of likeness were to be found in the inner depths of the thing. Hence, it is evident that like and unlike are equally joined together.

121. A fourth point follows from the same and from what was said previously. Something colored is colored formally by color alone and as a consequence is at the same time similar to everything colored and dissimilar to what is not colored. The more it becomes like colored things, the more it is unlike noncolored ones. But the forms of things, which give things name and species, are formally in the things themselves and in no way in God. On the contrary, the forms of things are not in God formally, but the ideas of things and of forms are in God causally and virtually.[284] These in no way denominate things, nor give name and species. The idea of a square is not and is not called a square, but is unlike a square. Thus, the created thing and the form through which it has a name exists in itself but in no way in God. The idea of the form, on the contrary, is in God, where it gives neither species nor name.[285] And so, every creature is unlike God from the viewpoint of each of the terms, that is, God and creature. God is not like the creature in that he does not have species and the name of a form, but only the idea which does not denominate it; the creature, for its part, does not have the form's idea nor the name as it is in God. Therefore, the unlikeness remains, and the foundation of the likeness is lacking in each term, that is, in God and the creature.

122. Yet, the forms of things would not be produced by God unless they were in him. Everything that comes to be comes to be from something similar.[286] Wine would as well come from a pear tree as from a vine, if it did not preexist in the vine and not in the pear tree, as the text in Matthew 7 says, "Do men gather grapes from thorns, or figs from thistles?" (Mt. 7:16).

It is necessary then that the forms of things which grant species and give name be in God. And so every creature is similar to God.

123. Now for three examples to clarify what has been said. The first concerns heat in fire and in the sun. Heat is in fire formally, so that it causes it and names it to be fire and to be called hot. In the sun heat is found not formally, but spiritually and virtually, so that it does not cause or give it the nature, existence or name of heat. Properly speaking, the sun is not and is not called "hot," since each thing takes its name from the form. For this reason, in order for something to be called hot it is not enough that heat be present in it in just any way; heat must be in it formally and as a form. This is not the case in the sun.

124. The second example, no less clear, concerns the color of a wall in itself, in its species (this is the medium),[287] in a mirror, in the eye, and especially in the intellect. If color did not exist in some way in its intelligible species, the eye would no more see color than it sees taste, nor would man be better understood in the species and likeness of man than would a stone. A color, such as white, is in the eye, without denominating the eye so that we call it a "white eye."

125. Again, unless there were color on the wall, we would not call the wall colored. The same thing, that is color, is on the wall and in the eye; but it endows the wall and exists in it as a form, while in the eye it does not exist as a form, but as an intention or likeness. Because form is ordered to existence, while intention or likeness are not ordered to existence nor made for its sake, but for knowledge and for the sake of knowing and seeing, a wall is colored but does not see color, while an eye on the other hand is not colored but sees color.[288] The consequence of this is that the wall is similar to everything colored and dissimilar to everything that is not, but the eye is similar to everything not-colored that sees color and dissimilar to everything colored. The less colored it is, the more it sees color and is dissimilar to all that is colored. Indeed, if it were colored in any way, it would not see any color, as Aristotle says.[289] Therefore, the same thing, that is, color, is both on the wall and in the eye, but under another existence, or better another mode of existence.

126. The third example is in the Godhead where the same essence and the same act of existence which is the Paternity is the Sonship: The Father is what the Son is. Nevertheless, the Father himself is not the Person who is the Son, nor is the Paternity the Sonship, but they are rather opposed [as relative terms]. Thus in the proposition under discussion the creature is similar to God because the same thing is in God and the creature, but it is dissimilar because it is under different aspects here and there. This finishes the

first issue, namely the command against making a likeness of God, for it says: ". . . and no likeness at all."

127. The second main issue is about the words "in heaven above or in the earth below." Augustine in the *Book of Eighty-Three Questions* says, "Nothing in the universe's body is really 'below.' Those who conceive of before and behind, right and left, above and below in the universe are deceived, because it is hard to oppose custom and the senses. . . . After we abolish these words, we have to make a real mental effort in order to see the point."[290] Remember that the six categories (before, behind, right, left, above, below) express terms that are related to some position or situation.[291] Situation and position of parts can be taken in two ways, either of the parts in the whole (and this does not belong to the category that is called situation), or in a second way as the position of parts not in the whole, but in a place (this belongs to one of the ten categories, that called situation).[292]

128. The reason for this is that the category situation takes its name from "place," just as the category "when" does from time. Therefore, if we consider heaven as far as its parts in the whole are concerned, since heaven is a simple body, there will be no place in it for above and below and the other four. But if heaven and its parts are compared with the whole universe (of which heaven is a part) as far as its place there is concerned, then we can talk about right, left, before, behind, up, and down in it. For example, in man the head is above, the feet below, the face before, the back behind, one hand is right, the other left. These do not vary among themselves insofar as they are related to man. Whatever direction a person turns, his face will always be in front, his back behind. If he stands on his head, his head will still be above and his feet below if we refer these parts to the whole person, but if the parts are referred to some exterior location, then the upside-down man is said to have his feet above and his head below. So the second point is clear, namely, how above and below are both found and not found in heaven, as Augustine has so well expressed it. This is why Avicenna well says that heaven exists and is moved in a "where,"[293] because "where" takes its meaning from place without any consideration of the order of parts in the place.

"Visiting the iniquity of the parents upon the children, unto the third and fourth generation of them that hate me" (v. 5).

129. In his *Questions on the Heptateuch* 5. 42, Augustine asks what it means when the sins of the parents are punished in those children "that hate" God, so that imitating ancestral crimes they are no longer being punished for their fathers' sins but for their own, according to the text, "The soul

which has sinned, the same shall die" (Ezk. 18:4). But in justice this should be not only unto the third and fourth generation, but unto all generations. Why then does it say here "unto the third and fourth generation"? Augustine asks a second time what it means to say "unto the third and fourth generation." Wouldn't it be better to have said "unto the first or second," since these are closer to the parents than the third, just as the fifth and sixth are closer to the parents' sins than the seventh?

130. To the first question he responds that the number seven, which is made up of three and four, frequently signifies the whole in scripture. To the second he answers that Moses did not put down the number seven under its own name, as if to say "unto the seventh," so that all generations would be understood; but he wished to signify the perfection of seven through "the third and fourth generation." This is because "it is made up from these two numbers, three which is the first uneven whole number, and four which is the first even whole number.[294] I think this is why we find that text so often repeated in the prophet, 'For three or four sins I will not turn away' (Am. 1:3, 6, 9, 11, 13; 2:1, 4, 6). Through it he wished all sins understood, rather than just three or four."[295] Note that when Augustine says "from the first uneven whole number and the first even whole number" the word "whole" is to be understood as a quota, that is, as part of a series whose repetition makes the whole.

131. It is evident that Augustine does not regard two as a number, but four is the first even number just as three is the first uneven one. Gregory agrees with Augustine in his *Morals on Job*,[296] but Avicenna in Book 3 of his *Metaphysics* disputes this and has another understanding.[297] The arguments seem to favor Augustine. First, two has the same role in the order of even numbers that unity does in uneven ones. But unity is not a number. Second, if two were a number, it would be the first number because unity is not a number. But the role of a first principle does not really belong to two, because a first ought always to be one and because division is proper to two but does not belong to a first. Therefore, the first uneven number, that is, three, ought to be the first number. 132. Third. Three, that is, the triangle, is the first of geometic figures, because two lines do not make a figure, according to geometry. But numbers and figures are judged by the same rules, both with respect to the genus of quantity, and with respect to the kinds of things they constitute (according to the Pythagoreans and Platonists),[298] or at least signify (as the astronomers and physiognomists say). Fourth, because quantity does not seem to exist where there is no divisible part. Size does not come from what has no size, and two does not have quantified parts.[299]

133. The fifth reason is that every number insofar as it is a quantity has

parts, but two does not have parts. The one and the part are opposed because the whole to which existence pertains is always one.[300] Existence does not belong to the part; the part always implies imperfection in its genus, and parts are always many. This is why Augustine in the *City of God* in dealing with the perfection of seven says "In the whole is rest, in the part labor."[301] Sixth, because according to theologians and jurists it does not belong to a part or party to make a judgment, or to measure or regulate either, as the tenth book of the *Metaphysics* says,[302] but this always pertains to the First, the Most Simple, and the One. All motion is from what is not moved.[303]

134. The seventh reason is because the One and being are convertible. What falls from the One falls from existence, but two of its nature and before all else falls from the One. Therefore, two as such neither exists nor is a number. There is no objection to this from the case of other numbers, even and uneven. Of its very nature the uneven number includes and smacks of unity and hence has something of the nature of the individual. This is why an uneven number is never divided in two equal parts while division is always naturally at first into two and into two different and particularly opposed parts. Privation and possession, two things, are the root of contraries.[304] The eighth reason is that two, as noted, is the privation of unity and privation as such gives existence to nothing.

135. The ninth reason is that God is not in what is equal and it is not in him. But everything in which God is not and which is not in God does not exist and is not a thing. Therefore, two does not exist and is not a number. The second proposition is proven both because God is in everything and everything is in him, and because anything in which God is not or which is not in him does not exist—it is not in existence, but outside existence and being. The first proposition is proved from Avicenna's *Metaphysics* 9.1, which shows that God has no equal. For then there would be two gods, and two gods are no God at all, as shown above in commenting on the text "You shall have no strange gods."[305] Augustine in his book on the Christian life says: "Peace and unity are a great virtue because God is one; therefore, those who are cut off from unity do not possess it."[306]

136. You should still remember that these arguments are probable, but not necessary, for two reasons. The first is because in what pertains to perfection the form or what is formal as such (i.e., what is perfect) must be the principle or what is first, while the opposite is true in what pertains to imperfection. In things of this kind what is perfect ought not be first, but on the same grounds it ought to be what it especially is, that is, imperfect. For example, form is the principle of all the operations and perfections of a composite being and in them is what it is supposed to be, namely, perfect. The

87

matter of a composite being is the root and principle of what the composite undergoes,[307] not its operations and perfections, and therefore it is what it is supposed to be, that is, completely imperfect.

137. This is why all forms are active in the Prime Mover, but passive in matter. God's action is completely perfect and begins from what is perfect. Deuteronomy 32: "God's works are perfect" (Dt. 32:4); and this is the reason why they are said to come down: "Every good gift and every perfect gift is from above, coming down" (Jm. 1:17). But nature's work or generation, on the contrary, begins from what is imperfect. The nearer it is to the end the more perfect it is; inversely, the nearer it is to the principle the more imperfect and impeded it is. Therefore, natural motion is slower and weaker in its principle but faster in its end.

138. The same is true in our discussion of how number and division belong to imperfection, so that two, insofar as it is the principle and first of numbers, ought not to be perfect in a simple sense, but should be posterior in what pertains to perfection and prior in what pertains to imperfection (e.g., division). Thus, just as every uneven number is indivisible because of the unity in it, as mentioned above,[308] every even number is divisible because of two. This is why God under the aspect of the One acts perfectly once and for all, doing nothing twice or for a second time, repeating nothing. "God speaks once and for all and does not repeat the same thing again" (Jb. 33:14). Nature, on the other hand, repeats, counts, and multiplies the same thing a second time because of its imperfection.

139. From what has been said the reason for the unity of form in every composite being and the solution of many arguments opposed to this is crystal clear. Unity and form are always to the fore in the act of existing because it is a perfection; but in becoming, which is an imperfection and transformation, it is the reverse—plurality and matter reign. Therefore, Plato attributed unity to form and duality to matter.[309] In the act of existence of a composite thing there is one form immediately informing and giving existence to the composite with no intervening medium. It immediately inheres in and totally penetrates the substance of the matter and the composite that it is joined to. On the contrary, when something is in the process of becoming, which always takes place in an imperfect thing that is transformable and not yet a being, there is always need for media that prepare the matter and the composite. From this comes what does not yet exist. Alteration is concerned with becoming and is a handmaid or servant; along with motion it serves the generation that looks to existence. "When what is perfect has come, that which is imperfect will be done away with" (1 Co. 13:10). This

is the natural meaning and fulfillment of the text "Cast out the servant and her son; he will not be an heir" (Gn. 21:10; Ga. 4:30), for the "son of alteration" is not an heir that inheres, but it adheres on the outside.[310]

140. This is just the case in our discussion. In the generation of fire alteration comes first in time, along with motion, labor, and a kind of natural "sadness." This requires a heat that alters and prepares. But in the kind of generation which is an end and is without motion, the existence of the thing is given through the form of fire; and then heating, motion, and time are not needed. This perfect inhering heat, now no longer imperfect as it was before, achieves and gains this form (not the prior form of fire); it attains to and adheres to the form of fire [itself], according to the text "A woman about to give birth has sorrow . . . , but when she has brought forth the child, she no longer remembers the anguish" (Jn. 16:21).

141. To return to the earlier discussion, I say a second time that the nine reasons given do not necessarily prove that two is not a number. You should know though that just as form and perfection are existence and good, and hence also one (which is convertible with these), so too division and number from their very nature by which they fall from the One fall also from goodness and from existence and hence from those things which belong to perfection. Therefore, division and number are not judged by the access they give to some positive principle of their own, but are measured and judged rather by their retreat from the principle. The further they are distant from it (that is, the One), the greater the number and division. Division, insofar as it is a fall from the One, is a privation of existence, of oneness and goodness, and is thus an evil of a kind and an accident in nature. Evil and the accidental are never reducible to something necessary, since they are not necessary,[311] but they are distinguished from what is necessary as opposites. Therefore, they are not reduced to something necessary that belongs to them, but to something outside themselves, such as being, the good, and the One.[312]

142. Jerome in a letter to Damasus explaining this passage "unto the third and fourth generation" says it is a sign of divine mercy that he punishes sins "unto the third and fourth generation," because, as often as he punishes by visiting the fathers' sins upon their progeny, he suggests penance for sin.[313] And since parents usually live into the third generation and see their progeny, and sometimes even into the fourth, thus we have the saying that the sins of parents will be punished "unto the third and the fourth generation." So, as often as the descendants are punished, the parents are mercifully moved to do penance for their sins. To visit parents' sin upon their

descendants beyond the fourth generation would be in vain, because then the parents would usually be dead and not able to see the punishments of their descendants and so be called back from sin and do penance.

This is the solution to the two questions posed by Augustine above, that is, why Moses did not say "unto the seventh generation," but said "unto the third and fourth generation"; and in the second place, why he did not say "unto the fifth and sixth, or even the second," but only "unto the third and fourth."

"You shall not take the name of your God in vain" (v. 7).

143. This passage is fully expounded by the saints and theologians commonly and well according to the letter. It wishes to prohibit God's name from being used to testify for or confirm anything vain, false, or lying, and generally from using God's name as testimony without a rational cause.

144. Because Maimonides says that this text concerns the name which is Adonai, we must note that in his [*Guide*], Book 1, Chapters 60–63, he treats of this name and others like it.[314] First, then, we must look at the name Adonai; second, at the name Tetragrammaton, the name of four letters; third, at the name of two letters; fourth, at the name of twelve letters; fifth, at the other name which has forty-two letters; sixth, at the name "Shaddai"; seventh, at the name "Who is."[315] Eighth and last, we must look at the other universal names generally attributed to God, such as "good," "wise," "bounteous," and the like.[316]

145. In relation to the first, know that the word Adonai "is the appellation of the other simple name . . . that signifies the Creator's substance in purity," that is, the Tetragrammaton, or name of four letters. Second, the word Adonai is interpreted "My Lord" in the singular, or "My Lords" plural, and it is derived from "adon."[317]

146. The name Tetragrammaton (whatever it is) is of four letters (whatever they may be) and takes its name from that fact. It is hidden and secret; it is the ineffable name of God. The term "Tetragrammaton" is not the name itself that we are treating, but it is a circumlocution for the four-letter name which is a sacred secret. Therefore, it is never expressed among the Jews, but is inexpressible in its nature and purity, just like the substance of God which it signifies.[318] Second, in this name there is nothing derived from God's works, and perhaps there is nothing in this name that is derived at all in the sense that with us compound terms are derived and deduced from simple and primitive ones. Even the term "Adonai," as mentioned above, is derived from "adon." Third, this name is "written, but not spoken nor ex-

pressed, save in the sanctuary by the holy priests at the priestly blessing and by the High Priest on the Day of Atonement."[319]

147. Fourth. "Great care and apprehension is taken in speaking this name because it signifies the Creator's substance in whose signification none of his creatures shares." This is why "the Hebrew sages say that this name is set apart simply for God," as one proper to him only.[320] Hence also Thomas in the [*Summa of Theology*] Ia, q. 13, a. 11 says: "The name Tetragrammaton is used to signify the incommunicable, and if we can speak this way, individual substance of God itself."[321] Earlier, in article 9, he says, "This name Tetragrammaton is used to signify God not from the viewpoint of nature, but from that of the supposit, according to which he is considered as an individual, and hence incommunicable in every way, just as if someone gives a person a name that means this individual." This is why some of the Hebrew sages say that before the world's creation there was only God and his name of four letters. Another of their sages says that "therefore the prophet promised people a mode of understanding that will remove improper, unfitting and imperfect denominations, when he said, 'In that day there will be one Lord and his name will be one' (Zc. 14:9)."[322] That means, when you understand God's simple substance, you will not have any name taken from divine works, but only the one true name that signifies his very substance. And this is the name of four letters.

148. Fifth. What this name is and "how it is pronounced and how its consonants are written, either in the short or long form, the sages receive from one another." They teach it only to the worthy, "and only once a week."[323] This is why, as I mentioned, it is not found clearly and openly in the scripture, but in concealed and secret fashion, as in Exodus 28: "You shall with engraver's work write 'Holy to the Lord' " (Ex. 28:36), which the *Gloss* says signifies the ineffable name of four letters.[324]

149. Then there is the "name of twelve letters," about which the Hebrews say that "its holiness is less than the name of four letters." This "is not one name, but is made up of many names whose letters together make up twelve." "The individual names signify different concepts that lead people to knowledge of the Creator's true substance." This was the name that used to be substituted for the Tetragrammaton, "just as with us today" the name Adonai is so used for the four-letter name that is very rarely spoken due to its purity and reverence. The name of twelve letters signifies "something more proper to God than the term Adonai."[325]

150. Fifthly, the sages would teach the name of twelve letters to anyone who wanted to learn it. Later on, when people had become quite evil, there was complete silence regarding the name of four letters, and in its place the

sages employed the name of twelve letters. This is why from that time "only the humble and the priests" taught in that name, "in order to bless the people with it in the sanctuary."[326]

151. Rabbi Moses writes four things about the fourth name of God, which is the name of forty-two letters. The first is that it is not one simple name, as is also the case in the name of twelve letters mentioned above. Just as that was one name composed of many which together made up twelve, so this is one name made up of many which all taken together equal forty-two letters.[327]

152. The second point is that each of these names indicates some perfection from whose concept there is a path leading to knowledge of the Creator's substance. Taken altogether they lead to a higher perfection than any of them taken individually, and this is signified in the name made up of them all. Let us give an example. The word "benediction" is one word made up of two: "bene" (i.e, well) and "dictio" (i.e., saying). Likewise, the Holy Spirit is one name made up of two, "sanctus" and "spiritus." The individual names in each of these also have their own meanings and the perfections proper to what they signify. The first word, benediction, taken together has ten letters; and the second, Holy Spirit, has fifteen. Each of these two words signifies a perfection that their individual components do not.

It is possible that not only the names (both as making up the compound and as in it when it is whole) but also the numerical value of the letters of the names (e.g., forty-two or twelve) signify some perfection in God. They could indicate perfections and properties of the divine nature with regard to the order of letters in the names, their nature and their shape, just as, for example, with us the secondary "stars" of the lower regions (whether in the air, the clouds, water, the earth and things growing on earth) point to the superior nature and properties of the primary heavenly stars. "Appearances in this world are subject to celestial appearances," as Ptolemy says in the ninth axiom of his *Centiloquium*,[328] because inferior things signify the nature, shape, order, and number of superior things, just as effects signify their causes. Alchemy, geomancy, pyromancy, and many similar sciences trust in this.[329] With us, for example, some letters are voiced, others unvoiced, others liquid insofar as they belong to the genus and species of letters.[330] Each letter has its own proper form. Some hold that the number and order of letters in nouns is perhaps not without meaning and a natural propriety so that neither the order nor the number is fortuitous.

153. The third point is that the things signified by these names are not to be taken "at face value," but according to the secret hidden thing they signify.[331] For example, with alchemists the name "sun" means gold, the

name "moon" silver, and so on. So too, Aristotle often attacks the surface meaning of Plato rather than the inner sense.

154. The fourth point is because this name, like the twelve-letter name, is a name set apart as dedicated and sacred to God. It approaches more closely the purity of the four-letter name without attaining it. This is why the sages have said: "The forty-two letter name is holy and sanctified and will only be given to a humble person of mature years who is not wrathful, nor a drunkard, nor subject to bad habits, and who is on good terms with people. Everyone who knows it, guards himself in it and keeps it pure, is beloved above and popular below. His reverence descends upon created things, and his instruction is always in his hand. He lives in two ages: this present one and that to come."[332] After this he adds: "What a distance there is between what people understand by these words and what is in the mind of the speaker, because many think that they are only letters pronounced, and that there is no meaning in them through which one gains promised higher levels," that is, "the grasp of the Agent Intellect."[333]

155. Fifth, there is another "name of two letters," whatever it is, which Rabbi Moses writes about. One point about it is that "it is derived from the four-letter name," the second is that it is settled and imposed on God "by reason of the stability of his essence."[334] This is why that name of itself does not directly signify God, but stability.

156. There is still a sixth name of God, namely "Shaddai," which is "derived from 'dai,' that is 'sufficiency.' "[335] Hence this name signifies sufficiency directly and immediately, but God only mediately, indirectly, and in a secondary way. In the same way the firmness, stability, and immobility of the divine essence is signified in or through the two-letter name, as in the text, "I am God and I do not change" (Ml. 3:6), and in Boethius, "Remaining stable, he gives movement to all."[336] The immensity and infinity of the divine essence is illuminated for our understanding through this, because the Infinite has nothing by means of which or from which it is moved since there is nothing outside it which could do so. It cannot be moved by itself, because nothing moves itself [in this way]. Even if you grant that the Infinite could be moved, it would still have no place to move from or to, since there is nothing outside it. This is clear from the first book of the *Physics*.[337]

157. Similarly, the name "Shaddai, which is derived from 'dai,' or 'sufficiency,' " signifies that the "divine essence is self-sufficient" in itself and in other things. I say that it is sufficient for itself in the realm of existence and in everything else—knowledge, will, power, operation, and universally all things. This belongs to it alone and nothing below it. In everything below it the essence is not self-sufficient in relation to all things, and therefore it

needs something else to help it. For example, the architect's essence does not suffice for the work of art, but above and beyond this habitual power, the habit of art, instruments, and other things are required.[338] The same is true of everything generated or created below God. What is second always depends on what is first and is not self-sufficient unless it is helped and moved by what is first.[339] Thus the perfection of the divine essence and its sufficiency is signified through the name "Shaddai" by which "its substance is self-sufficient" in everything and hence has no accident. There is no place for an accident where the essence is totally self-sufficient.

158. Consequently, the name "Shaddai" signifies that God is Existence Itself and that his essence is Existence Itself.[340] He is what he is and who he is. "I am who I am," and "He who is sent me" (Ex. 3:14). "Through him and in him" (Rm. 11:36) as Sufficiency Itself is everything that is; in him and through him and from him there is enough for all—"Our sufficiency is from God" (2 Co. 3:5). He it is who gives rest to himself in himself, and in him and through him all things come to rest, following Augustine's saying in Book 1 of the *Confessions*, "Our hearts are restless until they rest in you."[341] Every effort of nature and of art pursues, desires, and seeks existence. Every agent and even the subject of action is restless, is not self-sufficient, does not rest from motion and from the labor of action and passion below or outside of existence. When it has achieved existence, it rests and is satisfied; the turbulence and conflict of action, passion, and motion are stilled.

159. This is the reason why the act of begetting that confers existence is nontemporal. It is the goal of time, because it is not in the motion that is measured by time.[342] It is different with the alteration which assists begetting, because this is in motion and hence in time. In it there is an angry murmur and struggle between the agent and the subject of action that is not silent, satisfied, or at rest until the motion is finished and the act of becoming has reached existence itself. I have noted this in expounding the Genesis text: "God rested on the seventh day" (Gn. 2:2).[343]

160. It is clear then that just as the stability and infinity of the divine essence is signified in the two-letter name which is taken from the "concept of firmness," so too the perfection of the divine essence is signified in the name "Shaddai," which is taken from the concept of sufficiency. This latter is existence: It gives rest to all things, is sufficient for them all. In it, as in existence, all things rest and have enough. What has been said about these two names generally holds for all the names used of God in the scriptures, save only for the "four-letter name which is not derived from a work and does not express any participation,"[344] as we said above.

161. As a consequence from what has been said, in the seventh place there is that other name of God, I mean the name "Who is." "He who is sent me" (Ex. 3:14). John Damascene in Book 1 says that this is the first name of God,[345] and Thomas gives three beautiful reasons for this in Ia, q. 13, a. 11.
162. This can be proven in another fashion here by the following four arguments. The first is this: No name is more proper to man than the name "man." Therefore, no name is more proper to Existence Itself than the name "existence." But God is Existence Itself, as we have said.[346]
163. The second argument is this. That name is most proper to a thing which encompasses everything that belongs to and is attributed to it. But Existence Itself has and possesses everything which is proper to God. Therefore, this name "Existence" is the first and most proper of all God's names.

The major is explained as follows. Not everything that exists is called "man," nor everything that lives or senses, because all these things are not proper to man, but are shared by other things. But everything which reasons and makes syllogisms is called "man," because reasoning is proper to the thing called man.

The minor is evident by means of a universal induction, for example as in the text, "From him, through him and in him are all things" (Rm. 11:36). The same is clear from the fact that God is everywhere, and from the fact that God is in everything created through power, presence, and essence,[347] totally in each thing—totally within and totally without. Therefore, he is not moved, nor changed, nor corrupted no matter what corrupts, just as the soul is not corrupted when the hand is cut off, because the whole soul is in the hand in such a way that it is also completely outside the hand. You must not think that existence is not totally in every being, but only some part of existence. A part of existence is no existence and consequently does not give existence, just as a part of a man is not a man, and so on. Further, existence belongs to and is attributed to God because he is said to be lasting and eternal, having no cause nor principle, but himself being the cause and principle of all things. The same can be said about everything that is generally spoken about God. All these statements more plainly and clearly appear to belong to God under the name of existence than under the name "God."
164. The minor and major premises of the second argument are clear, and so the conclusion follows, that is, that of all the names of God existence is the first and proper one. This is why Avicenna very frequently, especially in his *Metaphysics*, speaks of God as "necessary existence." Rabbi Moses and many others rightly do the same. Only God's existence is "necessary existence."[348] Someone might perhaps think that existence is the name of four

letters itself, because the term "existence" [*esse*] has literally four letters and many hidden properties and perfections. It also does not seem "to be derived from a work nor express any participation." But this is enough.

165. The third argument for the thesis is this. In every being there are three things to consider: genus, species, and supposit.³⁴⁹ Because a thing is constituted in existence, known and hence named from these three, it follows that any created thing receives its name from genus, species, and the property of supposit. For example, Martin truly is and is called an animal by virtue of genus; he is truly called a man by virtue of species, and he is truly and properly called Martin by virtue of the property of his supposit. The names taken from the genus and species belong to many others and by nature are common and communicable to other beings besides Martin. Therefore, only the proper name that is taken from the property and the idea of the supposit (whatever it is) belongs to Martin and is incommunicable to other beings and proper to Martin alone. In God alone, if we could speak this way about the Godhead, the supposit is totally identical with the nature of the species and genus, and existence is the selfsame simple thing, as Thomas says in the second book of his *Quodlibetal Questions*.³⁵⁰ Therefore, the term existence is the proper name of God himself. This is what is said in the Psalm: "His name is in the Selfsame" (Ps. 33:4); and Augustine in the ninth book of the *Confessions* when he discusses Psalm 4 ("In peace, in the selfsame": Ps. 4:9) says: "Oh in peace, Oh in the Selfsame . . . You, O Lord, who do not change, are completely the same, because there is no other like you."³⁵¹ To say "in the selfsame" three times is important for referring to genus, species, and supposit. If someone says that God's name is "the Same," following the Psalm text, "But you are the same" (Ps. 101:28)—that is, "the same thing"—then the first part refers to the nature and the second to the supposit.³⁵²

166. The fourth argument for the main thesis is this. That which is above every name excludes no name, but universally includes all names and in an equally indistinct way. None of these names will consequently be proper to it save that which is above every name and is common to all names. But existence is common to all beings and names, and hence existence is the proper name of God alone.

167. The major is evident from the nature of what is essentially superior which always includes everything that is beneath it totally in itself, even in its least part. Thus, the whole of time and its differences are found in equal fashion in the now of eternity, the past and future no less than the present. The minor is explained thus. What does not participate in existence is not a being or a name. Wisdom, power, and each of these things either are

not names or participate in that which is above every name. But that is existence alone. What is without existence does not exist, is not a name, but a false, empty, phony name. It is not a name, because it does not give knowledge. "Name" is derived from "knowledge," in that it is the mark of some concept in the intellect making that concept known to others.[353] Therefore, it is a messenger by which a concept is announced to others. This is why nothing impossible deserves to be called a name or word, as the text says: "No word is impossible with God" (Lk. 1:37). 168. With the major and the minor set forth, the conclusion follows, namely that existence is the proper name of God alone. This is what is said in the Psalm, "You have magnified your holy name above all" (Ps. 137:2), and Philippians 2, "He has given him a name which is above every name" (Ph. 2:9). The twenty-second proposition of the *Book of Causes* says, "The First Cause is above every name by which it is named."[354]

169. According to Avicenna, "the first thing that comes into the intellect" and what is most general in understanding "is being."[355] This is the reason why the metaphysician in treating the primary beings and the first principles of things presupposes being,[356] and why being is and is said to be his subject in that it underlies and is presupposed by everything, even the first act of knowing and grasping. Every noun and word is a mark and sign of a preceding apprehension. Hence the meaning of the passage about "everything that is impossible with God" (Lk. 1:37) is that anything whose existence is impossible will not be and is not a "word."

170. Finally, in the eighth place we must take a look at the universal names of God, such as when he is called steadfast, generous, good, wise, and the like. On these you have [what I said] above on the fifteenth chapter concerning the text "Almighty is his name."[357] I still have something to note here, first about affirmative terms, like wise and others, and second about negative ones.

171. Rabbi Moses in [*Guide*] 1.59 says: "Nothing is in the Creator but the true, perfectly realized simplicity."[358] Therefore, anyone who "attributes positive denominations to the Creator sins in four ways." First, because the intellect and the apprehension of the one grasping something of this sort about God is "limited." Second, because such a person "makes God participate," that is, he understands him as having parts, and not as perfectly realized simplicity, or else as "participating," that is, he makes him participate and share something with the creature. Third, because "he apprehends God other than he is"; and fourth, because such a person removes "God's existence from his heart," even if he does not know it.

172. He proves the premises in this chapter with the following words:

"The explanation of this matter is that everyone who is limited in apprehending the truth of something grasps some part of its truth, but does not know how to grasp the other part, e.g., as when a person understands that man is living, but not the truth of his rationality. In the Creator there is no multiplicity in the truth of his essence that would enable you to know one part and be ignorant of another. Similarly, one who shares something with someone knows the truth of some substance as it is and attributes the truth of the substance to something else. . . . Likewise, one who apprehends a thing otherwise than it really is cannot do this without apprehending something of what it is. Concerning someone who thinks that taste is a quantity, I do not say that he thinks of the thing otherwise than it is, but that he does not know the essence of taste and does not know to what the term applies." Later on he says, "Anyone who attributes a denomination to the Creator . . . thinks that the name applies to him. This is not in the nature of things, but is a useless thought, as though one were to use that name about something that did not exist, because there is no being like that." 173. He says, "An example would be of a man who has heard the name elephant and knows that it is something alive. He wants to know its shape and truth, and someone responds who leads him astray, saying 'It is something having one foot and three wings that lives at the bottom of the sea. Its body shines like clear light, its face is like a human face, and sometimes it flies through the air, other times it swims in the sea like a fish.' Such a person would have the wrong idea of an elephant and would be limited in his apprehension; the way he conceived an elephant would be vain, because there is nothing like this among real beings. It is only a privation to which the name of a being is attributed."[359]

174. This is why he says in another chapter that the sages find it is dangerous, harmful, and unfitting to hear someone piling up words about God even in prayer, due to the imperfection which names and words entail and their distance from God's simplicity.[360] Thus the text of the sage, "God is in heaven, you are upon the earth, therefore let your words be few" (Qo. 5:1); and in Psalm 4 according to another version it says, "Speak in your hearts and on your beds and always be silent" (Ps. 4:5).[361] Again, in another Psalm where we have "A hymn is fitting for you, O God," (Ps. 64:2), the text of Rabbi Moses has, "Silence is praise for you," or "To be silent is praise for you." Therefore, he concludes that "our every affirmative apprehension of God . . . is defective for drawing near to understanding him. . . . Whatever we say of God in praise and exaltation . . . diminishes what belongs to him and is a defect," or withdrawal from knowing him.[362] This is how to explain the verse of 1 Kings 2: "Do not multiply to speak lofty things" (1 K.

2:3). Rabbi Moses also says, "Let the Creator be praised. In the apprehension of his essence the inquiries of the sciences receive their limit, wisdom is held to be ignorance, and elegance of words is foolishness."[363] The Savior himself says, "When you pray, do not say many words" (Mt. 6:5); and Proverbs 10 says, "Where there are many words sin is not lacking" (Pr. 10:19).

175. A threefold reason can now again be given for what has been said. The first point is this. Everything which with us is found in things is in them in a formal sense, but in God they are in no way formally found, because they do not inform him, but [they are there] virtually.[364] To grasp these things or to affirm them of God is false and unfitting, just as if we were to call God a circle or changeable. There is no circle or changeableness in God, but rather the idea of the circle and the idea of changeableness. The idea of circle is not a circle itself, nor is the idea of changeableness changeable, just as there is no stone in the soul, but the [intelligible] species of a stone.[365] 176. The second reason is this. Reason in its essence belongs to intellect and to truth, for truth is only in the intellect, not outside it. Therefore, the perfections in exterior things are not true perfections, and to attribute them to God is to apprehend him imperfectly and as not being totally pure Intellect himself, but as being something external, at least with some part of him, as is the case in created intellects.[366] 177. The third reason is this. Existence receives nothing, since it is last,[367] and it is not received in anything, since it is first.[368] But God is existence, "the first and the last" (Is. 44:6). Therefore, nothing is positively received by God nor apprehended truly in him, but it is empty and incorrect. So much for the affirmative names applied to God.

178. In the second place we need to look at what is negatively said about God. The first thing to recognize here is that "a negative statement provides no truth about the thing to which the statement applies"—nor about anything that is in it.[369] Therefore, "from negatives nothing follows,"[370] is known, or established in existence. A twofold question remains. First, according to the saints and doctors in general how is it that negations in the Godhead or in God are true?[371] Hence, even Rabbi Moses himself, as mentioned above,[372] says about the passage in Exodus 15 "Almighty is his name" (Ex. 15:3): "Know that a negative proposition concerning the Creator is true; there is nothing doubtful in it, nor does it detract from the Creator's truth in any way. But an affirmative proposition about him is partly equivocal and partly imperfect." Later he says, "We do not have any way to speak about God except through negatives."[373] Further, what is the difference between Moses, Solomon, Paul, John, and the other wise men and any nincompoop whatever in knowing God if the only things they know about him are pure negations?

179. There is still the second question. How do negatives spoken about God differ from affirmatives if the latter posit nothing, and the former, that is, the negatives, do not posit either, but only deny? [In answer to this,] know that affirmations of their nature produce knowledge of something that is either the substance of what is being talked about, or what belongs to it, such as a property or an accident. Negations, on the other hand, are not so by nature, but as negative terms they signify only the removal or privation of a perfection. Negation surely takes away the whole of what it finds and posits nothing. Blindness, as Anselm says, does not posit anything more in the eye than it does in the stone.[374] Therefore, the negations that are said of God only show that nothing of what is found in external things and grasped by the senses is in him.

180. To make this clearer, let us look at an example.[375] Someone sees "a person far off," and asks what it is. Somebody answers and says that what he sees and asks about is "a living thing." Someone else responds that what he sees is not metal nor a stone. The first respondent, though he did not fully and exactly say what it was that was seen, still brought something to mind which in some way belongs "to the universe" that one sees. The second, however, who said that what was seen was not a stone, said nothing at all about the substance or anything in the substance, except by way of negation. This is the solution to the second question.

181. As far as both parts of the first question are concerned, we can say that just as a negation in law is not a direct but an indirect proof (e.g., "Martin did not commit adultery at Thebes," if he was seen at Athens on that day and at that hour),[376] so in our proposition the manifest works of God prove that he is not material, and therefore it is an evident conclusion that he is free from every imperfection that accompanies the property of matter, such as ignorance, capacity to change, and the like. Because privation necessarily follows possession,[377] and negation is based on affirmation,[378] it can be decisively concluded that something exists in God, whatever it is, that excludes ignorance, capacity to change, and this sort of thing, just as light does darkness and good evil.

182. Here note that "negative names are not attributed to the Creator save in the way in which one denies something of a thing that is not fittingly found in it, for example, when we say that a wall does not see."[379] In the same way we say that the heavens are not "composed of the matter and form" found in things that corrupt, and that "the heavens are neither light nor heavy, nor 'made,' nor do they receive passing influences. Nor do they have a flavor or odor, or anything of the sort." We say all these negative things, "because we are ignorant of their nature."[380] As Wisdom 9 says, "Who will

investigate what is in heaven?" (Ws. 9:16) This is the answer to the first part of the first question.

183. As for the second part, know that "whatever you add by way of negative names with respect to the Creator, you come nearer to grasping him and will be closer to him than the person who does not know how to remove from God the perfections and attributes that have been proven to be far from him. It will be a conclusion and advance for knowledge to prohibit and remove from the Creator by way of negative names those things that have been proven to be meaningless when applied to him."[381] Let us give an example. Say there is someone who does not know how to prove that God is not a body. Therefore, when he thinks of God, he imagines him to be a body, having the qualities and properties he sees in bodies. Another person knows through demonstration that God is not a body and does not possess the things that are perfections in bodies, and that to posit them in God is impossible because they have many imperfections. There is a third person who knows by demonstration that not only corporality, but also all matter is far from God, and consequently all the properties of matter, such as corruptibility, the capacity to change, and the like, are also distant from him. Even the things that seem to be perfections in material things, but are really only remedies of imperfections, for example, motion, generation, corruption, alteration, and things of the sort, are not in God in any way.[382] There is a fourth person who knows how to prove universally that nothing that is created or limited or determined to some genus of being is in God. Hence, in God himself there is nothing which signifies an end or a limit, like definition, or demonstration, existence from another, the possibility of nonexistence, all changeableness, instability, and anything of the sort.

How great the perfection in knowledge of the second person is in relation to that of the first, the third to the second and the fourth to the third is clear. This is sufficient for the other part of the first question. The stronger the argument by which a person removes these attributes from God, the more perfect he is in divine knowledge. The same holds for one who knows how to deny many such things of him by means of the removal that happens through negative names.

184. Rabbi Moses says, "Therefore, the sages agree that the sciences do not grasp the Creator, and only he himself understands himself. Our understanding in his case is a distancing rather than an approach to grasping him."[383] Hence Plato, as Macrobius says,[384] when "he was inspired to speak about God did not dare to say what he is, but only knew that no one can know what he is." This supports the axiom of Socrates: "I know that I don't know,"[385] which is like saying, "The one thing I know about God is that I

do not know him." Algazel toward the end of the third tractate of his *Metaphysics* agrees with all this, as do many of the ancient philosophers.

"Honor your father" (v. 12).

185. 1 Timothy seems to be against this when it says, "Honor God alone" (1 Tm. 1:17), but it is not, for he from whom we possess everything we have from without, our very bodies and souls, is surely our father. Deuteronomy 32: "He who possessed, made and created you, is he not your father?" (Dt. 32:6) Malachy 1: "If I am your father, where is my honor?" (Ml. 1:6) Therefore, the statement "Honor your father" is most fitting, because no one else except the father is owed honor. Even the honor owed to God himself is owed only under the concept and property of father, just as one only knows under the concept of the intellect. The reason for the first conclusion is that begetting is a property of a father.[386] Begetting of itself has existence alone as its goal and looks to it. That from which something has existence is and is termed a father, but everything that exists has the whole of its existence from God alone. Therefore, "God is the father of all" (Ep. 4:6), ". . . from whom all paternity in heaven and earth comes" (Ep. 3:15). A poem says:

Creation itself calls the highest king father.[387]

Creation and generation both look to existence.

186. Moreover, every perfection of something that has been caused, in that it comes to it from something else, especially from the First, that is, God, is an honor for its cause whose power shines out in and from the perfection of the effect. Proverbs 14 says, "Where there is much grain, there the strength of the ox is manifest" (Pr. 14:4). There is an example in the servant who wears his master's cloak on his shoulders and follows him along the street.[388] This is the reason why "Honor your father" follows immediately after the commandments ordering us toward God. God himself is certainly our Father, according to the text in Matthew 6: "Our Father who art in heaven" (Mt. 6:9); and again, "Do not call anyone on earth father" (Mt. 23:9). Honor is owed, as we have said, to the idea of Paternity, which is the principle of generation and creation. "Honor your father," it says.

187. The inferior is universally the honor of its superior. If the inferior does not honor the superior, by that very fact it ceases to be an inferior and hence it is capable of receiving no perfection from its superior. Just as the superior's role is to influence naturally only what is inferior to it, so too the

inferior receives only from its superior.[389] This is why "pride is the beginning of all sin" (Si. 10:15). Pride is linked with every sin both because it is opposed to humility which subordinates the soul to God and so makes it able to be influenced by him, and also because pride by its very name usurps for itself the name and property of the superior by denying its own inferior status whose sole task is to receive the superior's gifts and perfections. It is the superior's job to give—"Children ought not to enrich their parents, but parents their children" (2 Co. 12:14). It is the inferior's job to give honor, and this is what is said here: "Honor your father"; and Deuteronomy 27, "Cursed be he that honors not his father" (Dt. 27:16).

"You shall not covet your neighbor's house" (v. 17).

188. This says first of all that a person ought to be content and thankful for the things God has given him, and not vainly strive for what belongs to others. Secondly, it says "You shall not covet," because only lust and covetousness in deeds are condemned, as Augustine says in the first book of *Free Choice.*[390]

189. Thirdly, it says "You shall not covet" (this belongs to the intellectual soul), because it is only "the will by which one lives rightly or sins," according to Augustine.[391] Ambrose in his *Duties* says, "Your motive gives the name to your deed,"[392] because it is by will and intent that evil deeds are distinguished according to law.[393] Everything that is meritorious or the opposite, praiseworthy or blameworthy, comes from within, from the heart, from the soul, as the Psalm says: "All the glory of the king's daughter is within" (Ps. 44:14). This is why Matthew 23 says, "Cleanse first what is within" (Mt. 23:26). The philosopher says that "we are not praised nor blamed because of passions," because they come in from outside.[394] In Matthew 15 the Truth says under a parable: "What goes into the mouth does not defile a man. . . . But the things that proceed out of the mouth come from the heart, and it is they that defile a man" (Mt. 15:11, 18).

190. Fourth. "Concupiscence when it has conceived brings forth sin" (Jm. 1:15). One must resist from the beginning. As the poet says:

. . . the medicine is too late
When evils have grown strong through long delays.[395]

On this point the Psalm says, "Blessed is he who shall take and smash his little ones" (Ps. 136:9), that is, the first stirrings of concupiscence; and in another Psalm, "He shall not be confounded when he shall speak with his enemies in the gate" (Ps. 126:5), that is, in the first encounter and attack of sin's concupiscence. 191. Fifth. It forbids coveting something that belongs to the neighbor, because the person who covets does not love his neighbor "like himself, but like a cow, or a bath, or a little colored talking bird, that is, as something from which some temporal pleasure or gain is had," as Augustine says in *True Religion*.[396] Against this the Apostle says, "I seek you, not what is yours" (2 Co. 12:14). 192. Sixth, and better on the same point. Someone who covets his neighbor's goods does not love his neighbor in God nor God in him. He does not love with the love of friendship, but with the love of concupiscence in a way that neither God nor neighbor is to be loved.[397] For the same reason, a person who loves God to enjoy him does not perfectly love the God who is to be loved in himself and for himself.

193. Seventh. Whoever loves something that belongs to or is in the neighbor, but that is not what the lover himself is, does not love his neighbor as himself. For example, if I love even my father and mother because they are my mother and father, I do not love them as myself, because I am not my father or mother. The same is even truer for everything that belongs to my neighbor and is not my neighbor himself.[398]

194. Eighth. Note that the person who loves what belongs to his neighbor and to another as other loves something temporal that is divided among owners. Divine things, insofar as they are divine, are not divided, just as God is not. Rather, the more they are shared and the more commonly they are divided among many things, the more they are divine and not divided among their particulars.[399] They unite the divided particulars and gather what has been scattered. In the *Gloss* on the Acts of the Apostles Augustine says, "Christ's brotherhood is better than blood brotherhood, for the former shares what they have with thanks, the latter divides what they share with envy."[400] In his Epistle 74 Seneca says, "Foolish avarice divides the property and possessions of mortals and does not believe that anything shared by all can belong to it, but the wise man thinks nothing more his own than what he shares with the rest of humanity."[401] Hence, Augustine in the passage cited above from *True Religion*[402] directly alludes to Seneca's words and to this text ("You shall not covet your neighbor's house," or anything that is his) [when he says], "To himself anyone is only a human being. . . . Therefore, anyone who loves someone like himself, ought to love what is human in him, that is, that he is 'to the image of God.' " And he adds: "The commandment 'You shall not covet anything of your neighbor's' supports this." He concludes, "Therefore, whoever loves anything in his neighbor other than the neighbor himself, does not love him as himself."[403]

195. In the ninth place it is said, "You shall not covet your neighbor's

house or possession," that is, nothing that is his own or that is appropriated [by him]. We have nothing that is our own save falsehood, evil, or sin, as Augustine says in treating the Psalm text, "Every man is a liar" (Ps. 115:11).[404] "When he says a lie, he speaks from his very nature" (Jn. 8:44).

196. Tenth, "You shall not covet" is said because Rabbi Moses in the [*Guide*] 3.9 says, "Thoughts about transgressing the law are worse than the transgression itself."[405] He gives two reasons for this along with examples. 197. The first is this. "When a person commits a sin, the sin arises from his animal nature. . . . But when he yields to the thought of doing sin, he has already sinned with the better of his powers."[406] When a wise man of greater station sins, it is worse than when an ignorant one of low degree does.[407] He gives an example when he says, "The sin of somebody who is helped by an ignorant slave is not as great as that of someone who gets the aid of an honored free person."[408] What Isidore says in Book 2 of his *On the Highest Good* in the chapter on "The Less Serious Sins" adds to this point: "Sins which are less serious for beginners are held grave for the perfect. The greater the position of the one who sins, the more serious the sin. The pile of sin grows in proportion to the order of merits [already gained], so that frequently what is passed over in lesser people, is imputed to more important ones."[409]

198. The second reason is this. It is a greater sin when a person who has been endowed by someone with better gifts than others abuses these gifts in contempt of his patron, both because he abuses better gifts and because he shows ingratitude toward his patron. Rabbi Moses's example here is of a man who is honored above others by a king and who receives gold, silver, and gems from him only to use them to plot against him, as it says in Osee 2: "I multiplied her silver and gold, which they have used in the service of Baal" (Ho. 2:8).

Rabbi Moses then addresses himself to the minor proposition of this second proof, saying that man has received nobler powers of soul than the other animals, such as reason and intellect, for the purpose of acquiring through them the perfections of the good deeds of virtue and of knowledge, and thus of being joined to God and not to things of sense and desire. Therefore, if he turns to the outside and desires inferior and carnal things, he sins more gravely, both because he abuses better gifts and because he [acts] against a generous patron. This is why he says that not a few students of the Law lived very temperately and by themselves, even in necessities, such as food and drink and the like. "Eating, drinking, and so forth, as well as desiring such things . . . and every imperfection found in man is the accomplice of matter; power and rule over matter is given to the human form, so that it may control it and suppress sensuality."[410]

199. "Therefore there are distinct grades of men." The first kind or grade of man is the one who always makes it his goal "to pursue moral integrity and eternal life as his noble form demands. In order to understand intelligible things he is separated from others by the intellect, which is poured out upon us. When such a person is pulled down by the forces in matter, he is distressed and ashamed by the wound inflicted on him. He strives, as far as he can, to lessen the illicit motion, like a man whose king is angry and who commands him to carry filth from one place to another to make him contemptible in the eyes of beholders and to cause him insult. The one on whom this burden is placed will try as hard as he can to remove and hide the shame and he will carry the filth bit by bit to a nearby place so as not to stain his hands or his clothes. He will try to be seen by nobody. The same thing is true for noble and honest men. But a slave will delight in such things and show they are no burden to him. He will plunge his whole body in filth and soil his appearance in the eyes of onlookers, and he will laugh and rejoice."[411] Proverbs 2 says, "They rejoice when they have done evil and delight in wicked things" (Pr. 2:14). This is the second kind of man, who is turned away from the nobility of his form and follows the passions and desires that accompany matter. Thus, the distinction of two kinds of men, the good and the bad.

200. The first kind of men "have as their end what ought to be the end of man as such, that is, as far as they can to grasp what is intelligible and to choose what is more honorable, for example, the knowledge of God, of the angels and of his other works. Such men will see God's face and not depart from his presence. It has been said of them, 'You are angels and sons of the Most High.' " (Or, as our version of the Psalm puts it, "You are gods and all sons of the Most High": Ps. 81:6.)

"It is necessary, then, that everyone who wishes to be human in truth, and not a beast bearing the figure of a man, labor as much as he can to lessen all the powers of matter in eating and drinking and in all the other vices that follow from concupiscence." These are the words of Rabbi Moses.[412] It alludes to this in the Psalm, "Man, when he was in honor, did not understand; he has been compared to the senseless beasts, and has been made like to them" (Ps. 48:21). Rabbi Moses adds: "Someone who is truly human in necessities, such as food and drink and the like, will be satisfied with what is useful and necessary, not with what pleases."[413] This is what Augustine says in the tenth book of the *Confessions:* "You have taught me this, O Lord, that I should come to take nourishment as a medicine. . . . Although health is the reason for eating and drinking, it has a dangerous pleasure that accompanies it and frequently tries to go beyond it, so that it becomes the cause of what I say I am doing for my health. . . . What is enough for health, is too little for pleasure." These are Augustine's words.[414]

201. In a brief resumé the tenth reason is this. Since sin is a privation, a stain, and an offense, its gravity is measured by the nobility of what it takes away and soils, as well as the dignity of the person offended.[415] But this is what we have in our proposition regarding the sin of concupiscence in the rational power in comparison with the exterior act of sin, as has been shown. Therefore, [the external sin is less serious].

202. In the eleventh place, note that both the affirmative and negative divine commandments we are treating here are not to be performed or avoided on the basis of a passionate motive, but from the love and prompting of reason. Abraham, the pattern of belief and obedience, is an example of this in not accepting or agreeing to fulfill the command to kill his son right away, but on the third day, as Genesis 22 says, "On the third day . . . he saw the place from afar" (Gn. 22:4). This makes it clear that he undertook God's command from the deliberation of reason and not from passion's bidding, as Rabbi Moses says in Book 3.25. This is what this commandment says, "You shall not covet."

203. Twelfth. Ambrose says that sin is a transgression or "violation of the divine law."[416] Rabbi Moses in Book 3, Chapter 33, says: "It is universally part of the perfection of the Law to do away with desires, to condemn them as far as possible, and to ask of them only what is necessary." This also agrees with the text "You shall not covet."

204. Thirteenth. The worse a sin is, the more good things it destroys and the more harm it does in more ways.[417] Hence Augustine after the middle of the third book of *Free Choice* says, "Because vice is opposed to nature, the more it diminishes the integrity of nature the worse it is."[418] But nothing destroys the good and nature as much as concupiscence. In the chapter cited above Rabbi Moses says, "Sensual desires take away the soul's ultimate perfections; . . . they corrupt city-dwellers and family life. The kind of pursuit of concupiscence that fools perform destroys speculation and holiness. It corrupts the body, causes death before its natural time, and multiplies troubles, jealousy and enmities. . . . Therefore, the Creator's love gave us the command that would take away sensual desires and prohibit everything that would arouse desire. This is great among the intentions of the Law."[419] These are Maimonides's words. This is our text, "You shall not covet." Seneca speaks of concupiscence under the name of avarice in his *Epistles:* "How sweet it is to have exhausted desires and have left them behind."[420] If they cannot be gotten rid of in any other way, the heart itself must be uprooted. Cicero in Book 1 of the *Highest Good* says, "Insatiable desires destroy not only

individuals but entire families; they even weaken the whole society. From desires come hatreds, dissensions, discords, seditions and wars. . . . Not only do they rush upon others in their blind attack, but kept locked within the soul they jostle and fight each other, so that life must needs become bitter indeed."[421]

205. Fourteenth. "You shall not covet." The first thing to recognize is that according to Augustine in Book 9 of the *Trinity*, generally a thing is conceived by concupiscence, but "is born by attaining," but there is a difference here between corporeal and spiritual things.[422] In corporeal beings conception or being conceived is one thing and birth or being born is another, as is evident in pregnant animals. The same is true in [mental] conceptions of corporeal things, because to conceive of and desire gold or worldly honors is not to possess them or have them in reality. In spiritual matters, however, such as in the case of justice and similar things, to desire is to possess and to have—the conception itself is the acquisition. He who truly desires and loves justice is a just person, as Augustine says in the same passage. Gregory says that he who loves God "already has what he loves."[423]

206. The second thing to note is that someone who apprehends something good or evil that he has seen, heard, thought, or in any way had presented to him has two possibilities regarding it. The thing is either pleasing to him and he can take delight in it, or it does not please him. If it is pleasing, then he will adhere to it, and it will stick to him, inhere in him, and so be conceived. If it is displeasing and disagreeable to him as he perceives it, he will turn away from it, not toward it. He will not adhere to it, nor will it stick to him nor inhere in him, and hence there will be no conception.[424] There is an example in someone eating or drinking. Food adheres to a healthy stomach; it is not rejected, but conceived, assumed, and retained. But it is different with a sick one, which does not conceive or retain the food, but rejects it. The same thing happens in similar cases. That is why it is a bad sign when a sick person does not retain food and accept comforts. These things are proven through the passage in Ecclesiasticus 22: "A tale out of time is like music in mourning" (Si. 22:6). On the other hand, weeping is sweet to one desolate, because it fits what he feels.

207. From what has been said, it is evident that both in good and evil matters the origin, or conception, is to adhere to or inhere in [something], and that conception exists in and through concupiscence. And because (as mentioned above) conception is identical with birth or bearing in spiritual matters, someone desiring what is evil is already evil by that fact. "When concupiscence has conceived, it brings forth sin" (Jm. 1:15). Augustine says that you are what you love: if evil, then you are evil; if good, then good.[425]

This is why Christ, the head and firstborn of all the good, as a type of this spiritual life was corporeally and spiritually born in a perfect way at one and the same instant in the womb in which he had been conceived by the Holy Spirit. "What is born in her, is of the Holy Spirit" (Mt. 1:20); and "You will conceive in your womb and will bear a son" (Lk. 1:31). "A woman shall encompass a man" (Jr. 31:22). Prior to and outside of concupiscence there is never any sin, neither small nor great. This is evident in the example of Adam's sin. There was nothing evil in the forbidden fruit, since it was "good, beautiful and sweet to eat" (Gn. 3:6). But the "woman," who signifies sensuality, was struck by this beauty and sweetness. She already conceived and at the same time brought forth sin by conceiving.[426] A sin which is already a true sin, because its conception is its birth, when it has been consummated by the "man's" consent brings forth death, because it is then finally mortal.[427] But make a special note that since the conception is the birth, when someone consents to the conception, as in an evil thought, the sin is already consummated, brings forth death, and hence is mortal.

208. This is the solution to a frequent question about this issue that causes scruples and doubts for many.[428] It solves a contradiction which seems to exist in Augustine's words in the *Trinity* 12.12.[429] Augustine seems to think there that a sin is not mortal as long as the "man," or reason, does not decide on an external action if the possibility for doing it is present. But he also at times seems to think that the "man" or reason eats the forbidden fruit at the same time as the "woman" and that the person sins mortally as often as he consents to the delight which is in the thought. Here Augustine's saying helps: Frequently although what is known is not pleasing or loved, the knowledge itself is pleasing, is loved and gives delight.[430]

209. With all this said, the argument can be thus summarized. Sin is conceived and born at the same time from concupiscence alone—conception is birth itself. Without concupiscence it is neither born nor conceived. Therefore, since God wishes to preserve man from all sin and to pull out the root of evil, our text says to our profit, "You shall not covet." 1 Timothy 6 says, "Covetousness is the root of all evils" (1 Tm. 6:10), the weeds choking the "good grain" which is "God's word" (Lk. 8:11), God in the soul. "Desires entering in choke the word" (Mk. 4:19). The Psalm says of sinners who desert God, "They coveted concupiscence in the desert" (Ps. 105:14); and Daniel 13 says, "Concupiscence has perverted your heart" (Dn. 13:56).

210. Further, in the fifteenth place, it should be noted that it is very significant that the commandment "You shall not covet" is made to man. The reason is because according to the teaching of the Philosopher all the soul's passions universally come and arise from concupiscence and return to

it, end in it, and are there quieted and take their rest. Hatred, strife, envy, fear, wrath, sorrow, and similar things arise from the lack of something desired which when present and acquired gives peace and extinguishes all passions.[431]

This is clear from the struggle of animals among themselves due to the desire for eating and mating, as Aristotle says.[432] It is also evident from the words of Cicero, Seneca, and Rabbi Moses cited in the thirteenth point. Therefore, if concupiscence is put in order in us the whole person and the whole human life is ordered. This is why Ecclesiasticus 18 says, "Go not after your concupiscences" (Si. 18:30). The *Decretals* of Gregory IX on the Constitution "Nam concupiscentiam" say: "It is a good law which prohibits all evil in prohibiting concupiscence."[433] What the *Legal Gloss* says about this law, [namely,] that ["all evil"] refers to "the varieties of individual sins," not to "individual sins of all kinds," is true, but not the whole truth.[434] For every sin, even the individual sins of each variety, is born from concupiscence, as evident from the text cited: "Each one is tempted by his concupiscence" (Jm. 1:14). Therefore, "He who prohibits concupiscence" by saying "You shall not covet" "prohibits every evil," as the *Decretals* say in a passage taken from Augustine.[435]

211. As evidence for the foregoing, we can note that on the basis of these points many passages from both testaments can be explained. They agree with and demonstrate what has been said. The first is that sacred scripture frequently tells a story in such a way that it also contains and suggests mysteries, teaches about the natures of things, and directs and orders moral actions.[436] 212. The second thing to recognize, as Dionysius says in the *Divine Names*, Chapter 4, is that the good of a human being is to exist according to reason, but evil is what is outside reason.[437] The explanation is that good is always from form, evil from matter and the material. 213. The third point is that a human being is composed of a double nature, that is, the sensitive and the rational parts, or flesh and spirit, matter and form. Matter and flesh are the sensitive part, its powers bound to, immersed in, and surrounded by flesh and matter. But reason is spirit and form, not immersed in or bound to any fleshly organ.

214. These premises clarify, explain, and prove the passage from Romans 7: "I know that in me, that is in my flesh, no good dwells. . . . I see another law in my members, warring against the law in my mind and making me a prisoner to the law of sin. . . . With my mind I serve the law of God, but with my flesh I serve the law of sin" (Rm. 7:18, 23, 25). And also Galatians: "The flesh lusts against the spirit and the spirit against the flesh" (Ga. 5:17).

What Rabbi Moses says in Book 3.23 also fits here: "Each person has a double creature joined to him, that is, a good and an evil one." What is rational and formal in man he calls the good creature, what is sensitive or material, or the matter of man, he calls the evil creature. In the same book in Chapter 9 he says: "Corruption takes place only on the side of matter, not on that of form, because the substance of form is eternal. Can you not see that every spiritual form is eternal? The corruption of form happens by accident, namely, because it is joined to matter. The nature of matter and its truth is that it never exists without being bound up with privation." Later he says, "Every corruption, loss or imperfection, all the sins of man follow from his matter, not his form. . . . Pull back on the bridle of concupiscence and everything that goes along with matter will follow after form. . . . Human form has been given power over matter to control it and to put down the sensuality that is in it,"[438] as said above. This is what the Apostle already says in the passages from Romans and Galatians.

215. Rabbi Moses proves this in six ways. The first is from the common teaching and tradition of the Jewish exegetes.[439] The second proof is that "scripture says that 'the creation of man's heart is evil from his adolescence' (Gn. 8:21)," where we have "the sense and thought of the human heart is prone to evil from his adolescence." This "evil creature" commences "in man at the hour of his birth, as scripture says, 'sin will forthwith be present at the door' " (Gn. 4:7). Ephesians 2 says, "We were by nature children of wrath" (Ep. 2:3). Augustine, in the first book of the *Confessions*, says, "Who can recall to me the sin of my infancy, because no one is free from sin in your sight, O Lord, not even an infant of a single day on earth? . . . What then was my sin? That I cried when I sucked at the breast? . . . Then I committed things that were reprehensible." Below he writes, "And so the weakness of the infant limbs is innocent, but not the infant heart. I myself have seen a child that could not yet speak and could be seen to be pale with envy at its milkbrother."[440] "The good creature is not found in man from birth, but after his intellect has been perfected."[441]

216. Thirdly, he proves the matter and explains it through his application of Ecclesiastes 9 to the issue. "A little city had a few men in it. There came against it a great king and invested it" (Qo. 9:14). And below, "Now there was found in it a man poor and wise, and he delivered the city by his wisdom" (Qo. 9:15). He says that "the evil creature," that is, sensuality, "is called the great king and the good creature is called the man poor and wise. This parable was spoken about the human body and the give and take of its powers," as he says. Sensuality is called the "great king" in this parable both because it is born together with the person and because so many people and

the greater part of humanity obey and follow the passions of concupiscence and so few live according to reason. As Matthew 7 puts it: "Broad is the way that leads to destruction, and many enter through it; narrow the way that leads to life and few there are who find it" (Mt. 7:13–14). This also can give a good explanation of the text from Ecclesiastes 4, "Better a child that is poor and wise than a king that is old and foolish" (Qo. 4:13), and the one that follows about the young man who rises up (Qo. 4:15), and other obscure parabolic statements found there.

217. Rabbi Moses's fourth proof is that according to the Hebrew sages as well as Jerome and our own authors, "Each person has two angels, one good and the other bad; one on the right, the other on the left. These are the good and the bad creatures."[442] Perhaps these good and bad angels, the sensitive part that inclines to and suggests evil, and the rational (i.e., synderesis)[443] that inclines to good, are the "good and bad tree" spoken of in Matthew 7:17–20. 218. Fifthly, Rabbi Moses says earlier in Chapter 9 of the same book that Solomon when speaking parabolically about the concupiscence of the sensitive part compares it to an adulterous woman: "Do not heed the deceit of a woman; . . . her steps are wandering and untrackable. . . . Remove your path far from her" (Pr. 5:2, 6, 8).[444] The sensitive part that is obedient to reason is compared to the strong woman in Proverbs 31: "Who shall find a strong woman?" (Pr. 31:10)—and the rest that follows there about the good woman. I mention this in commenting on Chapter 31 where I interpret the "strong woman" as the heavenly bodies.[445]

219. Sixthly, Rabbi Moses explains and proves what has been said about the sensitive part (the evil woman) and the part that is rational by participation (the good woman) through the text in Isaiah 11: "The wolf shall dwell with the lamb, and the leopard shall lie down with the kid. The calf and the lion and the sheep shall abide together, and a little child will lead them" (Is. 11:6). This is fulfilled when the sensitive part obeys and consents to reason, according to the text in Ecclesiasticus 25: "Approved before God and men . . . are the man and wife that agree together" (Si. 25:1–2). The man and the woman are the sensitive and rational parts because of what has been said.

220. The eleventh chapter of Isaiah is best taken as literally applied to Christ, in the sense that the sensitive appetite in him was completely subject to reason.[446] The text from Jeremiah 31 can be explained in the same way: "The Lord has created a new thing upon the earth, a woman shall encompass a man" (Jr. 31:22); and from Apocalypse 12: "A woman clothed with the sun, and the moon under her feet" (Rv. 12:1).

221. In the seventh and last place it seems to me that all that has been

112

said about concupiscence, the sensitive and rational parts, the good and the evil creature, the adulterous and the strong woman, is very beautifully and significantly set forth in a figural way in Genesis 16 and 17 through Hagar and Sarah, the servant and the mistress. It says there that Hagar, the Egyptian, that is, the black servant, "perceiving she was with child, despised her mistress" (Gn. 16:4). But she was told, "Return and humble [yourself] under your mistress's hand" (Gn. 16:9). Everything written there [treats] clearly and at length of the sensitive part (i.e., Hagar) and of the rational (i.e., Sarah) and of the children born to them. Galatians 4 touches on the same. According to St. Augustine's interpretation, the Savior demonstrates the same thing about the evil of the sensitive part and the perfection of the rational in John 4 when he reproaches the woman who had the five husbands (i.e., the sensitive part with the five senses) because the one she now has (i.e., the rational part or reason) is not her husband in that she does not live according to reason and reason does not rule her, nor make her fruitful, nor does she obey and agree with it.[447] This is why he says to her "Go," leaving the concupiscence of the sensitive part, "call your husband," that is, reason, so that it may rule you and make you bear and be fruitful (Jn. 4:16).

222. What is read in Genesis 4 about Adam having had two sons, Cain and Abel, agrees in a mystical way with what has just been said about the evil of the sensitive part and its concupiscence and the perfection of the rational part. The firstborn Cain signifies the sensitive part; Abel, the second born, signifies reason. The same goes for "the Lord looked with favor upon Abel and his gifts, but did not upon Cain and his gifts" (Gn. 4:4–5); and also for "Cain was exceedingly angry and his face fell" (Gn. 4:5), and he slew Abel his brother. [These] and the other things put down there agree in a beautiful figurative way with the sensitive and rational parts, which are genuine brothers in the constitution of a human being.

223. The same thing is quite finely portrayed in Genesis 25 in the brothers Esau and Jacob, the sons of Isaac, where Esau the firstborn signifies sensuality, and Jacob, born second, the rational part. That Esau is born first, that he is called the elder, that it is said "the elder shall serve the younger" (Gn. 25:23), that he was "red and hairy" (Gn. 25:25), and the like, all agree with the sensitive part in us. This part and its actions appear first in us— "For what is spiritual is not first, but what is animal" (1 Co. 15:46). The greater part of humanity lives according to it, which is why above it was called the "great king." That Jacob was born second, that "he held his brother's foot in his hand" (Gn. 25:25), and all the rest that is narrated about him in the scripture either there or in other places, agrees with the rational part that is the blood-brother of the sensitive part in us. The statement to their

113

mother, "Two nations are in your womb" (Gn. 25:23), denotes the two kinds of people whom I noted above in the example from Rabbi Moses, of whom some delight "and exult in the worst things" (Pr. 2:14), while others detest the concupiscences of the flesh, of matter and of sensuality, and rejoice and delight in what belongs to reason.

224. These two things in us, that is, the sensitive and the rational parts, are the old man, external and terrestrial, who corrupts because he is temporal (cf. Rm. 6:6; 1 Co. 15:47; 2 Co. 4:16; Ep. 4:22). "Time makes old," as the Philosopher says;[448] and "There is nothing new under the sun" (Qo. 1:10). This is why the Old Testament promises temporal and corruptible things. The New Law which does not corrupt succeeds it, and will be succeeded by no other. It promises not what can be seen and is temporal, but what is eternal and invisible, following the text "The eye does not see without you, O God" (Is. 64:4). The rational part or reason is the new, interior, celestial man, who does not corrupt, but "is renewed from day to day" (2 Co. 4:16). Therefore, it is necessary that the eternal man is above the sun, is divine, is a "treasure in earthen vessels" (2 Co. 4:7).

225. There are many passages of this sort in scripture that both literally and figuratively give a beautiful and proper teaching about the evil of the concupiscence of our sensitive part. Therefore, "the law prohibits all evils because it prohibits concupiscence"—and all mortal sins. "The wages of sin is death" (Rm. 6:23). It prohibits the source from which all evils come, as Augustine says [in commenting] on Romans 7.[449] This is what it says here: "You shall not covet."

226. The final thing to note in evidence of what has been said is that in scripture the name concupiscence is used and understood properly of the concupiscence of the sensitive part and not of the rational part. This is proven in three ways: first by authority, second from the very name, and third by reason. The first argument is this. John Damascene near the end of Book 2, Chapter 12, says, "What is obedient to reason and capable of being persuaded by it is divided into concupiscence and wrath. What is obedient to reason is called the irrational part of the soul."[450] This is why in the first book of his *Ethics* the Philosopher says that this is rational by participation, not by essence.[451] 227. The second proof of the proposition comes from the name "concupiscence" itself. Concupiscence implies and names some kind of association of two things.[452] From this it is evident that it does not belong to the soul alone nor to the powers separate from the body, as the intellect and intellectual reason do; but it is the act of a power joined to a bodily organ, as is true of every sensitive power.

228. Thirdly, the proposition is proved by reason. "We know the cause

through the effect," and this is why we give it a name. "When something that is loved is not possessed," this lack makes the love felt outside in the body. Therefore, "the first among all the passions of desire (or of a thing desired) is that sensible concupiscence" which is found in the sense power. This is the reason why the sensible power receives its name from concupiscence itself.[453] What is said in the Psalm ("My soul has coveted to long for your justifications": Ps. 118:20) is not in opposition to this, in that this is said "because of a kind of similarity," or because the rational concupiscence spreads over into the inferior sensitive appetite to inform, affect, and draw it up to the spiritual good which of its own nature it cannot attain.[454] This accords with the Psalm verse, "My heart and my flesh have exulted in the living God" (Ps. 83:3). Hence it is clear that when it says "You shall not covet," God is speaking of and prohibiting the concupiscence of the sensitive part.

When it is put in order under the power of the "man," that is, reason, the whole kingdom of the soul is at peace, as the text in Luke 11 has it, "When the strong man, fully armed, guards his courtyard, his property is undisturbed" (Lk. 11:21). Literally [interpreted], the sensitive part is the rational soul's courtyard. This is why the Savior teaches us to pray to the Father that "your will be done," and fulfilled, "on earth," that is, in the soul's sensitive part, "as it is in heaven," that is, in reason (Mt. 6:10). "This is the will of God, your sanctification" (1 Th. 4:3)—"sanctification" from the uncleanness of carnal concupiscence. Hence, the first "agreement and alliance" (Gn. 17:13, 22:18) involving the distinction of the elect and perfect was given to Abraham in his seed in which all nations were to be blessed. [This was] circumcision, which literally consisted of the cutting off of all concupiscence, as I have remarked at length in commenting on the text "All of your males shall be circumcised" (Gn. 17:10).[455]

229. Finally, I would like to make four points about the commandments that are treated here in Exodus 20. The first is the distinction of divine precepts into moral, ceremonial, and legal. The second is the distinction of the moral among themselves; the third, the distinction of the ceremonial; the fourth, the subdistinction of the legal.

230. On all four points you should know that Rabbi Moses in Book 3, Chapter 36, reduces "all the negative precepts, which are said to be three hundred and sixty-five according to the number of days in a year, and the affirmative precepts, which are said to be two hundred and eighteen according to the number of parts of a human body, to fourteen sections. The first contains the precepts that are the main articles of belief dealing with conversion to God. The second contains the precepts forbidding idolatry,

and so on."[456] Friar Thomas makes a more rational and much clearer distinction of all the commandments of the old law into three groups—moral, ceremonial, and legal.

231. This pertains to the first of the four points mentioned above. It is based on the [*Summa of Theology*] Ia IIae, q. 99, a. 4, and accords with the text in Romans 7: "The commandment is just, and holy and good" (Rm. 7:12). "It is 'just' in relation to legal matters; 'holy' in relation to things ceremonial ('holy' is said of things dedicated to God); it is 'good,' that is morally correct in relation to moral matters."[457] The text in Titus 2 also bears on this: "Rejecting ungodliness, may we live temperately, and justly and piously" (Tt. 2:12). The first reason is that the divine law not only sets a person in relation to himself "temperately," and in relation to his neighbor "justly," but also in relation to God "piously." The second reason is that "sin is transgression of the divine law and disobedience of heavenly commands," as Ambrose says.[458] There are three kinds of sins—against oneself, against one's neighbor, and against God, as Isidore says in Book 2 of *On the Highest Good*.[459] This is enough on the first of the four points, namely, the distinction of commands into three, that is, moral, ceremonial, and judicial.

232. The second point, about the distinction or subdistinction of the moral precepts, follows. Moral precepts are divided into ten, "three ordered to God, and seven ordered to our neighbor," and consequently also to ourselves. Thomas writes of this in Ia IIae, q. 100, a. 3, ad 4. This is enough for the second. 233. In relation to the subdistinction of the ceremonial precepts, we must first look at the name "ceremonies." In Book 3, Chapter 27, Rabbi Moses says that "the precepts whose usefulness is known by the people are called legal, but those whose usefulness is unknown are called ceremonial." Thomas discusses this in Ia IIae, q. 101, a. 1, in both the body of the article and the objections. So much for the name "ceremonial." As far as the subdistinction of the ceremonial goes, there is a fourfold division into sacrifices, sacred things, sacraments, and observances. In the six articles of q. 102 in the same part [of the *Summa*] Thomas gives a sufficiently extended and notably fine treatment of this fourfold subdistinction and the reasons behind it. So much for the third point.

234. Therefore, only the fourth point on the subdistinction of the legal precepts remains. These are divided into four. Some of these belong to the person of the ruler or rulers of the people, some belong to the subjects, both to the "foreigners," and to the "members of the household, as father to son, wife to husband, and servant to master." The fourth category concerns the relations of subjects to each other, as Thomas says in q. 104, a. 4. This is enough for the commandments for the present.

"Moses went into the darkness, wherein God was" (v. 21).

235. Literally, the cloud and darkness covered the mountain (cf. Ex. 19:9, 16). You can also say that "Moses drew near" to God in the darkness, because in darkness, that is, in tribulation, man is compelled to have recourse to God and to invoke his help. The Psalm says, "Fill their faces with shame, and they will seek your name, O Lord" (Ps. 82:17). Or through the same words we can learn in another interpretation that God is present to those who suffer, according to the Psalm: "I am with him in tribulation" (Ps. 90:15). In his interpretation of this text Bernard prays: "O Lord, if you are with us, grant that I may always have tribulation so that I may always merit to have you with me."[460]

236. Or thirdly, by means of this same text ("He went into the darkness, wherein God was") he wants to say that there are many who indeed go to God and follow him when he calls them to honors and prosperity, but if he calls them to burdens, trials, and difficulties, then they retreat and do not draw near, according to the text in John 6: "You seek me . . . because you have eaten of the loaves" (Jn. 6:26). "Many said, 'This is a hard saying' " (Jn. 6:61), and below, "From this time many of his disciples turned back" (Jn. 6:66). The perfect always go to the God who calls no matter where he calls, whether to prosperity or adversity. "I will follow you wherever you go" (Mt. 8:19); "They follow the Lamb wherever he goes" (Rv. 14:4). As a type of the imperfect it says, "Peter was following at a distance" (Mt. 26:58).

237. Further and fourth, the "darkness" can be understood as the immensity and surpassing excellence of the divine light, according to the text in 1 Timothy 6: "He dwells in light inaccessible" (1 Tm. 6:16).[461] In Book 3, Chapter 10, Rabbi Moses says: "When our intellect strives to apprehend the Creator, it finds a great wall dividing him [from us]." Below he says, "God is truly hidden from us in cloud and darkness. This is what is said, 'Cloud and darkness are round about him' (Ps. 96:2),and again, 'He made darkness his secret place' (Ps. 17:12). . . . It is known to all that the day Moses stood on Mount Sinai was a cloudy and dark one. . . . The intention in speaking of darkness and cloud is not [to say] that obscurity covers God, because with him there is no obscurity, but clear light according to the saying, 'The earth was illumined by his glory' (Ezk. 43:2)."[462] (Here the Vulgate has "The earth shone with his majesty.") "The earth was illumined by his glory" (Rv. 18:1); "God is light and there is no darkness in him" (1 Jn. 1:5). The meaning is then "Moses went into the darkness wherein God was," that is, into the surpassing light that beats down and darkens our intellect. We see the same thing when our eyes are beaten down and darkened by the rays

from the sun's disk. This is also what Dionysius says in the first chapter of the *Mystical Theology:* "The simple, hidden and unchangeable mysteries of theology are covered over by the surpassingly splendent darkness of hiddenly learned silence that causes the Supersplendent to shine forth in surpassing fashion in that which is most dark." The first Letter to Gaius says, "Perfect ignorance is the knowledge of him who is over all that is known." John Sarracenus in his *Prologue to the Mystical Theology* says, "Since man ascends to knowledge of God through removal, what God is remains hidden and covered at the end."

238. Finally, note in this text that one who wishes to draw near to see God ought to be taken away and removed from the "waters," that is, from everything changeable which water signifies. "He drew me out of many waters" (Ps. 17:17). "Moses" means "drawn from the waters."[463]

"You shall make an altar of earth unto me" (v. 24).

239. Thomas explains this passage in Ia IIae, q. 102, a. 4, ad 7. It can also be said that the meaning is "You shall make an altar of earth unto me," because every sacrifice made in humility and kindness is acceptable to God. "A sacrifice to God is an afflicted spirit; a contrite and humbled heart, O God, you will not despise" (Ps. 50:19). Earth is "humus" from which "humility" is derived.[464]

240. Or there is this meaning. "An earthen altar" is made for God because even in and from the least work there can be fitting homage to God, who weighs the motive not the cost, as Gregory says.[465] "Whoever gives a cup of cold water to one of these little ones . . . shall not lose his reward" (Mt. 10:42). This also pertains to the text from chapter 16, "Nor did he find less who had provided less."[466] God's will is done "on earth as it is in heaven" (Mt. 6:10). This is what is said here, "You shall make an altar of earth unto me."

241. Thirdly, "an altar of earth" is made for God when a person blesses God in and through difficulties and bears them with patience. "In the nights lift up your hands to the holy places and bless the Lord" (Ps. 133:2). "Light and darkness," darkness is dark earth, "bless the Lord" (Dn. 3:72). "Blessed are those who suffer persecution" (Mt. 5:10).

242. You can also see from what has been said how valuable humility and patience are which make heaven "from earth" by making "an altar unto God." An altar is a high table.[467] God lives in the heights. "He dwells in the heights and looks down on the low things in heaven and on earth" (Ps. 112:5–

6). In humble folk earth is heaven, the lowest is the highest, for the height and the depth are the same. Humility is depth and earth; height is heaven. God dwells in heaven, as the Psalm says: "I have lifted up my eyes to you who dwell in heaven" (Ps. 122:1). Earth is the center of everything;[468] heaven, which is the circumference and outer limit of everything, is spherical. If you imagine a sphere projected onto a flat surface, each pole of the axis will become the center; and inversely, if you imagine a circle becoming a cone, the center will become the tip.

243. Concerning the fact that he says "unto me" ("You shall make unto me") note first of all that God claims as done for him everything good that we do—or rather, that he does in us. God "works all things in all" (1 Co. 12:6); "He works miracles among you" (Ga. 3:5); and "God works in us both the will and the performance" (Ph. 2:13). Augustine says that God crowns his gifts in us.[469]

244. Secondly, he says "unto me" because God rejoices and delights as much as we do in any work of ours: indeed, much more! It is certain that a just work is more pleasing to justice itself than to the just person, because the just work pleases the just person only through the justice that is in him.[470] But "that because of which something possesses some characteristic has more of it itself."[471] "This is my Beloved Son in whom I am well pleased" (Mt. 3:17). Origen says: "There is a festival for the Lord in each person who is converted. God makes a feast when an impure person becomes chaste and when an unjust one cultivates justice."[472] 245. From this note in the third place how much we ought to exert ourselves over a good work, which is of such merit and worth that God is well pleased with it, indeed, that God as Word may be pleased in himself. He says, "in whom I am well pleased." Fourthly, he says "to me," and you should note that only every work in which there is nothing intended save God alone, God's honor, is done for God. "You shall make unto me." 1 Timothy 1: "To God alone be honor and glory" (1 Tm. 1:17). Anyone who in his work seeks something outside and apart from God does not give glory to him nor make an altar to God.

246. He says, "You shall make an altar unto me," not to you, to serve your convenience or anything of yours. Such people are mercenaries. They do not serve God, but they sell God in order to gain or acquire something else.[473] They make that their goal; they make God a means to another end, higher, prior, and more pleasing than God himself. This they make their God. They make God a non-God, depriving him of his deity as far as they can. Therefore, they are justly deprived of peace, according to the text in Isaiah 33: "Woe to you that despoil, shall you not also be despoiled?" (Is.

119

MEISTER ECKHART

33:1). Luke says, "Glory to God in the highest and peace to men on earth" (Lk. 2:14). These people deprive God of his glory, and therefore it is fitting that they be deprived of their peace.

247. There is a second [main] point. It is proper to God that he have no "why or wherefore" outside or apart from himself.[474] Therefore, every work that has a "why and wherefore" as such is not a divine work and is not performed for God. "He has made all things for himself" (Pr. 16:4). He who does anything that is not for God's sake does not have a divine work, since it has a "why and wherefore" which is foreign and different from God. It is not God and is not divine. This is what is said here, "You shall make an altar of earth unto me," not to another or for some other, but to me alone and for my sake alone.

248. This fits what Augustine says on the Psalm verse, "I will not be confounded because I have called upon you" (Ps. 30:18). He says, "You call on God . . . to give you a reward. Therefore, you call on the reward, not on God. . . . You make God the minister of your reward; you have cheapened him. Do you wish to call upon God? Do so freely. Is it not enough for you that God fills you? Don't you want him unless he comes to you with gold and silver? If God himself is not enough for you, how can any of the things he has made suffice?"[475] This is the meaning of the words preceding our text, "You shall not make gods of silver or gold along with me" (Ex. 20:23). "The idols of the gentiles are silver and gold" (Ps. 113:4).

"You shall offer upon it your holocausts and peace offerings" (v. 24).

249. Recognize that "there are three kinds of sacrifice.[476] The first which is totally burned, and this is called 'holocaust' from 'holon' or 'holos,' that is, 'whole,' and 'cauma,' that is, 'fire'—thus 'totally burned.' This is offered to God especially as reverencing his majesty and because of love of his goodness. It matches the state of perfection in the fulfillment of the counsels,[477] so that just as the whole animal is reduced to smoke and rises above, so too the whole person and what belongs to him is made subject to God." This agrees with the text "Seek the things that are above" (Col. 3:2). It seems to coincide with the members of religious orders in the New Dispensation.

250. The second kind is "the sacrifice for sin, which is offered for the remission of sin and fits the state of penitents. It is divided into two parts, one burned, the other given to the priests, signifying that the remission of sins comes from God through the ministry of priests. Still, when a sacrifice is offered for the sin of the whole people or for the sin of a priest, it is totally

burned." It would not be fitting to give over to the priest's use what was offered for his own sin, and it is also a sign that no sinful stain should remain in him. 251. The third kind was the "peace offerings" mentioned here. These "are offered to God either in thanks or for the health and prosperity of those offering because of some benefit received or hoped for. This kind fits the state of those progressing in the fulfillment of the commandments. This is why it is divided in three parts: one burned in God's honor, another given to the priests, and a third for the use of the offerers to show that man's salvation is given by God with the cooperation of his ministers and also of those who are saved. 252. It must always be observed that neither the blood nor the fat comes to the use of the priests or offerers, but the blood is poured out on the base of the altar in God's honor and the fat is burned to exclude idolatry. Idolaters drink the victim's blood and eat the fat, according to the text, 'Of whose victims they ate the fat and drank the wine of their libations' (Dt. 32:38)."[478]

253. He also says, "The Israelites were forbidden the use of blood so that they should tremble to shed human blood. This is what Genesis 9 says, 'You shall not eat the flesh with the blood, for I will require the blood of your lives at the hand of every beast . . .' (Gn. 9:4). The eating of fat is forbidden to avoid sexual excess, according to the text 'What is fat, you have killed' (Ezk. 34:3). 254. The third reason for the prohibition of blood was out of respect for God, because blood is particularly necessary for life. Life and the soul that gives life is said to be in the blood, and fat shows an abundance of food. In order to show that life and all good things come to us from God, the blood is poured out and the fat is burned. The fourth reason is because this is a type of the pouring out of Christ's blood and the 'fat' of charity by which he offered himself to God for us."

255. "The priests are given the breast and the right arm of the peace offerings (cf. Lv. 7:31–32) to exclude the kind of divination called 'spatula-mantia,' that is, divination with the shoulder blades and breast bones of sacrificed animals. These things are taken away from the offerers so that they cannot make divination with them. The breast and the right arm are given to the priest to signify that he ought to possess wisdom within, in the breast that covers the heart, so that he may teach the people. He also ought to be strong to resist vices and support the weaknesses of others—this is signified through the right arm."

256. It is also to be noted that "the holocaust is the most powerful of all sacrifices. The sin offering, which is eaten only in the vestibule [of the temple] by the priests on the day of sacrifice, holds the second place. The peace offerings of thanksgiving hold the third place; these are eaten on the

same day, but everywhere in Jerusalem. The fourth place is held by the peace offerings based upon vows, which can be eaten on the following day. The basis for the order is because humanity is first under obligation to God for the sake of his majesty; secondly, for the remission of sins committed; third, because of good things received; and fourth, because of those hoped for."[479] The text given here ("You shall offer holocausts and peace offerings"), by expressing the first and last kinds of sacrifice, intends every kind of sacrifice to be understood.

257. The holocaust that is discussed above signifies that sacrifices are to be offered in love and not in fear, following the text "The fire on my altar will always burn" (Lv. 6:12). Fire is a conflagration; holocaust means "totally consumed." Love offers itself totally, burns totally, strives upward totally, and totally transforms itself into the one loved, that is, into God. It lives for him, not for itself, according to the text, "It is now no longer I that live, but Christ in me" (Ga. 2:20); and, "For me to live is Christ" (Ph. 1:21). It lives for him and lives in him—"My beloved is mine and I am his" (Sg. 2:16); "She leaned upon her Beloved" (Sg. 8:5), so that she could say, "It is good for me to adhere to God" (Ps. 72:28).

258. What is said here about the breast and right arm fits the fact that the two horns of the bishop's mitre signify knowledge of the two testaments, and the two lappets hanging down the shoulders indicate the fulfillment of the law of each testament through observing the commandments.[480] There once was a man who was asked [about the meaning] by a ruler who saw someone with a mitre celebrating [the liturgy] who had little knowledge of the two testaments. He answered that the two horns signified the two testaments, as we said, but that the lappets showed that he knew nothing of either of them, as Jeremiah says: "You are near their mouth, but far from their reins" (Jr. 12:2).

269. [481]You can get enough from the *Gloss* and especially from the lengthy treatment of the priest's garb in the letter Jerome wrote to Fabiola concerning the other allegorical meanings, whether they pertain to natural or moral truths. This is especially so about the ceremonial commands and the things that are written about the tabernacle and the priestly garments here and there up to Chapter 32.[482] Friar Thomas also treats them beautifully and well in the treatise on the divine commands in the Ia IIae.[483]

Chapter 22. "If anyone shall have stolen" (v. 1) begins the twenty-second chapter. And below, "He shall restore four sheep for one sheep," which agrees with the text "If I have defrauded anyone of anything, I restore it fourfold" (Lk. 19:8).

259. Seneca in his *Excerpts* 5.6 says: "He who knowingly inflicts an injury shall repay fourfold; who does so unknowingly only once."[484] These are the words of the law which Seneca gives, and he provides the following case to illustrate them. "A rich man asked his poor neighbor to sell him a tree which he said got in his way. The poor man refused. The rich man burned this tree and the house burned with it. For the tree he had to give fourfold recompense, but only one for the house." This is enough for a case based on the law for injury simple or fourfold which Seneca's *Excerpts* treat for both cases. On the text treated here ("Four sheep for one"), see [*Summa of Theology*] IIa IIae, q. 62, a. 3, ad 2.

Chapter 23. "You shall not receive the sound of a lie" (v. 1) begins Chapter 23, and below, "You shall not boil a kid in its mother's milk" (v. 19).[485]

260. This command is well explained in Ia IIae, q. 102, a. 6, ad 4, and also ad 8. We can also say that the command is from God either because a kid is not yet fit for human consumption, or because it is ordained for excess rather than for nourishment, and the law intends to restrict excess in these matters and not encourage it. Furthermore, when it says here that the kid is not to be cooked "in its mother's milk," one possible fitting explanation is that "in the milk" [means] "under the milk," thus signifying that a kid is not to be cooked or eaten as long as it sucks its mother's breast for nourishment. This agrees with the text "They knew him in the breaking of the bread" (Lk 24:35)—"in the breaking," that is, when they broke the bread, namely, ate it. Eating is called breaking because food is broken with the teeth when it is eaten. Scripture commonly uses the term "bread" for every kind of food, as in the text of Luke 14: "He entered the house of one of the rulers of the Pharisees on the Sabbath to eat bread" (Lk. 14:1). The truth is that bread broken is naturally more healthy and tasty than that cut with a knife. The term "breaking" means eating.

Chapter 24. "And he said to Moses" begins Chapter 24. Below it has: "Come up to me on the mountain, and be there" (v. 12).

261. Note that he says "Come up." There are two points here. First, no one ascends who is not below, that is, humble, according to the text "He

who ascended is the one who first descended" (Ep. 4:9–10), and "Descend, because I must stay in your house" (Lk. 19:5). Augustine in Book 9 of the *Confessions* says, "O how exalted you are, Lord, and [yet] you dwell in the hearts of the humble."[486]

262. Second, he says "Ascend" because God is on high. He dwells in the heights according to Ecclesiasticus 24:7. Literally, that alone is God which is most high; God dwells only in what is most high. Everything which has something above itself, has God above itself. The Psalm says, "You are eternally Most High, O Lord" (Ps. 91:9). It says "you" in the discrete sense, because [it pertains to God] alone.[487] It is there that he is to be sought. He summons us to this when he says "Ascend." The good is always on high—the higher, the better. What is Most High is the best. On the contrary, evil is always below, and the deeper, lower, more inferior and more subject, or subject to many things it is, the worse it is. This is evident from the treatise "On the Nature of the Superior,"[488] and the argument is briefly thus. What is superior is always prior and consequently "rich in itself."[489] What is inferior, insofar as it is inferior, is needy, naked, and indigent. Everything which without interruption exists and possesses [anything], exists and possesses it from its superior.[490] Therefore, he says "Ascend," first, because God is in the heights (there he exists, there he hears, there he teaches, there he works), and second, since God cannot descend, it is necessary that we ascend to him. If he were to descend in any way at all, he would no longer be God; he would have descended from deity. Anything [that became] higher than him as he descended, whatever it might be, would be God for him.

263. In the third place he says "Ascend" so that he may give [us] greater and sweeter and diviner gifts more copiously and more purely. It is impossible for us to receive these below while we are fixed and bound by what is inferior. Therefore, the Psalm says, "You have put all things under his feet" (Ps. 8:8). Only what is above all things can receive all things, just as nothing temporal exists forever and nothing local exists everywhere. Matthew 24 says of the faithful servant, "He will set him over all his goods" (Mt. 24:47).

264. There follows "to me." He says "to me" against the many who do not seek and aim at God, but rather at themselves and their own convenience, wealth, honor, and the like. Against this Augustine in *On the Psalms* says, "If God himself is not enough for you, how can any of the things he has made suffice?"[491] It would surely be unworthy for God to be received by someone for whom God himself was worthless. [This is the kind of person] who holds something other than God dearer and more worthwhile than God, while he prays to God not for himself, but for something else which

is not God, but made by him. The term "me," because it is a pronoun, signifies the pure substance,[492] and because it is this particular pronoun (that is, "me"), both "purity" and "me" are expressed as related or mutual terms. Therefore, he says "to me," so that one should only aim at God purely and absolutely.

265. There follows, "on the mountain." Note that he does not say "to the mountain." The reason seems to be that love and the will look to the thing itself, and they take their stand and are at peace in it. But the intellect does not take its stand in the reality of the thing itself,[493] but according to its name of "intellect," it enters into the principles of the thing and there receives the thing in its principles, in its root and origin.[494] It receives God "in the bosom of the Father" (Jn. 1:18)—the Word with God, the Word in the Principle, the Word himself the Principle. "In the Principle was the Word" (Jn. 1:1).[495] The intellect does not receive things themselves, but their ideas. "In the Principle was the Word," which is the Logos and Idea. As a figure of this we have what is said about the intellect under the parable of the eagle in Ezekiel 17: "A large eagle with great wings, long-limbed . . . came to Lebanon and took away the marrow of the cedar. He cropped off the top of its foliage" (Ezk. 17:3–4).[496]

266. There follows, "and be there." "Be" by persevering; "be" not behind, not to the side, nor looking to something outside [God]. "Be" by being, according to the text in Matthew 17: "It is good for us to be here" (Mt. 17:4). "Be" comes from the word "Being" [or Existence]. This is why he first says "Ascend," then "to me," third "to the mountain," and fourth "and be there."

Chapter 31.   "And the Lord spoke to Moses" begins the chapter. Below at the end it has "two tables written with the finger of God" (v. 18).

267. Rabbi Moses in Book 1, Chapter 65, says: "The tables were the work of the Lord, and their essence was natural, not artificial, since all the works of nature are called works of the Lord." And later he says, "The writing was attributed to the Creator, as is said 'the writing was written by the finger of God,' which is like the Psalm text 'I will see your heavens, the works of your fingers' (Ps. 8:4). Of the heavens it also says 'By the Lord's word the heavens are made firm' (Ps. 32:6). Therefore, he wishes that the word of scripture, [God's] saying and speaking, be understood of the creation of something. Thus, when it says 'written by the finger of God,' it is the same as saying 'written by the will and word of God.' "[497]

268. Rabbi Moses does not approve of what Onkelos, one of the sages,[498] said, namely, "that the finger was called a kind of power joined to

the Creator, like 'the mountain of God' (Ps. 23:3), or 'the staff of God' (Ps. 22:4), as if the 'finger' were a created instrument that made the tables by God's will." Just as "the stars of heaven were made by the primal will of God, and not by means of an instrument, so too was the writing on the tables. This is why the sages said that ten things were created through God's agency of which one was the writing on the tables. This proves that the writing on them is a work of nature along with all the other works."[499]

Chapter 32. *"But the people seeing . . ." begins chapter 32, and below it says, "Forgive them this trespass . . . or strike me from your book" (vv. 31–32).*

270. This can be explained according to the passage "I could wish to be anathema from Christ for the sake of my brethren" (Rm. 9:3). I have written on this.[500]

Chapter 33. *"And the Lord spoke to Moses" begins Chapter 33, and below it has "Show me your face that I may know you" (v. 13).*

271. Augustine in the *Trinity* 2.17 treats this passage and says: "This is the face whose contemplation all sigh for who try to love God with their whole hearts and souls and minds." Below he writes, "This is the face which draws every rational soul by a desire for it that is stronger the purer it is, and is purer the more it lifts itself to spiritual things, and lifts itself to spiritual things the more it dies to carnal ones."[501] In Book 9 of the *Confessions* he says, "We will mentally behold a visage in comparison with which everything else is repulsive, though they are beautiful by its generosity."[502] Book 3 of the *Fountain of Life* writes thus: "What will aid us in gaining this noble visage?" The answer given is "You must separate first from all sensible things and mentally immerse yourself in the intelligible and be totally dependent on the giver of goodness. When you have done this, he will gaze upon you and be generous to you, as is his wont."[503]

272. Note that he says "Show me your face" against the many who do not seek God's face, that is, the things that are prior, more powerful and eternal, but rather seek what is posterior to God, those things which come after him and are on the outside, namely temporal and transitory. This agrees with the text in Genesis 16: "I have seen the back parts of him who sees me" (Gn. 16:13). These are the words of Hagar, the Egyptian servant who is the type of the imperfect, of servants, and of those who are dark. Matthew 7 says against them, "First seek God's kingdom . . . and all these things will be given to you" (Mt. 6:33), that is, exterior and temporal things

insofar as they are necessary. Jerome says of such things in a homily that Zebedee's wife "with feminine greed sought after present things and forgot those of the future" (cf. Mt. 20:20–21).[504]

273. He also says "Show me your face" according to the Psalm text, "My face has sought you; I will seek your face, O Lord" (Ps. 26:8). [This is] against those who "adulterate God's word" (2 Co. 2:17). These people do not seek God to know him or to possess him, but [want] to know something outside God, like pleasure, wealth, honor, and so on. Wisdom 8 says against them, "I have become a lover of her form" (Ws. 8:2). (The form is the face.) Such people adulterate divine science or knowing God; they place it among the mechanical sciences which leave behind the legitimate goal of science, which is to know—the soul's perfection—to pursue their lovers (cf. Ho. 2:5), following the body's gain and its perfections rather than the soul's.[505] What is written about Lot's wife will happen to them—"Looking back, she was turned into a pillar of salt" (Gn. 19:26). I have written on this text.[506]

274. Again, in the third place "Show me your face so that I may know you." This is said against those who even today put knowing God, seeing his face, under something else, like delight or pleasure. Like Epicurus they order operation to pleasure, when on the contrary delight exists for the sake of operation as a maidservant for the mistress,[507] or as the pleasing good does for the moral good.[508] This is what Cicero teaches in his *Duties* and the *Highest Good and Evil*.[509] Against such people it says here, "Show me your face that I may know you." "To know you is perfect justice, and to know you is the root of immortality" (Ws. 15:3). "This is eternal life that they may know you the only true God" (Jn. 17:3). "Blessed are the clean of heart, for they shall see God" (Mt. 5:8). Augustine in the *Morals of the Church* says: "It may be asked what eternal life itself is. Let us rather heed what its giver says. He says 'This is eternal life that they may know you the true God.' " He concludes, "Therefore eternal life is the very knowledge of truth."[510] In his *Epistle to Dardanus* Augustine himself says: "They are most blessed for whom having God is knowing him. That knowledge is truly most full, most true, most happy."[511] This is why when the Lord asks in Luke 18 "What do you want me to do for you?" the cautious response is "O Lord, that I may see" (Lk. 18:41). The same holds in the text from Matthew given above, "Blessed are the clean of heart, for they shall see God." Augustine says, "The vision is the total reward."[512]

"Show me your glory" (v. 18).

275. The reality of glory is the fulfillment of grace or "grace consummated."[513] According to its name, it is the same as brilliance—"glory" means the same as "things that are brilliant."[514] We can also note that this teaches us that the light of glory is necessary for the essential vision of God.[515] This is what is treated above ("Show me your face"), and now he says, "Show me your glory."

276. Because he says "to me," he teaches that the vision is given to the pure and clean of heart, for a pronoun signifies the pure substance to the exclusion of anything else. But he also says "to me," that is, to Moses. Moses means "taken from the waters," and signifies someone who is above everything that is mutable. The person who wishes to see God's face ought to be like this.

277. Again and in the third place, it says "to me." Man is man through the intellect; to have an intellect is part of him and is proper to him,[516] and the property of the intellect is to see the glory of God.[517] "Show me your glory," he says. In Book 3, Chapter 52, Rabbi Moses says, "The intellect which is poured out upon us . . . binds us to the Creator insofar as we grasp him with the light of the intellect, just as David said: 'In your light we will see light' (Ps. 35:10). Likewise, he looks upon us with the same light and through it is always with us."[518]

"I will show you every good" (v. 19).

278. Rabbi Moses in [his *Guide*], Book 3, Chapter 53, treats this passage when he says, "You should know that Moses, the first among all the sages, requested two things and got an answer to both. One thing he asked the Creator was that he would show him his substance and truth; the second, which he asked for first, was that he would show him his ways.

279. "The Creator responded on both counts. First, he promised that he would make his ways, that is, his works, known." This is what is said here, "I will show you every good." "Every good," that is, "everything created," as the passage in Genesis 1 says, "God saw all the things he had made, and they were very good" (Gn. 1:31). "He gave him knowledge of their nature and powers, the joining of part to part, and of the relations and divisions of all beings. This is to say that he understood the essence of the whole world both truly and securely."[519]

280. On the other point, [namely], that "Moses asked the Creator that he show him his substance," God answered him "that his substance could

not be comprehended as it is." This is what follows below, "You cannot see my face" (Ex. 33:20). Note that our authorities agree with this interpretation of Rabbi Moses.[520] They say that prior to sin the first man was so created that he had knowledge of everything that was virtually contained in the self-evident first principles. This concerns Moses' request to be shown "the Lord's ways." The theologians say that in that state of perfection, "at least according to its usual mode, the first man did not see God's essence."[521]

"You cannot see my face" (v. 23).

281. In Book 1, Chapter 4, of the *Fountain of Life* Avicebron asks, "Is there any way to understand the first essence?" His response is that "this is not impossible, but it is not possible in any way whatever. It is impossible to know the first of essences apart from the created things that come from it; it can be known from its works. . . . He adds that [full] knowledge of the essence of the First, that is, God's essence, is impossible, because it is above all things, because it is infinite, because it is not like the intellect, and because the First Essence and the intellect do not agree and have a mutual bond."[522] In Book 1, Chapter 58, Rabbi Moses says, "The sages agree that the sciences do not apprehend the Creator; only God himself can grasp his essence." Nevertheless, Moses knew everything that we can know about him to the limit of our apprehension. What he knew, no one before or after him knew, as Rabbi Moses says in the same chapter. To bring everything said thus far to a summary, we can conclude that the essential vision of God is impossible for a created intellect on the basis of its natural powers, but possible by supernatural aid.[523] Thus when Moses begs, "Show me your face," it is significant that he prefixes it with "If I have found grace in your sight" (Ex. 33:13).

Chapter 34. The chapter begins with "And after this," and later it says, "You render the iniquity of the fathers to the third and fourth generation" (v. 7).

282. This is treated above under Chapter 21.[524] What remains down to the end of Exodus is well handled in the *Gloss* and by the theologians, especially by Jerome in his *Letter to Fabiola* on the priestly garb,[525] and by Thomas in [the *Summa of Theology*] Ia IIae, especially q. 102.

This is the end of the interpretation of some famous and useful authoritative interpretations on the Book of Exodus.

MEISTER ECKHART

Notes

The text translated here may be found in LW II, pp. 1–227.

1. The *Table of Contents* (*Tabula auctoritatum* in LW II, pp. 1–8) merely lists the verses to be treated under their respective chapters and occasionally summarizes the exegesis. With the exception of the introduction, it has been omitted here.
2. Eckhart is referring to both the "marginal" and the "interlinear" *Glosses* developed in the twelfth century, which, as the *Ordinary Gloss*, was a standard part of theological education at his time.
3. Augustine, *Words of the Heptateuch* 2.2.
4. *Ordinary Gloss* on Ex. 1:19.
5. A quotation from an antiphon for the Feast of St. Augustine as found in the Dominican breviary (cf. 2 Co. 5:1).
6. Jerome, *Commentary on Isaiah* 65.21.
7. Augustine, *Questions on the Heptateuch* 2.1.
8. *Ordinary Gloss* on Ex. 1:21, citing Gregory the Great, *Morals on Job* 18.3.6.
9. Thomas Aquinas, *STh* Ia IIae. 88.6.
10. See *Ordinary Gloss* on Ex. 1:21.
11. On the relation of interior motive (*affectus interior*) and exterior act in Eckhart, see *Essential Eckhart*, pp. 58–59.
12. The passage is actually *STh* IIa IIae. 110. 4. ad 4.
13. Thus, Eckhart's determination seems to be that the two midwives actually did not lie when they said that Jewish mothers bore their children without outside help.
14. See *Comm. Wis.* n. 1 (LW II, p. 323).
15. These two quotations are from Gratian's *Decretum*, the standard law book of the Latin church.
16. Aristotle, *Soul* 3.2 (426b).
17. *Soul* 3.2 (425b).
18. Cf. *Comm. Wis.* nn. 2, 77 (LW II, pp. 324, 408–09).
19. Aristotle, *Soul* 2.4 (415a).
20. Augustine, *Dialogue of Sixty-Five Questions with Orosius* q. 65.
21. Bernard, *On Consideration* 3.3.
22. Moses Maimonides, *Guide* 1.5.
23. Ibid.
24. Ibid., citing Aristotle, *Heaven and Earth* 2.12 (291b).
25. An abbreviated quotation from a long passage in *Guide*, ibid.
26. Most of these texts appear in *Guide* 1.32, but Eckhart appears to have used a Latin translation and possibly abridgement that differed from the text available in modern editions and translations.

27. Avicenna, *Metaphysics* 9.7.
28. Boethius, *Consolation of Philosophy* 1. poem 7.
29. Aristotle, *Soul* 2.10 (422b).
30. E.g., a stick appears bent in water.
31. Following Aristotle and many philosophers, Eckhart held that there were "animating principles," or souls, responsible for the movement and actions of the heavenly bodies.
32. In medieval cosmology the *primum mobile* was the highest movable sphere responsible for the movements of all the lower spheres.
33. See below n. 74 (p. 68).
34. Eckhart follows Priscian, *Grammatical Institutes* 17.9, on the "distinguishing pronoun" (*pronomen discretivum*).
35. The phrase "without this or that" (*sine hoc aut illo*) is equivalent to the often used phrase *sine hoc et hoc* and might also be translated as "without anything particular." See the Glossary under *esse hoc et hoc.*
36. The grammatical particulars here are also from Priscian. For the "Substantive Word," see *Comm. Jn.* n. 8 (*Essential Eckhart*, p. 125).
37. On the importance of "second position" (*secundum adiacens*) predication in Eckhart's thought, see B. McGinn, "Meister Eckhart on God as Absolute Unity," pp. 130–31; and A. de Libera, "A propos de quelques théories logiques de Maître Eckhart," pp. 17–19.
38. *Quidditas*, or "what-it-is," was a widely used term among the scholastics; *anitas*, or "that-it-is," is a term that comes from Avicenna, whose *Metaphysics* 8.4 is being cited here. The identity of essence and existence in God was the foundation of Thomistic metaphysics, taken over by Eckhart, but adapted to his own Neoplatonic perspective. See *Essential Eckhart*, pp. 32–38.
39. The "reflexive turning back" (*reflexa conversio*) or "complete return" (*reditio completa*) of the Intelligible Principle upon itself is something that Eckhart took from the *Book of Causes*, prop. 14 (15). See, e.g., Sermon XLIX. 2, n. 510 (p. 236). The "boiling" within (*bullitio*) is the way in which Eckhart expresses the dynamic life of the Trinity giving rise to the three divine Persons who are identical with the divine nature. For comparable texts, see Sermons XXV. 1, n. 258 (p. 218), and Sermon XLIX. 3, n. 512 (p. 237). See also the discussion in the Introduction to *Essential Eckhart*, pp. 37–38.
40. From the *Book of the Twenty-Four Philosophers* prop. 1.
41. The "boiling over" (*ebullitio*) is the divine external activity of creation that follows the model of the inner divine *bullitio*. The term is used in a similar way by Dietrich of Freiburg in his *Treatise on the Intellect and the Intelligible* 8.
42. See *Comm. Gen.* n. 7 (*Essential Eckhart*, pp. 84–85) for Eckhart's development of this central teaching.
43. Augustine, *Trin.* 8.3.4.
44. *Book of Causes* prop. 14(15).
45. Priscian, *Grammatical Institutes*, citing Vergil, *Aeneid* 6.864.

46. Aristotle, *Met.* 4.7 (1012a).
47. This proposition was attacked during the Cologne proceedings against Eckhart, but he defended himself by citing Avicenna and Albert the Great and it did not form a part of the final condemnation (cf. Théry, pp. 176, 195).
48. Augustine, *Trin.* 8.2.3.
49. Bernard, *On Consideration* 5.6.13.
50. Maimonides, *Guide* 1.61. The "Tetragrammaton," or name of four letters (YHWH), was never pronounced by the Jews, who substituted "Adonai" (i.e., Lord) for it.
51. See below nn. 146–48 (pp. 90–91).
52. *Guide* 1.63.
53. Boethius, *On the Trinity* 2. See Sermon XXV. 1, n. 251 (p. 216).
54. *Book of Causes* prop. 21(20).
55. Maimonides, *Guide* 1.63 in modern versions.
56. Augustine, *Immortality of the Soul* 8.15.
57. Augustine, *Book of Eighty-Three Questions* 33.
58. E. g., Avicenna, *Metaphysics* 8.1.4.
59. Cf. Anselm, *Monologion* 15.
60. The twenty-sixth article of the Bull "In agro dominico" condemned the proposition "All creatures are one pure nothing" (see *Essential Eckhart*, p. 80).
61. The text cited in the *Ordinary Gloss* and in Peter Lombard's *Sentences* I, d. 8, c. 1, n. 79, is not actually by Jerome, but is a conflation of a number of patristic texts.
62. Bernard, *On Consideration* 5.6.13.
63. Augustine, *On the Psalms* 1.6.
64. *On the Psalms* 5.7.
65. *True Religion* 36.66.
66. John Damascene, *Orthodox Faith* 1.9 (in modern editions). This was a favorite text of Eckhart's.
67. This part of the *Work of Questions* has not survived, but see below the two long treatments on the divine names in nn. 34–78 and 143–84 (pp. 53–70, 90–102).
68. The first point is treated in nn. 28–33, the second in nn. 34–78.
69. Cf. *Comm. Jn.* n. 30 (*Essential Eckhart*, p. 131).
70. "God has power over everything" (*Deus omnia potest*) can also be translated as "God can do everything." Both translations are used throughout this part of the commentary. Cf. *Comm. Wis.* nn. 156–57 (pp. 170–71).
71. These examples are commonplaces of Aristotelian thought.
72. Augustine, *Book of Eighty-Three Questions* 46.2.
73. E.g., Thomas Aquinas, *STh* Ia. 41. 5.
74. Gregory the Great, *Morals on Job* 16.37.45.
75. Augustine, *Lit. Comm. Gen.* 8.12.

76. Avicenna, *Metaphysics* 1.6.
77. Aristotle, *Post. Anal.* 2.19 (100b). See Thomas Aquinas, *STh* Ia. 16. 3, and elsewhere on the convertibility of being and truth, an important principle for Eckhart.
78. The word rendered as "might" (*potentia*) can also be translated as "power" and "potency." The wordplay that Eckhart uses with the different forms of *potentia* is difficult to convey in English.
79. Aristotle, *On Interpretation* 2.14 (24b).
80. "Goal," literally *terminus in quem* in the Latin. The doctrine is Aristotelian; cf. *Phys.* 5.1 (224b).
81. See Aquinas, *STh* Ia. 25. 3.
82. A frequent teaching of Eckhart; cf. *Comm. Jn.* n. 52 (*Essential Eckhart*, p. 140); *Comm. Wis.* n. 15 (LW II, p. 336).
83. Aristotle, *Top.* 4.5 (126a).
84. Actually, *STh* Ia. 25. 3. ad 4.
85. Eckhart takes this from Aristotle, *Nicomachean Ethics* 7.3 (1145b) and possibly Augustine's *City of God* 9.5.
86. K. Weiss in his note on this passage (LW II, p. 39) interprets "the thing he is talking about" (*de re dicti*) as the stories about the goings on of the Olympian gods.
87. See below, *Comm. Wis.* n. 157 (pp. 170–71).
88. None of the three treatments referred to here survives.
89. See nn. 170–77 (pp. 97–99).
90. The first three points provide the structure for the lengthy treatise on the divine names in the following way: (a) the positions of the philosophers and Jewish scholars (nn. 35–53); (b) the views of the Catholic writers (nn. 54–61); and (c) the question of substance and relation (nn. 62–78). The treatment of the "Tetragrammaton" is postponed to nn. 146–48.
91. *Book of Causes* props. 5(6) and 21(22).
92. *Book of the Twenty-Four Philosophers* prop. 16.
93. See *Comm. Jn.* nn. 63 and 86 (*Essential Eckhart*, pp. 145, 154).
94. The characterization of God as "omninameable" originates in the Hermetic text known as the *Asclepius* 6.20, and was widely used by Eckhart.
95. Augustine, *Sermons on John* 13.5.
96. Eckhart summarizes a passage in Avicenna's *Metaphysics* 8.7.
97. *Book of the Twenty-Four Philosophers* props. 7, 19, 22.
98. Actually *Guide* 1.58 in modern editions.
99. A summary of a long treatment in *Guide* 1.52.
100. *Guide* 1.56.
101. Both quotations are from *Guide* 1.52.
102. Ibid.
103. That is, each individual must be said to be the same as itself and not merely *like* itself.

104. See note 61.
105. These texts are from *Guide* 1.52.
106. *Guide* 1.53.
107. Ibid.
108. Ibid.
109. This is a summary of reflections in *Guide* 1.54.
110. The avaricious ant is a well-known medieval topos that Eckhart probably took from Odo of Cheriton's *Fables*.
111. *Book of Causes* prop. 20(21).
112. Actually, *Guide* 1.55 in modern editions.
113. The reasons that follow are a summary of *Guide* 1.51.
114. "That by which something is," or its source, here translates the Boethian term *ex quo*. See Sermon XXV. 1, n. 251 (p. 216).
115. Boethius, *On the Trinity* 2.
116. Eckhart is indulging in a wordplay between *aeternitas* and *extra terminos*.
117. See *Comm. Wis.* n. 146 (p. 167).
118. Boethius, *On the Trinity* 2.
119. Maimonides, *Guide* 1.51 (cf. below n. 58).
120. Aristotle, *Met.* 5.20 (1022b).
121. E.g., Thomas Aquinas, *STh* Ia IIae. 49. 4.
122. *Book of Causes* prop. 20(21).
123. Aquinas, *STh* Ia. 12. 5.
124. Aristotle, *Met.* 5.1 (1013a).
125. See *Comm. Jn.* n. 100 (*Essential Eckhart*, p. 160).
126. An important Thomistic principle to which Eckhart always adhered.
127. Maimonides, *Guide* 1.53.
128. E.g., Augustine, *Trin.* 6.4.6.
129. *Guide* 1.57.
130. *Trin.* 5.1.2.
131. Aristotle, *Met.* 5.7 (1014a).
132. *Met.* 7.1 (1028a).
133. *Met.* 4.2 (1003a).
134. Both of these examples of the extrinsic character of analogy are found elsewhere in Eckhart, e.g., *Comm. Ecc.* n. 52 (p. 178), and Sermon XLIV. 2, n. 446 (LW IV, p. 372). The first is a standard Thomistic example (e.g., *STh* Ia. 16. 6); the second is Eckhart's own.
135. I follow K. Weiss's rendering of the curt phrase *sed in obliquo, puta entis*.
136. The verb "analogatur" is translated here as "have an analogical relation to."
137. What Eckhart is saying is that relation is defined not by causal dependence or analogical relation, but by mutual opposition. This is why it has a special place in the doctrine of the divine names, as the subsequent discussion of substance and relation will show.
138. E.g., man and dog are univocal in being both animals, though they differ in

species; man and rock are different things from this perspective and therefore equivocal.

139. Aristotle, *Interpretation* 1.1 (16a).
140. The proper visible object is color; the common visible object the quantified being. See Aristotle, *Soul* 2.6 (418a).
141. This is the teaching of Thomas Aquinas, e.g., *STb* Ia. 42. 4. ad 2.
142. *Book of Causes* prop. 17(18).
143. Augustine, *Dialogue of Sixty-Five Questions with Orosius* q. 6.
144. Bernard, *On Consideration* 5.12.
145. Aristotle, *Post. Anal.* 1.18 (81a).
146. Boethius, *On the Trinity* 2.
147. "A particular perfection"—literally "this or that" (*haec vel illa*).
148. As pointed out in the "Introduction," pp. 19–20, Eckhart here disagrees with Thomas Aquinas (e.g., *STb* Ia. 13. 2–4).
149. Ibn Gabirol, *The Fountain of Life* 5.23. This work by a medieval Jewish philosopher was translated in the twelfth century and was well known to the scholastics.
150. Boethius, *On the Trinity* 2.
151. Maimonides, *Guide* 1.51.
152. These two sentences and the last sentence from n. 60 below form Article 23 of the bull of condemnation; cf. *Essential Eckhart*, p. 79.
153. This sentence brings Eckhart closer to the position of Aquinas that he seemed to reject in n. 58 (see note 148 above), but important differences still remain.
154. Bernard *On Consideration* 5.7.17.
155. Eckhart here seems to be echoing the words of Aquinas, *In I Sent.* d. 2, q. 1, a. 3.
156. Augustine, *Trin.* 5.11.12.
157. Boethius, *On the Trinity* 4, 5.
158. Aristotle, *Cat.* 5 (3b).
159. Based on Aquinas, *Commentary on the Metaphysics* 7.1 (lecture 1).
160. Avicenna, *Logic* 1.
161. Thomas Aquinas, *In I Sent.* d. 33, q. 1, a. 1.
162. "Inheres," "exists in" (Latin *inesse*) is the characteristic mode of being of an accident.
163. Aquinas, *In I Sent.* d. 12, q. 1, a. 1.
164. Augustine, *Trin.* 5.5.6.
165. Aquinas, *STb* Ia. 28. 2.
166. The identity of essence and existence in God is the keystone of Thomistic metaphysics, e.g., *STb* Ia. 3. 4.
167. *STb* Ia. 28. 2. E.g., the relation of filiation in a son receives its reality insofar as it is a relation not from the subject, i.e., the son, but from the father to whom the son is related.
168. This was the opinion of some twelfth-century theologians, especially Gilbert

of Poitiers. The formulation was rejected, at least in part, by Thomas Aquinas (e.g., *STh* Ia. 28. 2, and *On God's Power* 8.2). Eckhart's citation of it without qualification seems to indicate another area of divergence from Thomas.

169. Aristotle, *Met.* 5.15 (1021a).
170. Aquinas, *On God's Power* 8.2.
171. That is, action signifies that there must be a principle of action in the agent. Eckhart is here following Thomas, e.g., *On God's Power* 9. 9. ad 4.
172. Aquinas, *STh* Ia IIae. 18. 4.
173. Aquinas, *In I Sent.* d. 33, q. 1, a. 1, ad 5.
174. Ibid.
175. Aristotle, *Met.* 10.7 (1057b).
176. "Imperfect"—*secundum quid* in the Latin.
177. That is, father as father is understood by relation to son as opposite, and not by anything else. See Aquinas, *STh* Ia. 28. 2, and Ia. 40. 2, etc.
178. Augustine, *Trin.* 5.8.9.
179. Boethius, *On the Trinity* 6.
180. That is, the S (subject) is really the P (predicate).
181. Aristotle, *Met.* 4.7 (1011b).
182. Augustine, *Soliloquies* 2.5.8.
183. On the negation of negation, see especially *Comm. Wis.* n. 147 (pp. 167), and Sermon 21 (p. 281).
184. *Book of Causes* prop. 14(15). See note 39 above.
185. When Eckhart says that "no negation belongs to God," he seems to be speaking of God *in himself* to whom only the negation of negation pertains. From our perspective, based on conceptions drawn from created reality, all language about God is negative (cf. nn. 44–45 and 78).
186. Augustine, *Immortality of the Soul* 7.15.
187. *Book of Causes* prop. 20(21).
188. Augustine, *Conf.* 10.6.10.
189. Augustine, *Sermons on John* 1.13.
190. *Sermons on John* 44.13.
191. That is, every affirmative sentence either contains "is" or can be reformulated to contain "is."
192. Pseudo-Dionysius, *Celestial Hierarchies* 2.3 (Eckhart is using the translation of John the Scot).
193. This and what follows is a paraphrase from Thomas Aquinas, *STh* Ia. 13. 3.
194. Augustine, *Questions on the Heptateuch* 6.29.
195. See below nn. 146–48 (pp. 90–91).
196. Augustine, *Trin.* 1.2.4.
197. *Book of Causes* prop. 2.
198. Traditional Christian theology taught that the angels had been created before time, and, like human souls, would last forever. Aristotle and those who followed him thought that the heavenly bodies and the universe itself were eter-

nal, and some theologians, like Thomas Aquinas, admitted that this view was not inherently contradictory.

199. This is based on Boethius's famous definition of eternity in the *Consolation of Philosophy* 5, prose 6: "total, perfect and simultaneous possession of endless life."

200. Boethius, ibid. Eckhart's criticism of *Proslogion* 20 is that it does not take up explicitly the issue of the eternal universe postulated by the Aristotelians.

201. Thomas Aquinas, *STh* Ia. 10. 2. ad 1.

202. Augustine, *Book of Eighty-Three Questions* 23.

203. Boethius, *Consolation of Philosophy* 3, poem 2.

204. Aquinas, *STh* Ia. 10. 2. ad 2.

205. Eckhart here cites the Old Latin version of Ex. 3:15, which has *Dominus regnabit in saeculum et adhuc* as compared with the Vulgate *Dominus regnavit in aeternum et ultra*.

206. The two Augustine texts are from the *Questions on the Heptateuch* 6.4 and 1.31. The latter cites Horace, *Epistle* 1.10.41.

207. *Ordinary Gloss* on Ex. 15:18, citing Origen, *Homilies on Exodus* 6.13.

208. Maimonides, *Guide* 2.29.

209. Aristotle, *Interpretation* 1.1 (16a).

210. See n. 55 (p. 61).

211. Aristotle, *Cat.* 5 (3b).

212. Aristotle, *Met.* 7.42 (1037b).

213. For the three modes of duration, especially the "aeon" (*aevum*), which measures the existence of the angels and heavenly bodies, see Thomas Aquinas, *STh* Ia. 10. 5.

214. That is, it is possible to conceive of the essence of some created thing (e.g., the dodo) without that thing actually existing.

215. One of Eckhart's favorite axioms; cf., e.g., *Comm. Jn.* n. 50 (*Essential Eckhart*, p. 139), and *General Prologue to the Three-Part Work* n. 19 (LW I, p. 163).

216. "Source" here translates the Boethian *quo est*, while essence translates *quod quid est*. Consult the Glossary under *essentia*.

217. This part of the *Work of Propositions* does not survive.

218. The text in Thomas is actually *STh* Ia. 14. 12. In his note on this passage, K. Weiss mentions the Dominicans John of Sterngassen and James of Metz as opponents of this view (LW II, p. 89, note 4).

219. E.g., *In I Sent.* d. 39, q. 1, a. 3; and *SCG* 1.69, where "knowledge of vision" (*scientia visionis*) extends only to really existing things, but the "knowledge of simple understanding" (*scientia simplicis intelligentiae*) embraces all possibles.

220. This is not extant.

221. The *Ordinary Gloss* takes the chapter in this way.

222. Boethius, *Consolation of Philosophy* 2, prose 5.

223. Augustine, *Conf.* 10.31.44.

224. Cicero, *Tusculan Disputations* 5.34.97 and 35.102.

MEISTER ECKHART

225. Aristotle, *Soul* 3.45 (432b).
226. See *Comm. Gen.* nn. 290 sq. (LW I, pp. 425 sq.).
227. See Pr. 5:2–6 and 7:6–15. Maimonides, *Guide*, Preface and 3.9, gives this interpretation.
228. Cf. n. 58 (p. 63).
229. Eckhart here combines propositions 2, 18, and 3 of the *Book of the Twenty-Four Philosophers*.
230. See *Comm. Jn.* n. 93 (*Essential Eckhart*, p. 157).
231. Augustine, *Questions on the Heptateuch* 2.68 sq.
232. *Ordinary Gloss* on Ex. 18:19.
233. Augustine, *Questions on the Heptateuch* 2.69.
234. Ibid. 2.68.
235. Ibid.
236. Ibid.
237. *Ordinary Gloss* on Ex. 20:2, and Thomas Aquinas, *STh* Ia IIae. 100.
238. Aristotle, *Nicomachean Ethics* 3.3 (1112b).
239. Cf. Sermon 9 (p. 256).
240. Aristotle, *Phys.* 2.9 (200a).
241. In what follows Eckhart is using Thomas Aquinas, *STh* IIa IIae. 22. 1.
242. John Chrysostom, *Unfinished Work on Matthew* 8.
243. Citations from *STh* IIa IIae. 22. 1.
244. Both quotations in this paragraph are from Maimonides, *Guide* 2.34.
245. Augustine, *Against Adimantus* 17.
246. The etymology of *filius* from *philos* is frequent in Eckhart, e.g., *Comm. Jn.* n. 115 (*Essential Eckhart*, p. 157).
247. Eckhart's wordplay between *tamquam* and *tantum quantum* does not come over in English.
248. E.g., Sermon XL. 1 (LW IV, pp. 335–37).
249. This exposition has not survived.
250. Cf. *Comm. Wis.* n. 146 (p. 167).
251. Cf. *Par. Gen.* n. 15 (*Essential Eckhart*, pp. 98–99), and *Comm. Wis.* n. 151 (p. 168).
252. *Comm. Wis.* n. 152 (p. 168–69).
253. *Comm. Wis.* n. 144 (p. 166).
254. No commentary of Eckhart on Deuteronomy survives, but he may be referring to Sermon XXIX (pp. 223–27).
255. See *Prologue to the Work of Propositions* nn. 5, 12–13, 15, 22 (LW I, pp. 168–69, 172–73, 175, 178–79).
256. John Damascene, *Orthodox Faith* 1.4.
257. Augustine, *Morals of the Manichaeans* 2.1.1.
258. See n. 58 below (p. 63); cf. also *Comm. Wis.* n. 144 (p. 166).
259. Cf. Sermon XXIX n. 296 (p. 224).
260. Thomas Aquinas, *Commentary on the Book of Causes*, lecture 1, n. 13.

261. *Book of Causes* prop. 1.
262. There is a Latin play on words here: *Alienum enim ab alio dictum est.*
263. See Sermon XXIX, ibid.
264. Cf. *Comm. Wis.* n. 145 (p. 166).
265. Augustine, *Conf.* 10.27.38.
266. Avicenna, *Metaphysics* 8.4. 5.
267. Augustine, *Questions on the Heptateuch* 6.29.
268. *Ordinary Gloss* on Jos. 24:23.
269. Gregory the Great refers to such views, which reflect the position of some of the Greek Fathers, in his *Morals on Job* 18.54.90. Thomas Aquinas condemns this position in his *Commentary on John*, chap. 1, lecture 11.1 (212). The term "theophany" was introduced into Latin theology by John the Scot in the ninth century. See *Comm. Wis.* n. 284 (p. 173).
270. Thomas Aquinas, *STh* Ia. 12. 2.
271. The dialectic of similar/dissimilar applied to God has its classic source in Christian theology in the Dionysian *Divine Names* 9.6. Eckhart's treatment here should be compared with his analysis of the distinct/indistinct dialectic in *Comm. Wis.* nn. 154–55 (pp. 169–70). In this treatment, the Latin *similis/dissimilis* is rendered at times by "similar/dissimilar," at others times by "like/unlike," depending on the context.
272. See above n. 104 (p. 79).
273. Cf. *Comm. Jn.* n. 103 (*Essential Eckhart*, p. 161).
274. Eckhart is following Thomas Aquinas, e.g., *On God's Power* 3. 5. ad 1.
275. Boethius, *Consolation of Philosophy* 3, poem 9.
276. Augustine, *Soliloquies* 1.1.3.
277. Thomas Aquinas, *STh* Ia. 7. 1. ad 3.
278. Augustine, *Christ. Doct.* 1.6.6.
279. Averroes, *Commentary on the Physics* 4.13 (222a).
280. Augustine, *Free Choice* 2.11.32.
281. "Ideas" (*rationes*) could also be rendered as "causes."
282. See n. 73 (p. 68).
283. A common example going back to Augustine. Cf. *Comm. Jn.* n. 12 (*Essential Eckhart*, p. 126).
284. See n. 175 below (p. 99). Emphasis on the virtual existence of all things in God is one of the cornerstones of Eckhart's thought; see *Essential Eckhart*, pp. 40–41.
285. Eckhart here reverses the dialectic to show that the forms are indeed in God, though virtually, not formally.
286. Thomas Aquinas, *SCG* 1.29.
287. This is the visible "species" of the colored wall that makes sight possible, and not the "species," which is a category of being (e.g., the species man). On the species as medium, cf. *Comm. Jn.* n. 25 (*Essential Eckhart*, p. 130).
288. Cf. *Comm. Jn.* n. 110 (*Essential Eckhart*, p. 160).

289. Aristotle, *Soul* 2.7 (418b).
290. Augustine, *Book of Eighty-Three Questions* 29.
291. See the *Book of Six Principles* 5.20, a work sometimes attributed to Gilbert of Poitiers.
292. Aristotle, *Met.* 5.19 (1022b).
293. Avicenna, *Metaphysics* 9.2.
294. According to Augustine, neither one nor two is a number, but they are the sources of numbers.
295. Augustine, *Questions on the Heptateuch* 5.42.
296. Gregory, *Morals on Job* 1.14.18.
297. Avicenna, *Metaphysics* 3.5.
298. Aristotle, *Met.* 13.6 (1080b).
299. That is, because the One has no size.
300. Aristotle, *Met.* 10.1 (1052a).
301. Augustine, *City of God* 11.31.
302. Aristotle, *Met.* 10.3 (1052b).
303. Aristotle, *Phys.* 8.10 (267b).
304. Aristotle, *Met.* 10.4 (1055a).
305. See nn. 100–03 (pp. 78–79).
306. Augustine, *Christian Struggle* 30.32.
307. Literally, "the passions of the composite" (*passionum compositi*).
308. See n. 134 (p. 87).
309. See Aristotle, *Met.* 1.6 (987b).
310. Eckhart is here playing on the words "heir" (*heres*), "inhere" (*inhaeret*), and "adhere" (*adhaeret*).
311. "Necessary" here translates "per se," that is, "through or by itself."
312. Thomas Aquinas, *STh* Ia. 11. 2. ad 1.
313. Not found among the letters to Pope Damasus, but see Jerome's *Commentary on Ezekiel* 4.18.
314. Maimonides, *Guide* 1.61–64 in modern versions.
315. These seven treatments take up nn. 145, 146–48, 155, 149, 151–54, 156–60 and 161–69 respectively.
316. The treatment of the affirmative and negative names in nn. 170–84 closes Eckhart's remarkable treatise on the divine names.
317. See Maimonides *Guide* 1.61.
318. A paraphrase of a passage in *Guide* ibid.
319. Ibid.
320. Ibid.
321. *STh* Ia. 13. 11. ad 1.
322. *Guide* 1.61.
323. Ibid.
324. *Ordinary Gloss* on Ex. 28:36, citing Bede.
325. This section is a pastiche of quotations and paraphrases from *Guide* 1.62.

326. Ibid.
327. Ibid.
328. The *Centiloquium* is a work pseudonymously attributed to Ptolemy.
329. Geomancy and pyromancy are forms of divination by signs taken from handfuls of earth and from fire.
330. Priscian, *Grammatical Institutes* 1.2.8–11.
331. Maimonides, *Guide* 1.62.
332. Ibid., citing the Talmud.
333. Ibid.
334. *Guide* 1.63 in modern versions.
335. Ibid.
336. Boethius, *Consolation of Philosophy* 3, poem 9.
337. Aristotle, *Phys.* 1.3 (186a).
338. See *Comm. Jn.* n. 30 (*Essential Eckhart*, p. 131).
339. See n. 20 above (p. 47). Cf. *Book of Causes* prop. 1.
340. See the *General Prologue to the Three-Part Work* n. 13 (LW I, p. 159).
341. Augustine, *Conf.* 1.1.1.
342. Aristotle, *Generation and Corruption* 1.7 (324b), and *Phys.* 4.11 (219b).
343. Cf. *Comm. Gen.* nn. 160, 163 (LW I, pp. 307–08, 310–11).
344. Maimonides, *Guide* 1.63.
345. John Damascene, *Orthodox Faith* 1.12.
346. Cf. nn. 158, 160 (p. 94).
347. E.g., Thomas Aquinas, *STh* Ia. 8. 3.
348. E.g., Thomas Aquinas, *SCG* 1.42, and 2.15.
349. The supposit is the concrete existing thing as the subject of predication.
350. Thomas Aquinas, *Quodlibetal Questions* 2.2.4.
351. Augustine, *Conf.* 9.4.11.
352. That is, "the same" will refer to the genus and species that comprise the nature, and "thing" will refer to the supposit that actually exists.
353. Cf. *Comm. Jn.* n. 110 (*Essential Eckhart*, p. 164).
354. *Book of Causes* prop. 21(22).
355. Avicenna, *Metaphysics* 1.2.
356. Aristotle, *Met.* 4.1 (1003a).
357. See nn. 34–61 (pp. 53–64).
358. *Guide* 1.60 in modern editions.
359. This is taken from *Guide* 1.60, but in a rather different form from that found in modern versions.
360. *Guide* 1.59.
361. Ibid.
362. Ibid.
363. *Guide* 1.58.
364. That is, "in power" (*virtute*). Cf. n. 121 (p. 83) and the parallels cited there.
365. See Aristotle, *Soul* 3.8 (431b); and Thomas Aquinas, *SCG* 1.53.

366. See Sermon XXIX n. 300 (p. 225).

367. See Boethius, *How Substances Are Good;* and Thomas Aquinas, *On the Soul* 1. 6. ad 2.

368. Thomas Aquinas, *In I Sent.* d. 8, q. 1, a. 1, citing Pseudo-Dionysius.

369. Maimonides, *Guide* 1.59.

370. Peter of Spain, *Logical Summaries* 4.

371. Cf. n. 78 below (p. 70).

372. Cf. n. 37 (p. 54), citing *Guide* 1.58.

373. Ibid.

374. Anselm of Canterbury, *Virginal Conception* 5.

375. Taken from Maimonides, *Guide* 1.58.

376. Cicero, *Invention* 1.36.62.

377. "Possession" here renders the Latin *habitus.*

378. Thomas Aquinas, *STh* Ia IIae. 72. 6. Cf. *Comm. Jn.* n. 75 (*Essential Eckhart,* p. 149).

379. Maimonides, *Guide* 1.58.

380. Ibid. The point is that the higher nature of the heavens, only partially understood by us, involves many negations of our own realm of experience and thus hints at the completely unknowable nature of God.

381. Maimonides, ibid.

382. Cf. nn. 44, 51 (pp. 56–57, 59).

383. Maimonides, ibid.

384. Macrobius, *Commentary on the Dream of Scipio* 1.2.15.

385. Cited, e.g., by Jerome in *Letter* 53.9.1.

386. Cf. n. 28 above (p. 50), and *Comm. Jn.* n. 43 (*Essential Eckhart,* p. 137).

387. Eberhard of Bethune, *Graecism* 9.3.

388. A similar example appears in *Par. Gen.* n. 25 (*Essential Eckhart,* p. 103).

389. Cf. *General Prologue to the Three-Part Work* n. 10 (LW I, pp. 154–55).

390. Augustine, *Free Choice* 1.4.9–10.

391. Augustine, *Retractations* 1.8.4.

392. Ambrose, *Duties* 1.30.147.

393. See, e.g., Justinian's *Digest* 48.8.14.

394. Aristotle, *Nichomachean Ethics* 2.4 (1105b).

395. Ovid, *Remedies of Love* 91–92.

396. Augustine, *True Religion* 46.87. Cf. Sermon 16b (p. 278).

397. On these two kinds of love, see Thomas Aquinas *STh* Ia IIae. 26.4.

398. Eckhart's insistence that perfect love must be indistinct (i.e., not based on distinctions) appears under many formulations throughout his works. See *Essential Eckhart,* p. 58, for some general remarks.

399. Cf. *Comm. Wis.* n. 144 (p. 166).

400. Actually from Maximus of Turin, *Homily* 95.

401. Actually Seneca, *Epistle* 73.7.

402. Cf. n. 191 (p. 104).

403. Augustine, *True Religion* 46.89.
404. Augustine, *On the Psalms* 115.3.
405. Maimonides, *Guide* 3.8 in modern versions, quoting the Talmud.
406. Ibid.
407. Thomas Aquinas, *STh* Ia IIae. 73. 10.
408. Maimonides, *Guide* 3.8.
409. Isidore of Seville, *Sentences* (i.e., *On the Highest Good*) 2.18.5–6.
410. Maimonides, *Guide* 3.8.
411. A paraphrase and partial quotation from Maimonides, ibid.
412. Ibid.
413. Ibid.
414. Augustine, *Conf.* 10.31.44.
415. Cf. Thomas Aquinas, *STh* Ia IIae. 73. 3 and 9.
416. Ambrose, *Paradise* 8.39.
417. Thomas Aquinas, *STh* Ia IIae. 73. 8.
418. Augustine, *Free Choice* 3.14.41.
419. Maimonides, *Guide* 3.8.
420. Seneca, *Epistle* 12.5.
421. Cicero, *Highest Good* 1.13.43–44.
422. Augustine, *Trin.* 9.9.14.
423. Gregory the Great, *Homilies on the Gospels* 2.30.1.
424. This and the following sentences are an extended wordplay on various forms of *haereo* (to stick to) and its cognates. It is based in part on Augustine, *Trin.* 9.9.14.
425. Augustine, *Commentary on the Epistle of John* 2.14. Cf. *Comm. Wis.* n. 34 (p. 153), and *Comm. Jn.* n. 48 (*Essential Eckhart*, p. 138).
426. The identification of the "man" of the Genesis account of the Fall with the higher reason directed to God and the "woman" with the lower reason directed to the senses (or sometimes with sensuality itself, as here) was something that Eckhart took over from Augustine, *Trin.* 12.30.20, etc. It appears in a number of places in the following comments, and also in Eckhart's remarks on Genesis 3, on which see *Par. Gen.* n. 135 sqq. (*Essential Eckhart*, pp. 108 sqq.). See also Sermons 16b and 40 (pp. 278, 302).
427. Cf. Peter Lombard, *Sentences* 2, d. 24, c. 12.
428. E.g., Thomas Aquinas, *STh* Ia IIae. 74. 8.
429. Augustine, *Trin.* 12.12.17–18.
430. Augustine, *Trin.* 9.10.15.
431. Aristotle, *Nichomachean Ethics* 3.13 (1118b). Cf. Thomas Aquinas, *STh* Ia. 81. 2.
432. Aristotle, *History of Animals* 6.18 (571b).
433. *Decretals* of Gregory IX (known as the *Liber Extra*), Book 1, Title 2, chap. 4.
434. I follow K. Weiss's version of this abbreviated reference to the *Gloss on the Decretals* (LW II, p. 177).

435. Augustine, *Spirit and the Letter* 4.6.
436. A fundamental principle of Eckhart's exegesis; cf. *Par. Gen.* nn. 1–3 (*Essential Eckhart*, pp. 92–95).
437. *Divine Names* 4.32.
438. The first quotation in this paragraph is from *Guide* 3.22; the second is an abbreviated form of two passages in 3.8.
439. *Guide* 3.22.
440. Augustine, *Conf.* 1.7.11.
441. Maimonides, *Guide* 3.22.
442. Ibid. Origen, *Homilies on Numbers* 20.3, has something similar.
443. Synderesis (i.e., rational conscience) is a term taken from Jerome, e.g., *Commentary on Ezekiel* 1.
444. Maimonides, *Guide* 3.8.
445. This commentary is lost.
446. Cf. Thomas Aquinas, *STh* IIIa. 15. 4.
447. Augustine, *Sermons on John* 15.21–22.
448. Aristotle, *Phys.* 4.12 (221a).
449. Augustine, as cited in the *Gloss on the Decretals* (see note 434).
450. John Damascene, *Orthodox Faith* 2.12.
451. Aristotle, *Nichomachean Ethics* 1.13 (1102b).
452. The "con" of *concupiscentia* signifies "together."
453. Based on a passage in Thomas Aquinas, *STh* Ia IIae. 25. 2. ad 1.
454. Thomas Aquinas, *STh* Ia IIae. 30. 1. ad 1.
455. Cf. *Comm. Gen.* nn. 236, 244–45 (LW I, pp. 380–81, 387–89).
456. Maimonides, *Guide* 3.35.
457. Aquinas, *STh* Ia IIae. 99. 4.
458. Ambrose, *Paradise* 8.39.
459. Eckhart here quotes Thomas Aquinas, *STh* Ia IIae. 72. 4, who is actually citing the twelfth-century *Summa of Sentences* rather than Isidore of Seville.
460. A paraphrase of Bernard of Clairvaux, *Sermons on Psalm 90* 17.4.
461. Cf. Pseudo-Dionysius, *Divine Names* 7.2, and *Mystical Theology* 1.1.
462. Maimonides, *Guide* 3.9.
463. See Jerome, *Interpretation of Hebrew Names* 14.1.
464. This derivation is frequent in Eckhart's writings, e.g., *Comm. Jn.* n. 9 (*Essential Eckhart*, p. 158).
465. Gregory the Great, *Homilies on the Gospels* 1.5.2.
466. See n. 92 (p. 75).
467. There is a play here between two words for altar (*ara*, which I have translated as "table," and *altare*). The derivation comes from Isidore of Seville, *Etymologies* 15.4.14.
468. Aristotle, *Heaven and Earth* 2.14 (296b).
469. Augustine, *Letter* 194.5.19.
470. Cf. *Comm. Wis.* n. 76 (LW II, p. 407), and *Comm. Jn.* n. 245 (LW III, p. 204).

471. Aristotle, *Post. Anal.* 1.2 (72a).
472. Origen, *Homilies on Numbers* 23.2.
473. Cf. Sermon 1 (p. 240).
474. That God lacks a "why or wherefore" (*quare* in the Latin) is one of Eckhart's constant themes. Cf. *Essential Eckhart*, pp. 59–60, and the Glossary under *âne war umbe*.
475. Augustine, *On the Psalms* 30.3.4.
476. The distinction of the three kinds of sacrifice found in nn. 249–55 is based on Aquinas, *STh* Ia IIae. 102. 3. ad 8, which Eckhart quotes and paraphrases extensively in what follows.
477. The traditional counsels of perfection are poverty, chastity, and obedience.
478. Thomas Aquinas's distinctions are based upon Lv. 4–7.
479. *STh* Ia IIae. 102. 3. ad 10.
480. Cf. Innocent III, *Holy Mystery of the Altar* 1.60.
481. K. Weiss, the editor, plausibly suggests that n. 269 was misplaced in the manuscripts and more properly belongs here (see LW II, p. 216, note 3).
482. Jerome, *Letter* 64.
483. Thomas Aquinas, *STh* Ia IIae. 98–105.
484. This is a reference to the elder Seneca, the father of the philosopher.
485. This problematic verse was one of the classic texts for illustrating the necessity for the spiritual interpretation of scripture.
486. Augustine, *Conf.* 9.31.41.
487. See n. 74 (p. 68).
488. A part of the *Work of Propositions* that has not survived.
489. *Book of Causes* prop. 21(20).
490. Cf. *Comm. Gen.* n. 25 (*Essential Eckhart*, p. 91).
491. Augustine, *On the Psalms* 30.3.4.
492. Cf. nn. 14 and 276 (pp. 45, 128).
493. Thomas Aquinas, *STh* Ia. 82. 3.
494. Cf. *Comm. Jn.* n. 9 (*Essential Eckhart*, p. 125). The etymology of *intellectus* according to the scholastics was from *intus legere* ("to read within").
495. The background to this passage is Eckhart's exegesis of Jn. 1:1 in *Comm. Jn.* nn. 4–51 (*Essential Eckhart*, pp. 123–40).
496. See *Comm. Jn.* n. 1 (*Essential Eckhart*, p. 122).
497. Maimonides, *Guide* 1.66.
498. This reference to the Targum Onkelos appears in ibid.
499. Ibid.
500. For an exposition of this text, see Sermon VI n. 67 (LW IV, p. 65), and Sermon 12 (p. 268).
501. Augustine, *Trin.* 2.17.28. The term *species*, here translated "face," can also mean both "beauty" and "splendor."
502. The text is actually from *True Religion* 52.101.
503. Ibn Gabirol, *Fountain of Life* 5.43.

504. Jerome, *Homilies on Matthew* 3.20.
505. On the status of the mechanical sciences, see Thomas Aquinas, *Commentary on the Metaphysics* 1, chap. 2, lecture 2.
506. Cf. *Comm. Gen.* nn. 259–61 (LW I, pp. 401–03).
507. This is the teaching of Aristotle, *Nichomachean Ethics* 10.4 (1174b), and Thomas Aquinas after him, e.g., *SCG* 3.26.
508. Thomas Aquinas, *STh* Ia. 5. 6. ad 3.
509. Cicero, *Duties* 3.33.116; and *Highest Good and Evil* 2.15.48.
510. Augustine, *Morals of the Church* 1.25.47.
511. Augustine, *Letter* 187.6.21.
512. Augustine, *On the Psalms* 90.2.13.
513. Thomas Aquinas, *STh* Ia. 95. 1. Cf. Sermon 21 (p. 282).
514. There is a wordplay here between two different Latin terms for divine glory, *gloria* and *claritas*.
515. Thomas Aquinas, *SCG* 3.53.
516. Cf. n. 163 (p. 95).
517. Aquinas, *STh* Ia. 12. 3.
518. Maimonides, *Guide* 3.54.
519. Ibid.
520. E.g., Thomas Aquinas, *STh* Ia. 94. 3.
521. Thomas Aquinas, *STh* Ia. 94. 1.
522. Ibn Gabirol here distinguishes between two kinds of knowledge of God, essential knowledge and imperfect knowledge by way of effects.
523. Thomas Aquinas, *STh* Ia. 12. 4.
524. Cf. nn. 129–42 (pp. 85–90).
525. Jerome, *Letter* 64.

II. SELECTIONS FROM THE COMMENTARY ON THE BOOK OF WISDOM, FROM THE SERMONS AND LECTURES ON ECCLESIASTICUS AND FROM THE COMMENTARY ON JOHN

Selection 1. "He created all things that they might be" (Ws. 1:14).[1]

19. Note that these words respond very aptly to what went right before, "God did not make death, nor does he rejoice in the destruction of the living" (Ws. 1:13). That God is not the cause of death, nor generally of nonbeing or privation, is evident from the fact that he is the cause of existence and "created all things that they might be"—to, in, and for the sake of existence.[2] This is what it says here, "He created all things that they might be."

The first point to be made is that becoming is from secondary causes, but the existence of everything, either natural or artificial, in that it is what is first and perfect, is immediately from God himself alone.[3] "God's works are perfect" (Dt. 32:4). The whole perfection of all things is their existence. John 1 says, "All things were made through him, and without him nothing was made" (Jn. 1:3). According to one explanation, the meaning is that everything made, whether by nature or art, is (that is, has existence) through him.[4] (The term "is" and the term "existence" signify the same thing, though as different parts of speech.) This is what follows, "without him nothing was made." For everything made, whether by art or nature as said before, is nothing without God who is the source of existence. This is the meaning of what is said here, "He created all things that they might be." Creation is the conferring of "existence after nonexistence."[5]

20. Secondly, note that no being has an efficient or final cause in relation to what it is.[6] The ground for this is that neither the metaphysician who considers being as being nor the mathematician demonstrates, teaches, or defines through these causes.[7] Thus the Philosopher says, "In mathematics there is [no question of] the good," in that the good and the end are the same.[8] Another ground of this is that the efficient and final causes are and are termed extrinsic causes.[9] A third argument for this is Avicenna's saying that a thing does not have what it is from another.[10] That a man or an animal exists comes from another, but that a man is an animal, or a body or a substance, he has from nothing other than himself. Either there is no man, or if there is one, he is also an animal. Hence [the statement] "man is an animal" is true even if no man really exists (and it is true in thought as well). According to the logicians, the predications in which the word "is" is the third term of the predicate do not involve a thing's existence, but the connection of the terms.[11] Even if no man existed, "man is an animal" would be no less true. But it is otherwise in the case of the existence or *esse* itself of things, for this looks to an outside cause as such. This is what it says here, "He created all things that they might be."

21. Thirdly, note that in its essential or original cause a thing has no existence, and the same is true of the art and intellect [of an artist].[12] The house in the mind is not a house; heat in the sun, in motion, or in light is not heat.[13] House and heat receive their respective formal existences insofar as they are produced and extracted from a cause and through an efficient cause. All things are in God as in the First Cause in an intellectual way and in the mind of the Maker. Therefore, they do not have any of their formal existence until they are causally produced and extracted on the outside in order to exist. This is why it says here, God "created all things that they might be."

22. Fourth. The ideas of created things are not created, nor creatable as such.[14] They are prior and posterior to things,[15] [as] their original causes, which is why mutable things are known through them as through [immutable] causes and by immutable knowledge, as is clear in natural philosophy. As far as its formal existence goes, any external thing is mutable, creatable, and created. Thus it says here, God "created all things, that they might be." In him things are their ideas—"In the Principle was the Word," or Logos, which is the Idea.[16] Augustine says that [the Word is] an "art full of all the ideas."[17]

23. Fifthly, one should know that every agent makes something like itself. But God is totally existence and works in creatures through Existence Itself and according to existence. Therefore, "the Trinity's works are un-

divided" in creatures,[18] because there is one existence of [all] three Persons. It is different in the uncreated realm, where the Father generates, not the Son, the Holy Spirit is "breathed forth," and does not "breath" [himself] in the notional sense.[19] This is why it expressly says here, God "created all things, that they might be." In existence alone is the creature properly assimilated to God its cause.[20]

24. The sixth point to note is that existence is the ground of creatability, according to the text: "Existence is the first of created things."[21] Hence something produced by God, although it is a being, and is living and intelligent, is creatable only by reason of its existence. This is why if something were living and intelligent, but had no existence above and beyond life and intelligence, it would be as such uncreatable.[22] Hence the subtle and significant text, "What was made in him was life" (Jn. 1:3–4), as if to say, what was made by God exists in itself, [but] in God was life, and as life [it is] uncreatable, just as God is uncreatable.[23] "He created that they might be," that is, by reason of existence, aptly signifies this. For example, an apple is colored, has taste and smell, is light or heavy and the like. However, it is by reason of color alone that it affects sight and is visible, and by no means by taste, or odor, and the rest.

25. Seventh, note that creation is the production of things from nothing.[24] A man is produced from what is not a man, and generally a particular being from something that is not that being, and in nature one opposite from another. So too the [act of] creation of the Agent that is first and higher than nature and nature's causes necessarily produces simply being, and, according to the property of its act of existence, simply from nonbeing or from nothing, the term opposed to it.[25] Existence and nothing are mutually opposed. This is the meaning of "He created that they might be."

26. We must remark in the eighth place that if someone asks why God "created all things," that is, the whole universe, the answer should be "that they might be." In Chapter 24 of *True Religion* Augustine, speaking generally of creatures, says: "Who made them? He who is in the highest way. Who is this? God. . . . Why did he make them? That they might be. . . . From what did he make them? From nothing." These are Augustine's words.[26] This is what the *Book of Causes* says, "Existence is the first of created things." According to one understanding, this means that the existence of created things itself is their first cause, that is, their goal. For the first cause of causes is the final cause. Therefore, the final cause for which all things were created is that they might be, namely, their existence itself. This is what it says here, "He created that they might be." Rabbi Moses treats this at length in Book 3, Chapter 14.[27]

27. To prove this we can cite the example that everything that generates and in general every agent has the existence of its effect as the necessary goal of its action. This is where it comes to rest: God "rested from all his work" (Gn. 2:2).[28] God is existence, and every [act of] existence comes from him. When the [act of] existence is received and accepted, every agent rests from its work and is pleased with it, according to the text in Proverbs 3, "The father is pleased in his son" (Pr. 3:12), and that in Matthew 3, "[This is] my beloved Son in whom I am well pleased" (Mt. 3:17). This is why joy in a work is the sign of a habit that has been generated. Every generation breathes love, rest, satisfaction, and delight, and is a kind of trinity of one who generates, one generated (or delight), and satisfaction or love. Once again, this is why in the change or disposition which precedes the act of existence that comes about through generation there is always labor, difficulty, resistence, motion, and unrest due to the absence of the existence which the agent intends as its goal. When it is received through generation, every motion ceases. Delight, love, and rest follow. The same can be seen in another example. The architect in his work labors at adaptation and change with no other end in mind insofar as he is an architect than the existence of the building. When it has achieved reality, if it is well made according to the skill and the form of the building in the mind, it pleases the architect. He loves it and rests satisfied with it; he does not look for anything more insofar as he is an architect. If he intends or inclines to anything beyond that the building be— its existence as building—this is completely accidental to his role as architect. An example would be wishing the building to be painted, or anything else like this.

28. Therefore, every action of nature, morality, and art in its wholeness possesses three things: something generating, something generated, and the love of what generates for what is generated and vice versa. A single generation, active in the one who begets and passive in the one begotten, breathes this love. The love breathed by both the begetter and the begotten Aristotle calls the "pleasure of the habit that has been generated."[29] Generation's purpose and final cause is existence—that what is generated should be. This is what is said here, "He created all things, that they might be," which is as if to say, "He created all things for the final purpose that they might be, intending nothing above and beyond this." And so nothing else remains save the pure trinity of the begetter, begotten, and the love breathed forth, which is and is called the spirit. What follows after (e.g., accidents, natural properties, and everything extrinsic), is related [to it] as creation or the production of created things is related to the Trinity of Father, Son, and Holy Spirit, [that is], to generation and spiration in the Godhead, according

to the text "In the Principle," that is, in the Son, "God created heaven and earth," and "God's Spirit was borne over the waters" (Gn. 1:1–2).[30]

29. Therefore, from all that has been said it is clearly evident that every agent of nature, morality, and art in general intends as the goal and repose of its whole action and "pilgrimage" that its effect exist and receive existence. He says, "He created them that they might be." Existence is through the substantial form and generation.[31] Everything which precedes that is dissimilar—the agent always finds something not its own in it. This is why it hates it and gets rid of it through the process of change until it finds itself in the offspring through generation.[32] This is the "Father's perfect image,"[33] having nothing dissimilar or foreign to the Father, and possessing everything which is his, if it is truly a "Son" and an image, as in the Godhead. "All the things that the Father has are mine" (Jn. 16:15). Therefore, the Father is well pleased in the Son, because he finds everything that belongs to him there, and nothing dissimilar. "This is my beloved Son in whom I am well pleased" (Mt. 3:17). Every agent and subject of generation intends [to make] another something like himself.

30. From this comes in the first place that only generation breathes forth love; alteration rather breathes forth pain. Second, comes the Psalm text "His place has been made in peace" (Ps. 75:3). Peace [is found] in generation where there is nothing dissimilar, displeasing, or contrary; conflict is found in alteration. Thirdly, there follows what the begotten Son says, "I am not of this world" (Jn. 8:23). The reason is that generation is not of this world, since it is not in time; but alteration, since it takes place with time, is of this world.[34] Fourth follows the text of John 16, "In the world you will have affliction, but in me peace" (Jn. 16:33)—"in me," that is, in the Son, through generation; "in the world affliction," that is, through alteration. "A woman about to give birth has sorrow; when she has brought forth, she no longer remembers the affliction" (Jn. 16:21).

31. There is a figure of this in the fact that Laban gave each of his daughters Lia and Rachel a maidservant when they were ready to bear children.[35] Alteration is a slave and serves nature for generation, and therefore as a slave it does not bear a free son and heir. But generation, as the free woman, bears a son "in virtue of the promise" (Ga. 4:23), a son [who is] principally intended and naturally promised through the one who generates. The one who generates, I say, naturally promises existence to the one generated, who is passive. This, that is, existence, essentially comes through the substantial form, which is brought about by generation and not by alteration.[36] Hence the text in Galatians 4, "Cast out the maidservant and her son" (Ga. 4:30). Alteration and its work are cast out through generation

151

when the Son has been born who is a second Father, similar to the Father in all things, having one existence with him.[37] "The Father and I are one" (Jn. 10:30). He says, "We are one"—we have one existence. "We are" is derived from "to be." And this is the sense of the words, "He created them that they might be," because existence is the goal even in creatures.

32. It must be noted that in each of the eight explanations given the text is arranged according to the common understanding so that it says God made "all things that they might be," that is, that they might have external existence in reality. Nevertheless, they were in him from eternity and eternally according to their ideas, that is, insofar as they are understanding and [exist in] an intellectual way.[38] Likewise, all things were in God insofar as they are living and are life, according to the text in John 1, "All things were made through him," and "What was made in him was life, and life was the light of men" (Jn. 1:3–4). The meaning is that "things made," that is, created (for what is eternal is not made), "are through him," that is, through God they have formal existence outside in reality under the proper forms by which they are. But in him they are not yet as they are, that is, as lion, man, sun, and so forth. They are not in him by reason of their existence as things of such a nature, but by reason of life and understanding. This is what John says, "In him was life," in relation to the idea of life and living, "and life was the light of men," in relation to understanding. The life of man as man is understanding and intellect.[39]

33. From what has been said note that God does not cause evil, death, and privations of that sort in any way, as the previous text says, "God made not death" (Ws. 1:13). It is evident first that evils, as nonbeing, are not from God nor is God in them, since there is no existence in them. They are evils in and only of the fact that they are not in God and he is not in them. This is why they do not exist, are not creatures, and have not been created. Second, it is clear that because existence belongs to supposits,[40] accidents, and the principles of things, in that they have no other existence than that of the supposit, are not said to be created, but "concreated."[41] Third, it is clear that the past and future as such are not in God nor is he in them, just as existence is not in them. "The past no longer exists, and the future does not yet exist."[42] Therefore, he did not create nor would he have created, unless what was created and had been created in the past were [really] created as something present, a real and actual being. In the first book of the *Confessions* before the middle Augustine in speaking to God says: " 'You are the same' (Ps. 101:28), and all tomorrows and beyond them and all yesterdays and what is behind them, you are making today and have made today. What is it to me if someone does not understand this?"[43] These are Augustine's words.

34. Fourth, it is evident that everything created is nothing of itself.[44] "He created them, that they might be," and prior to existence there is nothing. Therefore, whoever loves a creature loves nothing and becomes nothing, because love transforms the lover into the beloved.[45] Augustine says, "You are what you love."[46] You love nothing. You are nothing. "In his sight the evil one is brought to nothing" (Ps. 14:4). Fifth, it is clear that one who prays for these things that are perishing prays for nothing, prays badly and for what is bad—for the evil from which we ask to be freed when we say at the end of the Lord's Prayer "Deliver us from evil," according to one explanation.[47] He says "He created all things," with no exception, so that you should love and desire nothing beyond him. Sixth, note from what has gone before that he says "He created all things that they might be." "He created," he says, against the lazy who do nothing; "that they might be," against sinners who do not [really] exist. "Let sinners and the unjust be consumed so that they are no more" (Ps. 103:35). [He says] "all things" against the indolent who do very little, "straining out the gnat, but swallowing the camel" (Mt. 23:24).

35. The final thing to remark is that the aforementioned words, "He created all things that they might be," can be arranged in another way, so that the sense is "God created, so that all things might be," that is, a universal multitude. In the first way of understanding and arranging the words the sense is that the very existence of things is the final cause of creation, and this is true; the sense of the other order ("He created, so that all things might be") is that the final cause of creation is the whole universe, namely everything, or "all things."

36. Here the first thing to note is that just as every agent of itself always intends the whole (e.g., the architect in relation to a house thinks of the parts only in and for the whole), so too God, the First Agent, of himself and first of all produces and creates the universe having all things, but [creates] individual things as parts of the universe and of the whole, and only for and in the universe. This answers the question and difficulty that has bothered many up to today about how a multitude can come immediately from the Simple One, which is God. There are those, such as Avicenna and his followers,[48] who think that from the First comes the Created Intelligence in a primary and immediate fashion, and that other things follow from this subsequently. Rather say that the whole universe as one totality (as the name implies, because universe means "one") comes from the Simple One, one from the One in a primal and immediate way. This is fitting. Just as God is one simple thing in existence in every way, but is "multiple in conceptuality,"[49] so too the universe is one thing ("The world is one"),[50] but is multiple

153

in parts and distinct things. Therefore, something that is one but multiple in parts comes from the one God who is multiple in conceptuality.[51]

37. The question about the cause of the inequality of things also vanishes. From what has been said it is clear that just as the first intention and final cause of creation is the one perfect universe whose perfection and unity consist in a multitude and diversity of parts, so too the equality that accompanies unity is the first goal of creation, but is still attended by an inequality in things without which one thing would not be better than another nor would all things exist.[52] Therefore, God is the primary and necessary cause of the one, of equality, and of the best, but these three (unity, equality, the best) are followed in a secondary way by multitude in relation to the first, inequality in relation to the second, and gradations in goodness in relation to the third. This is why according to a common interpretation it says "it was good" of each created thing (Gn. 1:4, 10, 12, 18, 21, 25), but that "they were very good" (Gn. 1:31) concerning all things.[53] It is also clear from the example given above about each and every natural agent: Neither form nor matter come to be or are generated, but [only] the whole composite, as the seventh book of the *Metaphysics* says.[54] In this way then a multitude descends and proceeds from unity and inequality from equality, and multitude is reduced to and returns to unity, inequality to equality, and opposition to harmony. This is why Boethius teaches at the beginning of the second book of his *Arithmetic* that "All inequality may be reduced to equality."[55] In Book 3 of the *Consolation of Philosophy* he reduces all things to the Good, the Good to the One, the One to Existence, with a fine allusion to the three points we have made about the existence, unity, and equality of created things.[56] "He created, so that they all might be" expresses them very well, for different and opposed things are united in inferiors and agree in higher and superior things.[57] "He makes agreement in the highest things" (Jb. 25:2).

38. It is still necessary to note that multitude and inequality are the properties and constant partners of creatures or created things, but unity and equality are proper to God and divine things insofar as they are divine.[58] In order to signify this it says, "God created, so that all things might be." He says "God" and "created"—see the unity; "he created all things"—see the multitude and inequality. By the fact that something is created, it is distinct and is unequal and many.[59] By its descent from the One and the Indistinct the created thing falls from the One and into distinction and hence into inequality.[60] The Uncreated, on the contrary, has no fall or descent and therefore remains and stands in the fountainhead of unity, equality, and indistinction. This is why the three Persons in the Godhead, although they are plural, are yet not many but one, even if they were a thousand persons.[61]

"The Father, the Word and the Holy Spirit, and these three are one" (1 Jn. 5:7).

39. Note further here that because creatures are many, distinct, and unequal, it follows that God is indistinct, not-multiple, and not-unequal. It also follows that everything created is in some way one, equal, and indistinct. The ground for all of this is that a superior in itself always affects its inferior and, vice versa, is in no way affected by it, as is clear in the treatise "The Nature of the Superior."[62] Therefore, God the creator affects everything created by his unity, his equality, and his indistinction, according to Proclus's text: "Every multitude in some way participates in the One."[63] Everything that is divided from other things is undivided in itself.[64]

40. All this agrees with what Seneca says in his *Letter 67*: "Divine things are of one nature," and "There is no difference among divine things."[65] In the third book of the *Consolation of Philosophy* Boethius says of God:

> You draw forth all things from the supernal exemplar;
> Most beautiful of all, bearing the beautiful world in your
> Mind and forming it by a like Image,
> And making a perfect whole by framing perfect parts.[66]

So, from Seneca you have that unity and equality belong to the nature of divine things, and hence multiplicity and inequality to the nature of creatures; and from Boethius you have that this world, the whole universe, is first of all intended and drawn forth in exemplary fashion from the Image of the Creator, but the parts, which are many, [come forth] in a secondary way insofar as the perfection of the one universe requires them. Or, to speak more properly, the perfect unity of the universe acts as the principle of parts of this kind. It is generally true that the parts of any whole whatsoever do not confer existence on the whole, but rather receive existence from, through, and in the whole.[67] Insofar as they are parts, outside the whole they have no existence at all, save only in a false, equivocal way.

Selection 2. "All good things came to me together with her" (Ws. 7:11).[68]

96. Note that the word "together" can be taken in three ways. First, when "together" means the same as "at the same time"; second, when the word comes from "equality," and third when it comes from the verb *pario, paris.*

As far as the first sense is concerned, "All good things came to me" together with Wisdom at the same time and quickly, without succession and division, according to the text: "The grace of the Holy Spirit knows no slow pace," as it says in the *Gloss* on "Suddenly there came a sound from heaven" (Ac. 2:2).[69] But think about the fact that he says "with her." All good things necessarily come to the person to whom God comes, both because every good insofar as it is good is from him alone, just as every being insofar as it is a being is from him alone (the good and being are convertible and proceed together), and also because [all good comes] in him and with him and through him, or rather he himself is all good and "the good of every good," as Augustine says in the *Trinity*, Book 8, Chapter 3. Therefore, all goods or none come with him. Either he does not come, or if he does, all good things come with him. All things are in him in equal fashion, and he is equally all things. All things are the One, although it is not received according to and by all things. "The sensual man does not perceive" (1 Co. 2:14), and "The light shines in the darkness and the darkness did not comprehend it" (Jn. 1:5). He does not say "apprehend" but says "comprehend" because "There is no one that can hide himself from his heat," as it says in the Psalm (18:7).[70] "The act of active processes is in the recipient that is ready for it,"[71] according to the text "He gave them his goods . . . , to one five, another two, another one, to each according to his own ability" (Mt. 25:14–15). This is why it says here, "All good things came to me," that is, at the same time, "with her." They are all connected in the One from which they come, in the One in which they are, and in the One that is their goal.

97. On this see what the philosophers, saints, and doctors say about all the virtues being connected, a point I have treated fully in the *Book of Questions*.[72] For the moment note that all the virtues are connected in love of the good. Anything that anyone does because it is good and from absolute love for the good is virtuous as long as it remains at this level.[73] On the contrary, anything that anyone does that is not for this reason, or aside from the fact that it is good, is not virtuous. The Psalm says, "I will confess your name because it is good" (Ps. 53:8).

98. This is why some theologians say the virtues are connected in charity.[74] Charity is the love of the good insofar as it is good, and this is God, the "good Good," "the good of every good," as Augustine said above.[75] A particular good,[76] the good of this or that thing, is already something created and beneath, beyond, and beside the Good. It is proper, not common; it excludes something, while charity excludes nothing. Augustine in the passage cited above [says], "Take away this or that!" This and that is a trap through which one is no longer free, but a captive. One does not do good for its own sake—it does not happen freely—but for this or that reason one

serves this or that thing as a mercenary, a slave, not a son of the good, because one is not acting from the love of the good.[77] Son comes from *philos*, that is, love.[78] The Psalm prays to be liberated from this trap of slavery and made free: "You will bring me out of this trap" (Ps. 30:5). This and that is a trap: "The trap has been broken and we have been freed" (Ps. 123:7). "We have been freed," that is, liberated. Prior to this it says, "Blessed be the Lord, who has not given us over to captivity" (Ps. 123:6). "Our soul has been delivered from the hunters' trap" (Ps. 123:7); "The Truth will set you free" (Jn. 8:32). "Truth" is God: "I am the Truth" (Jn. 14:6). The good insofar as it is good and not this or that is God. "No one is good but God alone" (Lk. 18:19). Charity, absolute love of the good, is God. "God is charity" (1 Jn. 4:8). This deals with the first point: "All good things came to me together with her"—"together," that is, at the same time.

99. Secondly, the term "together" [is derived from] "par," [that is, equal]. In God unequal things are equal, unlike things like. This is why the doctors say that in God the ideas of unequal things are equal,[79] and according to Augustine the ideas of corruptible things (e.g., a bronze circle) are incorruptible and eternal.[80] "Eternal," that is, "without boundaries"; outside the snares of this and that, as mentioned above. Certainly charity loves all equally and on a par. One and simple in every way is the one God whom charity loves in all things—nothing else outside him or beyond him! Therefore it is necessary that it have as much love for the one as for the other, for the other as for itself, for the one as for all, for anyone as for God, because it is God alone and nothing else whom it loves in anyone and in all, as we said above on the verse "She goes about seeking those worthy of her" (Ws. 6:17).[81] This will appear more clearly below.[82] So much for the second point in which the term "together" is derived from equality.

100. Thirdly, "together" is derived from the verb *pario, paris*, when it says, "All good things came to me with her through generation." You know that what belongs to fire does not come to anyone, nor meet anyone, nor agree with anyone (he says, "Came to me") who does not have the form and act of existence of fire. When fire's form has been received [in something] by generation everything that belongs to fire comes along with it. Fire's form and its existence come about through generation; the goal of generation is the existence and the form of the thing generating, or bearing, or giving birth.[83] What is born and begotten is the offspring and son. "If a son, then also an heir" (Ga. 4:7), an heir, I say, of everything which the one bearing or the father has. "The Father has given all things" to the Son (Jn. 3:35). Romans 8 says of the Son, "He has given us all things with him" (Rm. 8:32). We see the same in the case of fire.[84] It communicates everything it has in

perfect fashion only to something that has received the form and existence of fire through birth and generation after all motion and alteration [has ceased]. Therefore, alteration is a path to the form and existence of fire, an imperfect and dissimilar one [that takes place] with something like the sounds of resistance and opposition. When [something] has received fire's form and existence, when the form of the fire giving birth is already fixed within [the thing] in silence and rest as if by hereditary right, it already has and does everything that belongs to fire. This is what John 14 says, "The Father dwells in me, he does the works" (Jn. 14:10). As the fire which generates, the father exists in alteration and in what is altered, but he does not remain there; he is a passing guest who does not inhere. Therefore, there is neither an heir nor a son of fire there. But he stays and inheres in the fire that has been generated and born, and there he performs not just the works of something that has been ignited, but the works of fire itself. He says, "The Father dwells in me; he does the works."

101. In the literal sense, the father as father is not in what has been altered, but in the son that has been begotten. On the other hand, the son as son is nowhere but in the father. "I am in the Father and the Father is in me" (Jn. 14:10). The Father and the Son are joined in nature, work, and intellect.[85] (Therefore, we have the sophistical saying: "If only the father is there, then not only the father is there.")[86] He says, "The Father remains in me" (Jn. 14:10). What does not remain and is not fixed is neither given a name nor praised. It is not a quality for change, but the very capacity to change.[87] "We do not give a name to or praise passions" insofar as they are transitory.[88] A person is not called ruddy-complexioned who blushes from shame,[89] just as the word "to blush" means "to become red on the outside," not within or from the inside. "All the glory of the king's daughter is from within" (Ps. 44:14).

102. This can also be seen in the area of morals, where we have an example in the habit of virtue, the disposition [to the habit], and the virtue itself.[90] These three are related like the form that gives birth or generates, the offspring brought forth, and the alteration [itself]. The habit (like the father remaining within) and the begotten offspring of the virtue perform works of virtue with delight and ease and without difficulty; but it is different with the disposition, which performs the father's works, that is, virtue's, [in such a way] that he does not remain within, but passes over to the outside. This is why such works take place with some difficulty and resistance, because they are not yet the works of a child begotten from the father, nor the works of a father giving birth, but rather of what changes and prepares. Therefore, all virtue's goods, properties, and perfections, such as being able

to act easily, promptly, and delightfully, have not yet arrived. These are the works of the father in the offspring or son, and also of the son who is brought forth and begotten. This is the meaning of the text "All good things came to me with her 'pariter,' " that is, through the birth or parturition by which a son is born and generated. In this act the father first remains, persists and inheres as a quality subject to change. It gives a name to and is praised in the agent who acts not from sorrow or necessity, but joyfully as with real delight. "A woman about to give birth has sorrow . . . , but when she has brought forth the child, she no longer remembers the anguish" (Jn. 16:21). "God loves a cheerful giver" (2 Co. 9:7), as a father loves his son. "The Father loves the Son" (Jn. 3:35); "My Father will love him . . . , and we will make our abode with him" (Jn. 14:23). I, the begotten Son, and the generating Father who remains in me [will do this], according to the texts: "I am in the Father and the Father is in me" (Jn. 14:23); "The Father remains in me, he does the works" (Jn. 14:10); "All the things the Father has are mine" (Jn. 16:15); "And all things that are mine are yours, and yours are mine" (Jn. 17:10). This is our text: "All good things came to me with her through generation."

103. Do you want to have all the Father's good things come to you, as it says here? Do you want to be established as an "heir of all things," as Hebrews 1:2 says? Do you want to be set up "over all his goods," as Matthew 24:47 says? Then be a son, be an offspring of God, as I explained above on the text from Chapter 5: "They were numbered among God's sons" (Ws. 5:5).[91]

A further, fourth point. God is "all in all" (1 Co. 15:28), and "works all things in all" (1 Co. 12:6). Therefore, it is clear that when and if he comes, all good things in the universal sense will come along to meet us with him, as it says here.

104. Again, in the fifth place note that all that is and is all things exists through and in the One, just as privation exists in a habit and negation in affirmation.[92] These pertain to one science,[93] and also have but one act of knowing and one act of existence. "God is one" (Ga. 3:20), and is the one existence in which all things are founded and made firm. Therefore, if and when he comes, as said above, all good things come along as well. In him all things are and are good; outside him nothing is and nothing is good. This is the meaning of what is said here, "All good things came to me together with her."

105. There is still a sixth way in which we can explain the passage "All good things came to me together with her." Note that according to the literal sense a person who loves something properly and formally thinks that he

possesses everything if he makes it perfectly his own, but on the contrary thinks that he has nothing good if he does not gain it. Second, note that someone who loves some one thing, such as justice, does not love anything else nor anything that is not just. He seeks therefore only to attain to justice in a perfect degree and to be transformed into it in its supreme point, in its source where, itself unbegotten, it is giving birth or bearing.[94] This fits the texts "Show us the Father and that is enough for us" (Jn. 14:8); and "Let him kiss me with the kiss of his mouth" (Sg. 1:1); and Isaiah 62 where the just man says, "For Sion's sake I will not hold my peace, and for the sake of Jerusalem I will not rest until her just one come forth as brightness" (Is. 62:1). But justice in its source, in its highest and full point, is "every virtue,"[95] and each and every perfection [is] a single perfection. In the supreme point all the things that below and in themselves are necessarily divided are one in the most perfect kind of unity.

106. Thus it is that along with any really perfect good "all good things together" come from the act of giving birth. Justice is begotten and born in the just person from the Unbegotten Justice, as the Son, the Father's brightness.[96] He says, "Until her just one come forth as brightness, . . . and the lamp be lighted" (Is. 62:1), that is, love, namely the Holy Spirit. This is why a person seeking only one real good, especially justice, at the same time and equally finds wisdom and other gifts which were not sought, considered, nor intended. This accords with Isaiah and Romans, "They found me who did not seek me" (Is. 65:1; Rm. 10:20), as I have fully explained in commenting on Romans 10.[97] Thus, in any single thing he finds everything and everything comes to him. [This happens], I say, in any single good whatever—in the One, where this and that good (justice, wisdom, and the like) are one. This is the One in which God dwells; the One in which and by which he unites us to himself. In this One God is found; there he teaches, and performs all things. Thus the Psalmist says, "How good it is and how pleasant for brothers to dwell in the One," and "for there the Lord has commanded a blessing and life evermore" (Ps. 132:1, 3), as I have explained more fully in my commentary.[98]

107. Literally speaking, in the realm of nature existence is always one and in the One.[99] Existence is God, or is immediately from him. God is united and is in all things under the covering of the One, and vice versa under the One's covering and property each thing grasps God. In that One God and the soul, indeed God and all things, come together. Other than the act of existence itself, there is nothing at all where being and existing, cause and effect, begetter and begotten can come together, find, see, and kiss each other, as it says in the beginning of the Song of Songs (Sg. 1:1). Existence

always stands in the One; multiplicity as such does not exist. This is why time, because it implies number, is not outside in things,[100] nor is God in time. (How would God, that is, existence, be in nonbeing, and the one God in number?) From the foregoing it is clear that "all good things together" come in the One, as it says here, and "He who offends against the One, is guilty of all" (Jm. 2:10).[101]

108. The passage that follows below, "I knew not that she was the mother of all" (Ws. 7:12), is explained in like manner. Someone seeking Justice neither intends, nor seeks, nor desires anything of Wisdom. He does not know that Justice in its perfection is Wisdom itself or Wisdom's mother. The person still seeking Justice and caught in an imperfect state of it says "I knew not" that Justice in its perfection is one with all good things until "she brought me into the wine cellar" (Sg. 2:4), "into her mother's house" (Sg. 3:4). An example from the sensible world would be a series of vases ingeniously connected so that it is impossible to fill one without filling all, and if one is filled all necessarily must be. Also, when a root is made fruitful the whole tree is fruitful, and when some substance is enriched everything that belongs to it enriched.

109. From all that has been said note for the present two things. First, the person who has God has all things. "We have all things in you, the One" (Tb. 10:5). "All things are yours" (1 Co. 3:22), and thus he is rich because all things are his. But he who does not have God is a pauper who has nothing: "I said that riches are nothing" (Ws. 7:8). "You say 'I am rich' . . . and you do not know that you are the wretched and miserable and poor and blind and naked one" (Rv. 3:17). Second, note that everyone who truly and properly loves God loves all things, and equally and on a par [loves] all things, and each thing like all, and all like himself, that is, as much as himself (this is what the word "like" means).[102] Again, [he loves] himself and each thing as much as God, as said in the second interpretation above. If he does not do that, he does not love God in all things nor all things in God, but something else in all things, and something else in and beyond God.

"Moral integrity not to be counted through her hands" (Ws. 7:11b).[103]

110. It is very significant that these two are joined: what cannot be counted and what is morally good. Everything that belongs to number by that very fact falls outside the idea of the moral good, and on the other hand everything that is morally good falls outside the concept of number and cannot be counted. This is why it says "Moral integrity not to be counted."

The reason and evidence in this context comes from three points. First, because every number falls from the One and hence from Goodness (these are convertible). Moral goodness is good in the proper and most perfect sense.[104] This is what Jerome says on the text, "Better a handful with rest than both hands filled with sorrow" (Qo. 4:6)—"A singular number is always taken in a good sense, a double one in an evil sense."[105] He means to say that the One bears a good sense, number an evil sense. According to one explanation this is what it says in Ecclesiastes 9: "He that shall have sinned against the One, will lose many goods" (Qo. 9:18); and James 2 says that he who offends "against the One, is guilty of all" (Jm. 2:10). (In both places the term "the One" is to be taken formally as a neuter substantive.) One who sins against and recedes from the One, which is convertible with the Good, falls from the Good, falls into multiplicity,[106] that is, into number, and consequently into evil. For just as the One is convertible with the Good and is good, so too multiplicity and all things fall into number and hence into evil and are convertible with evil. It is a rule of the *Topics* that "the opposed sentence in the opposed sense" is like the "proposed sentence in the proposed sense," [and so] good is in the One and evil in number.[107]

111. The second reason for the expression here, "Moral integrity not to be counted" is because number always comes from imperfection.[108] Among beings those things which are more imperfect and corruptible and cannot be conserved and prolonged in life are more frequent and numerous. The more perfect and incorruptible things stand in the One and are not numbered. This is why there is only a single angel in each nature and species.[109] It is useless to do through many and much what can be done through fewer and through the One.[110] "God and nature" possess and "work nothing in vain."[111] Thus we see in corporeal things that there is one sun, one moon, and so on. Therefore, the argument can be formed and summarized thus: Number and division is from imperfection. Moral goodness is always a perfect good. (Dionysius says, "The Good comes from the one total Cause."[112]) Therefore, the moral good is unnumbered or innumerable. And this is "Moral integrity not to be counted."

112. The third reason is closely allied with the second already given and it is this. Privation is the root of number and negation is the root of multiplicity.[113] The sign of this is that number, the "*nutus memeris*, that is, the sign of division,"[114] is properly in corporeal things, but multitude (not number) is found in created spiritual things in which there is no privation, but negation as a formal distinction.[115] But in God there is no number, nor multitude, nor negation, but pure affirmation and fullness of existence according to the text "I am who am" (Ex. 3:14).[116] Therefore, there is neither number

nor multitude in him, and the three Persons are not many, but one God— even if there were a thousand persons![117] "These three are one" (1 Jn. 5:7).

113. What has been said is proven from Job 25: "Is there any numbering of his soldiers?" (Jb. 25:3) This is like saying, "There is no numbering his soldiers, that is, his spirits." Apocalypse 7 says, "I saw a great crowd which no one could number" (Rv. 7:9). "A great crowd" is a multitude which still cannot be numbered because it does not fall under number. This is what Dionysius clearly says, "The multitude of angels exceeds the number of all corporeal things."[118] It exceeds the number in that it is without number and above number, and not, as many wrongly say, "exceeding the number of corporeal things" because it is greater in number (this is properly not to exceed number, but to be subject to it). In this sense there is a perfect explanation for the Psalm text "Who numbers the multitude of the stars" (Ps. 146:4). According to one interpretation, this is to say that the multitude in spirits later degenerates in the first corporeal bodies, that is, the stars, into number, just as light in the superior bodies degenerates into color and heat in the lower bodies. Therefore, in summary the argument says: Number proceeds from privation and "is caused by division [of a continuum]."[119] Moral goodness excludes privation; otherwise it would no longer be a moral good, which is the apex of goodness. "The Good is from one total Cause," as said above. Therefore, moral goodness is unnumbered. It is "Moral integrity that cannot be numbered."

114. There is still a fourth proof that goes like this. According to Cicero, the moral good is what attracts by its own power.[120] Everything that is of that nature is always one and single and so is outside number, or unnumbered and innumerable. The minor is proven in this way. Everything that belongs to me insofar as I am this man cannot pertain to someone who is not me or the one who I am. If anything belongs to someone who is not me, it no longer pertains to me insofar as I am this man. Hence, if I were [both] a man and this man by reason of the same thing, I would necessarily be one man and the only man.[121] This is why God, since he is "God and this God" by one and the same thing in that he is simple, can be shown to be one God, as Avicenna proves in his *Metaphysics* 1.8 and 8.5. Therefore, since the moral good attracts by its own power, that is, by its moral goodness, it must be one and not many insofar as it is morally good. Thus, as is said here, "Moral integrity not to be counted."

115. Again, fifthly, the same can be proven more from the properties [of moral goodness] in this way. Everything which attracts by number, size, or duration does not attract by its own power, but by the power of number

or multitude, or of size or of time. For example, a penny is of small value and does not attract or draw much. But if there were as many as a thousand thousands, and this a thousand times, then it would attract and draw many people greatly, not by its own power, but by the power of number. With gold too, the larger the amount, the more it attracts and draws, not by its own power, but by the power of size. The longer a house has lasted, the more it attracts and is loved by its owner; and the same goes for similar things. Things like this do not attract by their own power, but by the power of multitude, size, and time. Therefore, the moral good, because it attracts by its own power and not by another's, cannot be counted. If the case were otherwise, it would attract by another's power, that is, number's. Therefore, moral good is beyond number. This is the meaning of "Moral integrity not to be counted."

116. This is why in his eighty-ninth Letter Seneca says of the blessed life, "Its quality not its size places it in the highest state," and below, "Anyone who appreciates it by its number, measure or parts takes what is most precious away from it."[122] This is why God is said to be one in opposition to number, simple in opposition to size and parts, eternal in opposition to time, so that we may recognize that he is good and sweet by nature and property, not by number, or size, or parts, or time—only by himself!

117. According to what has been said there is a fine explanation of the Psalm verse "How great is the multitude of your sweetness, Lord, which you have hidden for them that fear you" (Ps. 30:20). That is like saying (according to one explanation fitting our point)[123] that the sweetness of divine Wisdom (he says, "of your sweetness"), drawn from you by your own power, covers over magnitude and multitude. When these have been hidden and excluded, not gazed upon, then Wisdom becomes sweet, delicious, and beloved in and through itself. This is why a meritorious or divine work which God instigates does not increase or decrease because of the number, size or duration of the exterior work.[124] If it were increased by any exterior thing, this would come about through the power of something else, not its own power. It would not be a moral good, because the morally good is what is drawn by its own power. Furthermore, nothing extrinsic or external, standing on the outside, changes the nature it stands outside of by increasing or decreasing. Such things are related only extrinsically, and consequently do not [really] affect one another.

118. You will find an example of this in the sacrament of the altar and its nature.[125] In the sacrament the dimensions of the bread, which existed there before, and the dimensions of Christ's body are related to each other extrinsically, and therefore are not measured against each other nor gov-

erned by the same laws. This is also found in nature. The substantial form and the properties accompanying it are from within; they follow the nature and its principle, which are the formal parts that are prior to the whole. The material accidents, because they follow the material parts which are posterior to the whole, stand on the outside. As posterior, they do not penetrate the subject's substance in a substantial way by an essential penetration. Therefore, they do not affect the subject in a substantial or essential way, but the subject's substantial form and material accidents are related extrinsically in the subject. Hence, fire's form and whole nature exists indifferently [and] whole in the whole [fire] or in the smallest or largest part of it; it does not grow or shrink or change due to the variation of material accidents.

119. This is what we are saying in this proposition: Virtue or moral integrity in like fashion is totally equal in one as in a thousand acts as far as number goes, and in the least act as well as the greatest as far as size goes. This is what Luke 16 says, "He who is faithful in a very little thing, is also faithful in something greater" (Lk. 16:10). Greater and less on the outside add nothing to and subtract nothing from fidelity. It only shows on the outside if the virtue is within, according to the text in Gregory: "Reproach inflicted brings out what a person is really like on the inside."[126] In his *Book of Resemblances* Anselm gives the familiar example of the copper coin gilded on the outside, which if it is thrown in the fire, is not made copper by the fire, but merely shown to be copper.[127] As a figure of this Exodus 16 says that "The children of Israel collected" the divine manna, "some more, some less. . . . Neither had he more that had gathered more, nor did he find less who had provided less" (Ex. 16:17–18).[128]

120. Directly related to what has been said is the Stoics' dictum that external goods add nothing to virtue for living well or happily.[129] I have given nine or ten reasons for this in the "Treatise on the Good" in the *Book of Propositions*.[130] Aulus Gellius treats this extensively in *Attic Nights* 20.1 in the disputation between the Stoics and Peripatetics, where he says "To relax the soul is to lose it."[131] There he also gives the example of a philosopher who was disturbed by a storm at sea.[132] On this, see Augustine on Genesis 30 in the *Questions on the Heptateuch*,[133] and more fully in the *City of God* shortly after the beginning of Book 9;[134] and also the *Gloss* on Genesis 15 on the verse, "A sleep fell upon Abram" (Gn. 15:12). (Augustine's text has "fear.") I have never seen this gloss corrected, perhaps because of its succinct brevity.

It is clear from everything that has been said that the good and the moral good do not consist in number, but in what is not numbered, as it says here "Moral integrity not to be counted." This is not contrary to what is said below in Chapter 11: "You have ordered all things in measure, and number and weight" (Ws. 11:21), as will become clear below.[135]

Selection 3. "And since it is one, it can do all things" (Ws. 7:27a).[136]

144. The wise man makes two statements about Wisdom: first, that it is one; second, a hint that because it is one it can do all things. As far as Wisdom being one is concerned, I have amply treated the matter [in commenting on] Deuteronomy 6 and Galatians 3, "God is one."[137] It should be noted in the case of this text that when God is said to be one by Moses speaking in God's name, this is not the only thing that God intended to teach Israel (that is, those who see God).[138] He intimated something deeper to us, beyond the fact that God is one and not many as the sun is one and not many, though this is also true.

We must understand that the term "one" is the same as indistinct,[139] for all distinct things are two or more, but all indistinct things are one.[140] Furthermore, there is an indistinction that concerns God's nature, both because he is infinite,[141] and also because he is not determined by the confines or limits of any genera or beings. But it is the nature of any created being to be determined and limited by the fact that it is created, as we read in Chapter 11, "You have ordered all things in measure, and number and weight" (Ws. 11:21). Therefore, saying that God is one is to say that God is indistinct from all things, which is the property of the highest and first existence and its overflowing goodness. For this reason later in the same eleventh chapter there follows, "You love all things which are" (Ws. 11:25).

145. A further, third argument. God is one which is indistinct. This signifies the highest divine perfection by which nothing exists or is able to exist without him or distinct from him. This is most clear if in place of the word "God" we use the word "existence." God is existence. It is clear that existence is indistinct from everything which exists and that nothing exists or can exist that is distinct and separated from existence.[142] John 1 says, "All things were made through him and without him nothing was made" (Jn. 1:3); and Augustine speaking to God says, "You were with me and I was not with you."[143] "You were with me," because indistinct from all things; "I was not with you," because I am distinct as something created. Therefore, here where the discussion concerns Wisdom which is "one," the fullness and purity of its own existence is shown, and also the goodness by which it loves all things, and thirdly its highest and primal perfection, as well as the imperfection of every created thing in that they are made from it and without it are nothing in themselves.

146. From these observations the common understanding according to the literal sense of the text "God is one" (Ga. 3:20) is well proven. This is the first way. It is impossible for there to be two infinite things. This is immediately evident to anyone who understands the terms, because the infinite is that outside of which there is nothing.[144] But God, as contained and limited by no genus or comprehended by no limits, is infinite, as said above. Therefore, he is one and unique. The second argument runs thus. It is impossible for there to be two or more indistinct things, for the indistinct and the One are the same, as was also said above. But God is indistinct and the Indistinct Itself. Therefore, it is impossible for there to be many gods.

Yet a third argument comes from the fact that God is Existence Itself (Ex. 3:14). Granted this, it follows that it is impossible for there to be two or more gods. Rather, if two gods are admitted, there will not be two gods: Either none or one of them will be God. Again, it would follow that there will be two acts of existence in any creature, and consequently any being will [actually] be two beings. The conclusion of all these premises will be clear enough to one who understands the terms. Nevertheless, the consequence has been demonstrated [in the explanation] of Galatians 3, "God is one" (Ga. 3:20).[145]

147. Again, the statement that Wisdom is one is proven from the nature of this term, that is, "one." Indeed, the first three proofs are derived from the nature of the term Wisdom or God. Therefore, it should be recognized now that the term "one" is a negative word but is in reality affirmative. Moreover, it is the negation of negation which is the purest form of affirmation and the fullness of the term affirmed.[146] Fullness, superabundance, and "what is said by way of superabundance belong to the One alone," as the Philosopher says.[147]

148. Still, the One descends totally into all things which are beneath it, which are many and which are enumerated. In these individual things the One is not divided, but remaining the incorrupt One,[148] it flows forth into every number and informs it with its own unity.[149] So, the One is necessarily found prior to any duality or plurality both in reality and understanding. Thus the term "one" adds nothing beyond existence, not even conceptually, but only according to negation. This is not so in the case of "true" and "good." For this reason it is most immediately related to existence in that it signifies the purity and core and height of existence itself, something which even the term "existence" does not do.[150] The term "one" signifies Existence Itself in itself along with the negation and exclusion of all nonbeing, which [nonbeing], I say, every negation entails. Every negation denies the existence of a thing whose very existence bespeaks privation. The

negation of negation (which the term "one" signifies) denotes that everything which belongs to the term is present in the signified and everything which is opposed to it is absent. This is necessarily the One. It is impossible for any being or nature to be multiplied unless something of its nature is either lacking to a second being or there is something added to the second being from another source, or both together, that is, there is both lack and addition.[151]

149. It is therefore evident from all the premises that unity or the One most properly belongs to God, even more than the terms "the True" and "the Good," and this is what is said here of Wisdom ("since it is one"), and in Galatians 3, "God is one" (Ga. 3:20). The sense is not only that God is one, but also that he is the only one or that he is alone. "God," he says, "is one," that is, he is the one God. Macrobius says this plainly in the first book of his *Commentary on the Dream of Scipio*, a good bit before the middle, in these words: "The One which is called the Monad, that is, unity, is not a number, but the source and origin of all number. The beginning and the end of all things, itself not knowing beginning nor end, it refers to the supreme God. You would seek it in vain in an inferior stage below God. Since it is one, it cannot be numbered itself; nevertheless, it creates innumerable kinds of genera from itself and contains them within itself."[152] Thus far the words of Macrobius, from which it is clear that God is one and is one Wisdom, as it says here, "since it is one, it can do all things."

150. From Macrobius's words, especially the last sentence, it is seen that the One, in that it is one, is formally distinguished from number as an opposed principle. This is the greatest distinction. Therefore Boethius in his *Trinity* says, "That is truly one in which there is no number,"[153] as if we were to say, "That is truly gold in which there is nothing foreign or opposed to gold."

151. The One itself also gives number existence, for number is a multitude composed of unities.[154] The One even conserves number and multitude in existence;[155] "Every multitude participates in the One," as Proclus says.[156] And this is what Macrobius states: "Unity cannot be numbered itself." Observe the opposition and distinction. There follows: "It creates innumerable kinds from itself and contains them within itself." Observe the indistinction.

152. From these two points I form two new arguments to prove from the nature of the One that God, Wisdom, is one. The first is this: "The One is that in which there is no number." But in God there is no number, as Macrobius says here.[157] The reason is that number is a falling away,[158] and falling away does not pertain to God, since he is the First and also since he

168

is existence. Therefore, God is one. This second [argument] is this. The One and the Many are opposed. But in God there is no number (as was said and proved above), because there is no falling away in him and because he is the First and is existence. Therefore, God is one.

153. What Augustine says in *True Religion*, Chapter 11, speaks to this: "All agree that what is preferred to everything else is God." Immediately prior to this he says, "All created things eagerly compete [in describing] the excellence of God."[159] From this it is evident that there is no falling away or retreat in him; consequently, there is neither number nor multitude. Therefore, God is one, for that is one in which there is no number. Again, [the same follows] because the One and the Many are opposed.

154. Accordingly, it should be noted that nothing is so distinct from number and the thing numbered or what is numerable (the created thing, that is) as God is. And yet nothing is so indistinct.

The first proof is because the indistinct is more distinguished from the distinct than any two distinct things are from each other.[160] For example, something not colored is further from a colored thing than two colored things are from each other. But indistinction belongs to God's nature; distinction to the created thing's nature and idea, as was said above.[161] Therefore, God is most distinct from each and every created thing.

Further, the second argument goes this way. Nothing is further from something than its opposite. But God and the creature are opposed as the One and Unnumbered is opposed to number, the numerated, and the numerable. Therefore, nothing is as distinct from any created being.

The third argument goes thus. Everything which is distinguished by indistinction is the more distinct the more indistinct it is, because it is distinguished by its own indistinction. Conversely, it is the more indistinct the more distinct it is, because it is distinguished by its own distinction from what is indistinct. Therefore, it will be the more indistinct insofar as it is distinct and vice versa, as was said.[162] But God is something indistinct which is distinguished by his indistinction, as Thomas says in Ia, q. 7, a. 1, at the end.[163] For God is a sea of infinite substance, and consequently indistinct, as Damascene says.[164]

155. On the other hand, it must be noted that nothing is so one and indistinct as God and every created being. There is a threefold reason for this, as proven before in the opposite sense.

First, because nothing is as indistinct as being and existence, potency and its act, form and matter. This is how God and every creature are related. Second, nothing is so much one and indistinct as a thing that is composed and that from which, through which, and in which it is composed and subsists. But, as said above, number or multitude, the numbered or the numerable as such, is composed and subsists from unities. Therefore, nothing is as indistinct as the one God or Unity and the numbered created thing. The third argument is this. Nothing is as indistinct from anything as from that from which it is indistinguished by its own distinction.[165] But everything that is numbered or created is indistinguished from God by its own distinction, as said above.[166] Therefore, nothing is so indistinct and consequently one, for the indistinct and the One are the same. Wherefore, God and any creature whatever are indistinct. The text of Romans 11 speaks to this: "From him, through him and in him are all things" (Rm. 11:36). Therefore, the first principle point is evident, namely that Wisdom is one, as it says here, "since it is one."

156. The second principle point follows, namely that because it is one "it can do all things." For it would not be able to do anything were it not one, much less do all things. It should be recognized that insofar as a thing is more simple and more unified, it is more powerful and more strong, able to do more things.[167] The reason is that every composite thing draws its power and strength from the other things composing it. Clearly, therefore, power and strength in a composite being are alien to it insofar as it is composite, but are proper to simple beings. This is what we want, because the simpler a thing is, the more powerful and strong it is, able to work in more things and upon more things. That with us the more composite beings are more perfect is not against our position, but in its favor. This happens not because they are more composite (for as such they are later and dependent), but because there are more simple things that compose them. A thing is more powerful, able to work more things, insofar as power descends upon it from many [simple] sources.

157. In summary, the argument may be briefly put in this way. The more a thing is one, the more powerful it is, as said. Therefore, what is simply one, and it alone, can do all things. The *Topics* say: "When more results in more, then what is simple results in simplicity."[168] But Wisdom is simply one, as it says here. Therefore, it can do all things. This is the meaning of "Since it is one, it can do all things."

Furthermore, the second argument—from the *Book of Causes*—runs thus, "Every unified power is more infinite,"[169] able to work more things and in more things. But the Wisdom which is God is especially one in that it is the First. Therefore, it is simply infinite and is able to do all things.

Further, the third argument runs this way. Form and act are always directed to one thing and exist in one thing. What is potential and material is in potency to many things, but in a passive and negative way. Each thing acts insofar as it is in act and is one.[170] Therefore, the more anything is one, the more it will be in act, as was said. Then the conclusion is as before. Divine Wisdom, "since it is one," has power and ability to act in that it is one and through the fact that it is one. Because it is simply and especially one, as being the First, it has the power to do all things. "It has the power," because it is one; "it has the power to do all things," because it is the First One. It also follows that nothing else can do all things.

Selection 4. "But to your saints there was a very great light" (Ws. 18:1). . . . For when quiet silence kept all things, and the night was in the midst of her course, your Almighty Word leapt down from heaven from your royal throne, as a fierce conquerer into the land of destruction" (Ws. 18:14–15).[171]

279. The literal sense says that the things spoken of here happened at an early hour after midnight when all things were at rest and in silence.

It can also be said that God's Wisdom, the Word, came into the world born according to the flesh in the middle of the night, following the text in Luke 2, "There were shepherds in the same district living in the fields and keeping watch over their flock by night" (Lk 2:8). And below, "A savior has been born to you today" (Lk. 2:11).

Again, thirdly, because no creature or offering or sacrifice was enough to sacrifice for sin (cf. Heb. 10:4–18), but all things were silent and rendered mute, at rest and asleep, then the Father sent the Son into the world, according to the Psalm text: "Sacrifice and oblation you did not want . . . and a holocaust for sin you did not ask for; then I said, 'Behold I come' " (Ps. 39:7–8), so that the Father's speech to the Son [might be heard].

280. Again, Wisdom comes into the mind when the soul rests from the turmoils of the passions and concern for worldly things, when all things are silent to it and it is silent to all.[172] This is what Augustine says in *Confessions* 4.9: "Be not foolish, my soul, and make not the ear of your heart deaf with the turmoil of your folly. Hear the Word itself; there is the place of imperturbable rest. . . . There fix your dwelling."[173] And in Book 9 he says: "What is like your Word, Our Lord, which remains unchanged in itself and yet renews all things?" There follows, "If to anyone the turmoil of the flesh be silenced, if the phantasies of the earth be silenced and the poles [of heaven], if the soul be silent to itself and by not thinking of itself transcend itself, if dreams and imaginary revelations are silent . . . he may speak alone through himself in order that we may hear his Word."[174] This is the meaning of "When quiet silence kept all things." And Aristotle says that the soul becomes prudent by sitting and being quiet.[175] Job 33 says, "In a night vision,

when deep sleep falls upon men and they sleep in their beds, then he opens the ears of men and by teaching gives them instruction" (Jb. 33:15–16). Each word must be weighed individually.

281. Further and fifthly, it is necessary that rest and "silence keep all things" so that God the Word can come into the mind through grace and that the Son can be born in the soul.[176] Thus all things must be silent, both in combination and separately. In combination, because the term "all" implies number or multitude. These are a fall from the One.[177] "God is one" (Ga. 3:20). Every number and multitude is silent and at rest in unity and the One. Therefore, it says in the Psalm, "I have asked for one thing from the Lord" (Ps. 26:4), that is, "the One" according to the Hebrew usage.[178] Again, "Behold how good it is and how pleasant for the brothers to dwell together in unity"; and below, "For there the Lord has commanded a blessing" (Ps. 132:1, 3).

282. Again, all things are silent separately when particular created distinct things are silent to the soul. Here note that there are four reasons why this is necessary for the soul which ought to receive God.

The first is that God himself is not particular,[179] but is above all things.[180] In *Metaphysics* 8.5 at the end Avicenna says, "It is clear that the First does not have a genus"; and below, "He is the highest and is glorious, . . . because everything that is, is from him, and what is from him has nothing in common with him. He is truly everything that is, and nevertheless is nothing of them all." Second, because each and every particular thing is created and God is uncreated. Third, because everything that loves the Indistinct and indistinction hates the distinct as well as distinction. But God is indistinct, and the soul loves to be indistinguished, that is, to be and to become one with God.[181] Every particular thing is distinct and denotes and reeks of distinction.

The fourth reason [is] that the soul is naturally borne to what is simply and absolutely good. No particular thing is simply and absolutely good, as Augustine says in the *Trinity*, Book 8.[182] This is the same as he says in Book 1 of the *Confessions* speaking to God: "You have made us for yourself, and our heart is restless until it rests in you."[183] An example of what has been said is that what is colored is the object of sight absolutely, simply, formally, and necessarily.[184] But any particular colored thing is only accidentally [the object of] the eye or sight.

283. There is still a sixth principal reason why it is necessary that "quiet silence keep all things" so that God the Son may be born in us by coming into our mind. The Son is the Father's image, and the soul is [created] according to God's image.[185] By its concept and property an image is

a formal production in silence of the efficient cause and the final cause which both properly look to the external creature and both signify "boiling over."[186] But the image insofar as it is a formal emanation properly smacks of "boiling."[187] This is what it says here, "When quiet silence kept all things"; and below, "Your Word," that is, your Son, the Word, O Lord, came.

284. You know that the church in the office expresses it in this way: "While the middle silence held all things."[188] According to this, you should know that at the Son's coming into the mind it is necessary that every medium be still. The nature of a medium shrinks from the [kind of] union that the soul desires with and in God.

The reason is, first, because existence of its nature is the First and the Last, the beginning and end, never the medium. Rather, it is the Medium Itself by whose sole mediation all things are, are present within, and are loved or sought. But God himself is Existence Itself. Again, second, we see the just man insofar as he is just loves Justice itself immediately, without a medium.[189] Indeed, Justice itself is the medium by means of which the just man's soul loves everything he loves, including himself. Hence, if anyone loves a medium or even beholds a medium, he does not love or see God. This is the reason why those who accept theophanies are in general rightfully condemned, and even those who believe that God is seen in some way by means of a likeness are condemned by the more subtle theologians.[190] Again, third, we see that every substantial form spurns a medium and without a medium affects everything it informs and to whom it gives its existence and operation.[191]

285. Still in the fourth place note that it is contrary to the concept of a medium that anything is silent or at rest in it, and therefore it is necessary that the very idea of a medium be removed, given up, be silent and at rest so that the soul can rest in God. This is what the church sings, "While the middle silence held all things," that is, while all things held the Medium Itself and every medium held silence, that is, was still. A medium as such is silence when you have stripped off the concept of medium, just as many things and all things are one in the One and in God. "We have all things in you, the One" (Tb. 10:5), and the Apostle says, "God will be one in all" (1 Co. 15:28).

Finally note that becoming and moving require a medium, but existing and possessing yield and are silent about any medium. The Psalm text agrees with this, "Silence is praise to you, God" (according to Rabbi Moses' text),[192] where we have, "A hymn is fitting for you, God" (Ps. 64:2). This is why Aristotle says in Book 2 of the *Soul* that if there were no medium we would see nothing.[193] In the same place Democritus [is cited] as saying that if there were no medium we could see an ant in the sky. This passage gives a sufficient hint about this when it says, "While quiet silence kept all things," and then, "held the middle course."

Selection 5. "They that eat me, shall yet hunger" (Si. 24:29).[194]

42. Note that hunger and thirst properly are the desire, appetite, and natural potency to act. For this reason every desire, appetite, and potency for something finite does not always hunger and thirst, but having gained the goal, they eat and drink and no longer hunger and thirst at all. Thus, when fire's form has been perfectly received, the heat that accompanies the form gains its goal.[195] John 16 says on this, "Ask, that your joy may be full" (Jn. 16:24). It is the opposite in things whose goal is infinite, for such things always hunger and thirst, and hunger more ardently and more avidly the more they eat. For example, prime matter is infinite in relation to all the infinite number of forms that can be generated. Therefore, even though it never exists without a form and thus always "eats," nevertheless, it always desires and hungers for one form after another because it does not find any form in which all forms exist. This is why Rabbi Moses in Book 3, Chapter 9, says that matter is described by Solomon in Proverbs 5 under the metaphor of an adulterous woman who has one husband but always wants another.[196] We also see that every part of the heavenly sphere, because it has a power and hence a thirst and desire in relation to each and every other position, for this reason is always both where it is and desiring and thirsting all other positions. This is the one true cause of the perpetual motion that is naturally in that body. On the contrary, light and heavy bodies, because they are related to one goal above or below, "eat" and are at rest when they have gained it; properly speaking, they no longer are thirsty. This is the reason why they are no longer moved; they do not seek, nor thirst, nor hunger any longer.

43. God, as infinite Truth and Goodness and infinite Existence, is the meat of everything that is, that is true and that is good. And he is hungered for. They feed on him, because they exist, are true, and are good; they hunger, because he is infinite. "All see him; each beholds from afar" (Jb. 36:25). "His going out is from the height of heaven . . . and there is no one that can hide himself from his heat" (Ps. 18:7). The Damascene in the beginning of his book says: "God has not left us in total ignorance of him, for knowledge of the being of God is naturally implanted in all things."[197] Thus God's Wisdom implies the infinity of his being, truth and goodness to us in these words when he says, "They that eat me, shall yet hunger." Thus, thirdly, we see

in every quantifiable thing that it is indeed quantified and divided or distinct, and nonetheless, because it is quantified, it always thirsts for [more] division, and always drinks and devours it. It always remains something divided.

44. Secondly, note that existence, both in nature and in art, is what everything thirsts and hungers for, seeks and desires. Art and nature labor to and for the end that an effect exist and possess existence. Without existence the whole universe is not worth a fly, nor the sun more than a piece of coal, nor wisdom more than ignorance.[198] This is what Avicenna says in *Metaphysics* 8.6: "What every being desires is existence and the perfection of existence insofar as it is existence. . . . Therefore, that which is truly desired is existence." No single being is existence, nor does any possess the root of existence. In *Confessions* 1 Augustine says, "Can anyone be his own maker? Or is there any vein by which existence courses into us from a source other than what you do, who are the Highest Existence?"[199] The reason is that everything that is common to many or to all is not able to have something from them that is the root or source of them all.[200] It would be the root and principle of itself, and would not be a principle above the things it is principle of, but would be on an equal level with them.

45. It is evident therefore that every being and everything that belongs to the number of beings does not possess the existence it thirsts for, hungers for, and desires from itself, but from some superior. Therefore, existence is not fixed and does not inhere or have its source in it, nor does it remain when the superior is absent, even if only conceptually. This is why it always thirsts for its superior's presence, and it is better and more proper [to say] that it continually receives existence than that it has existence itself in a fixed or even initial way. Thus every being, in that it is empty in and of itself,[201] thirsts for and desires existence, as matter does form "and the shameful the good."[202] This is the meaning of "They that eat me" (who am existence: "I am who am," and "Who is has sent me" [Ex. 3:14]), "shall yet hunger," in that they are empty in themselves and in potency to existence. This potency is a desire and thirst for Existence Itself.

46. A clear example and an argument for what has been said is [found in] light and heat in a medium.[203] Heat and the form of fire with which it goes take root in the medium (air) because of the agreement and identity of the matter on both sides. Thus, when air has been warmed, fire's form already has a root and is fixed, and something like fire begins. It is otherwise with light, because it is an active quality that accompanies the form of the sun or the sphere or heaven and has no material agreement with the elements. This is why the form of the sun and its consequent quality, that is,

light, do not take root nor commencement in any way in the medium. Thus, when the sun has gone down, heat remains rooted and everywhere begun in the air, but light leaves and departs from the air, because it has not the slightest root in the form it accompanies, but only a thirst or appetite.

Therefore, [being] receives existence through thirsting, and this is why it always hungers and thirsts, because through hunger it receives the existence by which it is and which it devours. It is different with everything else which does not thirst for Existence Itself and the Cause, but for a particular existence. In thirsting after and desiring this, it does not receive Existence, but particular existence. Through this such a thing is not a being, but a particular being. So it is significant that he says, "They that eat me," namely, me alone, Existence and the Cause of Existence, "shall yet hunger."

47. There is a third explanation for "They that eat me, shall yet hunger" through the fact that God is the beginning and end (cf. Rv. 1:8), the flower and fruit, as explained above.[204] Fourth, note that the Philosopher says that we are and we are nourished from the same things.[205] But we are through existence. Therefore, insofar as we are and are beings, we are fed and nourished by existence. Thus every being feeds on God in that he is existence; every being thirsts after Existence Itself, as said above. This is what is meant in the fourth sense by "They that eat me, shall yet hunger."

48. Fifthly, note that causes other than the First Cause, which is God, are not the cause of the existence of things or of a being, but rather the cause of becoming. This is why, when the effect has been finished and perfected, they no longer have influence on it. Therefore, the effects of such causes drink and eat their causes, but they do not thirst after them, nor seek and desire them. For example, a building drinks and feeds on the architectural form impressed on it by the builder, but once it has received it, it no longer seeks it nor thirsts after the art and the artificer. In nature we also see that animals feed and cherish their young with motherly care, and on the other side that the young thirst after their mothers and have recourse to them. But after they reach maturity, parents and offspring on each side no longer treat each other differently than other animals of the same species. The First Cause, which is God, does not have less influence on its effect by conserving it in existence than the influence it has or had in its becoming. On the other hand, the effect, even though complete, does not depend on the First Cause any less for its existence than it does for its becoming. This is why every effect eats and drinks the First Cause. Therefore, in the person of the First Cause we have the very fitting saying, "They that eat me, shall yet hunger."

49. Further, in the sixth place, you should know that every secondary

cause produces an effect from itself, but not in itself. This is why the effect drinks such a cause, but does not properly thirst after it. But the First Cause produces every effect from and in itself. The reason is that outside the First Cause there is nothing, for what is outside the First Cause, that is, God, is outside existence (God is existence). Because of both premises, namely, that everything created is from it and in it, and that it is from and in God himself, it is well said, "They that eat me, shall yet hunger." Bring each of the parts together. Augustine in *Confessions* 4.10 says: "God made all things. He did not make them and go away, but what is from him is in him."[206]

50. Again and seventh, know that the First Cause, God, differs from all things that are after him because the First Cause acts in all others and works in them.[207] Besides, its action is prior in nature to the actions of all secondary causes and it is consequently the Final Cause, for the ultimate goal always corresponds to the first action. Further, thirdly, the forms through which the secondary causes act have [their being] as forms and acts from God, who is the First Formal Act. Again, these forms by which the secondary causes act can be moved to act only by God as the Prime Mover, just as, for example, the forms of fire and heat cannot warm unless they are moved by the heavenly mover.[208] This is why effects drink the secondary agents, but properly speaking they thirst after the First Cause in them. Its power in comparison with a mediated agent is more immediate, more intimate; it is first and last in comparison with all. Hence all things thirst and hunger after it; they intend it and desire it. It is drunk by all because it is in them, but it is still thirsted after by all because it is outside them, in that it is not grasped by them. "The light shines in the darkness, but the darkness did not comprehend it" (Jn. 1:5). This is the meaning of "They that eat me, shall yet hunger."

51. Further, in the eighth place one should know that according to the Philosopher sense and intellect differ because from frequent and heavy use sense becomes weaker and less able to act, while intellect, on the other hand, the more often and the higher it understands, the more able to act it becomes.[209] Therefore, sight when exercised always eats and drinks the sensible object, but it does not always thirst for it because "too much of sensible objects harms the sense faculty."[210] The intelligible object is not so, but it strengthens the intellect the more sublime it is, and for this reason the intellect hungers and thirsts for it. This is what one of the twenty-four philosophers says, "God is the love the more it is had the more it pleases."[211] Augustine in the book of the *Sentences of Prosper* says that perfect charity always increases, becoming greater with use and richer through generosity.[212]

Therefore, "The First Intellect and the First Intelligible,"[213] God, under the appearance and form of Wisdom pertaining to the intellect, says, "They that eat me, shall yet hunger."

52. Again, note in the ninth place that these three are to be distinguished: "the univocal, the equivocal and the analogous. Equivocals are divided according to different things that are signified, univocals according to various differences of the [same] thing."[214] Analogous things are not distinguished according to things, nor through the differences of things, but "according to the modes [of being]" of one and the same simple thing. For example, the one and the same health that is in an animal is that (and no other) which is in the diet and the urine [of the animal] in such a way that there no more of health as health in the diet and urine than there is in a stone. Urine is said to be "healthy" only because it signifies the health, the same in number, which is in the animal, just as a circular wreath which has nothing of wine in it [signifies] wine.[215]

Being or existence and every perfection, especially general ones such as existence, oneness, truth, goodness, light, justice, and so forth, are used to describe God and creatures in an analogical way.[216] It follows from this that goodness and justice and the like [in creatures] have their goodness totally from something outside to which they are analogically ordered,[217] namely, God. This is what Augustine says about existence near the middle of the first book of the *Confessions*, that there is no "vein by which existence comes from a source other" than God who is the Supreme and "the Highest Existence,"[218] as was said above in the second explanation. In the third book of the *Confessions* the same Augustine says of justice that [it is] "everywhere and always [the same], not something else in another place, or otherwise upon another occasion; according to it, all the just are praised by the mouth of God."[219] He often says the same about light, life, and truth, as is clear from his comment on John 1, "The true light illuminated every man" (Jn. 1:9).[220]

53. The proof can be briefly summarized and formulated thus. Analogates have nothing of the form according to which they are analogically ordered rooted in positive fashion in themselves. But every created being is analogically ordered to God in existence, truth, and goodness. Therefore every created being radically and positively possesses existence, life, and wisdom from and in God, not in itself as a created being. And thus it always "eats" as something produced and created, but it always hungers because it is always from another and not from itself.

Note also that even until today there are some who are in error because they understand the nature of analogy poorly and reject it.[221] According to our understanding of the truth of analogy as declared in the first book of the *Book of Propositions*,[222] we say that the text "They that eat me, shall yet hunger" is perfectly fitted to signify the truth of the analogy of all things to God himself. They eat because they are; they hunger because they are from another.

54. Also in the tenth place note that the foregoing passage can be explained in this way. God is inside all things in that he is existence, and thus every being feeds on him. He is also on the outside because he is above all and thus outside all. Therefore, all things feed on him, because he is totally within; they hunger for him, because he is totally without. Thus, the whole soul is in the hand and outside the hand.[223] This is what is said, "They that eat me, shall yet hunger."

55. Again and eleventh, note that eating is never tasty without hunger and drinking without thirst. The more hunger and thirst decrease, the more in every way the taste and pleasure in eating and drinking do too. Near the beginning of the eighth book of the *Confessions* Augustine says, "There is no pleasure in eating and drinking unless the distress of hunger and thirst came first."[224] This is why drunks eat salted things to increase their thirst. "Wherever there is greater joy, greater distress came first."[225] In Book 5 of the *Tusculan Disputations* Cicero says: "Who doesn't see that all things are flavored by desires? When Caius Marius in flight drank dirty water stained with the blood of corpses he said that he had never tasted anything better because he had never been so thirsty when he drank."[226] Later, after many similar examples, he says that hunger and thirst "flavor banquets."[227] This is the way it is in corporeal things, but in divine and spiritual things it is the opposite. For now one reason is that the First Act universally and primarily separates [each thing] from its contrary or opposite, that is, its privation.[228] Therefore, the substantial form is more perfect than any other formal thing, and prime matter desires and hungers after it alone through its own material essence. This is because it is the form alone that separates it from nothing. This is a second reason why it receives such a form without a medium, without a sound, without time and motion, in an instant, and why one simple being comes to be from the matter itself and such a form.

56. When the body drinks, the first sip tastes the best—it is drunk more avidly and sweetly because in the first moment when it is drunk the beverage is the most distant from its harmful contrary, thirst. The next gulp is not as far removed from such total thirst, nor from simple thirst, but [is distant] from a smaller, less contrary and severe thirst, and so on down the line until thirst is quenched. What goes beyond that comes from evil; it is evil and disgusting. In spiritual and divine things it is different on both ends. First,

because every act first causes a separation from its bitter opposite. Here there is nothing prior and posterior; each and every act is first for this reason. Forward progress then is not to leave the First [i.e., God], but to draw near to it, so that the Last is the First. The reason is progress brings one nearer the End, and the End in the Godhead is the Beginning. "I am the beginning and the end" (Rv. 1:8, and 22:13). Therefore, an approach toward the end is always joined with its beginning if it is God and the pure divine that is eaten and drunk. But if it is anything else, however great or small, things are otherwise, according to the text in John 16, "A little bit, and you will no longer behold me" (Jn. 16:16).[229]

57. Thus in corporeal things eating ultimately brings on disgust, but in divine things as such eating causes hunger. The more and the purer the eating, the greater and purer the hunger. Eating and hunger proceed apace. Consequently and accidently, on the second point, every form of disgust is taken away and removed, following the text: "Her conversation has no bitterness" (Ws. 8:16), if "no defiled thing comes into her" (Ws. 7:25), that is, a nondivine thing. But if something other than God comes in or is introduced, it is different, for then already it is doubtless necessary that bitterness, labor, penalty, and disgust enter because God as such is not eaten. A work whose goal is something other than God does not have God as its beginning because the same God is end and beginning. A work that does not have God as its beginning is not a divine work. As a figure and example of this John 14 says, "The Father remaining in me, he does the works" (Jn. 14:10).

58. From what has gone before it is clear that "they that eat" God, "shall yet hunger." It is also clear that they still hunger not because they are not satiated (as is commonly said), but on the contrary they are not satiated because they hunger and because eating and hungering are the same. He who eats gets hungry by eating, because he consumes hunger; the more he eats, the more hungry he gets. There is no greater and less, prior and posterior in these things. This is the meaning of "They that eat me, shall yet hunger." By eating he gets hungry and by getting hungry he eats, and he hungers to get hungry for hunger.[230]

59. Nevertheless, Thomas explains it well in two other ways in the [*Summa of Theology*] Ia IIae, q. 33, a. 2. Bernard in his *Epistle on Charity* [discussing] "My soul has longed to desire" (Ps. 118:20) says: "Only the person who has longed to desire cannot be satiated by desire. Desire is the soul's hunger. The soul that truly loves God is not satiated by love. Because the God he loves is love, he loves love, and to love love is to make a circle so that there is no end to love." And later, "He comes aflame in desires. Even if

they were given in fullness, they can never be given to satiety."²³¹ This is what it says here, "They that eat me, shall yet hunger." Take the example of someone who is said to run for the sake of running. He always eats up the road as he runs; nonetheless he always hungers for it, because he runs for running and loves the road for itself. Thus, he loves what he loves for itself—love for love's sake. Augustine in the *Trinity* 9.1, and especially in 15.2, treats the Psalm verses, "Let the heart of them rejoice that seek the Lord," and "Seek his face forever" (Ps. 103:3–4), and there explains this passage, "They that eat me, shall yet hunger."

60. There is still one final point to make. Thirst and hunger, desire and appetite are taken in a double way: "In one way as meaning the appetite for something not possessed; in another way as meaning the exclusion of disgust."²³² Beware of thinking that the latter sense, that is, the exclusion of disgust, is the principle or first meaning. Many do this and thus crudely explain our text, "They that eat me, shall yet hunger," as though they eat without satiety.²³³ This seems to give too little to divine Wisdom, that is, to God, especially speaking of himself, teaching about himself, and recommending his excellence. Furthermore, nothing is truly taught by negation, and negation posits nothing, but is fixed and made firm in affirmation, having no perfection in itself.²³⁴ That is why negation has no place at all in God himself; he is "Who is" and "He is one," which is the negation of negation.²³⁵ Therefore, hunger as the exclusion of satiety is not to be accepted in divine matters.

61. Again, when hunger is taken as "the appetite for something not possessed," formally speaking, hunger or appetite is not defined on the basis of the thing that is not possessed. This is only a negation or privation and is something material. But the essence of hunger is formally an affirmative appetite, the root and cause for the exclusion of satiety which accompanies it. As such it belongs to something possessed and is a thing in some way positive. A clear and true example is privation, one of the three principles of natural things.

Therefore, it is better to interpret the aforementioned words as explained above. Each and every one of these explanations is based on some of the supreme attributes of the Godhead, such as infinity, simplicity, purity, priority, and so forth. They teach the weakness, or rather the nothingness, of creatures in themselves in relation to God.

Selection 6. "Lord, show us the Father, and it is enough for us" (Jn. 14:8).[236]

546. This passage can be interpreted in two ways: first, by taking the word "Father" for the One which is appropriated to the Father by the saints and teachers;[237] and second, by taking the word "Father" as it sounds and is.

First then, the case where the One is taken as appropriated to the Father can be explained in many ways, any one of which has a message and is a sufficient interpretation of the text "Show us the Father, and it is enough for us."

547. The first is thus. Unity is attributed to the Father. But every desire and its fulfillment is to be united to God, and every union exists by reason of unity and it alone, just as every whitening exists by reason of whiteness and it alone. Therefore, when he says "Show us the Father, and it is enough for us," he asks us to be united to God and for this to be enough.

Secondly, he says, "Show us the Father, and it is enough for us." Unity is appropriated to the Father and is more immediately related to existence than goodness or truth are,[238] according to the text in Wisdom 6: "Incorruption brings near to God" (Ws. 6:20). Corruption is always a departure from the One; therefore, on the opposite side, incorruption stands and subsists in the One. And the One is near God in that it adds nothing positive beyond existence even from viewpoint of reason. Existence is the first, the One is next, the True third, the Good last among the four things common to all.[239] Therefore, ["Show us the Father, and it enough for us"].

548. The third argument. Unity, as was said, is attributed to the Father. But our consummation and happiness consist in the One.[240] For this reason the Father, the Son, and the Holy Spirit beatify insofar as they are one. In the One there is no distinction at all.[241] Therefore, the relations of the Persons are not distinct in the essence or from the essence,[242] according to the figural passage in Genesis, "He saw three and adored one" (Gn. 18:2).[243] Hence Philip says, "Show us the Father," that is, unity and that the three are one, "and it is enough for us." This is what below in Chapter 17 the Son asks for those who will believe in him: "That they all may be one, as you, Father, in me, and I in you, and that they may be one in us" (Jn. 17:21).

549. Fourth. The One, as often said, is appropriated to the Father. Now you know that every creature below man has been made to God's likeness and is an idea of something in God. But man has been created to the image of God's entire substance, and thus not to what is similar, but to the One.[244] "God is one" (Dt. 6:4; Ga. 3:20), the ideas are many. What is similar

belongs to many things. Thus we have the text "The rivers return to the places from whence they flow" (Qo. 1:7), just as Boethius in the third book of the *Consolation* says, "All things rejoice in their return."[245] Every creature below man goes forth into existence according to the idea of similarity, and therefore seeks God again. It is enough for it to be similar to God. But man, because he has been made to the image of the one whole substance of God and has been brought forth into existence according to the idea of the One Whole, is not satisfied by a return to what is similar, but returns to the One from which he came forth. Thus alone is he satisfied.[246] This is what is said here: "Show us the Father," that is, the One, "and it is enough for us." Below, in Chapter 16 [it says], "I came forth from the Father . . . and I go to the Father" (Jn. 16:28); and the Psalm, "His going out is from one end of heaven, and his circuit even to the other end" (Ps. 18:7).

550. Fifth. The cause of every evil (if evil has a cause) is [either] that a thing is divided in itself—"Every kingdom divided against itself will be desolated" (Mt. 12:25; Lk. 11:17), and "Their heart is divided, now they will perish" (Ho. 10:2)—or, that [the thing] is not divided from other things, for that is not good gold which is mixed with silver or copper. The One excludes the whole cause of evil because in that it is one it is undivided in itself and divided from everything else.[247] Therefore, he well says, "Show us" the One, "and it is enough for us." Sixth, all things hope for the good, as the Philosopher [says] in the first book of the *Ethics*,[248] but the good consists in and is reduced to the One, as Boethius shows in the *Consolation*.[249]

551. Seventh. Potency and matter are [related] to many things, act and form to one.[250] Every capacity for change, privation, defect, and evil in things comes from matter, as Rabbi Moses says in Book 3, Chapter 9.[251] But good and perfection in things is from form. This is why it says here, "Show us" the One, "and it is enough for us."

Eighth, you should likewise know that all form and nature avoids and, as it were, detests matter. The reason is that evil comes from matter, as was said, and that matter is almost nothing according to Augustine,[252] or is nothing according to Plato,[253] and [also] that matter is potency or possibility. Potency and act, possibility and existence are opposed. Existence is desired by all things,[254] and hence matter, potency, and possibility, since they are nothing, are avoided and hated by all things and in all things. For example, what does someone love in health except "to be" healthy or "being-healthy?" What is hated in illness except "not being" healthy, or the privation, lack, and nothingness of some form of existence which is health or "to be" healthy?

552. According to what has been said, note that matter and multitude

(which is number) come from one root, flow from one stream of a single source, from which they have a single origin. They are in the world or the things of this world by accident. The things that are more perfect, higher, closer to God, can exist, subsist, and remain in themselves; other things, since they are remote from God, according to the scale of beings in the universe are not able to exist, nor subsist, nor be perpetuated in themselves because of their imperfection. As it says in Book 2 of the *Soul*,[255] this is why God has completed them and will perpetuate them in another way, namely, by being multiplied numerically through generation so that one comes from and after the other. Generation requires matter and matter requires extension. Touch, which the act of one generating presupposes, and division, which is a number, do not exist without quantity. Thus, inferior beings only receive an existence and self-subsistence that is shadowy, thin, and divided, just as in our sensible world a weak and ruined wall needs and requires something to support it because of its imperfection.

553. This is another reason why every being avoids, hates, and is, as it were, ashamed of matter. Every being is naturally ashamed of its defect and imperfection. Matter and number, [which] belong to the same species, as was said, reveal the imperfection of their forms and are medicines for these imperfections—[something] which the more perfect forms do not need, according to the text "The healthy do not need a doctor" (Mk. 2:17). A figure of this is Genesis 3 where it says that our first parents "were not ashamed" before sin, but after sin "sewed fig leaves and made themselves loincloths" (Gn. 3:7).

554. A sign and argument for what has been said is that the form of every composite thing surpasses and is distanced from matter; it has some operation that surpasses matter, as when a magnet attracts iron, and the like. The higher and more perfect the form, the more it is separate from and exceeds matter and the less it is immersed in it, up to the [level of] the human intellect. The same with the powers of the soul—the more perfect one is, the more it is separate and abstracts from matter. Even in the elements themselves, what has less of matter, such as fire, is higher, more noble and active; what has more of matter, such as earth, is low, ignoble, and is called the dregs of the elements. Therefore, he says, "Show us" the One, "and it is enough for us." The One is opposed to matter, in that it is many and evil, or nothing, as said above. Hence the author of the *Fountain of Life* in 2.9 and 10 and 3.4 denies that any bodies composed of matter have activity, but [says] they are only passive due to matter.[256] On this see Thomas in the [*Summa of Theology*] Ia, q. 115, a. 1.

555. Ninth. What is essentially rational in us is one, what is rational

by participation is two and has many senses. What is good in us is to exist according to reason, what is evil is to exist outside reason, as Dionysius says in the *Divine Names*,[257] following the text in Galatians, "The flesh lusts against the spirit" (Ga. 5:17). Therefore in saying "Show us" the One, he wishes the gift of being able to live according to reason.

Tenth. As Macrobius says, "The One which is called the Monad, that is, unity, is not a number, but is the source and origin of all number. The beginning and the end of all things, itself not knowing beginning nor end, it refers to the supreme God. . . . It creates innumerable kinds of genera from itself and contains them within itself. . . . When it pours itself into the immensity of the universe, it undergoes no separation from its unity." Thus far the words of Macrobius.[258] What is superior as such is always one, is always first, and is always rich for its every inferior.[259] It is not divided in the inferior, but unites it in itself. It influences it, but is not influenced by it, according to text above at the beginning, "The light shines in the darkness and the darkness did not comprehend it" (Jn. 1:5). Therefore, Philip fittingly says, "Lord, show us the Father," that is, the One, "and it is enough for us."

556. Eleventh. The One itself is the negation of negation—of the negation, I say, which every multitude that is opposed to the One includes.[260] The negation of negation is the core, the purity, and the repetition of the affirmation of existence. "I am who am" (Ex. 3:14). That is why it is fittingly said, "Show us the Father," that is, the One, "and it is enough for us." Negation always denies and removes some existence and thus does not please, but displeases; it is not satisfactory, but dissatisfactory and makes unsatisfactory what it exists in.[261]

Twelfth. Note first that just as all inequality is born from equality, as Boethius says at the end of the *Arithmetic*,[262] so too equality itself is born from unity. Hence the saints and the teachers appropriate equality to the Son, just as they do unity to the Father.[263] Each and every form of production cannot be understood without the mutual pleasure and love that is the bond of the producer and the thing produced and is of the same nature with them, as was shown above.[264] From this it follows that where equality proceeds from unity, the Son from the Father, by that very fact necessarily and immediately there is the Holy Spirit, the bond of the Father and Son.

557. Here note further in the third place that equality of its nature proceeds from unity in such a way that it remains in unity itself and unity in it, according to the passage that soon follows, "I am in the Father and the Father is in me" (Jn. 14:10–11). But inequality does not descend or proceed from unity in this way without the mediation of equality, according to the passage spoken in Chapter 1 about the Son, the Father's equal: "All things were

made through him, and without him nothing was made" (Jn. 1:3). Further, inequality does not proceed from equality in such a way that it remains in it formally and vice versa (the unequal is not the equal). Nevertheless, it remains in it by its power.[265] The case is different with equality and unity, for equality itself is a kind of unity, according to the text in Chapter 10, "The Father and I are one" (Jn. 10:30). This is why inequality and everything that smacks of it, like mutability, defectability, and the like, do not belong to the Son in the Godhead since he is equality proceeding immediately from unity; but they belong to all created things since they descend from unity by the mediation of equality and for that reason as unequal from what is equal. Therefore, Philip says, "Lord, show us the Father," that is, the One, "and it is enough for us."

558. The thirteenth point is from what has already been said. Equality rests only in unity, because there is no equality [anywhere else], just as the just man born of Justice, insofar as he is just, rests only in Justice itself, the just man's "father," because only there is he just.[266] This is what is said here, "Show us the Father, and it is enough for us." Accordingly, note in the fourteenth place that anyone who truly loves someone or something is not concerned or thinking of being loved by him in return, but only thinks totally of him. It is enough for the person to love the loved one totally. This is what is said here, "Show us the Father, and it is enough for us."

559. Further, the fifteenth point follows from what has been said. What descends from equality and unity draws near and falls into inequality and consequently into mutability and defectability and multitude. All these things do not belong to the One and Uncreated, with whom (that is, the One) Existence, the True, and the Good are convertible. Essentially, they belong to God alone in himself: he alone who is enough for the soul. Near the beginning of the first book of the *Confessions* Augustine speaking to God says: "You have made us for yourself, Lord, and our hearts are restless until they rest in you." And in Book 2, "I have flowed away from you, my God, and have become to myself a region of destitution." And in Book 13, "This alone I know, that woe is mine outside you, not only outside myself, but even in me. Every plenty which is not my God, is destitution to me."[267] This is what is said here: "Show us the Father, and it is enough for us." "Our sufficiency is from God" (2 Co. 3:5).

560. Sixteenth. Philip prays that the Father, that is, the One, be shown to us, so that in all our works we should simply have only one thing in mind, namely God. "His conversation is with the simple" (Pr. 3:32). Because the properties spoken of belong to the One, Philip prays, "Show us the Father," because unity is appropriated to the Father. Perhaps this why the Apostle

betroths and promises us to the One: "I have betrothed you to one spouse" (2 Co. 11:2).

561. Finally, I prefix two points for understanding the passage "Show us the Father, and it is enough for us." The first is how the four convertible terms common to all things (namely, being, one, true, good) relate to each other; the second is that there is a double enjoyment or reward of the blessed, the essential and the accidental.

562. As for the first, know that these four terms are the same and in relation to a supposit or subject are convertible in reality, but are distinguished from each other by their own idea or the property of each. The idea of being is something commonplace and indistinct and distinguished from other things by its very indistinction. This is the way God is distinguished by his indistinction from any other distinct things.[268] Therefore, the essence itself or existence in the Godhead is unbegotten and not begetting.[269] On the basis of its own property, the One itself points to distinction, for the One is indistinct in itself, distinct from other things, and therefore is personal and belongs to a supposit which is capable of acting.[270] This is why in the Godhead the saints attribute the One or unity to the first supposit or Person, the Father. It is clear from this that the One or unity after being is the first Principle of all emanation, adding nothing to being except the negation of negation. Therefore, it is and is called "the Principle without principle."[271] Hence, we have being or Existence, neither begotten nor begetting, and the One, not begotten but begetting, as Principle without principle.

The True from its property as a kind of equivalence of thing and intellect and the offspring begotten of the known and the knower[272] pertains to the Son, begotten indeed, but not begetting. Thus in the Godhead the saints rightly attribute equality to the Son. The Son himself is the Logos, or Idea, or Word: "In the beginning was the Word" (Jn. 1:1).[273] The Idea or Word by means of the principal activity of the Intellect is in charge of the whole universe,[274] and truth is in the soul according to the second book of the *Metaphysics*.[275] On the basis of its property the Good no longer looks within, but without, for the Good is not in the soul, but in external things, as it says in *Metaphysics*, Book 6.[276] As *Metaphysics* 4 says, the good is not in mathematical things.[277] Therefore, according to this, the Good itself is properly the principle and source of creatures—in that anything created is good, and vice versa. This is why Genesis 1 says of each thing insofar as it is created "God saw that it was good" (Gn. 1:10, etc.). In this sense the ancients were right in saying that the Good is not in God (much less in mathematicals),[278] but that he is called good inasmuch as he is the cause, the idea, and the principle of the good.[279]

563. Second, note that a double reward of the blessed is distinguished, the essential and the accidental.[280] The essential reward consists in the knowledge of divinity, the accidental in the knowledge of creatures, according to the text in Chapter 17, "This is eternal life, that they know you the one true God," on the first point, "and him whom you have sent, Jesus Christ," on the second (Jn. 17:3). The text in Matthew 6 can also be referred to this: "Seek first the kingdom of God," and then follows, "and all these things will be given to you besides," on the second point (Mt. 6:33). In Chapter 10 above it says, "Anyone who enters through me will be saved; he will go in and out and find pasture" (Jn. 10:9). "He will go in" in relation to knowledge and enjoyment of divinity; "he will go out" in relation to knowledge and enjoyment of creatures.

564. Two things are clear from the premises. The first is that being or Existence is unbegotten and neither begetting nor begotten; without a principle and not from anything. The One is without a principle, unbegotten, but begetting. The True is begotten and not begetting, having its principle from another. The Good is from another, having a principle, not begotten and not begetting, but creating [and] producing external created things in existence. Hence Augustine in Book 1 of *Christian Doctrine* says, "Because God is good, we exist."[281] The second point evident from what has been said is that the One is the primal source of the first emanation, namely of the Son and of the Holy Spirit from the Father by way of eternal procession.[282] The Good is the source of the second, as we may say, the temporal production of the creature. The reward or joy of the blessed is drawn from both sources—"You will draw waters in joy from the Savior's fountains" (Is. 12:3).

565. The sufficiency of beatitude comes from the first source, that is, from unity. "Our sufficiency is from God" (2 Co. 3:5); "But God is one" (Ga. 3:20). This is what is said here, "Show us the Father," that is, the One, "and it is enough for us." Speaking to God in the *Confessions* Augustine says: "Happy is he who knows you, even if he is ignorant of these things" (that is, created things); "yet whoever knows you and them is not happier because of them, but is happy because of you."[283] Again, in the first book of *On Order*, not far from the beginning, Augustine says, "The soul which proceeds into many things, follows after poverty and want with a hunger. . . . The more it turns toward the many, the more it suffers from want, because its nature makes it seek the One which multiplicity does not allow it to find." He gives the example of the circle and its center there.[284] This is what Ecclesiasticus 11 says, "Let not your acts be in many things" (Si. 11:10). Jerome

on this passage says, "Better a handful in peace than a full house with conflict."[285] Ecclesiastes 4 says, "A singular number is taken for good, a plural one for evil" (Qo. 4:6). This is the meaning of "Show us the Father," that is, the One, "and it is enough for us."

These points are enough in taking the word "Father" for what is appropriated to it, namely the One.

566. Taking the word "Father" properly, it can still be explained similarly in many ways. Therefore, note that Philip asks that the Father be shown to us for eighteen reasons.

First that God, insofar as he is Lord and God, is the Principle of the creature, as the Father is Principle of the Son. "I confess to you Father, Lord of heaven and earth" (Mt. 11:25). Second, that although the Son is equal to the Father in all things, and there is nothing greater or less there, still the idea of Paternity is greater than that of Filiation as that of a producer is greater than that of what is produced. [See] below in the same chapter, "The Father is greater than I" (Jn. 14:28).

567. Thirdly, he asks that the Father be shown to us so that nothing save God may be our father in order that we may be born from the one God only and not from many things.[286] "The only-begotten who is in the Father's bosom has revealed him" (Jn. 1:18). "Only-begotten" [means] "born from the One." "I have come to set a man against his father" (Mt. 10:35); and in Chapter 23, "Do not call anyone on earth father; one is your Father who is in heaven" (Mt. 23:9). Hence we have in Chapters 10 and 17 here, "This is eternal life, that they know you alone" (Jn. 10:28, 17:3).

The fourth reason is that according to the idea of existence and essence God is, as it were, resting and concealed, hidden in himself, neither begetting nor begotten, as said above. But according to the idea of Father or Paternity he first takes on and receives the property of fecundity, germination, and production.

568. Fifth. The intellect by its idea and property receives a thing in its principles according to the name "intellect."[287] "The Father is the Principle of the whole divinity," as Augustine says.[288] The intellect is only satisfied when it knows things in their principles. This is what is said figuratively in Ezechiel 17: "A large eagle . . . came to Lebanon and took away the marrow of the cedar and cropped off the tops of the foliage" (Ezk. 17:3 sq.).

Sixth. The Father is the "Principle without principle," the being that is not from another. This is the property of existence, namely, of the First, for "The First is rich of itself,"[289] having nothing from anything else. This is why Lucifer in trying to have from himself what he had or could have from another is said to have desired equality with God.[290] The Father in the Godhead is the being who is not from another (either in the masculine or neuter sense), and therefore when the Father is shown to us it is enough.

569. Seventh. The intellect and the will move toward the totality of all being. But the Father as Father gives all things. "All things have been given to me by my Father" (Mt. 11:27), and in Chapter 13 here: "Knowing that the Father had given all things into his hands" (Jn. 13:3). Indeed, what the Father gives the Son is something greater than all things. He gives him existence as Son, which is greater than all things—"What my Father has given me is greater than all" (Jn. 10:29). Hence Augustine says that it is greater than all things to be his Word, his only-begotten Son, the splendor of his light. And so in the same place there follows "The Father and I are one" (Jn. 10:30). This is what is said here, "Show us the Father, and it is enough for us." "He will set him over all his goods" (Mt. 24:47).

Eighth, as the poet says, waters are sweeter when drunk from the source.[291] The Father is the source and Principle of each and all emanation. The Psalm says, "Lord, with you is the fountain of life and in your light," which is the same as you, as explained above,[292] "we will see light" (Ps. 35:10). "My spirit is sweeter than honey and my inheritance above honey and the honeycomb" (Si. 24:27). Therefore, there follows "They that eat me, shall yet hunger" (Si. 24:29).[293]

570. Ninth. Being shown through creatures is not sufficient; therefore, he asks that [the Father] be shown to him in himself, in the Son. "Let him kiss me with the kiss of his mouth" (Sg. 1:1), and not with the kiss of the mouth of some creature. "In divers ways he spoke to the fathers, last of all in these days he has spoken to us in the Son" (Heb. 1:1–2). This is why when the Lord said to Moses, "I will show you everything good," Moses was not content and said, "Show me your face" (Ex. 33:19, 13).[294] This is the meaning of "Show us the Father, and it is enough for us." We have an example in natural things, where matter is not content with an alien act of form, but seeks the very substance of the form itself, just as sight seeks the very existence of the visible thing itself insofar as it is visible, as said above.[295]

Tenth. The Father is the Principle of generation, but what is unbegotten and begotten along with us remains with us as qualities capable of change, and we are praised because of them if they are good.[296] But what occurs accidentally, like the passions, does not remain; these things pass away in that they are passions. We are not praised for them, even if they are good. (No one is praised if his face gets red from anger.) Therefore, in saying "Show us the Father," he asks that our works do not proceed from passion, but from habit of virtue, according to the later text in the same chapter: "We will come to him and make our abode with him (Jn. 14:23), and that in Chapter 15: "He who remains in me and I in him will bear much fruit" (Jn. 15:5). On this point note that which comes from passion is not divine; God does everything without passion. Near the beginning of the *Confessions* Augustine says to God, "In loving you do not burn, in being sorry you do not grieve, in being angry you remain at peace."[297]

571. Eleventh. The Father is owed love, the Lord fear—love is related to the good, and fear to evil. Therefore, one who prays to be shown the Father prays that he may have the gift to work from the love of God, not from the fear of evil. "You have not received a spirit of bondage in fear, but the spirit of adoption of the children of God" (Rm. 8:15). Augustine [says]: "Better people are those whom love directs, the majority are those whom fear corrects."[298] Seneca [says]: "More people abstain from what is forbidden through shame of sinning than through good will"; and again, "A good horse is ruled by the shadow of the whip, and a bad one cannot be urged on even by spurs."[299] Therefore, the Father is shown when we do divine works through love as children, not through fear as slaves. Twelfth. The Father is shown when everything that is in us is totally concerned with God. The Father and the Son are the same in nature, kind, and understanding, as Aristotle says,[300] according to the text "You shall love the Lord, your God, with you whole heart, etc." (Dt. 6:5, etc.).

572. Thirteenth. Existence is the necessary goal of generation whose Principle is the Father.[301] Existence is properly a repose; it is above time, and consequently nothing grows old there, nothing passes away, nothing changes. Fourteenth. The nature or substance of a thing, and nothing foreign [to it], necessarily is communicated through generation whose Principle is the Father. But because the essence is the source and the cause of all the properties of a thing, it is what communicates everything. Therefore, the Father is shown when God is manifested through essence. "I will manifest myself to him" (Jn. 14:21), and with him all things. "All good things came to me together with her" (Ws. 7:11)—"together," "Father," and "birth" all have the same root.[302] "He has given us all things with him" (Rm. 8:32); "Nothing is covered that will not be revealed" (Mt. 10:26).

573. Fifteenth. The Father is shown to us when we are joint fathers of God,[303] fathers of the one Image, as we said above in relation to the knower and the known.[304] This is clear from the generation of an echo [treated] in the second book of the *Soul*,[305] and from things of this sort. What anyone meditates, thinks upon, and loves, becomes in him, and from him (and from

it and in it and out of it), a mental species, an image, a single offspring common to both.[306] Therefore, one who says "Show us the Father," prays that he may always think upon, meditate, and love God.

Sixteenth. The Father is the first Person in the Godhead, "And the First is rich in itself,"[307] supreme, best, and most pure as it is the Idea precontaining all things in itself. Therefore, it is enough for the soul, whose irascible part seeks what is supreme or difficult, whose desiring part seeks what is best, and whose rational part seeks what is most pure, namely the Idea of all things.[308]

574. Seventeenth. The principles of knowing and being are the same; things are related in [the realm of] truth the way they are in that of reality. From the fact that a thing is, a concept and true expression is spoken; from the fact that it is not, a false one.[309] Therefore, what is from another will be known by means of that other; but what is not from another will be properly known through itself, and whatever is from it will be known through it. In the Godhead the Son is from another, the Father is not from another. Therefore, he says, "Show us the Father, and it is enough for us."

Eighteenth. The Father is not shown insofar as he is Father except by [his] generating. No perfection is enough or pleasing or delightful for a person, nor does God himself perfectly delight a person, unless that person has become a child of God, as I noted on the passage "For Sion's sake I will not keep silence" (Is. 62:1).[310] In natural things we see in sensible fashion that what is passive is never satisfied or at rest as long as the begetting "father," that is, what is active, is bestowing and showing its form, the principle of generation, to the passive thing in the bestowal. Hence, alteration which disposes what is passive to the form of what is active is restless with motion and the murmur of resistance until fitting form which is the principle and "father" of generation takes over.[311] When it takes control, it has sufficiency and repose. This is also why the acts that precede a virtuous habit are difficult, but when the habit has been acquired, as the "father" of a virtuous act, it is sufficient and it makes the acts delightful. Aristotle says that the sign of a habit that has been born is delight in the work.[312] This is the meaning of what is asked for here, "Lord, show us the Father, and it is enough for us."

Altogether these eighteen explanations are enough to understand the text "Lord, show us the Father, and it is enough for us."

575. There are still moral meanings for "Show us the Father, and it is enough for us." 1 John 3 says: "We are God's children, but it has not yet appeared" (1 Jn. 3:5).[313] Genesis 37 writes, "The child does not appear" (Gn. 37:30). We can see an example when an image is sculpted from wood or stone

by changing nothing, but only by clearing away, cutting off and drawing out. When these things have been taken away by the artist's hand, the image appears and shines forth. So too what has been overlaid and scribbled upon us does not allow what we are to appear, nor let us conceive it. He says, "We are God's children," but it does not appear. "Whose are this image and inscription?" (Mt. 22:20).[314] Clearly, the image of God, the inscription of the flesh, the world, and the devil—"An enemy has sown tares" (Mt. 13:25). Therefore, we ask God that he who is a Father through generating may show himself a Father through regenerating and taking away the inscription that "the enemy has sown."

Again, it is proper to the Father to have mercy and to spare—"Father of mercies and of all consolation" (2 Co. 1:3). Therefore, we ask God that in work and effect he show that he is the "Father of mercies" by having mercy on us so that what we are by nature may appear "to the image," and [what we are] through grace "to the likeness" (Gn. 1:26). This is what John says: "When he appears, we will be like him"; he says, "God's children" through the image (1 Jn. 3:2). "Man passes in the image" (Ps. 38:7), even when sinning; "but it does not appear," because veiled with sin. "When he appears, . . . with his face revealed" (2 Co. 3:18), "we will be like him" with our image reformed through grace. The statement in Genesis 1 is significant, "Let us make man to our image and likeness" (Gn. 1:26). The image pertains to the nature in which "man passes," even when sinning; likeness [pertains] to the grace through which the image is reformed, as will appear.[315]

576. In the first book of the *Trinity* Augustine explains our text through the Psalm passage, " 'You shall fill me with joy with your countenance, at your right hand are delights' (Ps. 15:11). That joy requires nothing more because there is nothing more to be sought. The Father is shown to us, 'and it is enough for us.' "[316] These are Augustine's words, and they are briefly touched upon in Thomas's *Gloss*.[317]

From what has been said, note that if you want to know about your every effort whether it is good and worthy of eternal life, whether God the Father works in you, then see what the goal of your intention in the work is—the goal and the good are the same.[318] The goal is God. He is the Principle and the Goal. "The rivers return to the place from whence they flowed" (Qo. 1:7). The principle of operation does nothing beyond its kind. Therefore, if God is the goal of your intention, and nothing besides him, the work is divine, good, worthy of eternal life, worthy of God. Its reward is God alone: "I am your reward" (Gn. 15:1). The Father is the Principle of the work in you, and he will finish it. (Ambrose in Book 9 of his *Duties* alludes to what has been said—"Your motive gives the name to your deed."[319])

193

NOTES

1. Translated from the edition of Josef Koch in LW II, pp. 339–62. In this important treatment of the final cause of creation, Eckhart distinguishes two ways of understanding the verse: (1) nn. 19–34 treat the common understanding (i.e., God created all things that they might have real external existence); and (2) nn. 35–40 treat the goal of creation as the whole universe itself.
2. Cf. *Comm. Gen.* n. 19 (*Essential Eckhart*, p. 89).
3. On the difference between the First Cause and secondary causes, see *Comm. Ecc.* nn. 48–50 (pp. 176–77).
4. Cf. *Comm. Jn.* n. 53 (*Essential Eckhart*, p. 141).
5. This is Avicenna's definition from *Metaphysics* 6.2. Cf. the "General Prologue" to the *Book of Propositions* n. 16 (LW I, p. 160).
6. *Quod quid est;* cf. Sermon XXV.1, n. 251 (p. 216), where Eckhart appears to say the opposite. The solution may be found in the perspective used: here, an abstract, formal argument; and in the sermon a more existential and theological position. See the Glossary under *essentia*.
7. That is, they make use of formal causality.
8. Aristotle, *Met.* 3.2 (996a). Cf. Thomas Aquinas, *STh* Ia. 5. 3. ad 4.
9. Cf. *Comm. Ex.* n. 52 (p. 60).
10. Avicenna, *Metaphysics* 1.7.
11. Aristotle, *Interpretation* 2.10 (19b). On two- and three-term predication, see, e.g., "Prologue" to the *Work of Propositions* n. 3 (LW I, p. 167), and *Comm. Ex.* n. 15 (p. 45).
12. Eckhart is speaking of external inhering existence (*esse formale*), not virtual existence, as what follows makes clear. Cf. *Comm. Jn.* nn. 45, 66 (*Essential Eckhart*, pp. 137, 145–46). See *esse virtuale-esse formale* in the Glossary.
13. Cf. *Comm. Jn.* n. 6 (*Essential Eckhart*, p. 124), and *Comm. Ex.* n. 123 (p. 84).
14. Cf. *Comm. Jn.* n. 29 (*Essential Eckhart*, p. 131).
15. Cf. *Comm. Jn.* n. 12 (*Essential Eckhart*, p. 126).
16. Cf. *Comm. Jn.* n. 31 (*Essential Eckhart*, pp. 131–32), and *Comm. Ex.* n. 120 (p. 83).
17. Augustine, *Trin.* 6.10.11.
18. Peter Lombard, *Sentences* 3, d. 5, c. 1. Cf. Augustine, *Sermons on John* 20.3.
19. Eckhart is using the technical vocabulary of scholastic trinitarian theology where "passive spiration" is the notional act that expresses the relation of the Holy Spirit to the Father and the Son, and "active spiration" is the reverse.
20. Cf. *Comm. Ex.* n. 115 (p. 82).
21. *Book of Causes* prop. 4.
22. Cf. Sermon XXIX nn. 301, 304 (pp. 225, 226).
23. See the exegesis of these verses in *Comm. Jn.* nn. 61–69 (*Essential Eckhart*, pp. 144–47).

24. This is the common definition, see, e.g., Maimonides, *Guide* 2.14, and Thomas Aquinas, *STh* Ia. 45. 1.
25. Cf. *Comm. Ex.* n. 31 (p. 52).
26. Augustine, *True Religion* 18.35.
27. Maimonides, *Guide* 3.14.
28. Cf. *Comm. Ex.* n. 158 (p. 94).
29. Aristotle, *Nichomachean Ethics* 2.3 (1104b).
30. Cf. *Comm. Gen.* n. 5, and *Comm. Jn.* n. 56 (*Essential Eckhart*, pp. 84, 142).
31. Cf. *Comm. Ex.* n. 52 (p. 59).
32. That is, the process of change, or discarding dissimilarity, continues until perfect similarity of begetter and begotten is achieved with generation completed.
33. Cf. Sermon XLIX 3, n. 512 (p. 237).
34. Cf. *Comm. Ex.* nn. 140, 159 (pp. 89, 94), and *Comm. Jn.* n. 8 (*Essential Eckhart*, pp. 124–25).
35. See Gn. 29. In a note on this passage J. Koch points out that since all the children of Rachel, Lia, and their servants had equal rights of inheritance, the different fate of the sons of Sara and Hagar (see Gn. 21) would be a better figure and may actually have been what Eckhart had in mind (see LW II, p. 351).
36. Cf. *Comm. Ex.* n. 139 (pp. 88–89).
37. Cf. *Comm. Jn.* nn. 5, 16, 67 (*Essential Eckhart*, pp. 124, 127, 146, points out that this is the case in the generation of univocal things).
38. See the whole of Sermon XXIX (pp. 223–27).
39. Cf. *Comm. Jn.* n. 139 (LW III, p. 117).
40. A supposit is a concrete existing thing insofar as it is the subject of predication.
41. Thomas Aquinas, *STh* Ia. 45. 4.
42. Augustine, *Book of Eighty-Three Questions* 17.
43. Augustine, *Conf.* 1.6.10, a favorite text that Eckhart also cited in defense of his doctrine of creation at the Cologne proceedings (see *Essential Eckhart*, p. 76).
44. Cf. *Comm. Ex.* nn. 29, 40 (pp. 51, 55).
45. Cf. *Comm. Ex.* n. 257 (p. 122).
46. Augustine, *Commentary on the Epistle of John* 2.14.
47. See Eckhart's *Treatise on the Lord's Prayer* n. 18 (LW V, p. 128).
48. Avicenna, *Metaphysics* 9.4. Cf. *Comm. Gen.* n. 10 (*Essential Eckhart*, p. 86).
49. Thomas Aquinas, *On God's Power* 3. 16. ad 13.
50. Aquinas, *STh* Ia. 47. 3.
51. Cf. *Comm. Gen.* n. 12 (*Essential Eckhart*, p. 87).
52. Cf. *Comm. Ex.* nn. 72 sqq. (pp. 67 sqq.).
53. Augustine, *Conf.* 7.12.18.
54. Aristotle, *Met.* 7.8 (1033b).
55. Boethius, *Arithmetic* 1.32 (in modern editions).
56. Boethius, *Consolation of Philosophy* 3 prosa 12.
57. Cf. *Comm. Ex.* n. 91 (p. 74).
58. Cf. Sermon XXIX n. 302 (p. 225).

59. See below n. 144 (p. 166).
60. Cf. *Comm. Gen.* n. 26 (*Essential Eckhart*, p. 91), and *Comm. Ex.* n. 101 (p. 78).
61. See below n. 112 (pp. 162–63).
62. This part of the *Work of Propositions* has not survived, but it is often cited by Eckhart.
63. Proclus, *Elements of Theology* prop. 1.
64. Thomas Aquinas, *On God's Power* 9. 7. ad 15.
65. Seneca, *Letter* 66.12.
66. Boethius, *Consolation of Philosophy* 3, poem 9.
67. See the "Prologue" to the *Work of Propositions* nn. 14, 18 (LW I, pp. 174, 176–77).
68. This section is translated from LW II, pp. 429–57. It begins with a treatment of three meanings of the Latin word *pariter:* (a) "at the same time as" (*simul*), (b) "equally," as if it were derived from *paritas*, and (c) "through generation," as if it were related to *pario*, "I bear."
69. *Ordinary Gloss* on Ac. 2:2, citing Ambrose, *Exposition on Luke* 2.20.
70. Eckhart's point is that divine illumination touches all creatures, but is comprehended only by the spiritual person.
71. Aristotle, *Soul* 2.2 (414a).
72. This part of the work has not survived.
73. See n. 105 below (p. 160).
74. Cf., e.g., Augustine, *Morals of the Catholic Church* 15.25.
75. Augustine, *Trin.* 8.3.4. Cf. *Comm. Ex.* n. 17 (p. 46).
76. "A particular good," that is, *bonum hoc et illud* in the Latin. Compare this with Eckhart's notion of particular being (*esse hoc et hoc*) as contrasted with the *esse absolutum* of God in, e.g., *Comm. Jn.* n. 103 (*Essential Eckhart*, p. 161), Sermon VI. 1, n. 53 (pp. 212–13), and Sermon XXV. 2, n. 266 (p. 221).
77. This is another version of Eckhart's famous notion of "acting without a why" (MHG "âne war umbe"). See the Glossary.
78. Cf. *Comm. Ex.* n. 98 (p. 78).
79. See Sermon 9 (p. 257).
80. Augustine, *Immortality of the Soul* 4.6. Cf. *Comm. Ex.* n. 120 (p. 83).
81. Cf. *Comm. Wis.* n. 75 (LW II, p. 406).
82. See n. 109 below (p. 161).
83. Cf. *Comm. Ex.* nn. 140, 185 (pp. 89, 102).
84. Eckhart frequently used the example of the generation of fire both in the Latin and MHG works, e.g., *Comm. Jn.* nn. 127–31 (LW III, pp. 109–13), and *Bened.* 2 (*Essential Eckhart*, pp. 221–22).
85. Cf. *Comm. Ex.* n. 64 (p. 65).
86. ". . . but also the son" needs to be added to complete the point. Eckhart knew this sophistical maxim, which may come from Boethius of Dacia, from the logical teaching of the universities. See Koch's informative note in LW II, p. 437.
87. "Capacity to change" = *passio*. See the Glossary under *actio-passio*.

88. Aristotle, *Nichomachean Ethics* 2.4 (1105b). Cf. *Comm. Ex.* n. 189 (p. 103).
89. Aristotle, *Cat.* 8 (9b).
90. Cf. *Comm. Jn.* nn. 570–74 (LW III, pp. 497–503).
91. Cf. *Comm. Wis.* nn. 55–57 (LW II, pp. 382–85).
92. Cf. *Comm. Ex.* n. 181 (p. 100).
93. Aristotle, *Top.* 1.14 (105b).
94. Cf. *Par. Gen.* n. 147 (*Essential Eckhart*, pp. 113–14).
95. Thomas Aquinas, *STh* Ia IIae. 100. 12.
96. Cf. *Comm. Jn.* n. 19 (*Essential Eckhart*, p. 128).
97. This comment does not survive.
98. This does not survive.
99. See n. 37 (p. 154).
100. Aristotle, *Phys.* 4.11 and 14 (219b, 223a).
101. Cf. *Comm. Jn.* n. 114 (*Essential Eckhart*, p. 166).
102. Cf. *Comm. Ex.* n. 99 (p. 78).
103. In the following commentary on Ws. 7:11b ("Innumerabilis honestas per manus illius") I translate *honestas* as "moral integrity" and *honestum* as "moral goodness."
104. Thomas Aquinas, *STh* Ia. 5. 6. ad 3.
105. Jerome, *Commentary on Ecclesiastes* 4:6.
106. Cf. *Comm. Ex.* n. 101 (p. 78).
107. Aristotle, *Top.* 2.8 (114a).
108. Cf. *Comm. Ex.* n. 138 (p. 88).
109. Thomas Aquinas, *STh* Ia. 50. 4.
110. Aristotle, *Phys.* 8.6 (259a).
111. Aristotle, *Heaven and Earth* 1.4 (271a).
112. Pseudo-Dionysius, *Divine Names* 4.30.
113. Privation is the root of number because number is always an imperfection; negation is the root of multiplicity (*multum*) insofar as the basic negation of all is the distinction between *unum* and *non-unum*. See J. Koch's note on this passage in LW II, p. 448.
114. This etymology of the word "number" is found in Alexander of Hales, Albert the Great, and Thomas Aquinas (e.g., *In II Sent.* d. 26, q. 2, a. 6, obj. 1). Its source and meaning are unclear, since *memeris* is otherwise unknown.
115. Eckhart's reference here to "formal distinction" is not Scotist, but depends on Aquinas's ideas about formal and material distinction, e.g., *STh* Ia. 47. 2.
116. Cf. *Comm. Ex.* n. 77 (p. 69).
117. See n. 38 above (p. 154).
118. Pseudo-Dionysius, *Celestial Hierarchy* 14.
119. Thomas Aquinas, *STh* Ia. 30. 3.
120. Cicero, *Invention* 2.52.
121. Thomas Aquinas, *STh* Ia. 11. 3.

122. Actually *Letter* 85.22 of Seneca.
123. See Sermon VIII nn. 85–90 (LW IV, pp. 81–87).
124. Cf. *Comm. Ex.* n. 189 (p. 103), and *Bened.* 2 (*Essential Eckhart*, p. 226).
125. Cf. *Comm. Ex.* n. 92 (p. 75).
126. Gregory the Great, *Dialogues* 1.5.
127. Eadmer, *Anselm's Book of Resemblances* 95. Both texts are also cited in *Comm. Jn.* n. 76 (*Essential Eckhart*, p. 150).
128. Cf. *Comm. Ex.* n. 90 (p. 74).
129. Augustine, *City of God* 9.4.
130. This does not survive.
131. Aulus Gellius, *Attic Nights* 18.1 in modern editions.
132. Ibid. 19.1.
133. Augustine, *Questions on the Heptateuch* 1.30.
134. Augustine, *City of God* 9.4.
135. Cf. *Comm. Wis.* n. 219 (LW II, pp. 553–54).
136. This selection is translated from LW II, pp. 481–94. On this famous "dialectical" text, see the Introduction, p. 5.
137. Eckhart commented on these texts in Sermon XXIX, translated below on pp. 223–27.
138. Jerome, *Book of Hebrew Names* 76.8 provided this etymology.
139. That is, "not-to-be-distinguished," on which see Sermon XXIX n. 298 (p. 224).
140. Cf. *Comm. Ex.* n. 102 (p. 79).
141. Cf. *Comm. Ex.* n. 61 (p. 64).
142. Cf. *Comm. Ex.* n. 106 (p. 80).
143. Augustine, *Conf.* 10.27.38.
144. Cf. *Comm. Ex.* n. 156 (p. 93).
145. Apparently a reference to Sermon XXIX n. 303 (pp. 225–26). Cf. *Comm. Ex.* nn. 101–03 (pp. 78–79).
146. On the negation of negation, see the Glossary, and such texts as *Comm. Ex.* n. 74 (p. 68), *Comm. Ecc.* n. 60 (p. 181), and Sermon 21 (p. 281).
147. Aristotle, *Top.* 5.5 (134b).
148. Cf. Sermon XXIX n. 299 (p. 224).
149. Boethius, *Arithmetic* 1.3. Cf. *Par. Gen.* n. 20 (*Essential Eckhart*, pp. 100–01).
150. Compare this discussion of the relation of the transcendental terms with those found in *Comm. Jn.* nn. 512–13 and 562 (LW III, pp. 443–45, and below p. 187); and Prologue to the *Book of Propositions* nn. 4–25 (LW I, pp. 167–82).
151. The meaning of this convoluted sentence is that there can be only one "One."
152. Macrobius, *Commentary on the Dream of Scipio* 1.6.7.
153. Boethius, *Trinity* 2.
154. Boethius, *Arithmetic* 1.3.

155. Cf. Sermon XXIX n. 297 (p. 224).
156. Proclus, *Elements of Theology* prop. 1.
157. See note 152.
158. Cf. *Comm. Ex.* n. 141 (p. 89).
159. Actually this text is from Augustine, *Christ. Doct.* 1.7.7.
160. Cf. *Comm. Ex.* n. 113 (p. 81).
161. See n. 144 above (p. 166).
162. To facilitate understanding this difficult dialectical text, one can substitute "transcendent" for "distinct" and "immanent" for "indistinct." For an application to the Trinity, see Sermon 10 (p. 265).
163. Thomas Aquinas, *STh* Ia. 7. 1. ad 3.
164. John Damascene, *Orthodox Faith* 1.9. Also cited in *Comm. Ex.* n. 24 (p. 49).
165. Eckhart uses "indistinguish" as a verb (*indistinguor*) only here and in *Comm. Wis.* n. 282 below (p. 172).
166. See n. 145 (p. 166).
167. *Book of Causes* prop. 17(16).
168. Aristotle, *Top.* 2.11 and 5.8 (115b, 137b).
169. *Book of Causes* prop. 17(16).
170. Aristotle, *Phys.* 3.16 (202a).
171. Translated from LW II, pp. 611–19.
172. Augustine, *Conf.* 9.10.25.
173. Ibid. Actually 4.11.16.
174. Ibid. 9.10.24.
175. Aristotle, *Phys.* 7.3 (247b).
176. The birth of the Son or Word in the soul appears very frequently in the MHG sermons (see *Essential Eckhart*, pp. 50–54), and rarely in the Latin sermons (e.g., Sermon VI. 2, n. 57 [p. 214]). See the Glossary under *geburt, gebern*.
177. See above n. 152 (p. 168).
178. Eckhart's point here is that the feminine accusative (*unam*) of the Psalm text in Hebrew is actually the equivalent of the neuter accusative (*unum*).
179. "Particular," literally "this or that" (*hoc aut hoc*).
180. Cf. *Comm. Ex.* n. 57 (p. 63).
181. Cf. n. 154 above (p. 169), *Comm. Ex.* n. 113 (p. 81), and *Comm. Jn.* n. 99 (*Essential Eckhart*, p. 160).
182. Augustine, *Trin.* 8.3.4.
183. Augustine, *Conf.* 1.1.1.
184. Aristotle, *Soul* 2.7 (418a).
185. Cf. *Comm. Jn.* n. 123 (*Essential Eckhart*, p. 170).
186. Cf. Sermons XXV. 1, n. 258 (p. 218), and XLIX. 3, n. 511 (p. 236).
187. For more on *bullitio* and *ebullitio*, see *Comm. Ex.* n. 16 (p. 46), as well as the Glossary.
188. This is the reading in the Vespers and Lauds antiphons for the Sunday within the Octave of Christmas.

189. On the just man and Justice, see the Glossary, especially *Comm. Jn.* nn. 14–26 (*Essential Eckhart*, pp. 126–30), as well as n. 105 above (p. 160).
190. The question whether God could truly be seen in this life by certain physical apparitions, as recorded in the Old Testament (e.g., Gn. 12:7, Ex. 3:2), was much debated in the schools in Eckhart's time. Meister Eckhart agrees with Thomas Aquinas (e.g., *STh* Ia. 12. 2) that no perfect vision of God (apart from a few miraculous exceptions) was possible in this life. Cf. *Comm. Ex.* n. 111 (p. 81).
191. Cf. *Comm. Ex.* n. 139 (p. 88).
192. Maimonides, *Guide* 1.59.
193. Aristotle, *Soul* 2.7 (419a). See Sermon 69 (p. 312).
194. Translated from the edition of J. Koch in LW II, pp. 270–90. This passage forms a part of the second lecture of the *Sermons and Lectures on Ecclesiasticus*.
195. Cf. *Comm. Ex.* n. 140 (p. 89), and *Comm. Jn.* n. 129 (*Essential Eckhart*, p. 172).
196. Maimonides, *Guide* 3.8 in modern editions.
197. John of Damascus, *Orthodox Faith* 1.1.
198. Cf. *Comm. Ex.* n. 158 (p. 94).
199. Augustine, *Conf.* 1.6.10.
200. Cf. Sermon 9 (p. 257).
201. Cf. *Comm. Ex.* n. 262 (p. 124), and *Comm. Jn.* nn. 63, 103 (*Essential Eckhart*, pp. 144–45, 161–62).
202. Aristotle, *Phys.* 1.9 (192a).
203. Cf. *Comm. Ex.* n. 140 (p. 89), and *Comm. Jn.* n. 18 (*Essential Eckhart*, pp. 127–28).
204. Cf. *Comm. Ecc.* n. 18 (LW II, p. 247).
205. Aristotle, *Generation and Corruption* 2.8 (335a).
206. Augustine, *Conf.* 4.12.18.
207. Thomas Aquinas, *STh* Ia. 103. 5, 105.5, and 116. 2.
208. This Aristotelian doctrine was also held by Thomas Aquinas, e.g., *STh* Ia. 115. 3.
209. Aristotle, *Soul* 3.4 (429a).
210. Ibid. 2.12 (424a).
211. *Book of the Twenty-Four Philosophers* prop. 8.
212. Actually Prosper of Aquitaine, *Sentences from Augustine* 95.
213. Thomas Aquinas, *SCG* 1.62.
214. Thomas Aquinas, *In I Sent.* d. 22, q. un., a. 3, ad 2. Cf. *Comm. Ex.* n. 54 (p. 61), and the Introduction, pp. 26–27.
215. A circular wreath is still used as a sign of wine in some German inns. This noted passage on Eckhart's concept of "extrinsic analogy," or the analogy of formal opposition, is discussed above (p. 26), and also in *Essential Eckhart*, pp. 32–33. Cf. *Par. Quest.* 1, n. 11 (LW V, pp. 46–47).
216. Cf. *Comm. Gen.* n. 128 (LW I, pp. 282–83), and *Bened.* 1 (*Essential Eckhart*, pp. 209–10).

217. "Analogically ordered" = *analogantur*.
218. Augustine, *Conf.* 1.6.10.
219. Ibid. 3.7.13.
220. Augustine, *Sermons on John* 2.6.
221. Eckhart's unusual teaching on analogy must have aroused opposition, and indeed was taken up in the Cologne proceedings (see *Essential Eckhart*, p. 73).
222. The surviving Prologue to the *Book of Propositions* does not deal explicitly with analogy, but its teaching on predication and the transcendental terms is an important resource for Eckhart's thought on this issue, see nn. 1–25 in LW I, pp. 166–82.
223. Cf. *Comm. Ex.* n. 163 (p. 95).
224. Augustine, *Conf.* 8.3.7.
225. Ibid. 8.3.8.
226. Cicero, *Tusculan Disputations* 34.97 tells the story of Darius, not Marius.
227. Ibid. 34.98.
228. Cf. *Comm. Ex.* n. 134 (p. 87).
229. Cf. *Comm. Jn.* n. 51 (*Essential Eckhart*, p. 139). See Sermons 69 and 70 (pp. 311–20).
230. This sentence is a tour de force of Eckhart's delight in wordplay: "Edendo enim esurit et esuriendo edit et esurire sive esuriem esurit" (LW II, p. 287).
231. *Letter on Charity* 2.9. This pseudo-Bernardine work is based on Richard of St. Victor's *Grades of Charity*.
232. Thomas Aquinas, *STh* Ia IIae. 33. 2.
233. Eckhart seems to include Thomas in this attack.
234. Cf. *Comm. Ex.* nn. 178–79 and 181 (pp. 99–100).
235. Cf. *Comm. Ex.* n. 74 (p. 68), and *Comm. Wis.* n. 148 (pp. 167–68).
236. Translated from the edition of Karl Christ, Bruno Decker, and Josef Koch in LW III, pp. 477–506.
237. E.g., Augustine, *Christ. Doct.* 1.5.5; Thomas Aquinas, *STh* Ia. 39. 8.
238. Cf. Prologue to the *Work of Propositions* n. 15 (LW I, p. 175).
239. On the relation of the transcendental terms in predications about God, see Introduction, pp. 25–26.
240. Cf. Sermon VI. 1, n. 52 (p. 212).
241. Cf. *Comm. Wis.* n. 144 (p. 166).
242. Cf. *Comm. Ex.* n. 57 (p. 62).
243. This text had been interpreted in a trinitarian sense by many of the Fathers.
244. See Sermon 24 (p. 284).
245. Boethius, *Consolation of Philosophy* 3, poem 2.
246. Cf. Sermon 10 (pp. 265).
247. See *Comm. Wis.* nn. 144–45 (p. 166). Cf. Thomas Aquinas, *STh* Ia. 11. 1.
248. Aristotle, *Nicomachean Ethics* 1.1 (1094a).
249. Boethius, *Consolation of Philosophy* 3, prose 11. Cf. *Comm. Wis.* n. 37 (p. 154).

250. Cf. *Comm. Wis.* n. 157 (p. 170).
251. Actually Maimonides, *Guide* 3.8.
252. Augustine, *Conf.* 12.7.7.
253. Cf. Aristotle, *Phys.* 1.9 (192a).
254. Cf. *Comm. Ecc.* n. 44 (p. 175).
255. Aristotle, *Soul* 2.4 (415b).
256. Ibn Gabirol, *Fountain of Life* 2.9, 10; 3.4.
257. Pseudo-Dionysius, *Divine Names* 4.32.
258. Macrobius, *Commentary on the Dream of Scipio* 1.6.7. Cf. *Comm. Wis.* n. 149 (p. 168).
259. *Book of Causes* prop. 21(20).
260. See the Glossary for other texts on the negation of negation.
261. This is an attempt to render Eckhart's wordplay: "non sufficit, sed deficit et inficit id in quo est."
262. Boethius, *Arithmetic* 2.1. Cf. *Comm. Wis.* n. 37 (p. 154).
263. E.g., Augustine, *Christ. Doct.* 1.5; Thomas Aquinas, *STh* Ia. 39. 8. Trinitarian analogies based on the Father as unity, the Son as equality, and the Holy Spirit as the bond or connection between them were popular in some schools of twelfth-century Platonism.
264. Cf. *Comm. Jn.* nn. 162, 437–38, 513 (LW III, pp. 132–34, 375, 444).
265. That is, virtually. On the virtual existence of all things in God, see *Essential Eckhart*, pp. 40–41, and *esse virtuale-esse formale* in the Glossary.
266. See especially *Comm. Jn.* nn. 14–22 (*Essential Eckhart*, pp. 126–29). See Glossary under *iustitia*.
267. Augustine, *Conf.* 1.1.1, 2.10.18, 13.8.9.
268. Cf. *Comm. Ex.* n. 114, *Comm. Wis.* nn. 144, 154 (pp. 81–82, 162, 169), as well as *Comm. Jn.* n. 99 (*Essential Eckhart*, p. 160).
269. This is Eckhart's hidden Godhead, the ground but not the subject of the act of generating that pertains to the Father.
270. In this passage Eckhart gives priority to *esse* over *unum* in the Godhead; in other places, such as *Comm. Jn.* n. 360 (LW III, pp. 305–06) and Selection 3 above, priority is given to *unum*. On these two patterns in Eckhart's trinitarian thought, see *Essential Eckhart*, p. 35; and B. McGinn, "The God beyond God," pp. 11–14.
271. See Augustine, *Against Maximinus* 2.17.4; Peter Lombard, *Sentences* I, d. 29, c. 1. Cf. *Comm. Jn.* n. 19 (*Essential Eckhart*, p. 128).
272. See Avicenna, *Metaphysics* 1.9; Thomas Aquinas, *STh* Ia. 16. 1, etc.
273. Cf. *Comm. Gen.* n. 3, *Comm. Jn.* n. 4 (*Essential Eckhart*, pp. 83, 123).
274. The phrase "by means of the principial activity of the Intellect" translates the Latin *principiante intellectu* (LW III, p. 490).
275. Actually, Aristotle, *Met.* 6.4 (1027b).
276. Ibid.
277. Actually, Aristotle, *Met.* 3.2 (996a).

278. Ibid.
279. On this, see Introduction, pp. 25–26.
280. See Thomas Aquinas, *STh* Ia. 95. 4.
281. Augustine, *Christ. Doct.* 1.32.35.
282. This is the equivalent of what is called *bullitio* in other contexts, e.g., *Comm. Ex.* n. 16, Sermons XXV. 1, n. 258, and XLIX. 3, n. 511 (pp. 46, 218, 236). Cf. *Comm. Gen.* n. 7 (*Essential Eckhart*, p. 84). The stress on the Father as the one source of the trinitarian emanations brings Eckhart close to traditional Orthodox formulations.
283. Augustine, *Conf.* 5.4.7.
284. Augustine, *On Order* 1.2.3.
285. Jerome, *Commentary on Ecclesiasticus* 11.10.
286. Cf. *Comm. Jn.* n. 109 (*Essential Eckhart*, p. 164).
287. That is *intus legere*, to read within. Cf. *Comm. Jn.* n. 9 (*Essential Eckhart*, p. 125).
288. Augustine, *Trin.* 4.20.29.
289. *Book of Causes* prop. 21(20).
290. Thomas Aquinas, *STh* Ia. 63. 3.
291. Ovid, *Letters from Pontus* 3.15.18.
292. Cf. *Comm. Jn.* n. 506 (LW III, p. 437).
293. See the comment on this verse in Selection 5 (pp. 174–81).
294. Cf. *Comm. Ex.* nn. 271–81 (pp. 126–29).
295. Cf. *Comm. Jn.* n. 505 (LW III, p. 435).
296. Cf. *Comm. Wis.* n. 101 (p. 158). Eckhart is referring to the natural powers of the soul, either innate and hence unbegotten (*ingenita*), or capable of change and development (*congenita*), like the ability to acquire virtues.
297. Augustine, *Conf.* 1.4.4.
298. Augustine, *Letter* 185.6.21.
299. Seneca, *Letter* 83.19. The second quotation is from Quintus Rufus Curtius, *History of Alexander* 7.4.18.
300. Aristotle, *Met.* 7.8 (1033b). Cf. *Comm. Ex.* n. 64 (pp. 64–65).
301. Cf. *Comm. Jn.* n. 8 (*Essential Eckhart*, pp. 124–25).
302. The Latin wordplay here (*pariter, pater, partus*) cannot be brought out in English. See the interpretation of this text in Selection 2 (pp. 155–61).
303. Cf. Sermon 14 (p. 273).
304. Cf. *Comm. Jn.* n. 505 (LW III, pp. 435–36).
305. Aristotle, *Soul* 2.8 (419b).
306. Cf. *Comm. Jn.* n. 109 (*Essential Eckhart*, pp. 163–64).
307. *Book of Causes* prop. 21(20).
308. On the three parts of the soul, see *Comm. Jn.* n. 111 (*Essential Eckhart*, pp. 164–65).
309. Three basic principles of scholastic thought drawn from Aristotle.
310. This may be a reference to *Comm. Wis.* n. 105 (p. 160).
311. Cf. *Comm. Wis.* n. 27 (p. 150).

312. Aristotle, *Nicomachean Ethics* 2.2 (1104b).
313. Cf. *Comm. Ex.* n. 107 (p. 80).
314. Cf. Sermon XLIX on this text (pp. 234–38).
315. Cf. *Comm. Jn.* n. 109 (pp. 163–64).
316. Augustine, *Trin.* 1.8.17.
317. Thomas Aquinas, *Commentary on John*, Lecture 17, 607b.
318. Cf. *Comm. Wis.* n. 20 (p. 148).
319. Ambrose, *Duties* 1.30.147. Cf. *Comm. Ex.* n. 189 (p. 103).

Part Two

Meister Eckhart the Preacher

Latin Sermons

translated by
Bernard McGinn

German Sermons

translated by
Frank Tobin

I. LATIN SERMONS

Sermon IV. The Feast of the Holy Trinity. On the Epistle according to the Roman Missal (Rm. 11:33–36).[1]

1. "All things are from him, and through him and in him" (Rm. 11:36).

20. Note that when it says "all things are through him," the sense of "through him" is that he is in all things.[2] Everything through which anything exists is certainly in him in a general way. For example, the whiteness through which anything is white is surely in it, for nothing is white by a whiteness that is in something else. The Apostle wants to say and teach that all things are in God, God is in all and all in him.

21. Secondly, note that he does not say or add "all things are" for his sake. [This is] first, because God and hence the divine man does not act for the sake of a why or wherefore.[3] Secondly, because all things do what they do in God from him and through him, but God himself does all things in himself. "In him" is not "for the sake of." Thirdly, because that person really works for the sake of God who works from God, through God, and in God, just as the just man does just things or works justly, but not for the sake of justice insofar as "for the sake of" is distinguished from "of," "through," and "in."[4] Therefore, all things are "from him, through him, and in him." What is written in Proverbs, "The Lord has done all things for his own sake" (Pr. 16:4), is explained from what has been said. He says, "for his very own sake," not for the sake of anything else, according to the text in Genesis, "I have sworn through my very own self" (Gn. 22:16).

Note that these three terms (from, through, and in) seem to be not only appropriated, but proper to the divine Persons.[5] Second, note that they are the same, as will appear below; and third, note that universally, even in creatures, that "from which" any single thing is, is the same as that "through" and "in" which it is. Fourth, note that the term "from" is properly not the efficient cause, but rather the idea of the efficient cause.

22. "All things are from him, through him, and in him"—"from him," the Father, "through him," the Son, "in him," the Holy Spirit. Concerning the term "in him," first remark that all things are in the Holy Spirit in such a way that what is not in him must be nothing. He says, "All things are in him." What is not among all things, but is outside all things, must be nothing.[6] Whoever says "all" excludes nothing, but "All things are in him." This is what John 1 says, "without him" (that is, not in him), "what was made is nothing" (Jn. 1:3).

23. On the second point, note that "All things are in him" in such a way that if there is anything not in the Holy Spirit, the Holy Spirit is not God. Just as if anything were white outside of or without whiteness, whiteness would not be whiteness, because all that is white is so by means of whiteness, so too what is not in existence, but is outside of or without existence, is nothing. How might there be or might something be that is beyond existence, or without existence, or not in existence? Existence is from God alone, and he alone is existence: "I am who am," and "He who is sent me" (Ex. 3:14).[7] If there were anything outside him or not in him, he would not be existence and consequently not God. This is why John 1 says again, "All things were made through him" (Jn. 1:3).

24. Third, "All things are in him" in such a way that the Father would not be in the Son nor the Son in the Father, if the Father were not one and the same as the Holy Spirit, or the Son [also] the same as the Holy Spirit. It is contrary to the property of the Father, that is, to the constitutive relation which is Paternity, to exist in another or in something else. Paternity alone is the "from which"—"From which all fatherhood in heaven and on earth is named" (Ep. 3:15). "From which," because nothing in any way possesses or is named "fatherhood" without the "from which."[8] But if this is in another or in something else, then as such it is no longer the Father, but as such is what the Holy Spirit is. "I am in the Father and the Father is in me," and "The Father and I are one" (Jn. 14:11, 10:30). This is why the church prays:

> Now [come] to us, Holy Spirit,
> One with the Father and the Son.[9]

"Existence in" in no way pertains to the Son by reason of his personal property, but only "existence from," or out of another. The Holy Spirit who is the "bond" (this is his personal property, the "bond") possesses "[existence] in which," and thus all other things "are in him."

25. Fourth. "All things are in" the Holy Spirit in such a way that God is not in us nor are we in God unless in the Holy Spirit. "Existence in" does

not belong to or agree with the Father or the Son, both because it does not fit the personal property of either, and also because it is special to the personal property of the Holy Spirit and thus agrees with it alone. If it were to fit either the Father or the Son, the Father would now be the Holy Spirit, and so would the Son. Hence 1 John 4: "God is love." I say, "God," the Holy Spirit, "is love," according to Augustine,[10] and thus, "he who remains in love," that is, in the Holy Spirit, "remains in God, and God in him" (1 Jn. 4:16). Romans 5: "God's love is poured out in our hearts through the Holy Spirit" (Rm. 5:5); and John 14: "If anyone loves me, my Father will love him," and what follows, "we will come to him and make our abode with him" (Jn. 14:23). Hence, the Father and the Son love us by the Holy Spirit, and we ought to love God in the Holy Spirit.

26. Fifthly, "All things are in him" in such a way that nothing is in the Father, nothing in the Son, except because the Father and the Son are what the Holy Spirit is. Just as the Father is not in another or in something else, and nothing else is in the Father, so too there is nothing in the Son as Son except insofar as it is what the Holy Spirit is.

27. "All things are in him." "All things" has three references. "All things in him," therefore, are [those of] nature, grace, and glory. Again, "all things," because of

The triple fabric of the world . . .
The three-fold fabric of things
Of heaven, of earth, and of below.[11]

Indeed, even "Hell and destruction are before God" (Pr. 15:11). In another sense, "all things," [because] things substantial, accidental, and artificial. And another sense: "all things," because the whole existence of what is uncreatable, what is creatable and what is makable. "All things," even those made by art, "are through him, and without him," [i.e.,] not in him, "nothing was made" (Jn. 1:3). Concerning these three Acts 17 says, "In him we live and move and have our being" (Ac. 17:28). Further, "All things are in him," namely, the work of creation, of distinction, and of adornment.

28. Here note that when we say that all things are in God [that means that] just as he is indistinct in his nature and nevertheless most distinct from all things, so in him all things in a most distinct way are also at the same time indistinct.[12] The first reason is because man in God is God.[13] Therefore, just as God is indistinct and completely distinct from a lion, so too man in God is indistinct and completely distinct from a lion, and likewise with other things. Second, because everything that is in something else is in it according

to the nature of that in which it is. Third, because just as God is totally indistinct in himself according to his nature in that he is truly and most properly one and completely distinct from other things, so too man in God is indistinct from everything which is in God ("All things are in him"), and at the same time completely distinct from everything else. Fourth, according to what has been said note that all things are in God as spirit without position and without boundary.[14] Further, just as God is ineffable and incomprehensible, so all things are in him in an ineffable way. Again, every effect is always in the cause in a causal way and not otherwise.[15]

2. *The Trinity.* "*All things are from him, through him, and in him*" *(Rm. 11:36).*

29. This text is commonly explained in terms of the Trinity. Say then that "all things" are "from" the maker, "through" the form, and "in" the end. Therefore, God is the "from whom" of all, that is, the maker of all; the "through whom" of all, that is, the form of all or what forms all; and the "in whom" of all, because [he is] the end of all things. In this connection note that many have a crude and false picture here, first, because they imagine that action, form, and end are taken away from created things by this.[16] (Look this up under "Action.")[17] Second, [they think] that the maker, the form, and the end in creatures along with God are two makers or efficient causes, two forms, two ends. That is crude, first, because no being can be counted alongside God.[18] Existence and being, existence and nothing, and also a form and what it informs make up no number. Existence is more intimate than any form and is not a source of number. Second, because every being, every maker, every form, every end that is conceived of outside or beyond existence or that is numbered along with existence is nothing—it is neither a being, nor a maker, nor a form, nor an end. This is because existence, that is, God, is within every being, every form and end,[19] and conversely every being, form, and end is in existence itself. Indeed, every maker works through its existence, form informs through its existence, and every end moves through its existence—through nothing else! And where one [acts] for the sake of the other, in both cases there is still only one. Furthermore, every number or duality takes one thing outside or alongside another;[20] but every maker, form, and end outside of existence is taken as nothing. Therefore, there are not two efficient causes, two forms, two ends.

30. In summary, note that everything that is said or written about the Holy Trinity is in no way really so or true. First, [this follows] from the nature of the distinction of terms, especially between the distinct and the indistinct, between temporal and eternal things, between the sensible and

the intellectual heaven, between the material body and the spiritual body. Second, [it follows] that since God is inexpressible in and of his nature, what we say he is, surely is not in him. Hence the Psalm text "Every man is a liar" (Ps. 115:11). It is true, of course, that there is something in God corresponding to the Trinity we speak of and to other similar things. Third, [it follows] because every name or in general everything that denotes a number or makes a number come to mind or be conceived is far from God. According to Boethius, "That is truly one in which there is no number,"[21] not even in conception.

In this matter two [final] remarks. First, the terms good, true, truth, goodness, and the like, are not properly spoken of God because they add [something] and cause a number in thought, concept, or idea.[22] Second, this is why [Mary] Magdalene, who sought the One (that is, God), grieved so much when she saw the number two, that is, the two angels (cf. Jn. 20:11–13).[23]

NOTES

1. Translated from LW IV, pp. 22–32.
2. Thomas Aquinas, *STh* Ia. 8. 1.
3. This is an appearance in the Latin works of the equivalent of the MHG notion of living *sunder* or *ane warumbe*. Cf. *Comm. Ex.* n. 247 (p. 120). See the Glossary.
4. Eckhart's point here is that the term *propter* ("for the sake of") seems to imply a means to an end, something excluded by *ex*, *per*, and *in*, which hence express more directly the idea of living "without a why."
5. Thomas Aquinas admits this of the term *per* in relation to the Son in *STh* Ia. 39. 8.
6. Cf. *Comm. Jn.* n. 53 (*Essential Eckhart*, p. 141).
7. Cf. *Comm. Ex.* nn. 14–25 (pp. 45–49).
8. That is, fatherhood implies a relation to what is born from a father.
9. From the Hymn for Terce.
10. Augustine, *Trin.* 15.19.37.
11. Quotations from two hymns are joined here, the Hymn for the First Vespers of the Trinity, and the Vesper Hymn for the Ascension.
12. Cf. *Comm. Wis.* nn. 144–46, 154–55 (pp. 166–67, 169–70), and *Comm. Jn.* n. 9 (*Essential Eckhart*, p. 160). Eckhart may be referring to this passage in Sermon 10 p. 265.
13. This formula may be based on Alan of Lille, *Theological Rules* 9: "Whatever is in God, is God."
14. Cf. *Comm. Wis.* n. 99 (p. 157).
15. Cf. *Comm. Jn.* nn. 44, 66 (*Essential Eckhart*, pp. 137, 145–46).

16. Thomas Aquinas, *STh* Ia. 105. 5. Cf. *Comm. Ecc.* n. 50 (p. 177).
17. This aside may be a reference to a lost part of the *Book of Propositions*, or to some philosophical glossary.
18. Cf. *Par. Gen.* n. 20 (*Essential Eckhart*, p. 100).
19. Cf. *Comm. Ecc.* n. 54 (p. 179).
20. Cf. *Par. Gen.* n. 15 (*Essential Eckhart*, pp. 98–99).
21. Boethius, *Trinity* 2.
22. Cf. *Comm. Ex.* nn. 58–60 (pp. 63–64).
23. For this interpretation of Mary Magdalene's vision of the two angels at the empty tomb, see *Comm. Jn.* n. 706 (LW III, p. 619), where a pseudo-Origenian homily is cited as the source.

Sermon VI.   The First Sunday after Trinity Sunday. A Sermon on the Epistle (1 Jn. 4:8–21).[1]

1. "God is love" (1 Jn. 4:8).

52. By the fact that God is called love absolutely, the first thing demonstrated is his purest and most complete simplicity, and from this his priority over all things. His existence is simple existence, as it says in Exodus 3: "I am who am" (Ex. 3:14).[2] From this it is clear that all things exist and are had in him—"We have all things in you alone" (Tb. 10:5). It further follows that he alone makes blessed, both because all things are in him alone and because they are all one in him. The third conclusion is that he is something eternal and not subject to time. Those wishing to be united with him must come to be outside time.

In the second place, you must tell why he is better called love, when he is in equal measure wisdom, beauty, and the like. The reason is that love is unifying and diffusive.[3] In the third place, love begins where intellect stops. (On this, expound the passage "You who sit upon the Cherubim" [Ps. 79:2].[4] Treat how charity or love is unifying, and how great the union is. Also treat how love taken absolutely diffuses itself entirely.)[5]

53. "God is love" first because love is common to all, excluding no one. From this joint possession two things follow. First, God is common: He is every being and the whole existence of all things ("In him, through him, and from him" [Rm. 11:36]). God is all the best that can be thought or desired by each and every person—and more so! But the whole of what can be

desired by all people in relation to the word "more" is really nothing. Hence the axiom "God is the opposite of nothing by means of the mediation of being."[6] Secondly, note that whatever is common insofar as it is common is God, and whatever is not common insofar as it is not common is not God, but is created. Every creature is something finite, limited, distinct, and proper, and thus it is already not love. God with his total self is a common love.

54. Second, God is and is said to be love principally because he is the one whom everything that can love loves and seeks. Again, he alone is the one who is loved and sought by all and in all. Also, everything that exists and can exist subsists in seeking and loving him. Again, it is he in whom everything that is unpleasant, contrary, sad, or nonexistent is sweet and beautiful. Without him anything pleasant is disagreeable and nonexistent. Furthermore, God is love because he is totally lovable and totally love.

55. In the third place, God is love because he loves totally. On God's love toward us note first how much he loves us who loves us totally with his whole being; second, how he loves us with the very same love by which he loves and cherishes himself, his coeternal Son and the Holy Spirit. Third, it follows that he loves us with the same glory in mind by which he loves himself, as the texts say: "that you may eat and drink at my table in my kingdom" (Lk. 22:30), and "where I am there also shall my servant be" (Jn. 12:26). Fourth, the love with which he loves us is the Holy Spirit himself. Fifth, Hugh says he loves us "as if he had forgotten everything else," or almost everything else.[7] Sixth, he loves us in such a way that it is as if his blessedness depended on it.[8] "I have loved you with an everlasting love" (Jr. 31:3), and "My delight is to be with the sons of men" (Pr. 8:31). Seventh, he loved us when we were still his enemies, and so he gave us himself before his gifts, as if he could not wait for preparations and arrangements. Eighth, he gives himself and everything he has. Nothing created gives its own, nor the whole of it, nor itself.

In the ninth place declare that God's nature, existence, and life consist in sharing himself and giving himself totally. "The First is rich in itself."[9] He is absolutely the Absolute.[10] Hence according to Dionysius, he gives himself without thinking about his loving, but as the sun shines forth.[11]

56. On the basis of what has been said three points can be made. First, do not thank God because he loves us—he must do so! But I thank God because he is so good that he must love. Second, note that the soul itself is the noble substance that God, who possesses and [virtually] precontains everything, loves in such a way. Third, note that the soul is within God and God within the soul, and that God, who loves nothing outside himself, un-

like or different from himself, loves it in this way. Again, remember not to pray to God to pour the light of his grace upon us or anything like that, but to pray that we may be worthy to receive it, because God either always gives or never, either to all or to none.

2. *"In this has the grace of God, love, appeared in us, that God sent his only-begotten Son into the world that we may live through him" (1 Jn. 4:9).*[12]

57. The first point is that "In this has love appeared," because according to Augustine this is the greater grace.[13] The second is that "he sent his Son into the world," because God sends his Son into a clean heart.[14] On the first point note that the Son assumed human nature, not a human person (on which see the exegesis of "The Word was made flesh" [Jn. 1:14]).[15] On the second, note that a clean heart is one that has nothing in common with nothing.[16]

The first thing to be noted is that God most truly sends and gives birth to his only-begotten Son in the pure soul, and "in him and through him all things" (Rm. 11:36) [and] himself. "We will come to him and make our abode with him" (Jn. 14:23).[17] Second, why does he speak thus, or how does the soul become clean? It is clean when it loves nothing created. Everything created is stained with nothingness and set apart from God, like night from day, darkness from light, nothingness from existence. (Here remark that nothing is more offensive than nothingness itself.)

58. Thirdly, explain "into the world." He does not say "into this world," but simply "into the world," therefore into the intellectual world, according to Plato.[18] (Discuss this world and its properties.) Fourth, "into the world," that is, God gives us "the power of becoming sons of God" (Jn. 1:12) even in this world—only-begotten sons, or rather the only-begotten Son, so "that we may live through him" (1 Jn. 4:9).

59. Here you should note that living comes from within, from us and from what is ours: that alone is alive and not dead. "God's grace is life" (Rm. 6:23). Furthermore, this alone, like living, has no "wherefore," but exists for itself as spontaneous and free. Hence John 8 says, "If the Son makes you free, you will be free indeed" (Jn. 8:36); and Matthew 11, "No one knows the Father save the Son" (Mt. 11:27); and John 5, "Just as the Father has life in himself, even so he has given to the Son also to have life in himself" (Jn. 5:26). "When he appears, we will be like him" (1 Jn. 3:2). That is why it says here, "In this has love appeared in us." The love that is God was always in us, even before we existed, but now it "has appeared in us," in the interior person. "The Holy Spirit will come upon you" (Lk. 1:35).

60. "God is love." Note how God's love in us accomplishes our every deed, and how all his commands are totally for our benefit and not his. Therefore, it is just that we should aim at him alone, especially so that we may be converted to this [truth] in us and that on this basis every work will take on the nature of a command and earn us a reward.

61. "God is love" in all creatures. Everything which implies any type of defect does not have God in itself. From this perspective, it does not exist, is not a creature, is not counted among all that exists. The second point is that it is not an imperfection on God's part that he acts only in the present and without a medium, not through a medium or on something removed from himself, as the more perfect creatures do. This results from the greatness of God's perfection, both because no creature however far away can subsist without him, and because there is no medium at all between him and any creature, and also because even nothingness is not at a distance from him. How could he act on something at a distance from him when there is nothing distant [from him]? Surely, he does not act on something outside himself when there is no such thing. And so it is from the greatness of God's perfection and the greatness of the creature's imperfection that God does not act through a medium, nor at a distance, nor on something outside.

NOTES

1. This sermon (LW IV, pp. 50–74) consists of four loosely connected pieces of which only the first two (pp. 50–60) are translated here.
2. See Eckhart's explanation of this verse in *Comm. Ex.* nn. 14–21 (pp. 45–48).
3. In the Latin *uniens* and *diffusivus*. Thus love is the power behind the two basic metaphysical processes—emanation or diffusion, and unification or return.
4. The Cherubim were traditionally identified with intellect, so that God seated above them would be pure love.
5. The sentences within the parentheses are a series of notes Eckhart made for himself to indicate themes that could be developed in the fuller preaching.
6. *Book of the Twenty-Four Philosophers* prop. 14.
7. Hugh of St. Victor, *Soliloquy on the Earnest Money of the Soul.*
8. A frequent theme in Meister Eckhart; cf. Sermon 5b (*Essential Eckhart*, p. 184).
9. *Book of Causes* prop. 21. An axiom frequently cited by Eckhart; cf., e.g., Sermon XXV.2, n. 268 (p. 221), and *Comm. Jn.* n. 88 (*Essential Eckhart*, p. 155).
10. In the Latin "Est ergo ipsi per se per se," an almost untranslatable technical phrase. The German translation in LW IV, p. 55, paraphrases thus, "For God, what he is by nature is truly something which he has through himself."
11. Pseudo-Dionysius, *Divine Names* 4.1.

12. In this text Eckhart has changed the Vulgate reading by inserting "the grace of God" in order to make his point about the equivalence of grace and love.
13. Apparently a reference to Augustine's *Sermons on John* 72.3, where the African doctor insists that God's love in Christ is greater than the "grace" of nature.
14. Eckhart is here playing on the words *mundus* (world) and *mundus* (clean).
15. Cf. Sermon 46 (pp. 304–05), and *Comm. Jn.* nn. 116–121 (*Essential Eckhart*, pp. 167–70).
16. "Nothing in common with nothing," that is, the clean heart does not share in the nothingness of creatures. Cf. *nihil* and *niht* in the Glossary.
17. The birth of the Word and the Father in the soul of the just person, one of the most common themes in Eckhart's vernacular preaching, occurs in only one other place in the Latin sermons (Sermon LV.2 in LW IV, pp. 455–56). See Sermon 5b for a comparable passage also using Jn. 1:14 (*Essential Eckhart*, p. 183). For other appearances, see the Glossary under *geburt*.
18. Plato's intelligible world is here understood as the interior world of the soul rather than the archetypal world of forms.

Sermon XXV.   Eleventh Sunday after Trinity. On the Epistle (1 Co. 15:1–10).[1]

1. "By God's grace I am what I am" (1 Co. 15:10).

251. Everything that exists praises what it is and proclaims its source.[2] "From it" efficiently, "through it" formally, and "in it" finally is "what is" and "what it is."[3] For this reason "what is" is always material, potential, and a subject [of accidents]; the source itself is never material, never a subject, is always a predicate.[4] Hence, according to true understanding, Boethius says, "The simple form cannot be a subject."[5] It is clear then that the source itself belongs to the order of predicates, and this is why the "Preacher and Doctor of Truth" praises and proclaims God's grace: "By God's grace I am what I am."

252. The source itself is more or less threefold: efficient as "that from which," form as "that through which," and goal as "that to which," according to Augustine's text, "everything is from it, everything through it, everything in it."[6] The efficient cause descends outwardly from the idea or property of the Father in the Godhead where there is neither cause nor efficient activity, but only the idea of causing and acting. This fits the text in Ephesians 3, "From whom is all fatherhood in heaven and earth" (Ep. 3:15).

253. Therefore the Son in the Godhead in John 10 says, "What the Father has given me is greater than all" (Jn. 10:29), because it is not among all things, but above them. The Psalm says, "You have put all things under his feet" (Ps. 8:8). "All things were made" (Jn. 1:3); they have an efficient cause, but they have no place in the Godhead. It is "greater than all," because it is not all, but the idea of all—"In the beginning was the Word" (Jn. 1:1), the Logos, the Idea.[7] After this comes, "All things were made through him" (Jn. 1:3). Again, it is "greater than all," because all things came into existence through creation, and the Son comes from the Father through generation. "I came forth from the Father and came into the world" (Jn. 16:28) through creation, and not only through Incarnation. "He was in the world, and the world was made through him" (Jn. 1:10), as if to say, "by his making the world he came into the world." "What was made, in him was life" (Jn. 1:3–4)—life is not in the world that was created and made, because "life was the light of men" (Jn. 1:4).

254. On this basis, the text cited praises and proclaims God's grace as a form ("By the grace"), as an efficient cause ("of God"), and as a goal ("I am what I am"). A thing's preciousness and beauty come from its form, its excellence from its maker, its fruitfulness from its goal. On the first of these Wisdom 7 says, "She is a vapor of the power of God and a pure emanation of God" (Ws. 7:25), and then, "She conveys herself into holy souls and makes them friends of God and prophets" (Ws. 7:27). This is "that most prudent and beautiful woman" who freed her husband from death, saved flocks and family, and appeased King David's wrath (1 K. 25). A "beautiful woman," because a thing's beauty comes from its form, as we have said. "She is more beautiful than the sun" (Ws. 7:29). Also, a thing's preciousness comes from the form. What is more precious than grace? "No one knows its price" (Jb. 28:13). The evil of simony is condemned because it sets a price on grace. Thomas teaches that the perfection of the grace of each person is worth more [than the creation of heaven and earth].[8] What is more beautiful than grace?

255. The following words ("of God") signify the effective cause of grace. This shows the nobility of the thing: "She glorified her nobility by having fellowship with God" (Ws. 8:3). In its very idea God's grace is heavenly and divine, solely and immediately from God. "Nothing defiled comes into her" (Ws. 7:25), because nothing created acts along with her.

256. "God's grace." It is grace because it is given freely and without merit. "By grace you have been saved" (Ep. 2:8). Wise men of old and some famous moderns held that substantial forms came from some divine bestower of forms, but that they were given according the characteristics of the

kinds of matter.[9] Therefore, form is not always given to matter, nor to every kind of matter. Nor is every form always given, and therefore it is not free. God, however, "gives" (against the first point), "to all" (against the second), "abundantly" (against the third) (Jm. 1:5).[10] Because God gives his gifts and grace without merit, freely and for nothing, Wisdom 8 says, "He reaches from one end to the other mightily and orders all things sweetly" (Ws. 8:1). "Sweetly," first because by his own power;[11] second, because it is for nothing; third, because he first gives himself; fourth, because what he works in us and for us is received passively from without; fifth, because he works the common good. (Here expand on how usefully and peacefully the universe would live if each part served the whole.)[12]

257. In the third place, grace is extolled on account of its goal—"I am what I am." This signifies the fecundity or, better, the fruitfulness of grace. Proverbs 3, "Her fruits are the first and purest" (Pr. 3:14). "The first," because what is prior to existence? "The purest," because what is purer than what a thing is? "What I am." Exodus 3 writes of God, "I am who am" (Ex. 3:14).[13] Note that in grace a person has at the same time a conformity and a distinction in relation to God, just as [in the case of being] an "image" and "to the image."[14] Therefore, "What I am, I am through God's grace." Every work of God in the creature is a grace, and the act or gift of God alone is called a grace. Therefore, it says "God's grace," and it is clear from the name [of grace] itself that such is the case.[15]

258. Grace is said to be "freely given," whether we use the word free abverbially or substantively. The first kind of grace is usually called "grace freely given," that is, without merits; the second, "saving grace." The first is common to good and evil and to all creatures; the second is proper only to intellective and good creatures.[16]

The first grace comes from God insofar as he is understood as a being, or rather as something good—as Augustine says, "Because he is good, we exist."[17] The divine essence as such neither generates nor creates, only the divine subject does.[18] The second grace comes from God as he is understood according to the property of "personal notion,"[19] for which reason only the intellective being which properly reflects the image of the Trinity can receive it. Further, God as good is the principle of the "boiling over" on the outside; as personal notion he is the principle of the "boiling within himself," which is the cause and exemplar of the "boiling over." Thus, the emanation of the Persons in the Godhead, the cause and exemplar of creation, is prior.[20]

259. The first grace consists in a type of flowing out, a departure from God; the second consists in a type of flowing back, a return to God himself.[21] Both first and second grace have in common that they are from God alone.

This is why the Apostle says, "God's grace." The reason is that it is of the nature of grace to be given without merits, freely, for nothing, without any disposing medium. That belongs only to what is First, no matter what it may be in the one who receives it; but what is first in each thing is what comes from God. Otherwise, God would not be the First Cause or God. The First is from nothing, and before it there is nothing. Thus, it is without merit, without a medium, without a disposition, and hence free. Therefore, every act of God in the creature is a grace.

260. Hence again note the text of Wisdom 8: "He reaches from one end to the other strongly and disposes all things sweetly" (Ws. 8:1). He acts "sweetly" by giving a habit.[22] A virtue or habit is born in us from actions that are still strange, and therefore come about with difficulty. It is different with an infused habit. Note that here below dimensions precede form, but it is different in heaven. There heaven [as such] is prior to any individual heaven, while here below, on the contrary, the individual man is prior to man [as such].[23] Nature works in hidden fashion in the actions of each thing. Another way to put it: Heaven [as such] is prior to a particular heaven, because heaven [as such] exists through form, a particular heaven through dimensions. The same "sweet work" will take place in us, if we are heavenly and divine, if "our citizenship is in heaven" (Ph. 3:20) by means of love, and not earthly through fear.

261. The text says "sweetly," because God first gives himself. It says "from one end to the other" because the beginning itself is the end, and the end is always sweet.[24] Or again, "from one end" attained to "the other end" left behind, and "there being born again" (Si. 1:5). This is why the text says "strongly," because it always revives and finds new strength. And it says "sweetly," because its action is always directed to Absolute Good, not this or that good in particular.

2. *"By God's grace I am what I am" (1 Co. 15:10).*

262. Grace is high above love, first, in the same sense as the soul is above its faculty; second, as existence is over action; third, as a principle or cause is over what is caused. Thus it is outside the category of genus, as you know, and consequently is above intellect. (Intellect is a faculty, and operates in the category of truth.) "By God's grace I am what I am"—that is, the self-same, as the Psalm says, "In the self-same I will sleep and rest" (Ps. 4:9).

263. "By God's grace I am what I am." Note first that grace is a kind of "boiling over" of the birth of the Son which has its root in the Father's inmost heart. It is life, not just existence—"his name is the Word" (Rv.

219

19:13), higher than nature. He is above, not among all good things. To the person who receives it grace is a confirmation, a configuration, or—better— a transfiguration of the soul into and with God. Secondly, it makes one have one existence with God, something that is more than assimilation. Remember how the Word assumed a nature which belongs equally to all men. In Christ there is no other act of existence but the divine one.[25]

264. "God's grace." Grace comes from God alone for the same reason that existence itself does. Furthermore, just as the entire air is immediately related to the sun from the viewpoint of its capacity to be illuminated, although the particles of air have their own order, so too every creature is immediately related to God as far as existence, grace, and all perfections, especially the common ones that are not determined to this or that, are concerned. This and that pertains to the creature; it is proper, it is a lie.[26] This is the reason why things of this sort, that is, general perfections and grace, are said to be given freely, given by God, given without merits, because no created thing can be related to them in an active way, or perhaps even as a proper disposition. And so grace is said to be supernatural.

265. Causality demands order. Creatures are ordered to each other only by their differences, not by their genus, because all species are found in a genus and have the same relation to the genus. They participate equally in their genus, and inequality comes from their differences, and so does order.[27] This is why they have an order toward each other, but not toward the genus. (The same is true of the way that the faculties relate to the soul, so that the order of living species follows the order of the soul's faculties.)

266. The point to make here is that no creature seems to be able passively to receive grace or any kind of perfection, especially a common one, insofar as it is a creature, or insofar as it is this and that; but only insofar as it is ordered to God, and thus excluded and removed from every order and relation either to itself or to another created thing—to a this or that. This is why Augustine says that the soul is open to such things only insofar as it is the image of God.[28] An image, as image, is totally related to what it is an image of, and is ordered to it and to nothing else. Hence the fitting saying that we should deny ourselves and renounce what belongs to us.[29] It says, "Unless a person renounces everything he possesses, he cannot be my disciple" (Lk. 14:33). And again: "Blessed are the poor" (Mt. 5:3); and "Let him deny himself" (Mt. 16:24); and "Forget your people and your father's house" (Ps. 44:11); and "Go forth from your country, and from your kindred, and from your father's house" (Gn. 12:1); and "He gave them the power of becoming sons of God, . . . who were born not of blood, nor of the will of the flesh, nor of the will of man, but of God" (Jn. 1:12–13). To deny what is

one's own is to deny the creature, or this and that, because "this and that" is what is proper, a creature.[30]

267. "By God's grace I am." Grace is not in a faculty of the soul, but in its substance, in its deepest part, or rather in the soul's very existence, because "I am what I am." The second thing to note is that it follows that if there is grace in the soul, it is the whole of grace. "In me is all grace" (Qo. 24:25). First, because such a soul possesses God, who is the source of all grace, illuminating everyone; and second, because it is all or nothing. "The light that enlightens everyone" (Jn. 1:9) is unique, the self-same in all things, and all things are one in that which it illuminates. The same is true of grace. The third reason is because nothing is absent from the soul's existence, which is the location of grace, due to the fact that nothing can be absent from or lacking to Existence Itself.[31] Existence is common to all things—not only common, but the same in all things. Therefore, nothing that belongs to grace is ever absent from the soul's very existence. Fourth, the virtues and every kind of grace are joined in existence. (See what is said on the "Connection of Virtues.")[32] Through its own act of existence the soul stands in God's act of existence, in God, though you should remember that everything is in God only by reason of its existence—and as such it is totally in him.

268. "God's grace." The work of grace, because it is supernatural, is superior to every created work. Because it is above nature as something higher, the first thing that follows is that it contains the whole of nature undividedly united in itself as though by its power. Second, no creature has any power over grace, because nothing acts upon what is above it ("The First is always rich in itself").[33] Third, the operation of God's grace is also unknown to an intellect that is based only on the natural light of reason. (And so children who die without baptism know nothing about the glory of the blessed, and this seems to be the real reason why they do not grieve that they have not received grace or the glory of the blessed.)[34]

NOTES

1. This sermon is translated from LW IV, pp. 230–44.
2. At the outset, Eckhart introduces three scholastic terms important for the early development of the sermon: (1) *quod quid est*, the Aristotelian term that signifies the "quiddity," or "whatness" of a thing; (2) *id quod est*, a Boethian term meaning much the same (here translated "what it is"); and (3) *quo est*, a term used in different senses by different authors, but here indicating God, Existence Itself, as the source of all things. See the Glossary under *essentia*.

MEISTER ECKHART

3. Eckhart here uses Rm. 11:36, one of his favorite texts, to indicate three causal relations all things have to God as source—efficient, formal, and final.
4. The paragraph contains a wordplay impossible to bring out in English between "preaching" or "proclaiming" (*praedicans*) and "predicating" (*praedicans*), i.e., affirming or denying something of the subject of a proposition.
5. Boethius, *On the Trinity* 2.
6. Augustine, *On True Religion* 55.113.
7. See *Comm. Jn.* n. 12 (*Essential Eckhart*, p. 126).
8. Thomas Aquinas, *STh* Ia IIae. 113. 9.
9. This is the view of Avicenna, *Metaphysics* 9.2. Sermon VI.3 (LW IV, p. 62) refers to it as Plato's view, but it is not found in his writings.
10. This passage shows an important characteristic of Eckhart's thought, his attempt to work out fully consistent parallels between creation and recreation.
11. This is based on a wordplay between "sweetly" (*suaviter*) and "by his own power" (*sua vi*).
12. Another of Eckhart's frequent notes for expansion.
13. See the explanation of this verse in *Comm. Ex.* nn. 14–21 (pp. 45–48).
14. *Imago* expresses conformity or identity; *ad imaginem*, distinction or difference. See *Essential Eckhart*, pp. 43–44, and *imago* and *bilde* in the Glossary.
15. That is, the divine name (*Ego sum qui sum*) reveals the meaning of Paul's statement, "*id quod sum, sum gratia Dei.*"
16. "Grace freely given" (*gratia gratis data*) and "saving grace" (*gratia gratum faciens*) are common scholastic terms. Eckhart's identification of the first with the grace of creation and the second with the grace of salvation (cf. *Comm. Jn.* n. 500 in LW III, pp. 431–32; and *Comm. Wis.* nn. 273–74 in LW II, pp. 602–04) contrasts markedly with that of Thomas Aquinas, *STh* Ia IIae. 111. 1. Cf. the Glossary, *gratia*.
17. Augustine, *Christ. Doct.* 1.32.35.
18. This translation is a paraphrase of a technical scholastic formula in which the word here rendered as "subject" is actually "supposit," i.e., the concrete subject of predication. See *Comm. Jn.* n. 6 (*Essential Eckhart*, p. 124). The divine essence as such is never the concrete subject of the predication of divine actions, within the Trinity or without, but only the divine Persons, taken singly or together.
19. The "personal notion" (*notio personalis*) invoked here is also found in Aquinas, *STh* Ia. 32. 2.
20. On *bullitio* and *ebullitio* see the Glossary.
21. The "flowing out" (*effluxus* or *origo*, MHG *ûzvliezen*) and "flowing back" (*refluxus* or *reditus*, MHG *durchbruch, inganc*) are Eckhart's terms for the essential metaphysical dynamic of the Neoplatonic worldview (cf. *Essential Eckhart*, p. 30). See the references on these terms in the Glossary.
22. The "second grace" of redemption was customarily analyzed by the scholastics as a supernatural habit, granting the soul a new, higher way of being and acting, e.g., *STh* Ia IIae. 109–14.

23. Eckhart typically offers natural examples to illustrate supernatural matters. The difference between form and dimension in the heavenly and earthly realms is explained in *Comm. Gen.* n. 38 (LW I, pp. 214–15).

24. Eckhart is playing with the terms *principium* (beginning, principle) and *finis* (end, goal); cf. the Glossary.

25. The teaching of Thomas Aquinas, *STh* IIIa. 17. 2. Cf. *Comm. Wis.* n. 45 (LW II, pp. 367–69).

26. See *Comm. Ex.* n. 195 (p. 105).

27. E.g., all animals are alike in belonging to the genus "animal," but man differs from the other animals in the species of "rational animal."

28. Augustine, *Trin.* 14.8.11.

29. The second part of this sentence is lacking in the manuscripts, but is supplied by the editors through references to similar passages elsewhere (cf. LW IV, p. 242, n. 4).

30. Cf. the use of *eigenschaft*, or "property," in Sermon 1 (p. 241).

31. Eckhart is here speaking of the soul's existence insofar as it is identified with the divine ground, and not of its particular existence (*esse hoc et hoc*).

32. Eckhart may be referring to some lost treatment of his own, or he may possibly be thinking of *STh* Ia IIae. 65. 1.

33. *Book of Causes* prop. 31.

34. Thomas Aquinas, *On Evil* 5.3.

Sermon XXIX. Thirteenth Sunday after Pentecost. On the Epistle (Ga. 3:16–22).[1]

"God is one" (Ga. 3:20; Dt. 6:4).

295. "God." Anselm says "God is that than which nothing better can be thought."[2] Augustine in Book One of *Christian Doctrine* says, "The God of gods is thought of as something than which nothing is better or higher"; and further on, "You can't find anyone who thinks that God is something which has a better."[3] Bernard in the fifth Book of *On Consideration* says, "What is God? That than which nothing better can be thought."[4] In the Prologue to the *Natural Questions* Seneca says, "What is God? The totality that you see and the totality that you don't see. His greatness belongs to him in such a way that nothing greater can be conceived."[5]

296. God is infinite in his simplicity and simple by reason of his infinity.[6] Therefore, he is everywhere and everywhere entire. He is everywhere

by his infinity, but entire everywhere by reason of his simplicity. God alone flows into all created beings, into their essences; nothing of other beings flows into anything else. God is in the inner reality of each thing, and only in the inner reality.[7] He alone "is one."

297. Note that every creature loves the One in God, loves him for the sake of the One and loves him because he "is one." The first reason is that everything that exists loves and seeks God's likeness, and likeness is a kind of unity or the unity of certain things.[8] The second reason is that in the One there is never pain, punishment, or distress, nor ability to suffer or die. Third, because all things exist in the One by the very fact that it is the One. Every multiplicity is one and one thing in the One and through the One.[9] Fourth, neither power nor wisdom nor goodness itself, nor even existence, would be loved unless they were united to us and we to them. 298. Fifth, who truly loves can love only one thing, hence to our text "God is one" there follows "You shall love the Lord your God with your whole heart" (Dt. 6:5). Certainly, whoever loves something totally does not want it to be more than one. Sixth, because he wishes to be united with what he loves and this is not possible unless it be one. Furthermore, God would not unite anything to himself except because he is one and by reason of being one. Also, by the fact that he is one he necessarily unites all things and unites them in and to himself. Seventh, because the One is indistinct from all things, and hence all things and the fullness of existence are found in it by reason of indistinction or unity.[10] Eighth, the One properly refers to what is whole and perfect, and so once again nothing is wanting to it. Ninth, note that the One essentially refers to Existence Itself or to unitary essence, for essence is always one. Union or the ability to be united belongs to it by reason of this unity.

299. On this basis, observe that a person who truly loves God as the One and for the sake of the One and union no longer cares about or values God's omnipotence or wisdom because these are multiple and refer to multiplicity.[11] Nor do they care about goodness in general, both because it refers to what is outside and in things and because it consists in attachment, according to the Psalm text "It is good for me to adhere to God" (Ps. 72:28).

Tenth, note that the One is higher, prior, and simpler than the Good Itself, and it is closer to Existence Itself and to God, or rather according to its name it is one existence in or with Existence Itself. Eleventh, God is unstintingly rich because "he is one." He is first and supreme by the fact that "he is one." Hence the One descends into each and every thing, always remaining one and uniting what is divided. (This is why six is not twice three, but six times one.)[12]

300. "Hear, Israel, your God is one God." At this point note that unity

or the One pertains to and is a property of the intellect alone. Material beings are both one and not one insofar as they have size or at least are composed of form and matter. Immaterial beings, such as intellectual ones, are also not one, either because their essence is not existence,[13] or perhaps rather because their existence is not understanding.[14] They are composed of existence and essence or of existence and understanding. (See the *Book of Causes*, the comment on the last proposition.[15]) And so the text says significantly "Your God is one God," the God of Israel, a God who sees, a God of those who see, a God who understands and is understood by intellect alone, who is totally intellect.

301. "God is one." This can be taken in two ways. First thus: "God is one," for by the fact that he is one, existence belongs to him, that is, he is his existence, he is pure existence, and he is the existence of all things.[16] Second thus: "Your God is one God," as if nothing else is truly one because nothing created is pure existence and totally intellect. For then it would no longer be creatable. Similarly, in the case of anything whatever I ask whether it has intellect or understanding or not. If not, it is clear that because it lacks intellect, it is not God or the First Cause of all the things ordered to definite ends. If it does have intellect, I ask whether there is any existence besides understanding in it or not. If not, I already have what is simply One, and what is uncreatable, first, and the like—and that is God. If it has some existence other than understanding, it is already composed and not simply One. It is very clear then that God is properly alone and that he is intellect or understanding and that he is purely and simply understanding with no other existence. Therefore only God brings things into existence through intellect because existence is understanding in him alone. Also, only he can be pure understanding. [Other things] have some form of existence that differs from understanding—otherwise they would not be creatures, both because understanding is uncreatable and because "existence is the first of created things."[17]

302. On the basis of what has been said, all the things that follow upon the One or unity (equality, likeness, image, relation, and the like) in the universal sense are properly only in God and in the Godhead. Augustine in *True Religion* speaks of "that true equality or likeness."[18] 303. The reason is, first, that they follow upon unity which is proper to God, as was said. Second, because all these things are spoken of as the One in many, the One which is found nowhere and at no time save in intellect. It does not exist, but it is understood. Where existence is not Understanding Itself there is never equality. Only in God is existence the same as Understanding. A third reason is that two things that are alike and equal cannot be likeness itself and

equality itself. The same is true for the others. Fourth, in the universe there are never two things completely equal and alike in all things, for then they would not be two or related to each other. Fifth, diversity, deformity, and the like are always found outside intellect, as the Psalm text says: "You are always the self-same" (Ps. 101:28). Identity is unity.

304. From what has been said you can understand the way in which one "who adheres to God is one spirit" (1 Co. 6:17). Intellect properly belongs to God, and "God is one." Therefore, anything has as much of God and of the One and of "One-Existence" with God as it has of intellect and what is intellectual. For God is one intellect and intellect is one God. Nowhere and never do we find God as God save in intellect. In the tenth Book of the *Confessions* Augustine says "Where I found truth there I found my God, Truth itself."[19] Rise up then to intellect; to be attached to it is to be united to God. To be united, to be one, is to be one with God. "God is one." Every kind of existence that is outside or beyond intellect is a creature; it is creatable, other than God, and is not God. In God there is nothing other.

305. Act and potency are divisions of the existence of all created being. Existence is the first act, the first division;[20] but in the Intellect, in God, there is no division. This is why Scripture always exhorts us to go out of this world, to go out of ourselves, to forget our house and the house of our origin, to go forth from our land and our relations so that we may grow into a great people, so that all nations may be blessed in such a person (see Gn. 12:1–3). This best takes place in the region of the intellect where without doubt all things, insofar as they are intellect and not other, are in all things.

NOTES

1. The text is translated from LW IV, pp. 263–70.
2. Anselm, *Proslogion* 2.
3. Augustine, *Christ. Doct.* 1.15–16.
4. Bernard of Clairvaux, *On Consideration* 5.7.15.
5. Seneca, *Natural Questions* 1, Preface 13.
6. Cf. *Comm. Ex.* n. 53 (p. 60).
7. Cf. *Comm. Ex.* n. 105 (p. 79).
8. This is based on Aristotle, *Met.* 5.20 (1021a), and Aquinas, *STh* Ia. 93. 9.
9. The participation of number and all multiplicity in the One is essential to Eckhart's metaphysics, cf., e.g., *Comm. Wis.* n. 151 (p. 168).
10. See *Comm. Wis.* n. 144 (p. 166).

11. See *Comm. Ex.* n. 58 (p. 63).
12. This is the teaching of Augustine, *Free Choice* 2.8.22; and Boethius, *Arithmetic* 1.3. See also *Comm. Wis.* n. 148 (p. 167).
13. The teaching of Aquinas, *STh* Ia. 3. 4.
14. See *Par. Quest.* q. 2 (LW V, pp. 49–54).
15. *Book of Causes* prop. 32.
16. The identification of God as the *esse omnium* is a formula that finds its origin in the writings of the Pseudo-Dionysius. Cf. *esse omnium* in the Glossary.
17. *Book of Causes* prop. 4.
18. Augustine, *True Religion* 30.55.
19. Augustine, *Conf.* 10.24.35.
20. Aquinas, *STh* Ia. 4. 1. ad 3; and *On God's Power* 7.2. ad. 9.

Sermon XLV. Twenty-First Sunday after Trinity Sunday. A Sermon on the Epistle (Ep. 6:10–17).[1]

448. "Receive the armor of God" (Ep. 6:13). "Receive instruction" (Pr. 8:10).[2] Those who interpret God's word need both knowledge that illumines the intellect and grace or charity that enflames the power to love. Both require instruction. Of the first Proverbs 12 says, "He who loves instruction loves knowledge" (Pr. 12:1); of the second Proverbs 1 says, "My son, hear the instruction of your father and forsake not the law of your mother that grace may be added to your head" (Pr. 1:8–9). The "head" is called the intellective part or the mind, or even the soul's substance which is the source of all the powers. Instruction is a kind of union of knowledge and love, because where the Psalm has "goodness" (Ps. 118:66) the *Gloss* explains "Teach me love and discipline and knowledge."[3]

449. But what is discipline? Bernard says: "How well does discipline order the whole bearing of the body and the state of mind! It bows the neck, modifies the expression, binds the eyes, controls laughter, restrains the tongue, subdues appetite, calms anger and governs the gait. Such are the pearls which ought adorn the garment of chastity."[4] Therefore because discipline deserves both knowledge and grace, Solomon's words "Receive instruction" fittingly introduce the word of God.

450. "Receive the armor of God." The cry "To arms!" is used when enemies approach and danger threatens. Today's epistle talks about nearby

enemies and very great danger, so the Apostle calls us to arms with the words "Receive the armor of God."

There are some who have arms, but in a closet or on a stand for show. These are those who have virtues in their notebooks or who only know and talk about them. This is not enough. It did little good for the foolish virgins that they had lamps and the money to buy oil for them, because "while they went to buy . . . the door was shut" (Mt. 25:10). So the Apostle, wishing us to be armed and prepared, says, "Receive the armor of God." Apply this to yourselves. Earlier he said "Put on the armor" (Ep. 6:11); and Matthew 25 says, "Be prepared, because you know neither the day nor the hour" (Mt. 25:13).

451. There are four things treated in today's epistle which ought especially to incite us to take up arms. Our enemies are the world in whose midst we are enclosed on all sides, our own flesh that is within our walls, the devil who among many other things is invisible (that is very dangerous). Also, the struggle is not for "the goods of this world" (1 Jn. 3:17), or for the earthly life of working for justice, but for heavenly things, for the eternal life we hope for in heaven.

452. God himself is our necessity, because "in him we move and live and have our being" (Ac. 17:28). This is the defense against the first enemy. And so according to Augustine God flows into the soul and is closer to the soul than the soul itself.[5] This is the defense against the second. He is also the one whom "no one has ever seen" (Jn. 1:18), so that the Apostle says "to the King of ages, the immortal, invisible, only God" (1 Tm. 1:17). As far as the fourth enemy is concerned, he is not only the Lord of heaven but also the Creator ("In the beginning God created heaven and earth" [Gn. 1:1]). Hence the Apostle expressly says "the armor of God."

453. First, he exhorts us to take up the armor ("Receive the armor"); then he talks about the kind of armor ("of God"), and third, he [gives] the reason for his exhortation ("so that you can resist").

In relation to the first point you should know that the word "receive" implies three things about these arms: the way of asking for them, the ease of possessing them, and the power they have for conquest.

454. "Receive." As for the way of asking, see John 16: "Ask and you shall receive" (Jn. 16:24), and Luke 11: "Everyone who asks receives" (Lk. 11:10). "Everyone," but not "all things." "Man" signifies all men, and yet each man is "all men," as in the final chapter of Ecclesiastes: "Fear God and keep his commandments, for this is all man" (Qo. 12:13).[6] Such a person doubtless shall receive. He ought make his petition with his whole self in every way, that is, "with his whole heart, his whole strength, his whole soul"

(Lk. 10:27), in opposition to those about whom the Lord complained: "This people honors me with their lips, but their heart is far from me" (Mt. 15:8). This is why in Luke 11 the Savior adds "he who seeks finds, and to him who knocks it shall be opened" to the phrase "he who asks receives." "He who asks" in prayer, "seeks" in living, "knocks" in persevering. "He asks" humbly, "seeks" ardently, "knocks" constantly; or "he asks" in prayer, "seeks" in holy meditation, "knocks" in desire and love. "He who asks receives."

455. God gives his whole self totally and in every way. It is wicked to hope for a separate half-reward from God, as John 7 says, "I have healed the whole man on the Sabbath" (Jn. 7:23). This is why he also wants us to receive "with our whole soul, whole mind, and whole strength." The universal rule is that every agent always intends the whole.[7]

456. The second thing to note is how easy it is to gain these arms. They are displayed and offered indiscriminantly. "Receive," he says. Augustine in treating of God's words says of this passage ("everyone who asks") that "human laziness ought to blush—God wishes to give more than we do to receive."[8] "More," that is, a greater amount and more truly. He wishes "more truly" because he takes the fact that we wish to receive for a grace too, as in John 1 where it says "from his fullness we have all received, grace for grace" (Jn. 1:16), that is, he considers our reception of grace to be for the sake of grace, or he gives us grace so that we can fully accept the fullness of grace. This is the meaning of "of his fullness . . . grace for grace," that is, that it may be received as full. ("Ask . . . that your joy may be full" [Jn. 16:24].) This fullness is prefigured in 2 Machabees 15 where we read that Jeremiah extended his hand to Judas and said: "Receive the holy sword, a gift from God" (2 M. 15:15–16). The extending of the hand signifies a spontaneous gift indiscriminantly offered.

457. The third thing to be noted through the word "receive" is the power of conquest in these arms. We receive these arms in the proper sense of the term, since they are not ours, nor do we possess them from ourselves nor of ourselves. That is why what is said in the text cited above about the gift from God is significant: "Receive," he says, "the holy sword, a gift from God," and there follows, "with which you shall overthrow the adversaries of my people Israel." And in our text it says "the armor of God." "For the weakness of God is stronger than men" (1 Co. 1:25). Boethius in Book 1 of the *Consolation of Philosophy* says: "We gave you such good arms that if you had not first thrown them away, they would have given you unconquerable protection."[9] If he says this about the virtue of philosophers, it is all the truer about the grace of saints, as in Romans 8: "I am sure that neither death, nor life . . . can separate us from the love of God" (Ro. 8:38–39); and Psalm 17:

"In my God I shall go over the wall" (Ps. 17:30); and 2 Maccabees 11: "They were ready to break through . . . walls of iron" (2 M. 11:9).

458. On this it is noteworthy that the theologians hold that the least grace is enough to resist sins,[10] for what is least with God is infinitely great in relation to every creature. A maxim says that "God is the intelligible sphere whose center is everywhere and whose circumference is nowhere."[11] Someone once asked: "What was God doing or what kind of life did he lead when he was alone before creation?"[12] The response given him was, "Would you lack anything or be less well off if there were no flies?" He said, "No, rather I would be better off." The response was, "The least of all flies means more to you and your very existence depends more on it than God's existence depends on the whole creation."[13] Someone else who asked an impudent question was told that God could not make the world either before or after, because there was no before or after in which the world did not exist. How could he who created it in the first instant of the now of eternity have made it previously? There is only one now of eternity, and it was the "then" when God was creating the world. Untaught people falsely imagine that some delay or suspense intervened when time did not exist.[14]

459. The second main theme follows, where Paul establishes the kind or specification of arms or armor by saying "the armor of God." Every kingdom has its arms—the arms of the Roman Empire is an eagle on a golden field, the arms of France lilies on a blue one. The arms of the kingdom of heaven and of Christians is the cross, not on a colored ground, but in light itself. "Let us put on the armor of light" (Ro. 13:12). [John] Damascene and Ambrose say that the cross is the weapon of Christians.[15] While he was hanging on the cross, the author of mercy divided up his inheritance, willing persecution to the apostles, peace to the disciples, his body to the Jews, his spirit to his Father, [John] the "best man" to the Virgin Mary, paradise to the thief, hell to sinners, and the cross to penitent Christians.

460. This is why it says in Matthew 16, "If anyone wishes to come after me, let him deny himself, take up his cross and follow me" (Mt. 16:24). "If anyone"—see, with no exceptions. In this everyone is on the same footing, servant and lord, poor and rich, noble and base. "Wishes"—because good will alone suffices. If there is something you are not capable of, leave it to God because the work must come from the will.[16] Since the good is the object of the will and God is Goodness Itself, it is right that a person who serves God does so in completely voluntary fashion. "I will freely sacrifice to you and praise your name" (Ps. 53:8), and "No one does good without willing to do it, even if what he does is good," because "it is the will by which we sin and live rightly," as Augustine says.[17]

461. "After me." Many wish to come along with Christ, but not after Christ. Thus "it was necessary for Christ to suffer and so to enter into his glory" (Lk. 24:26). Such people certainly wish to enter into glory, but they do not wish to suffer. Also "after me" is used because he is "the way, the truth, and the life" (Jn. 14:6). To come after him is to live for truth and to truly live. Third, he says "after me" by inspiring us to follow, since he goes before us, struggling in our behalf. In a sermon Cyprian says that Christ, who conquered for us once and for all, is always conquering in us.[18]

462. "Let him deny himself," so that a person who once lived for the world may now live for Christ, who once lived a sensual life may now live by reason and intellect. In John 4 Jesus says, "You have had five husbands, and the one you now have is not your husband" (Jn. 4:18). And he told the women, "Go, call your husband and come here" (Jn. 4:16). Augustine explains that this husband is the intellect, the other five are the five senses.[19] (Take, for example, the story of the cleric who, moved by a sermon, threw out his concubine. He met her afterward and when she asked him, "Isn't it me that you used to love so much?" he answered, "You're the one, but I'm not the same man.")[20]

463. "Let him take up his cross." Here note that many carry the cross, but not really, because they carry it unwillingly under compulsion. In Matthew 27 we read that the soldiers of the guard "compelled a man of Cyrene to carry the cross" (Mt. 27:32). Inanimate objects and brute beasts act under compulsion; a human being ought to raise and exalt his cross freely. "God forbid that I should glory save in the cross" (Ga. 6:14). The virtuous person ought to rejoice to suffer for Christ,[21] as in Acts 5 where it says, "The apostles departed . . . rejoicing that they had been counted worthy to suffer disgrace for the name of Jesus" (Ac. 5:41). Pleasure is a sign of a virtuous habit.[22] Hence the *Gloss* on the text "God forbid that I should glory" says: "Where the philosopher of this world is ashamed, the apostle finds a treasure; what seems to him foolishness, is something holy to the apostle, it is wisdom and glory." It goes on to say, "The Lord has given us the cross that he carries on his shoulder as the scepter of his kingdom so that we may glory in it by our suffering in mind and heart." "His own." There are those who exalt and praise Christ's cross and those of others, but will not touch one "with their own finger" (Mt. 23:4). Against such people he says "his own."

464. In a collation on this point I would note that we ought to carry Christ's cross and our own in four ways.[23] First, by frequent and devout remembrance of the Lord's passion, as in 1 Peter 4: "Since Christ has suffered in the flesh, do you also arm yourselves with the same intent" (1 P. 4:1). Bernard says, "Consider with the mind's eye, man, what a great debt

231

binds you to the suffering Lord. Consider the indignity of the blows, the force of the scourges, the crown of thorns, the labor of the cross, the mockery of spitting, gall as food, bitter drink and the most heinous reproaches."[24] Origen teaches how great the effectiveness and usefulness of carrying the cross is when he says: "The power of Christ's cross is so great that if a person faithfully keeps it in mind no lust and no attack of sin can prevail over him, but immediately on remembering the passion the whole army of sin and death will take flight."[25]

465. In the second place, we ought to carry the cross by hatred of sin, as it says in Galatians 5: "They who belong to Christ have crucified their flesh with its passions and desires" (Ga. 5:24). There are those who certainly avoid some sins of greater notoriety, like the carnal ones, while they care little about others of greater malice, like spiritual ones. Paul says "with passions" to indicate carnal sins, "with desires" to indicate spiritual ones. Or you can say that passions are exterior acts, the desires interior ones. Ambrose comments thus on Galatians 6:14: Through Christ's cross "the desires of the world have no power over me nor does the world any longer force itself upon me; I am strong against it."[26]

466. Four things are needful for someone who is attacked: fortitude, circumspection, armor, and good trust. Thus the verses:

Let the brave man be strong and armed and cautious;
Faith and love make him brave, and fear brings caution.[27]

Avicenna claims and proves by cases that trust is more important for a cure than the doctor and his instruments.[28]

467. In the third place, the cross is carried by giving up the world's pleasures. In a Sermon for Lent cited in the *Gloss* on Galatians 5:24, Augustine says: "It is consistent with our devotion that we who celebrate the passion of the crucified Lord ought to make ourselves a cross of fleshly pleasures to be repressed." There follows, "On this cross . . . the Christian ought always to hang in this life," so that he is fixed with nails.[29] One nail by which we are fixed is the thought of eternal punishment; the second is the examination and anticipation of reward. On the first, Bernard in *On Consideration* Book 5 says, "I shudder at the gnawing worm and enduring death; I shudder at falling into the hands of living death and dying life."[30] On the second, Romans 8 says, "The sufferings of the present time are not worthy to be compared with the glory to come" (Ro. 8:18). "For our present light affliction prepares for us an eternal weight of glory that is beyond all measure" (2 Co. 4:17), because "eye has not seen nor ear heard, nor has it entered into

the heart of man, what things God has prepared for those that love him" (1 Co. 2:9).

468. Fourth, the cross is borne by mortification of the flesh and compassion for our neighbor. Gregory in his explanation of the text in Matthew 16 ("Let him bear his cross") says, "The cross is borne in two ways, when we either afflict the body through abstinence or afflict the soul by compassion for our neighbor."[31]

Therefore, it is clear what the armor of God is: It is the cross of Christ. This is the "armor of light" (Ro. 13:12). Light is an active quality of the heavens that has no contrary,[32] and what is more, the different kinds of contrary colors are not contrary in light, but lose their opposition in the medium. And so every contrary and everything hostile thing loses its evil and ill-nature in the soul that has been clothed with the armor of light, so that the soul no longer feels it, but rejoices and delights in suffering for the love of Christ.

NOTES

1. Translated from LW IV, pp. 374–87.
2. "Instruction" is the Latin *disciplina*. The first part of this sermon is constructed around a series of biblical texts using the term *disciplina*, which can mean variously discipline, instruction of any kind, a branch of study, a method, orderly conduct, a way of life (e.g., monastic or religious), or penance.
3. This is the explanation given in the *Interlinear Gloss* to the text of Ps. 118:66, "Teach me goodness (*bonitas*) and discipline (*disciplina*) and knowledge (*scientia*)."
4. Bernard of Clairvaux, *Letter* 113.5.
5. Augustine, *Trin.* 8.7.11.
6. Eckhart's point in this somewhat cryptic statement seems to be that what is a necessity for any individual Christian (i.e., asking for God's armor) is obligatory for all.
7. A principle based on Aristotle, *Met.* 7.27 (1033b).
8. Augustine, *Sermon* 105.1.
9. Boethius, *Consolation of Philosophy* 1, pr. 2.
10. Thomas Aquinas, *STh* IIIa. 70. 4.
11. This famous definition of God first appeared in the *Book of the Twenty-Four Philosophers* prop. 2.
12. This question was discussed by Augustine in *Conf.* 11.10.2, but Eckhart seems to be speaking of an incident in his own life.
13. In *Comm. Jn.* n. 220 (LW III, pp. 184–85) Eckhart says that he used this response in answering a layman in front of other laity.
14. The second response, for which Eckhart frequently cited support in Augustine, *Conf.* 1.6.3, was a constant part of the Meister's teaching on creation, and was

the source for the first three condemned propositions in the Bull "In agro dominico." See *Essential Eckhart*, pp. 40–41, 77–78.
15. John Damascene, *Orthodox Faith* 4.4. No such passage has been found in Ambrose.
16. What Eckhart means is that God will effect in our cooperating will what lies beyond its own powers to achieve. Cf. Aquinas, *STb* Ia. IIae. 109. 6, 111. 2.
17. The first Augustine text is from *Conf.* 1.12.19, the second from the *Retractations* 1.8.4.
18. Pseudo-Cyprian, *On the Twofold Martyrdom* 7.
19. Augustine, *Sermons on John* 15.18.
20. Apparently a homiletic *exemplum*, or moral story used in preaching.
21. See, e.g., *Bened.* 1 (*Essential Eckhart*, pp. 229–30).
22. Aristotle, *Nicomachean Ethics* 2.3 (1104b).
23. Collations were evening talks given to students in the Mendicant houses.
24. This passage in Bernard has not been found.
25. Not found verbatim in Origen, but a passage in *Homilies on Exodus* 3.3 is somewhat similar.
26. The quotation is from the *Gloss*.
27. The author of these verses has not been identified.
28. Avicenna, *Soul* 4.4.
29. Augustine, *Sermon* 205.1.
30. Bernard, *On Consideration* 5.12.25.
31. Gregory the Great, *Homilies on the Gospels* 2.32.
32. See Thomas Aquinas, *Commentary on the Soul* 2.7, lecture 14.

Sermon XLIX. Twenty-third Sunday after Trinity. On the Gospel (Mt. 22:15–21).[1]

1. "Whose are this image and inscription?" (Mt. 22:20)

505. The Apostle Paul answers this question thus: "the image of the invisible God, the firstborn of every creature" (Col. 1:15). Note two things. First, according to Augustine, the image is to be sought where the soul is truly light, not extinguished by the body's contagion.[2] That means where nothing having "the figure of this world" (1 Co. 7:31) is allowed; where the higher part in the soul, the apex of the soul, is joined to the angelic light.

Second, note that an image as such cannot be separated from that of which it is an image, even by the intellect.

On the first point, observe that nothing can enter into where the image is except God, and, according to some,[3] the theological virtue [of charity] which is God's work. "I saw the gate of the Lord's house closed" (Ezk. 44:1–2). 506. "Of the invisible God" (Col. 1:15). "No one has ever seen God" (Jn. 1:18). "No one," that is, no human ("No human may see me and live" [Ex. 33:20]); "ever," that is, not in time, because "ever" is a word that indicates time. There follows, "The only begotten, who is in the Father's bosom, has revealed him" (Jn. 1:18).[4]

"The first born of every creature," that is, he who is set before every creature as the exemplar to whom they are to be patterned, just as a painter sets a picture before an apprentice for him to copy. This is why Augustine says that likeness is found in every creature, but image only in intellectual beings.[5] He is also "first born" before all created things.

507. It is clear "whose image this is," namely, of "the invisible God." It is clear where it is to be sought, namely, in the highest part of the soul. We must now see how we are conformed to it. Paul teaches this in 1 Corinthians 11: "A man ought not to cover his head because he is the image and glory of God" (1 Co. 11:7), and in 2 Corinthians 3 near the end: "As with unveiled face we gaze upon God's glory, we are being transformed into the very image from glory to glory as though by the Lord's Spirit" (2 Co. 3:18).

508. "We are being transformed" in two ways: first, because the earlier form is vanishing; and second, because the image transcends and is higher than any form. "From glory to glory" means from the natural light into the supernatural and from the light of grace finally into the light of glory. It can also be understood in another way. Sometimes the soul receives divine illuminations sent down under bodily forms. The soul wishes to pass from this "glory" to the "glory" that rests in itself until finally it can ascend in that glory to the one that "dwells in light inaccessible" (1 Tm. 6:16). Hence in the text given it says "as though by the Spirit of the Lord."

There follows [in the Gospel text the words] "and inscription." The third chapter of the Apocalypse says: "He who overcomes, I will make him a pillar in the temple of my God, and he shall not leave it anymore; and I shall write upon him the name of my God and the name of the new city Jerusalem." And right below, ". . . and my new name" (Rv. 3:12). (Carefully treat each text, as well as you know.)[6]

2. "Whose image is this?"

509. Note that the image is first of all similar.[7] "We will be similar to him" (1 Jn. 3:2). He is similar to God, who is assimilated to no creature; this is the person who left all things and was transfigured with Christ on the mountain.[8] It is proper to God to have nothing like him and no likeness.

Second, the image ought to be similar in nature and species,[9] and indeed, as far as possible, even in individual reality and in nothing else so that who it is an image of can be recognized in it. It was formed for this purpose. Third, according to Augustine equality belongs to the perfection of the image.[10] Fourth, the image ought to be the expression and emanation of its source.[11] Fifth, everything that is alien or other is outside the notion of the image (e.g., that it is a stone, or its color, etc.). Hence according to Aristotle and against Plato, a thing is known through its [intelligible] species and not through an Idea.[12]

510. From the fifth and second points above it follows that the image and its exemplar are not separately numbered as two substances, but the one is in the other. "I am in the Father, and the Father is in me" (Jn. 14:11). Furthermore, the just person depends on Justice formally, not like something from outside oneself, different and alien.[13] This is the sixth property of the image. Seventh, it is consequently necessary that the image be found only in intellectual nature where the same reality returns to itself in a "perfect return,"[14] and where the one that gives birth is one and the same with the child or offspring, finding oneself in the other and the other in oneself. Eighth, note that for the image truly to represent what it images it is necessary that it lack nothing that is in what it images and that there is nothing related to it or in it that pertains to anything else. Therefore, it can lack nothing that is in God, and can possess nothing that is in anything created.

3. "Image."

511. Note that an image properly speaking is a simple formal emanation that transmits the whole pure naked essence.[15] The metaphysician considers it in abstraction from the efficient and final causes according to which natural scientists investigate things.[16] The image then is an emanation from the depths in silence, excluding everything that comes from without. It is a form of life, as if you were to imagine something swelling up from itself and in itself and then inwardly boiling without any "boiling over" yet understood.[17]

There are three stages in the production of existence. The first, the one just mentioned, is that by which something from itself, out of itself, and in itself produces a pure nature, pouring it forth formally without the cooperation of the will, but rather with its concomitant activity.[18] This is the way the Good diffuses itself.[19] This is also how the power of willing can be a principle even if the end is not yet grasped. The second stage is like the "boiling over" in the manner of an efficient cause and with a view toward an end by which something produces something else that is from itself, but not out of itself. This production is either out of some other thing (and then it is called "making"), or it is out of nothing (and then it is the third stage of production which is called "creating"). See Augustine, *Nature of the Good*, Chapters 25–26,[20] and Avicenna, *Metaphysics*, Book 8, Chapter 6 near the beginning.

512. From what has been said it is clear first that the image properly speaking exists only in what is living, intellectual, and uncreated, inasmuch as we abstract from and do not consider efficient and final causality. Second, the image has the character of a birth, an offspring, and a son inasmuch as it comes forth in the same nature and is equal and similar in everything to what produced it. Hence the Son, the Image, is in the Father and the Father is in him; he is one in the Father (Jn. 10:38, 30). Fourth, it is evident that the Son "is not made or created."[21] Also, the Son does not exist nor is he produced by will, but by nature or naturally. Sixth, the Son, as the perfect likeness, breathes forth love, the Holy Spirit, who is also truly uncreated inasmuch as he remains in the image and the image in him, as Augustine teaches in the ninth book of the *Trinity*.[22] Seventh, it is clear how the Image, the Son, the "Firstborn," with the Father and the Holy Spirit, is the one Principle "of every creature." For it is necessary for something first to "boil" itself totally and then finally to "boil over" so that it can be completely perfected in itself while overflowing [with a fruitfulness] that is more than perfection. (See Avicenna, *Metaphysics* 8.6 at the beginning.) This is why nature first nourishes, then gives increase, perfects, and thus produces another being like itself.

Notes

1. This sermon is translated from LW IV, pp. 421–28.
2. Augustine, *Trin.* 14.8.11.
3. According to the editors, this alludes to the opinion of Peter of Tarantaise, a well-known Dominican theologian who briefly ruled the church as Pope Innocent V in 1276.

4. Eckhart, in typical fashion, gathers together a series of scriptural texts that all bear on the same point.
5. E.g., Augustine, *Trin.* 6.10.12, 11.5.8. Cf. *Comm. Jn.* n. 31 (*Essential Eckhart*, pp. 131–32).
6. This is Eckhart's note to himself, indicating that we are dealing with a sermon outline in part 1, rather than a finished text.
7. On the notion of image in Eckhart, see the Glossary under *imago* and *bilde*. For some other texts in this volume, see, e.g., *Comm. Wis.* n. 283 (pp. 172–73), and Sermon 69 (pp. 314–15).
8. Eckhart is referring to the Apostle John as an example of one who perfected his image by participating in Jesus' transfiguration (Mt. 17:1–2).
9. This is also the teaching of Thomas Aquinas in *STh* Ia. 93. 2.
10. Augustine, *Trin.* 6.10.11.
11. See especially *Comm. Jn.* n. 24 (*Essential Eckhart*, p. 129).
12. Aristotle, *Soul* 3.9–11 (429b).
13. On the importance of formal causality in Eckhart, see, e.g., Sermon IV.2, n. 29 (p. 210).
14. The "perfect return" (*reditio completa*) is an important technical term for Eckhart (see the Glossary under *reditus*). The source of the notion is in the *Book of Causes* prop. 15. See also *Comm. Wis.* n. 5 (LW II, pp. 326–27).
15. See *Comm. Jn.* n. 25 (*Essential Eckhart*, pp. 129–30), and *Comm. Wis.* n. 283 (pp. 172–73).
16. The stress on the investigation of formal causality as the primary task of metaphysics is one of the cornerstones of Eckhart's thought; see, e.g., *Comm. Gen.* n. 4 (*Essential Eckhart*, p. 83).
17. On "boiling" (*bullitio*) and "boiling over" (*ebullitio*), see the Glossary.
18. On this passage, see the Introduction, p. 26.
19. "*Bonum est diffusivum sui,*" one of the fundamental axioms of Neoplatonic thought, was well known to the scholastics, especially through the Dionysian writings, e.g., *Divine Names* 4.1.
20. The text in Augustine is actually *Nature of the Good* 26–27.
21. A quotation from the Athanasian Creed.
22. Augustine, *Trin.* 9.10.15.

II. GERMAN SERMONS

Sermon 1:   Intravit Jesus in templum et coepit eicere vendentes et ementes (Mt. 21:12).

We read in the holy gospel that our Lord went into the temple and was throwing out those who were buying and selling, and he said to others who had doves and the like for sale: "Get rid of this, put it away!" (Jn. 2:16) Why was Jesus throwing out those who were buying and selling and why did he tell those who had doves to get rid of them? His intention was none other than to have the temple empty,[1] just as though he were to say: "I have a right to this temple and want to be in it and to rule in it alone." What does this mean? This temple in which God wants to rule mightily according to his will is the human soul which he formed and created exactly like himself, as we read that our Lord said: "Let us make man according to our image and likeness" (Gn. 1:26). And he did this, too. So like himself did he make the human soul that neither in heaven nor on earth, of all the wonderful creatures that God made so attractive, are there any as like him as the human soul. This is why God wants to have this temple empty—so that no one is in it but him alone. And this is why this temple pleases him so much: because it is so exactly like him and he is so very comfortable in this temple when he is in it alone.

Now note carefully! Who were the people who were buying and selling there, and who are they still? Now understand me correctly! I am not preaching now about anyone but good people. Still, I want to show who the sellers there were and still are—people who thus bought and sold and still do—people whom our Lord struck and drove out. And he still does this to all those who buy and sell there in this temple. He does not want to let a

239

single such person remain inside. Look! Those people are all businessmen who guard against serious sins, would like to be good people, and perform their good works for God's glory, such as fasting, vigils, praying, and whatever other good works there are. But they do them so that our Lord might give them something in return, or so that God might do something to please them. These are all businessmen. This can be seen to be something unrefined because they want to give one thing in return for another, and thus want to make a business deal with our Lord. But this business deal deludes them. For everything that they have and everything that they can accomplish—if they were to give all this for God's sake and do it completely for God's sake, God would still not be in the least obliged to give them anything or to do anything for them, if he did not want to do it willingly and freely. What they are, they are from God; and what they have, they have from God and not from themselves. Therefore God is not at all indebted to them for their works or for their giving, unless he freely and gratuitously wants to do something, but not because of their works or gifts because they are not giving what belongs to them nor are their works their own.[2] Christ himself said: "Without me you can do nothing" (Jn. 15:5). These are very foolish people who thus want to make business deals with our Lord. They know the truth very little or not at all. This is why our Lord struck them and drove them out of the temple. Light and darkness cannot exist side by side. God is the truth and a light in himself.[3] When then God comes into this temple, he drives out ignorance, which is darkness, and reveals himself in light and truth. Then the businessmen are gone insofar as the truth becomes known. Truth does not like business deals. God seeks nothing of his own. In all his works he is empty and free and works them out of genuine love. This is how the person acts who is united with God. He, too, is empty and free in all his works and he does them only for the glory of God, seeking nothing of his own, and it is God who is working this in him.

I will make a further claim. As long as a person in any of his works seeks anything at all of all that which God can or shall give, he is like these businessmen. If you want to be so completely free of making business deals that God permits you in this temple, you should do everything that you can in all your works purely to praise God, and you should be as empty as that nothing is empty which is neither here nor there.[4] You should desire nothing at all for this. When you so act, your works are spiritual and divine. Then the businessmen have been driven out of the temple completely, and God is alone within because this person has nothing but God as his intention. See, this is how the temple is free of businessmen. Look! The person who does not regard himself or anything else but God alone and God's honor is truly

240

free and rid of all mercantilism in all his works and seeks nothing of his own, just as God is free and unencumbered in all his works and seeks nothing of his own.

I have already mentioned that our Lord said to the people who were selling doves: "Put that away, get rid of that!" These people he did not drive out or punish very much. Instead he spoke very kindly: "Put that away!" as though he wanted to say: This is not really bad, but it does cause obstacles for pure truth. These people are all good people who perform their works purely for God's sake and seek nothing of their own in them, and yet they still do them with possessiveness, in time and in number, with a before and after.[5] In these works they are kept from the best truth, that they should be free and empty as our Lord Jesus Christ is free and empty, receiving himself continually anew without interruption and outside of time from his heavenly Father. And in this same "now"[6] he gives birth to himself in return fully and with grateful praise into the eminence of the Father in equal dignity. This is how that person should be who wants to receive highest truth and dwell in it without a before and after, and without being impeded by all the words and all the images which he ever was conscious of, empty and free in this "now," receiving anew divine gifts and giving birth to them in return un-impeded in this same light with thankful praise in our Lord Jesus Christ. Then the doves would be gone, that is, the obstacles and possessiveness attached to all those works which are otherwise good in which a person seeks nothing of his own. This is why our Lord said very kindly, "Put that away, get rid of it!" as though he wanted to say: It is good but does cause obstacles.

When this temple is thus free of all obstacles, namely, possessiveness and ignorance, then it sparkles so beautifully and shines so purely and bright *above* everything that God created and *through* everything that God created that no one can be compared to it in brightness but the uncreated God alone. And truly no one is like this temple but the uncreated God alone. Everything that is beneath the angels is not in the least like this temple. The highest angels themselves are like this temple of the noble soul to a large extent, and yet not completely. That they are like the soul to some degree is based on knowledge and love, but a limit is set for them beyond which they cannot go. The soul can go much further. If the soul of a man still living in time were standing on the same level as the highest angel, this person could reach immeasurably higher in his free capability above the angel in every "now," new beyond number, that is, and beyond manner and above the manner of the angels and any created intellect.[7] God alone is free and uncreated, and therefore he alone is like the soul with respect to being free, but not with respect to uncreatedness because the soul is created.

241

When the soul enters the unmixed light, it plunges into its utter nothingness so distant from its created somethingness in its utter nothingness
that it can in no way through its own power come back again to its created
somethingness. But God sustains its utter nothingness with his uncreatedness and holds the soul in his utter somethingness. The soul dared to become
nothing and cannot on its own return to itself—so far did it go out of itself
before God sustained it. This must of necessity be so. For, as I said before,
"Jesus went into the temple and was throwing out those who were buying
and selling there, and he said to the others: 'Get rid of this!' " Now watch
as I take up the phrase "Jesus went in and began to say, 'Get rid of this!' "
and they got rid of it. See, then there was no longer anyone there but only
Jesus, and he began to speak in the temple.[8] Now you should realize this is
true: If someone else but Jesus alone speaks in the temple (that is, the soul),
then Jesus keeps silent as though he were not at home. And he is not at home
in the soul then because it has other guests with whom it is conversing. But
if Jesus is to speak in the soul, it must be alone and must itself remain silent
if it is to hear Jesus speak. Yes, then he enters in and begins to speak. What
does the Lord Jesus say? He says what he is.[9] And what is he? He is the
Word of the Father. In this same Word the Father speaks himself and the
whole divine nature and everything that God is, as he knows it; and he
knows it as it is. And because he has perfect knowledge and power, he also
is perfect in his speaking. When he speaks the Word, he speaks himself and
all things in a different Person and gives to it [i.e., the Person] the same nature that he has himself. And he speaks all intelligent spirits in this same
Word, like this Word as to image insofar as it exists remaining within, but
not like this Word in every way as it shines forth, as each individual exists
in itself. Rather, they have received the capacity through grace to receive
likeness with the Word; and this same Word, as it exists in itself, the Father
has spoken totally—the Word and everything that is in the Word.[10]

Since the Father has spoken *this*, what then is Jesus speaking in the soul?
As I have said, the Father speaks the Word and speaks in the Word and
[speaks] in no other way, and Jesus speaks in the soul. The manner of his
speaking is that he reveals himself and everything the Father has spoken in
him in the manner that a spirit can receive. He reveals the fatherly dominion
in this spirit in equal, immeasurable power. When the spirit receives this
power in the Son and through the Son, it becomes powerful in every action
so that it becomes like to and powerful in all virtues and in the most perfect
purity so that neither happiness nor sadness nor anything that God created
in time can destroy this person. Rather, he remains standing mightily within
it, as within a divine power compared to which all things are small and weak.

Secondly, Jesus reveals himself in the soul in the immeasurable wisdom which he himself is and in which the Father knows himself with all his fatherly dominion and [in which he knows] this same Word, which is wisdom itself, and [knows] everything that is in it as this is one. When this wisdom is united with the soul, all its doubts, all illusions, and all obscurities are totally removed from it; and it is placed in a pure bright light which is God himself. As the prophet says: "Lord, in your light one shall know light" (Ps. 35:10). There in the soul God is made known to God. Thus with this wisdom the soul knows itself and all things, and it knows the same wisdom with him [God] himself. And with this wisdom it knows the fatherly power in its fruitful capacity to give birth, and [it knows] original being in its simple oneness,[11] void of all difference.

Jesus reveals himself also with an immeasurable sweetness and abundance, pouring forth from the power of the Holy Spirit and spilling over with an overabundant fullness of sweetness and richness, pouring into all receptive hearts. When Jesus reveals himself with this sweetness and with this abundance, uniting himself to the soul with this abundance and with this sweetness, then the soul flows into itself and out of itself, overflowing itself and [flowing out] over all things through grace with force without a medium back again to its first beginning. Then the exterior man is obedient to the interior man until death and is constantly in the state of peace in the service of God.[12] May Jesus also come into us, throw out and get rid of all obstacles, making us one as he is one with the Father and the Holy Spirit— one God. That we so become one with him and remain so eternally, may God help us. Amen.

NOTES

Translated from DW I, pp. 4–20.

1. The MHG word *ledic* means both "empty" and "free of," an ambivalence the preacher often uses to advantage. See the Glossary under *lûterkeit*.
2. See Sermon XXV.1, n. 256 (p. 218).
3. God is a light in himself in that the light shines forth from him and is not merely reflected light, as is the case with creatures.
4. The last part of this sentence may be corrupt. However, if it is not, this is one of the preacher's references to a nothing that is not *less* but *more* than being.
5. The defects of works done by these people rests on their being performed *mit eigenschaft*, which has been translated here as "with possessiveness." However,

mit eigenschaft can also imply that these works are done "with limiting characteristics"; that is, that they are not free of the limitations of human actions but are restricted as to time, place, etc. Thus they have not yet reached the level of divine actions, which are free of all limiting characteristics.

6. That is, in the "now" (*nû*) of eternity in which God exists. See the Glossary.
7. By "manner" *(wîse)* here Eckhart means a limited manner of existing that characterizes the existence of creatures and is contrasted to God's infinite existence. For more on this, see the Glossary.
8. With this mention of "temple," Eckhart resumes his allegorical interpretation of Jesus' speaking in the temple, that is, the soul.
9. This sentence is ambiguous in MHG. It could also be an allusion to Exodus 3:14, that God is simply existence (*esse*). Thus one could also translate it: "He says that he is."
10. In the foregoing sentences Eckhart is describing both the trinitarian relationship of Father and Son and the relationship of creatures, especially those endowed with intelligence, to the Son, whose image they are.
11. "Original being" (MHG *weseliche istikeit*) might also be translated "essential Existence." See the Glossary.
12. This sentence appeared on the lists of the Cologne censors (cf. Théry, pp. 180, 258).

Sermon 3: Nunc scio vere, quia misit dominus angelum suum (Ac. 12:11).

When Peter had been freed from the bonds of his imprisonment through the power of the exalted and sovereign God, he said, "Now I know truly that God sent his angel to me and saved me from the power of Herod and the hands of the enemy."

Now let us change the words around and say: because God sent his angel to me, I know truly.[1] *Peter* has the meaning *knowledge.*[2] I have often said: Knowledge and intellect unite the soul in God. Intellect penetrates into pure being; knowledge runs ahead, leading the way and breaking through so that God's only-begotten Son is born there. Our Lord says in Matthew that no one knows the Father but the Son (Mt. 11:27). The masters maintain that knowledge depends on similarity.[3] Some masters say that the soul is composed of all things since it has the potentiality of knowing all things.[4] This sounds silly, but it is true. The masters say: Whatever I am to know has to be completely present to me and like my knowledge.[5] The saints say that power is in the Father, likeness in the Son, and union in the Holy Spirit.[6] This is true because the Father is totally present to the Son, and the Son is completely like him. Thus no one knows the Father but the Son.

Now Peter says, "Now I know truly." What causes one to know truly here? It comes from a divine light that deceives no one. Secondly, it happens because one knows here immediately and purely, not covered by anything. Thus Paul says, "God dwells in a light to which there is no access" (1 Tm. 6:16).[7] The masters say that the wisdom we learn here [on earth] will remain with us there [in heaven].[8] But Paul says it will pass away (1 Co. 13:8). One master says that pure knowledge, even in this life, involves such great pleasure that the pleasure from all created things is as good as nothing in comparison with the pleasure it brings with it.[9] No matter how noble it is, it is nonetheless accidental; as small as one small word is compared to the whole world, so small is all the wisdom that we can learn here compared to the naked, pure truth. This is why Paul says that it will pass away. Even though it may still remain, it turns out to be real foolishness and as though it were nothing compared to the naked truth one learns there. The third reason why one learns truly there is that the things one sees here subject to change one knows there [as] unchangeable, and one perceives them there completely undivided and together. What here is far away is there close by, because there all things are present. Whatever happened on the first day and will happen on the last day is all present there.

"Now I know truly that God sent his angel to me." When God sends his angel to the soul, it knows truly. It was not in vain that God entrusted the key to St. Peter (Cf. Mt. 16:19), because *Peter* means *knowledge*.[10] Knowledge has the key, unlocks, penetrates, breaks through, and finds God naked. Then it tells its playmate, the will, what it has come into the possession of, although it had the will already, for what I want, I go searching for.[11] Knowledge goes on ahead. She is a queen seeking to rule over the most lofty and most pure, and handing it over to the soul. The soul in turn passes it on to its nature and its nature [passes it on] to all the bodily senses. The soul is so noble at its highest and purest that the masters can find no name for it. They call it "soul" because it gives being to the body. Now the masters say that, after the first breaking-out from the Godhead (where the Son "breaks out" of the Father), an angel is the thing formed most closely to God.[12] This is certainly true. The soul is formed like God as to its highest part, but an angel is a closer image of God. Everything belonging to an angel is formed like God. Therefore, an angel is sent to the soul to bring it back to the same image according to which it [the angel] has been formed, for knowledge

245

arises from similarity. Because the soul has the potentiality of knowing all things, it never rests until it comes to the first image where all things are one. There it rests, there in God. In God no creature is nobler than another. The masters say being and knowing are completely one.[13] What does not exist cannot be known either. What has the most being is also the most known. Because God has an overflowing being, he transcends all knowledge. As I said the day before yesterday in my most recent sermon,[14] the soul is formed into the highest purity, into the mold of pure being where it gets a taste of God before he takes on truth or intelligibility, where all possibility of naming has been cast off.[15] There it knows most purely; there it takes being on its [being's] own level. Therefore Paul says: "God dwells in a light to which there is no access" (1 Tm. 6:16). He is a subsisting in his own pure being, to which nothing [added] is clinging. Whatever is contingent must disappear. He is a pure abiding within himself, where there is no this or that; for whatever is in God *is* God.[16] A pagan master says that the powers that hover beneath God are dependent on God; and although they reside purely within themselves, they nevertheless are dependent on him who has neither beginning nor end, for nothing alien can enter into God.[17] The sky is a proof of this. It cannot receive an impression from without in a manner foreign to it.

This is what happens: Whatever comes to God is changed. However worthless it may be, if we bring it to God, it is emptied of itself. Here is a comparison. If I have wisdom, I am not myself wisdom. I can gain wisdom and also lose it. But whatever is in God, *is* God; it cannot be removed from him. It is fixed in the divine nature, and the divine nature is so powerful that whatever is put into it is completely established there or it remains completely outside. Now hear something wondrous! Since God transforms such worthless things into himself, what do you suppose he does with the soul which he has honored with his own image?[18]

That we may attain this, may God help us. Amen.

NOTES

Translated from DW I, pp. 48–57.

1. This "changing the words around" or playing with words is based on the ambiguity of the Latin conjunction *quia*. In the Vulgate it can mean "that" (as in "I know *that* God sent his angel . . ."). This is how Jerome uses it in this passage.

However, it can also mean *because* or *since*. This is how Eckhart wants it understood here. Later in the sermon he uses it again as Jerome wanted it understood.

2. Eckhart explains why *Peter* means *knowledge* later in the sermon.

3. Cf. Thomas Aquinas, *Commentary on the Soul* 1.4.

4. Cf. Aristotle, *Soul* 3.8 (431b).

5. Cf. *Book of Twenty-Four Philosophers* prop. 23, in the commentary.

6. Cf. Thomas Aquinas, *STh* Ia. 39.8, citing Augustine, *Christ. Doct.* 1.5.

7. For more on this quotation from 1 Timothy, see Sermons 29 and 69 (pp. 290, 314).

8. Cf. Thomas Aquinas, *STh* Ia. 89.5,6.

9. Cf. Aristotle, *Nichomachean Ethics* 7.11(1152b).

10. *Peter* does not, of course, mean *knowledge* etymologically. The preacher gives it this meaning here because of Peter's possessing the key that "opens up."

11. This last "although" clause is unclear. It seems to mean that the preacher is correcting his own oversimplified comparison of intellect and will with playmates by conceding here that the will is immediately aware of what the intellect possesses and does not have to be told anything. Also, according to what follows, the will precedes the intellect in a sense.

12. Cf. Thomas Aquinas, *In I Sent.* d. 3, q. 3, a. 1, and ad 4; and Albert the Great, *In II Sent.* d. 1, a. 1.

13. Cf. *Comm. Jn.* n. 26 (*Essential Eckhart*, p. 130), and Thomas Aquinas, *STh* Ia. 16.3, and *Commentary on the Metaphysics* 2.1.

14. It is difficult to know if this refers to a surviving sermon or not.

15. For God as unnameable, see, e.g., *Comm. Ex.* nn. 37–53 (pp. 54–60).

16. This is taken by some to be a doctrine objected to by the censors in Cologne. However, the Latin formulation of the Cologne censors is quite different. Its translation: "Everything that is, is God" (cf. Théry, p. 252).

17. *Book of the Twenty-Four Philosophers* prop. 16(15).

18. For more on the soul as God's image, see *Par. Gen.* nn. 138–40, 143, 154 (*Essential Eckhart*, pp. 109–10, 112, 116–17), and *Comm. Jn.* nn. 84, 119–20, 123 (ibid., pp. 153, 168–71). See both *imago* and *bilde* in the Glossary for more complete references.

Sermon 4: Omne datum optimum et omne donum perfectum desursum est (Jm. 1:17).

St. James says in the epistle: "The best gift of all and perfection descend from above from the Father of lights."[1] Now note carefully! You should realize that people who abandon themselves to God and seek only his will with all diligence—whatever God gives to such a person is the best. You may be as certain of this as you are that God lives—that it must of necessity be the best thing of all, and that no other way could be better. Even though something else might seem better, it would nevertheless not be good for you because God wants it this way and not a different way, and this way must of necessity be the best for you. Whether it be sickness or poverty, hunger or thirst, or whatever it might be—whatever God has ordained or not ordained for you, or whatever God gives you or does not give you, all this is the best for you. Be it that you have no sense of spiritual devotion or the interior life, or whatever you have or do not have,[2] if you really direct yourself toward intending God's honor in all things, then whatever he does with you is the best.

Now you could perhaps say: "How do I know whether it is God's will or not?" Know this: If it were not God's will, it would not be happening. You cannot be sick nor can anything at all happen unless it is God's will. And since you then know that it is God's will, you should have so much delight and satisfaction in it that you do not consider any pain as pain. Even if it were the most excruciating of all pain, if you then were to feel any pain or suffering, this would be completely wrong. You should accept it from God as the best thing of all because it must of necessity be the best thing for you. God's being depends upon his [always] willing the best. Therefore I, too, should always will it and nothing should suit me better. If there were a person that I wanted to please at all costs, and if I know for certain that I pleased this person in gray clothes better than in any other no matter how good they were, without a doubt I would find these clothes more enjoyable and would prefer them to any others no matter how good they might be. In trying to please anybody, if I knew that he liked something, be it in words or deeds, I would do it and not something else. Now take a look for yourselves how things stand with your love. If you loved God, then nothing could be more delightful for you than what would please him most of all and [to see] that his will in our regard be accomplished. No matter how great the suffering or distress might seem, if you do not have just as much enjoyment from it, something is wrong.

I say quite often (and it is true): Every day we raise our voices and exclaim in the Our Father, "Lord, your will be done!" (Mt. 6:10) And when his will comes about, we get angry and are not at all satisfied with his will. Yet whatever he does should please us best of all. Those who really do take this for the best remain in all circumstances fully at peace. Now sometimes a thought comes to you and you say: "Alas, if it had only turned out differently, things would be better." Or, "If it had not happened this way, things might perhaps have turned out better." As long as you think this, you will never gain peace. You should take it [God's will] as the best. This is the first meaning of these words.

There is another meaning which you should carefully note. He says "every gift." The best of all and the highest things are truly gifts in the most proper sense. God does not like to give anything as much as big gifts. I once said on this very spot that God likes to forgive big sins better than small ones. The bigger they are, the more freely and quickly he forgives them. This, too, is how it works with grace, gifts, and virtue. The bigger they are, the more freely he gives them because his nature depends on his giving big things. And so, the better things are, the more there are of them. The noblest of creatures are the angels. They are completely intellectual beings lacking corporality. There is the greatest quantity of them and there are more of them than the sum of all material things.[3] Big things are properly called gifts and are his [God's] domain in the most real and proper sense.

I once said whatever can be expressed properly in words must come forth from within and must have movement from an inner form; it cannot enter in from without but must come out from within. It lives actually in the innermost [part] of the soul. There all things are present to you, are living within and seeking, and are in their best and highest [state]. Why do you not notice any of this? Because you are not at home there. The more noble a thing is, the more common it is. The senses I have in common with animals; life I have in common with trees. Being is still more interior to me and I have it in common with all creatures. The sky has greater expanse than everything beneath it. This is why it is also nobler. The nobler things are, the more widespread and common they are. Love is noble because it is common.[4]

What our Lord commanded seems difficult: that one should love one's fellow Christians as oneself (Mk. 12:31). Unknowing people generally say it goes like this: one should love them for the same good as in loving oneself.[5] This is not the case. One should love them as much as oneself, and this is not difficult.[6] If you consider it correctly, love deserves a reward more than a commandment. The commandment seems difficult, but the recompense is desirable. Who loves God as he should and must love him (whether he wants to or not), and [who loves him] as all creatures love him, such a person has to love his fellow man as himself and has to rejoice at the other's joyous good fortune just as much as at his own. He must desire the other's honor as much as his own and [must love] a stranger as he does someone close to him. Such a person experiences joy constantly, as well as honor and advantage. He is just as he would be in heaven, and he experiences joys more frequently than if he were just feeling joy about his own success. Be aware of this in truth: If your own honor is more satisfying to you than that of another, this is not right.

Know that when you seek anything of your own, you will never find God because you do not seek God purely. You are seeking something along with God, and you are acting just as if you were to make a candle out of God in order to look for something with it. Once one finds the things one is looking for, one throws the candle away. This is what you are doing: Whatever else you are looking for in addition to God, it is nothing, no matter what it might be—whether it be something useful or reward or devotion or whatever it might be. You are seeking nothing, and so you also find nothing.[7] The reason why you find nothing is that you are seeking nothing. All creatures are a pure nothing. I do not just say that they are insignificant or are only a little something: They are a pure nothing.[8] Whatever has no being, *is* not. Creatures have no being because their being depends on God's presence. If God were to turn away from creatures for an instant, they would turn to nothing. I once said (and it is true), if someone were to have the whole world and God, he would not have more than if he had God alone. All creatures have nothing more without God than a gnat has without God—[they are] just the same, neither less nor more.

Now consider this true fact. If a person were to donate a thousand marks of gold to build churches and monasteries, this would be something great. However, a person who could consider a thousand marks as nothing would have given much more. This latter person would have accomplished much more than the former. When God created all creatures, they were so insignificant and confining that he had no freedom to move in them. Then he made the soul so like himself and so similar in order to give himself to the soul because, whatever else he could give it, it did not value at all. God has to give himself to me as my own as he really is himself, or I have nothing and have no taste for anything. The person who is to receive him thus must have surrendered himself completely and have gone out of himself. Everything that God has, such a person receives from him equally and just as much his own as what one has oneself, and [just as] our Lady and all those who are in heaven. This is all theirs and theirs equally. Those who have gone out of themselves like this and have surrendered themselves shall also receive like this, and not less.

The third phrase is "from the Father of lights" (Jm. 1:17). The word *father* implies *sonship*, and the word *father* [also] signifies simply *begetting* and is life for all things. The Father gives birth to his Son in the eternal knowledge, and the Father gives birth to the Son in the soul just as [he does] in his own nature.[9] He gives birth in the soul as its own, and his being depends on his giving birth to the Son in the soul whether he likes it or not. I was once asked what the Father does in heaven. I answered: He gives birth to his Son and this activity pleases him so much and is such a delight to him that he never does anything else but give birth to his Son, and the two of them cause the Holy Spirit to blossom forth. Where the Father gives birth to his Son in me, there I am the same Son and not a different one. We are, of course, different with respect to our humanity, but there I am the same Son and not a different one. "Where we are Sons, there we are true heirs" (Rm. 8:17).[10] Who knows the truth knows well that the word *father* contains in it pure begetting and having sons. This is why we are present in this Son and are the same Son.

Now concentrate on the phrase: "They descend from above" (Jm. 1:17).[11] I told you a short time ago: If a person wants to receive from above, he must of necessity be below in true humility. And know this in truth: If a person is not completely below, nothing whatsoever will work out for him and he will receive nothing, however small it might be. If you have your regard fixed on yourself or any thing or person, then you are not below and you are not receiving either. But if you are completely below, you are receiving completely and abundantly. It is God's nature to give, and his being depends on his giving to us if we are below. If we are not and if we are receiving nothing, we do him violence and kill him. And if we cannot do it to him, we still do it to ourselves to the extent that it is in our grasp. So that you really give him everything, see to it that you lower yourself under God in true humility and that you raise God up in your heart and in your understanding. "God our Lord sent his Son into the world" (Ga. 4:4). I once said right here: God sent his Son in the fullness of time to the soul—when it had traversed time.[12] When the soul is rid of time and place, then the Father sends his Son into the soul. This is the meaning of the words: "The best gift of all and perfection descend from above from the Father of lights." That we become prepared to receive the best gift, may God the Father of lights help us. Amen.

NOTES

Translated from DW I, pp. 60–74.

1. In translating this verse Eckhart changes "perfect gift" to "perfection."
2. This whole paragraph up to this point but excluding the initial quotation from James was on the list of articles of the Cologne censors (cf. Théry, p. 245).
3. Cf. Thomas Aquinas, *STh* Ia. 50. 3.
4. Part of the force of this passage arises from the ambiguity of the MHG adjective *gemein* (common), which means both "widespread" and "lowly," the opposite of "noble."
5. This "same good" would seem to be God. Eckhart seems to be objecting to the thought that we should love fellow Christians and ourselves because of God, that all love is ordered to him.
6. This teaching concerning love of neighbor found its way onto the list of the Cologne censors (see Théry, p. 287).
7. In seeking a creature, one finds nothing because creatures are in themselves "a pure nothing," as the preacher then notes. See the Glossary under *niht*.
8. These statements on the nothingness of creatures became article 26 of the papal bull "In agro dominico" (*Essential Eckhart*, p. 80).
9. For more on the birth of the Son, see the Glossary under *geburt*.
10. The last three sentences are very similar to a formulation found on the lists of the Cologne censors (cf. Théry, p. 176).
11. "They" are "the best gift of all and perfection." See the beginning of the sermon.
12. That is, when and to the extent that the soul achieves timelessness.

Sermon 7: Populi eius qui in te est, misereberis (Ho. 14:4).

The prophet says, "Lord, have mercy on the people that is in you." Our Lord responds, "All that is infirm I shall make whole and I shall love them willingly" (Ho. 14:5).[1]

I shall treat the text, that "the Pharisee desired that our Lord dine with him," and in addition, "our Lord said to the woman: '*vade in pace:* go into peace' " (Lk. 7:36–50).[2] It is good to go from peace to peace; it is praiseworthy. Still, it is a defect. One should *run* to peace, not *begin* in peace. God wishes to say that one should be put into peace and pushed into peace and should end in peace. Our Lord said, "In me alone do you have peace" (cf.

Jn. 16:33). To the extent that one is in God, one is in peace. Whatever of a person is in God has peace; whatever of a person is outside of God has turmoil. St. John says, "Everything that is born of God overcomes the world" (1 Jn. 5:4). Whatever is born of God seeks peace and runs to peace. Therefore he said, "*vade in pace:* run into peace." A person who is in a race, a continual race, and is in peace, such a person is a heavenly person.[3] The heavens are constantly running around [i.e., revolving] and in running they seek peace.

Now take note: "The Pharisee desired that our Lord dine with him" (Lk. 7:36). The food that I eat is united with my body, just as my body is with my soul. My body and my soul are united in one being, not just in one act, as my soul unites itself with the eye in the act of seeing. Thus the food that I eat has one being with my nature; it is not united to it [just] in one act. It signifies the great oneness we should have with God—in one being, not in one act. This is why the Pharisee asked our Lord to dine with him.[4]

Pharisee means someone who is detached and does not recognize any boundary.[5] Whatever is attached to the soul must be totally removed. The nobler the powers are, the greater their ability to detach. Some powers are so high above the body and so separated that they peel off and sever completely. A master puts it nicely: "Whatever in any way touches something material never enters in there."[6] Secondly, [*Pharisee* means] that one be detached, drawn away, and drawn inward.[7] From this one learns that an unlettered person can, with love and desire, attain knowledge and teach. The third meaning is that one can have no boundary, not be closed in anywhere, nor cling anywhere, and be so established in peace that one knows nothing of turmoil. [Thus it is] when such a person is established in God with powers which are totally detached. This is why the prophet said, "Lord, have mercy on the people that is in you" (Ho. 14:4).

A master says that the highest work God has ever performed in all creatures is mercy. The most intimate and secret work, even what he has worked in the angels, is carried up into mercy, the work of mercy as it is in itself and in God. Whatever God works, the first breaking forth is mercy, not in the sense of his forgiving someone their sin or of one person's showing compassion for another person. Rather, the master's meaning is that the highest work which God performs is mercy. A master says that the work of mercy is so closely related to God (granted that truth, abundance, and goodness name God), that one [such name] names him better than the others. The highest work of God is mercy, which means that God places the soul into the highest and purest that it can attain: into vast regions, into the sea, into unchartered depths. There God works mercy.[8] Thus the prophet said, "Lord, have mercy on the people which is in you."

Which people is in God? St. John says, "God is love, and whoever lives in love lives in God and God in him" (1 Jn. 4:16). Although St. John says that love unites, love does not place us into God. At most it binds. Love does not unite, not at all. It fastens together and binds what has already been united. Love joins [things] in an act, not in one being.[9] The best masters say that the intellect peels everything away and takes God bare, as he is pure being in himself. Knowledge pierces through truth and goodness, coming upon pure being and taking God bare as he is without names.[10] But I maintain that neither knowledge nor love unites.[11] Love takes God just as he is good. If the name *goodness* were removed from God, love would be at a loss what to do. Love takes God with a coat on, with a garment on. The intellect does not do this. The intellect takes God as he is known in it, but it can never encompass him in the sea of his unfathomableness. I maintain that above these two, knowledge and love, is mercy. In the highest and purest that God can work, there is where he works mercy.

A master puts it well when he says that there is something completely mysterious and hidden in the soul existing far above where the powers intellect and will burst forth. St. Augustine says that just as the first breaking-out of the Son from the Father in the first breaking-out is inexpressible, so, too, there is something completely mysterious [in the soul] which is above the first breaking-out where intellect and will break out. A master, who has spoken best of all about the soul, says that all human ingenuity can never discover what the soul is in its ground.[12] [To discover] what the soul is requires supernatural understanding. We know nothing of where the powers go out from the soul into works; or we know perhaps a little bit, but it is scant.[13] What the soul is in its ground, no one knows about this. What one can learn of it has to be supernatural; it must happen through grace. And there is where God works mercy. Amen.

NOTES

Translated from DW I, pp. 117–24.

1. "Willingly" has no manuscript backing and is a conjecture by Quint since it is much closer to the Latin original (*spontanee*) than the obvious corruptions in the manuscripts.
2. Eckhart translates the Latin *in pace* (in peace) as "into peace" (*in pacem*) for purposes of interpretation.

3. The union of action and contemplation hinted at here suggests the presentation of the figure of Martha in Sermon 86 (pp. 338–44).

4. The type of union Eckhart is advocating between human beings and God is what scholastic thinkers would call *substantial* union, a union in one being. This is evident from the analogy he uses of the union of soul and body because in *Comm. Jn.* n. 93 (*Essential Eckhart*, p. 157) Eckhart shows he conceives of the union of soul and body in the traditional manner of one substance, with the soul being the form of the body. This was attacked at the Cologne proceedings (cf. Théry, pp. 249–50).

5. The etymological foundation of the preacher's use of *Pharisee* is that it means "one set apart" or "separated." This was also the traditional meaning.

6. That is, into the noblest powers of the soul. Cf. Augustine, *Trin.* 14.8.11.

7. For more on detachment, see *abegescheidenheit* in the Glossary.

8. As this paragraph makes clear, the preacher's presentation of mercy in this sermon has little in common with the usual sense of the word, but rather signifies God's overflowing being.

9. For the distinction between union in act and union in being, see note 4 above.

10. Concerning the intellect's superiority over the will (love), see, e.g., *Comm. Ex.* n. 265 (p. 125). For more on seeing God as nameless, see *Comm. Ex.* nn. 37–53 (pp. 54–60).

11. For another passage in which union or beatitude is said to surpass knowing and loving, see Sermon 53 (*Essential Eckhart*, p. 201).

12. Cf. Augustine, *Lit. Comm. Gen.* 6.29.40.

13. That is, we know very little of the ground of the soul. We know of the soul mainly through the works or activities of its powers, intellect and will. What is behind this is hidden from us.

Sermon 9: Quasi stella matutina in medio nebulae et quasi luna plena in diebus suis lucet et quasi sol refulgens, sic iste refulsit in templo dei (Si. 50:6–7).

"As the morning star through the mist and as the full moon in its days and as the resplendent sun, so did this man shine in the temple of God."

First I shall take the last phrase: "temple of God." What is "God" and what is "temple of God?"

Twenty-four philosophers came together and wanted to discuss what God is.[1] They came at the appointed time and each of them gave his definition. I shall now take up two or three of them. One said: "God is something compared to which all changeable and transitory things are nothing, and everything that has being is insignificant in his presence." The second said: "God is something that is of necessity above being; that in himself needs no one and that all things need." The third said: "God is intellect living in the knowledge of himself alone."[2]

I shall leave aside the first and the last definition and speak about the second, that God is something that of necessity must be above being. Whatever has being, time, or place does not touch God. He is above it. God is in all creatures, insofar as they have being, and yet he is above them.[3] That same thing that he is in all creatures is exactly what he is above them. Whatever is one in many things must of necessity be above them. Some masters maintain that the soul is only in the heart. This is not so, and learned masters have gone astray here. The soul is complete and undivided at the same time in the foot and in the eye and in every part of the body.[4] If I take a segment of time, it is neither today nor yesterday.[5] But if I take "now," that contains within itself all time. The "now" in which God made the world is as near to this time as the "now" in which I am presently speaking, and the last day is as near to this "now" as the day that was yesterday.

One authority says: "God is something that works in eternity undivided in himself; that needs no one's help or instrumentality, and remains in himself; that needs nothing and that all things need, and toward which all things strive as to their final end."[6] This end has no limited manner of being. It grows out beyond manner and spreads out into the distance. St. Bernard says: "To love God is a manner without manner."[7] A physician who wants to make a sick person healthy does not have any degree of health [to measure] how healthy he wants to make the sick person. He certainly has a manner by which he wants to make him healthy, but how healthy he wants to make him—that does not have a manner: as healthy as he can![8] How we should love God has no manner: as much as we at all can, that is, without manner.

Everything works in being; nothing works above its being.[9] Fire cannot work except in wood. God works above being in vastness, where he can roam. He works in nonbeing. Before being was, God worked. He worked being when there was no being.[10] Unsophisticated teachers say that God is pure being. He is as high above being as the highest angel is above a gnat. I would be speaking as incorrectly in calling God a being as if I called the sun pale or black. God is neither this nor that. A master says: "Whoever imagines that he has understood God, if he knows anything, it is not God that he knows."[11] However, in saying that God is not a being and is above being, I have not denied being to God; rather, I have elevated it in him. If I take copper [mixed] with gold, it is still present and is present in a higher manner than it is in itself. St. Augustine says: God is wise without wisdom, good without goodness, powerful without power.[12]

Young masters say in the schools that all being is divided into ten modes of being and they deny them completely of God.[13] None of these modes touches God, but neither does he lack any of them. The first mode, which has the most of being and in which all things receive being, is substance; and the last mode, which contains the least of being, is called relation, and in God this is the same as the greatest of all which has the most of being. They have equal images in God.[14] In God the images of all things are alike, but they are images of unlike things. The highest angel and the soul and a gnat have like images in God. God is neither being nor goodness. Goodness adheres to being and is not more extensive. If there were no being, neither would there be goodness. Yet being is purer than goodness. God is neither good nor better nor best of all. Whoever would say that God is good would be treating him as unjustly as though he were calling the sun black.[15]

And yet God says: No one is good but God alone. What is good? Good is that which shares itself. We call a person good who shares with others and is useful. Because of this a pagan master says: A hermit is neither good nor evil in a sense because he does not share and is not useful. God shares most of all. Nothing [else] shares itself out of what is its own, for all creatures are nothing in themselves. Whatever they share they have from another. Nor is it themselves that they give. The sun gives its radiance yet remains where it is; fire gives its heat but remains fire. God, however, shares what is his because what he is, he is from himself. And in all the gifts he gives he always gives himself first of all.[16] He gives himself as God, as he is in all his gifts, to the extent that the person who can receive him is capable. St. James says: "All good gifts flow down from above from the Father of lights" (Jm. 1:17).

When we grasp God in being, we grasp him in his antechamber, for being is the antechamber in which he dwells. Where is he then in his temple, in which he shines as holy? Intellect is the temple of God. Nowhere does God dwell more properly than in his temple, in intellect, as the second philosopher said: "God is intellect, living in the knowledge of himself alone,"[17] remaining in himself alone where nothing ever touches him; for he alone is there in his stillness. God in the knowledge of himself knows himself in himself.[18]

Now let us understand this in the soul, which has a drop of understanding, a little spark, a sprout. The soul has powers which work in the body. One such power is that through which one digests. It works more at night than during the day. Because of it one gains weight and grows. The soul also possesses a power in the eye, because of which the eye is so delicate and refined that it does not perceive things in the coarse condition in which they exist. They have to be previously sifted and refined in the air and the light. This is because the eye has the soul within it. There is another power in the soul with which it thinks. This power forms things within itself which are not present, so that I know the things as well as if I were seeing them with my eyes; even better. I can call to mind a rose just as well in winter. And with this power the soul works in nonbeing and so follows God who works in nonbeing.

A pagan master says: "The soul that loves God loves him under the coat of goodness."[19] All these words which have been quoted up to now are those of pagan masters, who knew only in a natural light; I have not yet come to the words of sacred masters, who knew in a much higher light. The pagan says: "The soul that loves God perceives him under the coat of goodness." The intellect pulls off the coat from God and perceives him bare, as he is stripped of goodness and of being and of all names.

I said in a lecture that the intellect is nobler than the will, and yet they both belong in this light. A professor in another school said that the will was nobler than the intellect because the will grasps things as they are in themselves, while the intellect grasps things as they are in it.[20] This is true. An eye is nobler in itself than an eye that is painted on a wall. Nevertheless, I say that the understanding is nobler than the will. The will perceives God in the garment of goodness. The understanding perceives God bare, as he is stripped of goodness and being. Goodness is a garment by which God is hidden, and the will perceives God in this garment of goodness. If there were no goodness in God, my will would want nothing of him. If someone wanted to clothe a king on the day when he was to be made king, and if one clothed him in gray attire, such a one would not have clothed him well. I am not happy because God is good. I shall never beg that God make me happy with his goodness because he could not do it. I am happy for this reason alone— because God is of an intellectual nature and because I know this. A master says that God's intellect is that upon which the being of an angel depends completely. One can pose the question: Where is the being of an image most properly? In the mirror or in the object from which it comes? It is more properly in the object from which it comes. The image is in me, from me, to me. As long as the mirror is placed exactly opposite my face, my image is in it. If the mirror were to fall, the image would disappear. An angel's being depends upon this: that the divine understanding in which it knows itself is present to it.

"As the morning star through the mist." I would now like to focus on the little word *quasi* which means "as." Children in school call this an adverb.[21] This is what I focus on in all my sermons. What one can most properly say about God is that he is word and truth. God called himself a word. St. John said: "In the beginning was the Word" (Jn. 1:1). He means that one should be an ad-verb to the Word. The planet Venus, after which Friday is named, has many names. When it precedes and rises before the sun, it is called the morning star; when it so follows that the sun sets first, it is called an evening star. Sometimes its path is above the sun, sometimes below the sun. In contrast to all the other stars it is always equally near the sun. It never departs farther from, nor approaches nearer to, the sun. It stands for a man who wants always to be near to and present to God in such a way that nothing can separate him from God, neither happiness nor unhappiness, nor any creature.

The sage also says: "as the full moon in its days" (Si. 50:6). The moon rules over all moist nature. The moon is never so near the sun as when it is full and is receiving its light directly from the sun. Because it is closer to the earth than any star it has two defects: It is pale and spotted, and it loses its light. It is never so powerful as when it is farthest from the earth, because then it causes the ocean to rise the most. The more it wanes, the less it causes it to rise.[22] The more the soul is raised above earthly things, the more powerful it is. Whoever knew but one creature would not need to ponder any sermon, for every creature is full of God and is a book. The person who wants to achieve what we have just spoken about—and this is the whole point of the sermon—should be like the morning star: always present to God, always with him and equally near him, and raised above all earthly things. He should be an ad-verb to the Word.

There is one kind of word which is brought forth, like an angel and a human being and all creatures. There is a second kind of word, thought out and not brought forth,[23] as happens when I form a thought. There is yet another kind of word that is not brought forth and not thought out, that never comes forth. Rather, it remains eternally in him who speaks it. It is continually being conceived in the Father who speaks it, and it remains within. The understanding always works internally. The more refined and immaterial a thing is, the more powerfully it works internally. And the more powerful and refined the understanding is, the more that which it knows is united with it and is more one with it. This is not the case with material things—the more powerful they are, the more they work outside themselves. God's happiness depends on his understanding's working internally, where the Word remains within. There the soul should be an ad-verb and work one work with God in order to receive its happiness in the same inwardly hovering knowledge where God is happy.

That we may be forever an ad-verb to this Word, for this may we receive the help of the Father and the same Word and the Holy Spirit. Amen.

NOTES

Translated from DW I, pp. 141–58.

The sermon receives its structure largely from the preacher's treatment of two words: *wesen* and *vernünfticheit*. *Wesen* has been translated as *being*, but Eckhart understands it here as a term restricted to creatures. It does not apply properly to God nor to what is of a purely intellectual nature. *Vernünfticheit*, which is not included under *wesen*, has been translated as *intellect*. Some might have preferred it rendered as *intelligence* or *understanding*.

1. *Book of the Twenty-Four Philosophers*, Prologue.
2. The first two definitions reflect aspects of the propositions in the *Book of the Twenty-Four Philosophers*, but only the third is found there explicitly as proposition 20.
3. Cf. *Comm. Ecc.* n. 54 (p. 179).
4. Cf. *Comm. Ex.* n. 92 (p. 75).
5. This sentence would seem to be more intelligible if it read: "If I take a segment of time, it is *either* today *or* yesterday." However, there is no backing for this in the manuscripts.
6. Eckhart appears to be citing himself here, and there are similar passages in the Latin works, e.g., *Comm. Ex.* n. 51 (p. 59).
7. Running through this paragraph and beyond is a play on the word *wîse*. Eckhart uses it here while thinking of Bernard's play with *modus*. Since *modus* in Latin means both (*limited*) *amount* or *degree* and *manner*, Bernard can use it to say that one must love God in a manner free from limitation (*modus sine modo* [*On Loving God* 1.1]). See also the Glossary.
8. Cf. *Comm. Ex.* n. 95 (p. 76).
9. That is, all created beings can only do what is possible for them to do according to their essences or the limited amount of being they possess.
10. Cf. *Comm. Ex.* n. 28 (p. 50).
11. Again, Eckhart appears to be citing himself.
12. Augustine, *Trin.* 5.1.2.
13. These "modes" are the ten categories of Aristotle. Actually Eckhart uses the word *wîse*, which was the focal point two paragraphs above.

14. Image (*bilde*) could here also be rendered as *form* or *idea* since *bilde* refers to things as they exist in the divine mind.
15. This sentence became article 28 (second appended article) of the bull of condemnation. See *Essential Eckhart*, p. 80.
16. Cf. Sermon VI, n.53 (pp. 212–13).
17. Actually, the third philosopher's definition.
18. On God as understanding or intellect, see especially Sermon XXIX. nn. 301–05 (pp. 225–26).
19. The source has not been identified.
20. This is the Franciscan theologian Gonsalvo of Spain, with whom Eckhart debated.
21. Actually *biwort*, which is translated here as *adverb*, can refer to just about any part of speech except to a noun or verb. It can also mean allegory. Etymologically it means *with-word* and, placed in a context with word, almost reproduces the *verbum-adverbium* word play possible in Latin. Since the morning star and the full moon function as allegorical figures for man, it seems best to see Eckhart using *biwort* here to mean both a part of speech and allegory.
22. Actually, the opposite is true.
23. Adopting the reading *unvürbrâht* (not brought forth) present in some manuscripts provides a better sense than *vürbrâht* (brought forth), which Quint chooses.

Sermon 10: In diebus suis placuit deo et inventus est iustus (Si. 44:16–17).

The words that I have spoken in Latin are from the epistle, and one can apply them to a holy confessor.[1] In German the words mean: "He was found to be just within in his days.[2] He pleased God well in his days." Justice he found from within. My body is more in my soul than my soul is in my body. My body and my soul are more in God than they are in themselves. And this is justice: the cause of all things in truth. As St. Augustine says, "God is nearer to the soul than it is to itself."[3] It is true: The closeness of God and the soul admits no difference [between them]. The same knowledge in which God knows himself is the knowledge of every detached spirit and nothing else.[4] The soul receives its being immediately from God.[5] For this reason God is nearer to the soul than it is to itself, and God is in the ground of the soul with all his divinity.

One master asks whether the divine light flows into the powers of the soul as purely as it exists in [the soul's] being since the soul has its being immediately from God and the powers flow immediately from the being of the soul. Divine light is too noble to have anything in common with the powers. Everything that touches or is touched is far from God and alien to him. And because the powers are touched and touch they lose their virginity.[6] Divine light cannot shine into them, but through the practice of renunciation they can be made receptive.[7] To this point another master says that the powers are given a light which is like the inner [light]. It is like the inner light, but it is not the inner light. From this light they receive an impression which makes them receptive to the inner light. Another master says that all the powers of the soul that work in the body die with the body except the intellect and the will. These alone remain to the soul. If the powers which work in the body die, they remain nevertheless in their root.[8]

St. Philip said: "Lord, show us the Father and it is enough for us" (Jn. 14:8). No one comes to the Father except through the Son (cf. Mt. 11:27). He who sees the Father sees the Son, and the Holy Spirit is their mutual love. The soul is so simple in itself that at any given moment it can only grasp one image. While it is grasping the image of a stone, it cannot grasp the image of an angel; and while it is grasping the image of the angel, it grasps no other [image]. This same image that it grasps it must love as long as it is present. If it grasped a thousand angels, this would be as much as [only] two angels; and it would really only grasp one. Now a person should be made one in himself. St. Paul says, "If you have now been made free of your sins, you have become servants of God" (Rm. 6:22). The only-begotten Son has freed us from our sins. But our Lord speaks much more exactly than St. Paul: "I have not called you servants, I have called you my friends. A servant does not know the mind of his master" (Jn. 15:15), but a friend knows everything that his friend knows. "Everything that I have heard from my Father I have made known to you" (Jn. 15:15), and everything my Father knows I know, and everything I know you know; for I and my Father have one spirit. The man who knows everything that God knows is a God-knowing man.[9] Such a person takes God in his proper self,[10] in his own oneness, in his own presence, and in his own truth. Such a person is living well. But a person who is not at home with inward things does not know what God is. It is just like a man who has wine in his cellar and, having neither drunk nor even tried it, does not know that it is good. This is exactly the situation of people who live in ignorance: They do not know what God is and they think and fancy they are [really] living. Such knowledge is not from God. One must have a pure and translucent knowledge of divine truth. For a person who has a good intention in all his works, the beginning of his intention is God, and the execution of the intention is God himself and is the pure divine nature, and [it] ends in the divine nature in [God] himself.[11]

Now a master says that no one is so foolish as not to desire wisdom. Why then do we not become wise? Much is necessary for this. The most important thing is that one go beyond and transcend all things and the cause of all things, and one begins to find this irksome. Because of this a person remains limited. Just being rich does not make me wise; but when the being of wisdom and its nature has one form with me, then I am a wise man.

I once said in a convent: The true image of the soul emerges when it has been formed and fashioned out of nothing that is not God himself. The soul has two eyes, one inward and one outward.[12] The inward eye of the soul is the one that sees into being and takes its being from God without anything else mediating.[13] This is its proper function. The outward eye of the soul is the one that is turned toward all creatures, taking note of them by means of images in the manner of a [spiritual] faculty. The person who is turned in on himself so that he knows God by his own taste and in his own ground is free of all created things and is enclosed in himself as in a veritable fortress of truth. I once said that our Lord came to his disciples behind locked doors on the day of Easter. It is the same with the person who has been freed of all otherness and all createdness. God does not come to this person. He is there already as being.

"He was pleasing to God in his days." One is speaking of more than one day when one says "in his days." There is the day of the soul and the day of God. The days that are six or seven days past and the days that occurred six thousand years ago are as near to today as yesterday is. Why? Because time here is in a present "now."[14] Because the heaven rotates, the first rotation of heaven causes it to be day. There in a moment the day of the soul takes place. In its natural light, in which all things are, a whole day takes place. There day and night are one. God's day is where the soul exists in the day of eternity in an essential now. And here God gives birth to his only-begotten Son in a present now, and the soul is born back again into the Father. As often as the birth comes about, the soul gives birth to the only-begotten Son.[15] This is why there are more sons born of virgins than of wives. Virgins give birth beyond time in eternity. However many sons the soul bears in eternity, there is still no more than one Son, because it happens beyond time in the day of eternity.[16]

Now a person living in virtue does well. As I said a week ago, the virtues are in the heart of God. He who lives in virtue and acts according to virtue does well. He who seeks nothing of himself in anything, neither in God nor creatures, lives in God and God lives in him. For such a person it is a pleasure to abandon and to scorn all things, and it is a pleasure to bring all things to their highest fruition. St. John says, *"Deus caritas est:* God is love," and love is God, "and he who lives in love lives in God and God lives in him" (1 Jn. 4:16). He who lives in God has certainly found a good dwelling and is God's heir, and he in whom God lives has worthy housemates in himself. Now a master says that the soul is given a gift by God by which it is moved toward inward things. And another master says that the soul is touched immediately[17] by the Holy Spirit because in the love in which God loves himself he also loves me, and the soul loves God in the same love in which he loves himself. And if this love did not exist in which God loves the soul, the Holy Spirit would not exist. Where the soul loves God there is a warmth and a flowering forth of the Holy Spirit.[18]

Now an evangelist writes: "This is my beloved Son in whom I am very pleasing to myself" (Mk. 1:11). But a second evangelist writes: "This is my beloved Son, in whom all things please me" (Lk. 3:22). And a third evangelist writes: "This is my beloved Son in whom I please myself" (Mt. 3:17).[19] Everything that pleases God pleases him in his only-begotten Son; everything that God loves he loves in his only-begotten Son. Now man should so live that he is one with the only-begotten Son and that he *is* the only-begotten Son. Between the only-begotten Son and the soul there is no difference.[20] Between servant and master there can never be equal love. As long as I am a servant, I am far from the only-begotten Son and am unlike him. It would not be right if I were to look at God with those eyes of mine with which I look at color, because this is temporal. And everything temporal is far from God and alien to him. In considering time, even if one takes it in the smallest amount, in a now, it is still time and exists in itself. As long as one has time and place, number, multiplicity, and amount, things are not right with him and God is far from him and alien. Hence our Lord says: "Whoever wants to become my disciple must leave himself" (Lk. 9:23). That is, "No one can hear my words or my teachings unless he has left himself." All creatures are in themselves nothing. Hence I have said: "Leave nothing and embrace the fullness of being where the will is as it should be." Whoever has left his will completely likes the taste of my teachings and hears my words. Now a master says that all creatures take their being immediately from God. This is why creatures according to their proper nature love God more than themselves. If the spirit knew its utter detachment, it could not incline itself toward any thing but would have to remain in its utter detachment. This is why he says, "He was very pleasing to him [God] in his days."

The day of the soul and God's day are different. When the soul is in its

264

natural day, it knows all things beyond time and place. Nothing is either close to it or far from it. Thus I said that all things are equally noble in this day. I once said that God is creating the world now and all things are equally noble on this day.[21] If we said that God created the world yesterday or to-morrow, we would be entertaining a foolish notion. God creates the world and all things in a present now, and the time which passed a thousand years ago is as present and near to God as the time which is now. As for the soul that remains in a present now, the Father gives birth to his only-begotten Son into it, and in this same birth the soul is born back into God. All this is one birth. As often as the soul is born again into God, the Father gives birth to his only-begotten Son into it.

I have spoken of a power in the soul which in its first outpouring does not take God as he is good and does not take him as he is truth.[22] It seeks the ground [of God], continuing to search, and takes God in his oneness and in his solitary wilderness, in his vast wasteland, and in his own ground. Thus it remains satisfied with nothing else, but keeps on searching [to dis-cover] just what it is that God is in his divinity and in the possession of his own nature. Now one says that no union is greater than that three Persons are one God. This aside, one then says that no union is greater than that of God and the soul. When the soul receives a kiss from the divinity, it enjoys full perfection and happiness.[23] Here it is embraced by oneness. In the first contact, where God has touched and is touching the soul [as it is] uncreated and uncreatable, here because of the touch of God the soul is as noble as God is himself. God touches it as he does himself. I once said in a Latin sermon on the Feast of the Trinity: The difference comes from the oneness, that is, the difference in the Trinity. The oneness is the difference and the difference is the oneness. The greater the difference, the greater the unity, because this is difference beyond difference. Even if there were a thousand persons, there would be nothing but oneness.[24] By looking upon creatures, God gives them their being; by looking upon God, creatures receive their being. The soul has a rational, intelligent being. Because of this wherever God is, there also is the soul; and wherever the soul is, there is God.

Now it says: "He was found within." That is within which dwells in the ground of the soul, in the innermost of the soul, in the intellect; it does not go out nor look upon any [external] thing. Here all powers of the soul are equally noble. Here within he was found just. That is just which is the same in happiness and sorrow, in bitterness and sweetness, and whom no object hinders from becoming one in justice. The just man is one with God. Like loves like. Love loves always what is like it. Hence God loves the just man like himself.

So that we find ourselves within on the day and in the time of intellect, in the day of wisdom, in the day of justice, and in the day of happiness, may we receive the help of the Father, the Son, and the Holy Spirit. Amen.

Notes

Translated from DW I, pp. 161–74.

1. This epistle is from the mass of a saint who was a confessor, i.e., a saint who was not a martyr, doctor of the church, or a virgin.
2. In translating the Latin *inventus* by *inne vunden* Eckhart is, as often, being original and arbitrary. The *in* of *inventus*, besides its usual function of turning "come" (*venire*) into "find" (*invenire*), is here made to mean also *within*. This latter meaning is utterly the preacher's invention.
3. Not verbatim in Augustine, but close to *Trin.* 8.7.11, and *On the Psalms* 74.9. Cf. Sermon XLV. n. 452 (p. 228).
4. This sentence found its way onto the list of objectionable doctrines compiled by Eckhart's censors in Cologne (see Théry, p. 263).
5. For the implications of *immediate* and *immediately*, see the Glossary under *âne mittel*.
6. That is, even the spiritual powers of the soul—the intellect and the will—because of their contact with material things do not remain spiritually pure.
7. "Receptive" (MHG *enpfenclîch*) also means "capable of conceiving." Thus the preacher is continuing to use the "untouched virgin" and "a virgin shall conceive" themes to explain how the soul does and should function.
8. Cf. Aquinas, *STh* Ia. 77. 8 and Ia IIae. 67. 1. ad 3.
9. Through the neologism "God-knowing" (MHG *got-wizzender*) and the context he creates for it here, Eckhart is able to express the fact that such a person both shares God's act of knowing and has God as the object of his knowledge as well.
10. "Proper self" = MHG *eigenschaft* (cf. the Glossary).
11. This sentence also was objected to by the Cologne censors (see Théry, p. 264).
12. Concerning these two eyes and man's cognitive powers, cf. *Par. Gen.* n. 138 (*Essential Eckhart*, p. 109).
13. "Without anything else mediating = MHG *âne allez mitel.*
14. For more on time and eternity, see the Glossary under *aeternitas* and *nû.*
15. For more on the birth of the Son, see the Glossary under *geburt.*
16. These last four sentences make up one impugned article on the list of the Cologne censors (cf. Théry, p. 264).
17. "Immediately" = MHG *âne mitel* (cf. the Glossary).
18. Cf. Sermon 69 (p. 315).

266

19. Eckhart's unusual translations of the three gospel texts here rely in part on the ambiguity in the dative used with the Latin verb *complacere* (to please).

20. These last two sentences were also objected to by the censors in Cologne (cf. Théry, p. 266).

21. On Eckhart's doctrine of the "now" of creation, see the Glossary under *nû*.

22. For more on this "power in the soul" and its source, see the Glossary under *vünkelîn* and *ûzbruch*.

23. Cf. *Par. Gen.* n. 146 (*Essential Eckhart*, p. 113).

24. A possible reference, though less developed, is found in Sermon IV.1, n. 28 (pp. 209–10).

Sermon 12: Qui audit me, non confundetur: et qui operantur in me, non peccabunt. Qui elucidant me, vitam aeternam habebunt (Si. 24:30–31).

The words that I have spoken in Latin are those of the eternal Wisdom of the Father. They mean: "Who hears me is not ashamed"—if he is ashamed of anything, he is ashamed of being ashamed. "Who works in me does not sin. Who reveals and radiates me shall possess eternal life." Each of these three statements I have just made would be enough for a sermon. I shall speak first of all to the point that eternal Wisdom says: "Who hears me is not ashamed." Whoever shall hear the eternal Wisdom of the Father must be within, must be at home, and must be one. Then he can hear the eternal Wisdom of the Father.

Three things hinder us from hearing the eternal Word. The first is corporality, the second multiplicity, the third temporality. If a person had passed beyond these three things, he would live in eternity, in the spirit, in oneness, and in the vast solitude; and there he would hear the eternal Word.[1] Now our Lord says, "No one hears my words nor my teaching unless he has forsaken himself" (cf. Lk. 14:26). Who would hear the Word of God must be totally detached. In the eternal Word, that which hears is the same as that which is heard. Everything which the eternal Father teaches is his being, his nature, and his total divinity. All this he reveals to us completely in his only-begotten Son and teaches us that we are this same Son.[2] A man who had so passed beyond [these three things] that he was the only-begotten Son would have everything that belongs to the only-begotten Son. Whatever

God works and whatever he teaches, he works and teaches in his only-be-gotten Son. God works all his works so that we might be the only-begotten Son. When God sees that we are the only-begotten Son, he is very quick to pursue us and acts as though his divine being were going to burst and completely vanish, so that he might reveal to us the utter abyss of his divinity and the fullness of his being and his nature. God hastens to make it all ours just as it is his. Here in this fullness God has delight and joy. Such a person stands in God's knowing and in God's love and becomes nothing other than what God is himself.[3]

If you love yourself, you love all men as yourself. As long as you love one single person less than yourself, you have never really loved yourself; [that is,] unless you love all men as yourself, loving all men in one man, and that man is God and man.[4] All is well for the person who loves himself and all men as himself; for him all is well. Now some people say: "My friend, from whom I experience good, I like more than another person." All is not well with such a person; it is imperfect. But one has to put up with it, just as some people travel across the sea with half a wind but still make it. Such is the case with people who like one person more than another. This is natural. If I loved a person as myself, then whatever happened to him, good or bad, death or life, I would be as ready for it to happen to me as to him: This would be true friendship.[5]

In regard to this St. Paul says, "I would be willing to be eternally separated from God for my friend's sake and for God" (Cf. Rm. 9:3).[6] To be separated from God for an instant is to be separated from God for eternity; to be separated from God is the pain of hell. What then did St. Paul mean in saying that he would be willing to be separated from God? The masters pose the question whether St. Paul was on the way to perfection or whether he was in the state of full perfection. I claim that he was in the state of full perfection. Otherwise he could not have spoken thus of himself. I shall now explain the words St. Paul spoke when he said that he would be willing to be separated from God.

The noblest and the ultimate thing that a person can forsake is that he forsakes God for God's sake. Now St. Paul forsook God for God's sake; he left everything that he was able to take from God and left everything that God was able to give him and everything that he was able to receive from God. When he had left all this, he left God for God's sake, and there remained for him God as God exists in himself, not as one might receive something of him or as one might attain something of him; rather, as in the isness that he is in himself.[7] He never gave God anything nor did he ever receive anything from God. It is a oneness and a pure union. In this state a person is a true human being, and such a man experiences no suffering, just as the divine being cannot experience it.[8] Similarly I have often said that there is something in the soul that is so closely related to God that it is one [with him] and not just united.[9] It is one and has nothing in common with anything, nor does anything created have anything at all in common with it. Everything created is nothing. But this is far distant from and foreign to all createdness. If a person were completely like this, he would be completely uncreated and uncreateable.[10] And if everything that is material and weak were comprehended in this oneness, it would be no different from this oneness itself. If I found myself for an instant in this being, I would be as little concerned for myself as for a dung worm.

God gives equally to all things; and as they flow from God, they are equal. In their first outflow angels, men, and all creatures flow forth from God equal. One who would take things in their first outflow would take them alike. If they are so much alike in time, they are much more alike in God in eternity. If one takes a fly in God, it is nobler in God than the highest angel is in itself.[11] Now all things are alike in God and are God himself.[12] Here in this sameness God finds it so pleasant that he lets his nature and his being flow in this sameness in himself. It is just as enjoyable for him as when someone lets a horse run loose on a meadow that is completely level and smooth. Such is the horse's nature that it pours itself out with all its might in jumping about the meadow. This it would find delightful; such is its nature.[13] So, too, does God find delight and satisfaction where he finds sameness. He finds it a joy to pour his nature and his being completely into the sameness, for he is this sameness himself.

There is a question concerning the angels, whether those angels that dwell with us here and serve us and protect us, whether their joys are less than those angels who are in eternity, or whether they are in any way diminished by their activities of protecting and serving us. I say no, not at all. Their joy is not that much less nor their equality because the work of an angel is the will of God, and the will of God is the work of an angel. Hence an angel is not impeded in its joy or its equality or in its work. If God were to command an angel to fly to a tree and pick caterpillars off it, the angel would be ready to go pick the caterpillars off, and this would be its beatitude and the will of God.[14]

A person who is so established in the will of God wants nothing else but what is God and what is God's will. If he were sick, he would not want to be healthy. All pain is a joy to him, all multiplicity is simplicity and unity, if he is really steadfast in the will of God. Even if the pain of hell were connected to it, it would be joy and happiness for him. He is free and has left himself, and he must be free of everything that he is to receive. If my eye is to see color, it must be free of all color.[15] If I see blue or white, the sight of my eye which sees the color, this very thing that does the seeing, is the same as what is seen by the eye. The eye in which I see God is the same eye in which God sees me. My eye and God's eye are one eye and one seeing, one knowing and one loving.[16]

A person who thus remains in God's love should be dead to himself and to all created things, so that he gives as little attention to himself as he does to something a thousand miles away. Such a person remains in equality and in unity and remains completely the same.[17] He experiences no lack of sameness. Such a person has to have forsaken himself and the whole world. If a person owned the whole world and if he left it for God's sake as naked as he had received it, God would give this person the whole world back again and eternal life as well. And if there were another person who had nothing but good will and if he were to think: Lord, if this world belonged to me and if I had another one and yet another so that there were three of them, and if he were to beg: Lord, I want to leave all of this and myself as bare as when I received it from you, [then] God would give this person as much as if he had actually given it all away with his own hand. Another person who had nothing material or spiritual to leave or to give would leave most of all. Whoever were to forsake himself for an instant would be given everything. And if a person had forsaken himself for twenty years and then took himself back for an instant, he had never really forsaken himself at all. The person who has forsaken all and remains in this state and never for an instant casts a glance toward what he has forsaken and remains constant and unmoved in himself and unchanging, only such a person is detached.

That we may remain as constant and unchangeable as the eternal Father, so help us God and eternal Wisdom. Amen.

NOTES

Translated from DW I, pp. 192–203.

This sermon is remarkable among other things for the number of passages that found their way onto the lists of articles collected by Eckhart's censors in Cologne. It must have been one of the sermons they scrutinized carefully.

1. On the desert theme in Eckhart, see, e.g., *Bened.* 2 (*Essential Eckhart*, p. 247).

2. For more on the birth of the Son, see the Glossary under *geburt*.
3. The last five sentences of this paragraph are contained in the lists of the Cologne censors (cf. Théry, pp. 176–77, 219–21).
4. On indifferent loving in Eckhart, see *Essential Eckhart*, p. 58.
5. Most of this paragraph is contained in the lists of the Cologne censors. See Théry, pp. 221–22, for the extracts and Eckhart's reply.
6. On this quotation from Paul, cf. *Bened.* 1 and *Comm. Jn.* n. 79 (*Essential Eckhart*, pp. 216, 151), and *Comm. Ex.* n. 270 (p. 126).
7. "Isness," i.e., MHG *istikeit*, on which see the Glossary.
8. Almost everything from the Pauline text (Ro. 9:3) to here is on the lists of the Cologne censors (cf. Théry, pp. 182, 222).
9. This is the "spark of the soul." For more on this, see the Glossary under *vünkelîn*.
10. This formulation of the "uncreatedness" of this "something" in the soul is similar to the first article of the papal bull *In agro dominico*, which was judged heretical but was one of the two separated from the first 26 articles on the grounds that Eckhart claimed never to have said it. See *Essential Eckhart*, p. 80. In fact, there are several similar formulations in Eckhart's works (cf. Quint, DW I, p. 198, note 1).
11. Cf. Sermon 52 (*Essential Eckhart*, p. 200).
12. Cf. Sermon IV n. 28 (p. 209).
13. Cf. *Comm. Ecc.* n. 59 (p. 181).
14. Cf. Thomas Aquinas, *STh* Ia. 64. 4. ad 3.
15. Aristotle, *Soul* 2.7 (429b). Cf. *Comm. Jn.* n. 100 and *Bened.* 1 (*Essential Eckhart*, pp. 100, 220).
16. Objected to by the Cologne censors. Eckhart replied by quoting Augustine, *Trin.* 9.2 (cf. Théry, pp. 224–25). Cf. *Comm. Jn.* n. 107 (*Essential Eckhart*, p. 163).
17. Objected to by the Cologne censors (cf. Théry, pp. 181, 225).

Sermon 14: Surge illuminare Ierusalem (Is. 60:1).

The words I have spoken in Latin are from the epistle which one reads in the mass. The prophet Isaiah says, "Arise, Jerusalem, stand up and become resplendent." There are three ways of interpreting this. Ask God for grace.

"Arise, Jerusalem, stand up and become resplendent." The masters and the saints commonly say that the soul has three powers by which it is like the Trinity. The first power is memory, which is an interior, hidden knowledge. It signifies the Father. The second power is called intelligence; this is

271

a bringing to mind, a knowing, wisdom. The third power is called will, a flow of the Holy Spirit. We do not intend to pause here since it is not new material.[1]

"Arise, Jerusalem, and become resplendent." Other masters also divide the soul into three. They call the highest power the irascible power; this they compare to the Father. It constantly is at war and is angry with evil.[2] Anger blinds the soul and love overcomes the senses. . . .[3] The first power functions in the liver, the second in the heart, and the third in the brain.[4] The first power never rests until it comes to the highest; and if there were something higher than God, it would not want God. The second power is not satisfied with anything but the best of all. If there were anything better than God, it would not want God. The third power is satisfied with nothing but one good. If there were something better than God, it would not want God. It finds rest only in constant goodness in which all good things are so contained that they are one. God himself does not rest there where he is a beginning of all being. He rests where he is both an end and a beginning of all being.

Jerusalem means the heights, as I said in the convent Mergarden. To what is high one says, "Come down!" To what is low one says, "Come up!" If you were down below and I were above you, I would have to come down to you. This is what God does. If you humble yourself, God comes down from above and enters into you. The earth is the farthest of all from the sky and has crept into a corner, being ashamed. She would like to flee the beautiful heavens from one corner to the other, but what would her refuge be? If she were to flee downwards, she would come to the sky. If she flees upwards, she cannot escape either.[5] It [the sky] chases her into a corner and presses his power into her, making her bear fruit. Why? The highest flows into the lowest. One star is above the sun. This is the highest star. It is nobler than the sun; and it flows [with its light] into the sun and illumines the sun, and all the light that the sun has it has from this star. What then does it mean that the sun does not shine during the night as it does during the day? This means that the sun all by itself is not powerful enough, that there is a certain lack in the sun, that, as you can well see, it is dark on one side, and at night the moon and the stars take its light and drive it somewhere else. Then it shines in a different land. This star not only flows into the sun; rather, it flows through the sun, through all the stars to the earth, making her fruitful.[6] And so it is with the rightly humble person who has subordinated all creatures to himself, and himself to God.[7] God in his goodness does not neglect to pour himself completely into this person. He is forced to do it; he must do it of necessity.[8] If you wish to be high and exalted, you must be lowly, [away] from the coursing of flesh and blood, for the root of all sin and stain is hidden, deceiving pride from which follows nothing but sorrow and pain.[9] But humility is the root of all good and what follows from it.

I said in Paris at the university that all things are accomplished in the truly humble person.[10] The sun corresponds to God. The pinnacle of his immeasurable Godhead responds to the depths of humility. The truly humble person does not have to beg God; he can order him. For the heights of the Godhead seek out nothing other than the depths of humility, as I said in the convent of the Maccabees. The humble person and God are one; the humble person has as much power with God as he [God] has himself. And everything that is in all the angels belongs to the humble person as his own. Whatever God works, the humble person works; and what God is, he is: one life and one being.[11] This is why our dear Lord said, "Learn of me, that I am meek and of a humble heart" (Mt. 11:29).

If a person were truly humble, God would either have to lose all his divinity and would have to abandon it completely or he would have to pour himself out and flow completely into this person. The thought came to me last night that God's majesty depends on my lowliness; by my lowering myself, God is exalted. "Jerusalem shall be resplendent," say the scriptures and the prophet. Further, it occurred to me last night that God should be brought down, not absolutely but rather interiorly. This "God brought down" pleased me so much that I wrote it in my book.[12] It says therefore: "a God brought down," not in everything, rather within [the soul], that we might be raised up. What was above is now within. You shall be united of yourself into yourself so that he is within you. Not that we take something from that which is above us; we must take into ourselves and take from ourselves into ourselves.[13]

St. John says, "Those who received him he gave the power to become sons of God. Those who are God's Son are not of flesh and blood; they are born of God" (Jn. 1:12–13), not outwardly but inwardly. Our dear Lady said, "How can that be, that I become the mother of God?" Then the angel said, "The Holy Spirit shall come into you from above" (Cf. Lk. 1:34–35). David said, "Today I have given birth to you" (Ps. 2:7). What is today? Eternity. I have born me you and you me eternally.[14] Yet it is not enough for the noble, humble person that he is the only-begotten Son whom the Father has given birth to eternally. He also wishes to be the Father, to enter into the very sameness with the eternal Fatherhood, and to give birth to him from whom I was eternally born, as I said in the convent Mergarden.[15] There God enters into his own. Acquire God for yourself, and God is your own, as he is his own very own. What is born in me remains. God never separates himself from such a person, wherever he may go. A person can turn away from God; but no matter how far a person goes from God, God stands there on the lookout for him and runs out to meet him unawares.[16] If you want God to be your own, you should be his own just as my tongue or my hand [is my own], so that I can do with him what I will. As little as I can do without him, that is how little he can do without me. If then, you want God to be your own in this way, make yourself his own and have as your intention nothing but him. Then he is the beginning and the end of all your activity, just as his Godhead depends on his being God. The person who in all his works considers nothing but God and loves nothing but God, to him God gives his divinity. Everything that a person does . . . ;[17] for my humility gives God his divinity. "The light shines in the darkness and the light grasps nothing of the darkness" (Cf. Jn. 1:5).[18] This means that God is not just the beginning of all our works and of our being; he is also the end and a resting place of all being.

That we may learn from Jesus Christ the lesson of humility, may God the Father, Son, and Holy Spirit help us. Amen. Thanks be to God.

NOTES

Translated from DW I, pp. 230–41.

1. This common comparison of the Trinity with the three powers of the soul—memory, intellect, will—goes back to Augustine. Cf. *Trin.* 12.11.18.
2. This division of the soul goes back to Platonic and Pythagorean traditions according to which the three powers are the irascible, the concupiscent, and the rational. This division was widely known and used in Eckhart's time. Cf., e.g., Albert the Great, *On Animals* 13.1.7.
3. There seems to be a lacuna in the text at this point. One would expect at least a short explanation of the other two powers of the soul.
4. Here a sentence fragment has been omitted that makes no sense at all in this context.
5. Cf. *Comm. Ex.* n. 242 (p. 119).
6. The source of this strange cosmology is obscure.
7. On humility, cf. *Comm. Jn.* n. 90 (*Essential Eckhart*, p. 156).
8. God's being *forced* to respond to humility did not escape the notice of the Cologne censors (cf. Théry, p. 218).
9. For pride as the root of evil and the advantages of humility, see *Comm. Ex.* n. 187 (p. 103).

10. A similar statement from Sermon 15 (DW I, p. 247) was on the list of the Cologne censors (cf. Théry, p. 249).

11. From the humble person's not having to beg God to this point in the sermon was objected to by the censors in Cologne (cf. Théry, pp. 218–19).

12. The thought that so pleased the preacher was that, contrary to the usual image of raising God up, he must actually be lowered—not with any loss of majesty—in order that he enter the soul.

13. That is, once God is within us, all our spiritual activity is immanent.

14. The translation is literal. *You* and *me* are both twice what is being born. For a similar passage, see Sermon 6 (*Essential Eckhart*, p. 187).

15. This also was attacked in the Cologne proceedings (Théry, pp. 178, 238, and 199–200 for Eckhart's reply).

16. This is an allusion to the father's actions in the story of the prodigal son (Lk. 15:11–32).

17. Here there is a lacuna in the text. Quint (DW I, p. 240) suggests the addition of "God does, or performs."

18. The turning around of *light* and *darkness* in the second half of this quotation from John is most likely a scribal error.

Sermon 16b: Quasi vas auri solidum ornatum omni lapide pretioso (Si. 50:10).

I have spoken words in Latin that one reads in today's epistle. One can apply them to St. Augustine and to any good and holy soul[1]—how they are like a vessel of gold that is solid and unchanging, and that has on it precious stones of all kinds. Because of the noble dignity of the saints it is impossible to characterize them through a single comparison, and so one compares them to trees, the sun, and the moon.[2] Thus St. Augustine is compared to a golden vessel that is solid and unchanging, and that has on it precious stones of all kinds. And this can truly be applied to every good and holy soul who has abandoned all things, taking them as they are eternal. Whoever abandons things as they are accidental possesses them as they are pure being and eternal.[3]

Every vessel has two characteristics: It takes in and it contains. There is a difference between spiritual vessels and material vessels. Wine is inside the vessel; the vessel is not in the wine, nor is the wine in the vessel in the sense that it is inside the boards. If it were in the vessel in this sense, one

275

could not drink it. It is different with a spiritual vessel. Everything that is taken into it is in the vessel and the vessel is in it and it is the vessel itself. Everything that the spiritual vessel takes in has the same nature [as the vessel]. It is God's nature that he gives himself to every good soul, and it is the nature of the soul that it takes God in. This can be said to be among the noblest things that the soul can do. Thus the soul wears the divine image and is like God.[4] One thing cannot be the image of another without similarity, but similarity can exist without one thing being the other's image. Two eggs are equally white, but the one is not the image of the other. For whatever is supposed to be the image of another must come out of [the other's] nature and must be born of it and must be like it.[5]

Every image has two characteristics. The first is that it takes its being immediately and of necessity from that of which it is an image.[6] It issues from it naturally, coming forth from its nature like a branch from a tree. When a face is placed opposite a mirror, the face has to be reflected in it, whether it wants to be or not. But nature does not form itself in the image in the mirror; rather, the mouth, the nose, the eyes, and all the configurations of the face take form in the mirror.[7] But God has reserved for himself alone that wherever he forms an image of himself, he forms completely and necessarily an image of his own nature and everything that he is and can do. This image is placed before the will, and the will follows the image. The image has the first bursting-forth from nature and draws into itself everything that nature and being can accomplish, and nature pours itself completely into the image and yet remains entirely in itself. The masters do not place the image in the Holy Spirit; rather, they place it in the middle Person because the Son has the first bursting-forth from nature.[8] This is why he is properly called an image of the Father, and the Holy Spirit is not. He is a blossoming-forth from the Father and the Son yet has one nature with them both. Still, the will is not a medium between the image and nature. What is more, neither insight nor knowledge nor wisdom can be a medium because the divine image bursts forth from the fecundity of nature without a medium. If there is here some medium of wisdom, it is the image itself. This is why the Son in the Godhead is called the Wisdom of the Father.

You should know that the simple divine image which is pressed onto the soul in its innermost nature acts without a medium, and the innermost and the noblest that is in nature takes form in a most proper sense in the image of the soul. Here there is no medium, neither will nor wisdom, as I mentioned in saying: "If here wisdom is a medium, then it is the image itself." Here God is without a medium in the image and the image is without a medium in God. Still, God is much nobler in the image than the image is in God. Here the image does not take God insofar as he is Creator. It takes him, rather, insofar as he is a being endowed with intellect,[9] and what is noblest in nature takes form in a most proper sense in this image. This is a natural image of God which God has imprinted in a natural manner on all souls. Now I cannot give anything more to this image.[10] But if I could give it more, it would have to be God himself, which it is not because then God would not be God.

The second characteristic of an image can be learned by concentrating on the image's similarity [to its object]. Here notice especially two things. First, an image is not from itself, nor is it for itself[11]—just like an image that is received in the eye is not from the eye and has no being in the eye, but depends upon and inheres in that of which it is an image. Hence it is not from itself and is not for itself, but it derives from that of which it is an image and belongs to this completely. From this it takes its being and it is the same being.

Now understand me correctly! What an image actually is you should know through four things (but perhaps there will be more of them). An image is not from itself nor is it for itself. It is completely from that of which it is an image and belongs to this totally with everything it is. It does not belong to nor is it from anything that is foreign to that whose image it is. An image takes its being exclusively and without a medium from that whose image it is and it has one being with it and is the same being.[12] I am not just talking about things that one should discuss at the university. One can certainly discuss them for instruction from the pulpit as well.

You often ask how you should live. Now please pay careful attention to this. In the same way as I have spoken about image, so should you live. You should be his and for him and should not be your own nor for yourself and should not belong to anyone. When I came to this convent yesterday, I saw sage and other herbs on a grave, and I thought: here lies the dear friend of some person and this is why he values this piece of earth more dearly. If someone has a very dear friend, he cares for everything that belongs to him, and whatever is repugnant to his friend, he does not like either. Take the case of a dog as a comparison, though it is not a rational animal. It is so loyal to its master that it hates everything that is disliked by its master, and whoever is the friend of its master it likes, not noticing whether the person is rich or poor. If there were a blind poor man who was on intimate terms with his master, it would like him better than a king or emperor whom his master disliked. I say truly, if it were possible for the dog to be half unfaithful, it would hate itself half.

Now some people complain that they do not have intense devotion nor sweet or special consolation from God. Such people are really not as they should be. One can tolerate them, but it is not the best. I say in truth, as long as something takes form in you that is not the eternal Word and does not derive from the eternal Word, no matter how good it might be, this is really not right. Hence only he is a just man who has annihilated all created things and stands without distraction looking toward the eternal Word directly and who is formed therein and is reformed in justice.[13] Such a person takes where the Son takes and is the Son himself. The scripture says: "No one knows the Father but the Son" (Mt. 11:27); and so, if you want to know God, you should not just be *like* the Son. Rather, you should *be* the Son himself.[14]

Some people want to see God with their own eyes, just as they see a cow; and they want to love God just as they love a cow. You love a cow because of the milk and cheese and because of your own advantage. This is how all these people act who love God because of external riches or because of internal consolation. They do not love God rightly; rather they love their own advantage. I say truly: Everything which you make the object of your intention which is not God in himself—that can never be so good that it will not be an impediment to the highest truth.

And as I said before that St. Augustine is like a vessel of gold that is sealed on the bottom and open on top, see, that is how you should be. If you want to stand by St. Augustine in utter and complete sanctity, your heart must be sealed to all createdness and you should take God as he is in himself. This is why males are compared to the highest powers—because they always have their head bare, while women are compared to the lower powers because their head is always covered.[15] The highest powers are above time and place and have their origin without mediation in the being of the soul. This is why they are like men because they always stand bare. Thus their acts are eternal. A master says that the lower powers of the soul, to the extent that time or place have touched them, have lost their virginal purity and can never be so completely stripped bare or shaken out [like a rug] that they can come into the highest powers. However, they are certainly given a similar imprint of an image.[16]

You should be solid and unchanging, that is, you should stay the same in joy and sorrow, in fortune and misfortune. And you should possess the value of all jewels; that is, that all virtues should be contained in you and should flow from you as from being. You must penetrate and transcend all the virtues and should take virtue only in the ground, where it is one with the divine nature. And to the extent that you are more united to the divine nature than an angel, it must receive through you. That we may become one, may God help us. Amen.

NOTES

Translated from DW I, pp. 263–76.

1. This verse is from the epistle of the mass for the feast of St. Augustine.
2. These are additional comparisons used in the passage from Ecclesiasticus that is the epistle for this feast.
3. For a similar thought, see Sermon 29 (p. 289).
4. On the soul as image (*bilde*) of God and related uses of *bilde*, see *bilde* in the Glossary.
5. The eggs are similar in their both being white, but the whiteness of one is in no way influenced by the whiteness of the other. Cf. Thomas Aquinas, *STh* Ia. 35. 1, depending on Augustine.
6. Cf. *Comm. Jn.* n. 23 (*Essential Eckhart*, p. 129). For "immediately," see *âne mittel* in the Glossary.
7. That is, the face in the mirror is not a real face but is just an image of the face. Cf. Sermon XLIX n. 512 (p. 237).
8. For clarification of this, see *ûzbruch* in the Glossary.
9. See Sermon 9 (p. 258) and Sermon XXIX n. 304 (p. 226).
10. That is, the preacher is saying that there is nothing more he can add to its description to make it more noble.
11. This sentence beginning with "First" seems to contain both characteristics of an image to be discussed, that it is not *from* itself nor is it *for* itself. This is probably the result of faulty transmission. The entire paragraph does not fit in well.
12. There are many close parallels between this discussion of *image* and a lengthy passage in the lists of the Cologne censors (cf. Théry, p. 180). Cf. Sermon XLIX n. 509 (p. 236) and *Comm. Jn.* n. 23 (*Essential Eckhart*, p. 129).
13. For more on justice and being formed in justice, see *Comm. Jn.* nn. 14–21 (*Essential Eckhart*, pp. 126–28).
14. For more on being the Son, see the Glossary under *geburt.*
15. For the higher and lower powers of the soul being represented by man and woman, see also Sermon 40 (p. 302), and *Comm. Jn.* n. 84 (*Essential Eckhart*, p. 153).
16. Cf. Avicenna, *Soul* 4.2(18vb).

MEISTER ECKHART

Sermon 21: **Unus Deus et pater omnium, qui est super omnes, et per omnia, et in omnibus nobis (Ep. 4:6).**

I have spoken words in Latin that St. Paul speaks in the epistle: "One God and Father of all, who is blessed above all and through all and in us all." I shall also discuss from the gospel words spoken by our Lord: "Friend, climb up farther, pull yourself up higher" (Lk. 14:10).

In the first text, the one spoken by Paul: "One God and Father of all," he leaves a word out that implies change.[1] When he says "one God," he means God is one in himself and separated from all else. God belongs to no one, and no one belongs to him; God is one. Boethius says, "God is one and does not change."[2] All that God has created he created changeable. All things from the time of their creation carry about with them their mutability.

This means that we should be one in ourselves and separated from all else, and permanently unmoved we should be one with God. Outside of God there is nothing, only nothing. Hence it is impossible that any change or transformation could occur in God. Whatever seeks another place outside him undergoes change. God has all things in himself in abundance, and so he seeks nothing outside himself except in abundance, as it is in God.[3] No creature can comprehend how it carries God within itself.

A second lesson he tells us: "Father of all, you are blessed." These words imply change. When he says "Father," a connection with us is implied. Since he is our Father and we are his children, the honor and scorn he receives goes to our hearts. When a child sees how dear it is to its father, it knows why it owes it to him to live purely and innocently. Thus we, too, should live in purity, for God himself says: "Happy are the pure of heart, for they shall see God" (Mt. 5:8). What is purity of heart? That is purity of heart: whatever is separated and detached from all material things, is recollected and enclosed within itself, and then out of this purity throws itself into God and is there united. David says that those works are pure and innocent that occur and are accomplished in the light of the soul; and those are more innocent still that remain within, inside, in the spirit and do not come outside.[4] "One God and Father of all."

The second text is: "Friend, climb up higher, pull yourself up farther." I shall make one text out of these two. When he says, "Friend, climb up higher, pull yourself up farther," that is a colloquy between the soul and

280

God; and the response to this is: "One God and Father of all." A master says, "Friendship is a matter of the will."⁵ Insofar as friendship is a matter of the will, it does not unify. I have also said that love does not unify. Certainly it does in an act, but not in being.⁶ For this reason it says, "One God," "Climb up farther, pull yourself up higher." Nothing can come into the ground of the soul but the pure Godhead. Even the highest angel, no matter how close and related to God it may be or how much of God it has in itself—and its works are constantly in God, and it is united to God in being, not just in work; it dwells within God and resides with him always—no matter how noble the angel is—and it is certainly a marvelous thing—still, it cannot enter into the soul. A master says: "All creatures that have difference are not worthy to have God work in them."⁷ The soul is so pure and delicate in itself, as it is apart from the body, that it takes in nothing else but the bare, pure Godhead. And even God cannot enter unless he is stripped of everything that is added to him. Thus the soul receives the answer: "One God."⁸

St. Paul says, "One God." *One* is purer than goodness and truth. Goodness and truth do not add anything [to God]; they add something only in the thought. When it is thought, it is added. *One* adds nothing to him as he is before he flows out into the Son and the Holy Spirit. Hence he says, "Friend, draw yourself up higher." A master says: "One is a negation of negation."⁹ If I say God is good, this adds something [to him]. *One* is a negation of negation and a denial of denial. What does *one* mean? One means something to which nothing has been added. The soul receives the Godhead as it is purified in itself, where nothing has been added, not even in thought. *One* is a negation of negation. All creatures have a negation in themselves; one creature denies that it is the other creature. One angel denies that it is some other angel.¹⁰ But God has a negation of negation; he is one and negates everything other, for outside of God is nothing.¹¹ All creatures are in God and are his very Godhead, and this implies an abundance, as I said previously.¹² He is one Father of the whole Godhead. I say "one Godhead" because here nothing is yet flowing out, nor is it touched at all or thought. By negating something of God—say, I negate goodness of him (of course, I cannot really negate anything of him)—by negating something of God, I catch hold of something that he is *not*. It is precisely this that has to be removed. God is one, he is a negation of negation.

A master says that the nature of an angel has no power and performs no work that does not aim exclusively at knowing God.¹³ Whatever else exists, it knows nothing about it. Hence he said, "One God, Father of all." "Friend, pull yourself up higher." Some powers of the soul take in from outside, like the eye: Even though it removes what is coarsest and draws into itself only what has been refined, it nevertheless takes in something from outside which is dependent on here and now. But the understanding and the intellect strip off completely and take in what is neither here nor now. On this plane it touches the nature of angels. Still, it takes in from the senses; what the senses draw in from outside the intellect takes in. The will does not do this, and in this regard the will is nobler than the intellect. The will takes in from nowhere except in pure understanding, where there is neither here nor now.[14] God wishes to say: However high or pure the will is, it must climb up farther. This is the response that God speaks: "Friend, climb up farther and you will receive honor" (Lk. 14:10).

The will seeks beatitude. I was asked what the difference is between grace and beatitude. Grace, as we are now in this life, and beatitude, which we shall have hereafter in eternal life, are related to each other as the blossom is to the fruit.[15] When the soul is completely full of grace and there is nothing remaining in the soul which grace is not causing or accomplishing, it is still the case that not everything which the soul through grace does comes to fruition as it is within the soul in such a way that grace does everything which the soul should bring about. I have also said that grace performs no work but rather pours all ornament into the soul. This is abundance in the realm of the soul. I say grace does not unite the soul with God. It is a bringing to completion; this is its work: that it bring the soul back to God. Then the fruit develops from the flower. The will, because it seeks beatitude and wants to be with God and is thus raised aloft—when it is in this pure state, God certainly slips into the will, and as the pure intellect perceives God as truth, so God certainly slips into the intellect. However, when he descends into the will, he must climb up higher. Therefore he says, "One God." "Climb up higher."

"One God." In being one, God perfects his Godhead. I maintain: God could never give birth to his only-begotten Son if he were not one. By being one God brings about everything that he works in creatures and in his Godhead. I say further: God alone has unity. God's property is unity. It is what makes God God; otherwise he would not be God.[16] Everything that has number depends on *one*, and *one* depends on nothing. God's wealth and wisdom and truth are completely one in God. It is not one, it is oneness. All that God has he has in one; it is one in him. The masters say that heaven revolves in order to bring all things into one; this is why it revolves so swiftly.[17] God has all abundance as one, and God's nature and the soul's beatitude depend on his being one. It is its adornment and honor. He said: "Friend, climb up farther and so receive honor." It is the soul's honor and adornment that God is one. God acts as though he were one only to please the soul and as though he adorns himself just to make the soul become infatuated with him alone. This is why a person wants now one thing, now another. At one time he practices wisdom, at another art. Because the soul does not have oneness, it never rests until everything becomes completely one in God. God is one; this is the soul's beatitude, its adornment, and its repose. A master says that in all his works God intends all things. The soul is all things.[18] Whatever is the noblest, the purest, and the highest in all things beneath the soul, God pours all this into it [the soul]. God is all and is one.

That we so become one with God, may we be helped by "one God, Father of all." Amen.

NOTES

Translated from DW I, pp. 357–70.

1. Because of the existence of a parallel text where this idea of a word left out is treated more elaborately, we can assume this word is the verb *est* (is), which the preacher interprets here as formal or inhering existence, thus implying mutability.
2. Boethius, *Consolation of Philosophy* 3, poem 9. Cf. *Comm. Ex.* n. 46 (p. 58).
3. Cf. *Comm. Wis.* n. 147 (p. 167).
4. This reference to David has not been identified.
5. Cf. Thomas Aquinas, *STh* IIa IIae. 24.1 on charity residing in the will.
6. Eckhart insists that essential union with God takes place in the intellect, not in the will. See, e.g., Sermon XXIX n. 304 (p. 226) and Sermon 7 (p. 254).
7. Cf. *Comm. Jn.* n. 99 (*Essential Eckhart*, pp. 159–60).
8. That is, God insofar as he is conceived of as having positive attributes such as goodness, truth, justice, and the like, cannot enter. *One* adds nothing positive to God and is the highest manner of describing him, as the preacher's further comments here make clear. See also *Comm. Wis.* n. 149 (p. 168).
9. Cf. Thomas Aquinas, *Quodlibetal Questions* 10. 1. 1. ad 3 and *In I Sent.* d. 24, q. 1, a. 3, ad 1. For more on *one* as the negation of negation, see *Comm. Ex.* n. 74; *Comm. Ecc.* n. 60; and especially *Comm. Wis.* nn. 147–48 (pp. 68, 181, 167–68). Cf. the Glossary under *negatio*.
10. That is, one creature or angel, because it is a distinct and thus limited being, excludes by this fact the possibility of its being other creatures or angels.
11. God as one is indistinct from everything else. Thus nothing exists outside of God. Cf. *Comm. Ex.* n. 74 (p. 68).
12. See above, the beginning of the sermon.

13. Cf. Thomas Aquinas, *STh* Ia. 112. 1.
14. That is, the will only has as its object things from which the intellect has stripped such accidental qualities as their existing in a definite place or at a definite time. Intellect remains higher than the will not insofar as it is dependent on the senses, but insofar as it becomes one with what it knows in the act of knowing.
15. Cf. *Comm. Ex.* n. 275 (p. 128).
16. Cf. *Comm. Wis.* n. 149 (p. 168). For "property," see *eigenschaft* in the Glossary.
17. This is possibly a reference to Aristotle, *Met.* 12.7 (1072a).
18. Cf. Aristotle, *Soul* 3.8 (431b).

Sermon 24: Induimini Dominum Jesum Christum (Rm. 13:14).

St. Paul says: "Put Christ into yourself; interiorize him to yourself."[1] By putting self aside, a person puts inside himself Christ, God, happiness, and holiness. If a young boy were to tell marvelous tales, one would believe him; but Paul promises great things and you hardly believe him. For putting yourself aside he promises you God, happiness, and holiness. It is marvelous, but if a person puts himself aside as he should, by so doing he puts Christ, holiness, and happiness into himself and is very great. The prophet was amazed at two things. The first: what God does with the stars, the moon, and the sun. The second marvel is about the soul, that God has done and does such great things with it and for its sake.[2] He does whatever he can for it: He does many great things for its sake and is always occupied with it, and this is because of its greatness in which it has been created. Consider how great it has been made. I form a letter of the alphabet according to a likeness which the letter has in me, in my soul, but not according to my soul. The same is the case with God. God generally made all things according to an image of all things that he has in himself, but not according to himself. He made some things differently, according to something that comes forth from him, such as goodness, wisdom, and other qualities one attributes to God. But the soul he made not just according to an image in himself, nor according to something coming forth from him, as one describes him. Rather, he made it according to himself, in short, according to all that he is in his nature, his being, his activity which flows forth yet remains within, and according to the ground where he remains within himself, where he constantly gives birth to his only-begotten Son, from where the Holy Spirit blossoms forth. God created the soul in accordance with this out-flowing, inward-remaining work.[3]

It is part of the nature of all things that those above constantly flow into those beneath to the extent that the lower things have the capacity for those above; but the higher things never receive anything from the lower things. Rather, the lower things receive from the higher.[4] Because God is above the soul, he is constantly flowing into the soul and can never slip out of the soul. The soul can, of course, slip away from him; but as long as a person holds himself under God, he is receiving direct divine inflowing, straight from God, and he is under nothing else: neither fear nor joy nor sorrow nor under any other thing that is not God. And so, throw yourself completely under God, and you will receive the divine inflowing completely and directly. How does the soul receive from God? The soul receives from God not as something foreign, as happens when the air receives light from the sun.[5] Air receives [light] as something foreign to it. But the soul receives God not as something foreign to it, nor as though it were beneath God. Whatever is under something is different from it and distant. The masters say that the soul receives [from God] as light receives from light, where nothing is foreign or distant.

There is something in the soul in which God is bare, and the masters say it is nameless, that it has no name of its own.[6] It exists, but has no being of its own because it is neither this nor that, neither here nor there. It is what it is in another and that [other] is in it; for it is what it is in that other and that other is in it. This other flows into it and it into this other, and here, he [Paul] urges: "Join yourselves to God, to happiness." Here the soul takes all its life and being, and from here it draws its life and being, because this is completely in God and everything else is outside. Hence the soul is always in God according to this [something], unless the soul carries it outside or extinguishes it within.

A master says that this [something] is so present to God that it can never turn from God and that God is always present to it and within it.[7] I say that God has been in it continually from eternity. For man to be one with God in it grace is not necessary because grace is a creature, and no creature belongs here;[8] for in the ground of divine being where the three Persons are one being, the soul is one according to the ground. And so, if you wish it, all things are yours and God as well. Therefore, abandon yourself, all things, and everything you are in yourself, and take yourself according to how you are in God.

The masters say that human nature has nothing to do with time and that it is completely untouched, being much more within and closer to a person than he is to himself.[9] Therefore God assumed human nature and united it with his Person. At this point human nature became God because he took on human nature and not a human being.[10] Therefore, if you want to be this same Christ and God, abandon all of that which the eternal Word did not assume. The eternal Word did not assume *a* man. Therefore, leave whatever is *a* man in you and whatever you are, and take yourself purely according to human nature. Then you are the same in the eternal Word as human nature is in him; for your human nature and his are without difference. It is one, and whatever it is in Christ, that it also is in you. Thus I said in Paris that in the just man is fulfilled whatever the holy scriptures and the prophets had ever said [of Christ].[11] If you are as you should be, everything that was said [of Christ] in the Old and the New Testament will be fulfilled in you.

When are you as you should be? There are two ways of understanding this according to the words of the prophet who said: "In the fullness of time the Son was sent" (Ga. 4:4).[12] "Fullness of time" is of two kinds. A thing is full when it has reached its end, as the day is full at evening. Thus, when all time drops away from you, time is full. The second: When time comes to its end, that is eternity because then all time has an end since "before" or "after" is no longer. There, whatever is, is all present and new, and you have present to your view whatever ever happened or ever shall happen. There, there is neither before nor after; it is all present there. And in this ever present view I hold all things in my possession. This is "fullness of time," and thus I am as I should be. And thus I am truly the only Son and Christ.

That we come to this "fullness of time," may God help us. Amen.

Notes

Translated from DW I, pp. 414–423.

1. Eckhart does not really translate the quotation from Paul that would have us "put on" Christ like a garment. Rather, partially at least on the basis of sound, he turns the Latin *induimini* (put on) into MHG *intuot* (put into). He then follows up by contrasting MHG *intuon* (put into) with MHG *entuon* (put aside).
2. Cf. Ps. 8:3–4.
3. Eckhart seems to be claiming a likeness between God and the soul that is not merely based on (1) being created according to a divine idea in the mind of God; (2) sharing in those positive attributes, such as *wise, good, just*, as they apply to

God. The soul is also like God as he transcends these positive attributes, as he is in his ground, being, etc. Cf. *Essential Eckhart*, p. 42.

4. For more on relationships of higher to lower, cf. *Comm. Ex.* n. 5 (p. 42) and *Par. Gen.* n. 146 (*Essential Eckhart*, p. 113).
5. Cf. *Comm. Jn.* nn. 70–73 and *Bened.* 1 (*Essential Eckhart*, pp. 147–49, 224).
6. For other passages concerning this "something in the soul," see *vünkelîn* in the Glossary.
7. Cf. Augustine, *Trin.* 14.7.9 and 14.18.
8. For more on grace, see Sermon 21 (p. 282) and Sermon XXV (pp. 219–21).
9. Cf. Thomas Aquinas, *On Being and Essence* 3.
10. That is, in assuming human nature God did not join himself to an already fully constituted individual human being. He retained his divine personality. On the role of this in Eckhart's thought, see *Essential Eckhart*, p. 46.
11. This statement is assumed to be the basis for article 12 of the papal bull "In agro dominico" (*Essential Eckhart*, p. 78) condemning some of Eckhart's doctrines. The "of Christ" is not in the text of the sermon and was added by Quint because of its presence in the bull. For more on the just man, see Sermon 39 (pp. 296–97); *Comm. Jn.* nn. 14–22 and Sermon 6 (*Essential Eckhart*, pp. 126–29, 185–89).
12. Perhaps Paul is called a prophet here because the text quoted has a *post hoc* prophetic ring to it.

Sermon 29: Convescens praecepit eis, ab Ierosolymis ne discederent, etc. (Ac. 1:4).

These words that I have spoken in Latin one reads in the mass for this feast day.[1] Our Lord spoke them to his disciples as he was about to ascend into heaven: "Remain together in Jerusalem and do not depart. Wait for the promise that the Father made to you—that after these days, that are not many or few, you shall be baptized in the Holy Spirit" (Cf. Ac. 1:4–5).

No one can receive the Holy Spirit unless he lives above time in eternity. In temporal things the Holy Spirit can neither be received nor given. When a person turns away from temporal things and turns within himself, he becomes aware of a heavenly light that has come from heaven.[2] It is under heaven yet is from heaven. In this light a person has his fill, and yet it is corporeal; they say it is material. Iron, whose nature it is to sink, rises contrary to its nature and attaches itself to a magnet because of the nobility of the impression the stone received from the sky. In whatever direction the stone is turned, the iron turns, too. This is what the spirit does:[3] It does not rest satisfied just with this light, but presses all the way through the firmament and pierces through the sky until it comes to the spirit that makes the sky revolve. Because of the revolving of the heavens everything in the world turns green and leafs out. Still, this does not satisfy the spirit until it penetrates to the pinnacle and into the source in which the spirit takes its origin. This spirit comprehends according to number beyond number, and no number [beyond number] is found in our frail temporal existence. In eternity no one has a different root; there no one is without number.[4] This spirit must transcend *all* number and break through *all* multiplicity, and it is broken through by God. And just as he breaks through me, I break through him in return.[5] God leads this spirit into the desert and into the oneness of himself, where he is pure one welling up in himself.[6] This spirit has no "why," and if it were to have a "why," oneness would also have to have its "why." This spirit exists in oneness and freedom.

Now the masters say that the will is so free that no one can force it but God alone.[7] God does not force the will, but places it in freedom in such a way that it wills nothing but what God himself is and what freedom itself is. And the spirit can will nothing but what God wills. This is not a deficiency in freedom; it is its true freedom.

Now some people say, "If I possess God and God's love, I can do anything I want."[8] They do not understand these words correctly. As long as you can do anything against God and his commandments, you do not have the love of God, although you may fool the world [into thinking] you have it. The person who is established in God's will and God's love finds it delightful to do all the things that are pleasing to God and to avoid doing those that are against God.[9] And it is just as impossible for him to avoid doing something God wants done as it is to do something against God. Just as impossible as it would be for someone to walk whose legs were bound, that is how impossible it is for a person who is in God's will to do something against virtue. Someone has said: "If God had commanded me to practice vice and to shun virtue, I still could not perform an act of vice." For no one loves virtue but he who is virtue itself. The person who has abandoned himself and all things, who seeks nothing for himself in things and performs all his works without a why and out of love, such a person is dead to the whole world and lives in God and God in him.[10]

Now some people say, "These are beautiful words you are speaking, but we don't notice any of it [taking place]." This is my complaint, too. This way of being is so noble and yet so common that you do not have to spend a nickel or a penny on it.[11] Just keep your intention proper and your will free, and you have it.[12] The person who has abandoned all things where they are lowest and transitory receives them again in God where they are truth. All that is dead here is life there, and everything that is coarse and material here is there spirit in God. It is just as if someone poured pure water into a clean barrel that was completely spotless and clean and let it become still; and if then a person put his face over it, he would see it on the bottom just exactly as it is as part of himself. This happens because the water is pure and clean and unmoving. This is how it is with all those people who exist in freedom and unity in themselves. And if they take God in peace and tranquility, so they should take him in disorder and turmoil.[13] Then all is as it should be. If they take him less in disorder and turmoil than in peace and tranquility, it is not right. St. Augustine says, "Let one who finds the day irksome and the time long turn to God where time does not hang heavy and where all things are at rest."[14] Whoever loves justice is taken hold of by justice, and he becomes justice.

Now our Lord said, "I have not called you servants but friends, for the servant does not know what his master wants to do" (Jn. 15:15). A friend, too, could know something that I did not, if he did not want to reveal it to me. But our Lord said, "Everything that I have heard from my Father I have revealed to you" (Jn. 15:15). Now it puzzles me that certain priests, who are certainly very learned and want to be important, are so easily satisfied and let themselves be fooled in how they take these words our Lord spoke: "Everything that I have heard from my Father I have made known to you." They want to interpret them thus saying that he has revealed to us "on the way"[15] as much as is necessary for attaining eternal happiness. I do not agree that it is to be thus understood; it just is not the truth. Why did God become man? So that I might be born the same.[16] God died so that I might die to the whole world and to all created things. This is how one should understand our Lord's words: "Everything that I have heard from my Father I have revealed to you." What does the Son hear from his Father? The Father can do nothing but give birth; the Son can do nothing but be born. All that the Father has and is, the abyss of the divine being and divine nature, all this he brings forth completely in his only-begotten Son. What the Son hears from the Father he has revealed to us: that we are this same Son.[17] All that the Son has he has from his Father: being and nature, so that we might be this same only-begotten Son.

No one has the Holy Spirit if he is not the only-begotten Son. The Father and the Son "spirit" the Holy Spirit when the Holy Spirit is made spirit; this is essential and spiritual.[18] You can, of course, receive the gifts of the Holy Spirit or the likeness of the Holy Spirit, but this does not remain in you. It is not lasting. Similarly, when a person turns red in shame or turns pale, this is accidental and passes. But a person who is ruddy and good-looking by nature remains that way always.[19] Thus it is with the person who is the only-begotten Son. The Holy Spirit remains in his being. This is why it is written in the Book of Wisdom: "I have brought you forth today in the reflection of my eternal light, in the fullness and brightness of all the saints" (Cf. Ps. 2:7, 109:3). He gives birth to him now and today. There, in the childbed in the Godhead, they are "baptized in the Holy Spirit." This is "the promise that the Father made to them after these days that are not many or few" (cf. Ac. 1:5). This is the "fullness of the divinity" (Col. 2:9) where there is neither day nor night. In it that which is more than a thousand miles away is as near to me as the spot where I am now standing. There is the fullness and abundance of the Godhead; there is oneness.[20] As long as the soul knows difference, things are not right with it. As long as anything peers out or peers in, there is no oneness. Mary Magdalene sought our Lord at the grave and sought a dead person but found two living angels; but she was still inconsolable. Then the angels said, "Why are you troubled? What are you looking for? A dead person, and you have found two alive." And she said, "That is exactly why I am troubled. I have found two but am looking for one" (Cf. Jn. 20:11–14).[21]

As long as any differences from created things can gaze into the soul, it is troubled. I maintain, as I have often said, that where the soul has its natural, created being, there is no truth. I say that there is something above the created nature of the soul. And some priests do not understand that there is something so closely related to God and so one. It has nothing in common with anything. Whatever is created or createable is nothing; and all createdness and createableness is far from this "something" and foreign to it. It is a single one in itself and receives nothing into itself from outside.[22]

Our Lord ascended into heaven beyond all lights, beyond all knowledge, and beyond all comprehension. The person who is thus carried up beyond all lights lives in eternity. Hence St. Paul says, "God dwells in a light to which there is no access," and he is in himself pure one (1 Tim. 6:16).[23] Thus a person must be killed and be completely dead, and must be nothing in himself, made dissimilar, and like no one. Then he is really like God. For this is God's property and nature: that he is dissimilar and is like no one.

That we may be one in the oneness that is God himself, may God help us. Amen.

Translated from DW II, pp. 73–89.

1. The quotation is from the epistle for the feast of the Ascension.
2. "Heavenly," "heaven": the redundancy occurs in the original. On this heavenly light, see Sermon 39 (p. 298).
3. This spirit would seem to be the "spark of the soul" or highest part of the intellect, which seeks what it is like, the divine intellect.
4. A difficult passage. That in eternity no one is "without number" must in this context refer to number as it applies to angels and the Persons of the Trinity; *i.e.*, in some sense multiplicity, but not quantifiable numbers (Sermon 40, p. 301). Cf. also Thomas Aquinas, *STh* Ia. 30.3 and 50.3. ad 1.
5. The MHG *durchbrechen* (breaking-through) is the same word that is used at the conclusion of the famous Sermon 52 (*Essential Eckhart*, p. 203), where it means one's complete return to God to become what one was, is, and will be. It is difficult to say whether it has exactly the same meaning here.
6. See *Bened.* 2 (*Essential Eckhart*, p. 247).
7. Cf. Thomas Aquinas, *STh* Ia. 105.4 and Ia. IIae. 10. 4. ad 1. Here Eckhart takes up the question of what true freedom really is: Not free choice between finite objects, but rather willing what God is, willing without a specific "why." Cf. Glossary under *âne war umbe*.
8. This is probably a reference to the "Love God and do what you will" doctrine of the Brethren of the Free Spirit, who claimed to be following the spiritual heritage of Augustine (e.g., *On the Letter of John to the Parthians* 7.8). Eckhart clearly distances his own view from theirs.
9. See the similar attack on false mysticism in the Eckhartian "Sister Catherine" treatise below, p. 368.
10. Cf. *Comm. Jn.* n. 68 (*Essential Eckhart*, p. 146).
11. In contrasting *noble* and *common* as ways of describing the being of one who is dead to the world and lives for God, Eckhart plays on the ambiguity of common (*gemein*), which means both *vulgar* or *ordinary* and *universal* or *widespread*.
12. Free will here means, of course, freedom from a "why" and thus freedom to unite with God's will.
13. The verb here translated as "take" (MHG *nemen*) could also be rendered "receive" or "perceive."
14. Augustine, *On the Psalms* 36.1.3.
15. "On the way" (Latin: *in via*), i.e., while we are here on earth.
16. That is, "the same as he" or "the same Son." Cf. *Comm. Jn.* n. 106 and n. 117 (*Essential Eckhart*, p. 162, 167–68).
17. For more on the birth of the Son, see the Glossary under *geburt*.
18. The MGH *geistent*, here "spirit" or "breath," is a translation of the technical Latin term *spirant;* cf. *Quest. Par.* 5 n. 7 (LW V, p. 82).

19. Cf. *Comm. Wis.* n. 101 (p. 158).
20. For more on time and eternity, see the Glossary under *nû*.
21. Cf. Sermon IV.2, n. 30 (p. 211).
22. For more on the uncreated "something" in the soul see "In agro dominico" (*Essential Eckhart*, p. 80, and also pp. 42–44).
23. The last part of the sentence could also mean that this light is pure one in itself. For more on inaccessible light see Sermon 71 (pp. 320–21).

Sermon 30: Praedica verbum, vigila, in omnibus labora (2 Tm. 4:2).

One reads a phrase today and tomorrow concerning my master St. Dominic.[1] St. Paul writes it in the epistle and in German it means: "Speak the word, speak it externally, speak it forth, bring it forth, give birth to the Word!"[2]

It is a marvelous thing that something flows out yet remains within. That a word flows out yet remains within is certainly marvelous. That all creatures flow out yet remain within is a wonder. What God has given and what he has promised to give is simply marvelous, incomprehensible, unbelievable. And this is as it should be; for if it were intelligible and believable, it would not be right. God is in all things. The more he is in things, the more he is outside the things; the more within; the more outside; the more outside, the more within.[3] I have said many times that God creates the whole world right now all at once. All that God created six thousand years ago and earlier when God made the world—all this he is creating now completely.[4] God is in all things; but God as divine and God as intelligent is nowhere so intensely present as he is in the soul and in the angels; if you will, in the innermost and in the highest [part] of the soul. And when I say "the innermost," I mean the highest; and when I say "the highest," I mean the innermost of the soul. In the innermost and in the highest of the soul: I mean them both in one.[5] There, where time never entered nor image shined in, in this innermost and highest [part] of the soul, God creates this whole world. Everything that God created six thousand years ago when he made the world and everything he will yet create in a thousand years (if the world lasts that long), all this he creates in the innermost and in the highest of the soul. Everything that is past, everything that is present, and everything that is future God creates in the innermost of the soul. Everything that God accomplishes in all the saints he accomplishes in the innermost of the soul. The Father gives birth to his Son in the innermost of the soul and gives birth to you with his only-begotten Son, not less. If I am to be the Son, I have to be the Son in the same being in which he is the Son and in no other.[6] If I am to be human, I cannot be a man in the being of an animal; I have to be a man in the being of a man. But if I am to be *this* man, I have to be this man in *this* being.[7] Now St. John says, "You are children of God" (Cf. 1 Jn. 3:1).

"Speak the word, speak it externally, speak it forth, bring it forth, give birth to the Word!" "Speak it externally." That something is spoken from the outside in is a common thing. This, however, is spoken within. "Speak it externally!" This means: Be aware that this is within you. The prophet says, "God spoke one thing, and I heard two" (Cf. Ps. 61:12). This is true. God has only ever spoken one thing. His speech is only one. In this one speaking he speaks his Son and, together with him, the Holy Spirit and all creatures; and there is only one speaking in God.[8] But the prophet says, "I heard two," that is, I understood God and creatures. Where God speaks it, it is God; but here it is creature.[9] People imagine that God only became man there [in Palestine]. This is not true. God has just as much become man here [in the soul] as there, and he has become man so that he might give birth to you, his only-begotten Son, and nothing less.

I was sitting someplace yesterday when I spoke a phrase from the "Our Father," which says, "Your will be done!" (Mt. 6:10). But it would be better thus: "May will become yours," [in the sense] that my will becomes his will, that I become he: This is the meaning of the *Pater Noster*.[10] The phrase has two meanings. The first is: Sleep [unaware] of all things; that is, that you know nothing about time or creatures or images. The masters say: If a person were really asleep for a hundred years, he would not know any creature and he would not know of time or images. [Only if you so sleep,] then you can hear what God is bringing about in you. This is why the soul says in the Book of Love: "I sleep and my heart is awake" (Sg. 5:2). Therefore, if all creatures are asleep in you, you can become aware of what God is bringing about in you.[11]

The phrase "Work in all things" (2 Tm. 4:5) contains three meanings. It is the same as if to say: Achieve your advantage in all things; which is: Take God in all things because God is in all things. St. Augustine says: "God created all things, not by letting them come about and then going on his way; rather, he remained in them."[12] People imagine that they have more if they have both things and God than if they have God but not things. But this is wrong because all things together with God are not more than God by himself. And if someone who had both Father and Son in him were to think that he had more than if he had the Son but not the Father, he would be wrong. For the Father together with the Son is not more than the Son by himself, and the Son with the Father is not more than the Father by himself. Therefore, take God in all things in this manner, and that is a sign that he has given birth to you, his only-begotten Son, and nothing less.

The second meaning of "achieve your advantage in all things" is: "Love God above all things and your neighbor as yourself" (Lk. 10:27), and this is a command from God. But I say that it is not just a commandment; rather, it is also what God has given and what he has promised to give. And if you love your own hundred marks more than someone else's, this is wrong.[13] If you like one person more than another, this is wrong. If you like your father, your mother, and yourself more than some other person, this is wrong. [Someone might say:] "My goodness! What are you saying? Should I not prefer my own happiness to that of another person?" There are many learned people who do not understand this and think it terribly difficult, yet it is not difficult but very easy. I shall show you that it is not difficult. Look! Nature has two purposes which each part of a human being pursues in its works, namely, that it serve the body as a whole and, secondly, [that it serve] each part [of the body] separately for that part's good not less than for its own good. But it [each part] does not consider itself more in its works than some other part.[14] How much more must this be true in the realm of grace. God should be the measure and the foundation of your love. The first intention of your love should be purely God and then your neighbor as yourself and not less than yourself. And if you love happiness more in yourself than in someone else, this is wrong. For if you love happiness in yourself more than in someone else, you [really just] love yourself; and where you love yourself, there God is not purely your love, and this is then wrong. If you like happiness in St. Peter and St. Paul as much as in yourself, you possess the same happiness which they also have. And if you like happiness in the angels as much as in yourself and if you like happiness in our Lady as much as in yourself, you enjoy the very same happiness that she does. It is yours as genuinely as hers. Thus one says in the Book of Wisdom, "He made him like his saints" (Cf. Si. 45:2).

The third meaning of "achieve your advantage in all things" is: Love God equally in all things. This means: Love God as much in poverty as in wealth; care for him as much in sickness as in health. Love him as much when being tried as when not, and as much in suffering as when free of suffering. Truly, the more the suffering, the less the suffering; like two buckets: the heavier the one, the lighter the other. The more a person renounces, the easier he finds it to renounce. A person who loves God would find it as easy to give up this whole world as [he would to give up] an egg. The more he renounces, the easier it is for him to renounce. This was the case with the apostles. The worse their sufferings were, the more easily they suffered.

"Work in all things!" (2 Tm. 4:5). This means: Whenever you find yourself in various kinds of things and not in bare, pure, simple being, let this be your work: "Work in all things, completing your service" (2 Tm. 4:5). This means: Lift up your head. And this has two meanings. First, put everything aside that is yours and lay claim to God. Then God will be your own as he is his own very own. He will be God for you as he is God for himself, and not less. What is mine I do not have from anyone. But if I have it from someone else, it is not mine but rather his from whom I have it. The other meaning of "lift up your head" is: Direct all your works to God. There are many people who do not understand this, and this seems to me hardly surprising. For the person who is to understand this must be totally detached and elevated above all things.

That we may arrive at such perfection, may God help us. Amen.

Notes

Translated from DW II, pp. 93–109.

1. This scripture text is from the feast of St. Dominic, the founder of the Order of Preachers, or Dominicans.
2. Here at the beginning of the sermon Eckhart treats only the first part of the text: *praedica verbum* (preach the word). He keeps paraphrasing it until he arrives at what he wishes to treat: the birth of the Son. Here and in the instance immediately below it is difficult to know whether to render it "the Word" or "word."
3. For a similar idea, see Sermon 9 (p. 256) and *Comm. Ecc.* n. 54 (p. 179).
4. For more on the relationship of time and eternity, see the Glossary under *nû.*
5. That is, "innermost" and "highest" both apply because neither applies. The ground of the soul is not a place and can only very inadequately be described at all.
6. For more on the birth of the Son, see the Glossary under *geburt.*
7. Cf. *Comm. Ex.* n. 102 (p. 79).
8. Because he is outside of time and because he is infinite and cannot change, God must be thought of as acting (eternally) only once. In his one action of speaking (begetting) the Son, the Holy Spirit and creation must also be said to come about. This interpretation of the Psalm verse was popular with Eckhart. See *Essential Eckhart*, p. 39.

9. In our cognition and as separated from God here on earth this one act of speaking is perceived as having two separate results: Son and creatures.
10. In the MHG original this wordplay is based on a change of word order: *dîn wille der werde* becomes *werde wille dîn*.
11. Cf. *Comm. Wis.* n. 280 (p. 171).
12. Augustine, *Conf.* 4.12.18.
13. A hundred marks was a considerable sum of money.
14. Cf. *Comm. Ex.* n. 88 (p. 74).

Sermon 39: Iustus in perpetuum vivet et apud dominum est merces eius (Ws. 5:16).

One reads a short saying in today's epistle spoken by the wise man: "The just lives in eternity."[1]

I have already spoken at times about what a just man is, but now shall explain it differently or in a different sense:[2] A just person is one who has been informed by and transformed into justice. The just man lives in God and God in him because God is born in the just man and the just man in God. In every virtue of the just man God is born, and he is filled with joy by every virtue of the just man. But not just by every virtue, rather, by every work of the just man, however small it may be, if it is performed by the just man in justice, it fills God with joy. He is delighted through and through because nothing remains in his ground that is not animated by joy. This fact is for the less discerning to believe and for the enlightened to know.

The just man seeks nothing in his works. Those that seek something in their works or those who work because of a "why" are servants and hired hands.[3] And so, if you want to be informed by and transformed into justice, have no [specific] intention in your works and form no "why" in yourself, either in time or in eternity, either reward or happiness, either this or that. Such works are, in fact, dead. Even if you form God within yourself, whatever works you perform for a [specific] purpose are all dead, and you ruin good works.[4] You do not just ruin good works; you also commit sin because you act just like a gardener who is supposed to plant a garden but only pulls out the trees and expects to get paid for it. This is how you ruin good works. And so, if you want to live and want your works to live, you must be dead to all things and have become nothing. It is a characteristic of creatures that

296

they make something out of something, while it is a characteristic of God that he makes something out of nothing.[5] Therefore, if God is to make anything in you or with you, you must first have become nothing. Hence go into your own ground and work there, and the works that you work there will all be living. This is why he says, "The just lives." Because he is just he works, and his works live.

Now he says, "His reward is with God" (Ws. 5:16). On this point only a few words. He says "with" because the just man's reward is where God himself is. The happiness of the just man and God's happiness are one happiness because the just man is only happy where God is happy. St. John says, "The Word was with God" (Jn. 1:1). He says "with," and this is why the just man is like God: God is justice. Therefore, whoever is in justice is in God and *is* God.[6]

Now let us say more about the word "just." He does not say "the just *human being*" or "the just *angel*"; he simply says "the just."[7] The Father gives birth to his Son the just and the just his Son.[8] All the virtues of the just and every work that has been performed by the virtue of the just is nothing else but the Son being born of the Father. This is why the Father never rests but spends his time urging and prodding, so that the Son be born in me,[9] as the scripture says: "Neither for Zion's sake am I silent nor for Jerusalem's sake do I rest until the just appears and shines forth like lightning" (Is. 62:1). Zion means the summit of life, and Jerusalem means the summit of peace.[10] However, neither for the summit of life nor for the summit of peace does God ever rest, but [he] urges and prods always that the just appear. In the just nothing should work but God alone. If it happens that anything from without moves you to work, the works are really all dead. And if it happens that God moves you from without to work, these works are all dead.[11] If your works are to live, God must move you from within, in the innermost of the soul, if they really are to live. There is where your life is; there alone is where you live.[12]

I say further: If one virtue seems greater to you than another and if you esteem it more than another, then you do not cherish it as it exists in justice and God does not yet work in you. As long as a person esteems or cherishes one virtue more [than another], he does not cherish or take them as they exist in justice, nor is he just. The just man takes and performs all virtues in justice, since they are justice itself.

The scripture says: "Before the created world I am" (Si. 24:14).[13] He says "before" and "I am." This means: Where man is above time in eternity, there he works one work with God. Some people ask: How can a person perform works that God worked a thousand years ago or a thousand years hence, and they do not understand it. In eternity there is neither before nor after. Hence what happened a thousand years ago or will happen a thousand years from now or is happening now is all simply one in eternity. Therefore, whatever God did or created a thousand years ago or a thousand years hence he is doing now; it is simply all one work. Thus a man who is above time in eternity works together with God whatever God worked a thousand years ago or a thousand years hence. And this is for wise people to know and for the less wise to believe.

St. Paul says, "We are eternally chosen in the Son" (Cf. Ep. 1:4). Hence we should never rest until we become that which we eternally have been in him; for the Father urges and prods that we be born in the Son and become the same thing that the Son is. The Father gives birth to his Son, and in giving birth the Father has so much peace and delight that he consumes his whole nature in it. All that is in God moves him to give birth. His ground, his essence, and his being all move the Father to give birth.[14]

Sometimes a light becomes perceptible in the soul, and a person thinks it is the Son; but it is only a light.[15] Whenever the Son appears in the soul, the love of the Holy Spirit also appears. Therefore, I say: The Father's being consists in giving birth to the Son; the Son's being consists in my being born in him and like him; the Holy Spirit's being lies in my catching fire in him and becoming totally melted and becoming simply love. Whoever is thus inside of love and is totally love thinks that God loves no one but him alone, nor can he love anyone nor be loved by anyone than by him [God] alone.

Some teachers claim that the spirit takes its happiness from love; others claim that it takes it in seeing God. I say, however, it takes it neither from love nor from knowing nor from seeing.[16] Now one could ask: In eternal life does not the spirit see God? Yes and no. Insofar as the spirit is born, it does not look up to or see God. But insofar as it is being born, it sees God. Therefore the happiness of the spirit consists in its having been born and not in its being born; for it lives where the Father lives: in oneness and in the nakedness of being.[17] Therefore, turn away from all things and take yourself purely in being, for whatever is outside of being is accident and accidents result in "why."[18]

That we live in eternity, may God help us. Amen.

NOTES

Translated from DW II, pp. 251–66.

1. This awkward translation has been chosen to point up the fact that Eckhart translates the Latin *iustus* with MHG *der gerehte*. Both the Latin and the MHG words are adjectives used as nouns. In other words, they imply but do not state the noun *man.* This will be a point of interpretation later in the sermon. Eckhart generally uses the adjective *just* for the just man throughout; however, because of the awkwardness of reproducing it literally, it will henceforth be translated "just man," except where its meaning as the "just *man*" is called into question.

2. The reference seems to be to Sermon 6 (*Essential Eckhart*, pp. 185–89), but in fact this sermon is considerably different. For more on the just man see also *Comm. Jn.* nn. 14–22 (*Essential Eckhart*, pp. 126–29), as well as *iustitia* in the Glossary.

3. For more on "why" and "without a why," see *âne war umbe* in the Glossary.

4. The reason why this second kind of works is dead would seem to be that the God which we "form" or construct for ourselves bears such slight resemblance to the reality, thus negating the value of the works done with him as final goal. See Sermon 52 (*Essential Eckhart*, p. 200) for a more elaborate development of this idea.

5. Cf. Sermon XLIX. 3, n. 511 (p. 237).

6. For a similar identification of man and God, see *Bened.* 1 (*Essential Eckhart*, p. 212).

7. See note 1 above.

8. *Just* here without the accompanying noun *man* underlines the union achieved with the Son. *Just* is thus made to include within it both creature and God. Cf. Sermon 6 (*Essential Eckhart*, p. 187).

9. Cf. Sermon 12 (p. 268).

10. Etymologies found in Isidore of Seville, *Etymologies* 15.1.5–6.

11. See note 4 above.

12. Cf. Sermon VI.2, n. 59 (p. 214).

13. This is another of Eckhart's original renderings. It is usually taken to mean "Before the ages (or world) I was created." However, the original (*ante saecula creata sum*) contains the ambiguity that allows the preacher's version. Cf. *Par Quest.* 1, n. 4 (LW V, p. 41).

14. For more on the birth of the Son, see the Glossary under *geburt*.

15. This is possibly a reference to the "spark of the soul," but here and in Sermon 29 (p. 287) Eckhart may also be referring to something not unlike the "light" experience found in many Orthodox mystics.

16. This is a reference to the question disputed between Dominicans and Franciscans as to whether love (Franciscans) or knowing (Dominicans) is the foundation of happiness. Cf. *Par. Quest.* 3 (LW V, pp. 55–71); *Comm. Jn.* n. 108; Sermon 52 (*Essential Eckhart*, pp. 163, 201).

17. Eckhart here qualifies the traditional view that the beatific vision is the basis of one's happiness in heaven to fit his own thought. This vision implies duality, a subject looking (creature) and an object being seen (God). To the extent that the creature is *already born* the Son, there is no longer any such duality between God and creature. This unity is really the essence of beatitude, the preacher tells us, and not the *still being born*, which implies a duality of the one seeing and the one being seen.

18. Whatever is accidental and changeable in the thing is what causes it to be sought for a specific "why."

Sermon 40: Manete in me (Jn. 15:4). Beatus vir qui in sapientia morabitur (Si. 14:22).

Our Lord Jesus Christ says in the gospel, "Stay in me!" and a phrase from the epistle says, "Happy the man who dwells in wisdom." These two quotations have the same meaning: the words of Christ, "Stay in me," and the words of the epistle, "Happy the man who dwells in wisdom."[1]

Now listen to what a person should have who is to dwell in him; that is, in God. He should have three things. The first is that he has renounced himself and all things and is not dependent on things which hold on to the senses from within,[2] nor should he dwell in any creatures that exist in time or in eternity. The second is that he not love *this* good or *that* good; he should love, rather, the good from which all good flows. For a thing is only enjoyable or desirable insofar as God is in it. Hence one should love something good only to the extent that one is loving God in it; and one should, therefore, not love God because of heaven or because of any other thing. Rather, one should love him because of the goodness that he is in himself. Whoever loves him because of something else does not dwell in him, but dwells in that because of which he loves him. Therefore, if you want to stay in him, love him for nothing other than himself. The third is that he should not take God as he is good or just; he should take him rather in that pure, naked substance where he is taking himself bare.[3] Goodness and justice are pieces of clothing; they cover him. Therefore, strip everything from God that clothes him and take him bare in the dressing room where he is uncovered and naked in himself. Then are you [really] staying in him.

Who thus stays in him has five qualities. The first is that between him

300

and God there is no distinction; they are one. The angels are many, beyond number. They do not add up to a specific number because they are beyond number; this arises from their utter simplicity. Concerning the three Persons in God: There are three of them without number, but they are a multiplicity. Between man and God, however, there is not only no distinction, there is no multiplicity either. There is nothing but one.[4] The second is that such a person takes his happiness in the same purity where God takes his and where he dwells. The third is that his knowing is one with God's knowing, that his working is one with God's working,[5] and that his consciousness is one with God's consciousness. The fourth is that God is continually being born in this person. How is God continually being born in this person? Now pay attention! When a person uncovers and lays bare the divine image that God created in him in creating his nature, then the image of God becomes visible. Giving birth is to be taken here as God's revealing self. That the Son is said to be born of the Father is due to the fact that the Father, as a father, is revealing to him his secrets.[6] And so, the more and the more clearly a person lays bare the image of God in himself, the more clearly God is born in him. And thus God's continual giving birth is to be taken to mean that the Father uncovers completely the image and is shining forth in him.[7]

The fifth is that such a person is continually being born in God. How is this person continually being born in God? Pay close attention! Through the uncovering of this image in himself, this person is becoming ever more similar to God because, by means of this image, a human being becomes like God's image, the image that God is according to his bare being.[8] And the more a person lays himself bare, the more he is like God; and the more he is like God, the more he becomes united with him. And thus the birth of the person taking place continually in God is to be taken according to how he shines with his image in God's image, which God is according to his bare being—with which a person is one. Hence the unity of God and man is to be understood according to the likeness of the image, because a person is like God according to this image. And therefore, in saying that man is one with God and *is* God according to that unity, one considers him according to that part of the image by which he is like God, and not according to his being created. In considering him as God, one does not consider him according to his being a creature, for in taking him as God, one does not deny his being a creature, as if this denial were so to be understood that his creatureliness came to an end; rather, it [the denial of creaturehood] is to be understood with regard to a statement about God, that is, that one denies it to God.[9] If one considers Christ, who is God and man, according to his humanity—in so doing one denies him his divinity (not that one can really deny him his divinity), or rather one denies it to him just because of how one considers him.[10] This is how the words of Augustine are to be understood when he says: "Whatever a person loves a person is. If he loves a stone, he is a stone; if he loves a human being, he is a human being. If he loves God—I dare speak no further. If I were to say that he was then God, you might stone me. But I refer you to scripture."[11] Therefore, in joining himself nakedly to God in loving, a person becomes unformed, informed, and transformed in the divine uniformity in which he is one with God. A person has all this in staying within.[12] Now regard the fruits which a person brings forth there. When he is one with God, a person brings forth all creatures with God and by being one with him, he brings happiness to all creatures.

Now the second text, that from the epistle, says, "Happy the man who dwells in wisdom" (Si. 14:22). It says, "in wisdom." Wisdom is a name for a mother. The characteristic of a motherly name is passivity, and in God both activity and passivity must be thought. The Father is active, and the Son is passive because of his function as the one being born. For the Son is Wisdom born from eternity in which all things are distinct. Thus it says, "Happy the man who dwells in wisdom."[13]

Now it says, "Happy is the *man*." I have often said that there are two powers in the soul: One is the man and one is the woman. And it says, "Happy is the man." The power in the soul that one calls the man is the highest power of the soul in which God shines bare; for into this power nothing enters but God, and this power is continually in God.[14] And so, if a person were to take all things in this power, he would take them not as they are *things*, but as they are in God. Therefore, a person should dwell continually in this power because all things are alike in this power.[15] Thus a person would dwell in all things alike and take them as they are all alike in God, and there a person would have all things.[16] One would remove what is coarsest from all things and would take them as they are gratifying and desirable.[17] There [in this power in the soul] he has them in this manner, for God according to his own nature cannot help but give you everything that he ever created and [he will give you] his very self.[18] This is why that person is happy who dwells continually in this power; he dwells continually in God.

That we may dwell continually in God, may we receive the help of our dear Lord Jesus Christ. Amen.

NOTES

Translated from DW II, pp. 272–81.

1. The "stay" in the first quotation and the "dwell" in the second are taken by the preacher as expressing the same idea.
2. Quint considers this last clause, "which hold on to the senses from within," very likely not to be the original text.
3. Here as elsewhere the preacher urges us to "take" God as he "takes" himself, beyond what can be apprehended by applying positive terms to him. One is tempted to translate *nemen* (take) by "apprehend," "perceive," or something similar. However, to do so seems to be interpreting more than translating, and it weakens the original. What Eckhart is demanding seems to be both more general and more intense than what happens through the normal use of human cognitive faculties. Hence the decision to translate *nemen* literally as "take."
4. The point of this passage on number is that creature and God achieve a unity beyond the unity of the angels or the unity of the Trinity, even though angels (countless as they are) and the three Persons in God achieve a degree of unity that does not allow us to apply numbers to them. Angels and the Trinity have a kind of multiplicity, but not one that can be grasped by the accidental category of number. Cf. Thomas Aquinas, *STh* Ia. 30. 3. ad 2.
5. Cf. Sermon 52 (*Essential Eckhart*, p. 202).
6. Cf. Thomas Aquinas, *STh* Ia. 42. 4. ad 2.
7. On the image of God, see under *bilde* in the Glossary.
8. The paradox of this "bared" image is that it is an image that is more similar to the reality of God than positive perfections like justice and goodness. In Sermon 70 (p. 318), Eckhart describes it as an "image without image." See also Sermon 70, note 11 (pp. 319–20), and *Comm. Jn.* especially nn. 23–27 (*Essential Eckhart*, pp. 129–30).
9. This passage is difficult and unclear at best. The following section concerning Christ helps clarify. The whole argument may be seen as an illustration of the importance of the *inquantum* principle (that is, formal abstract predication) in Eckhart's thought (cf. *Essential Eckhart*, pp. 53–54).
10. That is, the "denial" occurs when one, by one's way of considering, abstracts from or prescinds from something one knows is really there, or, in other words, when one speaks of Christ formally, only insofar as (*inquantum*) he is man.
11. Augustine, *On the Letter of John to the Parthians* 2.14. Cf. *Comm. Wis.* n. 34 (p. 153).
12. This "staying within" is a reference to the scripture text of the sermon (Jn. 15:4).
13. Wisdom, a feminine noun in Latin and MHG, is identified with the Son, who is the Wisdom of the Father. In the Book of Wisdom, wisdom is called the mother of all these good things (Ws. 7:12). The Son's (motherly) passivity in his relationship to the Father consists in his *being born*. The Son is also the "place"

in the Trinity where the (distinct) images of created beings, their exemplary causes, exist.
14. For more on the "man" and the "woman" in the soul, see, e.g., *Par. Gen.* nn. 135–60 (*Essential Eckhart*, pp. 108–20).
15. One should note the use of *dwell* here. *Dwelling* in this power is made parallel to dwelling in the Son and "staying in me" (Jn. 14:3). All things are alike in this power as they are in God. See Sermon 12 (p. 269).
16. Cf. *Comm. Wis.* n. 99 (p. 157).
17. By *coarse* Eckhart usually means what is material or corporeal in a thing. One then takes it according to its image or form and leaves aside its matter or material.
18. Cf. Sermons VI.1, n. 56; and XLV n. 455 (pp. 213–14 and 229).

Sermon 46:   Haec est vita aeterna (Jn. 17:3).

These words are in the holy gospel and our Lord Jesus Christ speaks them: "This is eternal life, that one know you alone as the one true God and your Son whom you have sent, Jesus Christ."

Now note well! No one can know the Father but his only Son since he says himself that "no one knows the Father except his Son, and no one knows the Son except his Father" (Mt. 11:27). And thus if a person is to know God (in whom his eternal happiness consists), he must be an only Son of the Father with Christ. Therefore, if you want to be happy, you must be one Son, not many sons; rather, one Son.[1] You should, of course, be different according to your corporeal birth, but in the eternal birth you should be one because in God there is only one natural fountainhead, and, therefore, there is only one natural flowing-out of the Son, not two; rather, one.[2] Hence, if you are to be one Son with Christ, you have to be a single flowing-out with the eternal Word.

How should a person arrive at the point of being an only Son of the Father? Follow carefully! The eternal Word did not assume *this* human being or *that* human being.[3] Rather, he assumed a free, undivided human nature which was bare, or without a [formed] image, for the simple form *humanity* does not have a [formed] image.[4] Thus, because in being assumed human nature was taken on by the eternal Word simply and without [individuating] images, the image of the Father, which the eternal Son is, became the image of human nature. Hence it is just as true that man became God as it is that God became man. This is how human nature was transformed: by becoming the divine image, that is, the image of the Father.[5] And so, if you are to be one Son, you must sever and abandon everything in yourself which causes distinction. Man is an accident of nature.[6] Therefore, abandon everything that is accident in you and preserve yourself as a free, undivided human nature. Since this same nature which you possess has become the Son of the eternal Father through its being assumed by the eternal Word, you become the Son of the eternal Father with Christ because you have the same nature which has become God. Therefore, be careful not in the least to hold onto yourself as you are *this* person or *that*, but preserve yourself as a free, undivided human nature.[7] And so, if you want to be one Son, separate yourself from all nothing because nothing causes distinction.[8] How is that? Note the following. That you are *not* a certain person, it is the *not* which differentiates you from this person.[9] If you want to be without distinction, rid yourself of *not*. There is a power in the soul which is separated from nothing since it has nothing in common with any things. Nothing is in this power but God alone. He shines naked into this power.[10]

Look! The person who is thus one Son has movement, activity, and everything that he has as his very own. That the Son of the Father is Son eternally, this he has from the Father. Whatever he has, however, he has in himself because he is one with the Father in being and nature. Hence he has being and existence totally in himself and thus says, "Father, as I and you are one, so I will that they are one" (Jn. 17:11). And just as the Son is one with the Father in being and nature, so are you one with him in being and nature, and you have everything in yourself just as the Father has it in himself. You do not have anything from God just on loan because God is your own possession. And so everything which you have, you have as your own; and whatever works you do not have as your own, these are all dead in God's eyes. These are the works to which you are moved by foreign things outside yourself. They do not proceed from life and are therefore dead because a thing is alive if it has movement on its own. Therefore, if a person's works are to live, they have to be taken from his very own [self], not from alien things nor from outside, but rather in him.

Now take note of this. If you love justice as it is related to you or in you, you do not love justice as it is justice; and thus you do not take it or love it as it is one, but rather as it is divided. Since, then, God is justice, you are not taking him or loving him as he is one. Therefore, take justice as it is justice because then you are taking it as it is God. Where then justice works, you are working, for then you are continually working justice. Even if hell itself were standing on the path of justice, you would be working justice and it would cause you no suffering but rather joy because you yourself would be justice and would therefore have to work justice.[11] For to the extent that a thing ascends to union, to that extent it is one with the simplicity of this union and the more simple it is.

May God help us to the simplicity of this truth. Amen.

NOTES

Translated from DW II, pp. 378–86.

1. The word "rather" here is actually *mêr* in MHG, and it also means "more." Thus Eckhart is playing with the paradox that in not being many sons but rather one Son we become more.
2. See note 1 concerning "rather."
3. That is, the Word did not assume a particular individual human person. Thus the economy of redemption in which Christ does not assume *this* or *that* human being, but human nature in general, mirrors the structure of reality in which God is not *this* or *that* being (*esse hoc et hoc*), but pure indistinct Existence.
4. In this context the fact that the Word assumed a human nature *sunder bilde* (without a formed image) seems to mean that it was a human nature not yet individualized in any way, so that it was not disposed toward being this or that individual human person.
5. That is, through the Incarnation human nature took on the divine image, the image of the Father, which the Son is.
6. That is, man is an accident of nature in the sense that what is individual and individuating in man, that which differentiates him from other human beings and keeps him from being simply one with human nature transformed by the divine image, is accidental. It changes and can be changed.
7. What has been translated in this passage as "preserve," "possess," and "hold onto" is really "take yourself" (*sich nemen*), the same verb Eckhart uses when he urges us to "take" God as he is one, etc. Thus "preserving," "holding onto," and the like seems to be in part, at least (and perhaps in great part), an intellectual activity.
8. Since God is being, nothing is what separates us from him. We must rid ourselves of all nothing.
9. In MHG *niht* can mean both "nothing" (as immediately above) and "not."
10. For more on this power in the soul, see *vünkelîn* in the Glossary.
11. On justice and the just person, cf. *Comm. Jn.* nn. 14–21 (*Essential Eckhart*, pp. 126–28).

Sermon 59:   Et nunc sequimur te in toto corde, et timemus te, et quaerimus faciem tuam (Dn. 3:41).

The prophet Daniel says, "We follow you with all our hearts and fear you and seek your countenance." This passage is in clear agreement with what I said yesterday: "I called out to him, bid him come, and enticed him; and the spirit of wisdom has come into me. I have valued this more highly than all the kingdoms, power, dominion, gold, silver, and jewels; and in comparison with the spirit of wisdom I considered all things as a grain of sand, as muck, and as nothing" (Ws. 7:7–9).

It is a clear sign that a person has "the spirit of wisdom" if he considers all things as a pure nothing.[1] Whoever values any thing at all does not have "the spirit of wisdom." When he said "a grain of sand," this was understated; when he said "muck," it was still understated. When he said "as nothing," this was well said because all things are a pure nothing compared to "the spirit of wisdom." "I called out to him, bid him come, and enticed him; and the spirit of wisdom has come into me." If a person calls out to him from his innermost being, "the spirit of wisdom" comes into him.

There is a power in the soul extending farther than this whole world.[2] It has to be utterly extended because God dwells within it. Some people do not bid "the spirit of wisdom" come in; they invite health, wealth, and pleasure. "The spirit of wisdom" does not come into such people. What they are asking for is more valuable to them than God—just as if someone offers a penny for a loaf of bread he considers the bread of more value than the penny. Such people make God their servant. "Do this for me, and make me healthy," a rich person might say. "Demand whatever you want, and I'll give it to you!" If the other were then to ask for a halfpenny, this would be foolish. If he asked for a hundred marks, the rich man would gladly pay it. This is why it is pure foolishness for someone to ask God for anything else but himself. He does not like it because he gives nothing with more pleasure than himself. A master says, "All things have a 'why,' but God does not have a 'why.' And the person who asks God for anything other than himself reduces God to a 'why.' "[3]

Now he says, "With the spirit of wisdom all good things came to me at once" (Ws. 7:11). The gift of wisdom is the noblest of the seven gifts.[4] God gives none of these gifts without giving himself first and foremost, [and he gives himself] equally and in the manner of birth. Everything that is good and can bring pleasure and comfort—all this I possess in "the spirit of wisdom," as well as all sweetness, so that not as much as the point of a needle is lacking. And yet this would be insignificant if one did not possess it completely, equally, and just as God enjoys it. Exactly so do I enjoy it, this very same thing in his nature. For in "the spirit of Wisdom" he works all things alike, so that the least becomes the most and not the most as the least; just as if one were to graft a superior branch onto a base stock, the fruit would turn out according to the quality of the branch and not according to the baseness of the stock. This same thing happens in the spirit: There all works become alike because the least becomes like the most and not the most like the least. He gives himself as in giving birth. The noblest work in God is giving birth (if one work in God can be nobler than another), because God takes all his pleasure in giving birth. All that I have by birth can be taken from me by no one, unless he takes me away from myself. All that I have by chance I can lose. This is why God gives birth to himself into me fully, so that I may never lose him. Everything I have by birth I cannot lose. God takes all his pleasure in this birth, and he gives birth to his Son in us so that we have all our pleasure in it and so that we give birth to this same natural Son together with him. For God has all his pleasure in this birth and for this reason he gives birth to himself in us, so that he might have all his pleasure in the soul and that we might have all our pleasure in him. Hence Christ said, as St. John writes in the gospel: "They follow after me" (Jn. 10:27). Really to follow God is good; that is, to follow his will. As I said yesterday: "Thy will be done" (Mt. 6:10). St. Luke writes in the gospel that our Lord said: "Whoever wants to follow me must deny himself, take up his cross and follow me" (Lk. 9:23).[5] If a person were really to deny himself, he would actually be God's and God his. I am as sure of this as I am that I am a man. For such a person all things are as easy to leave behind as a lentil is; and the more one leaves, the more one likes it.

St. Paul desired for God's sake to be separated from God on behalf of his brethren (Rm. 9:3). This causes the masters much distress and grave doubts. Some say he meant [separation] only for a while. This cannot be the case. [Paul wanted this] as little for an instant as for an eternity, or as gladly for eternity as for an instant. If he put God's will first, then the longer it lasted, the happier he would be; and the greater the pain were, the more he would like it. It is just like the case of a businessman who knew for certain that what he was buying for one mark was really worth ten to him. He would spend all the marks he had and would do whatever work was necessary to be sure that he would make it home alive and with so much profit. All this would be enjoyable for him. So it was with St. Paul. Whatever he knew to be God's will—the longer, the nicer; the greater the suffering, the greater the joy. For to fulfill God's will is heaven; and the longer this will lasts, the more heaven it is; and the greater the suffering in God's will, the more happiness there is.

"Deny yourself and offer up your cross!" (cf. Lk. 9:23). So speak the masters: Suffering is fasting and other penance. But I say this is relief from suffering, for nothing but joy follows from such conduct.[6] Then he [Christ] says, "I give them life" (Jn. 10:28). Many other things pertaining to rational creatures are accidents. Life, however, is as much the property of every rational creature as being is. Therefore he says, "I give them life," because his being is his life. God gives himself completely when he says "I give." No creature has the power to give life. If it were possible for a creature to give life, God loves the soul so tenderly that he could not allow it. He wants to give it himself. If a creature were to give it, it would not be of value to the soul. It would consider it of as little worth as a gnat. It is just as though an emperor were to give a man an apple. The man would value it more than a coat given him by someone else. So, too, the soul cannot bear to receive it [life] from anyone else than God. Thus he says, "I give," so that the soul might have perfect joy in this giving.

Now he says, "I and the Father are one" (Jn. 10:30), the soul in God and God in it (cf. Jn. 17:21). If one were to pour water into a barrel, the barrel would encompass the water; but the water would not be inside [the planks of] the barrel, nor would the barrel be inside the water. But the soul is so completely one with God that the one cannot be understood without the other. One can think heat easily enough without fire and the shining without the sun, but God cannot be understood without the soul nor the soul without God; so utterly are they one.

There is no difference between the soul and our Lord Jesus Christ, except that the soul has a coarser being, since his [Christ's] being is connected to the eternal Person. To the extent that the soul divests itself of its coarseness (and if it could only completely divest itself of it!), it would be completely the same; and everything one could say about our Lord Jesus Christ, one could say about the soul.[7]

A master says that creatures are full of the least of God and that his magnitude is nowhere.[8] I want to tell you a story. Someone once asked a virtuous person why it was that he sometimes had an urge for devotion and prayer and at other times he had no urge at all. He replied thus: "The hound that catches sight of a hare, catches its scent, and comes upon its tracks, and so chases the hare. Then the others see this one giving chase, and they take up the chase, too. But they quickly tire and give up. So it is with a man who has caught sight of God and has caught his scent. He does not give up but keeps up the chase." David says about this: "Taste and see how sweet God is" (Ps. 33:9).⁹ Such a man does not tire; but others tire quickly. Some people run in front of God, some next to God, and some follow behind God. Those who run in front of God are the ones who follow their own will and do not want to acknowledge God's will. This is simply base. Those who go beside God say, "Lord, I want only what you want." But if they are sick, they beg that God might want them healthy. This one can let pass. The third group follows behind God; wherever he wishes they follow him willingly, and these are perfect. About this St. John says in the Book of Mysteries, "They follow the lamb wherever he goes" (Rv. 14:4). These people follow God wherever he leads them: in sickness or in health, in fortune or misfortune. [10] St. Peter went in front of God and our Lord said, "Devil, go behind me!" (Mt. 16:23) Now our Lord said, "I am in the Father and the Father is in me" (Jn. 14:11). Just so is God in the soul and the soul is in God.

Now he says, "We seek your countenance" (Dn. 3:41). Truth and goodness are God's garments; God is above everything we can put into words. Intellect "seeks" God and takes him in the root, from whence the Son and the whole Godhead come forth. The will, however, remains outside and clings to goodness. Goodness is God's garment. The highest angels take God in his dressing room, before he is clothed in goodness or anything else that one can express in words. [11] Hence he says, "We seek your countenance," because the countenance of God is his being.

That we grasp this and possess it willingly, may God help us. Amen.

NOTES

Translated from DW II, pp. 623–36.

1. This is one of several references the preacher makes to all things being "a pure nothing." However, although it was condemned by papal authority (see article 26 of "In agro dominico," *Essential Eckhart*, p. 80), its context here makes it sound less extreme than usual.
2. For more on this "power in the soul," see under *vünkelîn* in the Glossary.
3. This may be one of those occurrences where Eckhart is quoting himself. For more on "why" and "without a why," see under *âne war umbe* in the Glossary.
4. This is a reference to the seven gifts of the Holy Spirit, which are wisdom, understanding, counsel, fortitude, knowledge, piety, and fear of the Lord.
5. For an extended exegesis of the parallel text in Mt. 16:24, see Sermon XLV nn. 460–68 (pp. 230–33).

6. That is, penitential practices are a joy and a relief from suffering.
7. For similar statements about the soul's similarity to Christ, see Sermon 76 (pp. 328–29).
8. Perhaps Eckhart wishes to express something about God here similar to his thoughts in *Comm. Ex.* n. 91 (p. 75), where he quotes from the *Book of the Twenty-Four Philosophers* a similar definition of God.
9. This "taste and see" is the equivalent of "seeing and catching the scent" in the anecdote because the MHG verb *smecken* can mean both "to taste" and "to smell."
10. A similar passage may be found in *Comm. Jn.* nn. 227 sq. (LW III, pp. 140 sq.).
11. For positive attributes such as *good* or *wise* as garments of God and the need to see him naked, see Sermons 7, 9, and 40 (pp. 254, 258, and 300). For more on the inadequacy of positive attributes in general, see *Comm. Ex.* nn. 170–171 (p. 97).

Sermon 69: Modicum et iam non videbitis me (Jn 16:16).

I have spoken a phrase in Latin which St. John writes in the gospel that one reads on this Sunday. These words our Lord spoke to his disciples: "A little or small bit and immediately you will not see me."

However small a thing it is which sticks to the soul, we shall not see God. St. Augustine asked what eternal life is and he answered and said: "Are you asking me what eternal life is? Ask and hear eternal life itself."[1] No one knows better what heat is than one who has heat. No one knows better what wisdom is than one who has wisdom. No one knows better what eternal life is than eternal life itself. Now eternal life, our Lord Jesus Christ, speaks: "This is eternal life that one know you alone, the one true God" (Jn. 17:3). Whoever were to know God from a distance as though in a medium or in a cloud would not remain separated from God for an instant more for the whole world. What do you suppose it is like then for one who sees God immediately, how great that is?[2] Now our Lord says: "A little bit or a small thing and immediately you will not see me." All creatures that God has ever made or could yet make if he so wished, this is all a little bit or a small thing compared to God. The sky is so large and so vast that if I told you about it you would not believe it. If someone took a needle and touched the sky with the point, the part of the sky which the point of the needle encompassed would be greater in comparison with the sky and the whole world than the sky and the world compared to God. Thus it is certainly well said: "A little

311

bit or a small thing and you will not see me." As long as anything from a creature shines into you, you will not see God, however small a thing it might be.[3] For this reason the soul says in the Book of Love: "I have gone around and looked for him whom my soul loves, and I did not find him" (Sg. 3:2). It [the soul] found angels and many things, but it did not find the one her soul loved.[4] She then said: "Afterwards, when I leaped over a little bit or a small thing,[5] I found him whom my soul loves." Just as though she were to say: "When I sprang over all creatures, which are 'a little bit' or 'a small thing,' then I found him whom my soul loves." The soul that is to find God must jump and leap over all creatures.

Know that God loves the soul so powerfully that it staggers the mind. If one were to deprive God of this so that he did not love the soul, one would deprive him of his life and being, or one would kill God if we may say such a thing. For that same love by which God loves the soul is his life, and in this same love the Holy Spirit blossoms forth; and this same love *is* the Holy Spirit.[6] Since God loves the soul so powerfully, the soul must be something very great.

A master says in the book *On the Soul:* "If there were no medium, the eye would see an ant or a gnat in the sky."[7] And he spoke the truth, for he was thinking of fire, air, and the many other things which are between the sky and the eye. The other master says: "If there were no medium, my eye would not see."[8] Both views are correct.

The first says: "If there were no medium, the eye would see an ant in the sky." And his view is correct. If there were no medium between God and the soul, it would at once see God. For God does not have a medium nor can he endure a medium. If the soul were completely laid bare and stripped of any kind of medium, God would be laid bare and stripped for the soul and would give himself to it completely. As long as the soul is not laid bare and stripped of every kind of medium, no matter how small it may be, it will not see God. And if there were any medium at all between body and soul—even so much as the breadth of a hair—there would never be any real union between them. Since this is the case with corporeal things, it is much more so with spiritual things. Boethius says: "If you will to know the truth utterly, then put away joy and sorrow, fear and expectation or hope."[9] Joy and sorrow are a medium; fear and expectation: These are all a medium. As long as you regard it and it regards you, you will not see God.

The other master says: If there were no medium, my eye would see nothing. If I put my hand over my eye, I cannot see my hand. If I raise it in front of me, I see it immediately. This is caused by the coarse [material] nature of the hand; and it has to be purified of this and refined in air and light and carried as an image into my eye. Note the case of the mirror: If you raise it up in front of yourself, your image appears in the mirror. The eye and the soul are such a mirror in which everything appears that is held up to them. Thus I do not see the hand or the stone; rather, I see an image of the stone. But I do not see this image in another image or in a medium; rather, I see it [the image] without a medium and without an image, for the image itself is the medium and there is not some other medium. And this is why image is without image and motion is without motion, although it makes something move. And size does not have size; rather, it causes something to have size.[10] So also image is without image; for it is not seen in another image. The eternal Word is the medium and the image itself that is without medium and without image, so that the soul may grasp and know God in the eternal Word without a medium and without an image.

There is a power in the soul, namely, the intellect.[11] From the moment it becomes aware of and tastes God, it has within itself five properties. The first is that it separates from here and from now. The second, that it is like nothing. The third, that it is pure and unmixed. The fourth, that it is operating or seeking within itself. The fifth, that it is an image.

The first: It separates from here and from now. *Here* and *now* mean the same thing as place and time. *Now* is the smallest segment of time; it is neither a piece of time nor a part of time. It is certainly a taste of time and a point of time and a boundary of time. And yet, however small it may be, it has to disappear. Everything that touches time or the taste of time must completely disappear. Also, it separates from here. *Here* means the same thing as place. The place on which I stand is very small. Yet however small it may be, it has to disappear if one is to see God.

The second: that it is like nothing. One master says: God is a being that nothing is like or can become like.[12] And yet St. John says: "We shall be called children of God" (Jn. 3:1). But if we are to be children of God, we have to be like him. How then can the master say God is a being that nothing is like? You must understand it thus: The very fact that this power is like nothing makes it like God.[13] Just as God is like nothing, so this power is like nothing. Consider this. All creatures strive and toil out of their very natures to become like God. The heavens would no longer revolve if they were not striving and searching for God or a likeness of God. If God were not in all things, nature would bring about or long for nothing in any things. For whether you like it or not, whether you know it nor not, nature in its most inner self seeks and strives secretly for God. Never has anyone been so thirsty that if someone were to offer him something to drink and something of God were not in it, he would want any part of it. Nature seeks neither

313

food nor drink nor clothing nor shelter nor anything else in things if there is nothing of God in them. It searches secretly and strives and struggles constantly toward that in which it finds God.

The third: that it is pure and unmixed. It is God's nature that it can allow no mixture or composition. And so this power, too, has no mixture or composition. There is nothing foreign in it, nor can anything foreign fall into it. If I were to say to a good-looking person that he was pale or black, I would be doing him wrong. The soul should be completely without mixture. If someone were to attach something onto my hood or to put something on it and he then pulled the hood, he would pull everything along with it.[14] When I go from here, everything that is on me goes along. Whoever pulls whatever the spirit builds on or sticks to pulls the spirit as well. A person who was resting on nowhere and was attached to nothing, if someone were to overturn heaven and earth, would remain unmoved. For he would be attached to nothing and nothing would be attached to him.

The fourth: that it is in all ways seeking within itself. God is a being that in all ways dwells in the innermost recesses. Hence the intellect is in all ways seeking within. The will, however, goes out to that which it loves. Thus, if my friend comes to me, my will with its love pours itself out onto him and is thereby satisfied. But St. Paul says: "We shall know God as we are known by him" (1 Co. 13:12). But St. John says, "We shall know God as he is" (1 Jn. 3:2). If I am to receive color, I have to have something about me that belongs to color. I will never perceive color unless I have the being of color in me. I shall never behold God except precisely in that in which God sees himself. Concerning this St. Paul says: "God dwells in a light to which there is no access" (Cf. 1 Tm. 6:15–16). No one should lose heart because of this. One may certainly dwell on the path or by an approach, and this is good. But it is far from the truth, for it is not God.

The fifth: that it is an image. Ah, now pay close attention and remember this well. In this you have grasped the whole sermon at once. Image and image are so completely one and joined together that one cannot comprehend any distinction between them. One can think of fire without heat and heat without fire. One can think of the sun without light and light without the sun. But one cannot understand any distinction between image and image. I say further: God in his omnipotence cannot understand any distinction between them, for they are born together and die together. If my father dies, I do not die because of that. When he dies, one can no longer say: He *is* his son; one would say: He *was* his son. If one paints the wall white, inasmuch as it is white, it is like all whiteness. But if someone were to paint it black, it is dead of all whiteness. Look, the same is true here. If the image that is formed according to God were to perish, God's image would perish, too.[15]

I want to say a word, two or three of them. Understand me correctly. The intellect looks inside and surveys all recesses of the Godhead and perceives the Son in the heart and in the ground of the Father and places him in its own ground. The intellect penetrates within. It is not satisfied with goodness or with wisdom or with truth or with God himself. In good truth, it is as little satisfied with God as with a stone or a tree. It never rests, it bursts into the ground from which goodness and truth come forth and perceives it [God's being] *in principio*, in the beginning, where goodness and truth are going out, before it acquires any name, before it bursts forth; [the intellect perceives God's being] in a much higher ground than goodness and wisdom are.[16] Further, its sister the will is satisfied with God insofar as he is good. But the intellect peels all this away and enters in and pierces through to the roots from which the Son pours forth and the Holy Spirit is blossoming forth.

To the end that we may grasp this and become eternally happy may the Father and the Son and the Holy Spirit help us. Amen.

NOTES

Translated from DW III, pp. 159–180.

This sermon and the two following (70 and 71) have in common that they all treat the question of "seeing God" and what can hinder this. In their diversity, however, they are also good examples of how Eckhart can approach a theme in several ways. The present sermon is a *tour de force* centered on the word *modicum*. In the gospel passage it means "a little while" (and you will no longer see me). The preacher starts by interpreting it as the "little bit" that prevents us from seeing God. It then becomes the *medium* that both causes and prevents sight. Finally as *medium* it becomes the *image* that makes knowledge possible—and we are an *image* of the Son, the divine image.

1. Augustine, Sermon 150, 8.10.
2. For an explanation of "immediately" or "without a medium," see the Glossary.
3. That is, because this little thing can block our ability to see God.
4. Cf. *Comm. Ecc.* n. 56 (p. 180).
5. *Paululum*, which is Latin for a "little while" in the verse from the Song of Songs, "When I had passed by them a little while," is identified by the preacher with

modicum and is also translated as the "little bit" that creatures are. See also Sermon 71, note 9 (p. 326).

6. Cf. Sermon VI.1, n. 55 (p. 213).
7. See Aristotle, *Soul* 2.7 (419a). This is the view of Democritus. Cf. *Comm. Wis.* n. 285 (pp. 173–74).
8. This is Aristotle's own view as stated in the reference given in the preceding note.
9. Boethius, *Consolation of Philosophy* 1, poem 7. Cf. *Comm. Ex.* n. 12 (p. 44).
10. Eckhart is attempting to demonstrate why an infinite series of images can be avoided in explaining how we know through images. So, therefore, the concept of motion or the concept by which we abstract the notion of size are both spiritual realities and hence lack motion or size.
11. This is one of the preacher's clearest explanations of the power in the soul, which is the intellect. For a good treatment in his Latin works, see *Par. Gen.* nn. 137–58 (*Essential Eckhart*, pp. 108–19) and Sermon XXIX (pp. 223–26). See also under *vünkelîn* in the Glossary.
12. Eckhart may have Maimonides in mind here, whose *Guide* 1.52 he quotes to this effect in *Comm. Ex.* n. 39 (p. 55).
13. Cf. Sermon XXIX n. 297 (p. 224).
14. Cf. *Couns.* 11 (*Essential Eckhart*, p. 260).
15. The distinction between the Son as "God's image" and man as the image made "to the image" is also found in Sermon XXV.1, n. 257 (p. 218). Cf. also *Essential Eckhart*, pp. 43–44.
16. Cf., e.g., Sermons 48 and 52 (*Essential Eckhart*, pp. 198, 203).

Sermon 70: Modicum et iam non videbitis me: et iterum modicum, et videbitis me (Jn. 16:16).

Our Lord spoke to his disciples: "A small amount, a little bit, a tiny thing and you will not see me; again a little bit and you will see me."[1] The disciples said: "We don't understand what he is saying" (cf. Jn. 16:17–18). St. John, who was present, writes this. When our Lord read their hearts, he said: "A little bit, and you will see me and your hearts will be glad; joy shall then never again be taken from you" (Cf. Jn. 16:22).

Now our Lord says: "A little bit, and you will not see me." The best masters say that the essence of happiness consists in knowledge. An important priest came to Paris recently. He disagreed with this, and shouted and

316

thundered exceedingly. Then another master spoke, probably better than all those in Paris holding the better opinion: "Master, you are certainly shouting up a storm. If it were not for the fact that this is God's word in the holy gospel, you would be [justified in] shouting and ranting as you do."[2] Knowledge touches bare what it knows.[3] Our Lord says: "That is eternal life, that one know you alone as the one true God" (Jn. 17:3). The perfection of beatitude lies in both: knowledge and love.

Now he says: "A little bit, and you will see me." In these words are contained four meanings, all of which sound very much alike and yet are really quite different. "A little bit, and you will see nothing of me."[4] All things must be small in you, as nothing. I once said that St. Augustine says: "When St. Paul was not seeing [other things] he saw God."[5] Now I shall turn the words around—it is better that way—and say: "When he saw nothing, he saw God."[6] This is the first sense of these words.

The second sense is: Unless the whole world and all of time becomes small in you, you will not see God. St. John says in Revelation: "The angel swore by eternal life that time would no longer be" (Cf. Rv. 10:5–7). St. John says openly[7] that "the world was made through him, and it knew nothing of him" (Jn. 1:10). Even a pagan master says that the world and time are a "little bit."[8] Unless you get beyond the world and time, you will not see God. "A little bit, and you will not see me."

The third sense is: As long as anything sticks to the soul, however small it is, sin or something related to sin, so you will not see God. The masters say that the heavens receive no impressions from outside. There are many heavens; each has a spirit and an angel ordered to it. If one were to work in a different heaven to which it was not ordered, it could not do it. A priest said, "I wish your soul were in my body." I replied, "Really? Then it would be a fool in it because it could do nothing with it, nor could your soul do anything in my body." A soul cannot function in a body except in the one to which it is ordered. The eye allows nothing alien in itself. A master says, "If there were no medium, one would see nothing."[9] If I am to see color on the wall, it must first be refined in the light and the air and its likeness carried into my eye. St. Bernard says that the eye is like the heaven.[10] It receives heaven into itself. The ear does not do this. It hears nothing from heaven, nor does the tongue taste anything of it. Secondly, the eye is formed round as heaven is. Thirdly, it stands high as does heaven. Hence the eye receives the impression of light because it has a property of heaven. The heavens receive no impressions from outside. The body does receive impressions from without, and the soul also receives such impressions, as long as it functions in the body. If the soul is to know anything outside itself, like an angel,

317

however immaterial a thing it might be, the soul has to do this by means of a little image without image.[11] Thus also an angel, if it is to know another angel or anything else that is lower than God, has to accomplish this with a little image without image, but not as images are here [on earth]. The angel knows itself, however, without this "little bit," without image, and without likeness. Thus also does the soul know itself, without a "little bit," without image, without likeness, and apart from anything that mediates. If I am to know God, this must also take place without images or any other mediating instrument. The best masters say that one knows God without a means. Thus does an angel know God, namely, as it knows itself—without images and without "a little bit." If I am to know God without means, without images, and without likeness, God actually has to become me and I have to become God. [We must become] so utterly one that I work together with him, not in the sense that I work and he finishes up; I work with what is mine.[12] I work with him as truly as my soul works with my body. This is a great comfort for us; and if we had nothing else [as a comfort], it should be a great incentive for us to love God.

The fourth sense is completely contrary to the preceding three. One must be great and raised aloft, if one is to see God. The light of the sun is little compared to the light of the intellect, and the light of the intellect is little compared to the light of grace. Grace is a light soaring above and transcending everything that God ever created or could create. Yet the light of grace, great though it be, is still little compared to the divine light. Our Lord chided his disciples saying, "In you there is but a little light" (Jn. 12:35).[13] They were not without light, but it was a "little bit." One has to ascend and become great in grace. As long as one is increasing in grace, it is just grace and a "little bit" in which one knows God from afar. But if grace is brought to its highest perfection, it is no longer grace; it is a divine light in which one sees God. St. Paul says, "God resides and dwells in a light to which there is no access" (1 Tm. 6:15–16). There is no access; there is only an approach. Moses says, "Man has never seen God" (cf. Ex. 33:20). As long as we are just human beings and as long as what is merely human resides near us and we are in the access, we do not see God. We have to be raised up, established in pure tranquility, and thus see God. St. John says, "We shall know God just as God knows himself" (cf. 1 Jn. 3:2). It is a property of God that he knows himself without a "little bit" and without this or that. Thus does an angel know God—as it knows itself. St. Paul says, "We shall know God as we are known" (cf. 1 Co. 13:12). But I say: We shall know him just as he knows himself—in that reflection that alone is the image of God and the Godhead, that is, to the extent that the Godhead is the Father.[14] To the degree that we are like the image in which all images have flowed forth and have left, and to the degree that we are reconstituted in this image and are carried directly into this image of the Father—to the degree that he recognizes this in us, to that degree we know him as he knows himself.[15]

Now he says, "A little bit and you will not see me; but again a little bit, and you will see me." Our Lord says, "This is eternal life that one know you alone as the one true God" (Jn. 17:3).

That we come to this knowledge, may God help us. Amen.

NOTES

Translated from DW III, pp. 187–98

1. This sermon, like the previous one, centers on the interpretation of *modicum* as a "little bit."
2. This incident may be related to Eckhart's dispute with the Franciscan Gonsalvo of Spain concerning the roles of the intellect and will in man's achieving beatitude. The Dominicans insisted on the primacy of the intellect and truth; the Franciscans insisted on the primacy of the will and love. Quint thinks that the Dominican master referred to here was the noted John Quidort (DW III, p. 189).
3. That is, it touches it directly, without anything else mediating.
4. Here Eckhart changes his MHG translation of the gospel text slightly from "not . . . me" to "nothing of me."
5. Augustine, Sermon 279.1. Cf. *Comm. Jn.* n. 73 (*Essential Eckhart*, p. 149).
6. See Sermon 71 (pp. 320–25) for more on God as nothing and for more on this scripture text.
7. That is, in his gospel as opposed to what he says in Revelation, a secret book of mysteries.
8. This reference has not been identified.
9. Aristotle, *Soul* 2.7. (419a).
10. Bernard, *Sermons on the Song of Songs*, 31.2. The MHG word *himel* used throughout means both heaven and sky.
11. This last phrase has been translated literally. As the continuation of this passage indicates, Eckhart is positing three kinds of knowledge: At one extreme is human knowledge of material things, which occurs through a mediating nonmaterial image that the soul abstracts from the physical object known. At the other extreme is divine self-knowledge, which is utterly without any mediating images. Angelic knowledge of beings that are spiritual but are not God is described as happening through a "small" image or "little bit" that is not really an image. Notice that with "little bit" the preacher connects this idea to the *modicum* of the

gospel verse he is explicating. For more on knowledge and images, see Sermon 69 (pp. 312–13).
12. On this manner of working with God, see Sermon 52 (*Essential Eckhart*, p. 202).
13. It is worth noting that the Vulgate uses *modicum* for "little" in this passage from John.
14. On the relation of Father and Godhead, see *Essential Eckhart*, pp. 35–37.
15. This image in which all images flow forth and which is the image of the Father is, of course, the Son.

Sermon 71: Surrexit autem Saulus de terra apertisque oculis nihil videbat (Ac. 9:8).

The words that I have spoken in Latin were written by St. Luke in the Acts concerning St. Paul, and they mean: "Paul rose from the ground and with eyes open he saw nothing." It seems to me that this little word [*i.e.*, nothing] has four meanings. One meaning is: When he got up from the ground, with eyes open he saw nothing, and the nothing was God; for when he saw God, he [Luke] calls this a nothing. The second: When he got up, he saw nothing but God. The third: In all things he saw nothing but God. The fourth: When he saw God, he viewed all things as nothing.

Previously he had told how a light came suddenly from heaven and struck him down to the ground (Ac. 9:3). Note that he says that a light came from heaven. Our best masters say that heaven contains light within itself, and yet it does not shine. The sun also contains light within itself but does shine. The stars also have light; however, it is brought to them.[1] Our masters say that fire in its simple, natural purity, in its highest state, does not shine. Its nature is so pure that no eye can perceive it in any way. It is so refined and at variance with the eye that, if it were down here in front of the eye, it [the eye] would not be able to make it out when looking at it. But on something else one can perceive it easily, as when it enkindles a piece of wood or coal.[2]

By the light of heaven we mean the light that is God which no human faculty can attain. Thus St. Paul says, "God dwells in a light which no one can reach" (1 Tm. 6:16). He says: God is a light to which there is no access. To God there is no access. No one still ascending and growing in grace and light has ever reached God. God is not a growing light. Certainly one has to come there by growing, but when growing one does not see God. If God is to be seen, it has to happen in a light that is God himself.[3] One master says: "In God there is neither less nor more, neither this nor that."[4] As long as we are still making our approach, we are not entering.

Now he says: "A light from heaven shone all around him" (Ac. 9:3). By this he means: Whatever was part of his soul was enveloped. A master says that in this light all the powers of the soul leap beyond themselves and lift themselves aloft, both the external senses by which we see and hear as well as the internal senses which we call thoughts. How far these latter reach and how limitless they are is a marvel. I can think of something existing across the sea just as easily as something right next to me. Above thoughts is the intellect insofar as it is still seeking. It goes all around and searches, looking here and there, taking in [images] and losing them again. Above this intellect which is seeking there is another intellect that does not seek but rather remains in its pure simple being which is enveloped by this light. And I say that in this light all the powers of the soul lift themselves aloft. The senses leap into thoughts. How high and limitless they are no one knows but God and the soul. Our masters say—and it is a difficult question—that angels do not experience thoughts unless the thoughts break out and leap into the intellect which is still searching, and unless the intellect which is searching leaps into the intellect which is not searching but is rather a pure light in itself.[5] This light embraces within itself all the powers of the soul. For this reason he says, "The light of heaven shone all around him."

A master says that all things that have a flowing out cannot receive lower things. God flows into all creatures, yet he remains untouched by them all.[6] He needs nothing from them. God gives to nature the capacity to work, and its first work is the heart. Because of this some masters maintained that the soul is completely in the heart and flows out into the other members giving them life. This is not the case. The soul is complete in each part of the body. It is certainly true that its first work is in the heart.[7] The heart is in the middle. It wants to be guarded all around, just as the sky suffers no alien influence nor does it take in anything. It contains all things within it, touching all things while remaining untouched. And fire, no matter how lofty it may be in its highest state, does not touch the sky.

In this enveloping illumination he was thrown to the ground, and his eyes were opened for him so that with eyes open he saw all things as nothing. And when he saw all things as nothing, he saw God. Now notice this. In the Book of Love the soul speaks a short verse: "All through the night I searched in my bed for him whom my soul loves, and I did not find him" (Sg. 3:1). The soul's searching in its bed can be interpreted to mean that

321

whoever clings to or depends on anything which is beneath God, that person's bed is too confining. Everything that God can create is too confining. The soul says, "I have searched for him all through the night." There is no night that does not have a light, but it is covered. The sun shines in the night but it is covered. During the day it shines and covers over all the other lights. This is what the divine light does; it covers over all [other] lights. Whatever we seek from creatures is completely night. By this I mean: Whatever we seek from creatures is all shadow and night. Even the light of the highest angel, no matter how exalted the light might be, touches nothing in the soul. Whatever is not this first light is all dark and is night. Hence the soul finds nothing of God there. "Then I arose and looked everywhere and ran through the highways and byways. Then the watchmen found me"—these were the angels—"and I asked them whether they had at all seen him whom my soul loves" (Sg. 3:2–3). They remained silent; perhaps they did not know what to call him.[8] "When I had gone a little bit farther, I found him" whom I was seeking (Sg. 3:4). I have already frequently spoken about the "little bit" and the "small amount" which led the soul astray so that it found no trace of him. A person who does not consider all transitory things as trifles and as nothing will not find God. For this reason the soul said: "When I passed by a little bit, I found" (Sg. 3:4) whom I was seeking.[9] When God forms himself and pours himself into the soul, if you perceive him as a light or as being or goodness, if you know the least little bit of him, that is not God. You must realize that one has to pass over the "little bit" and must remove all additions and know God [as he is] one.[10] Hence the soul says: "When I passed by a little bit, I found whom my soul loves" (Sg. 3:4).

We frequently say "whom my soul loves." Why does the soul say "whom my soul loves"? Well, he is very far above the soul and it could not begin to name him whom it loves. There are four reasons why the soul did not name him. The first reason is that God is nameless. If it were to give him names, that would have to be [positively] thought. God is above all names. No one can so closely approach him that he can utter "God."[11] The second reason why it did not give him names is that when the soul has completely flowed into God through love, it knows nothing else but love. It thinks that everyone knows as it does. It is surprised that anyone knows anything else but God alone. The third reason: It did not have enough time to name him. It cannot turn away from loving long enough. It cannot properly form any other word but "love." The fourth reason: Perhaps the soul thought that he has no other name but "love." In saying "love" it names him with all names.[12] For these reasons the soul says "I arose and went through

322

the highways and byways. When I passed by a little bit, I found" whom I sought.

"Paul rose from the ground and with eyes open he saw nothing." I cannot see what is one. He saw the nothing which was God.[13] God is a nothing and he is a something. Whatever is something is also nothing.[14] Whatever God is he is completely. The illumined Dionysius speaks of this when he writes of God: "He is above being, he is above life, he is above light."[15] He does not attribute this or that to him and he thinks that he is an I-know-not-what that is utterly above this. Whoever sees anything or if anything comes to your attention, it is not God, because he is neither this nor that. If anyone says that God is here or there, do not believe him. The light that is God shines in the darkness. God is a true light (Jn. 1:5, 9). Whoever is to see this must be blind and must completely remove all "something" from God. A master says: "Whoever speaks of God through a simile speaks of him in an impure fashion; but whoever speaks of God by [using the term] *nothing* speaks of him properly."[15a] When the soul comes into the One and there enters into a pure rejection of itself, it finds God as in a nothing. It seemed to a man as though in a dream—it was a waking dream—that he became pregnant with nothing as a woman does with a child, and in this nothing God was born; he was the fruit of the nothing. God was born in the nothing. Hence he says: "He rose from the ground and with eyes open saw nothing." He saw God, where all creatures are nothing. He saw all creatures as nothing because he [God] has the being of all creatures in himself. He is a being that has all beings in itself.[16]

He has a second reason for saying, "he saw nothing." Our masters say that whoever has any knowledge of external things, something [from the thing] must be taken in, at least an impression. When I want to take in an image of some object, for example, of a stone, I draw into myself what is most [material and therefore] coarse. This I then strip away [from it] externally. However, when it is in the ground of my soul, it is at its highest and noblest. There it is nothing but an image. Whatever my soul knows of an external object, something alien enters in. Whatever I know of creatures in God, nothing enters in but God alone; for in God there is nothing but God. When I know all creatures in God, I know nothing. He saw God, where all creatures are nothing.

The third reason why he saw nothing: The nothing was God. A master says that all creatures exist in God as nothing. He has in himself the being of all creatures. He is a being that has all beings in itself. A master says that there is nothing beneath God, however near it might be to him, into which something [alien] does not enter.[17] Another master says that an angel knows itself and God without a medium. Something alien enters into whatever else it knows. It is at least an impression, however small it may be. If we are to know God, it must happen without a medium. Nothing alien can enter into it. If we know God in this light, it must be independent and self-contained without the intrusion of created things. Then we know eternal life without a medium.

When he saw nothing, he saw God. The light that is God flows out and darkens all [other] light. In the light in which Paul was seeing, he saw God and nothing else. Job says of this: "He commands the sun not to shine and holds the stars together beneath him as under a seal" (Jb. 9:7). Because he was surrounded by this light, he saw nothing else. Everything in his soul was concerned and occupied with the light that is God, so that he was able to perceive nothing else. This is a good lesson for us. When we are concerned with God, we are little concerned with things outside.

The fourth reason why he saw nothing: The light that is God is not mixed with anything, no mixture enters in. This was a proof that he saw the true light that is nothing. This light means simply that with eyes open he saw nothing. In seeing nothing he saw the divine nothing. St. Augustine says: "When he saw nothing, he saw God."[18] Whoever sees nothing else and is blind sees God. For this reason St. Augustine says: "Because God is a true light, a support for the soul, and is nearer to it than it is to itself, it happens of necessity that God glimmers and flares up in it when the soul is turned away from all created things."[19]

The soul can feel neither love nor perturbation without knowing where from. When the soul does not go out after things outside, it has come home and dwells in its simple, pure light. Here the soul feels neither love nor perturbation nor fear. Knowledge is a solid bedrock and foundation for all being. Love has no place to inhere except in knowledge.[20] When the soul is blind and sees nothing else, it sees God and this has to be the case. A master says: "The eye in its purest state, when it is free of all color, sees all color."[21] It is not just the case that the eye taken in itself must be free of color. It must also be free of color as a part of the body if one is to recognize color. Whatever is free of color enables one to see all color, even if it were down below as part of the foot. God is that kind of being which contains within itself all beings. If God is to become known to the soul, it must be blind. Hence he says: He saw the "nothing" whose light is all lights, whose being is all beings. This is why the bride says in the Book of Love: "When I passed by a little bit, I found whom my soul loves" (Sg. 3:4). The "little bit" that she passed by was all creatures. Whoever does not reject them will not find God. She also states that however fine and pure that thing is by which I gain knowledge of God, it must be removed. Even if I take the light that is God as it touches my soul, this is wrong. I have to take it from where it bursts forth. I could not really see the light as it shines on the wall, unless I turned my eye to where it bursts forth. And yet, if I take it as it bursts forth, I still have to be freed from this bursting forth. I must take it as it is hovering in itself. Nevertheless I say that this is wrong, too. I must take it neither as it is touching nor as it is bursting forth nor as it is hovering in itself because these are all definite modes [of existence]. One must receive God as he is a mode beyond measure, a being beyond being, for he has no limited mode.[22] Thus St. Bernard says, "Whoever would know you, God, must take measure of you beyond measure."[23]

Let us ask our Lord that we might come to that knowledge that is completely beyond limitation and manner. May God help us achieve this. Amen.

NOTES

Translated from DW III, pp. 211–31.

The sermon receives its structure from Eckhart's interpretations of two words: (1) the *light* from heaven that enveloped Saul/Paul (Ac. 9:3), and (2) the *nothing* that he saw after he rose from the ground (Ac. 9:9). In the first half the preacher elaborates on this light as demonstrating the purity and the freedom from creatures our knowledge must achieve if we are to see God. The second half treats the nothing Paul saw whereby *nothing* is given four different meanings: (1) The nothing is God. (2) He saw nothing but God. (3) He saw in all things nothing but God. (4) In seeing God he saw all things as nothing. Thus *nothing*, depending on the context, has positive or negative value, and refers now to God and now to creatures.

A few times for clarity I have inserted a noun where the MHG text has a pronoun, e.g., I have occasionally inserted *soul* for "it."

1. For a possible source of this doctrine of light see Albert the Great, *Concerning Heaven and Earth* 2.3.15, 1.1.11.
2. Cf. *Comm. Jn.* n. 74 (*Essential Eckhart*, p. 149).

3. Cf. Sermon 70 (p. 318).
4. Possibly, as often, Eckhart is here referring to himself as the authority. Cf. for example, Sermon 9 (p. 256) and *Comm. Ex.* n. 90 (p. 74).
5. Angels, as pure spirits, experience thought differently from the way human beings do. Angels do not rely on data from the external senses nor does their intellect search, since it is in full possession of its knowledge. Cf. Thomas Aquinas, *STh* Ia. 58. 4. ad 1.
6. Cf., e.g., *Comm. Wis.* n. 39 (p. 155).
7. This is the teaching of Maimonides, *Guide* 1.72.
8. This is one of Eckhart's references to God's being nameless or above all names.
9. Here, as in Sermon 69 (p. 312), Eckhart is playing with the Latin word *paululum*, which is generally translated "a little while," but which he renders "a little bit" so that the passage (Sg. 3:4) can be interpreted to mean that one must pass by or transcend this "little bit," which creatures are, before one can find God. Thus *paululum* is identified with the *modicum* of Sermons 69 and 70.
10. For Eckhart to perceive God as one (*unum*) is to perceive him in the highest manner of which we are capable. One adds no falsifying positive attributes to him but grasps him only negatively. The following lines clarify this. See also *Comm. Wis.* nn. 144–55, *Comm. Ex.* nn. 58–61 (pp. 166–70, 63–64).
11. That is, no one can give the word *God* a content that is both positive and adequate for the reality the word represents.
12. That is, the name *love* includes all other divine names.
13. Here Eckhart begins the second part of the sermon, in which he interprets the second of the four meanings of nothing he announced at the beginning of the sermon.
14. That is, creatures are made up of being (something) and nothing.
15. Pseudo-Dionysius, *Mystical Theology* 5.
15a. This seems to depend on Pseudo-Dionysius, *Celestial Hierarchies* 2.3.
16. This is the equivalent of the Latin formula *esse omnium*, on which see the Glossary.
17. Eckhart may be thinking of Augustine, e.g., *Christ. Doct.* 1.6.7, *Trin.* 8.2.3.
18. Augustine, Sermon 279.1.1.
19. Augustine, *Trin.* 8.7.11.
20. This is a reference to the question hotly debated by the Franciscans and Dominicans as to which is the superior faculty: the intellect or the will. Eckhart here takes the Dominican position that the intellect is superior. He sometimes takes a different view. See, for example, Sermon 52 (*Essential Eckhart*, p. 201).
21. See Aristotle, *Soul* 2.7 (418b).
22. See under *wise* in the Glossary.
23. Cf. Bernard, *On Loving God* 1.1.

Sermon 76: Videte qualem caritatem dedit nobis pater, ut filii dei nominemur et simus (1 Jn. 3:1).

One should know that to know God and to be known by God, to see God and to be seen by God, are in reality one and the same. To know and to see God [is to know and see] that he is the one who causes us to see and know.[1] Just as the air which is illuminated is nothing other than air which lights up (and it lights up by being illuminated), so too do we know that we are known and that he [God] makes us knowers.[2] Hence Christ said, "Again you will see me" (Jn. 16:16), which means: Through my causing you to see, you know me. Thereafter follows: "And your heart shall be made glad" (Jn. 16:22), which means: Because you see and know me, "no one will take your joy from you" (Jn. 16:22).

St. John says, "See what love God has given us, that we are called and are children of God" (1 Jn. 3:1). He does not just say "are called"; rather, we "are."[3] Thus I say: just as a person cannot be wise without knowing, so he cannot be Son without the filial being of the Son of God, only if he has the same being of the Son of God that he [the Son of God] has, just as being wise cannot happen without knowing. Therefore, if you are to be the Son of God, you cannot be it unless you have the same being of God that the Son of God has.[4] But this "is now hidden from us"; and then it says: "Dearly beloved, we are sons of God" (1 Jn. 3:2). And what do we know? To tell us this, he adds: "And we shall become like him," that is, the same as he is: the same being, consciousness, understanding, everything the same as he is "when we see him as he is God" (Cf. 1 Jn. 3:2). Therefore, I say that God could not bring it about that I were the Son of God without my having the being of the Son of God. This is just as impossible as for him to make me wise without my having a wise being. How are we God's children? We do not yet know; "it has not yet appeared to us" (1 Jn. 3:2). We only know of this as much as he tells us: "We shall be like him." There are some things in our souls which hide this from us and cover over this knowledge.

The soul has something in it, a spark of intelligence, which never goes out, and in this spark, as the highest part of the mind,[5] one places the image of the soul. There also exists in our souls a capacity for knowing external things. This is a knowing through the senses and through reason, that is, a knowing through sensible images and through concepts. Such knowing conceals this other knowing from us.[6] How are we sons of God? By having one being with him. But in trying to understand something about this, that we are the Son of God, one has to distinguish between outward knowing and inward knowing. Inward knowing is that which has its foundation, as pertaining to the intellect, in the being of the soul. However, it is not the being of the soul. It is, rather, rooted in this and is something of the life of the soul. In saying that knowing is something of the life of the soul, we mean the intellectual life, and in this life a person is born the Son of God and born for eternal life. This knowing is beyond time and place, beyond here and now. In this life all things are one; all things together, all and all united in all and all.[7]

I shall give you a comparison. In the body all parts of the body are united and one in such a way that the eye belongs to the foot and the foot to the eye. If the foot could speak, it would say that the eye which is located in the head belongs to it more than if it were located in the foot; and the eye would say the same thing reversed.[8] This is what I am saying: All the grace that is in Mary belongs more, and more properly, to an angel and is in it— that is, the grace that is in Mary—than if it were in the angel or in the saints. For whatever Mary has, the saint has completely and it belongs to him more [than what is in him]; and the grace that is in Mary delights him more than if it were in him.

This interpretation is still too simplistic and unrefined because it depends on similarities with material reality.[9] And so I shall give you another interpretation that is more refined and more spiritual. In the kingdom of heaven all is in all, all is one, and all is ours. Whatever our Lady has in the way of grace all belongs to me (if I am there!), but not as though it were streaming forth and flowing out of Mary; rather, [this grace exists] as in me and my own and not as though coming from outside. And so I say, whatever one person has the other has it, too, but not as *from* the other or *in* the other but as in oneself in such a way that the grace in one person is just as completely in the other person as his own grace is in him. This is the way that spirit is in spirit. And thus I say that I cannot be the Son of God unless I have the same being the Son of God has; and by having the same being we become like him, and we see him as he is God. But "it is not yet revealed" what we shall become. Hence I say that in this sense there is no [mere] like or difference. Rather, without any difference we become the same being, substance, and nature that he himself is. But "this is not yet evident"; for it will be evident "when we see him as he is God" (Cf. 1 Jn. 3:2).

God causes us to know him and makes us know him [as a being that is] knowing, and his being is his knowing. His causing me to know and my knowing are the same thing. Hence his knowing is mine, just as what the teacher teaches and what the pupil is taught are one.[10] And because his knowing is mine and because his substance, his nature, and his being are his knowing, it follows that his being, his substance, and his nature are mine. And because his substance, his nature, and his being are mine, I am the Son of God. "See, brothers, what love God has given us, that we are called and are the Son of God" (Cf. 1 Jn. 3:1).[11]

Consider the origin of our being the Son of God: We have the same being that the Son has. How is one the Son of God, or how does one know that one is, since God is like no one? This is true. Isaiah says: "To whom do you compare him, or what kind of image do you give him?" (Is. 40:18) Since it is God's nature that he is like no one, we must of necessity come to the point that we are nothing in order to be placed into the same being that he is himself. Therefore, when I come to the point that I form myself into nothing and form nothing into myself, and if I remove and throw out whatever is in me, then I can be placed into the bare being of God, and this is the bare being of the spirit. Everything must be driven out that is [merely] likeness, so that I can be placed above into God and become one with him, one substance, one being, one nature, and the Son of God. And after this has happened, nothing in God is hidden that does not become revealed or that does not become mine. Then I become wise, powerful, and all that he is—and one and the same with him. Then Zion shall become a "true-seer," a "true Israel," that is, a God-seeing man, for nothing in the Godhead is hidden from him.[12] Then a person is led into God. However, so that in God there remains nothing hidden from me that is not revealed to me, there may not be revealed in me anything [merely] like or any image, for no image reveals to us the Godhead or its being. If any image or any "similar" were to remain in you, you would never become one with God. Therefore, so that you may be one with God there may not be in you anything formed from within or without;[13] this means that there may not be anything covered over in you that cannot be revealed and thrown out.

Consider what deficiency is. It comes from nothing.[14] Therefore, whatever there is of nothing in a person must be eradicated. As long as there is deficiency in you, you are not the Son of God. That a person complains and is sad is totally the result of deficiency. Hence everything must be eradicated and driven out, that a person may become the Son of God and that there be no more laments or sorrow. Man is neither stone nor wood; these are totally insufficient and nothing.[15] We shall not become like him if this nothing is not driven out so that we become all in all, as God is all in all.

Man experiences two kinds of birth: one *into* the world and one *out of* the world, that is, this [second] is a spiritual birth into God. Do you want

329

to know whether your child is being born and whether it is stripped bare, that is, whether you have been made God's Son?[16] As long as you have sadness in your heart because of any thing, even if it is because of sin, your child has not been born. If you have sadness of heart, you are not a mother.[17] Rather, you are in the process of giving birth; the birth is near. Therefore, do not be troubled if you are sad on your own account or because of a friend. It is not yet born, but the birth is near. It is then completely born when a person feels no sadness in his heart because of any thing. It is then that a person has the being, nature, substance, wisdom, joy, and everything that God has. It is then that the very being of God's Son becomes ours and comes about in us, and we enter into this same being of God.

Christ says: "Whoever wishes to follow me, let him deny himself, take up his cross, and follow me" (Mt. 16:24).[18] This means: Throw out all sadness from your heart so that nothing but constant joy is in your heart. Then the child has been born. And if the child has been born in me and if I were to see my father and all my friends killed before my eyes, my heart would not be moved by it. But if my heart were moved by it, then the child would not have been born in me. Yet perhaps the birth would be near. I say that God and the angels have such great joy from every single work of a good person that no other joy could be compared to it. Thus I say: If the child is born in you, you will have such great joy in every single good work that is done in this world that your joy becomes constant and never changes. This is why he says, "No one will take your joy from you" (Jn. 16:22). Once I have really been transported into the divine being, God becomes mine and whatever he has. Hence he says, "I am God, your Lord" (Ex. 20:2).[19] Then I shall have true joy which neither sadness nor pain can take from me, because then I have been established in the divine being where suffering has no place.[20] For we see that in God there is neither anger nor gloom, but rather love and joy. Even though it may appear that he sometimes becomes angry with the sinner, this is not anger but love because it comes from great divine love. Those he loves he punishes, for "he is love" (cf. 1 Jn. 4:16), which is the Holy Spirit. Because God's anger arises out of love, he gets angry without passion.[21] And so if you come to the point that you experience neither suffering nor despondency because of any thing, and suffering is not suffering for you, and all things are pure joy for you, then in truth the child has been born. And so, strive intently, so that the child is not just *being* born in you, but rather that it *has been* born, as the Son has always been born in God and is constantly being born.[22]

That we may experience this, may God help us. Amen.

Notes

Translated from DW III, pp. 310–29.

1. The words in brackets are assumed by Quint to have been part of the original text despite no backing for this in the manuscripts. Eckhart expresses similar thoughts elsewhere in his works. Cf. Sermon 12 (p. 270) and *Comm. Jn.* 107 (*Essential Eckhart*, pp. 162–63). Cf. also Aristotle, *Soul* 3.4 (430a).
2. On the nature of illumination see *Comm. Jn.* n. 74 (*Essential Eckhart*, p. 149).
3. Cf. Sermon VI.2, n. 58 (p. 214).
4. For more on being the Son, see the Glossary under *geburt*.
5. "Mind" here renders the MHG *gemüete*, which is not just a capacity to feel, as the modern equivalent is, but includes the ability to think as well. Hence the preacher can use it, as he seems to here, for one's intellectual capacities in general.
6. That is, knowing through the senses and concepts hides or covers over the knowing happening in the spark of the soul where we learn how we are like God.
7. This sentence has been translated literally. It seemed better to let the reader ponder it than to attempt an interpretive translation.
8. Cf. Sermon 30 (p. 294) and *Comm. Ex.* n. 88 (pp. 73–74).
9. Even though the foregoing comparison centered on the spiritual entity grace, it still concerned itself with *where* grace was and thus dealt with the accident of place, an accident of material reality.
10. Cf. Thomas Aquinas, *On the Unity of the Intellect* n. 113, and Albert the Great, *On the Soul* 3.2.11.
11. Notice that the preacher has now changed the original "sons of God" to "Son of God."
12. Eckhart is playing here with the traditional etymologies of Zion and Israel. Zion meant *seeing* or *contemplation* and Israel is a *man who sees God*.
13. This would seem to mean that the images of external things as well as images concerning interior things of the soul must be eliminated.
14. Notice how the meaning of *nothing* has changed. In the previous paragraph it was a goal to be sought, establishing the possibility of oneness with God. Eckhart now switches from the nothing beyond being to the nothing that is less than being.
15. The idea seems to be that creatures whose total nature is material, like stone or wood, are the most deficient in being and can be called nothing.
16. The birth of the child who is "stripped bare" might be a reference to the Christmas story. In medieval iconography the Christ child is often portrayed naked resting on a torn piece of cloth, which is to remind one of the loincloth of the crucifixion. Naked he came into this world and naked he left it.

17. On the soul as virgin and mother, see Sermon 2 (*Essential Eckhart*, pp. 177–78).
18. For the interpretation of this verse, see also Sermon XLV nn. 460–68 (pp. 230–33).
19. To understand why Eckhart quotes this passage from Exodus here, one must focus on the "your." He is *your* Lord because everything he has is yours.
20. The notion of being "established in the divine being" (MHG *gesast in daz götlich wesen*) is central to the Pseudo-Eckhartian "Sister Catherine" treatise (cf. pp. 357, 360, 361–62, 368). Cf. Sermon 52 (*Essential Eckhart*, p. 200).
21. For more on God's passionless anger, see *Comm. Ex.* n. 44 (p. 57).
22. For more on "being born" as opposed to "having been born," see Sermon 39 (p. 298 and note 17), although the thought here seems to be slightly different and includes the idea that the birth of the Son in God is more adequately explained by representing it *both* as a process *and* as an accomplished state.

Sermon 80: Homo quidam erat dives, qui induebatur purpura, et bysso: et epulabatur quotidie splendide (Lk. 16:19).

"There was a rich man, who was arrayed in silk and satin, who ate delicacies every day, and who did not have a name."[1] This can be understood in two ways: as referring to the unfathomable ground of the Godhead and to every delicate soul.[2]

"There was a rich man." "Man" denotes an intelligent being according to a pagan master.[3] In this passage "man" is to be understood as God. St. Gregory says that if one could claim that in God anything were nobler than another thing, it would be his intellect; for in intellect God stands revealed to himself; in intellect God flows into himself; in intellect God flows out into all things; and in intellect God created all things. If God had no intellect, the Trinity could not exist and creatures would never have flowed forth.[4]

"He had no name."[5] Thus the unfathomable God is without names, for all the names that the soul gives him it takes from its own knowledge. Concerning this a pagan master speaks in the book called the *Light of Lights:* "God is above being, above comprehension, and above knowledge, insofar as this is natural."[6] I am not speaking of knowledge aided by grace, because a person could be so carried up by grace that he would understand as St. Paul did, who was transported into the third heaven and saw such things as one may not and cannot articulate completely.[7] Also, he could not express them as he saw them because whatever is understood must be understood from its causes, its manner [of existence], or by its effects. This is why God remains uncomprehended because he was caused by no one. He is always the First. He is also without a [specific] manner of being in his incomprehensibility.[8] He is also without effects, that is, in his hidden stillness.[9] This is why he remains without names. What about all the names which have been given him? Moses asked him his name, and God said: "He who is sent you" (Ex. 3:14).[10] Otherwise he could not have understood because God could not ever make himself comprehensible to creatures as he is in himself, not because of some inability on his part, but because creatures could not understand it. Hence the master says in the book called *Light of Lights:* "God is above being, above praise, above comprehension, and above knowledge."

This man was also "rich." Thus God is rich in himself and in all things.[11] Now take note! God's wealth is based on five things. First, he is the first cause and hence constantly pours himself forth into all things.[12] Second, he is simple in his being and hence is the innermost [part] of all things. Third, he is the source and hence spreads himself over all things. Fourth, he is unchangeable and hence is the most constant. Fifth, he is perfect and is hence the most desirable.

He is the first cause and hence pours himself forth into all things. Concerning this a pagan master says that the first cause pours itself more into all the other causes than the other causes pour themselves into their effects.[13] Also, he is simple in his being. What is simple? Bishop Albert says, "Something is simple which is one in itself separate from all else, and that is God. All unified things are sustained by that which he is. There creatures are one in the One and are God in God; in themselves they are nothing."[14] The third, he is the source and therefore flows out into all things. About this Bishop Albert says: "In three ways he flows out into all things commonly: with his being, with his life, and with his light; and [he flows out] in a special way into the soul endowed with intelligence in its power of knowing all things and in its leading back of creatures into their primal origin."[15] This is the light of lights, for "every gift and perfection flows from the Father of lights," as St. James says (Jm. 1:17).

Fourth, because he is unchangeable, he is the most constant. Now take note of how God unites with things. He unites himself with things and yet stays one in himself and [makes] all things one in him. Of this Christ says: "You shall be changed into me, but not I into you."[16] This is due to his immutability and immensity, and to the smallness of things. Concerning this a sage says that all things compared to God are as small as a drop is compared to the vast sea (Ws. 11:23). If one were to throw a drop into the sea, the drop would change into the sea and not the sea into the drop. Thus it happens with the soul: In drawing God into itself it is changed into God, so that the soul becomes divine. God does not become the soul. Then the soul loses its name and its power, but not its will or existence. Here the soul remains in God as God remains in himself. About this Bishop Albert says that a person shall remain forever in the will that he dies in.[17] Fifth, because he is perfect he is the most desirable. God is the fulfillment of himself and all things. What is fulfillment in God? That he is his own good and the good of all things.[18] For this reason all things desire him, for he is their good.

That we may attain this good which is God himself and that we may enjoy it eternally, may God help us. Amen.

NOTES

Translated from DW III, pp. 378–88.

1. Eckhart's justification for considering "and who had no name" part of the gospel passage is the Latin indefinite adjective *quidam* (certain). It was a certain (unnamed) rich man. This is essential for his interpretation of the quotation.
2. The preacher is certainly original in identifying the selfish rich man of Luke's gospel with God and delicate souls.
3. Cf. Aristotle, *Nichomachean Ethics* 10.7 (1178a).
4. Cf. Sermon XXIX n. 301 (p. 225). See the Glossary under *ûzganc.*
5. For more on God's namelessness see especially *Comm. Ex.* nn. 44–53 and 170–84 (pp. 56–60, and 97–102).
6. Cf. *Book of Causes* prop. 5.
7. Cf. 2 Co. 12:2–4.
8. For more on God as something beyond a specific mode or manner of existence, see under *wîse* in the Glossary.
9. For Eckhart's views (following Moses Maimonides) on what kind of knowledge we have of God by looking at his effects (creatures), see especially *Comm. Ex.* nn. 41–43 (pp. 55–56).
10. For more on God as "he who is" see *Comm. Ex.* nn. 14–25 (pp. 45–49).
11. Cf. *Comm. Ex.* n. 74 (p. 68).
12. Cf. *Comm. Jn.* n. 88 (*Essential Eckhart*, p. 155).
13. Cf. *Book of Causes* prop. 1.
14. Bishop Albert is Albert the Great. The quotation has not been traced. That creatures are nothing in themselves was a frequent statement of the preacher and was condemned as article 26 of the papal bull "In agro dominico," (*Essential Eckhart*, p. 80).

15. This quotation is also untraced.
16. This is closer to a quotation from Augustine, *Conf.* 7.10.16, than to Jn. 6:57.
17. Cf. Albert the Great, *On Matthew* 7:2.
18. Good is often defined by medieval philosophers as that which the will always desires. It seems to have such a meaning here.

Sermon 84: Puella surge (Lk. 8:54).

Our Lord said to the girl: "Arise!" With this single word our Lord Jesus Christ teaches us how the soul should rise up from all material things. And as the Son is the single Word of the Father, he thus teaches the soul with one word how it should arise and how it should raise itself up above itself and dwell above itself. The Father spoke a Word; this was his Son. In this single Word he spoke all things. Why did he only speak one Word? Because all things are present to it [the Word]. If I could encompass in one thought all the thoughts I ever had or ever shall have, I would have but a single word; for the mouth utters what is in the heart (Cf. Mt. 12:34).[1] But for now I do not want to talk more about this.

There are four reasons why the soul should "arise" and dwell above itself. The first is because of the many and various joys it finds in God, for God's perfection cannot contain itself but lets pour forth from him creatures with whom he can share himself, who can receive his likeness. Such immeasurable numbers flow out as though he were completely emptied: And there are more angels than pieces of gravel, blades of grass, or leaves. Through them all there flows down to us light, grace, and gifts.[2] And these same things that are flowing through all these creatures or natures God bids the soul receive, and all that God can give would be too little for one soul if God did not give himself in the gifts.

The second reason why the soul should "arise" is because of the purity it finds in God, for all things are pure and noble in God. As soon as they flow out of God into the highest creature, they are as unlike as something is to nothing. In God are light and being, and in creatures darkness and nothing. What is light and being in God is darkness and nothing in creatures.[3]

The third reason why the soul should "arise" is because of the completeness it finds in God, where there is no difference.[4] Wisdom and goodness are one in God. That same thing that is wisdom is also goodness, and that same thing that is mercy is also justice. If in God goodness were one thing and wisdom another, the soul could never find fulfillment in God. The soul is by nature inclined to goodness, and by nature all creatures desire wisdom. If goodness were one thing and wisdom another, the soul, in pouring itself completely into goodness,[5] would have to suffer the pain of leaving wisdom. And if it wanted to pour itself into wisdom, it would have to suffer the loss of goodness. Hence St. Augustine says, "Souls in heaven are not yet completely happy because they still have an inclination to the body."[6] Thus the soul finds rest in no one but God, because in him it finds the totality of all goodness.

If the soul is to grasp God, the soul must also dwell above itself. All things fashion themselves; each thing fashions its nature.[7] Why does the apple tree's nature not produce grapes nor the grapevine apples? Because it is not its nature. The same is true for all other creatures. Fire produces fire; if it could turn everything around it to fire, it would. Water would do the same. If it could turn everything to water and drench everything around it, it would do so—so intensely does a creature love its own being that it has received from God. Even if one were to heap upon the soul all the pains of hell, it would not want *not* to exist. So much does a creature love its own being which it has received without mediation from God.[8] The soul must dwell above itself if it is to grasp God. However much it works with that power with which it grasps everything that has been created (and if God had created a thousand heavens and a thousand earths, it would comprehend them all easily with this power),[9] it still cannot comprehend God. The immeasurable God who is in the soul is the one who comprehends the God who is immeasurable. There God comprehends God, and God fashions himself in the soul and forms it like himself.

The fourth reason why the soul should "arise" is because of the boundlessness it finds in God. All things are ever new in God, are beyond time. Therefore, St. John says in Revelation, "He who sat on the throne said: 'I shall make all things new' " (Rv. 21:5). All things are new in the Son because he is being begotten by the Father today as though he were never born before.[10] And as God flows into the soul, so does it flow also into God. And just as one can die of fright before the blow is struck, so too can one die of [anticipated] joy. This is how the soul dies in itself before it strides into God. The soul strides into God with four steps. The first stride is when fear, hope, and desire grow in it. It strides further when fear, hope, and desire are brought to an end. Thirdly, it comes to a state of forgetting all temporal things. Fourthly, the soul strides into God where it will remain forever, reigning with God in eternity; and then it never thinks of temporal things or itself. Rather it is completely dissolved in God and God in it. What it does then, it does in God.

That we may so stride and die here that we can enjoy him in eternity, may God help us. Amen.

NOTES

Translated from DW III, pp. 454–65.

1. Behind the last few sentences is the idea that the Son or the Word is the "place" in the Trinity where the divine ideas of all things are "located." Thus when the preacher says of himself that all his thoughts could be formulated in a single word that is in his heart, he means *the* Word.
2. This line of thought implies a kind of chain or ladder of being by which the lower natures receive in some sense not directly from God but from higher finite natures. Eckhart's point, however, is that these gifts only satisfy the soul if God himself is in them.
3. Here Eckhart combines the "existence is God"/"creatures are nothing" themes with traditional light-darkness imagery.
4. "Difference," that is, *underscheit*, on which see the Glossary. One finds all things in God; yet there is complete identity and oneness of all things in God.
5. "Pour self into" has the sense of "giving self completely to."
6. Cf. Augustine, *Lit. Comm. Gen.* 12.35, and Thomas Aquinas, *STh* IIIa. suppl. 78. 3. ad 2 and 3.
7. That is, everything's capabilities for performing acts is determined by the potentialities contained in its nature. Each one's nature "activates" itself. Cf. Sermon 9 (pp. 257–58), *Comm. Jn.* n. 4 (*Essential Eckhart* pp. 123–24), and Thomas Aquinas, *STh* IIIa. 2. 1.
8. For an explanation of "without mediation" (here: *unmittelîche*), see under *âne mittel* in the Glossary.
9. That is, with the intellect.
10. That is, as a timeless event the birth of the Son can be said to be taking place now as freshly as at any other time.

Sermon 86: **Intravit Jesus in quoddam castellum, et mulier quaedam, Martha nomine, excepit illum in domum suam (Lk. 10:38).[1]**

St. Luke writes in his gospel that our Lord Jesus Christ entered a little town where a woman named Martha received him. She had a sister named Mary who sat at the feet of our Lord and listened to his words; but Martha hurried about, serving our dear Lord. Three things caused Mary to sit at the feet of Christ. The first was that God's goodness had embraced her soul. The second was ineffable longing: She longed for she knew not what, and she wanted she knew not what. The third was the sweet consolation and delight she drew from the eternal words which flowed from the mouth of Christ.

Martha, too, was drawn by three things which caused her to go about and wait on our dear Christ. The first was her respected age and a ground very rich in experience. This made her think that no one could do the work as well as she. The second was a mature power of reflection which enabled her to accomplish external works with the perfection that love demands. The third was the great dignity of her dear guest.

The masters say that God is disposed to satisfy completely what anyone desires, both in the realm of the intellectual and in that of the senses. That God satisfies us intellectually and satisfies also our senses and feelings can be seen variously in God's dear friends. God satisfies our senses and feelings by granting us comfort, pleasure, and fulfillment; but to be pampered in this with regard to the lower senses is not something that happens to God's dear friends.[2] But intellectual satisfaction is a matter of the spirit. I call that intellectual satisfaction when the highest part of the soul[3] is not drawn down by any pleasure, so that it does not drown in pleasures, but stands sovereign above them. A person is only then intellectually fulfilled when the joys and sorrows of creatures cannot pull the highest part [of the soul] down. I call "creature" everything that one feels and sees lower than God.

Now Martha says, "Lord, tell her to help me" (Lk. 10:40). Martha did not say this out of spite. Rather, she said it because of endearment; that is what motivated her. We might call it affection or playful chiding. Why? Note what follows. She realized that Mary had been overwhelmed by a desire for the complete fulfillment of her soul. Martha knew Mary better than Mary Martha, for Martha had lived long and well; and living gives the most valuable kind of knowledge. Life knows better than pleasure or light what one can get under God in this life, and in some ways life gives us a purer knowledge than what eternal light can bestow. Eternal light gives us knowledge of self *and* God, but not knowledge of self apart from God. Life, on the other hand, gives knowledge of self apart from God. Seeing oneself alone makes it easier to recognize what is like or unlike. St. Paul and pagan masters confirm this. St. Paul saw in an ecstasy God *and* himself in God in the manner of the spirit, but he did not discern clearly in God through images each individual virtue (cf. 2 Co. 12:2–3). This was the case because he had not exercised them in actions. The masters achieved such lofty knowledge through the practice of virtue that they knew each individual virtue more distinctly than Paul or any saint in his first rapture.

This was the case with Martha. When she says, "Lord, tell her to help me," it was as though she were saying: "My sister thinks she can do what she pleases while she sits by you filled with consolation. Let her find out whether this is true, and tell her to get up and leave you." This last remark was said with tender regard, but this could not be gathered from the words themselves. Mary was so full of longing. She longed for she knew not what, and wanted she knew not what. We harbor the suspicion that dear Mary was sitting there more for enjoyment than for spiritual profit. Therefore Martha said, "Lord, tell her to get up," because she feared that she would remain stuck in this pleasant feeling and would progress no further. Then Christ answered her, saying, "Martha, Martha, you are careful, you are worried about many things. One is necessary. Mary has chosen the best part, which can never be taken from her" (Lk. 10:41). Christ did not speak these words to Martha to chasten her. Rather, he responded by giving her the comforting message that it would turn out for Mary as she desired.

Why did Christ say, "Martha, Martha," calling her name twice? Isidore says, "Without a doubt, none of those persons whom God named explicitly before he became man and after he became man were damned. Regarding those whom he did not call by their name there is some doubt."[4] This "being called by name by Christ" I call his eternal knowledge, namely, unequivocally to be inscribed before the creation of all creatures in the living book: "Father, Son, and Holy Spirit." Whatever has been named in it and Christ spoke the name in words, never was any such person lost. Moses to whom God himself said, "I knew you by name" (cf. Ex. 33:12) is witness to this, and Nathaniel to whom our dear Christ said, "I knew you when you were lying under the leaves of the fig tree" (Jn. 1:48). The fig tree signifies God in whom his name had been eternally inscribed. And thus it is confirmed that none of these people was or will be lost whom dear Christ named with his human mouth out of the eternal Word.

Why did he name Martha twice? He wanted to indicate that Martha possessed completely everything of temporal and eternal value that a creature should have. When he said "Martha" the first time, he indicated her perfection in temporal works. With his second calling out, "Martha," he affirmed that she lacked nothing of all that is necessary for eternal happiness. Hence he said, "You are careful,"[5] by which he meant: You stand in the midst of things, but they do not reside in you; and those are careful who go about unimpeded in all their daily pursuits. Those people are unimpeded who perform all their works properly according to the image of eternal light, and such people stand in the midst of things, but not *in* things. They stand very near and yet do not have less of it than if they stood up above, at the rim of eternity. "Very near," I say, because all creatures act as means. There are two kinds of means. One kind (without which I cannot come to God) is work and activity in time, and this does not lessen eternal happiness. By *work* I mean when one practices externally works of virtue, but *activity* is when one practices them internally with full rational consciousness.[6] The other kind of means is to be rid of this. We have been put into time for the purpose of coming nearer to and becoming more like God through rational activity in time. This is what St. Paul meant when he said, "Redeem time, for the days are evil" (Ep. 5:16). One "redeems the time" by ascending continually by means of the mind to God, not according to different images; rather, by means of living intellectual truth.[7] And "the days are evil" means that day implies night. If there were no night, there would not be day nor would one use the word. It would all be one light, and this is what St. Paul means because a life of light is insufficient if there can still be enough darkness to cast a veil and a shadow over eternal happiness for a noble spirit. This is what Christ meant when he said: "Continue to walk while you have light" (Jn. 12:35). He who works in light ascends to God free and stripped of all means. His light is his activity and his activity is his light.

This is how it was with dear Martha. Thus he said to her, "One thing is necessary," not two. You and I, once embraced by the eternal light, are one; and this two that is one is a flaming spirit standing above all things (yet under God) on the rim of eternity. It is two because it does not see God without something mediating. Its knowing and its being, or its knowing and the image that it knows, will never become one. They do not see God, for there God is only seen spiritually, free of all images. One becomes two, two is one; light and spirit, these two are one in the embrace of eternal light.

Now take note what the rim of eternity is. The soul has three paths to

God. One is to seek God in all creatures through all kinds of activity and with flaming love. This is what King Solomon had in mind when he said, "In all things I sought rest" (Si. 24:11). The second path is a pathless path, free yet bound, raised aloft and wafted off almost beyond self and all things, beyond will and images. However, it does not stand firmly on its own. This is what Christ meant when he said: "Happy are you, Peter. Flesh and blood have not enlightened you," rather, "your being raised up into the intellect" [did]. In this you called me God ("My heavenly Father revealed it to you") (Mt. 16:17). St. Peter did not see God bare [directly], but he had certainly been drawn up by the power of the heavenly Father above all created powers of comprehension to the rim of eternity. I say he was clasped by the heavenly Father with tempestuous strength in a loving embrace, his spirit gaping upwards unawares, carried beyond all human comprehension in the power of the heavenly Father. Then Peter was addressed from above in tones created and sweet, yet free from all sensual pleasure, in the simple truth and unity of the God-man in the person of the heavenly Father-Son. I dare to say: If St. Peter had seen God without a medium in his nature as he did afterwards and as Paul did when he was transported into the third heaven, conversation with the highest angel would have seemed to him too vulgar. In this state he spoke many endearing words of which dear Jesus had no need because he sees into the heart and into the ground of the spirit where he remains in the immediate presence of God in the freedom of true "theirness."[8] St. Paul had this in mind when he said, "There was a man carried up into God who heard secret words which are unutterable for all human beings" (2 Co. 12:3–4). Thus you should understand that St. Peter just stood on the rim of eternity and was not seeing God in unity [as he is] in his "ownness."[9]

The third path is called a path and yet is a being-at-home. It is to see God immediately in his ownness. Dear Christ says, "I am the way, the truth, and the life" (Jn. 14:6). One Christ, one Person; one Christ, one Father; one Christ, one Spirit; three, one; three: way, truth, and life; one beloved Christ in whom all this is. Outside this path bordering it are all creatures acting as means. To be led into God on this path by the light of his Word and to be embraced by the love of the Spirit of them both—this is beyond anything one can express in words. Now listen to something astounding. How wondrous to be within and without, to grasp and to be embraced, to see and to be what is seen, to hold and to be held: This is the final end where the spirit remains at rest in the unity of blissful eternity.

But now back to our explanation of how dear Martha, and, together with her, all of God's friends are *near* care but not *in* care. Here a work done in time is as valuable as any joining of self to God, for this [work in time] joins us as closely as the most sublime thing that can happen to us, except for seeing God in his pure nature. [10] Hence he says, "You are near things and near care," and he means that she certainly was worried and concerned in her lower senses because she was not pampered by the sweetness of the spirit. She was near things, not *in* things; she stood apart, . . ." [11]

Our works should have three qualities: One should work orderly, with discrimination, and with contemplation. I call that "orderly" which at all points answers the highest. I call that done "with discrimination" when one at the time knows of nothing better [to do]. And I call that done with contemplation when one feels in the good works the gratifying presence of living truth. Wherever these three things are, they join [us to God] as closely and are as useful as all the joys of Mary Magdalene in the wilderness. [12]

Now Christ says, "You are bothered by many things," not about one thing. This means that when she is in a purely simple state performing no activities and is focusing her attention on the rim of eternity, she is bothered when something acts as an [interfering] means, so that she cannot remain there above in consolation. A person is bothered by something who descends and stands in the midst of concern. But Martha stood in lordly, well-founded virtue with a free spirit unimpeded by anything. Hence she wished for her sister to be put in this same state because she saw that she was not standing firmly. It was a splendid ground out of which she wished that she [Mary] might be established in all that is necessary for eternal happiness. This is why Christ said, "One thing is necessary." What is the one thing necessary? It is the One that is God. That is necessary for all creatures. If God were to withdraw all that is his, all creatures would turn into nothing. If God were to withdraw what is his from the soul of Christ, where their Spirit is united to the eternal Person, Christ would remain a mere creature. Thus this One is certainly necessary. Martha was afraid her sister would remain clinging to consolation and sweetness, and she wished her to become as she herself was. This is why Christ said, "She has chosen the best part," as if to say, "Cheer up, Martha; this will leave her. The most sublime thing that can happen to a creature shall happen to her: She shall become as happy as you."

Now listen to some instruction on virtue. To live virtuously depends on the will in three ways. First, one must give up one's will to God. This is necessary in order that one rightly know whether to perform or avoid an action. There are three kinds of will. The first is *sensible* will, the second *rational* will, the third *eternal* will. The sensible will demands instruction, demands that one hear truthful teachers. The rational will sees to it that one follows in the footsteps of Jesus Christ and the saints in all one's works. This means that one's words, conduct, and activity are all equally directed to and ordered by what is highest. When all this has been achieved, God bestows something else on the ground of the soul—an eternal will with the loving command of the Holy Spirit. Then the soul says: "Lord, speak into me, that your eternal will may come about." And if the soul has achieved the condition just described sufficiently and if God so pleases, then the dear Father speaks his eternal Word into the soul.

Now our dear people maintain that one should become so perfect that nothing pleasant can move us and that one be untouched by pleasure or suffering. They are wrong in this. I say that a saint never became so great that he could not be moved. I declare, on the other hand, that it certainly does happen in this life, in the case of a saint, that absolutely nothing can cause him to move away from God. Do you think that you are imperfect as long as words can move you to joy and sorrow? This is not so. Christ was not like that. He made that clear when he said, "My soul is sorrowful unto death" (Mt. 26:37). Words caused Christ pain and, if the sufferings of all creatures were to befall one creature, this would not be as much as this pain was for Christ. This was due to the nobility of his nature and to the sacred union of divine and human nature. And so I say that a saint never reached nor can reach the state where suffering does not hurt him and pleasure not please him. This sometimes happens through favor, love, or grace; namely, that someone comes and says that so and so is a heretic or something like that, and that the other person is then flooded with grace so that he bears equally well and with indifference joy and suffering. But this certainly happens to saints that nothing can move away from God. Even if their hearts are made to suffer (if they are not in grace), their will remains utterly steadfast in God, and they say, "Lord, I belong to you and you belong to me." Whatever then happens does not conflict with eternal happiness, as long as it does not spill into the highest part of the spirit,[13] up there where it remains in unity with God's dearest will.

Now Christ says, "You are bothered by many cares." Martha was so grounded in being that her activity did not hinder her. Work and activity led her to eternal happiness. Granted, her happiness was somewhat impaired by mediation; but her noble nature, her constant striving, and the aforementioned virtue stood her well. Mary was a Martha before she became a Mary, for when she sat at the feet of our Lord, she was not Mary. She was, of course, Mary in name but not in her being because she was sitting there in joy and sweetness but had just begun to be schooled and to learn about life. But Martha was very steadfast in her being and hence she said, "Lord tell her to get up," as if to say, "Lord, I would wish that she were not sitting there just for the pleasure of it. I would like her to learn life so that she might possess it in being. Tell her to get up, so that she might become perfect." Her name was not really Mary as she sat at Christ's feet. This is what I call Mary: a well-disciplined body obedient to a wise soul. Obedience is when the will satisfactorily carries out what insight commands.

Now our dear people imagine they can bring things to a point where their senses are utterly unaffected by the presence of sensible objects. They cannot achieve this. That a painfully loud racket be as pleasant to my ears as the charming tones of a stringed instrument—that I shall never achieve. This, however, one should attain, that one's will, formed to God in understanding, is free of all natural pleasure, and, whenever insight on the alert commands the will to turn away, that the will say: "I do it gladly." See, then conflict turns to pleasure, because whatever a person has to obtain by great struggle and toil turns into heartfelt joy, and then it bears fruit.

Now some people want to go so far as to achieve freedom from works. I say this cannot be done. It was not until after the time when the disciples received the Holy Spirit that they began to perform virtuous deeds. "Mary sat at the feet of the Lord and listened to his words," and learned, for she had just been put into school and was learning to live. But afterwards, when she had learned and Christ had ascended into heaven and she received the Holy Spirit, then she really for the first time began to serve. Then she crossed the sea, preached, taught, and became the servant and washerwoman of the disciples.[14] Thus do the saints become saints; not until then do they really begin to practice virtue. For it is then that they gather the treasure of eternal happiness. Whatever was done before covers guilt and turns away punishment. We find testimony for this in Christ: From the very beginning of God's becoming man and man God, he undertook to achieve our eternal happiness, [continuing at it] to the end, when he died on the cross. There was no part of his body that did not practice its own proper virtue.

That we may truly follow him in the practice of true virtue, may God assist us. Amen.

NOTES

Translated from DW III, pp. 481–92.

1. Sermon 2 (*Essential Eckhart*, pp. 177–81) treats this same text from Luke; however, the sermons have otherwise very little in common. The present sermon is atypical in many ways, especially in the vocabulary the preacher chooses. Lin-

guistically it is among the most difficult, if not the most difficult, and the least clear of the sermons. One wonders what the reasons for this might be. It seems more likely that it is due to its being preached to an atypical audience or to some other external circumstance than to its not being genuine. There are frequent echoes of Eckhartian thought, and who else would be so original and antitraditional in interpreting the Mary-Martha story?

2. Several commentators assure us that Eckhart's use of the words "friends of God" in no way connects him to the sect that employed this term to refer to its members. The term appears frequently in pseudo-Eckhartian works, such as the "Sister Catherine" treatise (see below, p. 384, note 3).

3. The phrase here *wipfel der sêle* (literally, "the [tree] top of soul") is an expression the preacher uses elsewhere for the "spark of the soul."

4. No one has been able to locate this in the writings of Isidore of Seville.

5. Martha is seen here as being worried about many things in the sense that she is careful not to let these many things impede her spiritual progress.

6. *Work* (MHG *werk*) seems to refer to acts of virtue as they can be perceived by the senses in their having effects in the material world. *Activities* (MHG *gewerbe*) are these same virtuous practices as they are full human acts carried out in the spiritual realm through the human intellect and will.

7. Intellectual ascent to God is contrasted to ascent through images that, given the abyss between any images and God's true nature, cannot be any real ascent.

8. The MHG word that has been translated as "theirness" is *iresheit*, which refers to the unity of Father and Son.

9. "Ownness" (*sînesheit*) is obviously to be understood in conjunction with "theirness" above and denies that there is a perfect oneness between Peter and God.

10. For similar remarks on the value of works in time, see Sermon 5b (*Essential Eckhart*, pp. 183–84).

11. The next few words seem to be corrupt and incomprehensible.

12. This last remark refers to a legend in which Mary Magdalene spends her later years as a hermit in the wilderness and experiences many unusual spiritual delights. See "Sister Catherine," pp. 372–75, 380–82.

13. Again, a mention of the highest *wipfel* (branch) of the spirit.

14. See "Sister Catherine," p. 373.

Appendix

The "Sister Catherine" Treatise

translated by
Elvira Borgstädt

THIS IS ABOUT THE CONFESSOR'S DAUGHTER

I

"You must recognize how often you have resisted the seven gifts of the Holy Spirit and that you did not practice the six works of charity for which God must condemn you scornfully on Judgment Day.[1]

"Now begin a new life, dear daughter, and better yourself in all aspects of your life, that God perforce may forget your weakness!"

This is the first advice of the respected father confessor, and the first way.

So she asks: "Father, is this the shortest way?"

And he says: "No, but what I have told you must necessarily all be."

She says: "Father, show me the fastest way!"

He answers: "Wait until you possess in your life all that I have advised you of. Wait until you have rid yourself of all your sins, and return to me often!"

II

The daughter does this and is obedient to her respected confessor. She returns to him again and again, and she says: "Father, I will do everything you bid me to do until my death, so that you help me to gain the kind of life in which I can boldly dare to die!"

He says: "Did you turn away from all of your sins?"

She says: "Yes father, as much as I am now able to, and I will [continue to] do so until my death!"

He says: "Now I will show you a new way and give you new advice.

349

Keep your mouth truthful and your body pure and your soul loving! Understand this advice and this way in the following manner:

"A truthful mouth means that you say with your mouth only what you mean with your heart. Thus, daughter, you will speak the truth. God is the truth; for this reason you shall always and only speak of God. When you can no longer pray and no longer contemplate God, then you shall speak of him. You shall take your entire entertainment from God.

"You must understand a pure body in such a way that you are pierced with the fear of God, so that you will not allow anything to live in you which is not God.

"A loving soul you must understand like this: that the [soul] loves what is like itself—which is God. You shall unite yourself with him in such a way that it will seem wrong to you that your heart does not break from overflowing love."

Here the daughter says: "How foreign this still is to me!"

She says: "Father, will it ever be familiar to me?"

He says: "Yes, so do as I tell you. Put aside all that makes your soul gloomy so that the light of truth may shine for you. Thus, the soul can indeed return on the path from which it flowed."[2]

III

The masters speak of hell. I will tell you what hell is: It is nothing other than a mode of being. Whatever your mode of being is here on earth, it will be the same eternally—that is hell. You should understand it like this, observe how the thief who has forfeited his life and is held captive feels much worse when he sees other people filled with joy. That is what happens to those who are in hell and who see God with all of his friends.[3] The masters consider this to be their greatest torment.[4]

The good daughter of whom we spoke earlier hears this and goes to her respected confessor.

She says: "Father, show me the fastest way to my eternal salvation!"

He says: "Daughter, be content [with what I have told you]!"

She says: "I will not be content as long as my eternal salvation is not assured!"

He says: "Daughter, you can be certain of eternal life!"

She says: "Father, have you shown me the shortest way?"

He says: "All creatures direct you to it. They all say 'Go forth, we are not God!'⁵ Daughter, in that you have instruction enough."

She says: "Father, that is not enough for me!"

He says: "If you do not want to believe me, then believe the words of our Lord Jesus Christ when he said, 'Take up your cross and follow me!' (Mt. 16:24) He did not say, 'Take up my cross and follow me!' You must understand it this way: As long as you do what you are capable of you can be content, knowing that it satisfies God."⁶

She says: "But have I done all that I am capable of?"

He says: "What more do you want to do?"

She says: "I want to leave behind honor and property, friends and family, and all exterior comfort that may be given to me by creatures."⁷

Here the confessor says: "Will you leave me behind, too?"

She says: "Yes father, when I leave all things behind I must also leave you."

He says: "Do not be presumptuous. It is not meant for women."

She says: "I know very well that women can never come into heaven; they have to become men first.⁸ It is to be understood like this: They must perform manly deeds and must have manly hearts with full strength so that they may resist themselves and all sinful things."

He says: "Now you believe yourself very strong! I wonder what makes you think that you are able to suffer more than you already have."

She says: "I can suffer everything that Christ has suffered through me."

He says: "That is mere talk!"

She says: "I speak the truth."

He says: "How will you explain that to me?"

She says: "Very well! I have heard it said that the Godhead never came to the aid of Christ's humanity in all the suffering Christ endured."

He says: "That is true. The Godhead is free from suffering. It has never suffered and shall never suffer because no one can touch it."

She says: "I truly can suffer everything Christ has suffered."

He says: "Explain that to me."

She says: "I will. I know very well that Christ is the noblest human being who was ever born; he descended from a royal line of seventy-two. I will say more. He was of the noblest blood Mary's heart could ever bring forth. You must understand it as I do: I shall rightfully suffer everything he has suffered for my sake. One distinguishes people according to their nobility—the nobler they are the more delicate they are. That indicates to me that I can suffer more than Christ. I want you to know that my heart would

351

break if I would speak of everything I know about the noble beginning and end of his life on earth, [which he spent] in a rightly chosen poverty!"[9]

He says: "Daughter, counsel yourself better!"

She says: "Father, I have already counseled myself very well. You must know that I will follow the advice of the Holy Spirit every day of my life."

He says: "What does the Holy Spirit advise you to do?"

She says: "It advises me to give myself into the mighty hand of God and to leave behind all support from creatures."

He says: "Your intent is evil!"

She says: "How is it evil?"

He says: "In that you will not follow my advice. You should know that obedience is a virtue."

She says: "I will be obedient until my death."

He says: "To whom?"

She says: "To Christ and the heavenly Father to whom John was obedient in the desert, and Mary Magdalene, and Mary of Egypt, and Mary Salome."[10]

He says: "It seems to me that you will no longer follow my advice!"

She says: "That is true. I regret with all my heart that I followed human advice for such a long time and that I resisted the advice of the Holy Spirit for so long."

He says: "Daughter, now tell me, why do you think that I have harmed you?"

She says: "You have prevented me from obtaining my eternal salvation."

He says: "How?"

She says: "In that you did not show me immediately the fastest way."

He says: "That meant obeying the Holy Spirit. I should never advise you other than as I have."

She says: "If you and other clerics had not prevented me, I would have spent my time more virtuously than I have done. I thought that everything the clerics preach is gospel!"

He says: "The gospel is brought forth in the Holy Spirit from the perfect life of our Lord Jesus Christ and his noble sayings. We read and preach the gospel publicly. Whoever wants to follow it can follow it to the highest [degree]."

She says: "God have mercy that I have not done so all of my days."

He says: "I am sorry that you blame me for hindering you!"

She says: "Yes, I put the blame on you and on all creatures!"

He says: "You are wrong. No one can hinder you but yourself. You should know that he who is touched by God no one can resist. All of the saints in heaven espouse his cause and the preachers and mendicants who are on earth cannot resist one who is touched by the truth. The word Christ spoke to the youth who sought the perfect life drives them away. Christ said, 'Keep the Ten Commandments!' The youth answered, 'Lord, I have kept them all of my days.' Christ said, 'If you want to become perfect, sell everything you have and give it to the poor and follow me' (Mt. 19:21). Thus, Christ has given us the truth through Peter and his other disciples whom he called to himself and into voluntary poverty. Daughter, you should know that what Christ has done in word and in deed must be true, because he is the Truth himself. Realize that he who wants to come to the Father must follow in the footsteps of Christ to the highest [degree]."

She says: "Why then, dear father, do you dissuade me from it so ardently?"

He says: "It is such a poor life that he who endures it successfully is in need of God's help."

She says: "I know very well that now and then God withdraws from us. But I also know that he who clings to him receives him in all his needs."

He says: "What will you do when you are despised by all creatures?"

She says: "I desire to become the least among all the creatures our Lord Jesus Christ has so that I may say with Paul, 'I am happy, all creatures are a cross to me and I am a cross to all creatures' (Ga. 6:14)."

He says: "Daughter, you are too young for that!"

She says: "Mary was younger than I when she went into the desert and into exile for the sake of thieves and murderers."[11]

He says: "God was with her."

She says: "I know well that God is with me [too]!"

He says: "He was present with her."

She says: "He is with me spiritually without interruption."

He says: "Mary had a great refuge in his presence. You don't have that, dear daughter."

She says: "Since I must be without consolation, I will also make do without his external presence. I desire that he bear himself within my soul without delay!"[12]

He says: "Reconsider before you take that on."

She says: "Be silent, enough of this kind of talk! You have hindered me by talking so much."

He says: "Consider this: If you were touched by the truth, you would neither act nor not act on my account. You know well enough that I am a creature. I want you to realize that you do not live for the truth as long as a creature can give or take from you. The truth has so many virtues that it directs the human being toward the highest without the help of any creature. Therefore, you cannot blame me. On the contrary, you should know that he who is touched by the truth has the Holy Spirit for his master. The [Holy Spirit] will send him who wants to follow to the highest school that was ever established. There one learns more in one moment than everything the masters can put into words."

She says: "You speak the truth."

IV

Once again the daughter comes to the respected confessor and **she says:** "Father, I don't know if I will ever find help."

He says: "Why is that?"

She says: "I still have to take up all the virtues. I don't know if I ever carried a virtue to its full perfection, as I should have."

He says: "Let it be enough that you do the best you can."

She says: "I have never accomplished all that I am capable of and I know very well that I am indebted to God in three ways. The first debt is amends for my sins."

He says: "People cannot make amends for even one sin, unless God forgives them out of love."

She says: "I know that well. Nevertheless, it is only right that I do my best and remain penitent until my death in grace."

He says: "What is the second debt?"

She says: "That I would like to be with the friends of our Lord, and that I have never lived as I should have. I know very well that he who wants to get there must accomplish it with his life in our Lord Jesus Christ."

He says: "You are right. Tell me about the third debt."

She says: "The third is that I should follow my beloved in true love, as he preceded me, even if there were neither hell nor heaven. I must follow him to the highest [degree] without a question.[13] I know this debt so well, but do not better myself as I should."

He says: "What more would you want to do? Did you not leave behind honor and property, friends and family, and all of the comfort you could and would gain from creatures?"

She says: "Father, that is only true in a matter of speaking. If I had everything God ever created and left everything on account of God, I would have left nothing because it was not mine, it was God's. Whatever we call possession belongs to God. Therefore, I know very well that I still have to leave that which I must leave."

He says: "What else must you leave behind?"

She says: "Myself![14] [Only] after I have detached myself from all the circumstances and situations in which I find myself can I say that I have left myself behind."

He says: "You are right. I am greatly amazed how you endure the shameful treatment that befalls you in spite of your tender years."

She says: "God knows that I do not feel it."

He says: "Does it not concern you that both your spiritual and worldly friends are sad because of your choice and that they believe you act excessively?"

She says: "What should that tell me? I know very well that Christ knew, as he sat in the temple, that his mother and Joseph were looking for him and that they were sad. The masters said to Christ, 'Your mother and father are looking for you!' (Lk. 2:48). Christ answered, 'Who is my father and my mother, and my sister and my brother? He who does the will of my father is my father and my mother, my sister and my brother!' (Mt. 12:48–50; Mk. 3:32–35; Lk. 8:21)."

He says: "You are right. I implore you to take your necessities because they are offered to you through God."

She says: "Instruct me what the right necessities are."

He says: "Will you be satisfied with the proper necessities?"

She says: "Yes."

He says: "They are water and bread and a frock—those are the proper bodily necessities."

She says: "Now instruct me about spiritual necessity."

He says: "That is to become the most scorned human being in Christ ever to live."

She says: "May God reward you! Pray for me, that God may give all creatures permission to judge me the lowliest [among them] and that all people may persecute me according to their inclinations."

He says: "That will happen to you often enough if you pursue the [life] you have decided on. A saint once said, 'If God knew a human being who could suffer everything that all of human kind has suffered, he would give all this to him to suffer, so that his honor would increase accordingly in eternity.' God does this out of pure love to everyone he has called to himself. A master says that no one is worthy of suffering except the one who desires it with all of his heart."[15]

He says: "Daughter, you are right. I implore you to remain in this land and busy yourself, but only if you want to."[16]

She says: "That I will not do! I will do my own bidding. I will go into exile and to all the places where I can be persecuted. You must understand that I have found more good in the least humiliation than in all the sweetness that was ever done to me by creatures."

He says: "I do not criticize that because it is true. Christ confirmed it for us with the words he spoke to his disciples, 'You shall go to all the places where you will be persecuted' " (Cf. Mt. 10:22–23; Jn. 15:20).

She says: "Father, may God bless you; leave my devotion to me and God!"

He says: "Come to me where you find me."

She says: "That I will gladly do."

(Here, the daughter goes off into exile.)

V

Now, the daughter mentioned above comes to her confessor father and addresses him: "Father, hear me for the love of God!"[17]

He says: "Where do you come from?"

She says: "From distant lands."

He says: "Where were you born?"

She says: "Father, don't you recognize me?"

He says: "God knows, I don't!"

She says: "That shows me that you have never known yourself."

He says: "That is true. I know very well that if I knew myself perfectly, the way I should, I would know all creatures to the highest [degree]."

She says: "That is true. Let us stop this conversation and hear me for God's sake!"

He says: "Gladly, please begin."

The daughter confesses her current state to the respected confessor so that his own soul rejoices.

He says: "Dear daughter, come to me soon."

She says: "God willing I shall gladly do so."

He goes to his brothers and says: "I have listened to [the confession of] a person and I'm not sure if she is a human being or an angel. If she is human, then you must realize that all her soul's powers reside with the angels in heaven, for her soul has received an angelic life and being. She knows and loves more than all the people I have ever known."[18]

The brothers say: "Praise be to God!"

The confessor father seeks the daughter out in church where he knows her to be and begs her sincerely to speak with him.

She says: "Do you still not recognize me?"

He says: "God knows that I don't."

She says: "Well, I will tell you out of love. I am the poor person whom you have drawn to God."

Thus, she reveals to him who she is.

He says: "Alas, poor man that I am. How ashamed I feel in the eyes of God that I had religious knowledge for such a long time and still have found so few of the divine secrets."

He says: "I implore you, dear daughter, by the love you have for God to tell me about the life and labor you had since I last saw you."

She says: "There would be much to tell."

He says: "It cannot be too much; I would like to hear it. You should know that I have heard many mysterious things about you."

The daughter begins to tell the confessor and **says:** "You shall never disclose it as long as I live!"

He says: "I give you my oath that I will reveal nothing about your confession as long as you live."

She bursts out and tells him about many wonderous things, so that he is astonished how a human being could ever suffer so much.

She says: "Father, I am still wanting. I found that I have surpassed everything my soul desired, except that I am not challenged about my belief."

He says: "Praise be to God that he ever created you!"

He says: "Now, you should let it be enough."

She says: "Never, as long as my soul does not dwell in the eternal state."

He says: "I would be quite content if my soul had experienced the ascent yours did."

She says: "My soul ascended without any obstacles, but it did not gain a permanent place. You must understand that a brief visit is not enough for me. If only I knew what I could do to be permanently established in eternity."

He says: "Is this your greatest desire?"

She says: "Yes."

He says: "That [desire] itself you must abandon, if you ever shall be granted [eternal bliss]."

She says: "I will gladly do so."

And she puts herself into a state of emptiness.[19] There God draws her into a divine light so that she thinks she is one with God as long as it lasts. Then she is driven back into herself with a superabundance of divine experience so that **she says:** "I know well that there is no help for me!"

The confessor goes to the daughter: "Tell me, how are you now?"

She says: "I am not well, both heaven and earth are too small for me!"

He implores her to tell him more.

She says: "I know none of the trifling things that I could tell you."

He says: "For God's sake, tell me something."

He wins her consent through love and she speaks with him about mysterious and deep things such as the unveiled experience of divine truth, so that **he says:** "Realize that this is foreign to all people. Were I not so learned a priest that I had myself read this about divine wisdom, it would also be foreign to me."

She says: "I'm sorry about that. I wished you had learned it with your life!"

He says: "I tell you that I have learned so much of it that I know it just as well as I know that I said mass today. But I will admit to you it grieves me that I did not learn it through life."

The daughter says: "Pray for me."

And consolation comes back to her and she enjoys God. But the moment does not last very long. She goes back to the door and fetches her respected confessor and **she says:** "Father, rejoice with me, I have become God!"[20]

Virtuously, **he replies:** "God be praised for it! Go back into your union, away from all people. If you remain God, I will rejoice with you."

She obeys the confessor and goes into a corner of the church. There it happens that she forgets everything that had ever been named, and she is drawn so far out of herself and away from all created things that they have to carry her from the church. She lies until the third day and they think she is surely dead!

The confessor said: "I do not think that she is dead." (Now you must know that if the confessor had not been there they would have buried her.) They examine her in every way they can, but it cannot be determined if the soul is in the body. So they say: "Surely she is dead!" The confessor says: "Surely she is not!"[21]

On the third day the daughter recovers.

She says: "Oh, poor me, I am here again!"

The confessor is at hand and he says to her: "Reveal your experience to me and let me benefit from the divine truth."

She says: "God knows that I cannot! I cannot tell anyone what I have experienced."

He says: "Now do you have everything you want?"

She says: "Yes, I am granted everlasting bliss. I have attained by grace what Christ is by nature. He has made me his joint-heir so that I shall never again lose it."[22]

He says: "Praise be to God! Dear daughter, now stay here and don't do your God injustice."

She says: "I will not remain in one place with my body; only my soul remains in one place. I will follow the example of our Lord Jesus Christ as long as I live in time."

He says: "You are right. He has led you the right way."

She says: "God knows that is true! You must understand that if the Father had not sent the Son to me I would neither have cared a Hail Mary about God nor about his entire Godhead. Praised and honored be the name of our Lord Jesus Christ, because he revealed to me that I can know and love God in him. He has been the example [through which I found] my salvation."

VI

Now the respected confessor comes and seeks out the daughter in a foreign land and begs her sincerely to speak with him for the love of God.

She says: "I will speak with you about exterior things."

He says: "Tell me what you think has benefited you most on the way to your eternal salvation."[23]

She says: "[First], that I detached myself where[ever] I found myself.

"Second, that I never defended myself against things said about me, as long as they concerned only me.

APPENDIX

"Third, that I never suffered so much pain that I did not desire to suffer more, and that I thought I should suffer it deservedly.

"Fourth, that I always submitted to being the least of all human beings, and poor, and severed from all comfort that could have come to me through creatures.

"Fifth, that I never saw a person's defects without rebuking them. I never listened to what went against the gospel or against the life of Christ— I will stake my life on it. You must understand that I am better versed in perpetual exercises and have suffered more because I rebuked people for their sins, which I recognized to be their eternal loss. You should know that I did it out of pure love for God [and] because I pitied them. You should also know that people have persecuted me with many humiliating words.

"Sixth, that I never avoided a place in which I was despised. Where they offered me honor I fled, and where they despised me I stayed.

"Seventh, that I never looked back after I was shown the path to my salvation, and that I never followed the advice of any creature, but that I underwent everything alone with the right determination.

"Eighth, that I was never satisfied with the light in which I was guided, nor with the visions in which I saw God. All of that was nothing to me until I was established.[24]

"The ninth is that I never resist God in anything he wants to accomplish through me or anything the Holy One wants to say through me.

"The tenth, that I am active to the highest [degree], with both my external and internal being."

He says: "Praise be to God! Now that you told me about external activity, tell me also about internal activity."

She says: "God knows that I am afraid you may not understand it."

He says: "Please tell me."

She says: "I will. Before I was established, all the works God had ever created in heaven and on earth were within me.[25] My dwelling place was in heaven and there I mingled with the household that dwells in the Trinity. Everything was as familiar to me as house and household are [familiar] to a good man who lives in it; and I knew the distinction of all creatures and all that was created by God. I distinguished them as well as I do the five fingers on my hand."

He says: "Explain the meaning of this better to me."

She says: "Gladly! I gathered and tamed all the powers of my soul. When I looked into myself I saw God within me and everything he has ever created in heaven and on earth. I will tell you more about it.

"You know very well [that] he who is turned toward God and toward

360

the mirror of truth sees everything that [is] reflected in that mirror, which is all things.

"That was my inner practice before I was established. Do you understand its meaning well enough?"

He says: "It must necessarily be so!"

He says: "Is your practice not the same now?"

She says: "No, I have nothing to do with angels nor with saints, nor with all creatures, nor with any of the things that were ever created."

She says: "Furthermore, I have nothing to do with anything that was ever spoken!"

He says: "Explain that to me better."

She says: "That I will do. I am established in the pure Godhead, in which there never was form nor image."

He says: "Are you there permanently?"

She says: "Yes!"

He says: "Let me tell you, dear daughter, I am glad to hear it. Please continue."

She says: "Where I am, no creature may enter in its creatureliness."

He says: "Explain it better."

She says: "I will. I am where I was before I was created; that [place] is purely God and God.[26] There are neither angels nor saints, nor choir, nor heaven, nor this nor that. Many people speak of eight heavens and of nine choirs. They are not where I am. You should know that everything stated in such a way and presented to people in images is but an incitement to seek God. Realize that in God is nothing but God. You must also understand that no soul may come into God before it has become God as it was God before it was created. No one may come into the naked Godhead except the one who is as naked as he was when he flowed out of God. The masters say that no one may enter here as long as he has any attachment to lower things, even if it is only as much as the tip of a needle can carry."[27]

He says: "Dear daughter, you are right. Now, for God's sake, give me your best advice on how I can come to possess this gift."

She says: "I will give you general advice. You know that all creatures are made from nothing and that they have to become nothing again before they can return to their origin."

He says: "I know it well."

She says: "That tells you enough. Take note of that which is nothing!"

He says: "I know very well what is nothing, and I also know what is less than nothing. It must be understood like this. All sinful things are nothing in sight of God. And the one who engages in sin is less than nothing."

She says: "That is true. Let yourself be governed by it if you want to attain your highest good. You must regard yourself as the least among all creatures so that you do not perceive what more you have to do, so that God can work in you."[28]

He says: "That is true. One master said, 'He who loves God as his God, and acknowledges God as his God, and worships God as his God, and lets it be at that, appears to me like a nonbeliever.' "[29]

She says: "Blessed be the master who said that. He recognized the truth. You must understand that whoever is satisfied with that which can be expressed in words alone (God is a word, heaven is a word), and will not come further with the power of his soul and with knowledge and love than what has been expressed in words, shall rightfully be called a nonbeliever. That which is expressed in words is understood by the lower powers of the soul, but it does not suffice for the highest powers of the soul. They press on until they come to the origin from which the soul flowed out. You must understand that no power of the soul may enter into the origin. The lower powers of the soul are all servants to the 'man' of the soul;[30] they help the man toward the origin and draw him away from lower things. Thus the soul stands in its might, above all created things in [relationship to] the origin, so that the 'man' of the soul penetrates the origin, and all the powers remain outside.

"Understand it this way, it is the soul, naked and empty of all expressible things, which stands [as] one in the One, so that it can go forward in the naked Godhead, just like oil on a cloth flows on and on.[31] In such a way the soul flows forward, and flows for ever and ever, as long as God has ordained that it give the body its being in time. Understand that as long as the good person lives on earth his soul advances in eternity. Therefore, good people are fond of life."[32]

He says: "Daughter, you are right. One master said, if two people lay on their deathbeds and both stood in identical esteem in the eyes of God, and both should die, and if one were to die before the other just long enough that the other could heave a sigh toward God, or think about the least bit of misery that God had suffered, or the least [important] word God ever spoke, this he would certainly gain as a valuable gift over and above the other who had died before him; as long as God is eternal."[33]

She says: "That is true. You must understand it like this: The number of good people who will ascend is the same as the number of the ones who will descend because they stand in sin."

He says: "Now, dear daughter, with the help of God tell me [about this]: We speak of hell, of purgatory, and of heaven, and we read much about it. We also read that God is in all things and all things are in God."

She says: "That is true."

He says: "Now tell me for God's sake how I shall best understand this!"

She says: "I will gladly do so, as far as I can express it in words. Hell is nothing but a state. Whatever is anyone's state of being here [on earth] remains their being forever, if they are found in this state [when they die]. Many people want to have a creaturely existence here and want to possess a divine being there. That cannot be. Now understand that many people are deceived by this. Purgatory is a [freely] accepted thing like repentance; it comes to an end. You must understand it like this: Some people honor God and the friends of God so much that he must necessarily be merciful toward them, even if they do not experience true remorse in love and knowledge before their end so that they lift themselves out of themselves and out of all created things. Then right love becomes their being for the rest of their lives so that they never want to sin again, and they suffer everything out of true love that our Lord Jesus Christ and his beloved friends suffered. These people receive this by grace. Yet, the people who adhere to their creatureliness must eternally remain in that mode of being which is called hell. In the same manner the ones who do not let anything else but God reside in their being retain their being as it is. God becomes their being and remains their being eternally.

"You shall understand it like this: One says of Judgment Day that God will preside over it. One also says that he will give judgment. That is true. But it is not the way people envision it. Every human being judges himself; as he appears there in his being, so will he remain eternally. Now many people say that the body will rise with the soul. That is true. But it is not the way people understand it. It has to be understood like this: The being of the body joins the being of the soul which then becomes one being.[34] The blessed, who spent all of their days in God and whose being has been God, will retain God as their being in body and soul for all eternity. That does not happen to the worthless who have spent their time with creaturely affairs or doings. This has been their being; it will remain their being and they will sink away from God and his friends eternally. That [is what] one calls hell. You must understand that the same people have their being from God even if they were not like this. In this manner they are in God and God is in them. And accordingly they have their being from God. Now let me explain what this means.

"The unworthy are in God like the man who has forfeited his life to a just king. [The man] has taken from the king his honor and property, his friends and family and has often plotted against the king's life,[35] [even though] the lord showed him nothing but kindness. He thought that the man would better himself, yet he got worse all the time and so the king saw very well that he would never improve. The king deals with the man in proper judgment and does not kill him. He does this because he wants to repay him the offense which he received from him. First [the man] is bound by hand and foot and is thrown into the filthy water among toads and snakes which usually gather at the bottom of the [castle] tower. After that he is taken out and put in a public place where all see his shameful disgrace and where he sees the happiness of all. This increases his pain. Thus, one disgrace after another is heaped upon him up to the ultimate disgrace that can be thought of—he is thrown back [into the tower] where he is constantly waiting to be destroyed.

"Hence, one may say that the man is in the king's court, because the tower is in the king's court just as much as the hall where the king is with his beloved friends. But it is well understood that their situation is not the same. This is what happens to the hellish folk about which we have just spoken.

"You should know that their misery lasts eternally. I greatly wonder how anyone who hears this dares to go on sinning.[36] [Furthermore,] you must understand that purgatory in itself is frightful; whoever recognizes this properly stays away from sin. Purgatory is something that comes after time and after judgment.

"When the soul separates from the body in the way I have mentioned before (i.e., in penitence and love and acceptance, [with] all things done through God and all sins left undone through God), it finds itself in great agony because it can do no more than wait until God is moved to pity. And even if that does not happen until Judgment Day, hope is the soul's [only] mode of being. But know that all of this stops on Judgment Day.

"Yet the people who stand in the divine presence remain untouched. When their souls separate from the bodies they remain in the being of the divine presence to the extent to which they have known and loved God. After Judgment Day the being of the body and the being of the soul become one being in the divine presence: That is how you must understand it.

"You shall not be guided by the sayings of even the best masters, because they speak of events such as John's coming into heaven with body and soul, along with other friends of our Lord about whom it is said that they are in God with body and soul for all eternity. That cannot be. Nothing can be in God but God. There is neither mouth nor nose, nor hand, nor foot, nor any of the created parts that belong to the body. From this it does not follow that they have come into God with their bodies. To grasp its meaning you must understand it like this:

"When the time came that John should go hence, God let happen to him what should happen to him on Judgment Day. He did it out of fitting love because he had been a pure vessel. Thus, with divine help the soul's being took with it the being of the body and was elevated. Understand it this way: The body which should have died on the earth was carried away in the air, so that none of it came into God except the being of the body which would have followed the soul on Judgment Day.

"The same thing happened to Mary and to all of whom it is said that they came to God with their bodies."

He says: "Truly, daughter, you are right. Let me tell you that our best masters have disputed this point heatedly."[37]

She says: "I will tell you how you must understand it. We shall approach it through our Lord Jesus Christ and examine his Ascension, as he went to heaven. You know well enough that food and everything coarse and material which Christ had taken into himself must be destroyed in the ascent. It remained in time. Thus, his being came back into the Father. With its divine essence Christ's soul carried the being of the noble humanity of our Lord Jesus Christ [up to God]. In this manner his person resides within the Father so that he is one with the Father. And in the same way, all who receive by grace what Christ has by nature stand within the Father. However, they do not take their materiality with them when they depart. The body remains theirs until Judgment Day when all things become nothing; then the soul receives its being for the first time according to the life [it has] lived. You know very well that for one whom God wants to pardon he will do the same as he has done for John."

He says: "I know it well. If I were to act like St. Dominic, I would become Dominic. St. Dominic sold his books and everything he had and gave it to the poor for the sake of God. Dear daughter, we neither practice that nor many of the virtues Dominic adhered to. On account of that, we remain what we are. We strive to become important clerics and do not live like him.

"St. Francis was a simple man, and because of it God showed him great mercy. In simplicity he went to God in a perfect life, and, thus, he became intimate with God.

"There was an important priest in the land who harbored great hostility within himself because a layman had such familiarity with God. [So] he went to him and said, 'Brother, how shall we understand this? The gospel teaches us to punish the people for their sins.' St. Francis said, 'That is so!'

The priest said, 'I want to punish them, [but] they will punish me twice in return.' St. Francis said, 'It shall not be like that! I can explain the gospel better to you: We must aspire to the purest life of truth with a perfect exterior and interior living, so that we punish all people for their sins with our life.'

"The priest was ashamed and said, 'Brother, God knows, you are telling the truth!' Realize therefore that he who acts like St. Francis becomes St. Francis. I will say more: If we remain distant to life, grace will remain distant to us."[38]

She says: "God be praised that you recognize it!"

He says: "I have known it a long time and know that it must be true, although I do not live accordingly."

She says: "I want you to know that it moves me to pity! You have told me about your saints, now tell me what I ask you: Advise me according to your best knowledge how I shall conduct myself, because you know my life better than all other people!"

He says: "That is true, I do it gladly. You should eat when you are hungry and drink when you are thirsty. You should wear a soft gown and sleep in a soft bed, everything your heart desires in food and entertainment you should take for yourself and live for no one but yourself. If you see everything that God has created go down right before your eyes do not prevent it with a Hail Mary; you should bid all creatures to serve you according to your will, for the glory of God. You shall wear a noble gown which is soft and reside in one place and raise everything up to God. If you want to enjoy all creatures you shall rightfully do so, because any creature you choose to enjoy is brought back to its origin. You know very well whatever you enjoy stands in God for the glory of God."[39]

She says: "I know that you speak the truth. However, you must know that I will never desire anything else but to be a poor person until my death!"

He says: "You are wrong!"

She says: "I will adhere to that wrong as long as I live. I will be outcast and poor, no one can take that from me."

He says: "By my soul, you are doing your God wrong!"

She says: "How so?"

He says: "Because you have everything you want."

She says: "God knows well that I do it for no other reason than to honor the path which guided me to my eternal salvation; as wrong as the path itself has been in time and in eternity, I shall be in eternity and in time. I want you to know that I will never diverge from the path of our Lord Jesus Christ!"

He says: "Understand that God grants you all of it."

She says: "I truly take enough rest now that I don't have as many severe [penitential] exercises as before. But you must know [that] if I can help along all good people who are on the way to their eternal salvation but are not yet confirmed, I will gladly do so. And if I could help all people overcome their sins, I would gladly do so on account of God. I want you to know that since our Lord Jesus Christ exerted himself until his death, it is appropriate that I do the same. My exterior actions will be taken up with the noble life and humanity of our Lord Jesus Christ and with his noble sayings. I shall live according to them in this life.

"I want you to know that the highest powers of my soul are active in the soul of Christ within the heavenly Father. In him they are one being so that they will never lower themselves. Through these powers the Holy Spirit flows from the Father into the soul and from the soul into God; and each power has its own activity in the Holy Spirit and in the Father with the Son, our Lord Jesus Christ. You must understand this in connection with the advice according to which I will live in this life. Furthermore, the 'man' of the soul stands in his confirmation above speech, [both] in work and in time. Furthermore, he stands in a being untouchable by all things. This is not the case with the powers, as we will verify with [the life of] Christ. Be aware that Christ never came out of the Father, not even for a moment. Yet he ate and drank like other human beings and accomplished all of the deeds that other human beings should do with the exception of sin. Christ stood within the Father in his might. He knew and loved his Father as he does now, and was neither more nor less within his Father than he is now. True human being and true God he was then and still is and must remain eternally, according to what we have said earlier. His powers had to operate in this way when he resided in time. Thus, the saying goes that the powers never acted outside the Father.

"Here, we will take the words Christ spoke: 'Put the light into the house, that all the people may see!' (cf. Mt. 5:15–16).

"It tells us that we must always stay in [the same] good image in time as we desire to be in eternity."

He says: "That is true!"

She says: "You must know that many people are led astray by parables and want to work all deeds in the same way.[40] That brings them to their eternal death. They intend to gain the good without toil and trouble, but that can never be. I pity the people who exhibit good behavior in front of others but are false in themselves. I will tell you what happens to them.

"They discipline themselves a little at first. And they are shown a spir-

367

itual light so that they contemplate creation. God does this because he wants
to draw them to their eternal salvation. It is only right that they should continue until they are established."

He says: "Dear daughter, there are few who are established as timely
as you."

She says: "Whose fault is that?"

He says: "The fault is that they do not have enough determination. God
knows that I have never seen the same determination in others as I have in
you."

She says: "God knows well that it is still in me! As far as I could go, I
never wanted to stop until I was established. I knew from the time when I
was a little child that I might obtain by grace what Christ has by nature.
With that knowledge I knew enough. You must understand that I never
wanted to delay; if I still had to do it I would yet obtain a true place with
Christ in the Father."

He says: "Dear daughter, that is [precisely] what I say: They lack the
right determination. They turn back to lower, temporal things and believe
that they have what will never be theirs. In this they are deceived."

She says: "That is true! Imagining and thinking, many wise men are
deceived by it.[41] Therefore, no one should delay before being confirmed in
eternal salvation, which happens in true understanding. You should know
that many people are deceived by the light about which we spoke earlier.
They believe that they are able to accomplish all works in an identical manner and they bring about their eternal death. They are false believers and
say, 'All things are in God. I do as I please and I know very well that I flowed
out of God and that I shall return to my origin.'

"Believe me, these people are true heretics; they do as they wish in time
and they say: 'We have nothing to do with it!' You should know that these
people are dangerous. Guard yourself well against them! They will engage
in all sinful behavior to the extent that they can or dare in front of people,
because they do not take sin for sin. You should know that he who bows to
sinful things, and by himself does his share to be inclined toward sin, never
has divine secrets revealed to him. And understand that he who does not
follow the example of our Lord Jesus Christ, his noble life and sayings to
the fullest extent is in a bad way.

"They say that God is in all things and all things are in God. That is
quite true according to one interpretation. I say that God is not in anything;
God is neither in heaven nor in hell nor on earth. To sum it up, [he is] not
in anything. You should understand it like this: All things are in God and
all creatures ever made take their being from God. (Heaven is created, the

angels are created, both hell and earth are created. In other words, every-thing that was ever named is created.) All these [things are] in God, but God is in them only to the extent to which the creatures have their being from him.

"Now you shall learn about the soul's being. The soul's being is found within. It remains in God eternally to the extent that it draws divine exis-tence toward itself from all creatures. This does not happen in unworthy people who stand in disbelief, about whom we have spoken before. They love their life in its corporeality and cling to vice as their mode of being. That being remains theirs eternally when all things turn to nothing. The existence which the soul brings with itself will be maintained for all eternity."

He says: "That is true. The masters confirm it and say, 'What the soul loves with its being becomes its being and if a soul loves a stone it will be-come a stone.'[42] Therefore, the soul will gladly go to its highest good and will gladly love the highest.

"Saint Augustine said that the soul resides more where it loves than where it gives life to the body.[43] It is a natural aspect of love that everything drawn to it is turned into love. We should therefore get to know and love the very highest so that it may become our own being. [It is] a being which is so noble in itself that the best masters say [about it]: The being of a little flower is better in itself than everything God has ever created. I will say more. The being of a stone is better than God with all of his power if one were to deprive him of his being.[44] I will say more. He who recognizes the being of a pear stem in its highest aspect knows God in all of his might and knows everything God has ever created according to being. Therefore, we must strive for the highest life [so] that God may become the essence of our being."

She says: "It amazes me that a wise soul can be blinded [to the point where] it does not recognize that from which it ought to benefit eternally."

He says: "It happens because of sin. The masters speak of five sins that God hardly ever forgives, neither here nor there. The first sin is to despair of God's mercy.

"The second is to regret a good work.

"Third, to desire the reward of good people in the eternal life. You must understand it like this. We should not desire what belongs to other people, instead we should desire that we benefit from good people. But, we should not desire to possess the place that has become bitter to another. If we wish to possess the state of eternal life we must accomplish it with our own life, as it was shown to us by the truth which is God himself.

"The fourth sin is sinning with the expectation of receiving God's mercy. Know that many people sin and continue in their shortcomings. They would never do so if they thought God was not merciful. That is a dangerous thing.

"The fifth sin is not to live in repentance and penance as called for by the priests and to forget to fear God and say, 'Since I will no longer sin, God has forgiven my sins.' Realize that it is not so. Yet it is true that God forgives the sins of those who seek mercy as they should. You must understand that all sins and all shortcomings must be corrected, either here or there, according to justice as the scripture tells us."

She says: "Why do you put such small penance upon the people?"

He says: "So that they will not despair."

She says: "God knows if I were in your place, I would tell people the truth privately and publicly."

He says: "You know very well that the people cannot understand it."

She says: "If no more than one person understood it you should help him to go forth."

He says: "God knows that if I knew one good person on the right path to his eternal salvation I would help him go forth rather than convert a thousand sinners."

She says: "Truly, you are right. That is confirmed with the words Christ spoke,

" 'What one does to the lowliest person in my name one does to me.' (Mt. 25:45)

"Now you shall learn who the lowliest people are. They are the ones who have a true understanding of the right belief and who stand in our Lord Jesus Christ in a perfect life. These are called the lowliest as it is understood by our Lord. You must know that only a few people followed our Lord Jesus Christ. Yet there were many who condemned and persecuted him. The same still happens to the ones who are in Christ; there are few who believe in him."

He says: "I trust it is true. About this the masters say, 'There are people of the kind who are indebted to God for everything they do, and there are people of another kind to whom God is indebted.'

"Now let us distinguish the [two kinds of] people. The ones who are indebted to God are good, spiritual people who are honored here [on earth] and who guard themselves against sin in everything they can do. They serve God diligently in true obedience until their death. These are the ones who are indebted to God.

"The others to whom God is indebted are those who leave behind honor and property, friends and family, themselves and all bodily comfort. They follow Christ into exile and poverty and go to the places where they are despised. These people do as the apostles did who maintained neither house nor household, nor a place to stay. Where they were despised they stayed; where they were honored they fled (cf. Lk. 10:1–11). These are the people to whom God is indebted. Would you like to know the debt? It is that he himself is that special good which he has reserved for his dearest friends. I know well that he who still wants to acquire it with his life will transcend everything God has ever created."

She says: "That was confirmed for us when Christ praised John and said:

" 'No greater son was ever born of woman!' (Mt. 11:11).

"But he did not say that no greater person shall ever be born. That reassures us that we may transcend all created things."

She says: "It grieves me that the people do not know this."

He says: "I do not find it unjust!"

He says in reply: "You know very well that Mary Magdalene loved Christ in a natural love. She loved his noble humanity in his actual presence and loved him so much that she abandoned all vices and took up all virtues, so that Christ would allow her to be with him and would love her. For Mary Magdalene this was a journey to God. It was not that she loved God, but rather that she specially loved Christ's presence."

She says: "God knows that she did it deservedly because Christ was the most lovable human being ever born. Take note of what it was that caused this.

"The divine truth which was in him and which he was himself shone through his noble humanity. Whoever had proper judgment would readily have recognized both God and human being in Christ. Mary Magdalene was right; she directed her love toward a noble lover. Mary Magdalene was a noble woman by birth and by nature, and therefore, she had a noble and loving heart. Because of it she had to love intensely whatever she loved. She loved the world and loved it so much that whatever love forced out of her had to be truly excellent. The noble sayings of our Lord Jesus Christ and his perfect life and his virtuous way of life and the kindness of his being expelled everything from Mary Magdalene which was not Christ, and thus was she united with Christ's noble humanity. She could no longer do evil, instead she practiced the virtues, so that her lover would stay with her. In this she disciplined herself until the virtues became her being. This is confirmed for us when Mary Magdalene was sitting at the feet of Christ and Martha complained about Mary:

" 'Lord, my sister is idle and will not help me!'

APPENDIX

"Christ said, 'Martha, Martha! You are concerned and worried about many things. Only one thing is necessary. Mary has chosen the better part; it will never be taken from her' (Lk. 10:41–42).[45]

"First, you must understand it like this: The reason Christ spoke twice, 'Martha, Martha!' was for emphasis as if to say, 'the extent to which you love as she does is the extent to which you shall have the benefit of it.'

"Second, Christ spoke twice 'Martha, Martha,' [because] you should know that one must love Christ in all who love him. He deems fitting that everyone should rightly be glad to serve those who love him. Therefore, he spoke twice: 'Martha, Martha, you don't know what I know!'

"Mary Magdalene remained silent for three reasons. The first was that she did not know anything trifling enough that she could have answered Martha with. Secondly, she wanted to use the hour better than to answer her. Thirdly, she wanted to let her lover answer, as should be done by all who love Christ. They should let the lover give instructions.

"You already know that Mary Magdalene performed heroic deeds through love as long as she had Christ in time. We may see it by her action as she sought him at his grave and said: 'If you know where he is show him to me, so that I may carry him with me. I do not mind carrying him' (Jn. 20:15).

"You must understand it like this. Mary thought that all people should know what she knew. This still happens to all of those who are drawn into the knowledge of the highest good. They assume that other people understand what they themselves understand, and [so they] often speak about things which only those who are on their way to a true understanding of eternal truth can comprehend. Concerning this, a saint [once] said: 'The words of lovers are like the words of fools.'

"Now let us say more about Mary Magdalene.

"When she sought Christ and found him, she wanted to touch him. But he withdrew from her and said, 'Mary, do not touch me! We have not yet been made whole in my Father's kingdom' (Jn. 20:17).

"You must understand it like this. Christ lacked nothing, [but] Mary was wanting. And realize that Mary would have fallen to her eternal death if she had not exerted herself earnestly after Christ's death.

"Now understand the [following] saying. After she had seen Christ she ran to the other two Mary's and said:

" 'I have seen my Lord and beloved. He is risen from His death!' (Jn. 20:18). Then she and the women ran [back] to the place, behaving like people who are mad and have suddenly lost their senses. But on the way Christ met them and said: 'Greetings!' And he let them touch him and spoke, 'Women, what are you doing!' Then he chastised them and said, 'Conduct yourselves more prudently!' Yet he could not quiet them [and] they told him everything they knew.

"Christ said: 'Mary!'

"She answered: 'Lord!' recognizing at once that it was Christ because his words were familiar to her heart. She fell to her knees before him in wondrous joy. Christ gave her his foot and let himself be touched (cf. Jn. 20:16; Mt. 28:9).

"You must understand it like this. Mary was made more perfect by the Heavenly Father in this short hour, and her faculties were drawn further into God, and she learned more about God than in the long time in which she had been in the presence of Christ. That is the reason Christ let himself be touched.

"Here Mary experienced her eternal salvation for the first time. Her soul began to lift itself up and began to know and to love God as a good and wise soul ought to know and love her rightful creator.

"This is verified by the fact that she went to all the places where she could proclaim that her creator had risen from his death and that he was both true God and human being. [She] preached the Christian faith as the apostles did and carried out everything a strong man should carry out. You have probably heard it said how Mary Magdalene converted a king and many nonbelievers.[46] But it did no good. She considered it all as nothing and went into the wilderness. There she knew and loved God to the highest degree. She gained sorrow for the first time because she let no barrier stand between her and God.

"Now you know what Mary's life was like in the beginning, when she knew and loved Christ and followed him and his noble sayings and his perfect virtues and his noble life to the very highest.

"Now hear what her life was like after his death. Christ was her guide to the Father. As soon as she recognized the Father in the Son, she went into the wilderness and knew and loved and enjoyed God according to her own will. You must understand that if she had wanted to gain the greatest bodily comfort she would not have made herself like the animals in the forest. Understand that one moment in the wilderness gave her more familiarity with God than the entire presence of Christ had offered her.

"And now hear: Meanwhile the noble humanity of our Lord Jesus Christ and his noble transformation were an obstacle to Mary, and to all of the friends of our Lord. He himself said, 'It is for your own good that I go from you!' (Jn. 16:7). I want you to know that external comfort hinders [all of] us.

"Many people say, 'I will gladly love and obey my confessor!' But [I ask you]: Who heard her confession in the forest? Whom did she obey? Who gave her God's body?[47] And who gave her any comfort?"

He says: "God!"

She says: "That is true. She received God from God; she reached union and was established. The reason Mary Magdalene was in the forest so long was that she had enjoyed so much exterior comfort here on earth that now she had to atone for it.

"There are still many people who serve God in exchange for reward, by which they cause themselves eternal harm.[48]

"Some of them serve God quite diligently so that he may preserve their property and honor and grant them friends and family and bodily health. Understand that they do not recognize Christ.

"Others implore God to appear to them as he was when he was a child, as he was when he walked here in time, and as he was on the cross. In other words, they beg God to appear to them in his external shape [so] that they may look at him with external eyes.[49] They beg for something created and that he make them understand what shall die or live in time, and what God wants to accomplish with his creatures, so that they can gossip about it and receive comfort from it. See, because of this they are accustomed to fast frequently. They pray, dress in [rough] wool, and go barefoot. They offer mass, burn candles, and give their alms. They practice all the virtues they are capable of and they are called and seen as good people.

"You must know that even if they accomplished in this way all of the works the friends of our Lord have accomplished together, God would still not give them eternal reward. However, you must know that God leaves no virtue unrewarded. He rewards the people with what they desire. He secures their honor and property and lets them have bodily ease with friends and with family so that they have their will for a little while. God permits it for two reasons.

"He wants to reward in this life those who serve because of reward. But you should know that those who pray for this are asking for their own damnation!

"The other reason why God permits it is that his own [people] are oppressed. He does it out of pure love so that they may better recognize what he suffered himself, and that he may by right give himself to them as eternal reward.

"The other people about whom we have spoken earlier, who want to see God with exterior eyes, are unbelieving people. Here the devil confirms them in their wrong belief so that they stay with him eternally. In the air he takes from the elements whatever shape he wants and appears to the people when and how he wants to: sometimes as a child with curly hair in the consecrated host; at other times, he appears to them as a youth of twelve or as a pious man of thirty. In other words, he appears to them as the Father and the Son; he appears to them in the shape they desire to see. He speaks with them and explains things to them the way they want [to hear it], as far as he knows how. And you should know that often he tells them the truth, so that he establishes their wrong belief. I tell you his listeners are the most accursed folk ever born. And I will tell you how they come to it in the first place.

"They always do their deeds externally and speak their words externally. What they ought to say to God in their souls they speak with their mouths. The devil knows this well and satisfies their eager desire in order to ensnare them so that they cannot escape him. He pursues them with much skill.

"Exterior works and exterior words: The devil knows them well. Therefore, interior practice is good when the soul raises itself internally to God and converses with God as intimately as it wants and God converses with the soul. The soul may well reach the point at which God reveals all of his secrets as far as the soul can understand them. The devil knows nothing about this, and he will not mingle here, nor can he deceive such people. These are righteous people. You should know that in a [single] moment they come to a point of knowing God in such a way that they can no longer be deceived.

"I know very well that since Christ went to his heavenly Father no one has seen him with exterior eyes. Worthless people say that our Lady appeared to them with her child.

"Understand, since our Lady ascended to heaven out of time, she does not appear to people in this life, nor did she ever appear to any of the saints who went to heaven from this life.[50] However, our Lord and our Lady and the friends of our Lord will come to our help with their mercy in the eternal life and also in this life; therefore, we shall rightfully call on them for everything we are in need of.

"Now I will say more about Mary Magdalene and about the disciples of our Lord. I will make clear to you that they never knew God as long as they were in the presence of Christ.

"You shall recognize it in the exchange in which our Lord asked his disciples: 'What do the people say about the Son of Man and about who I am?' (Mt. 16:13).

"Peter said, 'Some of the people say you are Elijah, others say you are John. And so the people say many things about you.'

"Christ said, 'What do you say about me, about who I am?'

"Peter said, 'I say, Lord, you are Christ, Son of the living God' (Mt. 16:14–16).

"This shows that Peter did not recognize that the great God was within the person of our Lord Jesus Christ. Yet Peter would have spoken the truth if he had said about himself, 'I am the son of the living God!' Understand it this way!

"Everything that was ever created may rightfully say, 'I am a child of God.' According to this, one may better call God a mother than a father because he eternally carried all things within himself. Had Peter known that the almighty God was in front of him, he would have said, 'I know well that you are my Creator, my God and my Lord, and my eternal Father.'

"I want to make this point still clearer to you. When our Lord was on the mountain with his disciples and let the light of the Godhead shine out of himself, they became as if they were so drunk that Peter said, 'Lord, let us remain here always!' And he wanted to make a house for each of them and he forgot himself (Lk. 9:32–33). Our Lord said,

" 'Peter, you have designated a house for each one. Where do you want to live?'

"He said, 'Where you are and where you live, there I also want to live!'

"From that you can recognize that Peter did not know Christ because Christ is perpetually within the Father. Peter lacked that insight.

"Furthermore, you understand that Peter did not know God when he said, 'Lord, let us live here!' Had he recognized the Father in the Son he would not have been satisfied with the joys of this life.

"I will explain it still better to you.

"Once the disciples went all together with our Lord and when Christ walked ahead of them, the disciples began to say evil things to each other about Bartholomew. It irked them that he acted according to his noble up-bringing. You must know that Bartholomew had not yet shed the refined behavior which he had acquired as a nobleman. I don't find this unreasonable.

"If one were to take a sparrow-hawk and a curlew and provided the same care and food for each of them and put them in a cage and wanted to tame them equally, you should know that the sparrow-hawk would quickly die. And so it is with noble people. They may bend and break their own nature so that their life in time is shortened.

"Now you must realize that Christ knew all about their talk and thoughts, but the disciples did not know this. By this you might see that they did not know almighty God. Yet Christ revealed enough miracles to them.

"He told them to go into a house and said, 'Ask to be given food for us for the love of God!'

"The disciples found nothing in the house but a dead man. They returned to Christ and said, 'There is no one inside but a dead man!'

"Christ said, 'Then go and eat him!' The disciples said, 'Alas, shall we eat a dead man?'

"Christ said, 'It is better that you eat the dead than the living.'[51]

"This proves that Christ knew all things and gave us true testimony that slander is harmful to people.

"Now consider what he said: 'It is better that you eat the dead than the living!' You must take care for God's sake to forgive all people whom you want to forgive you.

"But now we understand that the disciples did not know the Father.

"Philip said, 'Lord, show us the Father' (Jn. 14:8).

"Had Philip known that the Father was present in the Son he would not have asked. By this we learn that they recognized nothing but Christ's presence.

"I will still better explain to you that they did not know the Father.

"When they sat at the Lord's Supper and he gave them his holy body and his holy blood, they were all ignorant people (cf. Mt. 26:26–29). They did not believe that a man sat among them and gave them his own body and his own blood. Now you shall learn about a wondrous love. Even though Christ knew that Judas would betray him, he gave him his holy body and his holy blood. Christ knew from the beginning that Judas would betray him, yet he still treated him as well as he did the others and made signs for his sake and performed all the works he did for the other disciples. He was as true an example for [Judas] as he was for John and for Peter and his other beloved disciples. But Judas remained evil; that was a fault in Judas and not in Christ.

"Thanks be to you, Christ, my Lord and my God, that you treated him so kindly while you had certain knowledge that he would betray you.

"Lord, you also knew that Judas was a thief and an unchaste man and full of all vices, and still you kindly let him be with you. With this you have given me a sign of love, that with my whole heart I shall truly love those who do me wrong in this life.

"You should know that there are many who are like Judas. They say, 'If God gave me as much grace as he gives to others, I would be as good as the other people!' They become true comrades of Judas. They do not admit that Christ has been as much an example to them as he has been to good people. Christ exemplified the truth for all who want to follow him. Christ did his part for all people so perfectly that no one can blame him. If we did as we should, God would do as we wished. Worthless people are in the habit of blaming God. They want to excuse themselves by blaming him and they punish God without knowing it. No matter how much good he does them, they find another excuse and say, 'If such and such would happen to me, I would become good.' They always want things to go according to their own will. These are the people who do not recognize God and do not know that all things are ordered in God according to the very best. They are the comrades of Judas and they continue in their misguided arrogance and self-satisfaction. Among them mingles the third fellow, Lucifer, who reassures them in their wrong belief so that they adopt the life of Judas and Lucifer as their own. Thus, it becomes their real being and their second nature so that they can seldom or never escape from it. You shall know that this manner of being and worthless company remains theirs eternally.

"Now we shall further say that if the disciples had recognized the Father in the Son, Peter would not have denied him on account of a maidservant (Jn. 18:25).

"From this we learn that if they had known the Father in Christ, they would not have fled (Mk. 14:50). They would have been glad to suffer their death with Christ. There are still many people like that who like to hear about Christ, but only with pain do they experience his life, discomfort, and the shameful treatment which should be endured rightfully and joyfully in his name. The reason for this is that they do not want to acknowledge what they are told.

"That the disciples did not know the Father can be seen in the fact that Thomas did not want to believe that Christ had risen (Jn. 20:24–25). Had he known the Father in the Son it would have seemed a small thing to him. Here Christ once more gave us a sign of his love, in that he showed kindness toward Thomas and let himself be touched as a true sign so that he might believe. He said:

" 'Thomas, you are blessed for you have seen and touched me. More blessed are those who have neither seen nor touched me and who still believe the truth in me' (Jn. 20:27–29).

"You can see that the disciples did not recognize the Father in the Son by the fact that they locked themselves in a house and dared not show themselves to anyone. Had they known the Father in the Son they would have wandered boldly among the people without any fear. But in this situation

378

Christ acted like a true friend and beloved. He had mercy on his disciples and comforted them in a friendly way. He appeared to them within their locked doors and said:

" 'Peace be with you!' (Jn. 20:19).

"You shall understand it like this. If Christ had had something better which would have given them more help at that time he would have given it to them. Do you know what kind of peace Christ meant? It is the peace in which the human being ascends by the powers of his soul and recognizes his Creator in all creatures and directs all his powers to the highest good until he is united with God. [He does this] so that he might remain untouched by everything that may happen to him within time and that he might accomplish all works without being hindered and stand godlike within our Lord Jesus Christ in order to receive all things directly in the Father without intermediary. You should know that these people possess the right peace. This was the peace Christ meant when he said, 'Peace be with you!' Christ knew well what they still had to suffer, but they did not know it. They still had to suffer more without any relief and without the help of any creatures.

"You must know that Christ had continued to be their abode until now. He told them what they should do, and with his own well-lived life he was an example to them in their pursuit of eternal salvation. Now, they had to do without this noble presence and all external comfort when he said [to them], 'I have to go from you, which is good for you. Now, the Holy Spirit of truth will be sent to you' (Jn. 16:7).

"Now for the first time you should understand the story.

"Because all exterior comfort was taken from them, their souls raised themselves internally with all of their strength, toward the Creator. Then the Holy Spirit flowed from the Father and the Son into their souls. They were illuminated in the Holy Spirit so that they might know the truth. They saw and recognized the Father in the Son and the Son in the Father and knew the Holy Spirit which flowed from the two persons into their souls. For the first time, they recognized who had gone before them, and now they followed Him for the first time with a perfect life. We can observe this in many ways:

"First, they became strong in the Holy Spirit so that they could withstand all that was not God.

"[Second], they became brave in the Holy Spirit [so] that they stood by the truth in every situation and never again left it for any reason, and overcame all fear.

"Third, they became wise and learned in the Holy Spirit to distinguish all things. The Holy Spirit taught them various languages so that they surpassed many wise priests with the truth. Now note this wonder: They who before had been fishermen and farmers became the princes of Holy Christianity in heaven and on earth.

"Fourth, they became so noble-spirited that they paid no attention to anyone's honor but to their Lord's. They proclaimed it publicly and preached the truth everywhere, before lords and servants, before Jews and heathens. No prince was so mighty in their eyes that they feared him, and so they did not stray from the truth on account of anyone."

He says: "That is true."

She says: "How do you understand it? Do you believe that Peter saw God with exterior eyes?"

He says: "God knows that I don't know the answer!"

She says: "I will explain it to you. Christ was in Peter, and Peter was in Christ with the power of his soul, and he saw God and read the book of life in the Godhead. Understand that Peter would never have come to that if he had remained attached to mediation. Do you recognize the final intermediary which Peter, and with him all of our Lord's disciples, had to give up before they reached their highest good?

"We can see the same thing in Mary Magdalene.

"She did everything the apostles did in a perfect life. She went into all the lands in which she could preach Christianity and reveal the truth. You must know that Mary Magdalene accomplished more in a shorter time than any of the apostles.

"Now I will explain to you why she went into the forest. It was because Mary was a loving woman and the people were very fond of her. She went into the forest so that she would not have any comfort from creatures and that she would stay solely in the eternal good, which is God. One says of Mary Magdalene that she was a wife. I say it is not so! I shall prove it to you with many examples:

"Mary Magdalene had neither husband nor child. That is the first thing. I will explain it to you still better. I am sure you are aware of the fact that like loves like naturally. You know that Christ would never have loved Mary Magdalene so sincerely if she had not been a pure maiden, nor would he have been so intimate with her, nor would Mary Magdalene have been able to love Christ as much as she did if she had not been a pure human being.

"Second, she was sincere and steadfast in her love.

"Third, she always had a heart full of love which could never be exhausted.

"Fourth, she stayed with Christ, whom she loved, and was faithful to him after his death. She knew her lover and loved him and followed him virtuously and never turned away from him.

"These are true signs of a maiden!"

He says: "Dear daughter, I would like to have this explained to me: One reads about her that Christ drove seven devils out of her as she lay at his feet (Mk. 16:9; Lk. 8:2). The masters say those were the seven deadly sins."

She says: "The masters are correct! I will explain it to you.

"The first one is pride, the second anger, the third avarice, the fourth gluttony and drunkenness, the fifth envy and hatred, the sixth idleness in God's service, the seventh lechery.

"You must understand it like this. One can be unchaste with many things without the help of any person. This happened to Mary Magdalene.

"She committed the sin that is called lechery [when] she loved herself excessively with words and adornments and public demeanor. She gave people a bad example, so that they were necessarily annoyed by her. These were the seven deadly sins which Christ drove from Mary Magdalene. He said:

" 'Magdalene, you are forgiven many sins because you have loved so much!' (Lk. 7:47).

"Thus, Christ became Mary Magdalene's lover as I have told you before, he was her noble guide to the Father and was her direct mediator as long as she had him in time, as it was with the disciples about whom you have already heard."

He says: "Dear daughter, may God reward you for your noble instructions."

She says: "I will tell you still more. I have told you all this so that you understand that one must go through all things and must be despised and tested before one achieves the next stage. Then this intermediary stage must cease so that we are in the mediator and that no mediation [any longer] remains between us and God.[52]

"This is the reason why I feel pity for the people who claim to see God with exterior eyes and who say that God has a mouth and nose, hands and feet. You must know if I had a God who could be seen with exterior eyes and comprehended with exterior senses and could be conversed with in exterior speech, and would thus be such a little God that he had hands and feet, I would never say a Hail Mary because of him!

"That is why I praise the worthy name of our Lord Jesus Christ who has revealed to me a steady and pure life so that I may know and love the great God in his person."

He says: "But how, dear daughter, could Christ ever hide himself from his disciples as long as he was with them, so that they did not recognize his divinity in spite of his accomplishments?"

She says: "I will tell you: if Christ would have revealed himself and would have let the great divinity which was in him shine forth, the disciples and all people would have been destroyed by the power of the great Godhead. Therefore, the Father hid himself in the Son so that the people could know and love him to the extent to which they were able to grasp him, some more and others less, according to their readiness. Christ recognized very well that the disciples were not ready to receive more than he gave them to understand.

"The reason for this was that they were not yet prepared, and the powers of their souls were not yet skilled. They viewed the noble intermediary externally and did not see what was in him. But because the mediator penetrated their external eyes they saw the great God inside the mediator with their inner vision, and they united with the great God through the mediator. Understand it like this: Afterwards, they stood raised up in the divine form of our Lord Jesus Christ and received from God all things out of the origin of divine truth without mediation.

"You should know [that] if God were to reveal himself in the consecrated host on the altar between the hands of the priest as he truly is, the eyes of the people would break; they could not endure it. I will say more: If God revealed himself as he truly is in the tiniest kernel of the consecrated host, everyone in the church would turn to nothing. Even if they had all the powers available to human beings, they could still not bear it. Thus, you can see that those who say they know God with external eyes are not right. God's splendor and might is unknown to them!

"One may recognize the body of God on the altar as true God and man in the hands of the priest. This, however, takes place [only] in the right belief, in understanding and in love. And thus, we are guided to our eternal salvation. This should be a certainty for us rather than a [mere] belief. Should I doubt that God, who can accomplish everything, is capable of this?"

She says: "God knows that I have known everything one may say about belief since the time I was able to distinguish good from bad."

He says: "Dear daughter, explain this to me for the love of God: The masters say, a thousand souls in heaven sit on the point of a pin.[53] Tell me how I shall understand it!"

She says: "The masters tell the truth and it should be understood in the following way. The soul which comes into God has neither place nor time, nor any nameable feature that one could formulate in words. Furthermore,

I tell you truly, if one were to mark the place which is occupied by a soul, it would be much larger than heaven and earth and everything that God ever created. I will say more:

"If God had created as many heavens and earths and as many worlds as he created creatures, it would still be less than the point of a pin compared to the place which is the alloted share of the soul that is united in God."

The daughter said more and came to talk of God. She was saying so much about God that the confessor said, "Dear daughter, speak on, speak on!" The daughter tells him so much about the greatness and power and the providence of God that he loses his senses and has to be helped to a sheltered cell where he lies for a long time before regaining consciousness.[54]

VII

As he regains his senses, he begs urgently that one should call the daughter to him. It is done and the daughter comes to the confessor, addresses him and **says:** "How are you now?"

He says: "I am very well! Praise be to God that he created you as a human being because you have guided me to my eternal salvation. I was drawn into a divine manifestation and have been given proof of everything I have heard from your mouth. O dear daughter, by the love you have for God, I urge you to help me with words and deeds so that I may win a place where I have now been!"

She says: "Understand that it cannot be, you are not prepared for it! Only when your soul and the powers of your soul are accustomed to the way up and down, like a member of the household who goes in and out of the house, and when you are able to distinguish the heavenly host and everything which God ever created, and you are lacking nothing in this regard, [and] you know everything as well as any good man knows about his household, then you shall recognize the difference between God and the Godhead.[55] Now you must learn the difference between the Spirit and Spirituality.[56] Only then shall you strive after permanence. You must not withdraw; you must seek activity with creatures by which you will not be harmed, as they themselves will remain without harm. With this you must gather your strength so that you will not go mad. This you must do often, until the powers of the soul are spurred on and you come into the knowledge of which I spoke earlier."

APPENDIX

Praised and honored be the sweet name of our Lord Jesus Christ. Amen.

Notes

Translated from Franz-Josef Schweitzer, Der Freiheitsbegriff der deutschen Mystik *(Frankfurt am Main: Peter Lang, 1981), pp. 322–70.*

1. See *STh* Ia IIae. 68. 4, on the seven gifts of the Holy Spirit. Mt. 25:31–46 is the scriptural source for the six works of charity.
2. The notion of the soul's return to the source from which it has "flowed out" (MHG *geflossen ist*) is characteristic of Eckhart's thought. Cf. *Essential Eckhart*, pp. 30, 37–42.
3. The "friends of God," or "friends of the Lord," appear frequently in the text (e.g., pp. 363, 364, 371, 373, 374, 375). This clearly relates the "Sister Catherine" to the circles of fourteenth-century German mystics who adopted such scriptural terms (e.g., Jn. 15:15, Jm. 2:23) as a self-identification. For an introduction, see A. Chiquot, "Amis de Dieu," *Dictionnaire de spiritualité* (Paris: Beauchesne, 1937–), Vol. 1, cc. 493–500.
4. The notion of the thief whose pain is increased by seeing others who are filled with joy is discussed in another mystical text of the same period. Cf. Josy Seitz, *Der Traktat des "Unbekannten deutschen Mystikers" bei Greith* (Rudolstadt: Mitzlaff, 1936).
5. Cf. Augustine, *Conf.* 10.7.9.
6. See Eckhart's comments on this verse in Sermon XLV nn. 460–63 (pp. 230–31).
7. Cf. another pseudo-Eckhartian treatise, "Von der edelkeit der sele," in F. Pfeiffer, *Deutsche Mystiker des Vierzehnten Jahrhunderts. Vol. 2. Meister Eckhart* (Leipzig: Göschen, 1857), pp. 382–94.
8. On "man" and "woman" in this sense, see *Par. Gen.* nn. 135–65 (*Essential Eckhart*, pp. 108–21).
9. Many of the nuns' lives of the thirteenth and fourteenth centuries deal with the "beginning and end" of the life of Christ. Compare this text also with "Regle des fins amans," which distinguishes among four ways of considering the beginning and end of Christ. Cf. Karl Christ, "Le Regle des fin amans—Eine Beginenregel aus dem Ende des 13. Jahrhunderts," *Philologische Studien aus dem romanischen-germanischen Kulturkreise. Festschrift für Karl Voretzsch*, ed. B. Schadel and W. Mulertt (Halle: Niemeyer, 1927), pp. 173–213.
10. This is the first appearance of female role models in the "Sister Catherine" text. Except for the brief reference to Mary of Egypt below (p. 353), the figure of Mary Magdalene will receive all the emphasis.
11. A reference to the late medieval German version of the popular legend of the

384

APPENDIX

converted harlot, Mary of Egypt; see "Von Sand Maria Egiptcitata," in chap. 16 of Erich Gierach, ed., *Das Märterbuch* (Berlin: Weidmann, 1928).

12. The notion of the "birth of the Word in the soul" appears to be the source of this formula. See *Essential Eckhart*, pp. 51–55.

13. "Without a question" (MHG: *sunder war vmbe*), a key theme of Eckhart's mysticism. See *Essential Eckhart*, pp. 59–60, and the Glossary.

14. The notion of leaving oneself behind is also found in the treatise "Von der edelkeit der sele" (Pfeiffer, *Deutsche Mystiker*, Vol. 2, p. 393).

15. See Adolf Spamer, ed., *Texte aus der deutschen Mystik des 14. und 15. Jahrhunderts* (Jena: Diederichs, 1912), p. 111, who notes that this saying is part of a collection of sentences attributed to Eberhart of Ebrach.

16. The translation "busy yourself" (MHG: *vbe dich*) can also mean "discipline yourself."

17. In the sense of "hear my confession."

18. This sentence strongly resembles a passage in the legend "Meister Eckhart's Daughter," Pfeiffer, *Deutsche Mystiker*, p. 625, lines 27–28.

19. The "state of emptiness" (MHG: *blosheit*) suggests Eckhart's notion of detachment (*abegescheidenheit*) and emptiness (*lûterkeit*). Cf. the Glossary.

20. This passage has been interpreted by many to mean that the "Sister Catherine" treatise either belongs to the "Free Spirit" heresy, or else is guilty of some form of pantheism. For an alternate possibility, see Introduction, pp. 12–13.

21. The parallel to Christ's three days in the tomb is unmistakable.

22. Cf. Rm. 8:17. The notion of "joint heirs" with Christ is frequent in Eckhart.

23. The following ten points may have been an independent short text absorbed into the "Sister Catherine." See R. E. Lerner, *The Heresy of the Free Spirit*, pp. 218–19.

24. On the importance of "being established," see Introduction, pp. 12–14.

25. The following exchange is based on Eckhart's notion of the identity of ground between God and the soul that allows for the soul's being described as "containing," or even "creating," all things. See the Bull of condemnation ("In agro dominico"), article 13 (*Essential Eckhart*, p. 79).

26. See Eckhart's famous Sermon 52 (*Essential Eckhart*, pp. 202–03).

27. See Eckhart, Sermon 20a (DW I, p. 328), and especially Sermon 69 (p. 311).

28. See Eckhart, Sermon 52 (*Essential Eckhart*, p. 202).

29. See Sermon 16b (p. 278).

30. Cf. Eckhart, Sermon 83 (*Essential Eckhart*, pp. 207–08).

31. The basic doctrine here is Eckhartian, e.g., Sermon 59 (p. 309), and *Bened.* 2 (*Essential Eckhart*, pp. 240–47). The image of oil on a cloth appears in Nicholas of Strassburg, Sermon 6, in Pfeiffer, *Deutsche Mystiker*, Vol. 1, pp. 276–77.

32. Cf. Eckhart, Sermon 26 (DW II, pp. 26–27).

33. Cf. Eckhart, *Couns.* 20 (*Essential Eckhart*, p. 273).

34. This notion of a purely spiritual resurrection is close to that argued by John the Scot in his *Periphyseon* 5.8. See Introduction, p. 14.

APPENDIX

35. The MHG text here can also bear the sense "the man has often sinned against his life."
36. Cf. Nicholas of Strassburg in Pfeiffer, *Deutsche Mystiker*, Vol. 1, p. 296.
37. "Our best masters" probably refers to Thomas Aquinas and Bonaventure, both of whom argued for a bodily ascension. See Introduction, p. 14.
38. The perfect union of exterior and interior living found in St. Francis and the admonition not to remain distant from life are reminiscent of the message found in Eckhart's Sermon 86 (pp. 338–44).
39. The confessor's advice here seems to hint at the antinomian tendencies ascribed to the "Free Spirit" heretics, but since this clashes with the general sketch of his character portrayed throughout the text, it seems better to take it as a form of test of the sincerity of the daughter's confirmation or establishment.
40. The MHG "das si wellen alle werck in einer gelicheit wircken" is vague.
41. The attack on false mysticism that follows should be compared with other attacks on the part of Eckhart's disciples, e.g., Henry Suso, *Little Book of Truth* 6; John Tauler, Sermon 54. Cf. also Jan van Ruusbroec, *Little Book of Enlightenment*.
42. Cf. Eckhart, Sermon 40 (p. 302).
43. The text is actually from Bernard of Clairvaux, *Precept and Dispensation* 20.60, and was often cited by Eckhart, e.g., Sermon 6 (*Essential Eckhart*, p. 186).
44. Cf. Eckhart, Sermon 8 (DW I, p. 134).
45. This traditional interpretation appears in Eckhart's Latin works, e.g., *Comm. Jn.* n. 130 (*Essential Eckhart*, p. 173), but not in his noted Sermon 86 (pp. 338–44).
46. For the legendary details of Mary Magdalene's career, see the account of her life (under July 22) in Jacobus de Voragine, *The Golden Legend* (New York: Arno, 1969), pp. 355–64.
47. The role of the Eucharist in the mystical life was the subject of much discussion at this time. See, e.g., Tauler, Sermons 32–33, 60f.; and the passages below on pp. 377, 382.
48. An important theme in Eckhart, cf. *Comm. Ex.* nn. 272–74 (pp. 126–27).
49. Eckhart condemns those who want to behold God with the same eyes with which they see a cow in Sermon 16b (p. 278).
50. Eckhart's indifference to visionary experiences is carried a step further here and in what follows.
51. This apocryphal story is obviously related to Mt. 8:22 and parallels ("Let the dead bury the dead"). There are also some texts in Gnostic sources that deal with the theme of eating what is dead—e.g., "In the days when you consumed what is dead, you made it what is alive" (Gospel of Thomas 11, in James M. Robinson, ed., *The Nag Hammadi Library* [New York: Harper and Row, 1977], p. 119); and "This world is a corpse-eater. All the things eaten in it themselves die also" (Gospel of Philip 73, *ibid.*, p. 144). The exact source, however, remains a mystery. (My thanks to Robert M. Grant and Hans-Dieter Betz for help in interpreting this passage.)

52. The notion of being united to God "without a medium" (MHG *âne mittel*) is important in Eckhart's mysticism. See *Essential Eckhart*, p. 56.

53. This is doubtless related to the famous question of how many angels could dance on the head of a pin. Thomas Aquinas in *STh* Ia. 52. 3 denies that many angels can be in one place at the same time, and there is no known medieval source for this famous example of scholastic quibbling. According to M. O'C. Walshe in "On Translating Eckhart," *German Life and Letters* 30 (1977):154–55, this is the earliest known example of something like the idea.

54. The confessor finally arrives at ecstatic union (though not "establishment") through the enlightenment given him by the Beguine. This may be taken as the dramatic culmination of the text.

55. The distinction between God and the Godhead is one of the more controversial aspects of Eckhart's thought; cf. *Essential Eckhart*, pp. 33–37.

56. "Spirituality" translates the MHG *geistlichhait*. This is obviously related to the God/Godhead distinction, but it is not found in Eckhart and its exact import is not clear.

A GLOSSARY OF ECKHARTIAN TERMS

Eckhart's linguistic and speculative genius is evident both in his MHG and in his Latin works. Indeed, one of the most fascinating aspects of the Meister's thought is the complex interplay between the two sides of his efforts to express the mystery of God and the soul. Many studies of Meister Eckhart's MHG vocabulary and usage exist, but relatively few of his Latin scholastic language. Still, some of the most illuminating contributions to the study of Eckhart have been attentive to this interaction between scholastic terms (many of which Eckhart uses in a highly personal way) and the rich and fluid MHG speculative vocabulary of his sermons and treatises.

As a contribution to the further study of Eckhart, the Glossary given here singles out some of the most crucial technical terms found in both the Latin and the MHG works and gives references to at least their appearances in this volume, as well as in the *Essential Eckhart*. Obviously, there are problems involved in using a Glossary keyed to Latin and MHG terms for the interpretation of the *Essential Eckhart* and *Meister Eckhart: Teacher and Preacher* (here abbreviated as *Teacher and Preacher*) both of which contain English texts without the facing originals. Nevertheless, the efforts made by the translators of both volumes to adopt, if not a standard, at least an arguably coherent translation procedure for such technical terms help to facilitate this move from the original languages to some of their possible modern equivalents and vice versa.

The limitations of the following Glossary need to be stressed. First of all, it is restricted to the texts translated in these two volumes and the linguistic decisions of the translators involved. Second, it chooses some key Latin and MHG terms to the exclusion of others. And third, it does not pretend to analyze the full range of meanings, nor to give all possible references to the terms, even in the texts translated here. With these important qualifications, we offer the following Glossary as a help for those who undertake the study of Meister Eckhart through these two volumes in the Classics of Western Spirituality.

GLOSSARY

In this Glossary we have tried to give bibliographical references to some of the most useful secondary studies of the terms surveyed. It may also be helpful at the outset to mention a few general works of major importance for the study of Eckhart's vocabulary.

The only useful general handbook of Eckhart's terminology is devoted to MHG terms, though it does not lack important references to Latin equivalents. This is the monograph of Benno Schmoldt, *Die deutsche Begriffsprache Meister Eckharts: Studien zur philosophischen Terminologie des Mittelhochdeutschen* (Heidelberg: Quelle and Meyer, 1954), a necessary tool for all Eckhart scholarship. Two articles by masters of German Eckhart research are worth mentioning as general pieces of value. Josef Quint's 1953 article, "Mystik und Sprache: Ihr Verhältnis zueinander, insbesondere in der spekulativen Mystik Meister Eckeharts," reprinted in *Altdeutsche und altniederländische Mystik*, edited by Kurt Ruh (Darmstadt: Wissenschaftliche Buchgesellschaft, 1964), pp. 113–51, is probably still the best short study of Eckhart's MHG language. Though it surveys the whole range of MHG and not just Eckhart's writings, Kurt Ruh's article, "Die trinitarische Spekulation in deutscher Mystik und Scholastik," *Zeitschrift für deutsche Philologie* 72 (1953): 24–53, is a major contribution worthy of consultation on anything relating to vocabulary on the Trinity. Among general works, also see Kurt Berger, *Die Ausdrücke der Unio mystica im Mittelhochdeutschen* (Berlin: Ebering, 1935).

In English the most helpful brief piece surveying the major terms of Eckhart's mystical vocabulary in MHG is John D. Caputo, "Fundamental Themes of Meister Eckhart's Mysticism," *The Thomist* 42 (1978): 197–225.

A. Latin Glossary.

actio—passio (also *actus—potentia, operatio;* and cf. *forma—materia*)
These are the Aristotelian terms that Eckhart uses to analyze any form of activity or work. *Actio* is easily translated as "action" or "act"; *passio* is much more difficult to render, since it can mean anything from the root "capacity to be acted upon" through a wide variety of more particular examples.
a. Major appearances: *Essential Eckhart*, pp. 73, 96, 101–03, 131–32, 146–47, 160, 162–63; *Teacher and Preacher*, pp. 55–56, 65, 69, 87–88, 170–71, 192.
b. Other places: *Essential Eckhart*, pp. 41, 73, 85, 90, 105, 109, 116, 126, 134–35, 139–40, 143–46; *Teacher and Preacher*, pp. 42, 47–48, 50, 51–53, 57, 59–

389

60, 62, 65, 72, 76, 93–94, 103, 109, 122, 127, 148, 150, 153, 156, 158–59, 162, 164, 169–70, 173, 175, 177, 180, 183–84, 190–91, 193, 210, 221, 226.

aeternitas (see MHG *nû*)
"Eternity," a crucial concept that was one of the major sources of controversy about Eckhart's thought.
a. Major appearances: *Essential Eckhart* p. 78; *Teacher and Preacher*, pp. 58, 70–73, 230.
b. Other places: *Essential Eckhart*, pp. 75, 84–85, 141; *Teacher and Preacher*, pp. 48, 50, 83, 96, 152, 157, 164.

analogia
"Analogy," one of Eckhart's tools for speaking about God, has been much studied by Eckhart scholars. See especially J. Koch, "Zur Analogielehre Meister Eckharts," *Mélanges offerts à Etienne Gilson* (Paris: Vrin, 1959), pp. 73–103; and Alain de Libera, *Le problème de l'être chez Maître Eckhart: logique et métaphysique de l'analogie*, Cahiers de la revue de théologie et philosophie 4, 1980.
a. Major appearances: *Essential Eckhart*, pp. 32–33; *Teacher and Preacher*, pp. 23–27, 178–79.
b. Other places: *Essential Eckhart*, pp. 73, 124, 159; *Teacher and Preacher*, p. 61.

bonum (also *bonitas*) (This term needs to be considered along with the other classic "transcendental" predications, *esse, unum, verum.*)
Easily translated as the "good," "goodness," or sometimes when referring to God as "Goodness Itself" (*ipsa bonitas*), it is more difficult to be sure just how far Eckhart thought the term applicable to divine things in themselves.
a. Major appearances: *Essential Eckhart*, pp. 32–37, 80; *Teacher and Preacher*, pp. 25–26, 27–30, 74, 155–61 (metaphysical good), 161–66 (moral good), 167, 187–88, 224, 237.
b. Other places: *Essential Eckhart*, pp. 44, 73, 106, 120–21, 149, 152, 159, 166; *Teacher and Preacher*, pp. 45, 63, 66–67, 69, 82, 89, 97, 107, 110, 120, 126, 127, 128, 148, 154, 166, 172, 174, 178, 182, 183, 185, 186, 193, 211, 218, 219, 230. (For a discussion in MHG, see *Bened.* 1 in *Essential Eckhart*.)

caritas (also *amor*)
Translated diversely as "charity" or "love." For some remarks on Eckhart's idea of love, see B. McGinn, "St. Bernard and Meister Eckhart," *Cîteaux* 31 (1980): 373–86.
a. Major appearances: *Essential Eckhart*, pp. 48–50, 58; *Teacher and Preacher*, pp. 76–78, 103–04, 122, 156–57, 180–81, 212–14.
b. Other places: *Essential Eckhart*, pp. 46, 76, 79–80, 152; *Teacher and Preacher*, pp. 74, 97, 127, 153, 161, 177, 186, 191, 209, 219, 224, 227, 235.

GLOSSARY

creatio (see MHG *nû*)

"Creation" is the mode of external activity proper to God. In order to understand it fully, the discussions of *creatio* need to be compared with those listed under *emanatio*, as well as in more general fashion with those under *actio—passio*.

    a. Major appearances: *Essential Eckhart*, pp. 39–45, 77–80, 83–91, 96–107; *Teacher and Preacher*, pp. 147–54.

    b. Other places: *Essential Eckhart*, pp. 75–76, 142, 148, 152; *Teacher and Preacher*, pp. 46, 51–52, 77, 187–88, 209, 218, 230, 237.

distinctio—indistinctio (adj., *distinctus—indistinctus;* see also *similis—dissimilis* and the MHG *underscheit*)

"Distinction" characterizes creatures, while "indistinction" is proper to God and things insofar as they are one with God. God is sometimes called *indistinctum*, that is, the Indistinct. These are the fundamental terms of Eckhart's language of dialectic, on which see especially V. Lossky, *Théologie négative et connaissance de Dieu chez Maître Eckhart* (Paris: Vrin, 1960); M. de Gandillac, "La 'dialectique' de Maître Eckhart," *La mystique rhénane* (Paris: Presses universitaires de France, 1963), pp. 59–94; and B. McGinn, "Meister Eckhart on God as Absolute Unity," *Neoplatonism and Christian Thought* (Albany: SUNY Press, 1982), pp. 128–39.

    a. Major appearances: *Essential Eckhart*, pp. 56, 160; *Teacher and Preacher*, pp. 63, 79–80, 166–70, 209–10.

    b. Other places: *Essential Eckhart*, pp. 36–37, 42, 44, 49, 58, 78, 94, 100, 161; *Teacher and Preacher*, pp. 5, 19, 22, 25, 55, 68, 79, 81–82, 96, 154–55, 172, 175, 182, 187, 210, 213, 218, 224.

emanatio (see MHG *ûzbruch*, and see also *generatio* and especially *imago*)

"Emanation" indicates the origin or "flowing out" of all things from the divine source, and can be used both of the processions of the Persons in the Trinity (*bullitio*) and of the production of all created beings (*ebullitio*). Eckhart employed several equivalent Latin terms for this process, e.g., *origo, fons, egressus, effluxus,* and we may even argue *quo est* (cf. *Teacher and Preacher*, pp. 58, 72, 216). On the trinitarian dimensions, see K. Ruh, "Die trinitarische Spekulation in deutscher Mystik und Scholastik."

    a. Major appearances: *Essential Eckhart*, pp. 30–31, 124–25; *Teacher and Preacher*, pp. 236–37.

    b. Other places: *Essential Eckhart*, pp. 37–38, 85, 94, 96, 99, 129–30, 134, 152; *Teacher and Preacher*, pp. 46, 71, 125, 160, 167, 172–73, 185, 187, 188, 190, 191, 217, 218, 236.

GLOSSARY

(*bullitio—ebullitio:* usually literally translated as "boiling" and "boiling over."
 a. Major appearances: *Essential Eckhart,* pp. 37–38, 51–52; *Teacher and Preacher,* pp. 46, 236–37.
 b. Other places: *Essential Eckhart,* pp. 31, 39, 41, 47; *Teacher and Preacher,* pp. 172–73, 218, 219.

esse (see MHG *wesen*)
 Translated as "existence" or the "act of existence" (the term *ens* is rendered as "being" or "a being"). This is the most important single term in Eckhart's vocabulary and he uses it in a variety of ways, of which some of the most significant are sketched below. There is a large body of literature devoted to the word, on which we can note: V. Lossky, *Théologie négative et connaissance de Dieu chez Maître Eckhart;* Karl Albert, *Meister Eckharts These vom Sein* (Saarbrücken: Universitäts-und Schulbuchverlag, 1976); Ruedi Imbach, *Deus est Intelligere: Das Verhältnis von Sein und Denken in seiner Bedeutung für das Gottesverständnis bei Thomas von Aquin und in den Pariser Quaestionen Meister Eckharts* (Freiburg, Switzerland: Universitätsverlag, 1976); A. de Libera, *Le problème de l'être chez Maître Eckhart.*
 a. *Major appearances: Essential Eckhart,* pp. 32–37, 89, 137, 144–45, 163; *Teacher and Preacher,* pp. 21–23, 25–26, 45–49, 95–97, 166–70, 187–88, 225–26.
 b. Other places: *Essential Eckhart,* pp. 54, 73, 75–77, 83, 86–88, 90–91, 94, 99, 103–05, 115, 124, 133, 135, 140, 150, 153, 156, 158–59, 166, 171; *Teacher and Preacher,* pp. 27, 50–51, 52–53, 54, 55, 57, 58–60, 63, 66–67, 68–70, 72, 74, 79–80, 82, 84, 87, 88–89, 93–94, 99, 102, 124, 125, 147–55, 159, 160–61, 173, 175–78, 182, 183, 184, 186, 189–90, 191, 208–09, 212–14, 218, 219–20, 221, 224, 236–37.

(*esse a se—esse ab alio:* "necessary existence" and "dependent existence," or "existence from another."
 a. Major appearances: *Essential Eckhart,* pp. 83, 87; *Teacher and Preacher,* p. 79.
 b. Other places: *Essential Eckhart,* pp. 140, 144, 159–60; *Teacher and Preacher,* pp. 46, 48, 95, 101, 102.

(*esse hoc et hoc* (or *esse tale, esse determinatum)—esse simpliciter* (or *esse absolutum*): "particular, or determined existence" as contrasted with God's "simple, or absolute existence." (See MHG *diz noch daz.*)
 a. Major appearances: *Essential Eckhart,* pp. 137, 140; *Teacher and Preacher,* pp. 172, 176.
 b. Other places: *Essential Eckhart,* pp. 33, 96, 161, 187; *Teacher and Preacher,* pp. 27, 45, 51, 166, 220–21 (cf. the comparable term *bonum hoc et illud* on pp. 156, 219).

GLOSSARY

(*esse virtuale—esse formale* (or *esse formaliter inhaerens*): "virtual existence" (of all things in God as Principle) as contrasted with the "formal existence" of created things in themselves.
    a. Major appearances: *Essential Eckhart*, pp. 40–41, 90, 137; *Teacher and Preacher*, pp. 22–23, 83–84, 99, 148.
    b. Other places: *Essential Eckhart*, pp. 33, 42, 106, 126; *Teacher and Preacher*, pp. 14, 26, 61, 64, 65, 67, 152, 157, 213, 216–17.

(*esse omnium:* God as "the existence of all things."
    Essential Eckhart, p. 33; *Teacher and Preacher*, pp. 212, 225 (cf. p. 210 where God is the *forma omnium*).

(*ipsum esse:* God as "Existence Itself" (a term Eckhart took from Thomas Aquinas, e.g., *STh* Ia. 3. 4).
    Essential Eckhart, pp. 143, 159; *Teacher and Preacher*, pp. 48, 51, 59, 65, 68, 79, 81, 94 95, 167, 173, 175–76, 224.

(*puritas essendi—plenitudo essendi:* "purity of existence" and "fullness of existence."
    Essential Eckhart, pp. 37, 91, 96; *Teacher and Preacher*, 46, 48, 58, 68, 78, 79, 162, 166, 167, 181, 224.

essentia
    "Essence," a term that is sometimes given more technical scholastic form as *quiditas*, literally the "whatness" or "definition" of a thing (e.g., *Essential Eckhart*, pp. 83, 105–06, 114, 126, 132; *Teacher and Preacher*, p. 46), or as *quod quid est* or *id quod est*, "that which is" (e.g., *Essential Eckhart*, pp. 105–06, 114; *Teacher and Preacher*, pp. 72–73, 75, 148, 191, 216).
    a. Major appearances: *Essential Eckhart*, pp. 105–06, 114; *Teacher and Preacher*, pp. 93–94, 236–37.
    b. Other places: *Essential Eckhart*, pp. 35–36, 72, 83, 94, 132, 137, 146, 158–59; *Teacher and Preacher*, pp. 46–48, 54–55, 59, 62, 65, 66–67, 72, 75, 80, 84, 93, 94, 98, 114, 128–29, 182, 187, 189, 191, 218, 224, 225.

finis
    "Goal, end, final cause," sometimes appears as *terminus* (e.g., *Teacher and Preacher*, pp. 52, 72, 174, 191).
    a. Major appearances: *Essential Eckhart*, pp. 136–37; *Teacher and Preacher*, pp. 76, 119–20, 148–55, 210.
    b. Other places: *Essential Eckhart*, pp. 121, 132, 139, 144, 163; *Teacher and Preacher*, pp. 52, 60, 65, 71, 72, 81, 88, 89, 102, 106, 124, 156, 172, 176, 177, 180, 185 193, 207, 216–17, 218, 219, 229, 236–37.

GLOSSARY

forma—materia (see *actio—passio*)
 "Form, matter," the basic constituents of material created beings.
  a. Major appearances: *Essential Eckhart*, pp. 103–05; *Teacher and Preacher*, pp. 59–60, 88–89, 210, 217–18.
  b. Other places: *Essential Eckhart*, pp. 56, 73, 86–87, 90, 95, 102, 109, 114, 116, 131, 136, 146, 157, 160, 171–72; *Teacher and Preacher*, pp. 47, 50, 61, 72, 74, 83–84, 87–88, 100, 105, 111, 150–51, 154, 157–58, 165, 169, 170, 173, 175, 177, 179, 183–84, 190, 192, 216, 217, 219, 225, 235.

generatio, generare (see MHG *geburt, gebern*)
 Translated as "generation, generating" (sometimes "begetting"), this can apply to: (a) the eternal generation of the Son from the Father; (b) the generation of the Son in the soul of the just person (see *iustitia*); or (c) to any kind of generation of form in the created realm. For meaning (b) as it relates to both Latin and MHG appearances, see Karl Kertz, "Meister Eckhart's Teaching on the Birth of the Divine Word in the Soul," *Traditio* 15 (1959): 327–63.
  a. Major appearances: *Essential Eckhart*, pp. 124–25; *Teacher and Preacher*, pp. 94, 150–52, 157–59.
  b. Other places: *Essential Eckhart*, pp. 73, 91, 109, 127, 148, 152, 160, 163, 170, 172–73; *Teacher and Preacher*, pp. 50, 60, 74, 88, 89, 102, 184, 190, 191–92, 217.

gratia
 "Grace" for Eckhart can mean both any kind of divine gift at all, and the special gift of supernatural life given to fallen man.
  a. Major appearances: *Essential Eckhart*, pp. 45–46; *Teacher and Preacher*, pp. 216–21, 229.
  b. Other places: *Essential Eckhart*, pp. 52, 112, 156, 158, 161–62, 171; *Teacher and Preacher*, pp. 45, 128, 129, 172, 193, 214, 227, 230, 235.

imago (see MHG *bilde, bilden*)
 The term "image" and the related term *similitudo* ("likeness") are central to both the Latin and the MHG writings. There is a rich literature relating mostly to the MHG uses, see especially Alois Haas, "Meister Eckharts mystische Bildlehre," *Sermo Mysticus. Studien zur Theologie und Sprache der deutschen Mystik* (Freiburg, Switzerland: Universitätsverlag, 1979), pp. 209–37.
  a. Major appearances: *Essential Eckhart*, pp. 43–44, 129–30, 169; *Teacher and Preacher*, pp. 172–73, 192–93, 220, 234–37.
  b. Other places: *Essential Eckhart*, pp. 38–39, 41, 53, 109–10, 112, 115–116, 153, 169–70; *Teacher and Preacher*, pp. 81–82, 84, 104, 151, 155, 182–83, 191–92, 218, 224, 225.

GLOSSARY

intellectus and *intelligere* (see MGH *vernünfticheit*, and also *verbum* and *verum*)
"Intellect" and "act of understanding." On these terms, see R. Imbach, *Deus est Intelligere;* and John Caputo, "The Nothingness of the Intellect in Meister Eckhart's 'Parisian Questions,' " *The Thomist* 39 (1975): 85–115.
    a. Major appearances: *Essential Eckhart*, pp. 86, 103; *Teacher and Preacher*, pp. 27–29, 125, 225–26.
    b. Other places: *Essential Eckhart*, 32, 34–35, 56–57, 79, 84, 91, 105, 108–10, 115, 125, 131–32, 135, 137, 144–45, 153, 160, 163; *Teacher and Preacher*, pp. 45, 51, 59, 63, 70, 77, 84, 93, 97, 99, 102, 105–06, 114, 117, 128, 129, 148, 152, 158, 177, 184, 187, 189, 212, 219, 221, 227, 231, 235, 236.

iustitia and *iustus* (see MHG *geburt, gebern,* and Sermon 39, pp. 296–98)
"Justice" and the "just man, or person."
    a. Major appearances: *Essential Eckhart*, pp. 113–14, 126–30; *Teacher and Preacher*, p. 160.
    b. Other places: *Essential Eckhart*, pp. 38, 51–52, 89, 97, 110, 120, 138, 146–47, 152, 154, 169; *Teacher and Preacher*, pp. 74–75, 108, 116, 119, 161, 173, 178, 186, 207, 236.

medium (see MHG *âne mittel,* and also *unio* below under *unum*)
Generally translated as "medium," that which comes between two things. Eckhart insisted that all true union, whether of form and matter in the created realm or of God and the soul in the spiritual realm, must take place "without a medium."
    a. Major appearances: *Essential Eckhart*, pp. 104–05, 158; *Teacher and Preacher*, pp. 59, 88–89, 173–74, 215.
    b. Other places: *Essential Eckhart*, pp. 84, 86–87, 90, 113, 147–58; *Teacher and Preacher*, pp. 14, 51, 62, 65, 81, 84, 153, 175–76, 179, 219, 233.

negatio—affirmatio (see *verum*)
"Negation, affirmation," the fundamental acts of the intellect. Of special interest is Eckhart's dialectical description of God as the *negatio negationis.*
    a. Major appearances: *Teacher and Preacher*, pp. 21–27, 97–102, 162, 167–68.
    b. Other places: *Essential Eckhart*, pp. 78, 129, 149; *Teacher and Preacher*, pp. 159, 181, 185.

(*negatio negationis:* "the negation of negation," i.e., the purest form of affirmation as applied to God.
    Essential Eckhart, p. 34; *Teacher and Preacher*, pp. 9, 21, 25, 68, 167–68, 181, 185, 187, and MHG Sermon 21 (p. 281).

GLOSSARY

nihil (see MHG *niht*)

"Nothing." In Latin this refers to the nothingness of creatures in relation to God; in MHG it can refer either to creaturely nothingness, or to God considered as "nothing" when existence is ascribed to creatures.

　　a. Major appearances: *Essential Eckhart*, pp. 79, 140–41; *Teacher and Preacher*, pp. 79, 149, 153.

　　b. Other places: *Essential Eckhart*, pp. 33, 44, 75–76, 128, 152, 156, 160–61; *Teacher and Preacher*, pp. 48, 52, 55, 59, 68, 69, 99, 147, 159, 166, 181, 183, 208, 210, 214, 215, 219.

potentia (also *virtus, facultas;* see also *intellectus*)

"Power," or "faculty" of the soul. In the MHG there is considerable discussion of the soul's powers, especially in relation to the terms *grunt, vernünfticheit,* and *vünkelîn*. Although the Latin works lack the emphasis given to the *vünkelîn,* or "spark of the soul" found in the MHG, there is occasional mention of a *supremum animae* or *vertex animae,* the "high point of the soul" (e.g., *Essential Eckhart*, pp. 111–12; *Teacher and Preacher*, pp. 234–35).

　　a. Major appearances: *Essential Eckhart*, pp. 108–21, 164–65; *Teacher and Preacher*, pp. 111–15.

　　b. Other places: *Essential Eckhart*, pp. 42–44, 90, 104, 107, 133, 153, 171; *Teacher and Preacher*, pp. 50, 56, 59, 108–09, 129, 184, 192, 219–21, 227.

primum or *prima causa*

"The First," or "First Cause." The former term reflects the influence of the *Book of Causes*. Eckhart also refers to the *primus actus formalis,* or "First Formal Act" (*Teacher and Preacher*, p. 177).

　　a. Major appearances: *Essential Eckhart*, p. 155; *Teacher and Preacher*, pp. 176–77.

　　b. Other places: *Essential Eckhart*, pp. 87–89, 91, 151, 157, 159; *Teacher and Preacher*, pp. 57, 59, 61, 63–64, 68, 72, 80, 86, 87, 94, 99, 102, 129, 147, 148, 149, 153, 166, 168–69, 170–71, 172–73, 179, 180, 181, 185, 189, 192, 212, 213, 218, 219, 221, 224.

principium (see MHG *grunt,* which sometimes bears a related sense)

The Latin term can mean either "beginning" or "principle" and Eckhart exploits this fluidity throughout. Though closely related to *primum,* the former term smacks more of efficient causality, while *principium* generally implies formal causality. On God as the Principle, see especially C. F. Kelley, *Meister Eckhart on Divine Knowledge* (New Haven: Yale University Press, 1977).

　　a. Major appearances: *Essential Eckhart*, pp. 37–40, 83–84, 89–91, 97, 123–40 (on Jn. 1:1–2, esp. p. 135), 142–43; *Teacher and Preacher*, pp. 125, 187.

　　b. Other places: *Essential Eckhart*, pp. 42, 52, 66, 88, 94, 100, 103, 105, 109, 121, 142–43, 148–49, 151–52, 157–58, 166; *Teacher and Preacher*, pp. 50–51, 54,

GLOSSARY

65, 72, 76, 86, 87–88, 89, 95, 97, 129, 148, 151, 152, 155, 165, 175, 180, 189–90, 191–92, 193, 218–19, 237.

proprietas, proprium (sometimes *qualitas*, see MHG *eigenschaft, eigen*)
"Property, characteristic, proper nature." The corresponding MHG term has more varied uses, but a comparison is fruitful. See Frank Tobin, "Eckhart's Mystical Use of Language: The Contexts of *eigenschaft*," *Seminar* 8 (1973): 160–68.
    a. Major appearances: *Teacher and Preacher*, p. 95.
    b. Other places: *Essential Eckhart*, pp. 73, 83, 86, 91, 94–96, 98, 103–04, 109, 115, 119, 123, 126, 128, 132–33, 135, 143, 154, 159, 165, 171; *Teacher and Preacher*, pp. 29, 54, 57, 62, 91, 92, 100–01, 102, 103, 120, 128, 149, 150, 154, 158–59, 160, 163–64, 166, 172–73, 186, 187, 189, 191, 207, 208, 216, 218, 221, 225, 236.

reditus (see MHG *durchbruch*)
"Return," signifying the return of all things to their divine ground or source. Eckhart uses a number of equivalent terms, such as *conversio* (*Teacher and Preacher*, pp. 46, 215) and *refluxus*, or *regressus* (*Teacher and Preacher*, p. 218). On this important theme, see Shizuteru Ueda, *Die Gottesgeburt in der Seele und der Durchbruch zur Gottheit* (Gütersloh: Mohn, 1965).
    Essential Eckhart, pp. 30–31, 47–57; *Teacher and Preacher*, pp. 182–83.

(*redditio completa:* "the complete return" of the divine intellectual nature upon itself, a concept taken from the *Book of Causes*.
    Essential Eckhart, p. 37; *Teacher and Preacher*, pp. 46, 68, 236.

relatio
"Relation" is an important term (along with *substantia*) for Eckhart's doctrine of speaking about God.
    a. Major appearances: *Teacher and Preacher*, pp. 19–20, 64–67.
    b. Other places: *Essential Eckhart*, pp. 38, 73; *Teacher and Preacher*, pp. 27, 51, 53, 60–61, 84, 208, 220, 225.

similis—dissimilis (see *distinctus—indistinctus*)
"Similar, dissimilar," or at times "like, unlike." These are major dialectic terms for Eckhart, and they are related to his understanding of *similitudo* (see under *imago*).
    a. Major appearances: *Teacher and Preacher*, pp. 81–85, 151.
    b. Other places: *Essential Eckhart*, pp. 78, 170, 173; *Teacher and Preacher*, pp. 55, 58, 80, 148–49, 151, 157, 173, 182, 236, 237.

GLOSSARY

simplicitas, simplex

"Simplicity, simple." This is related to *unum,* but is formally diverse in stressing lack of composition of parts rather than lack of distinction.

    a. Major appearances: *Teacher and Preacher,* pp. 79, 97, 170–71.

    b. Other places: *Essential Eckhart,* pp. 86, 91, 146; *Teacher and Preacher,* pp. 58, 78, 87, 90, 98, 157, 163, 164, 181, 212, 223, 224–25.

substantia (see *esse; essentia*)

"Substance" is one of the most common scholastic terms. Eckhart's use is not idiosyncratic, but the term is significant for his general metaphysical position.

    a. Major appearances: *Teacher and Preacher,* pp. 60–61, 64–67.

    b. Other places: *Essential Eckhart,* pp. 76, 104, 125, 157; *Teacher and Preacher,* pp. 18–21, 27, 45, 47, 49, 53–54, 55–57, 58, 60, 61, 72, 90–91, 98, 100, 125, 128–29, 148, 161, 165, 169, 182, 190, 191, 209, 213, 221, 227, 236.

unum (see MHG *ein*)

In the neuter as a substantive this is translated as "the One," or sometimes as "Absolute Unity," and signifies formally the "not-to-be-distinguished" (see *indistinctus*) and efficiently God as the source of all that is in any way distinguished. The term also is used adjectivally in many contexts. Finally, *unum* is the metaphysical ground for the key terms *unio* and *unitas.* On the importance of this transcendental predicate in Eckhart's thought, see V. Lossky, *Théologie négative et connaissance de Dieu chez Maître Eckhart;* and B. McGinn, "Meister Eckhart on God as Absolute Unity."

    a. Major appearances: *Essential Eckhart,* pp. 32–37, 55–56, 97–101, 165–66; *Teacher and Preacher,* pp. 19, 62–64, 160–61, 166–71 (the relation to indistinction), 182–89 (the One and the Father), 223–26 (the One and Intellect).

    b. Other places: *Essential Eckhart,* pp. 41–42, 79, 87, 91, 138, 146, 159; *Teacher and Preacher,* pp. 5, 20, 25, 54, 58–59, 68, 74–75, 77, 78–79, 86–89, 153–54, 156, 157, 159, 160, 161–64, 172, 173, 178, 210, 211, 212, 236.

(*unio* (see MHG *einicheit*): "union."

    a. Major appearances: *Essential Eckhart,* pp. 55–57, 78; *Teacher and Preacher,* pp. 172–73, 220, 224, 226.

    b. Other places: *Essential Eckhart,* pp. 43, 47, 50, 75, 76, 91, 105, 113; *Teacher and Preacher,* pp. 76, 104, 160, 182, 212, 221.

(*unitas:* "unity," used in a more general sense than "union," which mostly refers to the bond of God and the soul.

    a. Major appearance: *Teacher and Preacher,* pp. 154–55.

    b. Other places: *Essential Eckhart,* pp. 91, 97–99; *Teacher and Preacher,* pp. 58, 63, 67, 87–88, 160, 167–68, 170, 172, 182, 185–86, 187, 188, 224–25.

verbum (see MHG *wort*)
"Word" is a rich term that spans the range from the Divine Word, the second Person in the Trinity, through the ideas of things in the divine mind, to any human word, or act of understanding. On the latter two meanings, see *ratio* below. For some background, see Emilie zum Brunn and Alain de Libera, *Maître Eckhart: Métaphysique du Verbe et théologie négative* (Paris: Beauchesne, 1984).

    a. Major appearances: *Essential Eckhart*, pp. 39–40, 123–47 (on Jn. 1:1–3), 167–73 (on the Incarnation).

    b. Other places: *Essential Eckhart*, pp. 45–46, 85, 149, 152, 159, 161; *Teacher and Preacher*, pp. 46, 51, 77–78, 83, 97, 109, 119, 125, 148, 171–72, 187, 217, 219–20.

(*ratio:* a rich term that can mean "reason," or "cause," but that frequently with Eckhart means "idea." As "idea" it is equivalent to *Logos, idea* (e.g., *Teacher and Preacher*, pp. 50, 182, 236), and *conceptus* or *conceptio* (e.g., *Teacher and Preacher*, pp. 97, 108, 192, 211).

    a. Major appearances: *Essential Eckhart*, pp. 83–84, 126; *Teacher and Preacher*, pp. 111–15.

    b. Other places: *Essential Eckhart*, pp. 86, 89, 91, 101–02, 123–24, 130–32, 141; *Teacher and Preacher*, 46, 61, 64, 66–67, 83, 99, 102, 109, 125, 148, 152, 153–54, 157, 169, 172–73, 187, 189, 192, 211, 216–17, 236.

verum (see *bonum, esse, unum*—the other transcendental terms)
"True," or "the Truth" especially as applied to God.

    a. Major appearances: *Essential Eckhart*, pp. 32–37; *Teacher and Preacher*, pp. 67–68, 167–68, 187–88.

    b. Other places: *Essential Eckhart*, pp. 28, 93–94, 106, 138–39, 159, 166, 171; *Teacher and Preacher*, pp. 25–26, 46–47, 49, 51, 56, 61, 64, 69, 75, 82, 99, 127, 128, 148, 157, 174, 178, 182, 186, 192, 210–11, 219, 226, 231.

B. Middle High German Glossary.

(This Glossary does not contain references to the "Sister Catherine" treatise.)

abegescheiden, abegescheidenheit, gelâzen, gelâzenheit
    "Detach, detachment, letting go." These terms indicate freedom from ties to creatures and all mundane concerns. For useful remarks, see Reiner Schür-

GLOSSARY

mann, *Meister Eckhart: Mystic and Philosopher* (Bloomington and London: University of Indiana Press, 1978).
    a. Major appearances: *Essential Eckhart*, pp. 285–94 (*Detach.*); *Teacher and Preacher*, pp. 264 (Sermon 10), 270 (Sermon 12).
    b. Other places: *Essential Eckhart*, pp. 47–50, 191, 197, 203, 249–50, 251–54, 276–77; *Teacher and Preacher*, pp. 253, 261, 267, 295.

âne mittel or mitel (see Latin *medium*)
    "Without a medium, without mediation, immediately, directly." This never has a temporal sense, but is used by Eckhart to describe an event or union that takes place with no means or medium intervening.
    a. Major appearances: *Essential Eckhart*, p. 56; *Teacher and Preacher*, pp. 261 and 264 (Sermon 10), 276–77 (Sermon 16b), 311–13 (Sermon 69).
    b. Other places: *Essential Eckhart*, pp. 182, 185, 187, 189, 191, 198, 208, 221, 244; *Teacher and Preacher*, pp. 243, 278, 317–18, 324, 336, 341.

âne war umbe, sunder war umbe
    "Without a why." Used in opposition to doing something for a specific or limited purpose. Living "without a why" unites one to God who is and who always acts "without a why." There is no precise verbal equivalent in the Latin works, but the theme occurs there also (e.g., *Teacher and Preacher*, pp. 120, 156–57, 180–81, 207, 214).
    a. Major appearances: *Essential Eckhart*, pp. 59–60, 183–84 (Sermon 5b).
    b. Other places: *Essential Eckhart*, pp. 186, 188, 201, 228–29; *Teacher and Preacher*, pp. 288, 296, 298, 300, 307.

bilde, bilden (there are many derived verb forms, e.g., *inbilden, überbilden;* see also *imago*)
    "Image, form; to form, inform, transform, etc." One of the most important Eckhartian terms. For an introduction, see A. Haas, "Meister Eckharts mystische Bildlehre."
    a. Major appearances: *Essential Eckhart*, pp. 43–44, *Bened. 1* (pp. 210–12, 216, 219, 222, 239); *Teacher and Preacher*, pp. 276–77 (Sermon 16b), 301–02 (Sermon 40), 304–05 (Sermon 46), 314–15 (Sermon 69), 317–19 (Sermon 70).
    b. Other places: *Essential Eckhart*, pp. 177, 182, 184, 187, 191, 193–94, 206, 208, 242–43, 245, 253, 261, 269, 274, 285, 293; *Teacher and Preacher*, pp. 242, 245–46, 257, 258, 262, 263, 284, 292, 293, 313, 323, 327, 329, 340–41.

diz noch daz (see *esse hoc et hoc*)
    "This or that," indicating the particularity and limits of all created being. God is *neither* this *nor* that, but Absolute Existence.
    Essential Eckhart, pp., 180–81, 241, 248, 287, 291; *Teacher and Preacher*, pp. 246, 256, 285, 296, 300, 304–05, 321, 323.

GLOSSARY

durchbruch, durchbrechen, widerruk, etc. (see *reditus*)

"Breakthrough, breaking through, return," etc. These terms indicate the soul's return to its primal source in God. For a study, see S. Ueda, *Die Gottesgeburt in der Seele und der Durchbruch zur Gottheit.*

    a. Major appearances: Essential Eckhart, pp. 55–57, 192 (Sermon 15), 198 (Sermon 48), 203 (Sermon 52); *Teacher and Preacher,* pp. 288 (Sermon 29), 336–37 (Sermon 84).

    b. Other places: *Essential Eckhart* pp. 47, 184, 196, 205, 253; *Teacher and Preacher,* pp. 244, 315, 319, 333.

eigenschaft, eigen (see *proprietas, proprium*)

"Property, characteristic" when used to translate the Latin term, but in MHG it also can mean "possessiveness," and at times "individuality." See F. Tobin, "Eckhart's Mystical Use of Language: The Contexts of *eigenschaft.*"

    a. Major appearances: *Essential Eckhart,* pp. 177–78 and 181 (Sermon 2), 280–82 (*Couns. 23*); *Teacher and Preacher,* p. 241 (Sermon 1).

    b. Other places: *Essential Eckhart,* pp. 183, 198, 217, 225, 227, 244, 288; *Teacher and Preacher,* pp. 262, 277, 282, 290, 296–97, 305, 309, 313, 317, 318.

ein, and derived terms like *einicheit, einung, einvaltic* (see *unum, unio, unitas,* and also *simplicitas, simplex*)

"The One, one, oneness, union, simple," etc. See the remarks under *unum* above, and the excellent discussion in B. Schmoldt, *Die deutsche Begriffsprache Meister Eckharts.*

    a. Major appearances: *Essential Eckhart,* pp. 32–37, 55–56, 194 and 196 (Sermon 22), 206 and 208 (Sermon 83), 244–47 (*Bened. 2*); *Teacher and Preacher,* pp. 253 and 254 (Sermon 7), 265 (Sermon 10), 269–70 (Sermon 12), 280–83 (Sermon 21), 288 and 290 (Sermon 29), 300–02 (Sermon 40).

    b. Other places: *Essential Eckhart,* pp. 179, 181, 182, 184, 187–88, 189–91, 197–98, 203, 205, 220–23, 227, 230, 234, 252, 271–73, 276, 286, 288, 293–94; *Teacher and Preacher,* pp. 243, 260, 262, 267, 272, 273, 278, 285, 293, 298, 304–06, 309, 312, 314, 318, 327–29, 333–34, 340–42.

geburt, gebern (see *generatio, generare*)

"Birth," especially the birth of the Son in the soul. See the remarks under *generatio,* and also note the rich secondary literature, especially S. Ueda, *Die Gottesgeburt in der Seele und der Durchbruch zur Gottheit.* For the history of the theme, see Hugo Rahner, "Die Gottesgeburt: Die Lehre der Kirchenväter von der Geburt Christi aus dem Herzen der Kirche und der Gläubigen," *Zeitschrift für katholische Theologie* 59 (1933): 33–418.

    a. Major appearances: *Essential Eckhart,* pp. 50–54, 178–79 and 181 (Sermon 2), 187–89 (Sermon 6), 226–29 (*Bened. 1*); *Teacher and Preacher,* pp. 250–51 (Sermon 4), 296–98 (Sermon 39), 327 and 329–30 (Sermon 76).

GLOSSARY

b. Other places: *Essential Eckhart*, pp. 183–84, 192–93, 194–96, 198, 205, 210, 232, 243; *Teacher and Preacher*, pp. 244, 263–65, 267–68, 273–74, 278, 289–90, 293–94, 301–02, 304–05, 307–08.

gotheit

"Godhead, divinity." See K. Ruh, "Die trinitarische Spekulation in deutscher Mystik und Scholastik."
Essential Eckhart, pp. 184, 190, 193, 196, 197, 206, 219, 221, 231; *Teacher and Preacher*, pp. 245, 265, 273, 274, 281–82, 290, 310, 315, 318, 329, 332.

grunt

"Ground," or "innermost depths," referring both to God and to the deepest level of the soul where it is identical with God. In referring to God, *grunt* has some of the implications of *principium*; in referring to the soul Eckhart occasionally uses terms like *supremum animae* or *abditus mentis*. See Bernward Dietsche, "Der Seelengrund nach den deutschen und lateinischen Predigten," *Meister Eckhart der Prediger* (Freiburg: Herder, 1960), pp. 200–58.
    a. Major appearances: *Essential Eckhart*, pp. 42–43, 182–84 (Sermon 5b); *Teacher and Preacher*, pp. 284–85 (Sermon 24), 296–98 (Sermon 39).
    b. Other places: *Essential Eckhart*, pp. 179, 190, 192, 198, 241–42, 245–46, 251, 258, 268; *Teacher and Preacher*, pp. 254, 261, 263, 265, 268, 278, 281, 315, 323, 332, 338, 341, 342–43.

isticheit

"Is-ness, existence, being," a rare term, but one of interest for the ways in which the Latin *esse* and related terms passed over into MHG. See M. S. Morard, "Ist, istic, istikeit bei Meister Eckhart," *Freiburger Zeitschrift für Philosophie und Theologie* 3 (1956); 169–86.
    Essential Eckhart, pp. 33, 51, 187, 207–08; *Teacher and Preacher*, pp. 243, 268.

lûterkeit, and the adjectival forms *lûter*, *ledic*, and especially *blôz* (cf. MHG *niht*)

"Purity, emptiness," and "pure, empty, bare, naked." This complex of terms is very frequent in Eckhart; it signifies both the primal purity of the divine nature and the purity and emptiness that the soul must achieve through detachment in order to be united with God.
    a. Major appearances: *Essential Eckhart*, pp. 177 and 180 (Sermon 2), 194–96 (Sermon 22), 200–03 (Sermon 52), 288 and 292 (*Detach.*); *Teacher and Preacher*, pp. 239–41 (Sermon 1), 253–54 (Sermon 7), 280–81 (Sermon 21), 313–14 (Sermon 69), 335 (Sermon 84).
    b. Other places: *Essential Eckhart*, pp. 47, 182, 191, 198, 203, 206, 210, 220–22, 228, 243, 245, 248, 254, 270, 274, 282, 286; *Teacher and Preacher*, pp. 244–46, 251, 256, 262, 263, 269–70, 275, 278, 282–83, 285, 289, 295, 298, 300–02, 304–05, 317, 320–21, 324–25, 329–30, 339, 342.

GLOSSARY

niht (rarely *nitheit;* cf. *nihil*)
"Nothing, nothingness." Eckhart uses *niht* both negatively (creatures are pure nothing) and positively (God is the *niht* beyond all being). See Minoru Nambara, "Die Idee des absoluten Nichts in der deutschen Mystik und ihre Entsprechungen im Buddhismus," *Archiv für Begriffsgeschichte* 6 (1960): 143–277.
    a. Major appearances: *Essential Eckhart*, pp. 199–203 (Sermon 52), 207–08 (Sermon 83); *Teacher and Preacher*, pp. 240–42 (Sermon 1), 280 and 281 (Sermon 21), 320–25 (Sermon 71).
    b. Other places: *Essential Eckhart*, pp. 177, 183–84, 187, 189–90, 197, 205, 233, 237, 244, 248, 263, 280, 286–87, 291–92; *Teacher and Preacher*, pp. 250, 256, 264, 269, 290, 297, 305, 307, 313–15, 317, 329, 333, 335, 342.

nû (see *aeternitas*)
"Now," used by Eckhart to describe what is beyond time, the "now" of eternity.
    Essential Eckhart, pp. 40–44, 177, 179, 202–03, 205, 228–29, 289; *Teacher and Preacher*, pp. 241, 251, 256, 263, 264–65, 273, 286, 290, 292, 297–98, 308, 313, 336.

underscheit (see *distinctus—indistinctus*)
"Distinction, difference." Not as developed in MHG works, but still important and at times used in dialectical fashion (e.g., *Teacher and Preacher*, p. 265, cf. pp. 281 and 292).
    a. Major appearances: *Essential Eckhart*, pp. 188–89 (Sermon 6), 244–45 (*Bened. 1*); *Teacher and Preacher*, pp. 265 (Sermon 10), 300–01 (Sermon 40), 305 (Sermon 46), 314 (Sermon 69).
    b. Other places: *Essential Eckhart*, pp. 191, 193–94, 198, 202, 222, 227, 234, 264, 272, 277, 285; *Teacher and Preacher*, pp. 261, 264, 281, 286, 290, 309, 328, 335.

ûzbruch, ûzvluz, ûzganc (sometimes also *ursprunc*) and the verbs *ûzbrechen, ûzvliezen, ûzsmelzen, ûzblüejen*, etc. (see *emanatio*)
"Emanation, going out, flowing out," etc. See K. Ruh, "Die trinitarische Spekulation in deutscher Mystik und Scholastik."
    a. Major appearances: *Essential Eckhart*, pp. 37–38, 189 and 191 (Sermon 15), 203 (Sermon 52); *Teacher and Preacher*, pp. 253–54 (Sermon 7), 276 (Sermon 16b), 281 (Sermon 21), 284–85 (Sermon 24), 321 and 325 (Sermon 71).
    b. Other places: *Essential Eckhart*, pp. 184, 187, 205, 221, 227, 282; *Teacher and Preacher*, pp. 245, 251, 265, 269, 273, 288, 292, 304, 310, 315, 319, 332–33, 335, 336.

GLOSSARY

vernünfticheit (see *intellectus*)
   "Intellect, understanding," sometimes "reason" (especially in *Essential Eckhart*). On this and the other terms listed below, see especially B. Schmoldt, *Die deutsche Begriffsprache Meister Eckharts.*
   a. Major appearances: *Essential Eckhart*, p. 191 (Sermon 15); *Teacher and Preacher*, pp. 254 (Sermon 7), 256 and 257–58 (Sermon 9), 313–15 (Sermon 69).
   b. Other places: *Essential Eckhart*, pp. 193, 200–01, 254–55, 275; *Teacher and Preacher*, pp. 241, 244, 249, 265, 277, 282, 292, 318, 321, 327–28, 341.

(*bekanntnisse:* "intellect, knowledge." Not really distinct from the above, but used more frequently of the divine mind.
   Essential Eckhart, pp. 188, 194, 201, 208, 245; *Teacher and Preacher*, pp. 244–46, 261–62, 271–72, 298, 301, 316–17, 324, 327, 328–29, 339.

(*verstantnisse:* another related term for "intellect."
   Essential Eckhart, pp. 202, 205, 208; *Teacher and Preacher*, pp. 250–51, 282, 310, 332.

vünkelîn, and related terms such as *bürgelîn; daz edele, oberste; wipfel; daz innigeste* (see also *grunt*)
   "Spark of the soul; the highest, noblest, innermost part of the soul." The "uncreated something" in the soul, as condemned in the Bull "In agro dominico" (*Essential Eckhart*, p. 80). On the history of this term (*scintilla animae, apex animae*), see "*Psychias Spinther.* Histoire d'une métaphore dans la tradition platonicienne jusqu'à Eckhart," *Revue des études augustiniennes* 21 (1975): 225–55; cf. also Hans Hof, *Scintilla animae: Eine Studie zu einem Grundbegriff in Meister Eckharts Philosophie* (Lund: Gleerup, 1952).
   a. Major appearances: *Essential Eckhart*, pp. 42–44, 180 (Sermon 2); *Teacher and Preacher*, pp. 313–15 (Sermon 69), 327–28 (Sermon 76).
   b. Other places: *Essential Eckhart*, pp. 194, 198; *Teacher and Preacher*, pp. 249, 257, 265, 269, 285, 288, 305, 307, 338, 342.

wesen (see *esse* and *isticheit*)
   Generally translated as "being" here, since the MHG term covers for a variety of Latin forms (e.g., *esse, essentia, ens, substantia*). See the literature cited under *esse*, as well as the material in B. Schmoldt, *Die deutsche Begriffsprache Meister Eckharts.*
   a. Major appearances: Essential Eckhart, pp. 190–91 and 195–96 (Sermon 15), 200–01 (Sermon 52), 206–07 (Sermon 83); *Teacher and Preacher*, pp. 256–57 (Sermon 9), 301 (Sermon 40), 323 (Sermon 71), 327–30 (Sermon 76).
   b. Other places: *Essential Eckhart*, pp. 186–88, 197–98, 205, 220, 226, 229, 233, 242, 244–46, 251, 288, 293; *Teacher and Preacher*, pp. 244, 246, 249, 251, 253, 254, 257–58, 261–62, 263, 264, 265, 268–69, 272, 274, 275, 277, 278, 281, 285, 289, 290, 293, 298, 305, 309, 312, 314, 322, 332–33, 336, 343.

GLOSSARY

wîse

"Manner, mode, way" (Latin *modus*), often implying limitation, or a particular manner of existing or loving as opposed to infinite existence or loving (cf. *diz noch daz*).

Essential Eckhart, pp. 180–81, 183, 185, 248, 252, 267, 278–79, 284; *Teacher and Preacher*, pp. 241, 256–57, 302, 325, 333.

wort (see *verbum*)

"Word," on which see the meanings given under *verbum*.

a. Major appearances: *Essential Eckhart*, pp. 203–05; *Teacher and Preacher*, pp. 259–60 (Sermon 9), 292–93 (Sermon 30).

b. Other places: *Teacher and Preacher*, pp. 242–43, 245, 249, 267–68, 278, 286, 304–05, 313, 335, 343.

INDEX TO PREFACE, INTRODUCTION, NOTES AND APPENDIX

INDEX TO TEXT

416

Other Volumes in this Series

Francis and Clare ● THE COMPLETE WORKS
Gregory Palamas ● THE TRIADS
Pietists ● SELECTED WRITINGS
The Shakers ● TWO CENTURIES OF SPIRITUAL REFLECTION
Zohar ● THE BOOK OF ENLIGHTENMENT
Luis de León ● THE NAMES OF CHRIST
Quaker Spirituality ● SELECTED WRITINGS
Emanuel Swedenborg ● THE UNIVERSAL HUMAN AND SOUL-BODY INTERACTION
Augustine of Hippo ● SELECTED WRITINGS
Safed Spirituality ● RULES OF MYSTICAL PIETY, THE BEGINNING OF WISDOM
Maximus Confessor ● SELECTED WRITINGS
John Cassian ● CONFERENCES
Johannes Tauler ● SERMONS
John Ruusbroec ● THE SPIRITUAL ESPOUSALS AND OTHER WORKS
Ibn 'Abbād of Ronda ● LETTERS ON THE SŪFĪ PATH
Angelus Silesius ● THE CHERUBINIC WANDERER
The Early Kabbalah ●